C0-AVO-000

**GORGIAS DISSERTATIONS 1**

**NEAR EASTERN STUDIES**

Volume 1

# Healing
in the
# Theology of Saint Ephrem

# Healing in the

in the

# Theology of Saint Ephrem

AHO SHEMUNKASHO

GORGIAS PRESS
2004

First Gorgias Press Edition, 2002.

Second Gorgias Press Edition, 2004.



**ISBN 1-59333-156-8 (Hardback)**

**ISBN 1-931956-14-6 (eBook)**

GORGIAS PRESS
46 Orris Ave., Piscataway, NJ 08854 USA
www.gorgiaspress.com

Printed and bound in the United States of America

# ACKNOWLEDGMENTS

I want to thank the Lord not only for enabling me to complete this work, but also for giving me such a joyful time throughout my study.

I would like to thank everyone who has made the research for this dissertation possible. First of all the Stiftung Pro Oriente, Vienna, who funded me generously for my study in Oxford, reading for the MSt and DPhil courses; the German Academic Exchange Service (DAAD), Bonn, for funding the first year of my DPhil; and Dolabani Trust, Oxford, which provided me with books.

Above all I want to express my sincere gratitude to my supervisor Dr. S. P. Brock for his tremendous support and help throughout my research. He has not only guided and encouraged me but has been wholly inspiring to work with. With the following lines, taken from the well known *mimro*, I would like to express my thanks to Dr. S. P. Brock:

ܐܠܗܐ ܗܒ ܝܘܠܦܢܐ
ܠܐܢܫܐ ܕܪܚܡ ܝܘܠܦܢܐ
ܘܠܪܒܐ ܕܡܠܦ ܫܦܝܪ
ܪܒܝܗܝ ܪܒܐ ܒܡܠܟܘܬܟ

God, [please] grant knowledge
to the one who loves knowledge
and the master who teaches excellently
make him great in Your kingdom.

I would also like to thank the staff of the Oriental Institute, particularly the library, for providing a lovely atmosphere in which to work. There are a number of special people who in one way or another have greatly enriched my life, and my study, and whom I would like to thank. These include my fellow students of Oriental Studies and those in Wolfson College with whom I have shared my time in Oxford. I also would like to thank my family for their continuing support and encouragement. My especial thanks to my wife Penelope who not only proofread this dissertation but was supporting and encouraging. Lastly, I want to thank Gorgias Press for making the publication of this work possible, and to George Kiraz for the time consuming work in preparing the final version of the text.

# CONTENTS

# PREFACE

Throughout his work, Ephrem presents a wide range of theological themes and images that are characteristic of Syrian Christianity in the fourth century. A significant one that no one has yet studied in Ephrem, or in any other Syriac writer is the concept of sickness and healing. In the course of six chapters, this thesis presents the significance of healing theology and the ways in which the healing of man, spiritually, mentally and corporally is highly valued by Ephrem.

The Introduction, chapter one, looks briefly at some modern studies done on the place of ancient medicine in society in relation to religion, philosophy and science. In particular, it looks at how Hellenistic and Graeco-Roman scientific medicine was seen in relationship to religion, first pagan, and later to Judaism and Christianity.

Chapter two considers the concept of healing and healing imagery in three selected Syriac works that are earlier than Ephrem; the *Odes of Solomon*, the *Acts of the Apostle Judas Thomas* and Aphrahat's *Demonstrations*.

Ephrem's healing terminology is presented in chapter three, which analyses the use of significant terms relating to sickness and healing To see how Ephrem's use differs from that of the Bible, the use of the same terms in the Bible is studied as well.

Chapter four focuses on Ephrem's exegesis of biblical passages dealing with healing It shows not only his knowledge of Scripture's references to healing and sickness, but further how he incorporates these in his theological language, how he develops and uses them in his arguments against heresies and false interpretations of God's word, i.e. (in his terms) spiritual sickness.

Chapter five, the main part of this book, deals with the causes of spiritual sickness and the process of healing, and the way in which Ephrem places these in the divine history of salvation. The cause of spiritual sickness is sin that is the result of the misuse of man's free will and the influence of man's enemy, i.e. Satan, the

Evil One. Ephrem understands Adam and Eve's expulsion from Paradise as a 'Fall' into a state of sickness. God provides heavenly medicine for humanity, first through His chosen people, the patriarchs and the prophets, and then through His Son Who is the Physician *par excellence* and the Medicine of Life that is also present in the Church's sacraments for the faithful.

Finally, in the Conclusion, chapter six, the results of this examination of Ephrem's healing terminology are summarised, and the implications of these are discussed. Some suggestions are made for further work needing to be done.

In the Introduction, selected secondary sources have mainly been used, whereas in the rest of the book, the work focuses on the Syriac sources, edited and published texts. For the *Odes of Solomon*, the edition used is that by J. H. Charlesworth;[1] whereas for the *Acts of Thomas* the Syriac quotations are taken from W. Wright,[2] and the English text cited is from A. F. J. Klijn[3] These translations have often been adapted and slightly altered. Aphrahat's *Demonstrations* are taken from 'Patrologia Syriaca',[4] and the translations are mine.

For Ephrem, the whole range of E. Beck's editions is used, as well as L. Leloir's edition of the *Commentary on the Diatessaron*, and Tonneau's edition of the *Commentary on Genesis* and Exodus.[5] Quotations from Ephrem's texts in English have been taken from existing translations, mainly the translations by Edward G. Mathews, Jr. and Joseph P. Amar,[6] Sebastian P. Brock,[7] Carmel Mc

---

[1] J. H. Charlesworth, *The Odes of Solomon* (Montana 1977).

[2] W. Wright, *Apocryphal Acts of the Apostles I* (London 1871).

[3] A. F. J. Klijn, *The Acts of Thomas* (Leiden 1962).

[4] J. Parisot, *Aphraatis Sapientis Persae, Demonstrationes*, PS I (Paris 1894), PS II (Paris 1907), 1 -489.

[5] See Bibliography. Also see the surveys in J. Melki, 'Ephrem le Syrien: bilan de l'édition critique', *PdO* 11 (1983), 3-88; and S. P. Brock, 'A brief guide to the main edition and translations of the works of St Ephrem', *The Harp* 3 (1990), 7-29.

[6] *Selected Prose Works, St. Ephrem the Syrian*; translated by E. G. Mathews, Jr. and J. P. Amar (Washington 1994); contents: Commentary on Genesis, Commentary on Exodus ,Homily on Our Lord, Letter to Publius.

Carthy,[8] Kathleen E. McVey[9] and Paul S. Russell.[10] As with the other translations, they have been often adapted or slightly altered. The other texts are based on my own translation. Ephrem's works that have survived only in Armenian, such as the *Commentaries on Acts and the Pauline Letters*, and the *Memre on Nicodemia*, have not been considered.

Many citations can be found in the book. The English versions of the most important passages are cited only once in the main text, and the respective Syriac version in the footnotes. Throughout the entire book, some Syriac passages are quoted more than once in the footnotes, in order to make it convenient for the reader, to remind him/her about the precise words or phrases and how they are used. This is not intended to be mere repetition or duplication.

When reading, comparing, studying and analysing Ephrem's texts, the question of authenticity cannot be avoided. What is Ephrem's genuine work? Which texts have been added later or been attributed to him? Is the Commentary on the Diatessaron authentically Ephrem's work? Or is it partly Ephrem and partly a later revision and extension by one of his disciples, or by a later author? Even though it is not the primary aim of this dissertation to answer these questions, I have been aware of this problem and had to decide which text to include or exclude. For this dissertation, I am basically following E. Beck's observations - although modern scholars have different opinions concerning the authenticity of specific texts. In general there is no doubt about the genuine authenticity of 'hymni de azymis', 'hymni de crucifixione', 'hymni de ecclesia', 'hymni de fide', 'hymni de contra haereses', 'hymni de ieiunio', 'hymni de nativitate' (apart from the last few hymns), 'carmina Nisibena', 'hymni de paradiso', 'hymni de

---

[7] S. P. Brock, *St. Ephrem the Syrian, Hymns On Paradise* (New York 1990).

[8] C. Mc Carthy, *Saint Ephrem's Commentary on Tatian's Diatessaron* (Oxford 1993).

[9] K. E. McVey, *Ephrem the Syrian Hymns* (New York 1989); contents: hymns On the Nativity, Against Julian, On Virginity, On the Symbols of the Lord.

[10] P. S. Russell, *Ephrem the Syrian, Eighty Hymns On Faith* [unpublished typescript] (1995).

resurrectione' and 'hymni de virginitate', as well as 'sermo de domino nostro' and 'sermones de fide', and the 'Commentary on Genesis' and the 'Commentary on Exodus'. Almost certainly the following texts are not by Ephrem: 'hymni de epiphania', 'sermones in hebdomadam sanctam', 'sermones III', 'sermones IV', 'Nachträge zu Ephraem Syrus' and 'Sogyatha'. Concerning the other works, there has been a long debate about how much is Ephrem and how much is later. These are the 'Commentary on the Diatessaron', 'hymni de Abraham Kidunaya et Juliano Saba', and texts in 'sermones I' and 'sermones II'

In studying all the texts mentioned above I have primarily analysed and compared the texts which are certainly genuine; I have also included the *Commentary on the Diatessaron* and the hymns on Epiphany, and referred to certain material from other texts which are not, or which may or may not be by Ephrem. Where the non-genuine material is cited, it is not always indicated as such, though sometimes I mention the problem of authenticity for the convenience of the reader.

Finally the aim of this dissertation is to present Ephrem's healing theology and terminology. It focuses on Ephrem's texts - with awareness of the problem mentioned above. There is no comparison made with later Syriac writers, nor with Armenian and Coptic, or with Greek and Latin Church Fathers. However, the present work opens up the way for such studies.

# LIST OF ABBREVIATIONS

**Syriac Texts**

| | |
|---|---|
| Abr Kid | hymni de Abraham Kidunaya, in: *Des Heiligen Ephraem des Syrers Hymnen auf Abraham Kidunaya und Julianos Saba*, ed. and tr. by E. Beck (CSCO 322/323; SS 140/141; Louvain 1972 ). |
| Acts of Thomas | *Apocryphal Acts of the Apostles* I-II, ed. and tr. by W. Wright (London 1871 ). |
| Aphr | *Aphraatis Sapientis Persae, Demonstrationes*, ed. and tr. by J. Parisot, PS I (Paris 1894); PS II (Paris 1907), 1-489. |
| Azym | hymni de azymis, in: *Des Heiligen Ephraem des Syrers Paschahymnen* (de azymis, de crucifixione, de resurrectione), ed. and tr. by E. Beck (CSCO 248/249; SS 108/109; Louvain 1964). |
| C | Codex Curetonianos. |
| CDiat | *Commentaire de L'Evangile Concordant* I-II, ed. and tr. by L. Leloir (Louvain 1963; 1990). |
| CGen | *Sancti Ephraem Syri in Genesim et in Exodum Commentarium*, ed. and tr. by R.-M. Tonneau (CSCO 153/153; SS 71/72; Louvain 1955). |
| CEx | *Sancti Ephraem Syri in Genesim et in Exodum Commentarium*, ed. and tr. by R.-M. Tonneau (CSCO 153/153; SS 71/72; Louvain 1955). |
| Crucif | hymni de crucifixione, in: *Des Heiligen Ephraem des Syrers Paschahymnen* (de azymnis, de crucifixione, de resurrectione), ed. and tr. by E. Beck (CSCO 248/249; SS 108/109; Louvain 1964). |
| Dom | *Des Heiligen Ephraem des Syrers Sermo de Domino Nostro*, ed. and tr. by E. Beck (CSCO 270/271; SS 116/117; Louvain 1966). |
| Eccl | *Des Heiligen Ephraem des Syrers Hymnen de Ecclesia*, ed. and tr. by E. Beck (CSCO 198/199; SS 84/85; Louvain 1960). |

| | |
|---|---|
| Epiph | hymni de epiphania, in: *Des Heiligen Ephraem des Syrers Hymnen de Nativitate (Epiphania)*, ed. and tr. by E. Beck (CSCO 186/187; SS 82/83; Louvain 1959). |
| Fid | *Des Heiligen Ephraem des Syrers Hymnen de Fide*, ed. and tr. by E. Beck (CSCO 154/155; SS 73/74; Louvain 1955). |
| H | Harklean. |
| Haer | *Des Heiligen Ephraem des Syrers Hymnen contra Haereses*, ed. and tr. by E. Beck (CSCO 169/170; SS 76/77; Louvain 1957). |
| Hebd | *Ephraem Syrus. Sermones in Hebdomadam Sanctam*, ed. and tr. by E. Beck (CSCO 412/413; SS 181/182; Louvain 1979). |
| Iei | *Des Heiligen Ephraem des Syrers Hymnen de Ieiunio*, ed. and tr. by E. Beck (CSCO 246/247; SS 106/107; Louvain 1964). |
| Jul Sab | hymni de Juliano Saba, in: *Des Heiligen Ephraem des Syrers Hymnen auf Abraham Kidunaya und Julianos Saba*, ed. and tr. by E. Beck (CSCO 322/323; SS 140/141; Louvain 1972). |
| Nachträge | *Nachträge zu Ephraem Syrus*, ed. and tr. by E. Beck (CSCO 363/364; SS 159/160; Louvain 1975). |
| Nat | *Des Heiligen Ephraem des Syrers Hymnen de Nativitate (Epiphania)*, ed. and tr. by E. Beck (CSCO 186/187; SS 82/83; Louvain 1959). |
| Nis | *Des Heiligen Ephraem des Syrers Carmina Nisibena* I-II, ed. and tr. by E. Beck (CSCO 218/219; 240/241; SS 92/93; 102/103; Louvain 1961; 1963). |
| Odes of Solomon | *The Odes of Solomon*, ed. and tr. by J. H. Charlesworth (Montana 1977). |
| P | Peshitta |
| Parad | *Des Heiligen Ephraem des Syrers Hymnen de Paradiso und contra Julianum*, ed. and tr. by E. Beck (CSCO 174/175; SS 78/79; Louvain 1957). |
| Resurr | hymni de resurrectione, in: *Des Heiligen Ephraem des Syrers Paschahymnen (de azymnis, de crucifixione, de resurrectione)*, ed. and tr. by E. Beck (CSCO 248/249; SS 108/109; Louvain 1964). |

| | |
|---|---|
| S | Codex Sinaiticus. |
| I Serm | *Des Heiligen Ephraem des Syrers Sermones I*, ed. and tr. by E. Beck (CSCO 305/306; SS 130/131; Louvain 1970). |
| II Serm | *Des Heiligen Ephraem des Syrers Sermones II*, ed. and tr. by E. Beck (CSCO 311/312; SS 134/135; Louvain 1970 ). |
| IIISerm | *Des Heiligen Ephraem des Syrers Sermones III*, ed. and tr. by E. Beck (CSCO 320/321; SS 138/139; Louvain 1972 ). |
| IV Serm | *Des Heiligen Ephraem des Syrers Sermones IV*, ed. and tr. by E. Beck (CSCO 334/335; SS 148/149; Louvain 1973 ). |
| SFid | *Des Heiligen Ephraem des Syrers Sermones de Fide*, ed. and tr. by E. Beck (CSCO 212/213; SS 88/89; Louvain 1961). |
| Sog | Soghyatha, in: *Des Heiligen Ephraem des Syrers Hymnen de Nativitate (Epiphania)*, ed. and tr. by E. Beck (CSCO 186/187; SS 82/83; Louvain 1959). |
| Virg | *Des Heiligen Ephraem des Syrers Hymnen de Virginitate*, ed. and tr. by E. Beck (CSCO 223/224; SS 94/95; Louvain 1962 ). |

**Other Abbreviations**

| | |
|---|---|
| AOF | *Altorientalische Forschungen*, Akademie der Wissenschaften der DDR. Zentralinstitut für Alte Geschichte und Archäologie. Berlin 1974. |
| Aram | *Aram Periodical*, Aram Society for Syro-Mesopotamian Studies. Oxford, 1989. |
| Bull Hist Med | *Bulletin for the History of Medicine*. 1968. |
| BZNW | *Beihefte zur Zeitschrift für die neutestamentliche Wissenschaft und die Kunde der Älteren Kirche*. Berlin/Giesen, 1923. |
| CSCO | *Corpus Scriptorum Christianorum Orientalium*. Paris/Louvain, 1903. |
| FMS | *Frühmittelalterliche Studien*. Berlin, 1967. |
| Gesnerus | Vierteljahresschrift herausgegeben von der Schweizerischen Gesellschaft für Geschichte der Medizin und der Naturwissenschaften. Aarau 1943. |

| | |
|---|---|
| JSPS | *Journal for the Study of the Pseudepigrapha*, Supplement Series. Sheffield. |
| NTS | *New Testament Studies*. Cambridge, 1954. |
| Numen | *International Review for the History of Religions*. Leiden, 1954. |
| OBO | *Orbis Biblicus et Orientalis*. Fribourg/Göttingen, 1973. |
| OCA | *Orientalia Christiana Analecta*. Rome, 1935. |
| OS | *Orientalia Suecana*. Stockholm, 1952. |
| PdO | *Parole de l'Orient*. Kaslik (Liban), 1970. |
| PS | *Patrologia Syriaca*. Paris, 1894-1926. 3 vols. |
| REA | *Revue des Études Arméniennes*. Paris, 1964. |
| SS | Scriptores Syri, CSCO. Paris/Louvain 1903. |
| ThLZ | *Theologische Literaturzeitung*. Leipzig 1876. |
| Traditio | *Studies in Ancient and Medieval History, Thought, and Religion*. Fordham University Press: New York, 1943. |
| ZKG | *Zeitschrift für Kirchengeschichte*. Gotha 1877-1930; Stuttgart 1931. |

# 1 INTRODUCTION

Looking at the whole of modern scholarly work on Syriac literature, we find hardly any publication on the concept of spiritual sickness and healing. Concerning natural medicine, drugs, diseases and ordinary physicians in Syriac literature we have the edition and translation of the Syriac 'Book of Medicines' by E. A. W. Budge,[1] the book of A. O Whipple,[2] and a few articles by R. Degen, M. Dols, R. F. Hau, M. Maroth, J. Nasrallah, M. Ullmann and S. A. Vardanyan.[3] The presence of healing imagery in early Syriac

---

[1] E. A. W. Budge, *Syrian Anatomy, Pathology and Therapeutics or 'The Book of Medicines"* I, II (London 1913). The anonymous author divides the 'Book of Medicine' in three sections. The first section, as lectures, is about human anatomy, pathology and therapeutics and contains prescriptions for the various related diseases. Budge points out that these lectures were translated from Greek into Syriac, and are based fundamentally on Hippocratic medicine. Some of the nearly one thousand prescriptions are of Egyptian, Persian or Indian origin, and others are attributed to Galen, Dioskorides, Solon, Philo, Theodoretus. Several parts have since been shown to be translations of Galen's medicinal works. The second section is astrological in character, containing for example omens, portents and divinations. The third section has four hundred prescriptions which 'illustrate the folk-lore of a part of Mesopotamia, and preserve a number of popular beliefs and legends about birds, animals, magical roots' (Budge, I. iii-ix).

[2] A. O. Whipple, *The Role of the Nestorians and Muslims in the History of Medicine* (Princeton 1967).

[3] R. Degen, 'Ein Corpus Medicorum Syriacorum', *Medizin historisches Journal* (Hildesheim) 7 (1972), 114-22; - 'Das Verzeichnis der Schriften des Hippokrates in der überlieferung des Barhebraeus. Ein kritischer Bericht', *Festgabe J. Assfalg*, 79-88. M. Dols, 'The origins of the Islamic hospital: myth and reality', *Bull Hist Med* 61 (1987), 367-90; - 'Syriac into Arabic: the transmission of Greek medicine', *Aram* 1:1 (1989), 45-52. R. F. Hau, ☞

Christianity has been recognized by certain scholars, such as R. Murray[4] and S. P. Brock,[5] and M. F. G. Parmentier has published an article about the aspect of 'non-medical ways of healing in Eastern Christendom',[6] but until the end of the twentieth century no research has been done on its outstanding significance.

This dissertation on Ephrem's healing theology is the first of its kind in Syriac literature. It presents Ephrem's theological healing imagery, prefaced by briefer accounts of the healing terminology of the *Odes of Solomon*, the *Acts of Thomas* and Aphrahat's *Demonstrations*. Among the early Syriac writers, Ephrem is doubtless the greatest. He uses healing terminology to describe the theological process of salvation, looking back at man's Fall from Paradise and looking forward to his eschatological restoration in good health by the divine economy. Indeed the concept of healing is not the only one through which the history of salvation can be explored and plausibly explained, but it is very significant, for it provides a convenient analogy - particularly for Ephrem - placing the divine salvation of humanity between the poles of the state of present sickness and eschatological good health. In this work there is no comparison made with the Greek and Latin Church Fathers whose medical imagery has been studied by a number of scholars. It is hoped that this book will contribute not only to the medical-theological understanding of the ancient writers and Church Fathers in general, but furthermore that it will provide material that will contribute to a healthy spiritual life today, considering Jesus

---

'Gondeschapur - eine Medizinschule aus dem 6. Jahrh. nach Chr.', *Gesnerus* 36 (1979), 98-115. M. Maroth, 'Ein Fragment eines syrischen pharmazeutischen Rezeptbuches aus Turfan', *AOF* 11 (1984), 115-25. J. Nasrallah, 'Médecins melchites de l'époque ayyubide', *PdO* 5 (1974), 189-200. M. Ullmann, 'Yuhanna ibn Sarabiyun. Untersuchungen zur überlieferung seiner Werke, Medizin-historisches Jahrbuch 6 (1971), 278-96. S. A. Vardanyan, 'Ancient Armenian traslationss of the works of Syrian Physicians', *REA* 16 (1982), 213-19.

[4] R. Murray, *Symbols of Church and Kingdom* (Cambridge 1975), 199-203.

[5] S. P. Brock, Spirituality in the Syriac Tradition, *Māran 'Ethā'* 2 (Kottayam 1989), 41-42.

[6] M. F. G. Parmentier, 'Non-medical ways of healing in Eastern Christendom', in *Fructus Centesimus: Mélanges offerts à G. J. M. Bartelink* (ed. A. A. R. Bastiaensen and others; Dordrecht, 1989), 279-95.

Christ as the Medicine of Life in the way that Ephrem understood the Saviour.

Health and sickness have been experienced by almost every human being. Medicine, healing and health care not only concern our world today, but also concerned the ancient world. The concept of health and disease has changed over time. New techniques and new approaches to health care have altered the relationship of medicine to medical ethics and religion. In the last few hundred years scientific knowledge about the nature of disease and the remarkable progress in the biological sciences, chemistry, physiology, etc., has professionalized medical technology more than ever. Particularly in the twentieth century, clinical academic departments and laboratories have been established in universities and hospitals for performing such research. The result of their work has improved the physical health of modern industrialised societies enormously.[7]

Furthermore, besides clinical medicine for physical diseases we also find some other highly qualified disciplines for treating invisible sicknesses, such as psychiatry, psychology and pathology. Having such skilled and specialised physicians, psychologists, sociologists, etc., for treating physical, mental and psychological disorders, what can be the role of spiritual medicine today, where can it be placed, and what is its relationship to the others?

The ancient world came to various answers concerning the place of medicine within society. This can be seen from numerous studies on the ancient texts, on medical treatises, the Bible and the

---

[7] The beginning of scientific medicine goes back to natural philosophy, and is associated especially with Isaac Newton and others, and their interpretations of the Aristotelean elements of earth, fire, and water. René Descartes considered a mechanical law behind all material things, including the human body. Based on this, the mechanical process of the body has been analyzed, and until today the cell, atoms, molecules and genes of the human body are a central object under microscopic research in laboratories. For scientific medicine, see C. Booth, 'History of science in medicine', in G. Teeling-Smith (ed.), *Science in medicine: how far has it advanced?* (London 1993), 11-22; I. Illich, *Limits to medicine. Medical nemesis: the expropriation of health* (Middlesex 1977); T. McKeown, *The origins of human disease* (Oxford 1988); D. J. Weatheral, *Science and the quiet art. The role of research medicine* (New York 1995).

Church Fathers. Both health and sickness can have their place in a religious, philosophical and medical sphere. In the ancient civilizations, health and disease were frequently associated with deities, and often magic and medicine went hand in hand. The Indian work 'Atharva-Veda' contains prayers against many diseases. In China, health and disease are incorporated into the philosophy of the Tao and the two polar principles, the *yin* and the *yang*. In ancient Egypt, men believed that pain and sickness are caused by the gods and goddesses, and evil spirits. For example, the Egyptian goddess Isis appears as a healer and her name is invoked against all kind of sicknesses.[8]

In 1924, W. R. Rivers discussed the inter-relationship of physicians, miracle-workers and magicians in the ancient world and observed that all three are seeking to overcome a disease by abstracting some evil factor from the physical body or by treating something external that has been connected with the body.[9] H. C. Kee studied the aspect of Medicine in Graeco-Roman culture and investigated the inter-relationship and difference between medicine, miracles and magic in New Testament times.[10] As Kee and O. Temkin emphasize, Galen's (130-200 A. D.) medical philosophy,[11] based on Hippocrates (460-370 B.C.), greatly influenced the

---

[8] Diodorus Siculus, Loeb Classical Library 1.25.3-7, tr. by C. H. Oldfather (London 1933). Diodorus Siculus attributes not only magical healing to the Isis cult, but says that according to the Egyptians 'she was the discoverer of many health-giving drugs and was greatly versed in the science of healing'. The Egyptian physicians were skilled in their medicine, had a certain scientific and anatomical knowledge. They were respected in the community and their position was one of great importance and dignity (Budge, cxxxii-cxxxiii.). However, Egyptian medicine, even though famous in the ancient world, did not develop as later Hippocratic medicine did.

[9] W. H. R. Rivers, *Medicine, Magic and Religion* (London 1924), vii.

[10] H. C. Kee, *Medicine, Miracle and Magic in New Testament Times* (Cambridge 1986).

[11] Galen, *Adhortatio ad Artes Addiscendas*, tr. by J. Walsh, 'Galen's Exhortation to the Study of the Arts, Especially Medicine', in *Medical Life* 37 (1930), 507-29; - *On Anatomical Procedures*, intr. and tr. by C. Singer (London 1956); - *Medical Experiences*, tr. by R. Walzer (Oxford 1944).

subsequent history of medicine, in both the medieval Arab world and in the post-medieval West.[12]

Hippocrates (460-370 B.C.), called the 'Father of Medicine', taught in the medical school in Cos. His disciples wrote nearly 60 treatises on clinical, theoretical and medical subjects which are reflected in the so called 'Hippocratic' corpus of medicine. Among the most famous are the treatises 'Airs, Waters, and Places', and 'Epidemics' and 'Regimen'.[13] At the time of Hippocrates, medicine was strongly related to the ministrations of the gods. The split between medicine and religion can be found later in the Hellenistic times.[14] Hippocrates developed a healing science (τεχνμ ιατρικμ) with an intellectual approach and methodology. His theory sought to explain the phenomena of health and illness. Disease was caused by an imbalance of the four bodily humors: blood, phlegm, yellow bile and black bile, or hot, cold, moist and dry. The physician's goal, using his skill, was to correct the imbalance, restoring a healthy balance through the use of diet, rest, exercise and and the prescribing of certain drugs. This healing 'techne' was secular, based on natural intellectual methods, and natural powers believed to exist in every human being and nature.[15]

---

[12] Kee, *Medicine, Miracle and Magic in New Testament Times*, 3; O. Temkin, *Galenism: Rise and Decline of a Medical Philosophy* (Ithaca, New York 1973). Galen's medicine was translated into Syriac, and then into Arabic. For Syriac translations of Galen, see R. Degen, 'Galen im Syrischen: eine Übersicht über die syrische Überlieferung der Werke Galens', in V. Nutton (ed.), *Galen: Problems and Prospects* (London 1981), 131-166. As an example of an Arabic translation, see P. Bachmann, 'Galens Abhandlung darüber, daß der vorzügliche Arzt Philosoph sein muß', in *Nachrichten der Akademie der Wissenschaften in Göttingen* (1/1965), 1-67.

[13] Hippocrates, tr. by W. H. S. Jones. Loeb Classical Library (London 1923); - *Concerning Airs*, 1, 71-117; - *Epidemics* I, 1, 146-211; - *Precepts*, 1, 313-33; - *On Regimen*, 2, 57-126.

[14] L. Edelstein, 'Greek Medicine in its Relation to Religion and Magic', in *Ancient Medicine* (Baltimore 1967), 217-46.

[15] For the 'Hippocratic Oath' see K. Deichgräber, *Medicus gratiosus* (Wiesbaden 1970); L. Edelstein, *The Hippocratic Oath* (Baltimore 1943); - 'The professional ethics of the Greek physician', in *Bull Hist Med* 30 (1956), 391-419; G. Harig and J. Kollesch, 'Der Hippokratische Eid', in *Philologus* 122 (1978), 157-76; W. H. S. Jones, *The Doctor's Oath* (Cambridge 1924). After the death of Alexander the Great in 323 B.C., Hippocrates'

☞

This system conflicts with that of ancient religious healers, physician-seers (*iatromanteis*) and in particular the cult of Asclepius who, from the fifth century onward, gradually became the god of medicine. Asclepius is mentioned in the *Iliad* (2.728-33), in Homer's description of the ships and their leaders assembling for the attack on Troy, and in Pindar's Pythian Ode. According to Pindar's *Pythian Ode* (III. 47-53), Asclepius was honoured as a divine healer, and at Pergamum and Cos there were medical schools as well as shrines where the sick awaited his divine visitations.[16] In the year 292 B. C, Rome and the surrounding countryside were struck by the plague. After they consulted their oracles, they went to Epidauros to bring Asclepius to Rome. Arriving in Rome, sacrifices, incense and perfumes were offered on altars, where Asclepius appeared in the form of a serpent.[17]

---

medicine was developed further in Alexandria, the chief cultural and commercial center. Here medical literature was added to the famous library of Alexandria, and famous scholars such as Herophilus of Chalcedon and Erasistratus of Cos carried out systematic medical research. Later Praxagoras of Cos pointed out the need for definition and an explanation of health and sickness and searched for theoretical knowledge in medicine. In contrast, the Empiricists, led by Herophilus doubted medical speculations and theories; instead, they had faith in practical experience at the bedside.

[16] Kee, *Miracle in the Early Christian World* (New Haven 1983), 78-108; see also the same author, *Medicine, Miracle and Magic in New Testament Times*, 27. For earlier works on Asclepius see E. J. and L. Edelstein, *Asclepius: Testimonies* (Baltimore 1945); W. A. Jayne, *The Healing Gods of Ancient Civilization* (New Haven 1925); C. Kerenyi, *Asklepios: Archetypal Image of the Physician's Existence* (New York 1959). See also L. Wells, 'The Greek language of healing from Homer to New Testament times', in *BZNW* 83 (Berlin 1998). Wells studied the healing cult of Asclepius from fifth century B. C. until fourth century A. D. in four famous places: Epidauros as pilgrimage; Athens as the state of cult; Cos and its famous medical school; and finally Pergamon as the place of Galen and a historical cult (see Wells, 34ff.).

[17] See Livy, *From the Founding of the City* 10.47; 11; Ovid, *Metamorphoses* 15.625-724. Kee says that 'Asklepios was viewed simultaneously as the patron of physicians and as the beneficient god who acted directly to heal suppliants' (Kee, *Medicine, Miracle and Magic in New Testament Times*, 4).

From the time of Homer onwards, the physician was considered as a craftman (δημιουϱγος, *Odyssey* 17.383) who performed his skill publicly for man's benefit.[18] In Rome, the most famous physician was Galen of Pergamon (130-200 A.D.) who carried out anatomical dissections and physiological experiments on animals. With his hundreds of treatises, Galen's medical knowledge, based on Hippocrates, was used until nearly the end of the Middle Ages. Side by side with the concept of spiritual healing in Christianity, physicians such as Oribasius (4th century), Aetius of Amida, Alexander of Tralles (6th century) and Paul of Aegina (7th century), compiled and preserved ancient medical knowledge, based on Galen's experiments.[19]

The Bible, even though not a scientific book, contains some valuable information about ancient sickness and medicine. In the early twentieth century, the medical doctor J. Preuss studied Biblical and Talmudic medicine.[20] His concern was not the theological medical imagery, but rather he looked at physical sicknesses, drugs and the role of ordinary physicians in biblical times. He points out that basically there is no 'Talmudic medicine' ('Medizin des Talmuds') to be compared to Galen's medicine, nor is there any 'Judaistic medicine' similar to Egyptian or Greek medicine. According to him, the first Jewish physicians who studied medicine were Arabs.[21]

In the Bible, scholars also looked at the aspect of spiritual healing and its relationship to ordinary medicine. S. Noorda finds a positive attitute to ordinary physicians and medicine for the first time in Ben Sira 38:1-15, where the function of a physician is incorporated within a religious context.[22] Ben Sira valued the role

---

[18] L. Cohn-Haft, *The Public Physician of Ancient Greece* (Northampton 1956), 11-18.

[19] Temkin, *Galenism: Rise and Decline of a Medical Philosophy* (Ithaca, New York 1973).

[20] J. Preuss, *Biblisch-talmudische Medizin* (Berlin 1911). He considered not only the results of others' work before him (see Preuss, iii-iv), but also the whole Bible and a wide range of Talmudic literature.

[21] *Preuss*, 3.

[22] S. Noorda, 'Illness and sin, forgiving and healing: the connection of medical treatment and religious beliefs in Ben Sira 38:1-15', in M. J. Vermaseren (ed.), *Studies in Hellenistic Religions* (Leiden 1979), 215-24.

of the ordinary physician for 'also him God has appointed' and 'from God the physician gets his wisdom' (Ben Sira 38:1-2). In Ben Sira, the physician has an intermediate function; healing can be achieved through faithful prayer and the physician's skill or wisdom. Noorda emphasises that having the physician's skill and wisdom added to faith is an 'impact of Hellenistic culture and sciences on traditional Jewish beliefs in second century Palestine'.[23] Ben Sira has not ignored Jewish tradition and biblical faith, that God's creation is good, and human freedom of choice is able to produce evil, that it is sin which causes illness, and forgiveness brings healing. However, certain injuries were allowed to be treated by an ordinary physician - even though there was a fear that ordinary medicine was associated with magic and foreign religion.[24]

L. P. Hogan points out that at the time of Ben Sira Israelite medicine must have gone far beyond the stage of the treatment of external wounds, and made use of Hippocratic medicine. In order to justify the role of the ordinary physician in Jewish society, Ben Sira portrays the ideal Jewish physician to be an instrument of God's healing purpose.[25] Hogan points out that illness was accepted as God's punishment for the sins of an individual or of the People, and that the ultimate healer is God. Only Job's critics and some of the Psalms (Ps 6; 28; 30; 38 41; 88; 103) objected 'that illness is always the result of sin'.[26] Furthermore, he refers not only to the healing aspect in Ben Sira, but to the whole of Hebrew Scripture in general, including the Apocrypha and Pseudepigrapha, and the New Testament, Dead Sea Scrolls, Philo of Alexandria and Josephus. He concludes, that in the second Temple Period there are five causes of illness: 'These five are 1) God, for His own purposes, 2) intermediaries of God, 3) evil spirits (devils, fallen angels, Satan), 4) the stars and their movements and 5) sin'.[27] Likewise he outlines five 'means' of healing, considering 'God as

---

[23] Noorda, 215.

[24] Cf. J. Hempel, 'Ich bin der Herr, dein Arzt', in *ThLZ* 82 (1957), 809-826.

[25] L. P. Hogan, *Healing in the Second Temple Period* (Freiburg 1992), 38-48.

[26] *Hogan*, 25. Hogan distinguishes between 'sickness' that can be 'healed' and 'illness' that can be 'cured' (see Hogan, 1-2).

[27] *Hogan*, 302-05.

the ultimate Source of healing as well as the ultimate Source of illness. These means are: 1) faith and prayer, 2) exorcism or apotropaic means, 3) virtuous living, 4) physicians, scientific and folk medicine and 5) magical means'.[28]

Studying the concept of spiritual healing in the Old Testament, H. C. Kee worked on the biblical stories of healing, signs and wonders, Jahweh's function as Healer and His relation to human physicians, including the patriarchs and prophets. Kee emphasises that healing, signs and wonders focus on the divine destiny of the covenant people, and they are identified as God's actions on behalf of Israel. Ezekiel's prophecy of the renewal of nature is 'healing' (Ez 47:8-12).[29] Kee compares Ben Sira's view of healing with that of Pliny. While Pliny attributes the power of plants to their nature as 'self-originating', Ben Sira accepts nature, and so the power of plants as medicine 'out of the earth', as God's creation, and consequently God as the provider of medicine.[30] Referring to G. Vermes, Kee also draws attention to the Book of Tobit where demons and exorcism are linked to sickness and death,[31] and he considers Josephus, who depicts the medical skill of the Essenes, as an author who manifests the influence of Hellenistic medical tradition and belief in the link between demons and sickness.[32] According to Josephus, there is no negative attitute towards medicine, as in the older biblical tradition, for the Jewish people were engaging in medicine, miracles and magic. The Essenes used two modes of healing: medicine and exorcism, whereby the factor of forgiveness of sins was included.[33]

D. W. Amundsen published eleven of his essays in the book 'Medicine Society, and Faith in the Ancient and Medieval Worlds'. Chapters 5 to 7 could be considered as the most important. In

---

[28] *Hogan*, 305-310.

[29] Kee, *Medicine, Miracle and Magic in New Testament Times*, 9-14.

[30] Kee, *Medicine*, 20-21. According to Pliny the Elder, Natural History xxiii.1, healing is provided by the right use of natural medicine, as the Greeks speak of 'sympathia' and 'antipathia'.

[31] Tob 2:10; 6:7-16; 8:1-3; 11:8-14. See G. Vermes, *Jesus the Jew* (New York 1973), 61; Kee, *Medicine*, 21.

[32] Kee, *Medicine* 23; see Antiquities 8.136.

[33] IQ GenAp 20:12-29; 4QOrNab; Kee has own definition of medicine, miracle and magic, see Kee's *Medicine*, 3-4; 24-25.

chapter five, 'Medicine and Faith in Early Christianity', Amundsen outlines the relationship between natural medicine and Christian theology, based on the doctrines of various Church Fathers. Some of them believed that diseases are a result of a natural cause, others considered the source of illnesses to be supernatural. However, the Christian writers' view differs from that of the pagans, for Christians believed in an omnipotent God Who loves everyone. Amundsen emphasises that the early Christian writers based their view on biblical tradition, but they - the Greek and Latin Church Fathers - approached it from their own Hellenistic-philosophical background. Therefore, there have been different ways of bringing these traditions together, and this can also be seen in the aspect of Hellenistic medicine and its incorporation into Christian belief. While Tatian and Arnobius (including Marcion) rejected medicine altogether, other early Christian writers accepted its place within Christianity.[34] However, they consider God, Who can also heal without the use of means, to be the Fountain of Healing. When ordinary physicians have failed, the Church Fathers draw attention to miraculous divine healing, such as the healing of Gregory Nazianzen's father[35] and Gregory of Nyssa's sister.[36]

Basil considers physical suffering, sickness and healing as a mirror for spiritual sickness and the medicine of the soul. God allows man to fall ill and suffer so that he may become aware of the need of spiritual healing. Physical sickness can be a punishment for man's sin and it calls for repentance, so that man does not sin further and become wounded spiritually, as, for example, through

---

[34] D. W. Amundsen, *Medicine, Society, and Faith in the Ancient and Medieval Worlds* (Baltimore 1996), 127-157. These are the writers to whom he refers: Clement (ca. 150 - 215), Origen (ca. 184 - 253); the Cappadocian fathers: Basil (ca. 329 - 379), Gregory Nazianzen (ca. 330 - 390), Gregory of Nyssa (ca. 335 - 394); John Chrysostom (ca. 349 - 407); Augustine (354 - 430), Ambrose of Milan (339 - 397), Jerome (ca. 345 - 420); Tertullian; Tatian, Arnobius, Marcion.

[35] Amundsen quotes from from Gregory Nazianzen, *On the Death of His Father*, 28-29.

[36] Amundsen refers to Gregory of Nyssa, *The Life of St. Macrina*; Jerome, *Life of St. Hilarion* 14,15; Augustine, *City of God* 22.8. Chapter six of Amundsen's book is on 'Tatian's «Rejection» of Medicine in the Second Century', 158-174.

pride.[37] Likewise Gregory Nazianzen, John Chrysostom and Jerome consider physical illness in the same way, and its benefit can be man's spiritual healing.[38]

H. J. Frings studied the aspect of medicine and the role of physicians in the early Greek patristic texts up to John Chrysostom.[39] He defines the function of medicine and physicians according to the patristic texts, and refers to the inter-relationship of theology and herbal medicine, as well as of spiritual healers and ordinary physicians. Medical art is considered to be good, and it is used as an argument against heresies, i.e. Manichaeans. Frings pointed out that medicine was seen as part of God's creation that is good and for man's benefit. God grants physical skills to man in order to make use of the power of medicinal herbs. Likewise He grants the gift of Healing (the physician's art) to certain people to show that human beings need and depend on each other.[40]

In his article 'Christus als Arzt. Ursprünge und Wirkungen eines Motivs', G. Fichtner argues very clearly against those who maintain that early Christianity had a hostile attitude towards scientific medicine, and that faith and science exclude each other in general.[41] In three sections, Fichtner shows how the early Christians understood sickness, the way they treated it, and how they incorporated Hellenistic medicine into the concept of theological healing. He points out that 'Christ as Physician' has been understood in two ways: metaphorically and in reality, as He is the Physician *par excellence.* Furthermore, Fichtner argues that Hippocratic medicine was not completely free from religious thought. Since Christianity has grown up in a Hellenistic culture where the role of a physician was highly respected, theological thought was influenced by Hellenism in general, as can be seen in John's prologue, Christ as the λογος. Galen's understanding of the

---

[37] Amundsen, 137. See Basil, *The Long Rules* 55.

[38] See Amundsen, 137-38, and the bibliography given there.

[39] H. J. Frings, *Medizin und Arzt bei den griechischen Kirchenvätern bis Chrysostomos* (Bonn 1959).

[40] Frings, 8-11.

[41] See G. Fichtner, 'Christus als Arzt. Ursprünge und Wirkungen eines Motivs', *FMS* 16 (1982), 1-18. By name, Fichtner only mentions the article of Matoušek, 'Zur Frage des Verhältnisses der Urchristentums zur Medizin' (1960).

cause of sickness differs from the biblical Jewish point of view: instead of sin, Galen sees the cause of sickness to be imbalance in the human body. Referring to the Gospel, such as Jn 9:1-3, Fichtner points out that the Christians did not look for the cause of sickness any more, but rather for its spiritual meaning. In order to show the significant role of sick people in the early Christian community, Fichtner draws attention to the Christians' charitable work, diakonia (Acts 6:1-7; Rom 16:1), which led to activities such as those of Bishop Basil who built a place for the sick (nosokomeion) in Caesarea around 370 A.D. Finally, Fichtner looks for biblical and early Christian sources (Ignatius of Antioch, the *Act of John*, Justin, Tertullian, Actantius, Arnobius, Clemens of Alexandria, Hieronymus, Augustine, Ambrosius) where healing terminology is used. As a result, Fichtner says that hardly anyone mentions Asclepius by name, but referring to K. H. Rengstorff (1953), he observes that there are some implications that conflict with Asclepius' healing cult and with Hellenistic philosophy, which resulted in the fully developed motif of Christ as the δωτηϱ and Healer in Christian theology.[42]

J. Hempel would agree with Fichtner that the concept of Jesus Christ as Healer and Physician has been understood in both ways, metaphorically and literally, but Hempel does not see such a Hellenistic influence in the Christus-medicus motif.[43] Hempel discusses the role of medicine in the religious culture of old Israel, and he looks at the conflict between demons and man's will to survive as well. Likewise, Hempel draws attention to Jahwe as the

---

[42] Fichtner, 11-12: 'So hat sich das Christus-medicus Motiv aus der einen Wurzel der zumeist verdeckten, selten offenen Auseinandersetzung zwischen dem Soter Asklepios und dem Heiland Christus heraus entwickelt und verselbständigt. ... Auch in der kynisch-stoischen Philosophie war der Arztvergleich sehr beliebt: so wie der Arzt die Leiden des Körpers heilt, so heilt der Philosoph die Leidenschaft der Seele. Voraussetzung dieses Vergleichs ist also eine dichotomische Anthropologie, eine strenge Teilung in Körper und Seele ([in the sense of] soma-sema, der Körper ist nur ein Grabmal, ein Gefängnis der Seele). ... Christus wird in der plastischen Kunst des 3. Jahrhunderts in Philosophentracht dargestellt.'

[43] J. Hempel, 'Heilung als Symbol und Wirklichkeit', in *Nachrichten der Akademie der Wissenschaften in Göttingen* (3/1958), 237-314.

One Who heals His People and the Good News of Jesus Christ as being the δωτηϱ Who saves and gives life. And, therefore, the Good News has been understood as being sound/healthy and demanding sound/healthy faith, as it can be found in the pastoral Epistles (1 Tim 1:10; 2 Tim 4:3; Tit 1:9; 2:1; 2:10ff) which imply the metaphorical sense of healing and its reality.[44]

In her recent publication *The Greek language of healing from Homer to New Testament times*, L. Wells has explored the use and meaning of Greek healing terminology in selected Greek sources from the fifth century B. C. until the fourth century A. D.[45] She studied the terms ʻυγιης, ιαομαι, θεϱαπευω, σωζω πασχω and their derivatives in the work of Homer, Septuagint, Philo of Alexandria, Josephus and the New Testament (Aramaic and Hebrew are excluded). Discussing Asclepius' healing cult in Epidaurus, Athens, Cos and Pergamon, Wells realised that these healing terms in literature and in inscriptions are uniform in meaning, and 'there shows a remarkable degree of consistency in the use of healing

---

[44] Hempel resumes (Hempel, 311): 'Was das biblische Schrifttum über Krankheit und Heilung berichtet oder erwartet, gehört nur am Rande in den Bereich rationaler Medizin. Fünfhundert Jahre nach Hippokrates verraten die Heilungserzählungen der Apostelgeschichte keinen Einfluß dieses Meisters auf den Verfasser, in dem doch die Tradition einen Arzt sehen will, und im Grunde steht es nicht anders, wenn wir die wissenschaftliche Medizin Ägypten zum Vergleich mit dem AT heranziehen. Die Heilkunde der AT gehört in den Zusammenhang mit der altorientalischen Volksmedizin, aber gerade auf deren Hintergrund zeigt sich ihre religionsgeschichtliche Sonderstellung. Sie konzentriert Krankmachen und Heilen auf ihren Gott, seinen Willen und seine (prophetischen) Werkzeuge, die sich im Töten und Heilen als solche legitimieren und seine souveräne Macht repräsentieren. Im eminenten Sinne gilt das für Jesus, in dessen Heilungen zugleich der Kampf Gottes gegen den (in der dualistischen Erweichung des strengen Monotheismus und seiner Ambivalenz Gottes tätig geglaubten) satanischen Gegenspieler sichtbar wird. Sie sind symbole des Gottessieges, wie die "Heilung" im AT bereits als Bild für die überwindung der "Krankheit" des Volkes in dem doppelten Sinne seiner Sünden und der durch sie bedingten äußeren, gottgewirkten Katastrophen genutzt wird.'

[45] L. Wells, *The Greek language of healing from Homer to New Testament times* (1998).

language by authors'.[46] However there is some difference in some of these words in Jewish writers, the Septuagint and the New Testament. In the Septuagint,[47] ειρηνη (peace) is used in preference to the Greek word ὑγίεια to describe health in order to include a strong spiritual emphasis in its notion of health and this 'appears to be akin to holistic health with a spiritual emphasis'.[48] In the Septuagint, θεραπεύω is not related to divine healing, except in Wisdom 16:12 when it refers to the healing λογος of God, but Philo of Alexandria uses it in the sense of 'to court and to worship, and it 'involves healing the soul as well as the body, incorporating spiritual mental, emotional and physical healing'.[49] Josephus uses the verb θεραπευω to mean 'to court' or 'flatter' in the context of bribery, political social life and human activity, but it can also mean 'to worship' and 'to serve' God, in a religious context.[50] Wells points out that Jesus' healing ministry (θεραπευω), along with that of teaching (διδασκων) and preaching (κμρυσσων) are evidence of His divinity. The synoptic authors prefer to use the term θεραπευω to describe Jesus' ministry and they link it to preaching and teaching. Wells says: 'Thus θεραπευω seems to be a description of a process which occurs when the gap between a human and God is closed, i.e. when an indivudual's sense of alienation and separation from God is destroyed, and that individual becomes aware of the presence of the kingdom (i. e. "God"), and inclusion in a new

---

[46] Wells, 100. For example, Wells says, 'υγιαινω is used in a holistic sense to indicate the general well-being and effective functioning of the state, family or individual' (Wells, 61).

[47] There is no difference in the use of ιαομαι that 'denotes the activity and nature of the Septuagint God, and on occasion, of his agents. It is the preferred verb in a healing context, and is the verb that is put into God's mouth when he speaks of healing. In this incidence and use it reflects the language of healing in the Greek world' (Wells, 108f.)

[48] Wells, 107.

[49] Wells 112-14: 'Thus to cure in the sense of θεραπευω is to strive for holistic health'. Philo understands θεραπευω primarily in a spiritual sense, referring to teaching or contemplating.

[50] Wells, 115-16. 'Thus Philo and Josephus' use of it (θεραπευω) in a secular context differs greatly from its use in a spiritual context. In a spiritual and teaching context the verb θεραπευω refers primarily to the health and well-being of the soul, and the nurturing of the God-human relationship.

spiritual community. In this way θεραπεύω is primarily a spiritual term, but it can have a holistic effect, affecting the physical, mental, and emotional state of a person, as well as a person's spiritual state.'[51] Wells argues that Luke, as a medical doctor, uses the term ἰάομαι more in a sense that could imply both a 'cure' and 'divine intervention' in its meaning, in order to avoid the notion of 'nature' or 'persuasion' implicit in θεραπεύω.[52] Otherwise, all four terms (υγιαινω, ιαομα, θεραπευω, σωζω) and their derivatives in the synoptic Gospels are used to depict the healing ministry of Jesus.

P. D. E. Knipp worked on the illustrations of the biblical healing miracles in the iconography of sarcophagi from the Theodosian era in the fourth and fifth centuries. He focuses on three miracles: giving sight to the man born blind (Jn 9), healing the woman with a haemorrhage (Lk 8:43-48), and healing the one who was sick for 38 years in Bethesda (Jn 5:1-9). The sarcophagi portray 'Christus medicus' in various ways, most probably based on different theological concepts - even though these cannot be identified precisely. According to Knipp, it is obvious that the Christian pictures are influenced by imperial language and art. The healing of the blind man is related to Jesus Christ as the Light of the world (φως, του κοσμου) and to Christian baptism (βαπτισμος).[53] The metaphor of light, sun (ηλιος), shows that healing means illumination of the soul, in contrast to darkness that is the cause of being spiritually sick. Thus, the healing of the man born blind is incorporated into the antique image of the light symbol in the myth and the cult of Helios and Sol. In the myth of Orion, Helios is the healer of the blind Orion.[54]

---

[51] Wells, 154-55.

[52] Wells, 155. It does not seem that Syriac can distinguish between ἰάομαι and θεραπευω (Syriac did not have the problem of Asclepius' religious cult as such), for basically both of these terms are rendered with ܐܣܝ. The Syriac verb equivalent to υγιαινω would be ܪܒܝ, and to σωζω it would be ܐܚܝ.

[53] P. D. E. Knipp, 'Christus medicus' in *der frühchristlichen Sarkophagskulptur: ikonographische Studien der Sepulkralkunst des späten vierten Jahrhunderts* (Leiden 1998), 34-39.

[54] Knipp, 34-53. For the healing of the woman with a haemorrhage whose iconography is greatly influenced by the theology of Ambrose, see Knipp, 90-139; for the healing miracle in Bethesda, see Knipp, 140-184.

R. Arbesmann, in his article 'The concept of «Christus medicus» in St. Augustine', points out that Augustine warns of the sickness of pride. God as the heavenly Physician humiliated Himself to heal man from the festering wound of pride which caused man's Fall from Paradise. Arbesmann argues that Augustine uses the image of the physician and healing for his salvation theology in order to emphasise the importance of the virtue of humility as the foundation of Christian life. Any disease can be healed by the 'cup of humility' which is drunk first by the divine Physician. God is able to heal and restore human nature, for He is its Creator. He wants to restore human nature to full health, even though He permits some after-effects of sin to cause pain to man's soul. From the second and third century onwards, Augustine's predecessors used the concept of healing to argue against the healing cult of Asclepius, the pagan healer and physician. Instead, based on the Gospel, the Church Fathers draw attention to Jesus Christ as the Healer of body and soul.[55]

O. Temkin has gone further and studied health and sickness in a specific Christian context, namely Asceticism.[56] He has looked at the relationship of the ascetic to his body, health and sickness. Referring to the life of St Antony, Temkin says: 'Antony's mode of life broke all the rules of Hippocratic hygiene. He and his fellow ascetics not only deviated from Hippocratic medicine but also believed that their deprivations returned man to his pristine condition before the Fall.'[57] Although the ascetics considered Jesus to be the perfect Healer of both soul and body, they did not have a hostile attitude towards the ordinary medicine and physician. In their opinion ordinary medicine and physical doctors were God's arrangements for the weak and for those without faith, because God does not want to destroy utterly sinful human beings. Temkin says: 'So far as ascetic doctrine can be summarized briefly, it can be said to have viewed complete reliance on God and Jesus in all disease, to the exclusion of all medical help, as ideal. The

[55] R. Arbesmann, 1-28.

[56] O. Temkin, Hippocrates in a world of Pagans and Christians (Baltimore 1991); chapter five is on 'Asceticism' (149-70), chapter six on 'Hippocratic Medicine and Spiritual Medicine' (171-177).

[57] Temkin, *Hippocrates in a World of Pagans and Christians*, 154.

fulfillment of this ideal could be expected of those who had reached perfection in their faith. For all others, laymen as well as monks, God had provided doctors and medicines as help in their weakness.'[58]

Finally, it can be said that Christianity adapted Hippocratic medicine to its theology and biblical belief. The function of pagan medicine has been altered in the light of faith. Medicine is considered to be given to mankind by God, and as the provider of medicine, both spiritual and physical, there remains God Who is the perfect Healer of humanity. It is in this sort of context that Ephrem developed his own understanding of healing.

---

[58] Temkin, *Hippocrates*, 160.

# 2 HEALING IMAGERY IN SOME OTHER WORKS

Before dealing with Ephrem's healing imagery, the concept of sickness and healing in three other Syriac works, all earlier than Ephrem, will be discussed. These are the *Odes of Solomon*, the *Acts of Judas Thomas the Apostle* and Aphrahat's *Demonstrations*. Among these the Odes of Solomon provides only a few references concerning our theme, whereas the *Acts of Thomas* and Aphrahat's *Demonstrations* are rich sources. *The Acts of Thomas*, which is basically a Christ-oriented missionary narrative, emphasises Jesus Christ as the Healer and Physician of mankind. Whereas the *Acts of Thomas* hardly makes use of any biblical text outside the Gospel, Aphrahat refers to the whole Bible and quotes a variety of references concerning sickness and healing.

## 2.1 The Odes of Solomon

The *Odes of Solomon*[1] do not provide any healing imagery, apart from twice when the terms 'sickness' (ܟܘܪܗܢܐ) and 'pain' (ܟܐܒܐ) are used, and once ܣܡ̈ܡܢܐ in the sense of 'poisons'.[2] The author uses the term 'sickness' once in the singular (ܟܘܪܗܢܐ) and once in the plural (ܟܘܪ̈ܗܢܐ). In Ode 18, the inspired Odist expresses his

---

[1] J. H. Charlesworth's edition and translation of *The Odes of Solomon* (Montana 1977) is mainly used here, but also following books have been taken in consideration: - H. Grimme, *Die Oden Solomos* (Heidelberg 1911); - J. R. Harris, *The Odes and Psalms of Solomon* (Cambridge 1911); - J. R. Harris and A. Mingana, *The Odes and Psalms of Solomon II* (London 1920); - M. Lattke, *Die Oden Solomos in ihrer Bedeutung für Neues Testament und Gnosis II* (Göttingen 1979).

[2] *Odes of Solomon*, 18.3; 19.7; 21.3; 25.9; 38.8.

joy about God who strengthened his 'limbs' (ܗܕܡ̈ܐ) and removed the 'sickness' (ܟܘܪܗܢܐ) from his 'body' (ܦܓܪܝ).

1 ܐܬܪܝܡ ܠܒܝ ܒܚܘܒܗ ܕܡܪܝܡܐ ܘܐܬܬܪܝ:
ܕܐܫܒܚܝܘܗܝ ܒܝܕ ܫܡܝ
2 ܐܬܚܝܠܘ ܗܕܡ̈ܝ:
ܐܝܟ ܕܠܐ ܢܦܠܘܢ ܡܢ ܚܝܠܗ.
3 ܟܘܪܗܢܐ ܐܬܪܚܩܘ ܡܢ ܦܓܪܝ:
ܘܩܡ ܠܡܪܝܐ ܒܨܒܝܢܗ:
ܡܛܠ ܕܫܪܝܪܐ ܗܝ ܡܠܟܘܬܗ.

1 My heart was lifted up and enriched in the love of the Most High,
so that I might praise Him with my name
2 My limbs were strengthened,
that they may not fall from His power.
3 Sicknesses fled from my body,
and it stood firm for the Lord by His will;
because His kingdom is firm/true.[3]

*Odes of Solomon, 18.1-3*

'Sicknesses' have been removed from the speaker's body and his limbs have received power. Both terms 'limbs' and 'my body' refer to physical sickness and healing, and do not specifically indicate spiritual healing. But, the fact that the Odist's heart is lifted up and he is pleased to praise the Lord by using his name, shows peace and health within.

The term 'body' (ܦܓܪܐ) also appears in Odes 22 and 39. While the former speaks positively about the dead bones that were covered with 'bodies' (ܦܓܪ̈ܐ) by the Lord's right hand,[4] the latter illustrates the negative effect of the Lord's power that snatches bodies and corrupts souls like strong rivers.[5]

---

[3] The verb 'and it stood for' (ܘܩܡ) is singular and refers to the term 'my body'. The other manuscript has the plural form 'and they stood for (ܘܩܡܘ) which refers to the 'sicknesses' (ܟܘܪ̈ܗܢܐ). See, R. Harris and A. Mingana, *The Odes and Psalms of Solomon* II, 295-98.

[4] *Odes of Solomon*, 22.7-9.

[5] *Odes of Solomon*, 39.1-3.

The word 'limbs' (ܗܕ̈ܡܐ) is used in seven further Odes.[6] The limbs, which are like the harp's strings, through which the Lord speaks, need to be restored and made healthy. If they collapse, they need the Lord's power and light to be strengthened,[7] for it is the Lord Who has formed man's limbs;[8] they belong to Him,[9] and need to be without pain and suffering.[10] Moreover, the limbs are elements that should rightly praise the Lord as the Odist says: 'I will praise and exalt Him with all my limbs'.[11] The singing and praising of the Lord affect the limbs, causing them to be pleased and anointed as with oil.[12]

In Ode 25, the Odist praises the Lord because of his personal experience of salvation and illumination. The Lord granted him redemption and honour, and He removed 'sickness' (ܟܘܪܗܢܐ) from him.

9 ܡܛܠ ܕܝܡܝܢܟ ܐܪܝܡܬܢܝ܆
ܘܐܥܒܪܬ ܟܘܪܗܢܐ ܡܢܝ.
10 ܘܗܘܝܬ ܫܠܝܛܐ ܒܫܪܪܟ܆
ܘܩܕܝܫܐ ܒܙܕܝܩܘܬܟ.

9 Because Your right hand exalted me,
and removed sickness from me,
10 and I became mighty in Your truth
and holy in Your righteousness.

*Odes of Solomon 25.9-10:*

6 *Odes of Solomon*, 3.2; 6.2,16; 8.14 (16); 17.16 (15); 21.4; 26.4; 40.3.

7 *Odes of Solomon*, 6.2: ܗܟܢܐ ܡܡܠܠܐ ܒܗܕ̈ܡܝ ܪܘܚܗ ܕܡܪܝܐ. ܘܡܡܠܠ ܐܢܐ ܒܚܘܒܗ. See also 6.16: ܘܗܕ̈ܡܐ ܕܢܦܝܠܝܢ ܗܘܘ܆ ܬܪ̈ܨܘ ܘܐܬܩܝܡܘ.

8 *Odes of Solomon*, 8.14(16): ܐܢܐ ܐܬܩܢܬ ܗܕ̈ܡܝܗܘܢ܆ ܘܬܕ̈ܝܐ ܕܝܠܝ ܛܝܒܬ ܠܗܘܢ܆ ܕܢܫܬܘܢ ܚܠܒܐ ܩܕܝܫܐ ܕܝܠܝ ܕܢܐܚܘܢ ܒܗ.

9 *Odes of Solomon*, 17.16 (15): ܡܛܠ ܕܗܘܘ ܠܝ ܗܕ̈ܡܐ܆ ܘܐܢܐ ܪܫܗܘܢ.

10 *Odes of Solomon*, 21.4: ܘܗܘܘ ܠܝ ܗܕ̈ܡܐ ܠܘܬ ܢܦܫܝ܆ ܟܕ ܠܐ ܐܝܬ ܒܗܘܢ ܟܐܒܐ܆ ܐܦܠܐ ܐܘܠܨܢܐ ܐܦܠܐ ܚ̈ܫܐ.

11 *Odes of Solomon*, 26.4: ܐܫܒܚܐ ܠܗܘܬܗ ܡܢ ܟܠ ܠܒܝ܆ ܐܫܒܚ ܘܐܪܘܪܒܝܘܗܝ ܡܢ ܟܠܗܘܢ ܗܕ̈ܡܝ.

12 *Odes of Solomon*, 40.3: ܘܠܒܝ ܚܠܐ [ܒ]ܬܫܒ̈ܘܚܘܗܝ܆ ܘܗܕܡܝܢ ܗ[ܕ̈ܡܝ] ܒ[ܫܠܝܘܬܐ ܕ]ܙܡܝܪ̈ܬܗ.

While Ode 18 provides a passive verb, 'sicknesses were held at a distance from my body' (ܟܘܪܗܢܐ ܐܬܪܚܩܘ ܡܢ ܦܓܪܝ), and sickness is attributed to the body, in contrast, Ode 25 mentions the person who causes the sickness to pass from the Odist: It is the hand of the Lord which removed sickness not just from a certain part of man, body or limbs, but from the entire person, 'from me' (ܡܢܝ). Likewise, Ode 18 speaks of 'my heart' (ܠܒܝ) that is lifted up, whereas in Ode 25 it is 'me' who is exalted. This indicates that the Odist speaks about his entire personality which is saved from sickness and is exalted. Being saved from sickness means being strong, holy and shining like light.[13] As at the beginning of Ode 25, the Odist also takes refuge in the Lord after being rescued from chains, so too in Ode 21, he praises the Lord who casts off his chains. He is saved, exalted and covered by light, for there is no 'pain' (ܟܐܒܐ), 'affliction' (ܐܘܠܨܢܐ) or 'suffering' (ܚܫܐ).

3 ܘܫܠܚܬ ܚܫܘܟܐ܆
ܘܠܒܫܬ ܢܘܗܪܐ
4 ܘܗܘܘ ܠܝ ܗܕܡܐ ܠܢܦܫܝ܆
ܟܕ ܠܐ ܐܝܬ ܒܗܘܢ ܟܐܒܐ܆
ܐܦܠܐ ܐܘܠܨܢܐ ܐܦܠܐ ܚܫܐ.
5 ܘܝܬܝܪܬܐ ܡܥܕܪܢܝܬܐ ܗܘܬ ܠܝ ܡܚܫܒܬܗ
ܕܡܪܝܐ܆
ܘܫܘܬܦܘܬܗ ܕܠܐ ܚܒܠܐ.

3 And I put off darkness,
and put on light.
4 And there became limbs to my soul,
while in them there was no pain,
neither affliction, nor suffering.
5 And abundantly helpful to me was the thought of the Lord,
and His incorruptible fellowship.

*Odes of Solomon 21.3-5*

13 For the term 'eye' (ܥܝܢܐ) and 'light' (ܢܘܗܪܐ) see *Odes of Solomon*, 5.5-6; 6.17; 7.14; 8.2; 10.1-6; 11.11-19; 12.3-7; 13.1; 14.1; 15.2-3; 16.9-15; 21.3-6; 25.5-7; 29.7; 32.1; 38.1; 41.6-14. For the word 'darkness' (ܚܫܘܟܐ) see *Odes of Solomon*, 5.5; 11.19; 15.2; 16.15-16; 18.6; 21.3; 42.16.

Obviously, thinking about the Lord and being guided by Him, means to be saved, restored and healthy. Inasmuch as suffering, affliction and pains are related to 'darkness' (ܚܫܘܟܐ), the thoughts about the Lord belong to the 'light' (ܢܘܗܪܐ). Coming out of the darkness is like no longer being sick or in pain (ܟܐܒܐ). Another form of the term 'pain' (ܟܐܒܐ) is used in Ode 19.7-8, where the author speaks about the Virgin giving birth without pain:

7 ܘܗܘܬ ܐܡܐ ܒܬܘܠܬܐ ܒܪ̈ܚܡܐ ܣܓܝܐܐ.
8 ܘܚܒܠܬ ܘܝܠܕܬ ܒܪܐ ܘܠܐ ܟܐܒ ܠܗ̇.
ܡܛܠ ܕܠܐ ܗܘܐ ܣܪܝܩܐܝܬ ܗܘܬ

7 So the Virgin became a mother with great mercies.
8 And she laboured and bore the son but without pain,
because it did not occur without purpose.

*Odes of Solomon 19.7-8*

When Eve transgressed the Lord's commandment, she was punished with pains in childbearing (cf. Gen 3.16). Here, in contrast, the Virgin gives birth without any pains. Both the Virgin giving birth and the childbearing free from pains are not natural. However, this can happen in agreement to the Lord's will through his 'mercies' (ܪ̈ܚܡܐ).

Finally, one might look at the term ܡܫܒ̈ܫܢܐ that is used once in Ode 38. This Ode, full of difficulties and obscurities, is about truth and error:

7 ܫܪܪܐ ܕܝܢ ܐܙܠ ܗܘܐ ܒܐܘܪܚܐ ܬܪܝܨܬܐ.
ܘܟܠܡܐ ܕܠܐ ܡܩܒܠ ܗܘܝܬ ܠܗ ܡܚܘܐ ܗܘܐ ܠܝ.
8 ܠܟܠܗܘܢ ܡܫܒ̈ܫܢܐ ܕܛܘܥܝܘܬܐ.
ܘܠܟ̈ܐܒܐ ܗܢܘܢ ܕܡܬܚܫܒܝܢ ܕܚܠܝܘܬܐ ܗܝ ܕܡܘܬܐ.
10 ܘܠܡܚܒܠܢܘܗ̇ ܕܡܚܒܠܐ.
ܚܙܐ ܗܘܝܬ ܟܕ ܡܨܛܒܬܐ ܗܘܬ ܟܠܬܐ ܕܡܚܒܠܐ.
ܘܡܫܬܘܝܐ ܕܡܚܒܠ ܘܡܬܚܒܠ.
11 ܘܫܐܠܬ ܠܫܪܪܐ ܕܡܢ ܐܢܘܢ ܗܠܝܢ.
ܘܐܡܪ ܠܝ ܗܢܘ ܡܛܥܝܢܐ ܘܛܘܥܝܘܬܐ.

7 But truth was proceeding on the upright way,
and whatever I did not understand He exhibited to me:

8 All the drugs/poison of error,
and pains of death which are considered sweetness;
9 and the destroyer of destructions.
I saw when the bride who was corrupting was adorned,
and the bridegroom who corrupts and is corrupted.
10 And I asked the truth, who are these?
And he said to me: This is the Deceiver and the Error.[14]

*Odes of Solomon 38.7-10*

Here the term ܣܡ̈ܡܢܐ has a negative sense, 'poisons'. The Odist realises who the deceiver (ܡܛܥܝܢܐ) is, and to whom the 'poisons' (ܣܡ̈ܡܢܐ) belong. In Ode 22, the term for 'venom' (ܡܪܪܬܐ) also appears once. The evil venom which was shown to the Odist is destroyed by the hand of the Lord: 'Your right hand destroyed the poison of Evil, and your hand levelled the way for those who believe in you.'[15]

To conclude, the Odist does not speak of an ordinary medicine or physician at all. On the one hand he attributes pains and sickness to the physical body and its limbs; on the other hand, terms such as pain, suffering, affliction, poison and venom are used in the context of error and darkness that reflect spiritual sickness. In both cases, God is the Lord of the body and the entire person, and so He strengthens the limbs and removes sickness. Likewise, He enlightens the Odist and saves him from his enemies, as well as from pain and suffering. As a response, the Odist gives thanks and praises the Lord for His caring and support.

---

[14] *Odes of Solomon*, 38.7-10.

[15] *Odes of Solomon*, 22.7: ܣܚܦܬ ܝܡܝܢܟ ܠܡܪܪܬܗ ܕܒܝܫܘܬܐ. ܘܐܫܘܝܬ ܐܝܕܟ ܐܘܪܚܐ ܠܐܝܠܝܢ ܕܡܗܝܡܢܝܢ ܒܟ. The terms ܣܚܦܐ or ܣܚܦ often occur in Odes; see 7.11; 8.23; 9.4; 11.12; 15.8; 17.2; 21.5; 22.7-11; 24.8; 28.5-15; 33.1-12; 38.8-14; 39.3-12; 40.6.

## 2.2 The Doctrine of the Acts of Judas Thomas the Apostle

The Syriac *Acts of Thomas* is one of the oldest apocryphal acts along with those of Paul and John. The Apostle's life, deeds, words and mission in India proclaim Jesus the Messiah Who became a man for the salvation of mankind. Whilst referring to Jesus Christ, His Life on earth and His divinity as the Son of God, the author refers to Him as 'the Healer of His creation' (ܐܣܝܐ ܕܒܪܝܬܗ) Who was sent for the 'healing of men' (ܐܣܝܘܬܐ ܕܒܢܝ̈ܢܫܐ).[16] Judas Thomas performs various healing miracles in the name of the Lord and indicates that Jesus is the Healer and Physician of bodies and souls. Almost all the healing imagery occurs in the context of miracles done through the Apostle, his prayer or through the prayer of those who believed the Apostle's preaching.

In the following, the first section presents the description and terms of physical and spiritual sickness. The second section draws attention to Jesus Christ and Judas Thomas as the healers and physicians. Finally, the relationship between healing and the holy sacraments is described, such as the healing power of the oil and water used in baptism, and the consecrated bread and wine used in Holy Communion.

### 2.2.1 The Sickness of Body and Soul in the Acts of Thomas

Although the *Acts of Thomas* speaks about the healing of the body and soul, certain passages show a difference between them. While the soul can be saved as it is incorruptible, the body cannot be saved since it is corruptible, and it dissolves.[17] But even though the

---

16 *Acts of Thomas*, ܪܠܐ-ܪܠܒ [62]; ܫܝܒ [143]. Quotations of the Syriac text are taken from W. Wright, *Apocryphal Acts of the Apostles* I (London 1871), and the page numbers are given in Syriac characters. His translation, *Apocryphal Acts of the Apostles* II (London 1871), is also edited in A. F. J. Klijn, *The Acts of Thomas* (Leiden 1962). Klijn divides the text into chapters which are given here between square brackeds.

17 *Acts of Thomas*, ܪܙ [35], ܪܢܚ [78]; for corruptibility see further pages ܪܠܘ [67], ܪܢܛ [79], ܪܦ [103], ܪܨܗ-ܪܨܘ [115], ܪܨܚ-ܪܨܛ [117], ܫܓ-ܫܗ [124], ܫܘ [126], ܫܝ [135], ܫܝܒ [143], ܫܟ [156].

body is considered to be dust and it will become dust again,[18] it is presented as the dwelling place of God's spirit.[19] Therefore, the contrast between body and soul does not imply that the former belongs to a world which is opposed to God for it is His creation.[20] Thus both the soul and the body can have fellowship with God, and they need to receive life[21] and healing.[22]

Several different terms are used to describe sickness of the body and soul and disease in this corporeal world. At the beginning of chapter 10, the author speaks of the 'sick souls' ( ܢܦܫ̈ܬܐ ܟܪ̈ܝܗܬܐ) in the context of the 'afflicted' (ܐܠܝ̈ܨܐ), 'poor' (ܡܣܟ̈ܢܐ) and 'feeble' (ܡܚܝ̈ܠܐ).[23] The text does not provide any information about what kind of sickness it is. Likewise, in chapter 20, the term 'sick' (ܟܪ̈ܝܗܐ) is used for sick people without any further definition of their sickness. In its context, this term can refer to any kind of sicknesses of both body and soul.[24]

Chapter 28 illustrates some of the consequences of leading an immoral life. While fornication, covetousness and the service of demons are considered as the three heads of wickedness: 'fornication blinds the intellect, and darkens the eyes of the soul; it confuses the steps of the body, and changes its complexion, and

---

18 *Acts of Thomas*, ܪܘ [37].

19 *Acts of Thomas*, ܪܨܐ [94].

20 *Acts of Thomas*, ܪܐ-ܪܕ [34].

21 *Acts of Thomas*, ܪܝܐ [42], ܫܟܚ-ܫܟܛ [156].

22 *Acts of Thomas*, ܩܥܛ [10], ܪܣܘ [49], ܪܨܚ-ܪܨܛ [95].

23 *Acts of Thomas*, ܩܥܛ [10]: ܘܫܪܝ ܗܘܐ ܕܢܠܦ ܘܢܐܡܪ ܗܟܢܐ. ܡܪܝ ܠܘܬܟ ܕܒܢ̈ܘܗܝ. ܘܗܕܝܐ ܘܡܕܒܪܢܐ ܕܐܝܠܝܢ ܕܡܗܝܡܢܝܢ ܒܗ. ܘܡܢܚ ܠܢܦܫܐ ܘܢܝܚܐ ܕܐܠܝ̈ܨܐ: ܘܡܣܒܪܐ ܕܡܫܥ̈ܒܕܐ: ܘܦܪܘܩܐ ܕܡܣܟ̈ܢܐ. ܘܡܐܣܝܢܐ ܕܢܦܫ̈ܬܐ ܟܪ̈ܝܗܬܐ. ܡܚܝܢܐ ܕܥܠܡ̈ܐ ܘܦܪܘܩܐ ܕܒܪ̈ܝܬܐ. Although the literal translation of ܢܦܫ̈ܬܐ ܟܪ̈ܝܗܬܐ is the 'sick souls', the term ܢܦܫ̈ܬܐ is synonym for man. Therefore, a better rendering would be 'the sick people'.

24 *Acts of Thomas*, ܩܨܘ [20]: ܐܠܐ ܡܬܟܪܟ ܗܘܐ ܒܡܕ̈ܝܢܬܐ ܘܒܩܘܪ̈ܝܐ: ܘܝܗܒ ܗܘܐ ܠܡܣܟ̈ܢܐ. ܘܡܠܦ ܗܘܐ ܠܗܘܢ ܐܠܗܐ ܚܕܬܐ. ܘܐܦ ܟܪ̈ܝܗܐ ܡܐܣܐ ܗܘܐ. ܘܫ̈ܐܕܐ ܡܦܩ ܗܘܐ. ܘܣܓ̈ܝܐܬܐ ܥܒܕ ܗܘܐ.

makes it sick'.[25] The term 'sick' (ܟܪܝܗܐ) is used for the body, but the effect of fornication is also mental, spiritual and physical sickness.

The term 'sick' (ܟܪ̈ܝܗܐ) appears in chapter 59. Thomas' reputation caused the people to meet him for they expected to be healed by him.[26] Together with 'sick people', there are mentioned those who are 'possessed by a spirit' (ܪܘܚܐ), 'lunatic' (ܕܒܪ ܐܓܪܐ) and 'paralytics' (ܡܫܪܝܢ ܗܘܘ ܦܠܓܝܗܘܢ). These sick people were suffering because of their 'grievous sicknesses' (ܟܘܪܗܢܐ ܚܝ̈ܠܬܢܐ) and 'hideous torments' ( ܘܒܬܫܢܝܩܐ ܣܢܝ̈ܐ). The term 'restored/healthy' (ܫܠܝܡܝܢ) describes the opposite of sickness. Although the term ܟܪܝܗܐ is used in the context of some physical diseases, it cannot be limited to these only. It seems that it can refer to any kind of sickness, as in chapter 143, the author speaks of 'all sickness/pains, hidden and visible'

---

[25] *Acts of Thomas*, ܨܝܕ [28]: ܐܬܦܪܣܘ ܡܢ ܙܢܝܘܬܐ ܘܗܝ ܡܘܒܕܢܝܬܐ. ܘܡܢ ܦܘܠܚܢܐ ܕܟܪ̈ܣܐ. ܒܗܠܝܢ ܓܝܪ ܬܠܬܐ ܪ̈ܫܝܢ ܗܘܐ ܟܠܗ ܪܘܫܥܐ. ܙܢܝܘܬܐ ܓܝܪ ܡܥܘܪܐ ܡܕ̈ܥܐ. ܘܡܚܫܟܐ ܥܝ̈ܢܐ ܕܢܦܫܐ. ܡܕܒܪܐ ܠܗܘܠܟܗ. ܕܦܓܪܐ. ܘܡܫܚܠܦܐ ܠܒܘܣܡܗ ܘܡܥܒܕܐ ܠܗ ܟܪܝܗܐ. For 'fornication' or 'adultery' see further ܩܦܐ-ܩܦܒ [12], ܪܢܛ-ܪܣ [84], ܪܨܗ-ܪܨܘ [126].

[26] *Acts of Thomas*, ܪܟܛ-ܪܠ [59]: ܘܐܫܬܡܥ ܗܘܐ ܛܒܗ ܒܟܠ ܟܦܪ̈ܢܐ. ܒܡܕ̈ܝܢܬܐ ܘܩܘܪ̈ܝܐ. ܘܟܠܢܫ ܕܐܝܬ ܗܘܐ ܠܗ ܟܪܝܗܐ ܐܘ ܕܐܝܬ ܗܘܐ ܠܗ ܪܘܚܐ ܐܘ ܕܒܪ ܐܓܪܐ: ܐܘ ܕܡܫܪܝܢ ܗܘܘ ܦܠܓܝܗܘܢ. ܐܝܬ ܡܝܬܝܗܘܢ ܕܒܪ̈ܘܫܬܐ ܡܝܬܝܢ ܗܘܘ ܘܡܣܝܒܝܢ ܗܘܘ ܠܗܘܢ ܒܐܘܪܚܐ. ܠܐܝܟܐ ܕܠܩܝܢ ܗܘܘ ܕܐܙܠ ܗܘܐ. ܘܗܘܘ ܠܟܠܗܘܢ ܒܚܝܠܐ ܕܝܘܒ ܡܢܗ ܡܬܐܣܐ ܗܘܐ ܘܡܬܐܣܝܢ ܗܘܘ ܟܪ̈ܝܗܐ ܕܟܪ̈ܝܗܝܢ ܗܘܘ ܒܟܘܪ̈ܗܢܐ ܚܝ̈ܠܬܢܐ ܘܒܬܫܢܝܩܐ ܣܢܝ̈ܐ. ܘܡܫܪ̈ܝܐ ܕܡܣܝܒܝܢ ܗܘܘ ܒܗ ܙܢ̈ܝܢ. ܘܡܫܒܚܝܢ ܗܘܘ ܟܠܗܘܢ ܡܢ ܚܕ ܦܘܡܐ ܘܐܡܪܝܢ. ܠܟ ܫܘܒܚܐ ܝܫܘܥ ܡܫܝܚܐ: ܕܝܗܒܬ ܠܢ ܐܣܝܘܬܐ ܒܝܕ ܥܒܕܟ ܘܫܠܝܚܟ ܬܐܘܡܐ. ܗܐ ܓܝܪ ܒܗ ܫܠܝܡܝܢ ܘܚܕ ܚܝܝܢ ܒܟܝܢ ܡܪܢ. ܕܐܢܬ ܗܘ ܐܦ ܣܡ ܒܢ̈ܝ ܕܢܝܟ. ܘܐܬܡܠܝܐ ܒܡܫܝܚܐ ܕܐܢܫܝܢ. ܘܟܠܝܢ ܡܢܟ ܘܠܐ ܛܥܝܢ ܠܟ ܫܠܝܡܝܢ ܘܡܫܒܚܝܢ:. ܕܐܠܐ ܒܝܕ ܡܫܝܚܐ ܡܚܝܢ ܐܢܫܐ. The report about the Apostle reminds about that of his Lord (cf. Mk 6:53-56; Lk 4:37-41), of Peter (cf. Act 5:14-16) and Paul (cf. Act 19:12).

(ܕܟܠܗܘܢ ܟܐܒ̈ܐ ܒܣܝ̈ܡܐ ܘܚܠܝ̈ܐ).[27] Later in the passage, paradoxically, Jesus the Physician of His creation is called 'sick' (ܟܪܝܗܐ) because of man's salvation. It is the only text where the term 'sick' (ܟܪܝܗܐ) refers to Jesus. This term is not just used in opposition to ܫܠܝܡܐ, but also to ܐܣܝܐ. Since Jesus humiliated Himself because of man's redemption, He has been despised (ܡܬܬܫܝܛ) and insulted (ܡܬܒܣܪ) for He became 'a slave and poor' (ܥܒܕܐ ܘܡܣܟܢܐ) and 'sick' (ܟܪܝܗܐ).[28] This text reminds us also of 1 Corinthians, when Paul says 'to the sick, I became sick, to win the sick'.[29]

The contrast between ܫܠܝܡܐ and ܟܪܝܗܐ is also found in the passage where Vizan was baptised and his wife had received healing.[30] Because of being 'sick' (ܟܪܝܗܐ) she is called 'feeble' (ܡܚܝܠܬܐ).[31] In this context the term 'sickness' (ܟܘܪܗܢܐ) is frequently used. In chapter 155 it appears together with the adjective 'grievous' (ܟܘܪܗܢܐ ܒܝܫܐ), as in chapter 59: 'grievous sicknesses' (ܟܘܪ̈ܗܢܐ ܒ̈ܝܫܐ).[32] The author also refers to the time and location with reference to the term 'sickness'. He speaks of 'the

---

27 *Acts of Thomas*, ܩܡܓ [143].

28 *Acts of Thomas*, ܩܡܓ [143]: ܘܐܡܪ ܬܘܒ ܝܗܘܕܐ. ܗܝܫܘܥ ܒܐܣܝܐ ܕܟܠܗܘܢ ܟܐܒ̈ܐ ܒܣܝ̈ܡܐ ܘܚܠܝ̈ܐ. ܘܡܚܝܠܢܐ ܕܢܦ̈ܫܬܐ ܐܠܝܡ ܕܟܝܡ ܒܘܕ̈ܝܠܐ ܡܠܗ. ܗܠܝܢ ܒܢܝ̈ܢܫܐ. ܘܒܪ ܡܠܟܐ ܕܗܘܐ ܥܒܕܐ ܘܡܣܟܢܐ. ܗܢܐ ܐܣܝܐ ܕܟܪܝܗܘܬܗ. ܘܟܪܝܗܐ ܡܢ ܥܒܕܘ̈ܗܝ. ܗܢܐ ܡܫܡܫܢܐ ܕܡܫܡܫܢܘ̈ܗܝ: ܘܡܬܬܫܝܛ ܘܡܬܒܣܪ ܡܢ ܐܝܠܝܢ ܕܠܐ ܥܒܕܘܗܝ. ܗܢܐ ܡܚܣܪ ܡܢ ܥܒܕܘܬܐ ܘܡܢ ܫܟܠܐ. ܘܡܢ ܥܘܒܕܐ ܘܡܢ ܚܘܫܒܢܐ ܠܡܬܢܝܢܘ̈ܗܝ.

29 1 Cor 9:22: ܗܘܝܬ ܥܡ ܟܪ̈ܝܗܐ ܐܝܟ ܟܪܝܗܐ܆ ܕܠܟܪ̈ܝܗܐ ܐܬܪ.

30 *Acts of Thomas*, ܩܢ-ܩܢܚ [150-158].

31 *Acts of Thomas*, ܩܢ [150]: ܘܡܫܡܠܢܐ ܐܠܐ ܫܠܝܡܐ ܗܘܬ: ܘܠܟ ܫܪܬ ܗܘܬ ܐܘ ܥܒܕܬ ܡܠܬܟ: ܠ ܗܘܐ ܗܘܐ ܢܝܫܐ ܗܘ ܚܝܐ ܗܘܬ. ܘܫܢܝܐ ܕܠܟܠܗ ܡܡܟܠܐ ܗܘܬ. ܒܐܘܠܨܢܐ ܒܢ ܙܒܢܐ ܐܝܬܝܗ̇: ܗܐ ܘܟܠܐ ܗܟܐܠܢܐ. ܕܟܘܪܗܢܐ. ܡܫܘܚܐ ܐܠܐ ܗܘܝܠ ܠܬܘܪܐ ܕܡܫܝ̈ܚܐ: ܐܝܟ ܗܘ ܕܡܬܥܘܕܐ ܐܝܬ ܠܟ ܕܬܐܠ ܒܟܝܢ ܠܫܝܬ: ܡܢ ܟܪ ܐܘ ܒܪܬܐ ܠܚܘܕܝ. ܒܪܡ ܐܢܐ: ܘܡܐܡܐ ܐܝܬ ܠܗ̇ ܠܡܚܝܠܬܐ ܕܟܪܝܗܐ ܗܝ܀

32 *Acts of Thomas*, ܢܛ [59], ܩܢܗ [155].

long time of sickness' (ܙܒܢܐ ܣܓܝܐܐ ܕܟܘܪܗܢܐ)[33] and of 'the place of sickness' (ܐܬܪܐ ܕܟܘܪܗܢܐ) which can be compared to 'the weary place' (ܐܬܪܐ ܠܐܝܐ), 'unclean place' ( ܒܐܬܪܐ ܛܢܦܐ) and 'place of the enemy' (ܒܐܬܪܐ ܕܒܥܠܕܒܒܐ).[34] The sickness dwells not only in some places at certain times, but it can also reside in man. When a certain bridegroom believed in Judas' preaching and consequently was healed, he praised God for he had been delivered from 'the sickness that was abiding' in him for ever.[35]

Since ܟܘܪܗܢܐ does not specify any particular physical sickness, the term ܟܐܒܐ is used to illustrate that kind of pain and suffering. As life on earth ends and the world is corruptible, the author prefers virginity to the married state. He cites some of the reasons for remaining a virgin, being saved from the 'hidden and visible sufferings/passions' (ܚܫ̈ܐ ܟܣ̈ܝܐ ܘܓܠ̈ܝܐ) and from 'the heavy care of children, the end of whom is bitter sorrow' ( ܘܡܢ ܝܨܦܬܐ ܝܩܝܪܬܐ ܕܒܢ̈ܝܐ ܗܠܝܢ ܕܚܪܬܗܘܢ ܟܡܝܪܬܐ ܗܝ). In particular, he assumes that most children have 'many diseases' (ܘܣܓܝܐܐ ܓܝܪ ܕܒܢ̈ܝܐ ܟܐܒ̈ܐ ܣܓܝܐܐ ܗܘܝܢ ܠܗܘܢ).[36]

---

33 *Acts of Thomas*, ܫܢܚ [150].

34 *Acts of Thomas*, ܥܢܠ [156]: ܘܗܘܝ ܠܗܘܢ ܡܐܣܝܢܐ ܒܐܬܪܐ ܕܟܘܪܗܢܐ. ܘܗܘܝ ܠܗܘܢ ܡܢܝܚܢܐ ܒܐܬܪܐ ܠܐܝܐ. ܘܢܛܪ ܐܢܘܢ ܒܐܬܪܐ ܛܢܦܐ. ܘܕܒܪ ܐܢܘܢ ܡܢ ܫܠܝܐ ܒܐܬܪܐ ܕܒܥܠܕܒܒܐ. ܘܗܘܝ ܐܣܝܐ ܠܦܓܪ̈ܝܗܘܢ ܘܐܚܝܐ ܠܢܦܫ̈ܬܗܘܢ. ܘܥܒܕ ܐܢܘܢ ܢܟ̈ܦܐ ܘܗܝܟܠ̈ܐ ܩܕ̈ܝܫܐ. ܘܬܫܪܐ ܒܗܘܢ ܪܘܚܐ ܩܕܝܫܬܐ܀

35 *Acts of Thomas*, ܡܦܠ [15]: ܘܗܕܝܢ ܐܦ ܚܬܢܐ ܗܢܐ ܘܐܡܪ. ܡܘܕܐ ܐܢܐ ܠܟ ܐܠܗܐ ܚܕܬܐ܆ ܕܒܝܕ ܐܟܣܢܝܐ ܐܬܐ ܠܟܐ. ܡܫܟܚ ܐܢܐ ܠܟ ܐܠܗܐ ܕܒܝܕ ܓܒܪܐ ܚܒܪܐ ܡܬܚܙܝܬ. ܗܘ ܕܐܪܚܩܢ ܡܢ ܫܠܝܐ܆ ܘܙܪܥ ܒܝ ܚܝܐ܆ ܗܘ ܕܦܪܩܢ ܡܢ ܟܘܪܗܢܐ ܕܡܟܬܪ ܗܘܐ ܒܝ ܠܥܠܡ.

36 *Acts of Thomas*, ܡܦܐ [12]: ܘܗܕܐ ܒܢ̈ܝ ܕܐܢܫ ܡܛܠ ܒܢܝܗܘܢ ܘܕܒܘ ܠܚܝܠܗ ܐܟܠܗܘܢ. ܘܕܒܘ ܕܡܚܝܐ ܕܡܬܦܪܥܝܢ ܐܝܬܝܗܘܢ ܡܢ ܗܕܐ ܫܘܬܦܘܬܐ ܓܝܪ ܐܬܐ. ܗܘܝܢ ܐܝܬܝܗܘܢ ܢܦ̈ܫܐ ܕܒܢ̈ܝܐ. ܘܡܬܦܪܥܝܢ ܐܝܬܝܗܘܢ ܡܢ ܚܫ̈ܐ ܟܣ̈ܝܐ ܘܓܠ̈ܝܐ܆ ܘܡܢ ܝܨܦܬܐ ܝܩܝܪܬܐ ܕܒܢ̈ܝܐ. ܗܠܝܢ ܕܚܪܬܗܘܢ ܟܡܝܪܬܐ ܗܝ. ܘܐܢ ܢܦܘܫܘܢ ܠܟܘܢ ܣܓ̈ܝܐܐ ܡܬܛܠܠܘܢ ܗܘܝܢ

☞

The term ܟܐܒ is also put in Charisius' mouth, for he was worried about his wife Mygdonia who left him.[37] Here the term ܟܐܒ describes Charisius' sympathy and compassion for his wife. He feels pain for her and is sorry. At the same time, she was also 'sorely grieved' (ܡܬܥܢܝܐ) and 'afflicted' (ܘܡܬܛܪܦܐ). As they are both hurt emotionally, Charisius begs her: 'torture not my soul by the sight of you, and pain not my heart by your care'.[38] Here the pains are within man's heart, whereas chapter 143 speaks of 'hidden and visible pains' (ܟܐܒ̈ܐ ܟܣ̈ܝܐ ܘܓܠ̈ܝܐ).[39] Obviously the term ܟܐܒܐ generally can be used for a particular pain as well as for interior and exterior suffering.

In two of Thomas' protection prayers the term ܓܪܒܐ appears without being attached to any specific disease or leprosy. In chapter 25 the apostle prays for the King and his brother to be 'cleansed/purified from their leprosy' ( ܘܕܟܝܐ ܐܢܘܢ ܡܢ ܓܪܒܗܘܢ).[40] Likewise, in chapter 67, Thomas asks the Lord to

---

ܐܢܬܘܢ ܓܠܒܝܢ ܘܕܒܝܢ ܘܡܣܝܢ ܠܡܪ̈ܥܐ. ܘܚܠܡܝܢ ܠܟܪ̈ܝܗܐ: ܘܡܫܬܠܡܝܢ ܐܢܬܘܢ ܗܟܢ ܒܫܘܦܪ̈ܝܗܘܢ. ܗܘܟܢܐ ܐܦ ܟܢ ܕܟܪ̈ܝܗܐ ܒܟܐܒ̈ܐ ܗܟܢܐ ܗܘܝܢ ܠܗܘܢ. ܐܘ ܕܟܠܟܐ ܢܦܠ ܥܠܝܗܘܢ: ܐܘ ܕܒܪ ܐܒܪܐ ܐܚܕ ܠܗܘܢ: ܐܘ ܕܦܠܓܐ ܢܦܠ ܥܠܝܗܘܢ. ܘܐܦ ܫܠܝܛܝܢ ܒܗܘܢ ܦܪ̈ܝܫܝܢ. ܐܘ ܒܟܐܪܐ ܐܘ ܒܟܐܒܘܬܐ. ܐܘ ܒܝܫܘܬܐ: ܐܘ ܒܡܚܠܘܬܐ. ܐܘ ܒܥܘܒܕܐ ܦܪܝܫܐ. ܘܡܫܠܡܝܢ ܗܘܦܢܝܐ ܡܫܬܠܡܝܢ ܐܢܬܘܢ ܒܗܘܢ.

[37] *Acts of Thomas*, ܨܛ [99]: ܠܐ ܟܢ ܟܪܝܐ ܠܝ ܕܐܬܦܪܫܬ ܡܢ ܫܘܬܦܘܬܗ ܕܡܬܓܘܪܘܬܐ. ܐܠܐ ܥܠܝܗ ܥܠ ܫܘܦܪܗ ܟܐܒ ܠܝ. ܕܗܘܢܗ ܪܒܐ ܘܚܠܦܬ ܡܪܝܐܘܬܗ: ܘܦܓܥܬܗ ܒܪܬ ܐܝܬܐ ܡܬܟܒܫܬ.

[38] *Acts of Thomas*, ܩܝܗ-ܩܝܘ [115]: ܘܟܕ ܫܠܡ ܫܒܚܐ ܕܒܗ ܕܒܪܝܫ ܒܥܠܗ ܗܘܬ ܡܬܬܪܦܐ ܘܗܘܬ ܡܬܛܪܦܐ. ܘܗܘ ܗܘܐ ܐܡܪ ܠܗ. ܡܢ ܟܕ ܐܣܬܠܩܬ ܒܐܠܗܐ ܕܠܥܠܡ ܚܝܐ ܪܒܐ ܐܬܦܢܝ. ܘܡܢܐ ܣܠܩܬ ܕܒܪܢܫܐ ܕܠܥܠܡ ܒܡܫܡܫܢܘܬܐ ܘܒܫܝܢܐ ܡܬܦܢܝ. ܒܟܐ ܐܢܐ ܡܢܟܝ ܡܛܠܬܝܢ: ܠܐ ܬܫܢܩܝܢܗ ܠܢܦܫܝ ܒܚܙܘܬܟܝ. ܘܠܐ ܬܟܐܒܝܢܗ ܠܠܒܝ ܒܒܛܝܠܘܬܟܝ.

[39] *Acts of Thomas*, ܩܡܓ [143].

[40] *Acts of Thomas*, ܟܗ [25]: ܡܟܝܠ ܠܡܠܟܐ ܘܠܐܚܘܗܝ. ܩܒܠ ܐܢܘܢ ܒܕܝܪܟ. ܘܡܫܘܚ ܐܢܘܢ. ܘܕܟܝܐ ܐܢܘܢ ܡܢ ܓܪܒܗܘܢ. ܘܢܛܪ ܐܢܘܢ ܡܢ

cleanse (ܘܕܟܝܗ̇) the flock of Xanthippus of 'its leprosy' (ܠܓܪܒܗ̇) through anointing it with the oil of life.[41] In both cases the verb 'to cleanse/purify' (ܕܟܐ) is used in connection with the term 'leprosy' (ܠܓܪܒܐ).

It is worth looking at the term ܡܪܪܬܐ, 'venom', which is mentioned several times. First, it appears in the context of the black snake that caused the death of a young man when he was 'struck/bitten' by him (ܕܐܬܢܟܬܗ). He was revived after the snake sucked from him the 'venom' (ܡܪܪܬܐ) which he had injected.[42] The serpent's venom reminds one of the garden of Eden and the Serpent persuading Eve. The snake symbolises the devil who is the enemy of men. The serpent, who is also called 'their disturber' (ܡܕܘܕܢܗܘܢ), is man's enemy who tries to poison mankind and to cause them pain (ܢܟܝܢܗܘܢ).[43] The enemy causes man to suffer physically (ܡܬܢܟܝܢ),[44] as is seen when a certain woman drew

---

ܕܐܣ̈ܝܐ. ܘܪܒ ܐܢܘܢ ܒܡܪ̈ܓܠܝܢ. ܘܐܣܝܐ ܐܢܘܢ ܡܢ ܡܟܐܒܝܢ ܕܠܐ ܡܬܕܠܚܝܢ. ܘܠܐ ܚܙܐ ܡܪ̈ܕܘܬܗ.

[41] *Acts of Thomas*, ܪܠ [67]: ܘܐܟܠ ܐܢܘܢ ܠܬܪ̈ܝܢ ܘܐܡܪ. ܡܪܝܐ ܕܥܠܡܘܢ ܚܠ̈ܦܐ ܕܠܗ ܡܫܡܫܝܢ: ܘܐܠܗܐ ܕܥܠܡܝܢ ܢܦܫ̈ܬܐ ܕܒܗ ܡܫܬ̈ܝܢ. ܘܦܪܘܩ ܡܢ ܛܘܦܝܢ ܠܒܢ̈ܝܢܫܐ ܕܠܗ: ܡܚܝܪ ܡܢ ܚܢܟܐ ܘܡܢ ܚܒܘܠܬܐ: ܠܐܠܝܡ ܕܐܬܬܟܝܒܘ ܠܗ ܘܐܬܐܘ ܠܬܚܝܬ ܠܥܘܗܕܢܐ. ܐܢܬ ܗܘ ܚܢ ܡܢܟܝܬܗ ܕܐܬܡܢܬܝܢܘܗ: ܘܡܥܘܒܣܝܗ ܠܒܝܬܗ ܡܢ ܡܥܕܝܢ ܕܚܛܐ. ܘܕܟܝܗ ܡܢ ܓܪܒܗ: ܘܠܛܘܪܝܗ ܡܢ ܕܐܒ̈ܐ ܘܡܢ ܚܛܘܦ̈ܐ: ܕܠܐ ܢܒܕܘܢܗ ܡܢ ܐܝܕܘܗܝ܀

[42] *Acts of Thomas*, ܪ [33]: ܘܡܨܐ ܗܘܐ ܡܪܪܬܐ ܡܢܗ. ܘܡܫܠܠ ܫܠܠ ܡܢܗ ܕܡܢ ܡܪܪܬܐ ܡܬܠܚܕܬܐ: ܠܚܘܝܐ ܕܗܘ ܚܘܝܐ ܕܚܒܫ ܗܘܐ ܐܝܟ ܐܪܓܘܢܐ ܚܘܪ ܗܘܐ. ܘܚܘܝܐ ܙܢܐ ܗܘܐ. ܘܚܢ ܚܠܘ ܡܪܪܬܗ ܠܒܪ ܡܢܗ ܕܗܘ ܚܘܝܐ. ܢܚܬ ܗܘܐ ܘܪܗܛ ܠܘܬ ܥܠܝܡܐ ܕܢܫܝܟܐ. ܘܢܦܠ ܦܫܛܪ ܠܗ܀. Cf. ܥܘܨ [148]: ܐܠܗܐ ܕܦܓܪܘܗܝ ܡܪܪܬܐ ܗܝ. In page ܥܒܕ [158] the text includes the term 'bitterness/venom' (ܡܪ̈ܪܬܐ) while Judas prays: ܢܗܘܐ ܠܝ ܦܪ̈ܘܩܢ ܠܒ̈ܢܐ. ܘܕܡܝܢ ܠܥܘܡܩ ܫܠܡܐ. ܘܚܠܦ ܡܪ̈ܪܬܗ ܕܐܬܬܠܝܛܘ ܫܠܝܡ: ܬܬܥܠܡ ܡܢ ܡܪ̈ܪܬܗ ܕܒܥܠܕܒܒܝܢ.

[43] *Acts of Thomas*, ܪܒ [34]: ܐܢܬ ܗܘ ܡܚܒܠ ܐܢܫܐ ܠܗܢܐ ܒܥܠܕܒܒܐ ܕܐܬܢܟܝܬ ܡܢ ܒܥܠܕܒܒܐ.

[44] *Acts of Thomas*, ܪܟ [42].

attention to her long suffering when she explained to the Apostle that she has been tormented by the enemy for five years.[45] In another context, Thomas prays to the Lord for some women to become as they had been before being struck by devils (ܫܐ̈ܕܐ).[46] Both verbs 'to torment' (ܫܢܩ) and 'to strike' (ܡܚܐ) are used with the 'devils' (ܫܐ̈ܕܐ) and 'enemy' (ܒܥܠܕܒܒܐ) who caused pains and suffering to mankind.

### 2.2.2 Jesus Christ and Thomas as Physicians and Healers

The missionary Apostle's deeds, acts and miracles caused people to believe that he was the 'physician' (ܐܣܝܐ), 'healer' (ܡܐܣܝܢܐ) and source of 'healing' (ܐܣܝܘܬܐ) that is sent by God to India. The author presents Thomas as the mediator of healing and indicates that Jesus the Messiah Himself is the real Physician and Healer.

The first report to King Gudnaphor about Thomas illustrates the Apostle's work as 'healing the sick' (ܟܪ̈ܝܗܐ ܡܐܣܐ ܗܘܐ), and 'driving out demons' (ܘܫܐ̈ܕܐ ܡܦܩ ܗܘܐ). Both sentences are paralleled to each other. Thomas' compassion and his healing are without recompense ( ܡܪܚܡܢܘܬܗ ܘܐܣܝܘܬܗ ܕܡܓܢ ܗܘܬ).[47] The term 'his compassion' is related to Thomas'

---

45 *Acts of Thomas*, ܪܢܐ [42]: ܘܐܡܪܐ ܐܢܐ ܠܟ. ܕܠܐ ܗܘܐ ܒܝܫܐܝܬ ܡܫܬܢܩܐ ܐܢܐ ܡܢ ܒܥܠܕܒܒܐ: ܗܐ ܙܒܢܐ ܕܫܢ̈ܝܐ ܚܡܫ.

46 *Acts of Thomas*, ܪܢܐ-ܪܢܒ [81]: ܬܐܣܝܢ ܘܬܩܘܡܢ ܗܠܝܢ. ܘܢܗܘܝܢ ܐܝܟ ܕܐܬܝܗ̈ܝܢ ܗܘ̈ܝ، ܥܕܠܐ ܢܬܡܚ̈ܝܢ ܗܘ̈ܝ، ܡܢ ܫܐ̈ܕܐ. See also ܪܢܐ [42].

47 *Acts of Thomas*, ܩܦܘ- ܩܦܙ [20]: ܟܕ ܕܝܢ ܐܬܐ ܡܠܟܐ ܠܡܕܝܢܬܐ. ܡܫܐܠ ܗܘ ܠܚܕ ܚܕ ܡܢ ܪ̈ܚܡܘܗܝ، ܥܠ ܒܝܪܬܐ ܕܒܢܐ ܠܗ ܝܗܘܕܐ. ܗܢܘܢ ܕܝܢ ܐܡܪܝܢ ܠܗ. ܕܠܐ ܒܝܪܬܐ ܒܢܐ. ܐܦܠܐ ܡܕܡ ܐܚܪܝܢ ܥܒܕ. ܐܠܐ ܡܬܟܪܟ ܗܘܐ ܒܡܕ̈ܝܢܬܐ ܘܒܩܘܪ̈ܝܐ: ܘܝܗܒ ܗܘܐ ܠܡܣ̈ܟܢܐ. ܘܡܠܦ ܗܘܐ ܠܗܘܢ ܐܠܗܐ ܚܕܬܐ. ܘܐܦ ܟܪ̈ܝܗܐ ܡܐܣܐ ܗܘܐ. ܘܫܐ̈ܕܐ ܡܦܩ ܗܘܐ. ܘܬܕܡܪ̈ܬܐ ܥܒܕ ܗܘܐ. ܘܡܣܒܪܝܢ ܕܫܠܝܚܐ ܗܘ. ܐܠܐ ܡܪܚܡܢܘܬܗ ܘܐܣܝܘܬܗ ܕܡܓܢ ܗܘܬ. ܘܒܟܐܢܘܬܗ ܘܕܫܝܢܘܬܗ ܡܣܒܪܐ ܟܠܗܘܢ، ܕܐܘ ܡܫܝܚܐ ܗܘ. ܐܘ ܫܠܝܚܐ ܗܘ ܕܐܠܗܐ ܚܕܬܐ. ܨܐܡ ܟܠ ܝܘܡ ܘܡܨܠܐ ܗܘ. ܘܠܚܡܐ ܠܚܘܕ ܐܟܠ ܘܡܠܚܐ ܘܫܬܐ ܡ̈ܝܐ.

☞

work of charity that consisted in ministering to the poor, giving them the King's silver and gold.[48] However, Thomas is a physician only for those who have faith in his mission. While Mygdonia believed in his healing and considered that visiting him was like visiting a physician's practice (ܠܒܝܬ ܐܣܝܐ), her husband Charisius neglected his healing capability.[49] Arguing, Mygdonia maintains her position and acknowledges Thomas as the healer and that his healing is different from that of other physicians:

And when it was evening, she came, and he met her and said to her: "Where have you been till now?" And she said to him: "I went to the physician's house". He said: "That strange conjurer is the physician?" She said to him: "Yes, he is the physician, and he is different from all [other] physicians, for all [other] physicians heal those bodies which shall be dissolved, but this physician heals bodies with the souls, which will never more be dissolved".[50]

---

ܘܠܟܠ ܚܕ ܐܝܟ ܣܘܢܩܢܗ. ܘܡܣܒܪ ܠܐ ܫܩܠ ܠܗ ܡܢ ܐܢܫ. ܘܡܣܒܪ ܕܐܝܬ ܠܗ ܠܐܚ̈ܝܢܐ ܝܗܒ ❖. The gratis healing is the fulfilment of the Lord's commandment: when He sent out the Twelve, he said: 'heal the sick, cleanse those who have leprosy, drive out demons. Freely you have received, freely give' (Mt 10:8: ܟܪ̈ܝܗܐ ܐܣܘ ܘܓܪ̈ܒܐ ܕܟܘ. ܘܕ̈ܝܘܐ ܐܦܩܘ. ܡܓܢ ܢܣܒܬܘܢ. ܡܓܢ ܗܒܘ).

48 *Acts of Thomas*, ܩܦܘ-ܩܦܙ [19].

49 Charisius considered the Apostle a poor sorcerer, who does not have enough to eat, drink or clothe himself. According to Charisius, Thomas does not take pay 'because he knows that he does not in reality heal any man'. *Acts of Thomas*, ܪܨܕ [96]: ܘܗܢܐ ܐܣܝܐ ܕܥܒܕ ܐܢܐ: ܚܪ̈ܫܬܐ ܠܡ ܡܣܟܢܐ ܕܡܣܟܢܐ. ܘܐܦ ܬܘܒ ܕܠܐ ܐܟܠ ܘܠܐ ܫܬܐ. ܠܐ ܬܘܒܥܝܢ: ܕܡܛܠ ܕܢܡܘܣܘܬܐ ܠܐ ܐܟܠ ܘܠܐ ܫܬܐ. ܐܠܐ ܡܛܠ ܕܠܐ ܩܢܐ ܡܣܒܪ. ܡܢܐ ܓܝܪ ܢܩܒܠ. ܗܘ ܐܢܫܐ ܕܐܦܠܐ ܠܣܘܟܐ ܠܡܥܒܪܐ ܐܝܬ ܠܗ. ܘܠܒܫ ܚܕܐ ܡܛܠ ܕܠܝܬ ܠܗ ܐܫܝܬܐ. ܘܕܠܐ ܫܩܠ ܐܓܪܐ ܡܢ ܐܢܫ. ܡܛܠ ܕܝܕܥ ܕܠܐܢܫ ܠܐ ܡܐܣܐ ܒܫܪܪܐ ❖

50 *Acts of Thomas*, ܪܨܒ-ܪܨܓ [95]: ܘܟܕ ܗܘܐ ܪܡܫܐ ܐܬܬ ܗܘܬ. ܘܗܘ ܐܪܥܗ ܘܐܡܪ ܠܗ̇. ܐܝܟܐ ܗܘܝܬܝ ܥܕܡܐ ܠܗܫܐ. ܗܝ ܐܡܪܬ ܠܗ. ܠܒܝܬ ܐܣܝܐ ܐܙܠܬ ܗܘܝܬ. ܐܡܪ ܗܘ ܗܘ ܐܡܣܝܢܐ ܢܘܟܪܝܐ ܐܣܝܐ ܗܘ. ܐܡܪܐ ܠܗ. ܐܝܢ ܐܣܝܐ ܗܘ. ܘܫܢܐ ܗܘ ܡܢ ܟܠܗܘܢ ܐܣ̈ܘܬܐ. ܟܠܗܘܢ ܓܝܪ ܐܣ̈ܘܬܐ ܦܓܪ̈ܐ ܗܘ ܗܠܝܢ ܕܡܫܬܪܝܢ ܡܐܣܝܢ. ☞

While the ordinary physicians heal only corruptible bodies, Thomas heals both bodies and souls. Obviously, Thomas' healing cannot be compared to that of other physicians. Healing both body and soul indicates a perfect healing. The body and soul belong to each other. Chapter 42 speaks of the 'giver of life to the souls' ( ܡܚܝܢܐ ܕܢܦ̈ܫܬܐ) and of 'the healer of the bodies' (ܡܐܣܝܢܐ ܕܦܓ̈ܪܐ). A woman in whom the devil lived said to Thomas: ܫܠܝܚܐ ܕܐܠܗܐ ܚܕܬܐ ܕܐܬܐ ܠܗܢܕܘ. ܥܒܕܗ ܕܐܠܗܐ ܩܕܝܫܐ ܕܒܟ ܡܬܟܪܙ: ܘܡܚܝܢܐ ܕܢܦܫܬܐ ܕܐܝܠܝܢ ܕܠܘܬܗ ܐܬܝܢ: ܘܡܐܣܝܢܐ ܕܦܓ̈ܪܐ ܐܝܠܝܢ ܕܡܢ ܒܥܠܕܒܒܐ ܡܫܬܢܩܝܢ: ܕܗܘܝܬ ܥܠܬܐ ܕܚܝܐ ܠܟܠܗ ܐܢܫܘܬܐ ܕܗܢܕܘ: ܐܦܣ ܕܢܩܪܒܘܢܢܝ ܩܕܡܝܟ: ܕܐܡܪ ܠܟ ܡܕܡ ܕܓܕܫ.[51] Following Wright, Klijn refers 'the giver of life' (ܡܚܝܢܐ) and 'the healer' (ܡܐܣܝܢܐ) to God (the Greek refers the former to God), as he translates:

> Apostle of the new God, who art come to India; servant of the holy God, who by thee is proclaimed both the Giver of Life to the souls of those that come unto Him, and the Healer of the bodies of those who are tortured by the enemy; (thou) who art the cause of life to the whole people of India; permit them to bring me before thee, that I may tell thee what has befallen me.[52]

Unfortunately, it is not clear whether these terms describe the Lord or His servant. The phrases '(thou) who art the cause of life to the whole people of India' might apply to Thomas, for the woman addressed her speech to him. The particle 'and' connects ܘܡܚܝܢܐ and ܘܡܐܣܝܢܐ with the first part of the sentence and is paralleled to ܥܒܕܗ ܕܐܠܗܐ. Therefore, it is likely that the woman accepted Thomas as the 'life giver of the souls' ( ܡܚܝܢܐ ܕܢܦ̈ܫܬܐ) and 'healer of the bodies' (ܡܐܣܝܢܐ ܕܦܓ̈ܪܐ). It is

---

ܗܢܐ ܕܝܢ ܐܣܝܐ: ܦܓ̈ܪܐ ܥܡ ܢܦ̈ܫܬܐ ܡܐܣܐ: ܐܝܠܝܢ ܕܬܘܒ ܠܐ ܡܬܚܒܠܝܢ.

[51] *Acts of Thomas*, ܡܒ [42].

[52] Wright, *Apocryphal Acts of the Apostles* II, 182-83. Cf. Klijn, *The Acts of Thomas*, 87 [42].

obvious that the author distinguishes theologically between Jesus as the Healer and His Apostle as the mediator. Thomas is the healer, as long as he heals with Jesus' power: 'he was healing them all by the power of Jesus his Lord'.[53] Since Jesus is the source of healing, Thomas himself is the servant through whom 'healing' ( ܐܣܘܬܐ ܐܣܝܘܬܐ]]) was granted to the people in India,[54] as they considered him as he who was sent 'for the healing of men' (ܠܐܣܝܘܬܐ ܕܒ̈ܢܝܢܫܐ).[55] Later, when a King's general, called Sifur, falsely identifies Thomas with Christ because of his healing miracles, Thomas corrects him and clarifies that he is not the one who heals, but Jesus:

> And when the Apostle had heard these things from the general, he was very sorry for him, and said to him: "If you believe in my Lord Jesus the Messiah that He can heal them, you shall see their recovery". The general, when he heard these things said to him: "I believe that you can heal them". The Apostle said to him: "I am not Jesus, but His servant and His Apostle. Commit then yourself to Him, and He will heal them and help them".[56]

---

[53] *Acts of Thomas*, ܪܟܛ [59]: ܘܗܘܐ ܠܟܠܗܘܢ ܒܚܝܠܐ ܕܝܫܘܥ ܡܪܗ ܡܐܣܐ ܗܘܐ.

[54] *Acts of Thomas*, ܪܟܛ-ܪܠ [59]: ܘܗܘܐ ܠܟܠܗܘܢ ܒܚܝܠܐ ܕܝܫܘܥ ܡܪܗ ܡܐܣܐ ܗܘܐ ܘܡܬܐܣܝܢ ܗܘܘ ܒ̈ܢܝܢܫܐ ܕܒ̈ܢܝܗܘܢ ܗܘܘ ܒܟܘܪ̈ܗܢܐ ܟ̈ܠܗ ܘܒܬܫ̈ܥܝܬܐ ܗܢܐ. ܘܡܫ̈ܬܥܝܢ ܕܡܣܝܒܝܢ ܗܘܘ ܒܗ ܒ̈ܢܝܢܫܐ. ܘܡܫܬܒܚܝܢ ܗܘܘ ܟܠܗܘܢ ܡܢ ܚܕ ܦܘܡܐ ܘܐܡܪܝܢ. ܠܟ ܫܘܒܚܐ ܝܫܘܥ ܡܫܝܚܐ: ܕܝܗܒܬ ܠܢ ܐܣܘܬܐ [ܐܣܝܘܬܐ] ܒܝܕ ܥܒܕܟ ܘܫܠܝܚܟ ܝܗܘܕܐ..

[55] *Acts of Thomas*, ܪܠܐ-ܪܠܒ [62]: ܘܟܕ ܝܗܘܕܐ ܒܟܠܗ̇ ܗܢܕܘ ܡܟܪܙ ܗܘܐ. ܪܒ ܚܝܠܐ ܕܡܠܟܐ ܚܕ ܐܬܐ ܠܘܬܗ ܘܐܡܪ ܠܗ. ܒܥܐ ܐܢܐ ܡܢܟ ܒܒܥܘܬܗ ܕܐܠܗܐ: ܘܐܦ ܕܚܙܐ ܐܢܬ ܕܐܝܟܐ ܩܘܡܟ ܐܬܬ ܠܬܡܢ: ܐܝܟ ܕܠܘܬ ܫܠܝܚܗ ܕܐܠܗܐ ܕܐܫܬܕܪܬ ܠܐܣܝܘܬܐ ܕܒ̈ܢܝܢܫܐ: ܕܫܡܥܬ ܠܓܒܪ̈ܘܬܐ ܕܒܐܝ̈ܕܝܟ ܡܬܥܒܕܢ ܠܗܘܢ.

[56] *Acts of Thomas*, ܪܠܗ [65]: ܘܟܕ ܗܠܝܢ ܫܡܥ ܫܠܝܚܐ ܡܢ ܗܘ ܪܒ ܚܝܠܐ: ܟܪܝܬ ܠܗ ܒܠܗܘܢ ܠܒܐ. ܘܐܡܪ ܠܗ. ܐܢܗܘ ܕܡܗܝܡܢ ܐܢܬ ܒܡܪܝ ܝܫܘܥ ܡܫܝܚܐ ܕܡܫܟܚ ܠܗܘܢ. ܚܙܐ ܐܢܬ ܚܘܠܡܢܗܘܢ. ܐܡܪ ܠܗ ܪܒ ܚܝܠܐ ܗܘ ܟܕ ܫܡܥ ܗܠܝܢ. ܡܛܠ ܕܐܡܪ ܠܗ ܕܗܘܝܘ ܝܫܘܥ. ܡܗܝܡܢ

☞

Later, Sifur gives witness to King Mazdai, that Thomas 'healed (ܐܣܝ) his wife and daughter, and he did not ask for reward, except 'faith' (ܗܝܡܢܘܬܐ) and 'purity/holiness' (ܩܕܝܫܘܬܐ).[57] In order to give a good report about the Apostle, Sifur recounts the healing as one of the good deeds which Thomas performed. After Vizan had asked Thomas to go with him and heal (ܢܐܣܐ) his wife Manashar,[58] she had a vision that a youth laid his hand upon her and she was healed (ܐܬܚܠܡܬ), and she went to the Apostle to be 'completely healed/restored' ( ܕܡܫܠܡܐܝܬ ܐܬܚܠܡ).[59] Here, the term 'restore' (ܚܠܡ) is used.[60] When Manashar saw Thomas, she recognised him as her healer. She says: 'Have you come, my healer from sore disease?'[61]

Thomas' grave and bones also had a healing effect. King Mazdai thought: 'I will go [and] open the grave of Judas, and take one of the bones of the Apostle of God, and will hang it upon my son, and he will be healed'. Searching for the Apostle's grave, the King did not find Thomas' bones. But he took some of the grave's dust

---

ܐܢܐ ܕܐܣܝܐ ܐܝܬ ܠܗܘܢ܀ ❖ ܐܡܪ ܠܗ ܥܠܝܡܐ ܠܐ ܗܘܝܬ ܐܢܐ ܚܘܒ ܐܠܐ ܒܪܗ ܘܥܠܝܡܗ. ܐܙܠ ܠܗ ܕܝܢ ܢܘܦܝܐ. ܘܗܘܐ ܡܐܣܐ ܠܗܘܢ ܘܒܪܟ ܠܒܝܬܗܘܢ. For the general visiting Thomas cf. the captain in Kapernaum visiting Jesus for healing his servant (Jn 4:46-54).

[57] *Acts of Thomas*, ܩܕ [104]: ܣܗܕܬ ܕܝܢ ܬܫܒܘܚܬܐ ܦܪܝܫܬܐ ܥܠ ܐܬܐ ܐܢܐ ܒܒܝܬܗ ܕܡܠܟܐ. ܘܐܦ ܗܘܝܐ ܡܦܣܩܢܐ ܗܘ ܘܫܡܥܢܘ ܠܕܪܐ ܗܘ ܡܠܟܐ ܐܡܪ. ܘܐܦ ܠܥܡܪܐ ܗܘ ܡܠܟܐ ܒܪܡ ܠܟܠܗܘܢ. ܘܐܣܝ ܐܢܫ ܠܐܢܬܬܝ ܘܠܒܪܬܝ ܘܗܘܐ ܫܠܝܚܐ. ܘܡܟܪܙ ܐܚܪܢܐ ܠܐ ܒܥܐ ܐܠܐ ܐܠܐ ܗܝܡܢܘܬܐ. ܘܐܦ ܩܕܝܫܘܬܐ. ܕܢܗܘܘܢ ܠܗ ܫܘܬܦܐ ܒܥܒܕܐ ܕܥܒܕ.

[58] *Acts of Thomas*, ܩܢ [150]: ܘܒܥܐ ܡܢܗ ܐܝܬ ܠܗ ܠܫܠܡܬܐ ܕܢܐܣܝܗ ܠܐܢܬܬܗ ܗܝ.

[59] *Acts of Thomas*, ܩܢܕ [154]: ܐܡܪܐ ܠܗ ܕܗܢܐ ܛܠܝܐ ܗܘ ܟܠ ܐܝܕܗ ܘܐܬܚܠܡܬ. ܘܣܡܬ ܒܫܠܡܐ ܕܐܙܠ ܠܘܬ ܗܘ ܐܟܣܢܝܐ ܐܝܟܐ ܕܢܫܒܩ ܕܡܫܠܡܐܝܬ ܐܬܚܠܡ ❖

[60] *Acts of Thomas*, ܢܛ [59], ܩܕ [104], ܩܢ [150], ܩܥ-ܥܩ [170].

[61] *Acts of Thomas*, ܩܢܗ [155]: ܘܟܕ ܚܙܬܗ ܠܬܐܘܡܐ ܕܝܢ܇ ܐܬܬ ܠܩܕܡܘܗܝ ܘܣܓܕܬ ܠܗ ܘܐܡܪܐ ܠܗ. ܐܬܝܬ ܡܐܣܝܢܝ ܡܢ ܟܘܪܗܢܐ ܒܝܫܐ. ܐܢܬ ܗܘ ܕܙܪܥܬ ܒܫܠܡܐ ܕܐܬܚܠܡܬ ܠܝ ܛܠܝܐ ܗܘܐ ܕܢܬܚܝܢ ܠܘܬܟ ܠܓܘܢܐ ܚܝܝܢܐ.

and hung it upon his son, and he was 'restored/healed' (ܐܬܚܠܡ).[62]

In his prayers, the Apostle makes clear that the Lord is the source of healing. He asks Jesus the Messiah to act as the 'Healer' (ܡܐܣܝܢܐ) and 'Physician' (ܐܣܝܐ) to grant 'His Healing' (ܐܣܝܘܬܗ) to mankind and 'heal' (ܐܣܝ̈ܗ) their bodies and souls from sickness, pain and wounds.[63] The term 'Healer' (ܡܐܣܝܢܐ) appears together with the title 'Life-Giver' (ܡܚܝܢܐ) and refers to the Lord. While in chapter 10, Thomas invokes Jesus the 'Healer of sick souls' (ܡܐܣܝܢܐ ܕܢܦ̈ܫܬܐ ܟܪ̈ܝܗܬܐ) and 'Life-Giver of the [two] worlds' (ܡܚܝܢܐ ܕܥܠ̈ܡܐ) to be beneficial for the King's daughter and her bridegroom,[64] in chapter 37, He is asked

---

62 *Acts of Thomas*, ܥܠܒ-ܥܠܓ [170]: ܘܐܬܚܫܒ ܗܘܐ ܡܙܕܝ ܡܠܟܐ ܒܪܚܫܘܗܝ ܘܐܡܪ. ܕܐܙܠ ܐܦܬܚ ܩܒܪܗ ܕܫܠܝܚܐ: ܘܐܣܒ ܓܪܡܐ ܡܢ ܓܪ̈ܡܘܗܝ ܕܫܠܝܚܐ ܕܐܠܗܐ: ܘܐܬܠܐ ܥܠ ܒܪܝ ܘܢܬܚܠܡ. ܘܐܬܚܙܝ ܠܗ ܬܐܘܡܐ ܒܚܙܘܐ ܘܐܡܪ ܠܗ. ܒܚܝܐ ܠܐ ܗܝܡܢܬ. ܒܡܝܬܐ ܗܐ ܡܗܝܡܢܬ ܕܬܗܝܡܢ: ܠܐ ܕܝܢ ܬܕܚܠ. ܝܫܘܥ ܠܝ ܡܪܝ ܡܪܚܡܢܐ ܡܛܠ ܒܡܪܚܡܢܘܬܗ. ܘܠܐ ܐܫܟܚ ܗܘܐ ܓܪ̈ܡܘܗܝ. ܓܢܒ ܗܘܐ ܐܢܘܢ ܚܕ ܡܢ ܐܚ̈ܐ. ܘܐܘܒܠ ܐܢܘܢ ܠܡܥܪܒܐ. ܘܢܣܒ ܗܘܐ ܕܝܢ ܡܙܕܝ ܡܠܟܐ ܡܢ ܥܦܪܐ ܕܗܘ̇ ܕܘܟܬܐ ܕܪܡܝܢ ܗܘܘ ܒܗ̇ ܓܪ̈ܡܘܗܝ ܕܫܠܝܚܐ: ܘܬܠܐ ܥܠ ܒܪܗ ܘܐܡܪ. ܗܝܡܢܬ ܐܢܐ ܒܟ ܡܪܝ ܝܫܘܥ ܡܫܝܚܐ. ܕܐܪܦܝܬ ܗܘ ܐܝܠܐ ܕܟܐܒܝܢ ܗܘܘ ܠܒܢܝ̈ܢܫܐ ܕܠܐ ܢܚܙܘܢ ܢܘܗܪܐ܀ ܘܟܕ ܬܠܐ ܥܠ ܒܪܗ ܘܗܘܝܢ ܐܬܚܠܡ.

63 *Acts of Thomas*, ܡܚܛ [10, ܡܦܛ [15], ܡܨܒ [25], ܪܛ-ܪܝܒ [34], ܪܘ-ܪܙ [37], ܪܢ [51], ܪܢܒ-ܪܢܓ [52], ܪܢܒ [54], ܪܢܛ [59], ܪܠܗ [65], ܪܠܙ [67], ܪܡܚ-ܪܡܛ [78], ܪܢܐ-ܪܢ [81], ܪܦܐ [281], ܪܨܐ [121], ܫܢܒ [143], ܫܣܒ [156], ܫܣܒ-ܫܣܛ [157], ܫܣܗ [158].

64 *Acts of Thomas*, ܡܚܛ [10]: ܘܫܪܝ ܗܘܐ ܕܢܨܠܐ ܘܢܐܡܪ ܗܟܢܐ. ܡܪܝ ܠܘܝܐ ܕܥܒ̈ܕܘܗܝ. ܘܡܕܒܪܢܐ ܘܗܕܝܐ ܕܐܝܠܝܢ ܕܡܗܝܡܢܝܢ ܒܗ. ܘܒܝܬ ܓܘܣܐ ܘܢܝܚܐ ܕܐܠܝ̈ܨܐ: ܘܣܒܪܐ ܕܡܣܟ̈ܢܐ: ܘܦܪܘܩܐ ܕܡܚ̈ܝܠܐ. ܘܡܐܣܝܢܐ ܕܢܦ̈ܫܬܐ ܟܪ̈ܝܗܬܐ. ܡܚܝܢܐ ܕܥܠ̈ܡܐ ܘܦܪܘܩܐ ܕܒܪ̈ܝܬܐ. 'Healer' (ܡܐܣܝܢܐ) and 'Life-Giver' (ܡܚܝܢܐ) are titles that appear in the context of some other titles, such as 'Companion' (ܠܘܝܐ), 'Guide' (ܗܕܝܐ), 'Conductor' (ܡܕܒܪܢܐ), 'Refuge' (ܒܝܬ ܓܘܣܐ), 'Repose' (ܢܝܚܐ), 'Hope' (ܣܒܪܐ) and 'Deliverer' (ܦܪܘܩܐ).

to be 'the Healer and Life-Giver for your bodies' ( ܡܐܣܝܢܐ ܘܡܚܝܢܐ ܠܦܓܪ̈ܝܟܘܢ).[65] In chapter 10, as well as in chapter 42, the term 'Healer' (ܡܐܣܝܢܐ) and 'Life-Giver' (ܡܚܝܢܐ) are separate. In the latter - if the terms are addressed to the Lord - the 'Life-Giver' refers to 'souls' (ܡܚܝܢܐ ܕܢܦܫ̈ܬܐ) and the 'Healer' to 'bodies' (ܡܐܣܝܢܐ ܕܦܓܪ̈ܐ).[66] In the former, the term 'Healer' is linked with 'souls' (ܡܐܣܝܢܐ ܕܢܦܫ̈ܬܐ), and 'Life-Giver' with 'worlds' (ܡܚܝܢܐ ܕܥܠܡ̈ܐ).[67] Moreover in chapter 156, the Lord has been asked to be 'the Healer in the place of sickness' (ܡܐܣܝܢܐ ܒܐܬܪܐ ܕܟܘܪܗܢܐ) and 'the Physician to their bodies' (ܐܣܝܐ ܠܦܓܪ̈ܝܗܘܢ),[68] whereas in chapter 143 He is acknowledged to be the 'Physician of all hidden and visible pains' (ܐܣܝܐ ܕܟܠܗܘܢ ܟܐܒ̈ܐ ܟܣ̈ܝܐ ܘܓܠ̈ܝܐ) and the 'Physician of 'His creation' (ܐܣܝܐ ܕܒܪܝܬܗ).[69] While Thomas proclaims Jesus

---

[65] *Acts of Thomas*, ܪܘ-ܪܙ [37]: ܐܠܐ ܗܝܡܢܘ ܘܫܡܥܘ ܒܡܪܢ ܝܫܘܥ ܡܫܝܚܐ ... ܘܢܗܘܐ ܠܟܘܢ ܗܕܝܐ ... ܠܡܐܬܐ ... ܡܒܘܥܐ ܕܡܝ̈ܐ ܚܝ̈ܐ ... ܣܠܐ ܡܠܝܐ ... ܢܝܚܐ ܠܢܦܫ̈ܬܟܘܢ. ܘܡܐܣܝܢܐ ܘܡܚܝܢܐ ܠܦܓܪ̈ܝܟܘܢ܀ Here the Apostle motivates people to believe in Jesus Christ so that He will become for them not only 'the Healer and Life-Giver' ( ܡܐܣܝܢܐ ܘܡܚܝܢܐ), but also 'the Guide' (ܗܕܝܐ), 'the Fountain of living water' (ܡܒܘܥܐ ܕܡܝ̈ܐ ܚܝ̈ܐ), 'Full Basket' (ܣܠܐ ܡܠܝܐ) and 'Rest' (ܢܝܚܐ).

[66] *Acts of Thomas*, ܪܝܐ [42].

[67] *Acts of Thomas*, ܩܦܚ [10]. For ܡܚܝܢܐ see also ܪܛ [39], ܪܝܗ [45], ܪܝܘ [47], ܪܟܒ [53], ܪܠ [60], ܪܠܗ [65], ܪܦܐ [281], ܫܝܒ [143].

[68] *Acts of Thomas*, ܫܟܒ [156]: ܘܗܘܝ ܠܗܘܢ ܡܐܣܝܢܐ ܒܐܬܪܐ ܕܟܘܪܗܢܐ. ܗܘܝ ܠܗܘܢ ܡܢܝܚܢܐ ܒܐܬܪܐ ܠܐܝܐ. ܘܥܕ ܐܝܟ ܒܐܬܪܐ ܠܗܘܐ. ܘܕܒܪ ܐܝܟ ܡܢ ܚܝܠܐ ܒܐܬܪܐ ܕܡܠܒܒܐ. ܗܘܝ ܐܣܝܐ ܠܦܓܪ̈ܝܗܘܢ ܘܐܚܝܐ ܠܢܦܫ̈ܬܗܘܢ. ܘܥܒܕ ܐܝܟ ܢܦܫܐ ܘܗܝܟ̈ܠܐ ܡܕܝܪ̈ܐ. ܘܬܬܒܪ ܒܗܘܢ ܪܘܚܐ ܡܕܝܪܐ ܀ Jesus Christ as 'the Healer in place of sickness' (ܡܐܣܝܢܐ ܒܐܬܪܐ ܕܟܘܪܗܢܐ) is not just the Healer of bodies, but also 'the Physician of bodies' (ܐܣܝܐ ܠܦܓܪ̈ܝܗܘܢ). In this chapter the term 'your souls' (ܢܦܫ̈ܬܟܘܢ) is not linked with Jesus as the Healer or Physician, but with Him Who is able 'to give life' (ܘܐܚܝܐ).

[69] *Acts of Thomas*, ܫܝܒ [143]: ܘܐܡܪ ܬܘܒ ܝܗܘܕܐ. ܗܝܡܢܘ ܒܐܣܝܐ ܕܟܠܗܘܢ ܟܐܒ̈ܐ ܟܣ̈ܝܐ ܘܓܠ̈ܝܐ. ܘܡܚܝܢܐ ܕܢܦܫ̈ܬܐ ܐܝܠܝܢ

☞

Christ's incarnation, he describes the Lord as the Physician, Life-Giver and Redeemer for those who truly repent.[70]

Even though Jesus Christ as a Physician without fee ( ܐܣܝܐ ܕܡܓܢ) was crucified for the sake of mankind,[71] He is glorified for his deeds and 'His healings' (ܐܣܘ̈ܬܗ).[72] While ordinary physicians heal corruptible bodies ( ܐܣܘ̈ܬܗ ܗܠܝܢ ܦܓܪ̈ܢܝܬܐ ܕܡܫܬܪ̈ܝܢ ܠܗܘܢ), the Lord, through His Apostle, offers an indissoluble healing (ܗܝ ܐܣܝܘܬܗ ܠܐ ܡܫܬܪܝܢܐ) to mankind.[73] But the Lord, as 'the Healer of His creation' (ܐܣܝܐ ܕܒܪܝܬܗ), grants His healing for both body and soul.[74] Therefore, the people praise God for giving them 'healing through His servant' (ܐܣܝܘܬܐ [ܐܣܝܘܬܐ] ܒܝܕ ܥܒܕܟ),[75] as a youth proclaimed his faith saying:

---

ܕܟܠܡ ܡܚܝܢܐ ܡܢܗ. ܗܘܝܘ ܒܪܢܫܐ. ܘܒܪ ܡܠܟܐ ܕܗܘܐ ܥܒܕܐ ܘܡܦܪܩܢܐ. ܗܘܝܘ ܐܣܝܐ ܕܒܪܝܬܗ. ܘܡܚܝܢܐ ܗܘ ܕܒܪܘ̈ܗܝ. ܗܘܝܘ ܕܡܒܛܠܐ ܕܡܬܡܠܠܘܗ̈ܝ: ܘܡܬܬܚܝܠ ܘܡܬܚܫܒ ܡܢ ܐܝܠܝܢ ܕܠܐ ܫܡܥܘܗ̈ܝ. ܗܘܝܘ ܡܚܪܪ ܡܢ ܥܒܕܘܬܐ ܘܡܢ ܚܛܝܬܐ. ܘܡܢ ܫܘܥܒܕܐ ܘܡܢ ܚܘܣܪܢܐ ܠܡܩܢܝܢܘܗ̈ܝ.. In chapter 143 one finds the term 'Life-Giver' again, used together with 'souls' (ܘܡܚܝܢܐ ܕܢܦ̈ܫܬܐ).

[70] *Acts of Thomas*, ܣܗ [65]: ܡܗܝܡܢ ܐܢܐ ܒܟ ܝܫܘܥ ܡܫܝܚܐ ܐܠܗܐ: ܕܐܢܬ ܗܘ ܚܝܐ ܒܪܗ ܕܚܝܐ. ܘܗܘܝܬ ܒܪܢܫܐ ܘܐܬܚܫܚܬ ܐܣܝܐ ܘܡܚܝܢܐ ܘܦܪܘܩܐ. ܠܟܠܗܘܢ ܐܝܠܝܢ ܕܒܫܪܪܐ ܬܝܒܝܢ ܠܘܬܟ.

[71] *Acts of Thomas*, ܥܣܪ [156].

[72] *Acts of Thomas*, ܣܗ [65]: ܒܥܒܕܘܗ̈ܝ ܘܐܣܘ̈ܬܗ ܡܫܬܒܚ.

[73] *Acts of Thomas*, ܥܚ-ܬܡܢܐ [78]: ܡܢܐ ܐܢܫ ܠܟ ܬܫܒܘܚܬܐ ܥܠ ܡܣܒ̈ܪܢܘܬܗ ܡܫܬ̈ܦܝܐ.. ܗܠܝܢ ܒܢܝ ܐܢܫܘܬܐ ܐܝܟ ܕܫܘܐ ܠܐܘܡܢܘܬܟ. ܘܐܦ ܗܘ ܕܬܫܒܘܚܬܐ ܥܠ ܡܫܠܡܢܘܬܐ ܕܡܣܬܒܪܢܘܬܗ: ܠܐ ܡܫܟܚ ܐܢܬ ܕܬܘܣܦܬܐ ܐܝܟ. ܡܢ ܡܬܕܡܪ ܐܢܬ ܥܠ ܐܣܘ̈ܬܗ ܗܠܝܢ ܦܓܪ̈ܢܝܬܐ ܕܡܫܬܪ̈ܝܢ ܠܗܘܢ. ܒܪ ܗܘ ܐܣܝܘܬܗ ܠܐ ܡܫܬܪܝܢܐ ܕܢܦܫܬܗܘܢ. ܒܗܕ ܐܢܬ. ܡܢܐ ܡܬܚܫܒܐ ܐܢܬ ܒܚܝ̈ܐ ܗܠܝܢ ܕܙܒܢܐ: ܘܥܠ ܚܝ̈ܐ ܕܠܥܠܡ ܗܘܐ ܠܥܠܡ ܡܬܚܫܒ ܐܢܬ.

[74] *Acts of Thomas*, ܥܣܪ-ܥܣܪ [157]: ܠܐܣܝܘܬܐ ܕܦܓܪ̈ܝܗܘܢ ܘܕܢܦ̈ܫܬܗܘܢ. See also ܥܣܪ [158]: ܘܠܐܣܝܘܬܐ ܕܦܓܪ̈ܝܢ ܘܕܢܦ̈ܫܬܢ.

[75] *Acts of Thomas*, ܪܚܛ-ܪܚ [59].

I have in truth believed in You my Lord Jesus the Messiah, the gifts of Your Father, that in You are all aids and in You all dispensation, and in You all healings, and in You life for the repentant, who in truth repent unto You with all their heart.[76]

Healing is from the Lord Who has all kinds of healing. He is capable of healing bodies and souls,[77] all hidden and visible pains,[78] suffering and wounds.[79] The requirement for healing is faith in Jesus Christ and repentance from sin.[80] Approaching the Lord in faith and receiving his gifts and sacraments is what restores and heals man.

### 2.2.3 Healing Imagery in Connection with Baptism and the Eucharist

The author of the *Acts of Thomas* links healing imagery with the sacraments of the Church. In four passages, Thomas the Apostle attributes healing to the oil and water of baptism and to the holy bread and wine of the Eucharist. The first time where the Eucharist is linked with healing occurs in Thomas' epicletic prayer when he let those whom he baptised take Holy Communion. Thomas begs Jesus' holy name to come and communicate with them 'that it [the holy body] may be unto them for the health of their soul and for the life of their bodies'.[81] While the term 'health' (ܚܘܠܡܢܐ) refers to the soul, the 'life' (ܚܝ̈ܐ) is related to bodies.

---

[76] *Acts of Thomas*, ܪܢܕ [54]: ܗܝܡܢܬ ܒܟ ܒܫܪܪܐ ܡܪܝ ܝܫܘܥ ܡܫܝܚܐ ܡܘܗܒܬܐ ܕܐܒܘܟܝ. ܕܒܟ ܗܘ ܟܠ ܥܘܕܪ̈ܢܝܢ. ܘܒܟ ܗܘ ܟܠ ܦܘܪ̈ܣܝܢ. ܘܒܟ ܗܘ ܟܠ ܐܣܘ̈ܢ. ܘܒܟ ܗܘ ܚܝ̈ܐ ܠܬܝ̈ܒܐ ܕܒܫܪܪܐ ܬܝܒܝܢ ܠܘܬܟ ܡܢ ܟܠܗ ܠܒܗܘܢ. See also ܪܢܐ-ܪܢܒ [52].

[77] *Acts of Thomas*, ܡܚܠ [10], ܪܘ-ܪܙ [37], ܪܟܐ [42], ܫܟܒ-ܫܟܠ [156], ܫܟܠ-ܫܟܕ [157], ܫܟܕ-ܫܟܗ [158].

[78] *Acts of Thomas*, ܫܟܒ [143].

[79] *Acts of Thomas*, ܪܠ-ܪܙ [34], ܪܦܐ [113], ܪܓܐ [121].

[80] *Acts of Thomas*, ܪܒ [34], ܪܠ-ܪܢ [51], ܪܢܕ [54].

[81] *Acts of Thomas*, ܪܢܚ [49]: ܘܐܬܐ ܫܠܝܚܐ ܩܡ ܠܥܠ ܡܢܗ ܘܐܡܪ ܗܘܐ. ܫܡܟ ܕܐܫܡܥܬܢ ܕܬܬܩܪܒ ܠܦܓܪܟ ܩܕܝܫܐ ܘܕܢܫܬܘܬܦ ܠܕܒܝܢ ܩܕܝܫܐ ... ܒܚܝܠ ܡܢܝ ܕܬܐܬܐ ܘܬܫܬܘܬܦ ܥܡܢ ܠܚܘܕܪܐ ܘܠܫܝܢܐ: ܘܠܡܬܦܢܝܢܘܬܗܘܢ ܕܒܒ̈ܝܢ ܠܗܘܢ. ܕܬܬܠܠܝܢ ܒܫܡܟ ܒܡܫܝܚܐ ☞

However, Holy Communion does not make everyone healthy. A young man that murdered a woman 'came and took the Eucharist, and was going to put it into his mouth, but both his hands dried up and it did not reach his mouth.[82] Seeing this, the Apostle inquired why this happened. Thomas was convinced that the gift of the Lord usually 'heals' (ܡܐܣܝܐ) those who take Holy Communion in 'love' (ܕܒܚܘܒܐ), 'truth' (ܘܒܫܪܪܐ) and in 'faith' (ܘܒܗܝܡܢܘܬܐ).[83] The 'withered' (ܟܘܒܫܘ ܐܘܒܫܬܟ) hand of the young man indicates that, while the Eucharist can heal, it can also cause sickness. After the young man confessed his sin, - for he was baptised - the Apostle prayed over the waters so that Jesus' 'power' (ܚܝܠܟ), 'healing' (ܐܣܝܘܬܟ) and 'mercy' (ܡܪܚܡܢܘܬܟ) might descend and abide with them. The Lord's healing restored the hands as they had been before. The Apostle invokes the healing of the Lord, as one of His gifts, to come and dwell in the water. Full of trust, the young man washed in the water and was healed.[84]

---

ܘܚܝܠܟ ܐܚܝܢ. ܘܢܗܘܐ ܠܗܘܢ ܠܣܘܠܩܢܐ ܕܦܓܪ̈ܝܗܘܢ ܘܠܚ̈ܝܐ ܕܢܦ̈ܫܬܗܘܢ ܒܥܠܡܟ ܚܝܐ ܀

82 *Acts of Thomas*, ܪܦ-ܪܦܐ [51]: ܐܬܐ ܗܘܐ ܕܝܢ ܬܘܒ ܥܠܝܡܐ ܚܕ: ܕܥܒܝܕܐ ܗܘܬ ܠܗ ܒܝܫܬܐ ܐܚܪܬܐ ܕܥܒܕ ܣܢܝܐ ܗܘܬ. ܘܐܬܐ ܘܢܣܒ ܐܘܟܪܝܣܛܝܐ. ܘܐܙܠ ܕܢܣܡ ܒܦܘܡܗ. ܘܝܒ̈ܫ ܗܘ̈ܝ ܬܪ̈ܬܝܗܝܢ ܐܝ̈ܕܘܗܝ. ܘܠܐ ܡܛ̈ܝ ܠܦܘܡܗ.

83 *Acts of Thomas*, ܪܦ-ܪܦܐ [51]: ܘܦܪܣܗ̇ ܫܠܝܚܐ ܘܐܡܪ ܠܗ. ܐܡܪ ܠܝ ܒܪܝ ܘܠܐ ܬܒܗܬ ܡܢ. ܡܢܐ ܥܒܕܬ ܘܐܬܝܬ ܠܟ ܗܪܟܐ. ܕܗܐ ܡܘܗܒܬܗ ܕܡܪܢ ܐܚܘܝܬܟ: ܗܕܐ ܕܡܐܣܝܐ ܟܠܗܘܢ ܕܒܚܘܒܐ ܘܒܫܪܪܐ ܘܒܗܝܡܢܘܬܐ ܩܪܒܝܢ ܠܗ̇ ܡܐܣܝܐ ܠܗܘܢ: ܠܟ ܕܝܢ ܕܠܟ ܟܘܒܫܘ ܐܘܒܫܬܟ.

84 *Act of Thomas*, ܪܦܐ-ܪܦܒ [52]: ܘܐܬܝܘ ܠܗ ܡ̈ܝܐ ܣܓܝܐ̈ܐ ܕܢܝܓܠܐ ܥܠܝܗܘܢ ܘܩܡ ܘܦܢܝ ܘܐܡܪ. ܡ̈ܝܐ ܕܡܢ ܡ̈ܝܐ ܚ̈ܝܐ ܐܬܝܬܘܢ ܠܢ: ܘܢܘܗܪܐ ܕܡܢ ܢܘܗܪܐ ܐܫܬܕܪܬܘܢ ܠܢ: ܫܠܝܐ ܕܡܢ ܫܠܝܐ ܐܫܬܕܪܬܘܢ ܠܢ: ܬܐܬܐ ܚܝܠܟ ܡܪܢ: ܘܐܣܝܘܬܟ ܘܡܪܚܡܢܘܬܟ ܬܫܪܐ ܘܬܫܪܐ ܥܠ ܡ̈ܝܐ ܗܠܝܢ ܕܒܫܡܟ ܢܣܒ ܚܝܠܐ ܐܬܪܬ ܥܠܝܗܘܢ. ܘܐܡܪ. ܡܗܝܡܢܘܬܐ ܕܪܘܚܐ ܕܩܘܕܫܐ ܬܫܪܐ ܒܗܘܢ ܀ ܘܐܡܪ ܠܗܘ ܥܠܝܡܐ. ܙܠ ܐܣܚܐ ܐܝ̈ܕܝܟ ܒܗܠܝܢ ܡ̈ܝܐ. ܘܐܙܠ ܐܣܚܐ ܐܝ̈ܕܘܗܝ ܘܗܘ̈ܝ ܐܝܟܢܐ ܕܐܝܬܝܗܝܢ ܗ̈ܘܝ. ܟܕ ܠܐ ܢܟ̈ܝܢ.

The next passage where the author links the holy sacraments with the power of healing is Thomas' song of praise.[85] It is only in this doxology[86] where the term 'Medicine of Life' (ܣܡ ܚ̈ܝܐ) occurs. The author addresses the doxology to the Father and to the Son in turn. While the verb 'to glorify' (ܡܫܒܚ) is used for the Father, 'to sing halleluja' (ܡܗܠܠܬ) is related to the Son. In the middle of the song, after glorifying and praising the Father and the Son for giving life and feeding everyone, the author writes:

To be praised are You, the beloved Son, Who gave (new) life to our deadness, and turned us back from going astray, and were to us a Medicine of Life through Your life-giving body and by the sprinkling of Your living blood.[87]

Through His death, when He was crucified and His blood was sprinkled for us, He became the 'Medicine of Life' (ܣܡ ܚ̈ܝܐ). The Lord gave us His 'life-giving body' (ܒܦܓܪܟ ܡܚܝܢܐ) and the 'sprinkling of His living blood' (ܘܒܪܣܣ ܕܕܡܟ ܚܝܐ) once on Golgotha, but this is present in the holy bread and wine in the Church. The verb 'tasted' (ܘܛܥܡܢܟ) in the next sentence addressed to the Father indicates that Jesus as the Fruit of the Father has been consumed sacramentally by the believers.[88] In the next sentence, the author praises Jesus as the 'Peace-Maker, Who

---

[85] *Acts of Thomas*, ܪܥܐ - ܪܦܗ (Wright tr. 245-51).

[86] While Wright includes this doxology in his edition (ܪܥܐ-ܪܦܗ) and translation (Wright tr. 245-251), Klijn excludes it for he considers it as secondary; cf. A. F. J. Klijn, *The Acts of Thomas* (Leiden 1962), 2. The doxology is available in Sachau's Manuscript only. See Sachau No. 222 (Berlin 1881), edited by P. Bedjan, *Acta Martyrum et Sanctorum* III (Parisiis 1892), 1-175.

[87] *Acts of Thomas*, ܪܦܐ (Wright tr, 248): ܡܗܠܠܬ ܒܪܐ ܪܚܝܡܐ. ܕܐܚܝܬ ܠܡܝܘܬܘܬܢ. ܘܐܦܢܝܬ ܠܛܘܥܝܘܬܢ. ܘܗܘܝܬ ܠܢ ܣܡ ܚ̈ܝܐ ܒܦܓܪܟ ܡܚܝܢܐ ܘܒܪܣܣ ܕܕܡܟ ܚܝܐ ܀

[88] *Acts of Thomas*, ܪܦܐ (Wright tr. 248): ܡܫܒܚ ܐܢܬ ܐܒܐ ܪܒܐ. ܡܢ ܟܠ ܦܘܡ̈ܝܢ ܘܡܢ ܟܠ ܠܫ̈ܢܝܢ. ܕܐܬܪܥܝܬ ܠܢ ܒܡܫܝܚܟ ܘܛܥܡܢܟ ܒܪ ܦܐܪܐ. ܘܗܘܝܢ ܒܢ̈ܝ ܚܝܝܢ܀

has healed our wounds' (ܕܐܣܝܬ ܫܘ̈ܚܬܢ).[89] In both sentences where healing imagery occurs, it is the Son Who is linked with healing. He is a Medicine of Life through His holy body and blood. The bread and wine of the Eucharist, consecrated as the Body and Blood, are the Medicine of Life which have the power of life-giving. In this context it is also the Son Who 'has healed our wounds' (ܐܣܝܬ ܫܘ̈ܚܬܢ).

The passage about Mygdonia's baptism makes the relationship between healing and the epiclesis clear. The Apostle calls Jesus 'the Life and Health and Remission of sins' ( ܚܝ̈ܐ ܘܚܘܠܡܢܐ ܘܫܘܒܩܢ ܚܛܗ̈ܐ), and begs Him to send His power 'to abide upon this oil' (ܘܬܫܪܐ ܥܠ ܡܫܚܐ ܗܢܐ) and His holiness 'to dwell in it' (ܘܩܕܝܫܘܬܟ ܬܫܪܐ ܒܗ).[90] Jesus Christ makes man healthy, and His holy power in the oil heals the wounds of those who will be anointed: 'And he cast [it] upon the head of Mygdonia and said: "Heal her of her old [previous] wounds, and wash away from her her sores and strengthen her weakness"'.[91] The verb 'to heal' (ܐܣܝܗ̇) is used in parallel with 'to wash' (ܐܫܝܓ). The result of the anointing and baptism is not just the re-birth, but also the healing of man from his wound. The 'previous wounds' ( ܫܘܚܬ̈ܗ̇ ܩܕܡܝ̈ܬܐ) refer to her individual sins and trespasses and is unlikely to be related to the Fall from Paradise.

Finally, healing aspects are also found in the baptism and Holy Communion of Vizan and his companions. When the Apostle cast the oil upon the head of Vizan and upon the others, he said: 'In Your name, Jesus the Messiah, let it be to these persons for the

---

[89] *Acts of Thomas*, ܪܦܐ-ܪܦܒ (Wright tr. 248): ܒܡܠܠܬܟ ܒܪܐ ܚܕ ܝܚܝܕܐ. ܕܐܣܝܬ ܫܘ̈ܚܬܢ ܘܐܦܝܣܬ ܟܠܝܠܬܢ: ܘܚܕܬܬ ܦܘܩܕܢܢ: ܘܐܪ̈ܝܪܬܢ ܒܥܒ̈ܕܝܟ ܘܢܬܚܡ ܒܟ ܠܐܒܘܟ ܀

[90] *Acts of Thomas*, ܪܟܐ [121]: ܐܢܬ ܗܘ ܡܫܡܠܝܢܐ ܕܗܕܪ̈ܐ ܡܦܝ̈ܩܐ. ܐܢܬ ܗܘ ܡܪܢ ܝܫܘܥ ܚܝ̈ܐ ܘܚܘܠܡܢܐ ܘܫܘܒܩܢ ܚܛܗ̈ܐ. ܢܐܬܐ ܚܝܠܟ ܘܬܫܪܐ ܥܠ ܡܫܚܐ ܗܢܐ. ܘܩܕܝܫܘܬܟ ܬܫܪܐ ܒܗ.

[91] *Acts of Thomas*, ܪܟܐ [121]: ܘܐܪܡܝ ܒܪܫܗ̇ ܕܡܓܕܘܢܝܐ ܘܐܡܪ. ܘܐܣܝܗ̇ ܡܢ ܫܘܚܬ̈ܗ̇ ܩܕܡܝ̈ܬܐ: ܘܐܫܝܓ ܡܢܗ̇ ܫܘ̈ܚܢܝܗ̇. ܘܚܝܠ ܡܚܝܠܘܬܗ̇ ܀

remission of offences and sins, and for the destruction of the enemy, and for the healing of their souls and bodies'.[92] The baptismal oil serves for healing (ܐܣܝܘܬܐ), the Eucharist for health/restoration (ܚܘܠܡܢܐ) and healing (ܘܐܣܝܘܬܐ) both of souls and body. The Apostle prays: 'Let this Eucharist be to you for life and rest and joy and health, and for the healings of your souls and of your bodies'.[93]

### 2.2.4 Conclusion

Much more strongly than the Odist, the author of the *Acts of Thomas* draws attention to the spiritual sickness of mankind. This is explicit in his use of healing terminology, such as 'sick' ( ܟܪܝܗܐ), 'sick souls' (ܢܦܫܬܐ ܟܪܝܗܬܐ) and 'all sickness/pains, hidden and visible' (ܟܠܗܘܢ ܟܐܒܐ ܟܣܝܐ ܘܓܠܝܐ). Spiritual sickness is also indicated in the metaphorical use of the serpent that poisons man with its venom, as a representative of the enemy of humanity, the devil, the Evil One and Satan.

Physical diseases and pains are not absent from the *Acts of Thomas* either. Spiritual and physical sicknesses often appear together, and they are related to each other. Sin and moral life could be the cause of both visible and invisible pains.

However, the source of healing is always the Lord Who is capable of healing man from every kind of sickness. Because of Jesus Christ's humiliation and descent into the world, the author speaks of Him as 'being/becoming sick' in order to serve as Physician and Medicine for His creation. Jesus Christ, as the main Healer and the Physician par excellence, was sent to heal humanity, as the healing miracles characterise His ministry. Likewise the Apostle Judas Thomas was sent to India to perform healing

---

92 *Acts of Thomas*, ܪܟܐ-ܪܟܒ [157]: ܘܐܪܫܡ ܒܪܫܗ ܕܘܢ. ܘܗܕܝܢ ܒܪܫܗܘܢ ܕܗܠܝܢ ܘܐܡܪ. ܒܫܡܟ ܝܫܘܥ ܡܫܝܚܐ. ܢܗܘܐ ܠܗܘܢ ܠܗܠܝܢ ܢܦܫܬܐ ܠܫܘܒܩܢ ܚܘܒܐ ܘܚܛܗܐ. ܘܠܚܘܒܠܗ ܕܒܥܠܕܒܒܐ ܘܠܐܣܝܘܬܐ ܕܢܦܫܬܗܘܢ ܘܕܦܓܪܝܗܘܢ ❖

93 *Acts of Thomas*, ܪܟܒ-ܪܟܓ [158]: ܘܐܡܪ ܬܗܘܐ ܠܟܘܢ ܐܘܟܪܣܛܝܐ ܗܕܐ ܠܚܝܐ ܘܠܢܝܚܐ ܘܠܚܕܘܬܐ ܘܠܚܘܠܡܢܐ. ܘܠܐܣܝܘܬܐ ܕܢܦܫܬܟܘܢ ܘܕܦܓܪܝܟܘܢ.

through the medicine of his Lord. The healing miracles of the Apostle are highly comparable and similar to those of Jesus Christ. Both of them provide medicine for body and soul, and generally healed any kind of sickness and drove out demons. Both their healing is without recompense, but it required faith and is different from that of the ordinary medical physicians.

It has to be emphasised, that the author - like Aphrahat and Ephrem - clearly distinguishes between Jesus Christ as the main Healer and Source of healing, and His servant Judas Thomas as the mediator through whom God's medicine is made accesible to the people in India.

The mission of the Apostle and his charitable work - like the ministry of his Master - are characterised by his healing miracles. People came to him in a similar way to going to see a medical doctor in his practice. He prayed for those who approached him with faith and God healed them. Also after his death, people approached his grave and bones in order to be healed.

Furthermore, the author makes clear that healing can be achieved by approaching the Lord, as well as His disciples and the divine sacraments in the Church with the right attitude, i.e. faith. The Lord's healing power is given to His disciples, and it dwells and abides in the eucharistic bread and wine, and is provided in the oil and water of Christian baptism. Baptism is capable of washing and healing man's wounds, transgressions and sins, whereas the Eucharist serves as divine medicine for mankind.

## 2.3 Aphrahat's Demonstrations

Aphrahat's *Demonstrations*, addressed to one of his friends in the first half of the fourth century, offer a wide variety of Biblical aspects of healing and healing terminology. The biblical references and citations illustrate Aphrahat's good knowledge of the Old Testament, as well as the New. While most Demonstrations include only a little healing imagery or a few relevant verses from the Bible (such as Demonstration 1 On Faith and 2 On Love, which mention Jesus' healing miracles), the theme of healing and healing terminology are primarily focused in the Demonstration 7 On Repentance where the sinners are compared to those wounded in the war. The Demonstrations 14 On Intercession and 23 On the Vinecluster (23) come second in importance as texts concerning healing.

After having discussed the biblical references that contain healing imagery, some of the significant terms such as 'physician', 'medicine' and 'wound' are studied mainly on the basis of three Demonstrations: Demonstration 7 On Repentance (ܬܝܒܘܬܐ), 14 On Intercession (ܦܝܣܐ) and 23 On the Vinecluster (ܛܘܛܝܬܐ).

### 2.3.1 Old Testament Healing Imagery in Aphrahat's Demonstrations

In his *Demonstrations*, Aphrahat includes a number of biblical references when he speaks about healing or sickness. This subsection considers references from the Old Testament. Firstly he relates the curse of Adam and Eve to disease and suffering (Gen 3:8-18). Secondly, some verses from Leviticus and 2 Kings are quoted when Aphrahat discusses the Law of purity and cleanliness, such as the commandments concerning food and leprosy (Lev 11:2; 13:45-46; 15:5). Gehazi and King Uzziah's leprosy, as well as Hezekiah's sickness and Uzziah's punishment, are included. Two Psalms are used in the context of healing (Ps 41:2-4; 69:27). Finally, Aphrahat's excellent knowledge of the Prophets enables him to use the prophecies which are linked to healing in different Demonstrations (Is 28:12; 53:3; 63:11; Jer 6:7-8; 33:10; Ez 13:4-5; 33:11; 34:2-19; Mal 1:14; 2 Macc 9:18).

#### *2.3.1.1 Adam and Eve's Fall (Gen 3:8-18)*

Adam and Eve's Fall is mentioned in Demonstrations 6.6, 7.8 and 23.3. Here the Fall is related to sickness, suffering, pain and death. In the Demonstration On Repentance, Aphrahat considers repentance as a medicine. Those who become injured in the battle of life, need to reveal their wounds in order to be healed. Unlike Adam, those who sin should not be ashamed to confess their sins:

I also advise you who are stricken not to be ashamed to say that we have been overpowered in the battle. Take the priceless medicine and repent and live before you get killed. I remind you, physicians, about what is written in our wise Physician's books that He has not stopped repentance. After Adam had sinned, He called him to repentance, saying: Where are you, Adam? And [Adam] hid his sin from the One Who examines the heart; and he laid the blame on Eve who had led him astray. And because he did not confess his transgression, [God] punished him and all his children by death (Gen 3:8-9).[94]

Even though the Demonstrations are addressed in general to one of Aphrahat's friends, here he addresses the 'physicians' (ܐܣܘ̈ܬܐ) who are the leaders, priests or bishops of the faithful people, and likewise the ܒܢ̈ܝ ܩܝܡܐ. Nevertheless, it is the Lord Who is 'our Physician' (ܐܣܝܢ) Whose 'priceless medicine' ( ܣܡܐ ܕܠܐ ܕܡܝ̈ܢ) is given in the Bible, as for example through the narrative about Adam. Although Adam was disobedient to the Lord's commandment, God offered him repentance when he asked him: 'Where are you Adam' (Gen 3:9: ܐܝܟܐ ܐܢܬ ܐܕܡ). If Adam had accepted repentance as the 'priceless medicine' ( ܣܡܐ ܕܠܐ ܕܡܝ̈ܢ), he would not have been punished with death. However, rejecting repentance from 'our wise Physician' ( ܐܣܝܢ ܚܟܝܡܐ) is a further sin that increases the wounds and pains.[95]

Demonstration 6 deals with the sons and daughters of the covenant (ܒܢ̈ܝ ܩܝܡܐ). In paragraph 5 where Aphrahat speaks about the consecrated life (ܩܕܝܫܘܬܐ = 'holiness'),[96] he

---

[94] *Aphr* 7.8: ܐܦ ܠܟܘܢ ܡܠܟ ܐܢܐ ܠܐܝܠܝܢ ܕܡܬܟܣܝܢ ܕܠܐ ܬܟܣܘܢ ܬܐܡܪ̈ܘܢ: ܕܐܬܥܩܠ ܒܐܝܟܢܐ. ܗܒܘ ܠܟܘܢ ܣܡܐ ܕܠܐ ܕܡܝ̈ܢ: ܘܬܘܒܘ ܘܚܝܘ ܒܗ ܠܐ ܬܬܡܠܠܘܢ.ܠܟܘܢ ܕܝܢ ܡܟܣܢܐ ܐܢܐ ܐܣܘ̈ܬܐ ܡܢ ܐܕܡ ܕܟܬܝܒ ܒܣܦܪ̈ܘܗܝ، ܕܐܣܝܢ ܚܟܝܡܐ: ܕܗܘ ܠܐ ܟܠܐ ܬܝܒܘܬܐ. ܟܕ ܚܛܐ ܓܝܪ ܐܕܡ ܗܘܐ ܠܗ ܬܝܒܘܬܐ ܟܕ ܐܡܪ ܠܗ: ܐܝܟܐ ܐܢܬ ܐܕܡ. ܘܗܘ ܛܫܝ ܚܛܗܗ ܡܢ ܒܚܢ ܠܒܐ: ܘܐܚܕ ܥܠܬܐ ܒܚܘܐ ܕܐܛܥܝܬܗ. ܘܥܠ ܕܠܐ ܐܘܕܝ ܒܣܟܠܘܬܗ ܓܙܪ ܥܠܘܗܝ ܡܘܬܐ ܘܥܠ ܟܠܗܘܢ ܝܠܘܕ̈ܘܗܝ.

[95] *Aphr* 14.42: ܐܕܡ ܟܕ ܚܛܐ ܩܪܐ ܠܗ ܡܪܗ ܕܢܬܘܒ: ܘܠܐ ܩܒܠ ܘܐܣܬܬܪ ܒܥܠܠܬܐ: ܕܚܘܐ ܗܝ ܐܛܥܝܬܢܝ: ܘܠܐ ܐܬܬܘܝ، ܘܠܐ ܬܒ (Gen 3:12). Cf. R. J. Owens, The Genesis and Exodus Citations of Aphrahat the Persian Sage (Leiden 1983), 63-62.

[96] The term ܩܕܝܫܘܬܐ reflects a life with sexual abstinence which required a special charism. Although Aphrahat and Ephrem were ܐܝܚܝ̈ܕܝܐ and lived the consecrated life, they affirm and approve marriage (*Aphr* 6.3-4; 18.8; Haer 45.6-10; Virg 5.14). For works on early Syriac monasticism see A. Adam, 'Grundbegriffe des Mönchtums in Sprachlicher Sicht', *ZKG* 65 (1953-54), 209-39; - E. Beck, 'Ein Beitrag zur

☞

emphasises the separation of certain prophets from women. Since the enemy approached man through a woman, and she is used as a 'weapon' (ܙܝܢܐ) and 'harp' (ܟܢܪܐ) by Satan, the prophets were served by male servants and not by a woman.[97] Therefore, the curse is blamed on women in the following paragraph: 'Because of her, the Law's curse came to exist; and because of her, the promise of death: with pains she will give birth to children and hand them over to death. Because of her, the earth was cursed to produce thorns and thistles (Gen 3:16-18)'.[98] The sentence 'with pains she will give birth to children' (ܒܟܐ̈ܒܐ ܓܝܪ ܝܠܕܐ ܒܢ̈ܝܐ) is paraphrased from Genesis 3:16. The pains, as a part of the curse, belong just to giving birth. But the curse of death, including the death of children, emphasises the pain and suffering of life until the coming of the Messiah. Through the coming of Mary's blessed Son, the thorns and thistles were uprooted and the curse and suffering were changed into joy. Furthermore, Aphrahat contrasts Eve's situation with that of those who give themselves to Jesus. Since with Mary and her Son a new age has started, the virgins who 'betrothe themselves to the Messiah are kept far from the Law's curse, and they are saved from the punishment of Eve's daughters, they do not become [married] to men so that they [the men] receive curses and they themselves are in pains'.[99]

---

Terminologie des ältesten syrischen Mönchtums', in *Antonius Magnus Eremita* (St. Ans. 38, Rome 1956), 254-67; 'Asketentum und Mönchtum bei Ephräm', *OCA* 153 (1958), 341-62; - A. Vööbus, *History of Asceticism in the Syirian Orient*, CSCO 184 (Louvain 1958), 97-108; - S. P. Brock, 'Early Syrian Asceticism', *Numen* 20 (1973), 1-19; - R. Murray, *Symbols of Church and Kingdom* (ܐܪ̈ܙܐ ܕܥܕܬܐ ܘܕܡܠܟܘܬܐ) (Cambridge 1975), 11-16; - S. AbouZayd, *Ihidayutha. A Study of the Life of Singleness in the Syrian Orient. From Ignatius of Antioch to Chalcedon 451 A.D.* (Oxford 1993), 51-107.

97 *Aphr* 6.5.

98 *Aphr* 6.6: ܡܛܠܬܗ ܓܝܪ ܐܬܬܣܝܡܬ ܠܘܛܬܐ ܕܢܡܘܣܐ: ܘܡܛܠܬܗ ܗܘܐ ܡܘܠܟܢܐ ܠܡܘܬܐ: ܒܟܐ̈ܒܐ ܓܝܪ ܝܠܕܐ ܒܢ̈ܝܐ ܘܡܫܠܡܐ ܠܡܘܬܐ. ܡܛܠܬܗ ܐܬܠܛܛܬ ܐܪܥܐ ܕܬܘܒܠܐ ܟܘ̈ܒܐ ܘܕܪܕܪ̈ܐ.

99 *Aphr* 6.6: ܥܠ ܐܝܠܝܢ ܕܡܟܝܪ̈ܢ ܠܡܫܝܚܐ ܡܢ ܠܘܛܬܗ ܕܢܡܘܣܐ ܪܚܝܩܝܢ ܘܡܢ ܡܘܟܣ ܒܢܬ̈ܗ ܕܚܘܐ ܦܪ̈ܝܩܢ: ܠܐ ܓܝܪ ܗܘܝܢ ܠܓܒܪ̈ܐ ܕܢܩܒܠܢ ܠܘ̈ܛܬܐ ܘܢܗܘܝܢ ܒܟܐ̈ܒܐ.

The virgins and those who live a consecrated life are not cursed. As the curse does not effect everyone necessarily, so too everyone has the opportunity to escape from it to a certain degree. Humankind suffered under the curse, but the curse was not performed completely. Although Adam and Eve were persuaded by the enemy and ate from the fruit and were cursed, they were saved from the promise of the curse. In the Demonstration On the Vinecluster, Aphrahat says:

> And for men who had previously taken hold of many scourges, because of disorderly and harmful knowledge, the curse's promise was torn apart through this resource of healing. When the enemy realised [this], he was ashamed a little in his mind, and his plots came to an end, and he was wroth about the fruit and those who ate it. And they received the annulment of the curse in their bodies. And the wisdom of truth overcame the Evil One's deceitfulness. And those who ate the fruit were preserved as a vinecluster in the bunch. And because of the blessing, the whole bunch was preserved until the time which is determined by the Most High will be fulfilled, and the fact that He was patient with them concerning the decree upon the rest of the bunch, [yet] they were not willing to repent through the power of the blessing so that they might ripen and become sweet from the bitterness that they had received, and would be partakers of the fruit's sweetness seeing that the plant is being cultivated by the Vinedresser's wisdom, though for a long time it had been deprived of the help and recognition of the gift of healing.[100]

[100] *Aphr* 23.3: ܘܒܢ̈ܝ ܐܢܫܐ ܡܛܠ ܝܕܥܬܐ ܕܒܘܕܪܬܐ ܘܡܣܟܠܢܘܬܐ ܕܡܚܒܠܘ ܐܚܕܘ ܗܘܘ ܒܢܝ̈ܪܐ ܡܚܝ̈ܢܐ: ܒܗܢܐ ܦܘܪܣܐ ܕܐܣܝܘܬܐ ܐܬܦܣܩ ܒܢܝܫܗܘܢ ܡܘܠܟܢܐ ܕܠܘܛܬܐ. ܘܟܕ ܐܪܓܫ ܒܥܠܕܒܒܐ ܒܗܬ ܩܠܝܠ ܒܬܪܥܝܬܗ ܘܫܠܡ ܢܟ̈ܠܘܗܝ ܘܪܓܙ ܥܠ ܦܐܪܐ ܘܥܠ ܐܟܘܠܘ̈ܗܝ. ܘܩܒܠܘ ܒܦܓܪ̈ܝܗܘܢ ܠܫܘܠܠܐ ܕܠܘܛܬܐ: ܘܙܟܬ ܚܟܡܬܐ ܕܩܘܫܬܐ ܠܢܟܝܠܘܬܗ ܕܒܝܫܐ. ܘܐܬܢܛܪܘ ܐܟܘܠܘ̈ܗܝ ܕܦܐܪܐ ܐܝܟ ܛܘܛܝܬܐ ܒܣܓܘܠܐ: ܘܥܠ ܕܒܘܪܟܬܐ ܐܬܢܛܪ ܟܠܗ ܣܓܘܠܐ ܥܕ ܢܫܠܡ ܙܒܢܐ ܕܦܣܝܩ ܠܥܠܝܐ. ܘܕܢܓܪ ܥܠܝܗܘܢ ܒܦܣܩܢܐ ܥܠ ܨܒܘ ܕܢܬܘܒܘܢ ܒܚܝܠܗ ܕܒܘܪܟܬܐ ܕܢܒܫܠܘܢ ܫܪܟܗ ܕܣܓܘܠܐ: ܘܠܐ ܘܢܚܠܘܢ ܡܢ ܡܪܝܪܘܬܐ ܕܩܒܠܘ ܘܢܗܘܘܢ ܫܘܬܦܐ ܠܚܠܝܘܬܗ ܕܦܐܪܐ ☞

The 'resource of healing' (ܦܘܪܣܐ ܕܐܣܝܘܬܐ) and the divine 'gift of healing' (ܕܡܘܗܒܬܐ ܕܐܣܝܘܬܐ) contrast with the curse and overcome the promise of the curse. Repentance is the way to turn bitterness to sweetness. God offered His fruit to man as a resource and charism of healing, so that man would overcome the evil of deceit and bitterness.

### 2.3.1.2 *Unclean Food and the Affliction of Leprosy*

Aphrahat refers to the Law when he comments on the commandments concerning unclean food and leprosy. At the beginning of the Demonstration On the Distinction of Food, Aphrahat considers those who argue about unclean and clean food as 'childish' (ܫܒܪ̈ܐ) and 'untaught' (ܗܕܝܘ̈ܛܐ) as people who 'become sick' (ܡܬܟܪܗܝܢ):

The thoughts of childish and untaught men are greatly confused concerning what enters the mouth, that cannot defile a man (cf. Mt 15:11). And those who are sick in this way say that God singled food out and showed to His servant Moses concerning unclean and clean foods (Lev 11:2f.).[101]

Those who misunderstand and misinterpret the Bible will become sick, but for those who are 'healthy in mind' ( ܠܚܠܝܡ̈ܝ ܪܥܝܢܐ) there is nothing difficult to understand.[102] Although the Old Testament speaks about unclean food (Lev 11:2f), according to the Gospel, it is not the food that defiles man, but what comes out of the mouth (Mt 15:11f). Since Aphrahat insists that nothing that enters the mouth makes man unclean, he draws attention to evil thoughts which dwell in man's heart and it is they which defile him, not food. Therefore, when he explains why Moses wrote

ܕܡܬܦܠܚܐ ܢܝܚܬܐ ܒܡܡܟܬ ܦܠܚܐ: ܘܕܒܠܐ ܣܘܓܐܐ ܐܬܝܠܕܬ ܡܢ ܡܪܕܘܬܐ ܘܡܢ ܡܫܘܕܥܢܘܬܐ ܕܡܘܗܒܬܐ ܕܐܣܝܘܬܐ.

[101] *Aphr* 15.1: ܣܓܝ ܕܝܢ ܡܬܕܘ̈ܠܚܢ ܬܪ̈ܥܝܬܐ ܕܐܢܫܐ ܫܒܪ̈ܐ ܘܗܕܝܘ̈ܛܐ ܥܠ ܡܕܡ ܕܥܐܠ ܠܦܘܡܐ ܕܠܐ ܡܫܟܚ ܠܡܛܡܝܘ ܠܒܪܢܫܐ: ܘܗܠܝܢ ܐܡܪܝܢ ܐܝܠܝܢ ܕܗܟܢ ܡܬܟܪܗܝܢ: ܕܐܠܗܐ ܦܪܫ ܘܚܘܝ ܠܡܘܫܐ ܥܒܕܗ ܥܠ ܡܐܟ̈ܠܬܐ ܛܡ̈ܐܬܐ ܘܕܟ̈ܝܬܐ.

[102] *Aphr* 12.12: ܡܛܠ ܕܬܩܝܦܢ ܘܬܩܝܦܢ ܠܐܢܫܐ ܒܡ̈ܠܝ ܕܟܬܒܐ ܕܒܥܝܢ ܥܠ ܗܢܐ ܕܒܥܐ ܕܦܫܝܩܐ. ܠܚܠܝܡ̈ܝ ܪܥܝܢܐ ܠܐ ܥܛ̈ܝܠܢ ܗܠܝܢ ܠܡܕܪܫ.

about unclean food, he speaks of the 'sick conscience' ( ܬܐܪܬܐ ܟܪܝܗܬܐ). Food is naturally 'clean', but man's thoughts and consciousness link food with making offerings to idols instead of to the true Creator of the world, and this makes it unclean.[103] Consequently, the Law was given to distinguish between idols and the living God; 'and the meek one meditates on His Lord's Law and he receives from it the medicine that he asks for'.[104] The Law's effect is like medicine and heals. Although the Lord gave His Law to the Israelites through the prophets, they ignored Him and worshipped their own idols, such as the calf. The Law served to keep man far from eating food that was offered to the idols, but also to cleanse man from 'leprosy' (ܓܪܒܐ), 'menstruation' (ܕܕܒܐ), 'menstruous discharge' (ܦܘܣܐ) and 'birthgiving' (ܝܠܕܐ) (cf. Lev 15:5f).[105] In the Demonstration 19, Aphrahat refers to Leviticus to illustrate the commandment of the Law concerning leprosy:

> And why did he say about the seers and diviners that they will be ashamed and cover their lips (Mic 3:7)? This is the wound without any healing. In the Law it is written: If there is a leper in Israel, he should cover his lips, and his clothes must be tattered and his head

---

[103] *Aphr* 15.2: ܘܗܕܐ ܕܐܡܪ ܫܠܝܚܐ ܣܓܝܐܐ ܠܘܩܒܠ ܒܢ̈ܝ ܥܡܡܐ ܐܡܪܗ̇ ܟܕ ܚܙܐ ܕܡܬܠܥܒܝܢ ܡܐܟܠܬܐ ܕܥܡܡ̈ܐ. ܡܛܠ ܕܒܢ̈ܝ ܐܢܫܘܬܐ ܠܐ ܡܬܚܫܒܝܢ ܒܝܕܗ ܓܒܗ ܒܟܠ ܡܐܟܠ ܕܥܡܡ̈ܐ ܒܒܝܬ: ܘܟܠ ܣܡܪܐ ܕܥܡܡ̈ܐ ܒܪܝܫ ܠܐ ܝܕܥܝܢ: ܡܛܠ ܕܥܡܡ̈ܐ ܣܓܕܝܢ ܠܟܠ ܟܠ ܡܒܪ̈ܝܢ ܘܟܠ ܟܠ ܐܕܪ̈ܝܢ ܕܒܢܝܢ ܘܡܥܒܕܝܢ ܥܒܕܗ̈ܐ ܕܦܬܟܪ̈ܝܗܘܢ. ܟܠ ܗܘ ܗܘ ܠܐ ܡܬܚܫܒܝܢ ܒܡܐܟܠܬܐ ܒܢ̈ܝ ܐܢܫܘܬܐ. ܘܗܕܐ ܗܝ ܬܐܪܬܐ ܟܪܝܗܬܐ. ܘܫܠܝܚܐ ܦܣܩ ܟܠܬܐ ܕܠܝܢ ܕܒܗܝܐ ܙܕܝܩܐ ܡܢܟܝܢ ܘܐܡܪ: ܕܟܠ ܡܐܟܠܝܢ ܡܬܡܪܩܝܢ ܒܡܠܬܐ ܕܐܠܗܐ ܘܒܨܠܘܬܐ.

[104] Cf *Aphr* 9.2: ܒܢܡܘܣܗ ܕܡܪܗ ܪܢܐ ܡܟܝܟܐ: ܘܡܢܗ ܢܣܒ ܐܣܝܐ ܕܒܥܐ.

[105] *Aphr* 15.8: ܘܟܕ ܒܥܘ ܠܗܘܢ ܥܠܬܐ ܘܦܫܛܘ ܡܢ ܒܬܪܗ: ܡܚܕܐ ܝܗܒ ܠܗܘܢ ܦܘܩܕ̈ܢܐ ܘܕܝ̈ܢܐ ܕܠܐ ܫܦܝܪܝܢ: ܦܘܪܫܢܐ ܘܬܕܟܝܬܐ ܕܓܪܒܐ ܘܕܕܒܐ ܘܕܦܘܣܐ ܘܕܝܠܕܬܐ: ܘܕܠܐ ܐܝܟ ܢܦܘܩ ܠܚܝܘܬܐ ܘܠܦܓܪܐ ܘܠܓܪ̈ܡܐ ܘܠܡܐܢ̈ܐ: ܘܕܟܠ ܟܠ ܚܛܗ̈ܝܢ ܢܦܩ ܦܘܪܫܢܐ ܘܟܠ ܟܠ ܠܓܡܐܘܬܗ ܕܐܕܡ: ܘܟܠ ܚܕ ܚܕ ܡܢܗܘܢ ܐܡܪ: ܢܗܘܐ ܗܘܐ ܠܓܡܐ ܕܕܒܐ. ܠܙܒܢܐ ܐܦ ܒܗ ܢܗܘܐ ܒܒܝܬܐ. (cf. Lev 15:5f).

> shaved; he must live outside the camp. As long as he has leprosy, he should call himself unclean (Lev 13:45-46). Therefore, the prophet who preaches any lies with his lips will receive leprosy's wound, and his lips will be covered all days: and he will sit in disgrace, like Uzziah the King of Judah. Because [King Uzziah] wished to usurp the priesthood, leprosy came from the Shekinah of the Holy One and smote him on his forehead. And he sat at home secretly, ashamed all the days (2 Chr 26:19-21; 2 Kgs 15:5). And a big earthquake occurred among all the people, as Zechariah said: You will flee as you fled from the earthquake in the days of Uzziah, King of Judah (Zech 14:5).[106]

It is a 'wound without any healing' (ܡܚܘܬܐ ܕܠܐ ܐܣܘܐ) to ask the seers and diviners for their advice and prophecy, instead of asking the living God. Since the theme of leprosy is not further developed here, it is used just as a reference to what the Law commands. Uzziah's leprosy is mentioned in the Demonstration On the Vinecluster as an example without any further comment:

> And Uzziah reigned after him and dared [to approach] the priesthood, but he did not listen to it. And the Holy One smote him with the wound of leprosy all his days (2 Chr 26:19-21; 2 Kgs 15:5).[107]

---

[106] *Aphr* 19.4: ܘܠܟܗܢܐ ܐܡܪ ܥܠ ܡܨܘܪ̈ܥܐ ܘܥܠ ܕܣܝܡ ܚܘܪܐ: ܕܒܗܬܘܢ ܘܬܬܟܣܘܢ ܥܠ ܣܦܘ̈ܬܗܘܢ: ܗܕܐ ܓܝܪ ܡܚܘܬܐ ܗܝ ܕܠܐ ܐܣܘܐ. ܟܬܒ ܓܝܪ ܒܢܡܘܣܐ: ܕܓܒܪܐ ܟܕ ܢܗܘܐ ܒܐܝܣܪܝܠ ܥܠ ܣܦܘ̈ܬܗ ܢܬܟܠܦ ܘܡ̈ܟܐܒܘܗܝ ܢܗܘܘܢ ܡܦܪ̈ܥܝܢ ܘܪܫܗ ܢܗܘܐ ܦܪܝܥ: ܘܠܒܪ ܡܢ ܡܫܪܝܬܐ ܢܗܘܐ ܡܘܬܒܗ: ܘܛܡܐܐ ܢܩܪܐ ܢܦܫܗ ܟܠܗܘܢ ܝܘܡ̈ܬܐ ܕܐܝܬ ܒܗ ܓܪܒܐ. ܡܛܠܗܢܐ ܢܒܝܐ ܕܡܟܪܙ ܒܣܦܘ̈ܬܗ ܕܓܠܘܬܐ ܡܩܒܠ ܡܚܘܬܐ ܕܓܪܒܐ ܘܡܬܟܠܦ ܥܠ ܣܦܘ̈ܬܗ ܟܠܗܘܢ ܝܘܡ̈ܬܐ ܘܝܬܒ ܒܒܗܬܬܐ ܐܝܟ ܥܘܙܝܐ ܡܠܟܐ ܕܒܝܬ ܝܗܘܕܐ ܕܒܠ ܕܢܓܒܐ ܠܟܗܢܘܬܐ ܒܡܠܟܘܬܐ: ܢܦܩ ܓܪܒܐ ܡܢ ܩܕܡ ܫܟܝܢܬܗ ܕܩܕܝܫܐ ܘܡܚܝܗܝ ܥܠ ܒܝܬ ܒܝܢ̈ܘܗܝ: ܘܝܬܒ ܒܒܝܬܐ ܡܛܫܝܐܝܬ ܟܕ ܒܗܝܬ ܟܠܗܘܢ ܝܘܡ̈ܬܐ. ܘܗܘܐ ܙܘܥܐ ܪܒܐ ܒܟܠܗ ܥܡܐ. ܐܝܟ ܕܐܡܪ ܙܟܪܝܐ: ܕܬܥܪܩܘܢ ܐܝܟ ܕܥܪܩܬܘܢ ܒܙܘܥܐ ܕܗܘܐ ܒܝܘ̈ܡܝ ܥܘܙܝܐ ܡܠܟܐ ܕܒܝܬ ܝܗܘܕܐ܀

[107] *Aphr* 23.17: ܘܡܠܟ ܥܘܙܝܐ ܒܬܪܗ ܘܐܡܪܚ ܥܠ ܟܗܢܘܬܐ ܘܠܐ ܫܡܥܗ: ܘܡܚܝܗܝ ܩܕܝܫܐ ܒܡܚܘܬܐ ܕܓܪܒܐ ܟܠܗܘܢ ܝܘܡ̈ܬܗ.

Although Aphrahat refers to Gehazi's leprosy in three passages, he does not include anything new, apart from emphasising that Gehazi's leprosy occurred as a result of his greed and desire for money and earthly wealth. In Demonstration 14, Aphrahat says: 'and his greed also covered Gehazi, Elisha's servant, with leprosy'.[108] In the other two passages where Gehazi is mentioned, leprosy not only aflicted Gehazi himself, but also his 'seed' (ܙܪܥܗ) and 'family' (ܫܪܒܬܗ) for ever: 'And through the desire for Naaman's money which Gehazi took, he put on leprosy, both he and his seed for ever'.[109]

In Demonstration 18, Aphrahat speaks about those prophets who were living a consecrated life, and he also mentions the prophets Elisha and Gehazi. As prophets, their minds should neither desire earthly wealth, nor marriage and a family. Gehazi and his family were afflicted with leprosy, because he wanted possessions and desired to have a wife and children:

> And behold, when Gehazi, Elisha's servant, inclined his mind toward this world and desired possessions, a wife and children, Elisha told him: Is this the time to gain wealth, vineyards and olive gardens? Because you did this, Naaman's leprosy will clothe Gehazi and all his family (2 Reg 5:26-27).[110]

### 2.3.1.3 *Jesus in Relation to the Prophet Elisha and to Hezekiah*

In the Demonstration On the Persecution, the prophet Elisha is compared to Jesus. While Elisha had only made one person come back to life, Jesus gave life to all humankind.[111] In the following

---

108 *Aphr* 14.23: ܘܠܓܚܙܝ ܬܘܒ ܬܠܡܝܕܗ ܕܐܠܝܫܥ ܥܠܘܒܘܬܗ ܓܪܒܐ ܐܠܒܫܬܗ.

109 *Aphr* 14.40: ܘܒܪܓܬ ܡܡܘܢܗ ܕܢܥܡܢ ܕܢܣܒ ܓܚܙܝ ܠܒܫ ܓܪܒܐ ܗܘ ܘܙܪܥܗ ܠܥܠܡ

110 *Aphr* 18.7: ܘܗܐ ܟܕ ܓܚܙܝ ܬܠܡܝܕܗ ܕܐܠܝܫܥ ܐܪܟܢ ܪܥܝܢܗ ܠܘܬ ܥܠܡܐ ܗܢܐ ܘܪܓ ܩܢܝܢܐ ܘܐܢܬܬܐ ܘܒܢܝܐ: ܐܡܪ ܠܗ ܐܠܝܫܥ: ܗܘ ܙܒܢܐ ܕܬܩܢܐ ܩܢܝܢܐ ܘܟܪܡܐ ܘܙܝܬܐ܀ ܡܛܠ ܕܥܒܕܬ ܗܕܐ ܓܪܒܗ ܕܢܥܡܢ ܢܠܒܫܝܘܗܝ ܠܓܚܙܝ ܘܠܟܠܗ ܫܪܒܬܗ ܠܥܠܡ.

111 *Aphr* 21.15: ܐܠܝܫܥ ܚܕ ܡܝܬܐ ܐܚܝ ܥܠ ܓܪܡܘܗܝ܂ ܘܥܠ ܓܪܡܘܗܝ ܕܝܫܘܥ ܐܬܩܪܒܘ ܘܚܝܘ ܟܠܗܘܢ ܥܡܡܐ ܕܡܝܬܝܢ ܗܘܘ ܒܚܛܗܝܗܘܢ.

paragraph, King Hezekiah's life is also paralleled to that of Jesus, while Hezekiah's sickness is compared to Jesus' suffering and death: 'And because Hezekiah became ill, the sun went back (2 Kgs 20:1-11); and because Jesus suffered, the sun withdrew its light (Mt 27:45)'.[112] Hezekiah's prayer restored him to life and granted him health, whereas Jesus' prayer rescued him in his rising from death:

> Hezekiah prayed and he was healed from his sickness, whereas Jesus prayed and He rose from the dead. Hezekiah added to his life, after he was cured of his sickness, whereas Jesus received great glory after His resurrection.[113]

When mentioning Jesus no healing imagery is used, whereas Hezekiah's sickness (ܟܘܪܗܢܗ) is mentioned. His praying not only granted him health, but also long life. The effect of prayer also appears in Demonstration 23 where prayer destroys Hezekiah's enemies and restores his health (2 Kgs 20:1-11):

> And Hezekiah became a righteousness king over all Judah in Jerusalem, and he prayed and found mercy in the presence of his God. And his prayer was heard and it destroyed his enemies. And he ministered chastely to the blessing of the righteous that was in himself. And when he became sick, he prayed and was restored from his sickness.[114]

The term 'to heal' (ܐܣܝ) that is used in 2 Kings does not appear here, whereas Aphrahat always uses the same terms 'his sickness/to be sick' (ܐܬܟܪܗ/ܟܘܪܗܢܗ) and 'to be restored'

---

112 *Aphr* 21.16: ܘܝܫܘܥ ܡܠܟܐ ܕܥܠܡܐ ܚܫ̈ܐ. ܡܛܠ ܕܐܬܟܪܗ ܚܙܩܝܐ ܗܦܟ ܫܡܫܐ ܠܡܥܠܢܗ: ܘܡܛܠ ܕܚܫ ܝܫܘܥ ܟܢܫ ܫܡܫܐ ܡܢ ܢܘܗܪܗ.

113 *Aphr* 21.16: ܚܙܩܝܐ ܨܠܝ ܘܐܬܚܠܡ ܡܢ ܟܘܪܗܢܗ: ܘܝܫܘܥ ܨܠܝ ܘܩܡ ܡܢ ܒܝܬ ܡܝ̈ܬܐ. ܚܙܩܝܐ ܡܢ ܒܬܪ ܕܩܡ ܡܢ ܟܘܪܗܢܗ ܐܘܣܦ ܥܠ ܫܢ̈ܘܗܝ, ܘܝܫܘܥ ܡܢ ܒܬܪ ܩܝܡܬܗ ܩܒܠ ܫܘܒܚܐ ܪܒܐ.

114 *Aphr* 23.17: ܘܗܘܐ ܚܙܩܝܐ ܡܠܟܐ ܙܕܝܩܐ ܥܠ ܟܠܗ ܝܗܘܕܐ ܒܐܘܪܫܠܡ: ܘܨܠܝ ܘܐܬܚܠܡ ܩܕܡ ܐܠܗܗ: ܘܐܫܬܡܥܬ ܨܠܘܬܗ ܘܚܪܒܬ ܒܥܠܕܒܒܘܗܝ: ܘܫܡܫ ܒܢܟܦܘܬܐ ܠܒܘܪܟܬܐ ܕܙܕܝ̈ܩܐ ܕܒܓܘܗ. ܘܐܬܟܪܗ ܘܨܠܝ ܘܐܬܚܠܡ ܡܢ ܟܘܪܗܢܗ܀

(ܐܬܚܠܡ/ܐܚܠܡܗ).[115] Both terms are also used in the next paragraph of the 23rd Demonstration. Aphrahat assumes that there are people who blame Hezekiah for worrying about his sickness and praying to be healed and to live longer. Hezekiah was afflicted with a serious sickness that would have killed him ( ܒܟܘܪܗܢܐ ܕܡܐܬ ܗܘܐ) if he had not prayed.[116] While in the previous texts, the passages concerning healing imagery were in the passive form, here God is the Healer: 'he did not praise the name of his God Who restored him from his sickness' ( ܘܠܐ ܫܒܚ ܫܡܐ ܕܐܠܗܗ ܕܐܚܠܡܗ ܡܢ ܟܘܪܗܢܗ; cf. 2 Chr 26:19-21: Zach 14:5). For God is capable of healing; Hezekiah prayed and was healed.

### *2.3.1.4 Uzzah and the Ark of the Lord (2 Sam 6:6-7)*

In Demonstration 14, Aphrahat refers to Uzzah who reached out his hand and took hold of the Ark of God. God struck him down for he dishonoured God's Ark (2 Sam 6:6-7). Aphrahat takes this event as an example of someone who acts presumptuously towards the Lord. Those who do not honour God's Ark will be afflicted with 'bitter pains' (ܟܐܒ̈ܐ ܡܪ̈ܝܪܐ) as the Philistines were struck by the Lord (1 Sam 6:1-7:14). The phrase 'bitter pains' ( ܟܐܒ̈ܐ ܡܪ̈ܝܪܐ) appears in parallel to 'evil wounds' ( ܘܡܚܘܬ̈ܐ ܒܝ̈ܫܬܐ).[117]

---

115 The term 'to restore' (ܘܡܬܚܠܡ) appers in 2 Kgs 20:7. 2 Kgs provides some more terms: verse 1 and 12 have 'become sick' (ܐܬܟܪܗ), whereas verse 5 and 8 has the term 'to heal' (ܐܣܝܐ) 2 Kgs 20:5: ܐܣܝܐ ܐܢܐ ܠܟ; 2 Kgs 20:8: ܐܣܝܐ ܠܝ.

116 *Aphr* 23.18: ܘܡܛܠ ܕܐܝܬ ܐܢܫܝܢ ܕܡܬܚܫܒܝܢ ܚܫܒܐ ܒܕܠܝܐ ܥܠ ܚܙܩܝܐ: ܕܠܡܢܐ ܒܥܐ ܠܗ ܒܟܘܪܗܢܗ ܕܡܐܬ ܗܘܐ ܕܗܘܐ ܕܢܬܘܣܦܬܐ ܙܒܢܐ ܦܠܚ ܗܘܐ ܐܠܗܗ: ܘܒܥܐ ܠܗ ܚܝܐ ܡܘܬܪܝܢ ܒܗ̇ ܬܘܣܦܬܐ ܕܬܬܘܣܦܢ ܒܗ ܫܢܝܐ ܒܗ̇ ܬܘܣܦܬܐ ܥܠ ܕܐܬܟܪܗ ܗܘܐ ܒܟܘܪܗܢܗ ܡܢ ܐܝܟܢܐ ܕܡܠܟ ܒܟܠ ܘܠܐ ܫܒܚ ܫܡܐ ܕܐܠܗܗ ܕܐܚܠܡܗ ܡܢ ܟܘܪܗܢܗ. (cf. 2 Chr 26:19-21; Zach 14:5).

117 *Aphr* 14.20: ܘܕܘܝܕ ܒܗ ܚܙܐ ܕܥܬܝܕ ܡܪ̈ܝܪܐ ܬܘܪܒܬܐ ܒܟܐܒܐ ܕܚܠ ܠܡܚܠܘ ܠܗܘܢ ܠܟܘܫܬܗ ܕܐܠܗܐ: ܗܝܕܝܢ ܐܟܠܘܗܝ ܠܚܝܠܬ ܒܥܒܪ ܐܝܕܐ ܚܬܐ: ܡܛܠ ܕܒܥܒܪ ܐܝܕܐ ܡܢ ܟܠ ܗܘܐ ܕܦܠܛܢܝ̈ܐ ܡܢ ܟܐܒܐ

### 2.3.1.5 *Jesus' Suffering in the Psalms (Ps 41:2-4; 69:27)*

When Aphrahat illustrates the prophecy concerning the Son of God, he quotes the Psalmist in the 17th Demonstration: 'and they persecuted the one whom you struck, and added to the pains of the slain one' (Ps 69:27: ܘܠܡܢ ܕܐܢܬ ܡܚܝܬ ܪܕܦܘ: ܘܐܘܣܦܘ ܥܠ ܟܐܒܗ ܕܩܛܝܠܐ). This Psalm is quoted here in order to show the real suffering and passion of Jesus on the cross.[118] Verse 27 quoted above has the term 'his pain' (Ps 69:27: ܟܐܒܗ), whereas verse 21 has a significant phrase that is not used by Aphrahat; 'heal the wound of my heart and bind it up' (Ps 69:21: ܐܣܐ ܬܒܪܗ ܕܠܒܝ ܘܚܒܘܒ).

The second Psalm, used in the context of healing, is Psalm 41 which is about giving help to the poor and the sick. Aphrahat quotes verses 2 and 4, when he emphasises the help that David gave to the weak, poor and sick:

David also took care of the needy, poor, weak, orphans and widows. And he established managers throughout Israel to provide for and distribute to the needy. While he sings psalms and gives praise before his God, he blessed those who provided for the poor. He said: "Blessed is he who has regard for the weak; in the day of trouble the Lord will deliver him. The Lord will protect him and grant him life and bless him in the Land, and not hand him over to the enemy. The Lord will sustain him on his sick-bed" (Ps 41:2-4).[119]

---

ܠܟܐܢܐ ܘܠܐ ܡܢ ܐܣܝܪܘܬ: ܘܦܩܕ ܗܕܐ ܕܡܢ ܕܠܐ ܚܣܝܪ ܠܡܒܥܬܗ ܕܐܠܗܐ ܥܠ ܒܟܐܒܐ ܟܪܝܗܐ ܘܒܡܚܘܫܬܐ ܒܢܬܢܐ ܐܝܟ ܕܥܠܘܗ ܠܥܠܬܐ̈ ܒܦܠܣܛܪܘܗܝ. While 1 Sam 6:3 has the term 'you will be healed' (ܬܬܐܣܘܢ) 2 Sam 6 does not provide any healing terms. However, in this context Aphrahat uses the term 'pains' (ܟܐܒܐ̈).

118 *Aphr* 17.10: ܬܘܒ ܐܡܪ ܒܗ ܒܟܬܒܐ: ܘܠܡܢ ܕܐܢܬ ܡܚܝܬ ܪܕܦܘ: ܘܐܘܣܦܘ ܥܠ ܟܐܒܗ ܕܩܛܝܠܐ. Cf. *Aphr* 14.20.

119 *Aphr* 20.4 (Ps 41:2-4): ܘܬܘܒ ܐܦ ܕܘܝܕ ܐܬܒܛܠ ܠܗ ܥܠ ܡܣܟܢܐ̈ ܘܒܨܝܪܐ̈ ܘܝܬܡܐ̈ ܘܐܪܡܠܬܐ: ܘܐܩܝܡ ܩܘܝܡܐ̈ ܒܟܠܗ ܐܝܣܪܐܝܠ ܕܢܗܘܘܢ ܐܝܠܝܢ ܘܡܦܪܢܣܝܢ ܠܡܣܟܢܐ. ܘܟܕ ܡܙܡܪ ܘܡܫܒܚ ܩܕܡ ܐܠܗܗ ܛܘܒ ܝܗܒ ܠܦܪܢܣܐ ܠܡܣܟܢܐ. ܐܡܪ ܓܝܪ ܕܛܘܒܘܗܝ ܠܡܢ ܕܡܣܬܟܠ ܥܠ ܡܣܟܢܐ: ܕܒܝܘܡܐ ܕܒܝܫܬܐ ܢܦܨܝܘܗܝ ܡܪܝܐ: ܘܡܪܝܐ ☞

The terms 'sickness' (ܒܟܘܪܗܢܐ) and 'his pains' (ܒܟܐܒܘ̈ܗܝ) are used here. Everyone who does charitable work and helps the needy and sick, will be comforted by the Lord when he is sick and 'the Lord will sustain him on his sick-bed' ( ܡܪܝܐ ܢܣܝܒܪܝܘܗܝ، ܥܠ ܥܪܣܐ ܕܟܐܒܘ̈ܗܝ).

### *2.3.1.6 Isaiah (Is 28:12; 53:5)*

Aphrahat uses two verses from Isaiah that include healing imagery. In the Fourth Demonstration On prayer, he describes visiting and looking after the sick.

He said through the prophet: 'This is my resting-place: let the weary rest' (Is 28:12). Therefore, oh man, do God's rest, and you will not be in need [to say] 'forgive me'. Give rest to the weary, visit the sick and provide for the poor; this is prayer.[120]

While here the term 'sick' (ܟܪ̈ܝܗܐ) is used, Isaiah speaks about the Lord's 'resting-place' (ܢܝܚܬܝ) for the 'weary' (ܠܡܠܐܝ̈ܐ) (Is 28:12). In the 17th Demonstration Aphrahat refers to Isaiah 53 when he speaks about the prophecy concerning Jesus' suffering:

And at the end of the sentence he said: "the One Who will be killed for the sake of our sins, will be humbled because of our iniquity; the discipline of our peace is laid upon Him, and by His wounds we will be healed" (Is 53:5). Through whose wounds have the people been healed?[121]

---

ܢܛܪܝܘܗܝ، ܘܢܚܝܘܗܝ، ܘܢܛܘܒ ܠܗ ܒܐܪܥܐ ܘܠܐ ܢܫܠܡܝܘܗܝ، ܠܒܥܠܕܪ̈ܐ: ܘܒܟܘܪܗܢܐ ܢܣܝܒܪܝܘܗܝ، ܥܠ ܥܪܣܐ ܕܟܐܒܘ̈ܗܝ. The next part of the Psalm that includes healing terms is not quoted: Ps 41:4-5: ܘܟܠܗ ܡܫܟܒܗ ܗܦܟ ܒܟܘܪܗܢܗ. ܐܢܐ ܐܡܪܬ ܕܐܢܬ ܗܘ ܡܪܝ، ܚܘܣ ܥܠ. ܘܐܣܝ̈ܗ ܠܢܦܫܝ ܡܛܠ ܕܚܛܝܬ ܠܟ.

120 *Aphr* 4.14 (Is 28:12): ܐܡܪ ܓܝܪ ܒܢܒܝܐ: ܗܕܐ ܗܝ ܢܝܚܬܝ: ܐܢܝܚܘ ܠܡܠܐܝ̈ܐ. ܥܒܕ ܗܟܝܠ ܢܝܚܗ ܕܐܠܗܐ ܐܘ ܒܪ ܐܢܫܐ: ܘܠܐ ܗܘܐ ܠܟ ܣܘܢܩܢܐ ܕܫܒܘܩ ܠܝ. ܐܢܝܚ ܠܡܠܐܝ̈ܐ ܘܣܥܘܪ ܟܪ̈ܝܗܐ ܘܦܪܢܣ ܠܡܣܟ̈ܢܐ: ܘܗܕܐ ܗܝ ܨܠܘܬܐ.

121 *Aphr* 17.10 (Is 53:5): ܘܐܡܪ ܒܚܪܬܗ ܕܦܬܓܡܐ: ܕܗܘ ܡܬܩܛܠ ܡܛܠ ܚܛܗ̈ܝܢ ܡܬܡܟܟ ܡܛܠ ܥܘܠܢ: ܡܪܕܘܬܐ ܕܫܠܡܢ ܥܠܘܗܝ، ܘܒܡܚܘ̈ܬܗ ܢܬܐܣܐ. ܒܐܝܠܝܢ ܡܚܘ̈ܬܐ ܐܬܐܣܝܘ ܒܢ̈ܝܢܫܐ.

Jesus' wounds and death are the real witness to the fulfilment of the prophecy that by His wound humankind has been healed. Not all of the healing imagery of the suffering Servant (Is 52:13-53:12) is included in Aphrahat's Demonstrations: as usual, Aphrahat selects just one significant phrase.

### *2.3.1.7 Jeremiah (Jer 6:8; 33:10)*

Aphrahat uses two references from Jeremiah that have to do with the Lord's care and love for mankind. In Demonstration 7, the author emphasises the healing effect of repentance referring to biblical events. God always offered healing to His people through His chosen people. The prophet Jeremiah proclaimed the Lord's healing, as Aphrahat quotes:

> And when the Lord called the children of Israel to repent because their sins had increased, and they did not accept [it], He called them through Jeremiah and said: "Penitent children, repent and I will heal your backsliding" (Jer 33:10).[122]

Because of the wickedness of the people, the Lord warns Jerusalem and speaks about the violence and destruction. Aphrahat quotes Jeremiah in the Demonstration On the Persecution: 'And he said to Jerusalem: "Jerusalem be disciplined with pains and wounds, lest I abhor you" (Jer 6:8)'.[123]

### *2.3.1.8 Ezekiel (34:1-21)*

In the Tenth Demonstration, where the author advises the shepherds to take care of their flocks, he refers to the book of Ezekiel. Ezekiel proclaims the word of the Lord to the shepherds whose sheep were scattered over the whole earth. The shepherds 'have not strengthened the sick or healed the infirm or bound up

---

[122] *Aphr* 7.9 (Jer 33:10): ܘܒ̈ܢܝ ܐܝܣܪܝܠ ܟܕ ܣܓܝܘ ܚܛ̈ܗܝܗܘܢ ܘܩܪܐ ܠܗܘܢ ܠܬܝܒܘܬܐ ܘܠܐ ܩܒܠܘ ܩܪܐ ܠܗܘܢ ܒܝܕ ܐܪܡܝܐ ܘܐܡܪ: ܬܘܒܘ ܒ̈ܢܝܐ ܬܝ̈ܒܐ ܘܐܣܐ ܬܘܒܘܬܟܘܢ. The phrase ܐܣܐ ܬܘܒܘܬܟܘܢ appears also in Hos 14:4(5): ܐܣܐ ܬܘܒܘܬܗܘܢ ܘܐܪܚܡ ܒܕܪ̈ܝܗܘܢ: ܘܢܗܦܘܟ ܪܘܓܙܝ ܡܢܗܘܢ.

[123] *Aphr* 21.7: ܘܠܐܘܪܫܠܡ ܐܡܪ ܠܗ: ܕܒܟܐܒ̈ܐ ܘܒܡܚܘ̈ܬܐ ܐܬܪܕܝ ܐܘܪܫܠܡ: ܕܠܡܐ ܬܣܢ ܢܦܫܝ ܡܢܟܝ.

the injured' (Ez 34:4: ܠܕܟܪܝܗܐ ܠܐ ܣܥܪܬܘܢ ܘܕܡܪܥܐ ܠܐ ܐܣܝܬܘܢ ܘܕܬܒܝܪܐ ܠܐ ܚܒܫܬܘܢ ). Aphrahat includes this text in his Demonstration On the Shepherds, but in a different sentence structure, when he says:

> Woe to [you], foolish shepherds; you clothe yourself with pure wool, you eat the meat of fatlings and you do not shepherd the flock: You have not healed the sick or bound up the injured; you have not strengthened the weak, and you have not gathered the lost and scattered (cf. Ez 34:2-4, 9-12, 18-19).[124]

Aphrahat does not include verse 16 where the Lord promises to bind up the injured and strengthen the sick.[125] However, the reason the sheep are sick and wounded is because of the shepherd. Therefore, he challenges the shepherds to follow the steps of the true Shepherd 'Who cared about His flock and gathered those who were far and returned the lost and visited the sick and strengthened the sick and bound up the wounded and protected the fatlings'.[126]

### *2.3.1.9 Malachi (Mal 1:14)*

The term **ܟܪܝܗ**, attributed to an animal and not to people, is used in Malachi. Aphrahat quotes it in Demonstration 4 saying: 'listen to the prophet what he is saying: "cursed is the cheat who has a good

---

[124] *Aphr* 10.3: ܘܐ ܪܥܘܬܐ ܣܟܠܐ: ܥܡܪܐ ܕܕܟܝܐ ܠܒܫܝܬܘܢ ܘܒܣܪܐ ܕܦܛܝܡܬܐ ܐܟܠܝܬܘܢ ܘܥܢܐ ܠܐ ܪܥܝܬܘܢ ܐܢܘܢ: ܕܡܪܥܐ ܠܐ ܐܣܝܬܘܢ ܘܕܬܒܝܪܐ ܠܐ ܚܒܫܬܘܢ: ܕܟܪܝܗܐ ܠܐ ܣܥܪܬܘܢ ܘܕܐܒܝܕܐ ܘܕܡܒܕܪܐ ܠܐ ܟܢܫܬܘܢ.

[125] Ez 34:15-16: ܐܢܐ ܐܪܥܐ ܠܥܢܝ: ܘܐܢܐ ܐܪܒܥ ܐܢܝܢ ܐܡܪ ܡܪܐ ܡܪ̈ܘܬܐ. ܕܐܒܝܕܐ ܐܒܥܐ: ܘܠܕܛܥܝܐ ܐܗܦܟ ܘܠܕܬܒܝܪܐ ܐܚܒܘܫ: ܘܠܕܟܪܝܗܐ ܐܚܝܠ. ܘܕܡܫܡܢܐ ܘܕܚܣܝܢܐ ܐܛܪ: ܘܐܪܥܐ ܐܢܝܢ ܒܕܝܢܐ.

[126] *Aphr* 10.4: ܐܬܕܟܪܘ ܐܘ ܪܥܘܬܐ ܠܗܢܐ ܪܥܝܐ ܚܦܝܛܐ ܪܥܝܐ ܕܚܠܦ ܡܪܥܝܬܗ: ܕܐܟܢܫܐ ܐܬܟܬܠ ܠܗ ܥܠ ܚܘܪܗ ܘܦܢܝ ܪ̈ܚܝܩܬܐ ܘܐܟܢܫ ܠܛ̈ܥܝܬܐ ܘܣܥܪ ܟܪ̈ܝܗܬܐ ܘܚܝܠ ܡܚܝ̈ܠܬܐ ܘܚܒܫ ܠܬ̈ܒܝܪܬܐ ܫܡ̈ܝܢܬܐ: ܢܦܫܗ ܐܫܠܡ ܥܠ ܐܦ̈ܘܗܝ ܕܥܢܐ ܘܢܛܪ. In Ez 34:21, the term ܟܪ̈ܝܗܬܐ is used for the sheep.

male in his flock and vows to sacrifice a sick one to the Lord" (Mal 1:14)'.[127]

### *2.3.1.10 Maccabees (Macc 9:5)*

In Demonstration 5, Aphrahat mentions Antiochus who was afflicted with 'heavy and evil sickness' ( ܟܘܪܗܢܐ ܚܛܠܐ ܘܒܝܫܐ).[128] In 2 Maccabees both terms, 'sickness' (ܟܘܪܗܢܐ) and 'pains' (ܟܐܒ̈ܐ) appear, but not with the adjectives 'heavy' (ܚܛܠܐ) and 'evil' (ܒܝܫܐ). Instead 2 Maccabees speaks of bitter and strong pain (Macc 9:5: ܟܐܒܐ ܡܪܝܪܐ ܘܥܫܝܢܐ).

## 2.3.2 New Testament Healing Imagery in Aphrahat's Demonstrations

In this section attention is drawn to Aphrahat's view on the healing of man by Jesus Christ Who performed healing miracles because of His love towards mankind. Just as Jesus' love is fundamental for His healing ministry, so too man's faith and prayer are essential for healing. Aphrahat refers to Jesus' healing miracles to highlight the significant role of God's love, as well as of man's faith and prayer. To these Aphrahat adds the importance of charity work in Christian social life, particularly visiting the sick which is based on Mt 25:32-45, the parable of the sheep and the goats. Referring to Rom 15:1, Aphrahat emphasises the duty of the shepherds to care about the sick and eventually heal them. Based on 1 Cor 15:42-56, at the end the resurrection will transform man from the state of sickness into a state of glory.

### *2.3.2.1 Jesus' Healing Miracles*

At the end of the First and Second Demonstration, Aphrahat mentions a few people whom Jesus healed. In the Demonstration On Faith, Aphrahat emphasises those who were healed because of

[127] *Aphr* 4.13: ܥܒܕ ܕܝܢ ܠܢܒܝܐ ܡܠܐܟܝ ܐܡܪ: ܕܠܝܛ ܗܘ ܟܠ ܡܢ ܕܐܝܬ ܠܗ ܒܓܙܪܗ ܕܟܪܐ ܛܒܐ ܘܢܕܪ ܘܡܕܒܚ ܠܡܪܝܐ ܕܟܪܝܗ.

[128] *Aphr* 5.20 (2 Macc 9:18): ܡܛܠ ܟܕ ܕܢܚܐ ܠܐܢܛܝܘܟܘܣ ܕܢܚܐ ܡܢ ܫܡܝܐ. ܘܐܬܟܪܗ ܒܟܘܪܗܢܐ ܚܛܠܐ ܘܒܝܫܐ: ܘܡܢ ܪܚܫܐ ܕܒܣܪܗ ܐܦ ܠܐ ܩܪܒ ܗܘܐ ܠܘܬܗ ....

their faith. Among them he mentions the blind man (Mt 9:27-31),[129] the healing of the son with the evil spirit (Mk 9:17-27), the centurion's servant (Mt 8:5-13), the reviving of Jairus' daughter (Mk 5:21-43) and Lazarus (Jn 11:1-43). Jesus' promise to His disciples is also included: everyone who believes will be able to heal the sick (Mt 10:1):

And our Saviour said this to everyone who drew near to Him: it should happen to you according to your faith. When the blind man drew near to Him, He said to him: do you believe that I can heal you (Mt 9:28)? The blind man responded: yes, my Lord, I believe. And his faith opened his eyes. And He said to the one whose son was sick: believe and your son will live. He answered Him: I believe, my Lord, help my weak faith (Mk 9:22, 26). And his son was healed through his faith. The centurion's servant was also healed when he approached Him in faith, since he said to our Lord: say Your word and my servant will be healed through it. And our Lord wondered at his faith, and it happened to him according to his faith (Mt 8:8-10). And also while the elder of the Synagogue besought Jesus concerning his daughter, He said to him: just believe and your daughter will live. And he believed and his daughter was revived and rose (Mk 5:23, 36). And when Lazarus died, our Lord said to Martha, if you believe, your brother will rise. Martha responded to Him: yes my Lord I believe. And He raised him after four days (Jn 9:23, 27).[130]

---

[129] Mt 9:27-31 speaks of two blind men to whom sight was granted. The healing of the man born blind in Jn 9 is not related to his faith.

[130] *Aphr* 1.17: ܘܐܦ ܡܚܝܢܢ ܟܠ ܡܢ ܕܡܬܩܪܒ ܗܘܐ ܠܗ ܕܢܬܐܣܐ ܗܟܢܐ ܐܡܪ ܗܘܐ ܠܗ: ܕܐܝܟ ܗܝܡܢܘܬܟ ܢܗܘܐ ܠܟ. ܘܟܕ ܣܡܝܐ ܩܪܒ ܠܗ ܐܡܪ ܠܗ: ܡܗܝܡܢ ܐܢܬ ܕܡܫܟܚ ܐܢܐ ܕܐܣܝܟ. ܐܡܪ ܠܗ ܗܘ ܣܡܝܐ: ܐܝܢ ܡܪܝ، ܡܗܝܡܢ ܐܢܐ. ܘܗܝܡܢܘܬܗ ܥܝܢܘܗܝ ܦܬܚܬ. ܘܠܗܘ ܕܒܪܗ ܟܪܝܗ ܗܘܐ ܐܡܪ ܠܗ: ܗܝܡܢ ܘܢܚܐ ܒܪܟ. ܐܡܪ ܠܗ: ܡܗܝܡܢ ܐܢܐ ܡܪܝ: ܥܕܪ ܠܡܚܝܠܘܬ ܗܝܡܢܘܬܝ. ܘܒܗܝܡܢܘܬܗ ܐܬܐܣܝ ܒܪܗ ܘܐܦ ܥܒܕ ܡܠܟܐ ܟܕ ܩܪܒ ܠܗ ܒܗܝܡܢܘܬܗ ܐܬܐܣܝ ܛܠܝܗ ܟܕ ܐܡܪ ܠܗ ܠܡܪܢ: ܕܐܡܪ ܒܡܠܬܐ ܘܢܬܐܣܐ ܛܠܝܝ. ܘܐܬܕܡܪ ܡܪܢ ܒܗܝܡܢܘܬܗ: ܘܐܝܟ ܗܝܡܢܘܬܗ ܗܘܐ ܠܗ. ܘܐܦ ܪܒ ܟܢܘܫܬܐ ܟܕ ܒܥܐ ܡܢܗ ܥܠ ܒܪܬܗ ܡܚܠܐ ܐܡܪ ܠܗ: ܒܠܚܘܕ ܗܝܡܢ ܘܬܚܐ ܒܪܬܟ. ܘܗܝܡܢ ܘܚܝܬ ܒܪܬܗ ܘܩܡܬ. ܘܟܕ ܡܝܬ ܠܥܙܪ ܐܡܪ ܠܗ ܡܪܢ ܠܡܪܬܐ: ܐܢ ܗܘ ܕܡܗܝܡܢܐ ܐܢܬܝ، ܢܩܘܡ ܐܚܘܟܝ. ܐܡܪܐ ܠܗ ☞

Faith is capable of everything. In the same way as Jesus heals sick people because of their faith, He also grants this healing gift to His disciples 'to lay their hands over the sick and they will be healed' (Mk 16:17-18).[131] Since the Lord healed those who drew near to Him with faith, Aphrahat feels able to say that the faith 'had healed the sick' (ܘܟܪ̈ܝܗܐ ܐܣܝܬ).[132] Healing is not attributed to faith only, but also to prayer in the case of barrenness (ܘܗܝ ܐܣܝܬ ܥܩܪܘܬܐ),[133] and to the love of God. In the Demonstration On Love, Aphrahat links healing with love. Even though the above mentioned people were healed or brought back to life because of their faith, the Lord is the One Who restored them to health and life because of His love towards mankind:

> And because of His abounding faith, He restored the wounds of the sick. He also healed the centurion's son because of his faith (Mt 8:8, 13). And he calmed the sea's waves from us through His power (Lk 8:24). He scattered from us the legion's devils because of His

ܡܪܬܐ: ܐܝܟ ܡܢ، ܒܗܝܡܢܘܬܐ ܐܬܐ. ܘܐܩܝܡܗ ܡܢ ܒܬܪ ܐܪܒܥܐ ܝܘܡ̈ܝܢ.

[131] *Aphr* 1.17: ܘܬܘܒ ܗܟܢܐ ܐܡܪ: ܕܗܢܐ ܐܬܐ ܬܗܘܐ ܠܐܝܠܝܢ ܕܡܗܝܡܢܝܢ: ܕܒܠܫ̈ܢܐ ܚܕ̈ܬܐ ܢܡܠܠܘܢ: ܘܚܘ̈ܘܬܐ ܢܗܘܘܢ ܕܚܩܝܢ: ܘܐܝܕ̈ܝܗܘܢ ܢܗܘܘܢ ܣܝܡܝܢ ܥܠ ܟܪ̈ܝܗܐ ܘܡܬܚܠܡܝܢ܀

[132] In *Aphr* 1.18, the author briefly put together what faith can achieve; faith is among them: ܢܬܘܪܒ ܗܒܝܠ ܢܣܒܝ ܠܗ ܠܡܗܝܡܢܘܬܐ ܕܗܒܠܐ ܩܘܪ̈ܒܢܝܢ ܫܠܝܡ. ܗܝܡܢܘܬܐ ܚܢܘܟ ܠܫܡܝܐ ܐܣܩܬ. ܘܡܡܒܘܠܐ ܢܘܚ ܦܨܬ. ܘܥܩܪܘܬܐ ܐܘܠܕܬ. ܘܡܢ ܚܪܒܐ ܦܨܬ. ܘܡܢ ܓܘܒܐ ܐܣܩܬ. ܘܠܡܫܒ̈ܝܢܐ ܐܗܦܟܬ. ܘܠܐܣܝ̈ܪܐ ܫܪܬ. ܘܠܝܪ̈ܕܢܐ ܦܠܓܬ. ܘܢܘܪܐ ܐܥܟܬ. ܘܝܡܐ ܦܠܓܬ. ܘܫܘܪܐ ܒܙܥܬ. ܘܡܝ̈ܐ ܠܨܗܝܢ ܐܫܩܝܬ. ܘܟܦ̈ܢܐ ܣܒܥܬ. ܘܡܛܪ̈ܐ ܐܚܬܬ. ܘܡܢ ܥܘܠ ܐܬܚܣܢܬ. ܘܟ̈ܠܐ ܥܬܩܬ. ܘܟܪ̈ܝܗܐ ܐܣܝܬ. ܘܚܝܠܐ ܙܟܬ. ܘܫܘܪ̈ܐ ܗܦܟܬ. ܘܦܘܡܐ ܕܐܪ̈ܝܘܬܐ ܣܟܪܬ. ܘܫܠܗܒܝܬܐ ܕܢܘܪܐ ܕܥܟܬ. ܘܠܫܒܗܪܢܐ ܡܟܟܬ. ܘܠܡܬܟܟ̈ܢܐ ܠܪܘܡܐ ܐܪܝܡܬ. ܗܠܝܢ ܟܠܗܘܢ ܚܝ̈ܠܐ ܒܗ̇ ܒܗܝܡܢܘܬܐ ܐܬܥܒܪܘ܀

[133] *Aphr* 4.1: ܒܗ̇ ܓܝܪ ܒܨܠܘܬܐ ܐܬܩܒܠܘ ܩܘܪ̈ܒܢܐ. ܘܗܝ ܬܘܒ ܐܦܩܬ ܡܡܒܘܠܐ. ܘܗܝ ܐܣܝܬ ܥܩܪܘܬܐ. ܘܗܝ ܦܫܛܬ ܡܫܪ̈ܝܬܐ. In the Demonstration On Prayer, various powers are attributed to the prayer. Some of them are the same as in the Demonstration On Faith (see *Aphr* 1.18).

> grace (Lk 8:32). And by His mercy He revived the daughter of the Head of the Synagogue (Lk 8:55). And He cleansed the woman from the impurity of her blood (Mk 5:29). And He opened the eyes of the two blind men who drew near to him (Mt 9:30). And He also gave power and authority to His Twelve over all pain and sickness, and to us through them (Lk 9:1; cf. Mt 10:8). And because of His abundant love, He listened to the Canaanite woman and revived her daughter from her sickness (Mt 15:28). And through the power of His Sender He stretched out the tongue of the mute man whose ear was deaf (Mt 7:35). And the blind men saw light and praised Him Who sent Him through Him (Mt 15:31).[134]

Jesus 'healed' (ܐܣܝ) the centurion's servant (Mt 8:8-13). He 'cleansed' (ܕܟܝ) the woman with the haemorrhage (Mk 5:29) and 'opened' (ܦܬܚ) the eyes of the blind (Mt 9:30). Concerning the disciples, in Demonstration 1.17 Aphrahat says: 'and they shall lay their hands over the sick, and they will be healed' (ܘܐܪ̈ܝܡܘܢ ܢܘܗܘܢ ܘܣܡܝܢ ܥܠ ܟ̈ܪܝܗܐ ܘܡܬܐܣܝܢ), whereas here the terms 'pain' (ܟܐܒܐ) and 'sickness' (ܟܘܪܗܢܐ) appear: 'they receive power and authority over every pain and sickness' (ܚܝܠܐ ܘܫܘܠܛܢܐ ܥܠ ܟܠ ܟܐܒ ܘܟܘܪܗܢ). This power is not limited only to the disciples, but is also given to 'us through them'.[135] The term 'sickness' (ܟܘܪܗܢܐ) is linked with the Canaanite woman's daughter (Mt 15:28). Concerning the man who was 'sick' (ܟܪܝܗ)

---

[134] *Aphr* 2.20: ܘܡܛܠ ܚܘܒܗ ܥܡܝܩܐ ܐܣܝ ܠܡ̈ܚܘܬܐ ܕܟܪ̈ܝܗܐ: ܐܣܝ ܟܢ ܐܦ ܠܒܪܗ ܕܡܠܟܘܢܐ ܡܛܠ ܡܪܚܡܢܘܬܗ. ܘܥܬܪ ܒܡܣܟܢܘܬܗ ܢܟܐ ܡܢ ܒܣܠܗ. ܘܪܕܦ ܡܢ ܒ̈ܢܝܐ ܕܠܟ̈ܐܒܐ ܡܛܠ ܛܝܒܘܬܗ. ܘܡܚܣܢܘܬܗ ܐܚܝ ܠܒܪܬܗ ܕܪܒ ܟܢܘܫܬܐ: ܘܕܟܝ ܬܘܒ ܠܐܢܬܬܐ ܡܢ ܛܡܐܘܬܐ ܕܕܡܐ: ܘܦܬܚ ܥܝ̈ܢܐ ܕܣܡ̈ܝܐ ܬܪ̈ܝܢ ܕܩܪܒܘ ܠܗ: ܘܝܗܒ ܐܦ ܠܬܪܥܣܪܬܗ ܚܝܠܐ ܘܫܘܠܛܢܐ ܥܠ ܟܠ ܟܐܒ ܘܟܘܪܗܢ ܘܐܦ ܠܢ ܒܐܝܕܝܗܘܢ. ܘܡܛܠ ܚܘܒܗ ܣܓܝܐܐ ܫܡܥ ܠܐܢܬܬܐ ܟܢܥܢܝܬܐ ܘܐܣܝܗ ܠܒܪܬܗ ܡܢ ܟܘܪܗܢܗ. ܘܒܫܘܠܛܢܐ ܕܫܠܘܚܗ ܦܫܛ ܠܫܢܗ ܕܥܠܓܐ ܦܐܟܐ ܕܐܕܢܗ ܗܘܬ ܐܛܝܡܐ. ܘܚܙܘ ܣ̈ܡܝܐ ܢܘܗܪܐ ܘܫܒܚܘ ܒܐܝܕܗ ܠܫܠܘܚܗ.

[135] *Aphr* 2.20.

for 38 years and the Lord 'healed him' (ܐܣܝܗ) (Jn 5:5), Aphrahat speaks of 'perfect healing' (ܐܣܝܘܬܐ ܓܡܝܪܬܐ).[136]

*2.3.2.2 'I became sick and you have visited me' (Mt 25:35-36)*

The phrase 'and I became sick and you have visited me' (ܘܐܬܟܪܗܬ ܘܣܥܪܬܘܢܢܝ) from Matthew appears in three Demonstrations (Mt 25:35-36). In the Demonstration On Prayer, Aphrahat attributes rest and healing to prayer. Prayer should help the needy and the sick, otherwise it does not fulfil its aim. Good deeds in social life reflect true faith and real prayer. In order to support this, Aphrahat refers to the parable of the sheep and the goats (Mt 25:32-46). He quotes: 'and I became sick and you visited me'.[137] While motivated for the good deeds and looking forward to the second coming of Christ, Aphrahat changes Matthew's words slightly when he uses it in the Sixth Demonstration: 'let us visit our Lord through the sick, so that He may call us to stand on His right hand'.[138] For it is essential for the faithful to help the poor, weak and sick people. Aphrahat uses the same quotation again in the Demonstration 20: 'and I was sick and you have visited me',[139] and it is clear that for him the sick and weak in the world play an important role in Christian social life. They ought to have a central place in the Christian community as the Lord does in the life of faithful people. In the three Demonstrations this healing imagery appears as an activity and work that Christians are obliged to do in order to be true disciples of Christ.

*2.3.2.3 Paul's Epistles (Rom 7:5; 15:1; 1 Cor 1:27-30)*

Aphrahat uses some verses from Paul's epistles to the Romans and to the Corinthians that include healing terms. When referring to Paul's epistles, he draws attention to the sick again. In the Seventh Demonstration where Aphrahat advises 'the keeper of heaven's

[136] *Aphr* 2.20: ܘܚܘܝ ܒܥܬ ܐܣܝܘܬܗ ܠܓܡܝܪܬܐ ܗܘܐ ܠܓܒܪܐ ܕܬܠܬܝܢ ܘܬܡܢܐ ܫܢܝܢ ܪܡܐ ܗܘܐ ܘܐܣܟܠ ܚܝܠܗ ܠܘܬܗ ܘܐܣܝܗ.

[137] *Aphr* 4.15 (Mt 25:35-36): ܘܐܬܟܪܗܬ ܘܣܥܪܬܘܢܢܝ.

[138] *Aphr* 6.1 (Mt 25:36): ܢܣܥܘܪ ܠܡܪܢ ܒܟܪܝܗܐ: ܕܢܩܪܝܢ ܘܢܩܝܡܢ ܡܢ ܝܡܝܢܗ.

[139] *Aphr* 20.5 (Mt 25: 32-45): ܘܐܬܟܪܗܬ ܘܣܥܪܬܘܢܢܝ.

keys' to open the door to the repentant, he refers to Paul saying: 'we who are strong ought to bear the sickness of the sick' (Rom 15:1: ܕܚܣܝܢܝܢ ܚܝܠ ܐܝܠܝܢ ܕܡܫܟܚܝܢ ܕܟܘܪܗܢܐ ܕܟܪ̈ܝܗܐ ܢܫܩܘܠ). This sentence is followed with the quotation from the Epistle to the Hebrews: 'the one who is lame shall not be disabled but healed' (Hebr 12:13: ܕܡܢ ܕܚܓܝܪ ܠܐ ܢܬܛܠܥ ܐܠܐ ܢܬܐܣܐ).[140] Helping a sick person is not just bearing with him his sickness, but more: he needs to be 'healed' (ܢܬܐܣܐ). For Aphrahat, repentance is a way of healing.[141]

Although the term 'sick' (ܟܪ̈ܝܗܐ) implies suffering and the stage that has to be passed, Aphrahat also uses it in a positive way. Here Aphrahat refers to 1 Cor 1:27-30: 'And the Apostle said: God chose the foolish people of the world in order to make the wise ashamed through them; and he chose the sick in order to make the strong ashamed through them.'[142] While strength, power and knowledge count in the eyes of this world, in the eyes of the Lord they are vain for they can harm man. Here Aphrahat mentions some biblical figures and what has happened to them because of their physical health and beauty: the result was spiritual sickness of pride and haughtiness.

In the Demonstration On the Resurrection of the Dead, Aphrahat speaks about the spirit and the body. Concerning the body and the pain it can experience, he quotes from Rom 7:5: 'when we were flesh, the pains of sin were at work in our limbs, so that we might be fruits for death'.[143] Even though pains, caused by sin, dwell in humankind, people are able to think about spirituality. Paul is used as an example: he thought and talked magnificently about the soul and the Spirit of God. As long as people dwell in

---

140 *Aphr* 7.11 (Rom 15:1; Hebr 12:13): ܬܘܒ ܐܡܪ: ܕܚܣܝܢܝܢ ܚܝܠ ܐܝܠܝܢ ܕܡܫܟܚܝܢ ܕܟܘܪܗܢܐ ܕܟܪ̈ܝܗܐ ܢܫܩܘܠ. ܬܘܒ ܐܡܪ: ܕܡܢ ܕܚܓܝܪ ܠܐ ܢܬܛܠܥ ܐܠܐ ܢܬܐܣܐ܀

141 *Aphr* 7.12.

142 *Aphr* 14.29 (1 Cor 1:27-30): ܘܫܠܝܚܐ ܐܡܪ: ܕܓܒܐ ܐܠܗܐ ܠܣܟܠܘܗܝ ܕܥܠܡܐ ܕܢܒܗܬ ܒܗܘܢ ܠܚܟܝ̈ܡܐ: ܘܓܒܐ ܟܪ̈ܝܗܐ ܕܢܒܗܬ ܒܗܘܢ ܠܚܝܠܬܢ̈ܐ...

143 *Aphr* 8.5 (Rom 7:5): ܘܬܘܒ ܐܡܪ: ܕܟܕ ܒܒܣܪܐ ܗܘܝܢ ܚܫ̈ܐ ܕܚܛܗ̈ܐ ܡܬܚܦܛܝܢ ܗܘܘ ܒܗܕ̈ܡܝܢ: ܕܦܐܪ̈ܐ ܢܗܘܐ ܠܡܘܬܐ.

flesh, they need to be changed: 'we have been sown in sickness, but have arisen in power' ( ܘܐܙܕܪܥܢ ܬܘܒ ܒܡܪܥܝܘܬܐ ܘܩܡܢ ܒܚܝܠܐ).[144]

*2.3.2.4 Repentance as the Medicine of 'Our Wise Physician'*

In the seventh Demonstration, On Repentance,[145] Aphrahat uses healing imagery in a unique way. Since Jesus Christ is the only One Who overcame sin and death, He was not injured or wounded in the battle with Satan. The Lord as 'our wise Physician' ( ܐܣܝܢ ܚܟܝܡܐ), is capable of healing any kind of sickness or pains, and binding up the wounds of the sinners who repent. Spiritual healing is discussed allegorically as the way of healing for those who have been injured in the war by their adversaries and enemies. In order to heal them, they ought to reveal their wounds without any shame to the wise physician (ܐܣܝܐ ܚܟܝܡܐ) or the physicians who are the disciples of our Lord and receive 'repentance as medicine' (ܣܡܐ ܬܝܒܘܬܐ) from Him.

Next, the terms associated with sickness and pains will be discussed. These terms, such as 'ulcers' (ܫܘܚ̈ܢܐ), 'wounds' (ܡܚܘ̈ܬܐ), 'gangrene' (ܣܠܥܬܐ) and 'pains' (ܟܐ̈ܒܐ) that imply the war, battle and agony of life, explain Aphrahat's understanding of life and human existence. Suffering because of sin and being subdued by it is not the final state of man. Healing of the wounds comes from God through Jesus Christ and repentance towards Him. Therefore, attention is drawn to the role of the Lord Who is the main Physician, to the function of the wise physician and the physicians of the Lord who are enabled to grant healing to the sick. Paragraphs 2 to 6 of the Demonstration On Repentance present the main healing imagery quoted below.

---

144 *Aphr* 8.10; cf. 1 Cor 15:42-52 and Gal 6:8.

145 There has been considerable discussion about the context of this Demonstration: see T. Jansma, 'Aphraates' Demostration VII.18 & 20. Some observations on the discourse on penance', *PdO* 5 (Kaslik-Liban 1974), 21-48, and R. Murray, 'The exhortation to candidates for ascetical vovs at baptism in the ancient Syriac Church', *NTS* 21 (Cambridge 1974), 59-80, and the literature cited there.

### 2.3.2.5 *The translation of Demonstration 7.2-6*

**7.2** All pains have medicines, and they can be healed, if the wise physician finds them. And those who are struck in our contest have repentance as medicine which they put on their ulcers and they will be restored. Oh physicians, disciples of our wise Physician, receive this medicine through which you will restore the wounds of the sick. When the wise physician is found for the fighters who have been stricken in the war by the hands of the one who fights against them, he devises their healing in order to restore the wounded. And after the physician has restored him who was stricken in the war, he will receive gifts and honour from the king. Likewise, my beloved, you ought to give repentance as medicine to the one who has laboured in our contest and the enemy overcame him and struck him, if the stricken one feels great contrition; because God does not reject the penitent. The prophet Ezekiel said: "I am not willing to let a sinner die, but wish he might repent from his evil way and be saved" (Ez 33:11; cf. 18:23, 32).[146]

**7.3** The one who has been stricken in the war is usually not ashamed to entrust himself to a wise physician's hands for the war has overcome him and he was stricken. And once he has been healed, the king does not reject him, but he will reckon and count him in his army. Likewise, the one whom Satan wounds ought not

---

146 *Aphr* 7.2: ܠܟܠ ܟܐ̈ܒܐ ܐܝܬ ܣܡ̈ܡܢܐ ܘܡܬܐܣܝܢ ܟܕ ܐܣܝܐ ܚܟܝܡܐ ܢܫܟܚ ܐܢܘܢ. ܘܠܕܡܬܡܚܝܢ ܒܐܓܘܢܐ ܕܝܠܢ ܐܝܬ ܠܗܘܢ ܣܡܐ ܬܝܒܘܬܐ ܕܣܝܡܝܢ ܥܠ ܟܘܪ̈ܗܝܗܘܢ ܘܡܬܚܠܡܝܢ. ܐܘ ܐܣܘ̈ܬܐ ܬܠܡ̈ܝܕܘܗܝ ܕܐܣܝܢ ܚܟܝܡܐ: ܣܒܘ ܠܟܘܢ ܣܡܐ ܗܢܐ ܕܒܗ ܬܚܠܡܘܢ ܡܚ̈ܘܬܐ ܕܟܪ̈ܝܗܐ. ܡܫܬܟܚܐ ܓܝܪ ܕܠܟܠܝܢ ܒܩܪܒܐ ܡܢ ܐܝ̈ܕܝ ܗܘ ܡܢ ܕܡܬܟܬܫ ܥܡܗܘܢ ܟܕ ܐܣܝܐ ܚܟܝܡܐ ܡܬܚܫܒ ܠܗܘܢ ܡܬܦܢܐ ܠܗ ܠܐܣܝܘܬܗܘܢ ܕܢܚܠܡ ܠܡܚ̈ܝܢܐ. ܘܡܢ ܕܡܚܠܡ ܠܗ ܐܣܝܐ ܠܗܘ ܕܒܠܒ ܒܩܪܒܐ ܡܩܒܠ ܡܘܗ̈ܒܬܐ ܘܐܝܩܪܐ ܡܢ ܡܠܟܐ. ܗܟܢܐ ܚܒܝܒܝ ܡܢ ܕܠܐܝ ܒܐܓܘܢܐ ܕܝܠܢ ܘܐܬܐ ܒܥܠܕܒܒܗ ܟܠܗܘܢ ܘܡܚܝܗܝ ܠܗ ܘܠܐ ܠܡܬܠ ܠܗ ܣܡܐ ܬܝܒܘܬܐ ܟܕ ܬܘܬ ܢܦܫܐ ܕܗܘ ܡܡܚܝܐ ܬܘܗܐ ܣܓܝܐܐ. ܡܛܠ ܕܐܠܗܐ ܠܐ ܡܣܠܐ ܠܬܝ̈ܒܐ. ܐܡܪ ܓܝܪ ܚܙܩܝܐܝܠ ܢܒܝܐ: ܕܠܐ ܨܒܐ ܐܢܐ ܒܡܘܬܗ ܕܚܛܝܬܐ ܣܛܠܝܐ ܐܠܐ ܕܢܬܘܒ ܡܢ ܐܘܪܚܗ ܒܝܫܬܐ ܘܢܚܐ܀

to be ashamed to confess his transgression and turn aside from it. Rather he should seek out repentance as medicine for himself. Whoever is ashamed to show his ulcer will get gangrene; and the harm reaches all his body. And who is not ashamed, his ulcer will be healed and he will return again to enter the contest. But whoever has gangrene is not able to be healed again; and the weapons that he put off he cannot put on again. Likewise, the one who will be overcome in our contest, has this way to be healed if he says: I have sinned; and asks for repentance. And whoever is ashamed cannot be healed for he is not willing to show his wounds to the Physician Who took two dinars with which he heals all those who are wounded (cf. Lk 10:35).[147]

**7.4** You, physicians, disciples of our glorious Physician, ought not to hold back healing from the one who needs to be healed. Whoever shows you his ulcer, grant him repentance as medicine; and whoever is ashamed to show his pain, advise him not to hide from you. And when he reveals [it] to you, do not expose him lest because of him, the victorious might also consider themselves as defeated by the adversaries and enemies. The battle-line from which the slain fall is considered by their enemies as defeat over all of them. And when those who have been wounded are to be found among those who have not been wounded, the latter heal their pains and do not reveal them to their enemies. But, if

---

[147] *Aphr* 7.3: ܠܐ ܓܒܪ ܒܗܬ ܗܘ ܕܡܚܐ ܒܩܪܒܐ ܕܢܣܒܗ ܢܬܠ ܠܐܣܝܐ܂ ܐܣܝܐ ܚܟܝܡܐ ܡܛܠ ܕܢܣܒܗ ܩܪܒܐ ܘܡܚܐ. ܘܡܢܐ ܕܐܬܐܣܝ ܠܐ ܡܣܬܠܐ ܠܗ ܡܠܟܐ: ܐܠܐ ܟܕ ܚܠܡ ܡܢܐ ܘܣܒܪ ܠܗ. ܗܡܟܢܐ ܠܐ ܘܠܐ ܕܒܗܬ ܒܪܢܫܐ ܕܩܛܠܐ ܡܚܝܐ ܠܗ ܕܢܘܕܐ ܣܟܠܘܬܗ ܘܢܥܒܪ ܡܢܗ: ܘܢܒܥܐ ܠܗ ܣܡܐ ܬܝܒܘܬܐ. ܡܢ ܓܒܪ ܕܒܗܬ ܕܢܚܘܐ ܫܘܚܢܗ ܡܛܐ ܠܗ ܠܣܪܛܘܬܐ: ܘܠܟܠܗ ܦܓܪܗ ܡܛܐ ܢܟܝܐ. ܘܡܢ ܕܠܐ ܒܗܬ ܡܬܐܣܐ ܫܘܚܢܗ ܘܬܘܒ ܗܦܟ ܠܡܥܠ ܒܐܓܘܢܐ. ܘܐܝܢܐ ܕܡܛܐ ܠܣܪܛܘܬܐ ܬܘܒ ܠܐ ܡܫܟܚ ܠܡܬܐܣܝܘ ܘܙܝܢܐ ܕܫܠܚ ܠܐ ܠܒܫ: ܗܟܢܐ ܡܢ ܕܡܙܕܟܐ ܒܐܓܘܢܐ ܕܝܠܢ ܐܝܬ ܠܗ ܗܢܐ ܦܘܪܣܐ ܕܢܬܐܣܐ ܟܕ ܢܐܡܪ ܕܚܛܝܬ ܘܢܒܥܐ ܬܝܒܘܬܐ ܘܐܝܢܐ ܕܒܗܬ ܠܐ ܡܫܟܚ ܕܢܬܐܣܐ ܡܛܠ ܕܠܐ ܨܒܐ ܕܢܘܕܥ ܡܚܘܬܗ ܠܐܣܝܐ ܕܢܣܒ ܬܪܝܢ ܕܝܢܪܝܢ ܕܒܗܘܢ ܡܐܣܐ ܠܟܠܗܘܢ ܕܡܬܡܚܝܢ܀

they were to tell everyone about them, the whole camp would receive a bad name. Also the king, the captain of the army, will be angry about those who expose his camp; and they will be beaten by him with worse blows than those by which they were struck in the war.[148]

**7.5** If those who have been stricken, are not willing to reveal their ulcers, the physicians do not deserve any blame for not restoring the sick who have been wounded. And if those who have been wounded wish to hide their pains, they will not be able any longer to put on armour for they possess gangrene in their bodies. And when, having gangrene, they make bold to put on armour, and they go down to make contest, their armour becomes hot on them; and their ulcers grow foul and fetid, and they will be killed. And when those from whom they had hidden their ulcers find their bodies, then it is that they will mock at their nakedness, since they hid the pains of their wounds. Neither will they give their bodies a burial for they consider them stupid, evil and headlong.[149]

---

148 *Aphr* 7.4: ܘܐܦ ܠܗܘܢ ܘܠܐ ܐܣܘ̈ܬܐ ܬܠܡܝ̈ܕܘܗܝ ܕܐܣܝܢ ܚ̈ܟܝܡܐ ܕܠܐ ܬܓܠܘܢ ܐܣܘ̈ܬܐ ܡܢ ܡܢ ܕܚܫܝܢ ܕܢܬܐܣܐ. ܡܢ ܕܡܚܘܐ ܠܗܘܢ ܫܘܚܢܗ ܗܘܐ ܠܗ ܫܡܐ ܠܡܫܪܝܬܐ: ܘܡܢ ܕܟܣܐ ܕܢܚܘܐ ܒܐܒܗ ܐܢܘܢ ܡܘܠܟܢܘܗܝ ܕܡܠܟܘܢ ܠܐ ܢܛܥܐ. ܘܡܢ ܕܓܠܐ ܠܗܘܢ ܠܐ ܡܬܦܪܣܝܢ ܕܠܐ ܡܬܬܠܝܗ ܐܦ ܪ̈ܫܝܐ ܢܬܚܫܒܘܢ ܠܗܘܢ ܗܘܘ ܣܟ̈ܠܐ ܡܢ ܗܢ̈ܝܐ ܘܒܥܠܕܒ̈ܒܐ. ܗܕܪܐ ܐܝܢܐ ܕܡܬܩܠܐ ܢܦܠܝܢ ܡܢܗ ܫܘܒܠܬܐ ܥܠ ܟܠܗܘܢ ܡܬܡܚܝܐ ܡܢ ܒܥܠܕܒ̈ܒܝܗܘܢ: ܘܟܕ ܐܝܠܝܢ ܕܡܚܝܢ ܢܬܚܒܘܢ ܒܗܘܢ ܗܠܝܢ ܐܝܠܝܢ ܕܠܐ ܐܬܡܚܝܘ ܡܐܣܝܢ ܒܐܒ̈ܝܗܘܢ ܘܠܐ ܓܠܝܢ ܟܠܗܘܢ ܠܒܥܠܕܒ̈ܒܝܗܘܢ. ܐܢ ܕܝܢ ܠܟܠܢܫ ܡܘܕܥܝܢ ܠܗܘܢ ܫܩܠܐ ܠܗ ܫܡܐ ܒܝܫܐ ܟܠܗ ܡܫܪܝܬܐ. ܘܐܦ ܡܠܟܐ ܡܕܒܪܢܗ ܕܚܝܠܐ ܪܓܙ ܥܠ ܗܠܝܢ ܐܝܠܝܢ ܕܡܦܪܣܝܢ ܡܫܪܝܬܗ ܘܠܩܝܢ ܡܢܗ ܡܚ̈ܘܬܐ ܕܒ̈ܝܫܢ ܡܢ ܕܗܠܝܢ ܕܠܩܘ ܒܩܪܒܐ܀

149 *Aphr* 7.5: ܘܐܢ ܕܝܢ ܐܝܠܝܢ ܕܐܬܡܚܝܘ ܠܐ ܨܒܝܢ ܕܢܓܠܘܢ ܥܠ ܫܘܚ̈ܢܝܗܘܢ: ܐܣ̈ܘܬܐ ܪܘܫܢܐ ܡܕܡ ܠܐ ܚܝܒܝܢ ܥܠ ܕܠܐ ܐܣܝܘ ܠܟܪ̈ܝܗܐ ܕܐܬܡܚܝܘ. ܘܐܢ ܨܒܝܢ ܐܝܠܝܢ ܕܡܚܝܢ ܕܢܛܫܘܢ ܟܐܒ̈ܝܗܘܢ: ܬܘܒ ܙܝܢܐ ܠܐ ܡܫܟܚܝܢ ܠܡܠܒܫ ܡܛܠ ܕܫܪ̈ܝܢܬܐ ܗܘܐ ܒܦܓܪ̈ܝܗܘܢ. ܘܟܕ ܫܪ̈ܝܢܬܐ ܐܝܬ ܠܗܘܢ ܘܡܡܪܚܝܢ ܠܡܠܒܫ ܙܝܢܐ: ܟܕ ܢܚܬܝܢ ܠܡܟܬܫ: ܐܝܟܢܐ ܙܝܢܗܘܢ ܡܚܡ ܥܠܝܗܘܢ ܘܣܪܝܢ ܘܡܬܡܣܝܢ ܫܘܚ̈ܢܝܗܘܢ ܘܡܬܩܛܠܝܢ. ܘܡܢ ܕܡܫܟܚܝܢ ܦܓܪ̈ܝܗܘܢ ܐܝܠܝܢ ܕܛܫܘ ܡܢܗܘܢ ☞

> **7.6** Also the one who shows his ulcer and is healed should take care about the place which has been healed so that he is not wounded there twice. Because it is difficult even for a wise physician to heal a person who is wounded twice, for any wound which has an ulcer cannot be healed; and even if it is healed again, he cannot put on armour. And if he should make bold to put on armour, he will take upon himself habitual defeat.[150]

### *2.3.2.6 The Pains and Sickness of the Wounded and Stricken People*

Considering life as a 'war' (ܩܪܒܐ) and 'contest' (ܐܓܘܢܐ), it does not surprise the author that men get 'wounded' (ܬܒܝܪܐ), 'stricken' (ܡܚܝܢܐ), 'scattered' (ܡܒܕܪܐ) and 'lost' (ܐܒܝܕܐ). The fight is against the 'enemies' (ܒܥܠܕܒܒܐ), 'haters' (ܣܢܐܐ), 'Satan' (ܣܛܢܐ) and 'sin' (ܚܛܝܬܐ). Since Jesus Christ is the only One Who has not been wounded, but instead overcame the world and crucified sin, mankind is advised to follow Him. Answering the question of how Jesus was victorious over the world, Aphrahat applies Malachi's words about Levi to Christ: Jesus Christ has not sinned for 'He has not committed wickedness and nothing false was found in His mouth' (Mal 2:6). Referring to Paul, Jesus Christ is the only One Who 'crucified sin and won the race in the stadium' (Col 2:14).[151] Although the author uses some terms that are

---

ܫܘܚܢܝܗܘܢ: ܡܚܘܝܢ ܗܘ ܠܣܝܡ ܥܠ ܟܠܗ ܦܘܪܣܝܗܘܢ ܥܠ ܕܬܒܝܪܘ ܟܐܒܐ ܕܡܚܘܬܗܘܢ: ܘܐܦ ܠܐ ܥܠܬܗܘܢ ܚܙܝܢ ܠܡܣܒܪܐ ܘܡܬܚܫܒܝܢ ܠܗܘܢ ܣܟܠܐ ܘܒܢܝܐ ܘܡܪܝܢܐ܀

[150] *Aphr* 7.6: ܘܐܦ ܡܢ ܕܡܚܘܐ ܫܘܚܢܗ ܘܡܬܐܣܐ ܢܙܕܗܪ ܡܢ ܗܝ ܕܘܟܬܐ ܕܐܬܐܣܝܬ ܕܠܐ ܢܬܚܒܠ ܒܗ ܕܬܪܬܝܢ ܙܒܢܝܢ: ܡܛܠ ܕܡܢ ܕܡܬܚܒܠ ܬܪܬܝܢ ܙܒܢܝܢ ܐܦ ܠܐܣܝܐ ܚܟܝܡܐ ܥܣܝܩܐ ܗܝ ܐܣܝܘܬܗ: ܡܛܠ ܕܟܠ ܡܚܘܬܐ ܕܒܫܘܚܢܐ ܗܘܝܐ ܠܐ ܡܬܐܣܝܐ: ܘܐܦ ܟܕ ܛܒ ܬܘܒ ܬܬܐܣܐ ܐܢܫ ܠܐ ܡܫܟܚ ܠܡܠܒܫ ܙܝܢܐ. ܘܐܦ ܟܕ ܐܢܫ ܢܡܪܚ ܘܢܠܒܫ: ܢܣܒ ܠܗ ܥܝܕܐ ܕܫܟܒܘܬܐ܀

[151] *Aphr* 7.1: ܘܡܢܐ ܚܕ ܗܘ ܒܠܚܘܕ ܡܢ ܟܠ ܝܠܘܕܐ ܕܠܒܫܘ ܦܓܪܐ: ܕܐܬܥܘܬܗܝ، ܡܢܗ ܢܨܘܚ ܡܚܣܢܐ ܐܝܟ ܕܗܘ ܗܘܐ ܥܠ ܢܦܫܗ. ܐܡܪ ܠܢ: ܕܐܢܐ ܙܟܝܬܗ ܠܥܠܡܐ. ܘܐܦ ܢܒܝܐ ܗܘܐ ܥܠܘܗܝ: ܕܠܐ ܥܒܕ ܥܘܠܐ ܐܦܠܐ ܢܟܠܐ ܐܫܬܟܚ ܒܦܘܡܗ. ܘܫܠܝܚܐ ܠܦܘܠܘܣ ܐܡܪ: ܕܗܘ

☞

associated with war and battle, it is obvious that his attention is drawn to the inner spiritual struggle[152] against sin and Satan. Jesus' victory over Satan and sin serves as an example for human beings.

Nonetheless, although the power of sin is defeated in Jesus' victory, something of it has remained. Since Adam's transgression, sin reigns on earth and 'wounds' (ܟܠܒܐ), 'strikes' (ܡܡܚܝܢܐ) and 'has killed' (ܩܛܠܬ) many. After sin has been killed on the cross, its power was at an end, but not its 'sting' (ܥܘܩܣܐ) that still exists and 'pierces' (ܕܒܝ) man. Sin's sting will finally be extinguished for ever on the last day of judgment.[153]

Although man's enemy is skilful and mighty, his weapon is weaker than the armour which men receive from the Lord.

---

ܕܠܐ ܝܕܥ ܗܘܐ ܚܛܝܬܐ ܡܛܠܬܢ ܚܛܝܬܐ ܥܒܕܗ. ܘܐܝܟܢܐ ܥܒܕܗ ܚܛܝܬܐ: ܐܠܐ ܡܛܠ ܕܢܩܛܠܝܗ̇ ܠܚܛܝܬܐ ܟܕ ܠܐ ܗܘܐ ܗܘ ܥܒܕܗ: ܘܩܒܥܗ̇ ܒܙܩܝܦܐ. Aphrahat's first quotation from Paul is from 2 Cor 5:21. Then in the loose allusion to Col 2:14, strictly what Christ nailed to the cross was not 'sin' but the ܫܛܪ ܚܘ̈ܒܝܢ.

152 The term ܐܓܘܢܐ is used in *Aphr* 6.1; 7.1-3; 7.5; 7.7-8; 7.18-22; 7.25; 14.6; 14.38. In the Epistles the term ܐܓܘܢܐ appears in the context of faithful people's life as a battle against the Evil One: cf. 1 Cor 9:25; Phil 1:30; Col 2:1; 1 Tim 6:12; 2 Tim 4:7; 1 Th 2:2.

153 *Aphr* 7.1: ܬܘܒ ܠܝܬ ܐܢܫܐ ܡܢ ܒܢ̈ܝ ܐܕܡ ܕܢܦܠ ܒܐܓܘܢܐ ܕܠܐ ܡܬܡܚܝܢܐ ܘܡܠܒ: ܡܛܠ ܕܐܡܠܟܬ ܚܛܝܬܐ ܡܢ ܕܥܒܪ ܐܕܡ ܥܠ ܦܘܩܕܢܐ. ܘܡܢ ܣܓܝܐ̈ܐ ܟܠܒܐ ܗܘܬ ܘܠܣܓܝܐ̈ܐ ܡܡܚܝܢܐ ܗܘܬ ܘܠܣܓܝܐ̈ܐ ܩܛܠܬ: ܘܐܦ ܡܢ ܣܓܝܐ̈ܐ ܠܐ ܩܛܠܬܗ̇ ܥܕܡܐ ܕܐܬܐ ܦܪܘܩܢ ܘܥܩܪܗ̇ ܘܩܒܥܗ̇ ܒܙܩܝܦܐ. ܘܐܦ ܟܕ ܒܙܩܝܦܐ ܩܒܝܥܐ: ܥܘܩܣܗ̇ ܐܝܬܘܗܝ ܘܠܣܓܝܐ̈ܐ ܕܒܝ ܟܕ ܗܘܝܐ ܚܪܬܐ ܘܡܬܬܒܪ ܠܗ̇ ܥܘܩܣܗ̇. In this context Aphrahat does not discuss what Jesus' victory precisely means. Nor is what sin's sting means widely illustrated. However, attention is drawn to the fact that people still suffer under sin and they, metaphorically speaking, get wounded and pricked. Aphrahat certainly knows 1 Cor 15:55-56: 'Where, O death, is your victory? Where, O Sheol, is your sting? The sting of death is sin and the power of sin is the Law' (ܐܝܟܘ ܥܘܩܣܟܝ ܡܘܬܐ. ܘܐܝܟܐ ܙܟܘܬܟܝ ܫܝܘܠ. ܥܘܩܣܗ ܕܝܢ ܕܡܘܬܐ ܚܛܝܬܐ ܗܝ ܘܚܝܠܐ ܕܚܛܝܬܐ ܢܡܘܣܐ ܗܘ). However, Paul does not use the verb ܕܒܝ along with ܥܘܩܣܐ as Aphrahat does. The term ܥܘܩܣܐ is further used in Act 9:4; 26:14.

Therefore, the faithful are enabled to enter the struggle and fight against Satan through Christ's armour.[154] Having said this, man still has to fight against sin for its presence cannot be denied. Consequently in this spiritual war people get injured and wounded.

However, Aphrahat challenges the people in authority, the ministers of the church, to provide help to the sick and repentance to sinners.[155] Repentance is the medicine provided by God to the penitent through his disciples. Aphrahat uses the phrase 'repentance as medicine' (ܣܡܐ ܬܝܒܘܬܐ) four times, implying the confessing of sin, and the resolve not do it again.[156] Spiritually, repentance serves as medicine if the penitent willingly wants it and reveals his 'iniquity' (ܣܟܠܘܬܗ), accompanied by 'contrition' (ܬܘܬ ܢܦܫܐ) and the confession: 'I have sinned' (ܕܚܛܝܬ).[157] The Lord does not reject the penitent repenting, wishing them to repent and be healed, as He offered repentance to Adam, Cain and Noah's contemporaries.[158] Confident in this, Aphrahat challenges the penitent to accept this repentance which he describes as healing: 'Also I am saying to you, penitent, do not hold back from yourselves this means that is given for healing'.[159] Aphrahat's confidence that God grants healing to the penitent is based on the Bible. He refers not only to Adam's fall, to the Ninivites' and the Israelites' sins,[160] but also to the Gospel and emphasises that 'our Lord did not come to call the righteous, but sinners to repent. Let

---

154 *Aphr* 7.7: ܐܘ ܠܒܢ̈ܝ ܐܝܠܗ ܕܡܫܝܚܐ: ܠܒܫܘ ܥܠܠܢ ܡܪܢܐ ܕܠܐ ܬܫܒܚܘܢ ܘܬܬܟܬܫܘܢ ܥܩܠܐ ܒܐܘܠܨܢܐ. ܢܨܚ ܗܘ ܘܐܘܟܡ ܒܟܠܗ̈ܝܢ: ܕܠܐ ܢܝܫܗ ܥܒܕ ܗܘ ܡܢ ܕܝܠܗ. ܘܠܐ ܠܗ ܡܣܒܠ ܠܬܟܬܫܘܬܗ ܒܟܡܗ ܘܠܡܫܟܚ ܢܝܫܗ ܕܡܟܬܫܐ ܒܟܪܝܘܬܐ. ܗܘ ܓܒܪ ܠܐ ܡܬܚܣܐ ܠܗ ܒܗ. ܡܢܘܪܒ ܒܒܡ. ܢܬܒܥܐ ܠܗ ܗܘ ܡܢ ܕܚܣܐ ܠܗ: ܕܒܬܠܝܩܘܗܝ ܡܢܡ.

155 *Aphr* 7.26: ܐܘ ܪ̈ܥܘܬܐ ܬܠܡܝ̈ܕܘܗܝ ܕܪ̈ܥܝܐ: ܪܥܘ ܥܢܐ ܘܕܒܪܘ ܥܒܪ̈. ܣܥܘ ܠܟܪ̈ܝܗܐ ܘܐܣܝܘ ܠܡܚ̈ܝܐ: ܚܒܘܫ ܠܬܒ̈ܝܪܐ ܘܐܗܦܘ ܠܚܫܝ̈ܠܬܐ ܘܗܦܘ ܡܛܥܝܬܐ ܕܥܪܩܐ. Cf. *Aphr* 10.3-4 along with Ez 34.

156 *Aphr* 7.2-4.

157 *Aphr* 7.2-3.

158 *Aphr* 7.8.

159 *Aphr* 7.12: ܘܐܦ ܠܟܘܢ ܬܝ̈ܒܐ ܐܡܪ ܐܢܐ: ܕܠܐ ܬܟܠܘܢ ܡܢ ܢܦܫܟܘܢ ܦܘܪܣܐ ܗܢܐ ܕܝܗܝܒ ܠܐܣܝܘܬܐ.

160 *Aphr* 7.8-9.

us take up some of the suffering of anyone of us who becomes sick, and where anyone stumbles, let us feel pain on his behalf'.[161] As the Lord gives help to mankind with penitence as medicine, men should also help each other. Like a body, if one limb suffers, so too the whole body suffers. Aphrahat, using the term **ܥܘܡܠܗ**, motivates people to work on the wound to heal it. He says: 'If one of our limbs receive a hurt, let us work on this wound until it is healed. When one of our limbs is praised, the whole body ought to glory; and when one of our limbs receives pain, the whole body will have fever.'[162] Here, the idea is that sinners and weak people should not be publicly blamed and disgraced. Instead, they should be encouraged and helped to find the way how to live and be healed. Referring to Matthew, Aphrahat goes further, saying: 'Anyone who causes one of these little ones [to sin] will be thrown into the sea with a millstone around his neck (Mt 18:6). The one who kicks his brother with his foot, will not be forgiven. The wound of the rebuker does not have any healing, and the trespasses of those who disgrace will not be forgiven.'[163]

In Aphr 7.4, the author speaks of the whole camp of the army as being comparable to the believer community. If some of them get injured and wounded, all of them should try to heal the wound and not reveal it to their enemy who is Satan. Again, this means sinners should not be blamed and disgraced for their wickedness, so that they will be caused to do further evil deeds. The defeat of

---

161 *Aphr* 7.23 (cf. Lk 5:32): ܠܐ ܐܬܐ ܡܪܢ ܕܢܩܪܐ ܠܙܕܝܩܐ ܐܠܐ ܠܚܛܝܐ ܠܬܝܒܘܬܐ. ܟܠ ܡܢ ܕܡܬܟܪܗ ܡܢܢ ܢܣܒܘܠ ܡܢ ܚܫܗ: ܘܡܢ ܕܡܬܬܩܠ ܢܬܟܐܒ ܚܠܦܘܗܝ. See also *Aphr* 28.8.

162 *Aphr* 7.24: ܟܕ ܠܚܕ ܗܕܡܝܢ ܢܬܡܚܐ ܟܐܒܐ ܚܠܡ ܢܥܡܠ ܒܟܐܒܗ ܥܕܡܐ ܕܬܬܐܣܐ: ܟܕ ܚܕ ܡܢ ܗܕܡܝܢ ܢܫܬܒܚ ܟܠܗ ܦܓܪܐ ܗܕܝܪ ܘܗܘܐ: ܘܟܕ ܠܚܕ ܡܢ ܗܕܡܝܢ ܢܬܡܚܐ ܟܐܒܐ ܠܟܠܗ ܦܓܪܐ ܠܚܡܝܬܗ ܐܫܬܐ.

163 *Aphr* 7.24: ܟܠ ܕܡܟܫܠ ܠܚܕ ܡܢ ܗܠܝܢ ܙܥܘܪܐ ܢܦܠ ܒܝܡܐ ܟܕ ܪܚܝܐ ܕܚܡܪܐ ܒܨܘܪܗ.. ܘܡܢ ܕܕܚܐ ܠܚܒܪܗ ܕܐܚܘܗܝ, ܒܪܓܠܐ ܕܝܠܗ ܗܘܐ ܬܒܪܗ. ܘܡܢ ܕܪܦܣ ܒܪܓܠܗ ܥܠ ܐܚܘܗܝ, ܠܐ ܢܫܬܒܩ. ܠܡܚܘܬܗ ܕܡܟܣܢܐ ܠܝܬ ܠܗ ܐܣܝܘܬܐ: ܘܡܚܣܕܢܐ ܣܟܠܘܬܗܘܢ, ܠܐ ܡܫܬܒܩܢ.

some people in the camp is like the pain of one limb which causes the whole body to suffer.[164]

Aphrahat uses different terms to describe the effect of sin on those who are either stricken or wounded in the battle of life. In particular, the following terms are found in Aphrahat's text: 'ulcers' (ܫܘܚ̈ܢܐ), 'wounds' (ܡܚ̈ܘܬܐ), 'gangrene' (ܫܠܕܝܬܐ), 'harm' (ܚܒܠܐ), 'pains' (ܟܐ̈ܒܐ), 'sick people' (ܟܪ̈ܝܗܐ), 'wound on a scar' (ܡܚܘܬܐ ܕܒܘܫܡܬܐ).

The term 'ulcer' (ܫܘܚܢܐ) is used in three demonstrations.[165] It appears often in the Demonstration On Repentance as something that needs to be healed. The 'ulcer' (ܫܘܚܢܐ) is the painful wound of the stricken and wounded people: 'and those who are struck in our battle have repentance as medicine which they apply to their ulcers and will be restored'.[166] The ulcers are the 'wounds of the sick people' (ܡܚ̈ܘܬܐ ܕܟܪ̈ܝܗܐ) and the 'pains of their wounds' (ܟܐ̈ܒܐ ܕܡܚ̈ܘܬܗܘܢ).[167] The verbs 'to be wounded' (ܡܚܐ) and 'to be struck' (ܒܠܥ) are used to describe the injury incurred by the fighter in the war against 'his enemy' (ܒܥܠܕܒܒܗ). While the author advises the fighter not to be ashamed to reveal his 'ulcer' (ܫܘܚܢܗ), he challenges 'the man whom Satan has struck not to be ashamed to confess his transgression, and leave it'.[168] Otherwise as Aphrahat emphasises, the consequence of the ulcer not being healed is 'gangrene' (ܫܠܕܝܬܐ) and 'harm' (ܚܒܠܐ) to the whole body.[169] Since the ulcer can be healed, the man can be enabled to fight against the enemy again without immediately being defeated; but the complicated healing of a gangrene disables a person from taking up his armour and entering

---

[164] *Aphr* 7.4.

[165] *Aphr* 7.2-6; 9.10; 20.7-8.

[166] *Aphr* 7.2: ܠܕܡܬܡܚܝܢ ܒܐܓܘܢܐ ܕܝܠܢ ܐܝܬ ܠܗܘܢ ܣܡܐ ܬܝܒܘܬܐ ܕܣܝܡܝܢ ܥܠ ܫܘ̈ܚܢܝܗܘܢ ܘܡܬܚܠܡܝܢ.

[167] *Aphr* 7.2; 7.5.

[168] *Aphr* 7.3: ܗܢܐ ܠܐ ܘܠܐ ܕܢܒܗܬ ܒܪܢܫܐ ܕܣܛܢܐ ܡܚܝܗ ܠܗ ܕܢܘܕܐ ܣܟܠܘܬܗ ܘܢܫܒܘܩ ܡܢܗ̇.

[169] The term ܫܠܕܝܬܐ is used only four times in *Aphr* 7.2 and 7.5.

the battle.[170] 'Our contest' (ܟܐܬܘܫܐ ܕܝܠܢ) is not the ordinary battle, but the invisible war against sin. Therefore, the consequence of any gangrene is death: 'their ulcers will become foul and fetid, and they will be killed'.[171]

The term 'ulcer' (ܫܘܚܢܐ) also appears in the Demonstration On Humility where Aphrahat presents 'anger' (ܚܡܬܐ) in contrast to 'humility' (ܡܟܝܟܘܬܐ). While humility causes man to live peacefully and bear good fruit, anger causes an 'ulcer' (ܫܘܚܢܐ). Therefore, the person addressed is advised not to become angry and express this anger on his lips.[172] The speech and words caused by anger are like an ulcer, and they make man unclean. While the singular is used metaphorically here, in Demonstration 20, the plural appears in its physical sense. When Aphrahat refers to the episode of the rich man and Lazarus (Lk 16:19-31) to explain the parable of the rich fool (Lk 12:13-31), he uses this term once in its simple plural form (ܫܘܚ̈ܢܐ) and twice with a suffix-ending (ܫܘܚ̈ܢܘܗܝ).[173] Both forms are taken from Luke. When Jesus speaks about Lazarus' ulcers, he says: 'even the dogs came and licked his ulcers'.[174] Aphrahat explains the parable allegorically. Referring to Moses (Dtn 4:7; 6:10-13), the Hebrews are identified with the rich man,[175] whereas Jesus is identified with the poor man

---

[170] *Aphr* 7.3; 7.5.

[171] *Aphr* 7.5: ܘܟܕ ܚܠܝܨܘܬܐ ܐܝܬ ܠܗܘܢ ܘܢܨܚܘܢ ܠܡܠܟܐ ܐܡܪ: ܟܕ ܢܦܠܝܢ ܠܡܚܕܐ: ܐܬܟܬܫܐ ܢܣܒܘܢ ܡܚܘܬ ܚܠܫܘܢ ܘܣܪܝܢ ܘܡܬܡܣܝܢ ܫܘܚ̈ܢܝܗܘܢ ܘܡܬܩܛܠܝܢ.

[172] *Aphr* 9.10: ܚܡܬܐ ܟܕ ܡܬܬܟܝܠܐ ܒܟ ܬܗܘܐ ܫܘܚܢܐ: ܘܠܐ ܬܦܩܝܗ ܠܠܫܢܟ ܘܠܐ ܬܬܠܝܗ ܠܣܦܘ̈ܬܟ: ܟܠ ܡܣܟܢ̈ܐ ܕܣܠܩ ܥܠ ܠܒܟ ܒܦܘܡܟ ܒܗܠܐ ܠܡܐܡܪ ܐܝܢ: ܠܡ̈ܠܬܐ ܕܒܠܒ ܠܒܟ ܗܘ ܠܠܫܢܟ.

[173] *Aphr* 20.7-8.

[174] Lk 16:20-21: ܡܣܟܢܐ ܚܕ ܐܝܬ ܗܘܐ ܕܫܡܗ ܠܥܙܪ. ܘܪܡܐ ܗܘܐ ܠܘܬ ܬܪܥܗ ܕܗܘ ܥܬܝܪܐ ܟܕ ܡܡܚܝ ܒܫܘܚ̈ܢܐ. ܘܡܬܪܓܐ ܗܘܐ ܕܢܡܠܐ ܟܪܣܗ ܡܢ ܦܬܬ̈ܐ ܕܢܦܠܝܢ ܡܢ ܦܬܘܪܗ ܕܗܘ ܥܬܝܪܐ. ܐܠܐ ܐܦ ܟܠܒ̈ܐ ܐܬܝܢ ܗܘܘ ܡܠܚܟܝܢ ܫܘܚ̈ܢܘܗܝ.

[175] *Aphr* 20.7: ܘܐܡܪ ܬܘܒ: ܕܟܠܒ̈ܐ ܐܬܝܢ ܗܘܘ ܘܠܚܟܝܢ ܫܘܚ̈ܢܘܗܝ. ܥܬܝܪܐ ܗܢܐ ܕܐܬܡܬܠ ܒܦܬ̈ܬܐ ܐܝܬܘܗܝ، ܗܘ ܥܡܐ ܕܐܟܠ ܘܣܒܥ ܘܒܥܛ ܘܐܦܠܚܐ ܠܡܪܝܐ ܘܢܫܝ ܠܐܠܗܐ.

and the gentiles with the dogs. Furthermore, Lazarus' ulcers (ܫܘܚ̈ܢܘܗܝ) are used in a positive sense since they signify the Lord's wounds (ܫܘ̈ܡܬܗ) which are His body given to the gentiles.[176] The term ܫܘ̈ܡܬܐ is also used in 1 Peter. When Peter refers to the healing imagery of Jesus' wounds, he says: 'He took all our sins and lifted them in His body on the cross, so that when we die to sin we might live for righteousness; by His wounds you have been healed'.[177] Along with the 'wounds' (ܫܘ̈ܡܬܐ) the dogs have a positive aspect too. The dogs are admired for their faithfulness and loyalty towards their owner. They love him and 'lick his wounds' (ܡܠܚܟܝܢ ܫܘ̈ܡܬܗ). Licking the wounds with the tongue indicates the partaking of Holy Communion.[178] Therefore, the tongue should not be used for evil thoughts and speak defiled words of hatred.[179] Jesus' wounds possess medical power and healing, so that man's wounds can be healed through them.[180]

However, Aphrahat, also uses the term ܫܘ̈ܡܬܐ in the sense of 'old scar' that is difficult even for a good physician to heal. Although the 'wound on a scar' (ܟܘܝܬܐ ܕܒܫܘܡܬܐ) might be healed, the 'scars' (ܫܘ̈ܡܬܐ) will stay.[181] It is not a disgrace to be injured, if the wounded person offers his wound to be healed. Morever, the king will not only accept him in his army again, but he

---

[176] *Aphr* 20.8: ܘܡܣܟܢܐ ܕܪܡܐ ܗܘܐ ܥܠ ܬܪܥܗ ܐܝܬܘܗܝ ܕܡܘܬܐ ܕܥܡ̈ܡܐ. ܘܐܝܟ ܗܘܐ ܘܡܬܚܫܚ ܕܢܣܒ ܡܢܗܘܢ ܦܬ̈ܘܬܐ ܘܢܛܠ ܠܡܣܒܪܘܬܗ: ܘܠܐ ܐܢܫ ܝܗܒ ܠܗ. ܘܕܐܡܪ ܕܟܠܒ̈ܐ ܐܬܝܢ ܗܘܘ ܘܠܚܟܝܢ ܫܘܚ̈ܢܘܗܝ: ܟܠܒ̈ܐ ܒܢܝ ܕܐܬܝܢ ܗܘܘ ܠܡܥܡ̈ܕܐ ܐܝܟܢ ܕܡܠܚܟܝܢ ܫܘ̈ܡܬܗ ܕܦܪܘܩܢ: ܦܓܪܗ ܕܥܡܠܐ ܘܡܣܝܒܪ ܥܠ ܚܝ̈ܘܗܝ. For the parable of the rich man and Lazarus (Lk 16:19-31) in Aphrahat, see: A. Valavanolickal, *The Use of the Gospel Parables in the Writings of Aphrahat and Ephrem* (Frankfurt am Main 1996), 288-296. See also the summary in R. Murray, *Symbols of Church and Kingdom* (Cambridge 1975), p. 60, n. 3.

[177] 1 Pet 2:24: ܘܥܡܠ ܚܛ̈ܗܝܢ ܟܠܗܘܢ ܟܠܗܘܢ ܘܐܣܩ ܐܢܘܢ ܒܦܓܪܗ ܠܙܩܝܦܐ. ܕܟܕ ܡܝܬܝܢ ܚܢܢ ܠܚܛܝܬܐ. ܒܙܕܝܩܘܬܐ ܕܠܗ ܢܚܐ. ܒܫܘ̈ܡܬܗ ܓܝܪ ܐܬܐܣܝܬܘܢ.

[178] *Aphr* 7.21.

[179] *Aphr* 9.10.

[180] *Aphr* 7.10; Is 53:3; see the previous section.

[181] *Aphr* 7.6; 7.17.

will also grant him gifts and honour. Aphrahat advises the wounded person to be aware of his wound so that he should not be wounded again on the same place. It is also difficult for a good physician to heal the 'gangrene' (ܣܠܕܝܬܐ).[182] Therefore, the ulcers need to be healed in their earliest state.

### 2.3.2.7 *The Medicine and Physician of the Wounded and Stricken People*

The term 'physician' (ܐܣܝܐ) appears in the singular and plural form as 'physician' (ܐܣܝܐ) and 'physicians' (ܐܣܘ̈ܬܐ); and with the adjectives 'wise' (ܐܣܝܐ ܚܟܝܡܐ), 'our wise' ( ܐܣܝܢ ܚܟܝܡܐ) and 'our victorious Physician' (ܐܣܝܢ ܢܨܝܚܐ). The phrases 'our wise Physician' (ܐܣܝܢ ܚܟܝܡܐ) and 'our victorious Physician' (ܐܣܝܢ ܢܨܝܚܐ) are used as titles for Christ, whereas the 'wise physician' (ܐܣܝܐ ܚܟܝܡܐ) is not only used for Jesus Christ, but also has a general meaning that could imply any good physician who understands his art and can be trusted. 'Our wise Physician' (ܐܣܝܢ ܚܟܝܡܐ) is used twice; both times it is linked to the term 'physicians' (ܐܣܘ̈ܬܐ) that is used for the disciples who are challenged to 'restore/heal the wounds of the sick' ( ܬܠܚܡܘܢ ܡܚ̈ܘܬܐ ܕܟܪ̈ܝܗܐ) through the medicine of penitence.[183]

[182] Cf. L. Haefeli, *Stilmittel bei Aphrahat dem Persischen Weisen* (Leipzig 1968), 168-169. He points out that in modern medicine too - according to his time at the beginning of this century - the full healing of a 'gangrene' is not easy even after being initially healed, but Aphrahat exaggerates it: Diese letzte Feststellung ist nach unseren heutigen medizinischen Kenntnissen und sicher auch nach der Heilpraxis der Alten übertrieben. Aber richtig daran ist, daß das Narbengewebe schlechte Heilungstendenz aufweist. Und diese schwere Heilbarkeit einer neuen Wunde auf der Narbe der alten ist wirklich ein gut gewähltes Bild dafür, daß die »letzten Dinge des rückfälligen Menschen schlimmer sind als die ersten«'.

[183] *Aphr* 7.2: ܐܘ ܐܣܘ̈ܬܐ ܬܠܡܝ̈ܕܘܗܝ ܕܐܣܝܢ ܚܟܝܡܐ: ܣܒܘ ܠܟܘܢ ܣܡܐ ܗܢܐ ܕܒܗ ܬܠܚܡܘܢ ܡܚ̈ܘܬܐ ܕܟܪ̈ܝܗܐ. Almost the same phrase, but slightly changed, is used in paragraph 7.4 where the author advises the 'physicians, the disciples of our glorious Physicians' ( ܐܣܘ̈ܬܐ ܬܠܡܝ̈ܕܘܗܝ ܕܐܣܝܢ ܢܨܝܚܐ) to grant healing to the needy. The adjective 'wise' (ܚܟܝܡܐ) is replaced with 'glorious' (ܢܨܝܚܐ). Finally, again the

☞

Obviously, the wise Physician is God, the Lord of the Old Testament and New Testament, Who provides healing to mankind through his chosen people, the physicians, and his written word. The Bible provides the medicine of the wise Physician that the physicians can use for binding up and healing wounds.

In paragraph 7.3, when the author refers to the parable of the Good Samaritan who took out two silver coins and gave them to the innkeeper (Lk 10:5), the term 'physician' (ܐܣܝܐ) is referred to Jesus Christ: the Samaritan, as the 'physician who took two dinars from which he heals all those who have been wounded' ( ܠܐܣܝܐ ܕܢܣܒ ܬܪܝܢ ܕܝܢܪ̈ܝܢ ܕܡܢܗܘܢ ܡܐܣܐ ܠܟܠܗܘܢ ܕܡܬܚܒܠܝܢ),[184] is identified with the Lord Who is called 'the Physician of all sick people' ( ܐܣܝܐ ܗܘܐ ܕܟܠܗܘܢ ܟܪ̈ܝܗܐ)[185] and the 'Physician of our pains' (ܐܣܝܐ ܕܟܐܒ̈ܝܢ).[186]

Since the Lord is 'our wise Physician' (ܐܣܝܢ ܚܟܝܡܐ) and in Him is 'healing' (ܒܗ ܐܣܝܘܬܐ), as well as 'peace' (ܫܠܡܐ), 'love' (ܚܘܒܐ) and 'purity' (ܕܟܝܘܬܐ),[187] the verb 'to heal' (ܐܣܐ) describes His healing deeds. The biblical healing miracles that are mentioned at the end of the first and second Demonstrations include the verb 'to heal', such as when Jesus asks the blind person: 'do you believe that I can heal you' ( ܡܗܝܡܢ ܐܢܬ ܕܡܫܟܚ ܐܢܐ ܕܐܣܝܟ ); or 'he healed the centurion's daughter' ( ܘܐܣܐ

---

phrase 'our wise Physician' (ܐܣܝܢ ܚܟܝܡܐ) appears in *Aphr* 7.8 along with the term 'physicians' (ܐܣܘ̈ܬܐ) where the author reminds the 'physicians what is written in the books of our wise Physician'. *Aphr* 7.8: ܠܟܘܢ ܕܝܢ ܡܟܬܒ ܐܢܐ ܐܣܘ̈ܬܐ ܡܕܡ ܕܟܬܝܒ ܒܣܦܪ̈ܘܗܝ ܕܐܣܝܢ ܚܟܝܡܐ: ܕܗܘ ܠܐ ܟܠܐ ܬܝܒܘܬܐ.

[184] *Aphr* 7.3. For the parable of the Good Samaritan (Lk 10:25-35 see K. A. Valavanolickal, *The Use of the Gospel Parables in the Writings of Aphrahat and Ephrem* (Frankfurt 1996), 247-48.

[185] *Aphr* 6.9.

[186] *Aphr* 23.52.

[187] *Aphr* 14.44: ܘܡܪܢ ܦܬܚ ܘܐܡܪ ܠܗܘ ܙܒܢܐ ܕܟܠܐ ܥܠ ܛܒ̈ܐ. ܒܗ ܚܘܒܐ: ܒܗ ܫܠܡܐ: ܒܗ ܙܕܝܩܘܬܐ: ܒܗ ܐܣܝܘܬܐ: ܒܗ ܕܟܝܘܬܐ: ܘܒܗ ܥܠ ܚܘܒ̈ܝܢ ܛܒ̈ܐ ܘܥܒ̈ܕܝܢ ܘܡܛܝ̈ܒܘܬܢ.

ܚܝܪ ܠܨܠܝܒܗ ܕܡܠܐܦܘܪܐ).[188] Aphrahat says that the healing comes through His crucifixion and restoration through His sickness and weakness.[189] In Aphr 17.10, healing is attributed to 'His wounds' (ܘܒܡܚܘܬܗ ܐܬܐܣܝܢܢ; 1 Pet 2:24). In order to make it clear that mankind is healed through the Lord's wounds, the author asks rhetorically when he refers to Is 53:3: 'Through which wounds were people healed?'[190] Also according to Aphr 23.11, the Lord's economy was for the healing of man: Since He was man like us, clothed with the 'sickness/weakness of body' (ܟܪܝܗܘܬܗ ܕܦܓܪܐ), His death and resurrection overcame death and sickness and are courage for mankind.[191] Thus, He as the 'Physician of our pains' (ܐܣܝܐ ܕܟܐܒܝܢ) granted His spirit to mankind as medicine for their bodies. His economy serves to heal man from pain and sickness.[192]

However, the verb 'to heal' (ܐܣܐ) is used more with the term 'physician' (ܐܣܝܐ). If the Samaritan who is called the physician can be identified with the Lord, then the term 'to heal' (ܠܡܐܣܐ) is related to the Lord as 'the Physician Who took two dinars by

---

188 *Aphr* 1.17 and 2.20; cf. the section before.

189 *Aphr* 14.31 ܦܬܚ ܟܘܪܐ ܘܐܣܠܝܗ ܟܪܝܗܐ: ܦܓܥ ܒܟܘܦܐ ܘܗܠܟܝܢ ܣܚܝܦܐ: ܥܡܠ ܒܐܟܝܢ ܘܐܣܠܝܗ ܠܡܣܟܢܘܬܗ ܘܐܣܝ ܟܪܝܗܘܬܗ: ܘܦܬܪ ܪܫܡܘܬܗ ܘܚܒܫ ܠܡܚܒܪܘܬܗ ܘܚܒܫ ܒܢܝ ܕܢܘܗ: ܐܟܚܕܐ ܒܡܫܡܠܝܘܬܗ ܘܒܟܪܝܗܘܬܗ ܐܣܠܝܗ: ܐܣܝ ܒܡܫܡܠܝܘܬܗ ܘܒܐܘܠܨܢܗ، ܪܘܚ.

190 *Aphr* 17.10 (Is 53:3): ܘܐܡܪ ܒܚܘܒܬܗ ܕܦܬܓܡܐ: ܕܗܘ ܡܬܡܚܠ ܡܛܠ ܚܛܗܝܢ ܡܬܡܟܟ ܡܛܠ ܥܘܠܝ: ܡܪܕܘܬܐ ܕܫܠܡܢ ܥܠܘܗܝ، ܘܒܡܚܘܬܗ ܐܬܐܣܝܢܢ. ܒܐܝܠܝܢ ܡܚܘܬܐ ܐܬܐܣܝܘ ܒܢܝܢܫܐ.

191 *Aphr* 23.11: ܠܒܢ ܒܡܘܬܗ ܘܚܝܢ ܒܩܝܡܬܗ. ܘܒܗܕܐ ܕܕܚܠ ܡܢ ܡܘܬܐ ܒܩܝܡܬܗ ܒܒܪ ܠܘܬܢ ܕܢܬܒܪ: ܕܚܣܝܐ ܦܓܝܥܘܬܐ ܠܟܠܗܘܢ ܒܢܝ ܐܢܫܐ ܟܪܝܗܘܬܗ ܕܦܓܪܐ ܕܠܒܫ ܐܟܘܬܢ ........ ܠܡܘܬܐ ܡܢܗ ܒܡܘܬܗ ܕܢܬܠܒܒ ܒܡܘܬܗ: ܘܡܢ ܒܚܝܠܐ ܪܒܐ ܕܠܐ ܟܪܝܗܘܬܐ ܟܕ ܙܟܐ ܠܡܘܬܐ ܘܩܛܠ ܡܢ ܐܬܪܗ ........ ܕܢܣܝܒ ܡܢ ܡܘܬܐ ܠܐ ܟܪܝܐ ܠܗ ܟܠܗܐ ܡܛܠ ܕܐܬܬܠܝ ܐܟܘܬܢ: ܘܠܐ ܦܠܚܐ ܠܗ ܒܟܘܪܗܢܝܢ: ܕܐܦ ܗܘ ܐܬܟܪܗ ܐܟܘܬܢ.......

192 *Aphr* 23.52: ܫܕܝܢ ܒܗ ܠܡܐ ܪܫܝܡܐ ܕܕܪܫ ܠܗ ܐܘܪܚܐ ܠܐܬܪ ܝܒܝܢ. ܡܕܝܢ ܠܗ ܐܣܝܐ ܕܟܐܒܝܢ ܕܫܒܩܬ ܒ ܪܘܚܗ ܣܡܐ ܠܦܓܪܝܢ.

which He heals everyone who is stricken'.[193] The object of healing is those who are stricken. Referring to Jr 33:10, God called His people through the prophet to 'heal their backsliding' ( ܘܐܣܐ ܬܘܒܬܗܘܢ).[194] Likewise the Lord as the Physician invites the sick who are in need of physicians. Referring to Lk 5:32, the author says: 'Jesus came for He wanted sinners to be righteous, because the healthy people were not in need of a physician for they did not have any sickness'.[195] Sinners are in need of the Physician: 'Our Lord did not come to call the upright, but sinners for repentance (Lk 5:32).[196] God never dishonours penitents[197] or holds back His people from repenting.[198] Therefore, the Lord offers His healing continuously to mankind, especially through His disciples whom the author calls 'physicians' (ܐܣܘ̈ܬܐ). The term 'His disciples' (ܬܠܡܝ̈ܕܘܗܝ) is not only used for the Twelve Apostles, but also for some of Aphrahat's contemporaries; probably the priests and bishops or the ܐܦܝܣܩܘܦ̈ܐ, ܡܕܒܪ̈ܢܐ and ܒܬܘ̈ܠܐ ܘܒܬܘ̈ܠܬܐ. Those physicians are also called shepherds (ܪ̈ܥܘܬܐ).[199] The term 'physicians' (ܐܣܘ̈ܬܐ) which appears four times is mainly used with reference to the Lord as 'our wise' or 'victorious' physician.[200] Aphrahat encourages the physicians to act as wise physicians or as our wise Physician. He offers them repentance as 'medicine

---

193 *Aphr* 7.3: ܘܐܝܢܐ ܕܡܚܘܬ ܠܐ ܡܫܟܚ ܕܢܬܐܣܐ ܡܛܠ ܕܠܐ ܝܕܥ ܕܢܘܕܐ ܡܚܘܬܗ ܠܐܣܝܐ ܕܢܣܒ ܬܐܪ̈ܝܩ ܕܚܟܝܡܘܢ ܡܐܣܐ ܠܟܠܗܘܢ ܕܡܬܟܪܝܢ.

194 *Aphr* 7.9.

195 *Aphr* 23.8: ܡܛܠ ܕܐܝܟܢܐ ܕܢܙܕܕܩܘܢ ܚܛܝ̈ܐ ܐܬܐ ܡܫܝܚܐ: ܡܛܠ ܕܠܝܬ ܗܘܐ ܠܗܘܢ ܡܕܡ ܣܘܢܩܢܐ ܠܚܠܝܡ̈ܐ ܥܠ ܐܣܝܐ: ܡܛܠ ܕܠܝܬ ܗܘܐ ܠܗܘܢ ܟܪܝܗܘܬܐ.

196 *Aphr* 7.23: ܠܐ ܐܬܐ ܡܪܢ ܕܢܩܪܐ ܠܙܕܝ̈ܩܐ ܐܠܐ ܠܚܛܝ̈ܐ ܠܬܝܒܘܬܐ. ܟܠ ܡܢ ܕܡܬܬܘܐ ܡܢ ܢܦܘܠ ܡܢ ܚܛܗ: ܘܡܢ ܕܡܬܬܟܠ ܢܬܠܐ ܫܠܡܘܗܝ܀

197 *Aphr* 7.2.

198 *Aphr* 7.23.

199 *Aphr* 7.6.

200 *Aphr* 7.2, 4, 8.

through which they shall heal the wounds of the sick'.[201] As wise physicians, when they come across a sick person, they should devise how to restore their health and heal their wounds.[202]

The physicians are not to hold back healing from those who need it. On the contrary, they should grant penitence as medicine to the stricken and encourage them not to be ashamed to show their ulcers.[203] The physicians' function is also to accept and respect the wounded without disgracing them or laughing at them. The example of the soldiers wounded in war clarifies what Aphrahat means. The king would not be content, if the situation of the wounded was revealed to his enemies. Instead, the physicians should keep the situation secret and do their best to restore the sick and wounded to health. The physicians of the Lord are blameless, if they do their duty, advising and healing those who want to be healed. If they offer repentance to sinners who do not accept it, they are free from judgement.[204] So if they do not heal the wounded, it is not their fault, but the fault of those who were not willing to repent.[205] These are deeds of a wise physician who is able to understand the sickness of his patients and give them medicine: offering repentance, advice and healing and restoring the wounded and sinners. The wise physician is capable of providing 'medicines' (ܣܡܡ̈ܢܐ) for all kinds of suffering. This can happen only if he meets the stricken people and finds their wounds. Aphrahat refers to this twice in paragraph 2 quoted above.[206] Usually in war the wounded reveal their ulcers to the wise physician. Taking this as an example, Aphrahat advises sinners to repent, and to entrust themselves to the wise physician so that they can be healed.

The wise physician can heal the wounds once easily, but the second time is more complicated.[207] Aphrahat also speaks of the

---

201 *Aphr* 7.2: ܣܒܘ ܠܗܘܢ ܣܡܐ ܗܢܐ ܕܒܗ ܬܐܣܘܢ ܟܘ̈ܝܬܐ ܕܟܪ̈ܝܗܬܐ.

202 *Aphr* 7.2: ܟܕ ܐܣܘܐ ܚܟܝܡܐ ܡܫܟܚܝܢ ܠܗܘܢ ܡܬܦܪܣܘ ܠܗ̇ ܠܐܣܝܘܬܗܘܢ ܕܚܠܝܡ ܠܡ̈ܟܐܒܢܐ.

203 *Aphr* 7.4.

204 *Aphr* 7.5.

205 *Aphr* 7.5.

206 *Aphr* 7.2.

207 *Aphr* 7.6.

'wise physician' in Demonstration 16. Firstly when he speaks metaphorically about the ruin of different places, he asks the question: 'and in these days who is the wise physician who will stand in the ruins and rebuild the walls?'[208] The Evil One who tempts mankind causes sinners to fall. He influences them and puts his claws like a 'lion on his flock'. Man's thoughts bring evil fruit in his heart and irritate his mind, but a wise physician is able to uproot the Evil One's claws from mankind through medicine.[209]

Finally, the term 'physician' is used twice more in Demonstration 7 and once in twenty-three. The first time it appears along with the verb 'to restore' (ܡܫܠܡ), the second time with the verbs 'to visit' (ܠܡܣܥܪ) the sick and 'to have need'.[210] The king honoured not the physician, but the wounded who have been healed. Because the physician is only for the needy and sick, those who are healed do not need to visit the physician.[211] They should be aware of their health and try to keep it so that they will not need a physician.[212]

---

[208] *Aphr* 14.16 (Ez 13:4-5): ܘܒܝܘܡܬܐ ܗܠܝܢ ܡܢܘ ܐܣܝܐ ܚܟܝܡܐ ܕܢܩܘܡ ܒܬܘܪܥܬܐ ܘܢܣܘܓ ܣܝܓܐ. ܕܠܐ ܬܬܥܠܡ ܐܦ ܒܠܝܡ ܡܠܬܐ ܕܢܒܝܐ ܗ̇ ܡܚܣܕ ܠܢ̈ܒܝܐ ܕ̈ܟܠܐ ܕܒܒܝܬܗ ܘܐܡܪ ܠܗܘܢ: ܕܐܝܟ ܬܥܠܐ ܒܚܘܪ̈ܒܬܐ ܗܘܘ ܢܒܝ̈ܝܟ ܐܝܣܪܝܠ. ܕܠܐ ܩܡܬܘܢ ܒܬܘܪ̈ܥܬܐ ܘܠܐ ܣܓܬܘܢ ܣܝܓܐ ܥܠ ܒ̈ܢܝ ܐܝܣܪܝܠ. ܦܬܓܡܘܗܝ ܠܐܣܝܐ ܚܟܝܡܐ ܕܢܣܒ ܡܣ̈ܡܢܐ ܘܢܬܠ ܒܡ̈ܚܘܬܐ. ܕܗܘܐ ܠܚܘܝܐ ܢܗܘܐ ܠܒܢܝܐ ܡܢ ܚܪܒܐ ܕܫܒܝܩܬܐ.

[209] *Aphr* 14.43: ܘܐܣܝܐ ܚܟܝܡܐ ܒܡܣ̈ܡܢܐ ܡܦ̈ܩܢܐ ܥܩܪ ܛܦܪ̈ܘܗܝ ܡܢ ܠܒܗ. ....... ܘܫܪ̈ܝܬܗ ܡܕܪܫܐ ܡܢ ܡܕܪܬܗ ܕܢܦܫܐ. ܘܟܠ ܡܢ ܕܐܬܐ ܐܢܫ ܒܠܒܗ ܡܣܒܐ ܠܐܘܣܝܬܗ ܠܝܬ ܐܠܐ ܚܟܝܡܐ.

[210] *Aphr* 7.2.

[211] *Aphr* 7.17: ܐܬܚܠܝ ܒܗ ܒܐܝܠܝܢ ܥܦܝܪ ܕܠܐ ܬܬܡܚܣܢܐ ܒܡܠܟܐ ܠܐ ܬܗܘܐ ܚܣܝܡܐ ܠܡܒܥܐ ܗܝܟܐ ܘܬܐܠܐ ܠܡܣܥܪ ܠܗ ܐܣܝܐ: ܘܒܪ ܠܒ ܬܬܐܣܐ ܗܠܝܢ ܫܘܝ̈ܬܐ ܗܘܘ ܡ̈ܬܒܝܢ. ܠܐ ܬܬܒܥܠ ܠܟ ܕܗܘܐ ܐܝܬ ܐܣܘܬܐ ܘܬܬܠ ܢܦܫܟ ܠܡܟܐ ܥܦܠܐ: ܐܠܐ ܗܘܝ ܢܛܪܐ ܡܢ ܬܒܥܘܬܐ..

[212] *Aphr* 23.18.

### *2.3.2.8 Conclusion*

Aphrahat shows clearly that he is not only familiar with both Old and New Testament, but is also aware of the biblical aspects of healing and sickness. He draws attention to a number of biblical passages which provide healing imagery and incorporates them in his Demonstrations in order to support his arguments.

In a Christian spirit, Aphrahat is basically concerned about the spiritual life of the faithful and their salvation. Based on holy Scripture, Aphrahat tries to provide a plausible explanation of a right way of life for Christians, and warns them to be aware of the invisible spiritual war against the enemy of humanity, Satan and the Evil One; i.e. sin. The metaphor of war, including wounding and healing, between nations and countries, serves as an ideal image for Aphrahat to place human life after the Fall. All pains, suffering, sicknesses and death experienced in human life are related to the curse of man's Fall from Paradise. Although the curse has never been performed completely, and sin has been killed on the Cross through Jesus' crucifixion, sin's sting is still present in human life and pierces man. Apart from Jesus Christ Who was not wounded and won the battle against Satan, death, and sin, everyone can be hurt to a certain extent in the fight against man's enemy.

Mankind gets wounded in the spiritual war, but God has provided repentance as medicine through His chosen people. In order to be healed, both the chosen people in authority, i.e. spiritual leaders, priests and bishops, and the wounded soldiers, are advised to make use of this heavenly medicine, that is freely given in the Bible and in the Church's sacraments. The spiritual leaders of the Christian community - in particular Aphrahat might be addressing those of the ܒܢ̈ܝ ܘܒ̈ܢܬ ܩܝܡܐ - are explicitly compared to ordinary medical physicians whose function is to heal the wounded wisely. Likewise they are compared to shepherds who care about the sheep, as this metaphor is used by Ez 34. In turn the wounded have to reveal their wounds to the wise physicians. Spiritually they will be healed if they confess their sin, repent with contrition (ܬܘܬ ܢܦܫܐ) and pray and have faith.

Aphrahat uses the term 'gangrene' to make an emphatic warning about the danger of being wounded twice in the same place. Even if this wound is healed, old scars will stay. This would be caused by repeated sinful acts and immoral life. Those who are baptised, or those who gave their vows to live a consecrated life (in the community of ܒܢ̈ܝ ܘܒܢ̈ܬ ܩܝܡܐ) should not sin repeatedly. Even though repentance can heal, repeated sinful acts may not be forgiven.

Aphrahat's concern is for the individual and whole community; both are related and cannot be separated. The faithful community is compared to the whole body, or, using the metaphor of a war, it is compared to a camp or army. If any of the body's limbs or army's soldiers is hurt and defeated, then the whole body or army is affected.

Thus, with these metaphors, Aphrahat echoes Christ's message to his contemporaries to take spiritual war seriously. He encourages spiritual leaders and individuals to make use of the spiritual medicine provided in Scripture and the Church's sacraments. In an unusual interpretation given to the parable of the Rich Man and Lazarus, receiving Holy Communion is compared to a loyal and faithful dog who licks his owner's ulcers.

# 3 EPHREM'S HEALING TERMINOLOGY

This chapter discusses the most significant terms related to sickness and healing. Basically it shows which terms Ephrem most frequently uses, what he employs with them and how he uses them. At the beginning of each term, attention is drawn to the appearance of these significant terms in the Bible, and it is emphasized where Ephrem refers to Scripture and how he develops the meaning and use of healing and sickness terminology.

## 3.1 Terms Related to Sickness

The following terms are studied here: all terms based on ܐܬܟܪܗ, 'to become sick', ܟܐܒܐ, 'pain', ܡܚܐ, 'to strike, wound', ܒܠܥ, 'to swallow, be struck' and ܬܒܪ, 'to break, fracture'. Some further terms are also dealt with: ܚܒܪ̈ܬܐ, 'bruises, sores', ܬܡܣܘܬܐ, 'pus', ܚܒ̈ܠܐ, 'hurts', ܫܘܚܢܐ, 'ulcer', ܫܘܡ̈ܬܐ, 'scars' and ܚܠܕܝܬܐ, 'gangrene'.

### 3.1.1 ܐܬܟܪܗ and Related Terms

In the Peshitta Old Testament, the verb ܐܬܟܪܗ appears frequently with the verb 'to die' (ܡܝܬ) and emphasises physical sickness in old age and consequent death. The phrase ܐܬܟܪܗ ܘܡܝܬ occurs first in relation to Abraham in Genesis 25:8 and 25:17; later it is used for Isaac (Gen 35:29), Jacob (Gen 49:33) and Elisha (2 Kgs 13:14).[1] While ܐܬܟܪܗ, along with ܡܝܬ, in these

1 Also with reference to Hezekiah, even though he did not die, it is said: 'Hezekiah became sick and was at the point of death'; 2 Kgs 20:1; 2 ☞

passages describes the natural end of man at a ripe old age (Gen 25:8: ܒܣܝܒܘܬܐ ܛܒܬܐ), in the case of Jehoram, King of Judah (2 Chr 21:15-19), it is the Lord who caused sickness and death because of Jehoram's evil deeds. In other passages[2] ܐܬܟܪܗ is used simply in reference to ordinary illnesses. It may apply to particular parts of the body (thus Asa's feet, 1 Kgs 15:23); the passive participle is also used in reference to sheep (Zach 11:16), or even figs (Ez 24:12). ܟܪܝܗܐ can also apply to an emotional, rather then a physical state, as Cant 2:5 and 5:8: ܟܪܝܗܬ ܪܚܡܬܐ.[3]

The noun ܟܘܪܗܢܐ always refers to physical sickness, and may be associated with ܡܚܘܬܐ (Dt 28:61; 1 Kgs 8:37) or ܟܐܒܐ (Hs 5:13); in Prov 16:18 it is the consequence of ܪܡܘܬ ܪܘܚܐ, 'haughtiness of spirit'. Dtn 29:22 uses ܟܘܪܗܢܐ in the context of the Lord's wrath and zeal that burn against His people in fierce anger. It is the Lord who causes ܟܘܪܗܢܐ since His people abandoned His covenant. Here, ܟܘܪܗܢܐ, along with ܡܚܘܬܐ, does not refer to the people, but to the land: 'they will see the wounds of that land and the sickness that the Lord brought on it'.[4]

Verbs of healing, restoration etc. used in association with ܟܘܪܗܢܐ and ܟܪܝܗܐ are ܐܣܐ,[5] ܐܬܚܠܡ[6] or ܡܬܚܠܡ[7] and ܐܚܝܠ ܚܝܠܐ[8] is used in Ez 34:16, whereas ܚܝܠܬܘܢ in Ez 34:4.[9]

---

Chr 32:24; Is 38:1. The terms ܟܪܗ and ܟܘܪܗܢܐ are consistently translated as 'to be sick' and 'sickness', although 'to be weak' or 'weakness' might be mor appropriate in some contexts for the English, particularly in reference to the New Testament where the Greek has ασθενμσ and ασθενεια.

[2] Gen 48:1; 2 Sam 13:5-6; 1 Kgs 14:1; 15:23; 17:17; 2 Kgs 1:2; 8:7; 20:12; 22:19; 2 Chr 11:18(11); 16:12; 32:25-26; Sa 9:5; 12:8; Is 14:10; 19:8(10); 33:24; Mi 1:12: Ez 19:5.

[3] In Hs 11:6, the verb ܐܬܟܪܗ is also used for 'blunting' the sword.

[4] Dtn 29:22: ܘܢܚܙܘܢ ܡܚܘܬܗ ܕܐܪܥܐ ܗܝ: ܘܟܘܪܗܢܐ ܕܐܝܬܝ ܡܪܝܐ ܥܠܝܗ.

[5] Sa 11:16: ܘܕܬܪܝܦܝܢ ܠܐ ܐܣܐܢܐ; 1 Chr 7:25: ܒܠܒ ܕܐܣܝܘܬܐ ܗܘܬ: ܘܒܐܣܝܘܬܐ ܟܪܝܗܝܢ; 2 Kgs 20:5: ܗܐ ܐܣܐ ܐܢܐ ܠܟ.

Throughout the Old Testament, the term ܟܪܝܗܘܬܐ, 'sick state', occurs only once, and it is paired with ܗܒܠܐ, 'vanity' (Ec 6:2). ܟܪܝܗܘܬܐ refers to the moral sick state concerning man's relationship to God. The author of Ecclesiastes considers the fact that a stranger enjoys wealth, possessions and honour, rather than the man who received them from God, as ܗܒܠܐ and ܟܪܝܗܘܬܐ.[10]

In the New Testament, the term ܐܬܟܪܗ or ܟܪܝܗ refers to various individual people such as Lazarus (Jn 11:1-6), the official's son (Jn 4:46), the centurion's son (Lk 7:10) and Trophimus (2 Tim 4:20); and it is used in the sense of a physical sickness. In Mt 26:41, where Jesus prays in Gethsemane, He says that the body is sick (ܦܓܪܐ ܕܝܢ ܟܪܝܗ). While in Mt 26:41 and in Mk 14:38 ܟܪܝܗ is attributed to the term ܦܓܪܐ, in 2 Cor 10:10 it refers to ܠܘܫܒܐ. Acts 28:8 speaks of a particular physical sickness when it says 'he was sick from fever and dysentery'.[11] As we saw above in the Pentateuch, also in Phil 2:25 ܐܬܟܪܗ leads to death: 'he was sick until death'.[12]

---

6 Is 39:1: ܡܛܠ ܕܫܡܥ ܕܐܬܟܪܗ: ܘܚܠܡ: ܘܐܬܚܠܡ.

7 2 Kgs 1:2; 8:8; (20:7).

8 2 Kgs 8:9; 20:1; 20:12; 38:9; Is 38:9: ܟܕ ܐܬܟܪܗ: ܘܚܝܐ ܡܢ ܟܘܪܗܢܗ.

9 Cf. 1 Sam 2:4: ܘܟܪܝܗܐ ܐܬܚܝܠܘ ܒܚܝܠܐ; Lm 1:14: ܘܐܬܟܪܗ ܚܝܠܝ.

10 Ec 6:2: ܓܒܪܐ ܕܢܬܠ ܠܗ ܐܠܗܐ ܥܘܬܪܐ ܘܢܟ̈ܣܐ ܘܐܝܩܪܐ. ܘܠܐ ܚܣܝܪ ܠܢܦܫܗ ܡܕܡ ܡܢ ܟܠ ܡܐ ܕܪܓܐ. ܘܠܐ ܐܫܠܛܗ ܐܠܗܐ ܠܡܐܟܠ ܡܢܗ. ܐܠܐ ܓܒܪ ܢܘܟܪܝ ܢܐܟܠܝܘܗܝ ܡܢ ܒܬܪܗ. ܗܢܐ ܗܒܠܐ ܘܟܪܝܗܘܬܐ ܗܝ. In the OT we come across: 'evil's sickness' ( ܟܘܪܗܢܐ ܕܒܝܫܬܐ, Ec 5:13); 'evil sickness' (ܟܘܪܗܢܐ ܒܝܫܐ, Ec 5:16; 2 Chr 21:19); 'much sickness' (ܟܘܪܗܢܐ ܣܓܝܐܐ, 2 Chr 21:15; 21:18); 'many sicknesses' (ܟܘܪ̈ܗܢܐ ܣܓܝ̈ܐܐ, 2 Chr 24:25).

11 Act 28:8: ܒܐܫܬܐ ܘܒܟܐܒ ܡܥ̈ܝܐ ܟܪܝܗ ܗܘܐ.

12 Phil 2:25: ܐܬܟܪܗ ܥܕܡܐ ܠܡܘܬܐ. For ܡܘܬܐ see further Act 9:37.

In Lk 4:40, the phrase 'the sick who were sick with various kinds of sickness'[13] could refer to both physical as well as spiritual sickness. In the sense of non-physical sickness ܐܬܟܪܗ or ܟܪܝܗ occurs clearly in the Epistles. Rom 4:19 speaks of Abraham who 'did not become sick in his faith' (ܘܠܐ ܐܬܟܪܗ ܒܗܝܡܢܘܬܗ) for he believed 'in hope against all hope' ( ܘܕܠܐ ܣܒܪܐ ܠܣܒܪܐ ܗܝܡܢ);[14] and he did not doubt the promise of God. Therefore, it says, 'he was strengthened in his faith' (Rom 4:20, ܐܬܚܝܠ ܒܗܝܡܢܘܬܗ), which contrasts with the phrase ܐܬܟܪܗ ܒܗܝܡܢܘܬܗ. 1 Tim 6:4 uses ܟܪܝܗ in the context of false doctrines: 'he is sick with controversies and quarrels' ( ܟܪܝܗ ܒܕܪ̈ܫܐ ܘܒܒܥܬܐ ܕܡ̈ܠܐ). Here, too, ܟܪܝܗ contrasts with ܚܠܝܡܬܐ of 1 Tim 6:3. Any other teaching which is not based on the 'sound/ healthy words of our Lord Jesus Christ' ( ܡ̈ܠܐ ܚܠܝܡܬܐ ܕܡܪܢ ܝܫܘܥ ܡܫܝܚܐ) corrupts the mind of the person who is then 'sick with controversies and quarrels'. In the context of food sacrificed to idols, Paul uses ܟܪܝܗܐ together with ܬܐܪܬܗܘܢ: 'for their defiled conscience is sick' (1 Cor 8:7, ܘܡܛܠ ܕܟܪܝܗܐ ܬܐܪܬܗܘܢ ܡܬܛܘܫܐ). Furthermore, 1 Cor 1:27 speaks of 'the sick of the world' (ܟܪ̈ܝܗܘܗܝ ܕܥܠܡܐ) and Hebr 5:11 of 'sick in obedience' (ܟܪ̈ܝܗܐ ܒܡܫܡܥܬܐ).[15]

---

[13] Lk 4:40: ܟܪ̈ܝܗܐ ܕܟܪ̈ܝܗܝܢ ܒܟܘܪ̈ܗܢܐ ܡܫܚܠ̈ܦܐ. For ܟܘܪ̈ܗܢܐ ܡܫܚܠ̈ܦܐ see further Mt 4:24; Mk 1:34.

[14] For ܗܝܡܢܘܬܐ see Rom 14:1; Jas 5:15.

[15] Mt 25:36; Lk 4:40; 10:9; Act 20:35; Rom 14:2; 2 Cor 11:29; 12:10; 13:9; Phil 2:26. While with ܟܪܝܗܐ terms such as 'demons' (ܕܝ̈ܘܐ, Mt 10:8; Lk 3:15), 'lepers' (ܓܪ̈ܒܐ, Mt 10:8), spirit (ܪܘܚܐ, Lk 13:11) or 'spirits' (ܪ̈ܘܚܐ, Act 5:16), 'blind, lame and paralysed' ( ܣܡܝܐ ܚܓܝܪܐ ܘܝܒܝܫܐ, Jn 5:3) and 'weak' (ܡܪ̈ܥܐ, 1 Cor 11:30) are linked; with ܟܘܪܗܢܐ terms such as 'pain' (ܟܐܒܐ, Mt 4:23; 8:17; 9:35; 10:1), 'spirits' (ܪ̈ܘܚܐ, Lk 6:18), 'death' (ܡܘܬܐ, Jn 11:4), 'wounds and evil spirits' ( ܡܚ̈ܘܬܐ ܘܪ̈ܘܚܬܐ ܒܝ̈ܫܬܐ, Lk 7:2; 8:2), 'insult and hardship' (ܨܥܪܐ ܘܐܘܠܨܢܐ, 2 Cor 12:10), 'devils' (ܫܐܕ̈ܐ, Lk 9:1; Act 19:2) and 'demons' (ܕܝ̈ܘܐ, Mk 1:34) are used.

The term ܟܘܪܗܢܐ can mean both spiritual and physical sickness. In the Gospel, it occurs in a general sense, such as 'He healed many from sickness and from wounds and evil spirits',[16] or 'He gave them strength and power against all devils and to heal all [kind of] sickness';[17] it also appears in the context of individual people, such as Lazarus (Jn 11:4), the man who was an invalid for 38 years (Jn 5:5) or the woman who was crippled for 18 years (Lk 13:11-12).[18] In this sense ܟܘܪܗܢܐ is associated with ܡܚܘ̈ܬܐ (Lk 7:21), ܪܘ̈ܚܐ ܒܝ̈ܫܬܐ (Lk 7:21; 8:2) and ܟܐ̈ܒܐ (Mt 8:17);[19] in 2 Cor 12:10 where Paul speaks of his sicknesses, it occurs also together with ܨܥ̈ܪܐ ܘܐܘܠܨ̈ܢܐ (2 Cor 11:30-12:10).[20]

The healer of ܟܪ̈ܝܗܐ or ܟܘܪ̈ܗܢܐ is usually the Lord;[21] or those who have received power from Him.[22] As agents of healing the ܟܪ̈ܝܗܐ, the laying on of the 'hand' (ܐܝܕܐ, Mk 6:5; 16:18; Lk 4:40; Act 19:12) and 'oil' (ܡܫܚܐ, Mk 6:13) are significant. The verb 'to strengthen' (ܚܝܠ) or the noun 'strength' (ܚܝܠܐ) may also be used in connection with ܟܘܪܗܢܐ,[23] ܟܪܝܗܐ[24] or ܟܪܝܗܘܬܐ[25]

---

[16] Lk 7:21: ܣܓܝ̈ܐܐ ܐܣܝ ܡܢ ܟܘܪ̈ܗܢܐ ܘܡܢ ܡܚܘ̈ܬܐ ܘܡܢ ܪܘ̈ܚܐ ܒܝ̈ܫܬܐ.

[17] Lk 9:1: ܘܝܗܒ ܠܗܘܢ ܚܝܠܐ ܘܫܘܠܛܢܐ: ܥܠ ܟܠܗܘܢ ܕܝ̈ܘܐ ܘܟܘܪ̈ܗܢܐ ܠܡܐܣܝܘ; see also Mt 4:23; 9:35; 10:1.

[18] ܟܘܪ̈ܗܢܐ are frequently attributed generally to people, such as 'women', ܢܫ̈ܐ, (Lk 8:2) or ܟܪ̈ܝܗܐ (Lk 4:40; Act 19:12); cf. Mt 4:24; 8:17; Mk 1:34; Lk 4:40; 5:15; 6:18; 7:21; 8:2; 9:1; Act 19:12; 2 Cor 11:30; 12:5; 12:9-10; 1 Tim 5:23; Hebr 11:34. Also the term ܟܪܝܗܐ refers to people, both to a particular person (Jn 5:7; Act 4:9), as well as, to people in general (cf. Mt 10:8; 25:39-44; Mk 3:15; 6:5; 6:13; 1 Cor 9:22).

[19] Cf. Mt 4:23; 9:35; 10:1.

[20] In Hebr 11:34 (hardly known to Ephrem), referring to some figures in the Old Testament, ܟܘܪ̈ܗܢܐ is used in parallel to ܢܘܪܐ, ܣܝܦܐ and ܚܪܒܐ, that has bad consequences for human life.

[21] For healing the ܟܪ̈ܝܗܐ see Mk 6:5; for ܟܘܪ̈ܗܢܐ Mt 4:23; 8:17; 9:35; 10:1; Lk 4:40; 5:15; 6:18; 7:21; 13:12.

[22] For ܟܪ̈ܝܗܐ see Mt 10:8; Mk 3:15; 6:13; Act 4:9; 1 Cor 9:22; for ܟܘܪ̈ܗܢܐ see Lk 9:1; Act 19:12.

[23] Lk 9:1; Rom 15:1; 2 Cor 12:9; Hebr 11:34.

While ܐܣܝ is often used with the terms ܟܪܝܗܐ[26] and ܟܘܪܗܢܐ,[27] the verbs 'to visit' (ܣܥܪ, Mt 25:36), 'to be restored' (ܐܬܚܠܡ, Lk 7:10; cf. Mk 16:8) and 'to heal' (ܐܣܝ, Lk 10:9) are only employed rarely in direct connection with the verb ܐܬܟܪܗ.

In the Pauline Epistles the term ܟܪܝܗܘܬܐ is used a number of times to denote the fallen human condition. Thus Paul speaks of the ܟܪܝܗܘܬܐ of the flesh (Rom 6:19; 8:26; Gal 4:13), and of 'our sick state' (ܟܪܝܗܘܬܢ, Rom 5:6; 8:26; Heb 4:15). Accordingly, Christ's incarnate state can be described as ܟܪܝܗܘܬܐ, when He was 'clothed in the sick condition' (ܠܒܝܫ ܟܪܝܗܘܬܐ, Heb 5:2). This metaphor for the incarnation is also found in 1 Cor 1:25 where 'God's [adoption of the human] sick condition' ( ܟܪܝܗܘܬܗ ܕܐܠܗܐ) is 'stronger than human beings'.

In Ephrem, ܟܪܝܗܘܬܐ is the general human condition of spiritual sickness after the fall (as in Paul); in Parad 11.9 it is specifically said to have been brought about by Eve; its opposite is ܚܠܝܡܘܬܐ.[28] By contrast, ܟܘܪܗܢܐ is a particular state of sickness, whether physical or spiritual; brought about by such things as 'paganism' (ܚܢܦܘܬܐ),[29] 'error' (ܛܘܥܝܝ)[30] etc. 'Error' (ܛܘܥܝܝ) is able to 'grow strong' precisely because of the general human condition of ܟܪܝܗܘܬܐ.[31] Those affected are, for instance, a person who 'has become sick' (ܐܬܟܪܗ), or 'fallen into sickness' (ܢܦܠ ܒܟܘܪܗܢܐ),[32] and is 'sick' (ܟܪܝܗܐ), or 'lying in sickness' (ܪܡܐ ܒܟܘܪܗܢܐ).[33] The verbs 'to press hard' (ܬܩܦ),[34] 'to fall

24 1 Cor 1:27; 4:10.

25 1Cor 1:25; 1 Cor 15:43; 2 Cor 12:9.

26 Mt 10:8; 14:18; Mk 3:15; 6:13; 6:15; Lk 9:2; Act 4:9; 28:9.

27 Mt 4:23; 9:35; 10:1; Lk 5:15; 6:18; 7:2; 8:2; 9:1.

28 Virg 4.10.

29 Nis 21.18.

30 Nis 34.9.

31 Fid 60.13; 75.18; Nat 3.1; Parad 3.11; 11.9; Virg 4.10; 39.7.

32 Nis 5.22; 21.18.

33 Parad 3.18.

34 Fid 68.22: ܬܩܦ ܟܘܪܗܢܐ.

into' (ܢܦܠ),[35] 'to lie' (ܪܒܥ),[36] 'to go astray' (ܛܥܐ),[37] 'to lengthen' (ܐܓܪ)[38] and 'to subdue' (ܟܒܫ)[39] emphasise the negative aspect of ܟܘܪܗܢܐ and its effect on human nature. In Ephrem's use, the term ܟܘܪܗܢܐ contrasts with 'health' (ܚܘܠܡܢܐ)[40] and 'strength' (ܚܝܠܐ),[41] while it appears along with the terms 'pains' (ܟܐܒ̈ܐ),[42] 'hunger' (ܟܦܢܐ),[43] 'sweetness' (ܚܠܝܘܬܐ),[44] 'freedom' (ܚܐܪܘܬܐ)[45] and 'paganism' (ܚܢܦܘܬܐ).[46] The ܟܘܪ̈ܗܢܐ are compared to the 'reapers' (ܚܨ̈ܘܕܐ)[47] and considered as 'fruit of the earth' (ܦܐܪܗ̇ ܕܐܪܥܐ)[48] and the 'hateful habit of the prodigal' (ܥܝܕܗ ܕܡܢ ܣܢܝܐ ܕܐܣܘܛܐ).[49] A different aspect of ܟܘܪܗܢܐ is found in Eccl 17.2 where the sickness overcomes cupidity.[50]

---

35 Nis 5.22: ܘܢܦܠ ܒܟܘܪܗܢܐ; Nis 21.18: ܒܟܘܪܗܢܐ ܪܒܥ ܢܦܠ ܗܘܐ.

36 Parad 3.11: ܕܐܬܐ ܕܡܢ ܒܟܘܪܗܢܐ ܗܘܐ ܪܒܥ.

37 Parad 8.5: ܐܢ ܛܥܐ ܒܟܘܪܗܢܗ.

38 Parad 11.10: ܗܝ ܟܠܬܐ ܐܬܚܙܬ ܒܫܘܒܚܬܗ ܕܗܘܢ ܟܠܒܐ ܒܪܢܐ ܕܐܓܪ ܒܟܘܪܗܢܐ; cf. Fid 47.11.

39 Virg 39.7: ܕܟܒܫܬܗ ܒܚܠܝܘܬܐ ܒܟܒܫܬܗ ܪܢܗܘܬܐ.

40 Parad 3.10; 11.9; Nis 5.22; 52.6; Vir 4.8-10; 39.7; Fid 86.4; Eccl 2.19; 19.11; 34.7; 39.15; 43.9-11; 43.20.

41 Nis 43.10.

42 CDiat 16.8: ܟܐܒ̈ܐ ܘܟܘܪ̈ܗܢܐ ܐܝܟ; Sog 1.29: ܠܦܐܪܗ̇ ܕܐܪܥܐ ܗܘܐ ܟܘܪܗܢܐ ܘܟܐܒ̈ܐ ܠܟܠܒܐ.

43 Eccl 32.8: ܟܠܗ ܗ̇ܘ ܕܟܒܫ ܟܦܢܐ ܘܟܘܪܗܢܐ.

44 Eccl 2.19; 2.22; Fid 35.4. Fid 42.1 uses the term 'honey' (ܕܒܫܐ).

45 Eccl 2.19: ܚܢܢܐ ܕܚܠܝܘܬܐ ܚܠܝܐ ܠܟܘܢ ܕܚܠܝܡ ܡܪܢܐ ܠܟܘܢ ܕܒܪܢܫܗ ܗܟܡ ܐܦ ܚܐܪܘܬܐ; 8.3.

46 Nis 21.18: ܦܫܛܬ ܒܟܠ ܚܢܦܘܬܐ ܕܗܝ ܗܝ ܟܠܬ ܟܘܪܗܢܗ̇.

47 Nis 36.8: ܗܢܐ ܚܨܕܐ ܕܐܪܡܝܢ ܒܗ ܒܠܝܘܬ ܟܘܪ̈ܗܢܐ ܐܝܟ ܚܨ̈ܘܕܐ.

48 Sog 1.29.

49 Iei 10.7.

50 Iei 10.7: ܐܘܟܝ ܕܓܠܝܗ̇ ܒܚܬܐ ܠܒܢܝܢܘܬܐ ܦܘܩܕܗ̇ ܒܟܘܪܗܢܐ ܦܩܕ ܠܗ.

Based on the Bible, Ephrem speaks of individual sick people too, such as Peter's mother-in-law because of her fever,[51] or Amnon for his deceitful plan.[52] In particular man's mind ( ܪܥܝܢܐ ܟܪܝܗܐ) and body (ܦܓܪܐ ܟܪܝܗܐ)[53] are affected. Some other individual limbs are also mentioned: both Saul's and Zion's ear (ܐܕܢܐ) indicates their spiritual sickness for disobeying the Lord's commandment;[54] the hand (ܐܝܕܐ) possesses healing power, even though it can be sick like Elisha's sick hand.[55] Because of sin and error in the world, Ephrem speaks of the 'sick People' ( ܥܡܐ ܟܪܝܗܐ),[56] or metaphorically of the 'sick flock' or 'sick sheep'.[57] He considers man's free will as sickness for sinners; even more, it is the cause of sickness.[58] The subject can also be the 'universe' (ܬܐܒܝܠ),[59] the world as a body,[60] [human] nature;[61] or, more specifically, the Virgin's womb.[62] The 'water' (ܡܝ̈ܐ) as an element within the natural world can be sick too,[63] likewise the 'winter' (ܣܬܘܐ).[64] As geographical places, along with Nisibis, Harran and Egypt are also described as sick.[65]

---

51 Virg 25.13-14; cf. Mt 8:14-15.

52 Virg 2.1; cf. 2 Sam 13:1ff.

53 For ܪܥܝܢܐ ܟܪܝܗܐ see Fid 2.16; 79.9; for ܦܓܪܐ ܟܪܝܗܐ see Dom 42; Fid 19.12.

54 For Saul' ear see Virg 30.2; Zion's ear Virg 19.2. In Fid 35.2, Ephrem refers the verb ܬܬܟܪܗܘܢ to ܫܡ̈ܘܥܐ in the context of understanding and interpreting the holy Scripture: those who listen to/obey the holy Scripture would not become sick.

55 Nis 43.9; Nis 11.3; cf. 2 Kgs 13:16.

56 Fid 86.4: ܘܕܪܫܐ ܥܒ̈ܕܐ ܥܡܡܐ ܟܪܝܗܐ ܠܟܠܗ ܣܘܠܓܡܐ.

57 For ܥܢ̈ܐ ܟܪܝܗܬܐ see Fid 59.12; ܢܩܝܐ ܟܪܝܗܐ Nis 19.4.

58 Eccl 2.19: ܚܐܪܘܬܐ ܟܪܝܗܐ ܠܚܛ̈ܝܐ; Eccl 8.3.

59 Nis 34.9.

60 Nis 21.18.

61 Nis 34.9; Virg 14.13.

62 Virg 25.8.

63 Parad 11.11; Epiph 11.7.

64 Nis 29.18.

65 For Harran and Egypt see Nis 34.1-8; for Nisibis Nis 4.16.

Verbs of healing associated with ܟܪܝܗܘܬܐ are 'to heal' (ܐܣܝ),[66] 'to visit' (ܣܥܪ),[67] 'to rest against/sustain' (ܣܡܣܡܢ)[68] and 'to give medicine' (ܣܡܣܡ).[69] In Nat 3.1 ܟܪܝܗܘܬܢ appears parallel to 'our need' (ܣܢܝܩܘܬܢ): while through the Lord 'our need' has been fulfilled, so too it is Him Who visited 'our sickness' (ܟܪܝܗܘܬܢ).[70] The Lord, as the Healer of ܟܪܝܗܘܬܢ is also emphasised in Fid 75.18, where 'in many ways He approached ܟܪܝܗܘܬܢ to heal it'.[71] In hymn 11 On Paradise, it is the healthy fragrance of Paradise that ܣܡܣܡ the ܟܪܝܗܘܬܐ as a physician,[72] whereas in Virg 4.10, it is the 'oil' (ܡܫܚܐ) that ܣܡܣܡܢ the ܟܪܝܗܘܬܐ, for it symbolises the Messiah (ܡܫܝܚܐ).

Even though the oil and fragrance of Paradise are used as agents because of their supernatural aspect, the Lord is the real Healer; no one else could heal humanity from its fallen state. While some prophets, such as Elisha,[73] Abraham and Joseph[74] are mentioned as agents of healing in some way ܟܘܪ̈ܗܢܐ or ܟܪ̈ܝܗܐ, the main agent is still the Lord,[75] the 'Physician' (ܐܣܝܐ),[76] the

---

66 Fid 75.18.

67 Nat 3.1.

68 Virg 4.10.

69 Parad 11.9.

70 Nat 3.1.

71 Fid 75.18: ܒܟܠ ܙܢ̈ܝܢ ܗܘ ܐܬܩܪܒ ܠܗ̇ ܗܘ ܟܡܣܝܒܪܢܐ ܠܟܪܝܗܘܬܢ ܐܝܟ ܕܢܐܣܝܗ̇.

72 Parad 11.9.

73 Nis 43.9.

74 Nis 34.1; 34.8-9.

75 Dom 42; Virg 25.13; 37.3; Fid 35.4; 36.1; 75.18; Nis 4.16; 34.5; 39.3; CDiat 16.8; Nat 3.1.

76 Nis 34.1; 39.4; 40.2; Virg 25.13; Parad 11.9.

'Healer of all' (ܡܐܣܝܐ ܟܠ),[77] 'Medicine' (ܣܡܐ),[78] or healing through His 'sweat' (ܕܘܥܬܐ)[79] and 'hand' (ܐܝܕܐ).[80]

Those before Jesus 'healed a little' (ܐܣܝܘ ܩܠܝܠ), whereas 'the Son descended to visit the servants because their sickness continued and lasted long.[81] The verb 'to heal' (ܐܣܐ),[82] 'to restore' (ܐܚܠܡ),[83] 'to visit' (ܣܥܪ)[84] and 'to bind up' (ܚܒܫ)[85] occur in direct connection with the term ܟܘܪܗܢܐ in the active, with the Lord as agent; only once is the passive ܐܬܐܣܝܐ used, in Nis 34.9. In direct connection with the term ܟܪܝܗܐ the verb 'to restore' (ܐܚܠܡ) is more often used, both in the active[86] and passive.[87] While in the former, the one who restores the ܟܪ̈ܝܗܐ is the Lord, in the latter, the medium of restoring can be 'the shadow of Jesus'/oil's name' (ܛܠܠ ܫܡܗ),[88] 'the salt' (ܡܠܚܐ),[89] 'the sweat' (ܕܘܥܬܐ),[90] but also the 'Healer of all' (ܡܐܣܝܐ ܟܠ).[91] The verb 'to heal' is used for the prophet Elisha who 'healed the sick water',[92] or for Abraham who 'visited' (ܣܥܪܗ), 'bound up and

---

77 Nis 4.16: ܐܝܬ ܗܘ ܡܐܣܝܐ ܟܠ ܡܣܥܪ ܒܡܪ̈ܥܝܢ; 34.5: ܚܝܘ ܠܚܣܝܪ̈ܝܢ ܟܪ̈ܝܗܬܐ ܕܐܬܐ ܐܬܚܠܡܬ ܒܡܐܣܝܐ ܟܠ.

78 Nis 19.11; Fid 19.11.

79 Crucif 8.1: ܠܘܩܒܠ ܠܟܪܝܐ ܕܒܕܘܥܬܗ ܒܐܣܘܬܗ ܘܕܒܪ̈ܝܗܐ ܐܬܚܠܡܬ ܕܒܗ ܕܥܬ ܒܗ ܚܝܐ ܡܬܥܒܕ ܠܟܪ̈ܝܗܐ ܕܐܬܚܠܡ ܒܕܘܥܬܐ ܕܠܐ ܕܠܗ.

80 Nis 11.3; 21.18; 43.9-10.

81 Fid 36.1.

82 CDiat 16.8.

83 CDiat 16.12; Fid 35.4.

84 Nis 4.16; Fid 36.1.

85 Virg 37.3.

86 Dom 42; Nis 39.3.

87 Virg 4.8; Parad 11.11; Crucif 8.1; Nis 34.5.

88 Virg 4.8

89 Parad 11.11.

90 Crucif 8.1.

91 Nis 34.5.

92 Epiph 11.7: ܡܝ̈ܐ ܟܪ̈ܝܗܐ ܐܣܐ ܠܢܝܚܐ; cf. 2 Kgs 2:19-22.

healed' (ܚܠܡ ܘܐܣܝ) the whole body of the sick Egypt,[93] and for Joseph and Moses who 'healed' (ܐܣܝ) Egypt that was likewise sick.[94] However, the Lord is the 'heavenly Physician' ( ܐܣܝܐ ܪܘܡܢܝܐ) Who 'hunts' (ܨܐܕ) the sick from death,[95] and He 'visited' Peter's mother-in-law;[96] medicine 'flows' from Him,[97] and He is able to 'give medicine' (ܣܡܡ), in a metaphorical sense, to the fruits that are sick.[98]

### 3.1.2 The Term ܟܐܒܐ

Already in the Syriac Peshitta the term ܟܐܒܐ is used in the Genesis narrative about the fall of man: as Adam and Eve were cursed, the term ܟܐܒܐ is used once for Adam's punishment, and twice for Eve's punishment. It is said to Eve: 'I will greatly increase your pains (ܟܐ̈ܒܐ) in your pregnancies, and with pains you will give birth to children';[99] and to Adam: 'all the days of your life you will eat through pains'.[100] Thus, while for Eve ܟܐܒܐ refers to a particular matter, namely pregnancies and birthgiving, for Adam ܟܐܒܐ is attributed to all physical toil and daily labour on earth.

Furthermore, in Gen 34:25, in the episode of Dinah and the Shechemites, the term ܟܐܒܐ appears in the context of circumcision: three days after the Shechemites have been circumcised, their 'pains were [still] sore...'[101] While in the whole

93 Nis 34.1; 34.7.

94 Nis 34.7-8; only in the the response of Eccl 38, the verb 'to heal' (ܐܣܝ) is attributed to the Lord (ܥܠ ܒܪ̈ܝܬܐ ܕܐܣܝ ܡܪܢ) in one manuscript.

95 Virg 5.11.

96 Virg 25.13.

97 Fid 19.11: ܣܡ̈ܡܢܐ ܦܐ̈ܝܐ ܪܕܘ ܡܢܗ; cf. Nis 19.11.

98 Nis 5.21.

99 Gen 3:16: ܡܣܓܘ ܐܣܓܐ ܟܐ̈ܒܝܟܝ ܘܒܛ̈ܢܝܟܝ: ܘܒܟܐ̈ܒܐ ܬܐܠܕܝܢ ܒܢ̈ܝܐ.

100 Gen 3.17: ܒܟܐ̈ܒܐ ܬܐܟܠܝܗ̇ ܟܠ ܝܘ̈ܡܝ ܚ̈ܝܝܟ.

101 Gen 34:25: ܘܗܘܐ ܒܝܘܡܐ ܬܠܝܬܝܐ ܟܕ ܚܫܝܢ ܟܐ̈ܒܝܗܘܢ.

Pentateuch, the term ܟܐܒܐ appears only another three times,[102] in Job,[103] Proverbs,[104] Isaiah[105] and Jeremiah[106] it is often used; and occasionally it appears in some other biblical books too, such as Hosea and Ezechiel.[107] In Proverbs, ܟܐܒܐ is directly connected with the 'soul' (ܢܦܫܐ),[108] 'heart' (ܠܒܐ)[109] and 'spirit' (ܪܘܚܐ).[110] The prophets use ܟܐܒܐ with the words 'broken state' (ܬܒܪܐ)[111] and 'wound' (ܡܚܘܬܐ).[112] The verb 'to heal' (ܐܣܝ) is only used twice along with ܟܐ̈ܒܐ that need to be healed: in Pr 14:23 it is the Lord Who 'heals all pains';[113] in Is 30:26 the verb ܐܣܝ has as its object the 'pain of his blow/smiting'.[114]

By contrast, the Syriac New Testament[115] uses healing verbs such as 'to heal (ܐܣܝ) and 'to restore' (ܐܚܠܡ) more often with ܟܐܒܐ or ܟܠ ܟܐܒܐ whose healer is usually the Lord.[116] The verb 'to heal' (ܐܣܝ) frequently has as object 'every pain and

---

102 Ex 3:7; Dtn 7:15; Dtn 28:59.

103 Jb 14:13; 14:22; 16:6; 17:7; 18:2; 18:7; 19:2; 31:18; 32:19; 33:19.

104 Pr 10:10; 10:22; 14:23; 15:13; 16:26; 17:22; 18:14; 19:29; 25:20; 29:13; 31:7.

105 Is 1:5; 17:11; 30:26; 40:29; 53:3-4; 57:15; 59:9; 61:3; 63:10; 65:14.

106 Jer 4:15; 4:19; 6:8; 10:19; 14:17; 15:18; 30:12; 30:14 (15); 45:3; 51:8.

107 Ez 13:22; 21:7; 28:24; Hs 5:13; 12:8 (9); 12:11 (12); and furthermore see 1 Sam 22:8; 2 Chr 6:28-29; Ec 1:18; 2:23; 10:9; Na 3:19; Mi 1:9; Lm 1:12; 1:18.

108 Pr 16:26; see Jb 14:22.

109 Pr 15:13; 25:20; se also 2 Chr 6:29; Jb 14:13; Is 57:17; 65:14. Jr 4:19.

110 Pr 15:13; 17:22; 18:14; Is 61:3. Ez 21:7 uses the plural ܪ̈ܘܚܬܐ and Is 63:10 speaks of ܪܘܚܐ ܕܩܘܕܫܗ.

111 Na 3:19; Jr 30:12.

112 Mi 1:9; Is 30:26; Jr 6:8; 10:19; 14:17; 30:12; Na 3:19.

113 Pr 14:23: ܟܠ ܟܐܒ ܡܪܝܐ ܡܐܣܐ.

114 Is 30:26: ܘܟܐܒܐ ܕܡܚܘܬܗ ܢܐܣܐ.

115 Mt 4:23; 8:17; 9:35; 10:1; Lk 14:21; Jn 5:4; Act 28:8; Rom 1:26; 7:5; 9:2; 1 Cor 12:26; Gal 5:24; Col 3:5; Rev 16:2ph; 16:10-11ph; 21:4ph.

116 Mt 4:23: ܟܠ ܟܐܒ ܘܟܘܪܗܢ (P); ܟܠ ܟܐܒܐ ܘܟܠ ܟܘܪܗܢ (S); ܟܠ ܟܘܪܗܢܝܢ ܘܟܠ ܬܫܢܝܩܝܢ (C); Mt 10:1; Mt 9:35: ܟܠ ܟܘܪܗܢܝܢ ܘܟܠ ܟܐܒܝ̈ܢ (P); ܟܘܠ ܟܐܒ ܘܟܠ ܟܘܪܗܢ (S); Jn 5:4.

sickness' (ܟܠ ܟܐܒ ܘܟܘܪܗܢ), e.g. 'He heals every pain and sickness among the People'.[117] The terms ܟܐܒܐ and ܟܘܪܗܢܐ are very close to each other. The difference can be described as following: while ܟܘܪܗܢܐ describes the kind of sickness from the physician's point of view, ܟܐܒܐ expresses the effect, experience and feeling of sickness from the patient's side, i.e. the pain and suffering. The verb 'to be restored/cured' (ܐܬܚܠܡ) is only used once with the term ܟܐܒܐ: 'every pain was cured'.[118] Based on Is 53:4, Mt 8:17 uses ܟܐ̈ܒܝܢ ܘܟܘܪ̈ܗܢܝܢ[119] in a moral and spiritual sense. Paul goes beyond the physical meaning of ܟܐܒܐ and speaks of 'the pain of sins' (Rom 7:5: ܟܐ̈ܒܐ ܕܚܛܗ̈ܐ). Because of sin, Rom 1:26 speaks of the 'shameful pains' ( ܠܟܐ̈ܒܐ ܕܨܥܪܐ); Col 3:5 draws attention to sinful deeds as ܟܐ̈ܒܐ.[120]

Ephrem frequently uses the term ܟܐܒܐ in the context of Jesus as the One Who 'heals' (ܐܣܐ),[121] 'binds up' (ܚܒܫ),[122] 'chases away' (ܪܕܦ),[123] 'cuts away' (ܓܙܪ)[124] and 'cuts off' (ܦܣܩ)[125] the ܟܐܒܐ or ܟܠ ܟܐ̈ܒܐ.[126] Terms such as 'sickness' (ܟܘܪܗܢܐ),[127] 'bruises/sores' (ܚܒ̈ܪܬܐ),[128] 'pains' (ܚܫ̈ܐ)[129] and

---

117 Mt 4:23: ܘܡܐܣܐ ܟܠ ܟܐܒ ܘܟܘܪܗܢ ܒܥܡܐ; cf. Mt 9:35; Mt 10:1; cf. Mt 8:17.

118 Jn 5:4: ܡܬܚܠܡ ܗܘܐ ܟܠ ܟܐܒܐ. Jn 5:4 is not included in C and the best Greek manuscripts.

119 Mt 8:17 (P): S has ܡܪ̈ܥܝܢ; C ܟܐ̈ܒܝܢ.

120 Rom 1:26; Col 3:5.

121 Dom 19; CDiat 16.8; Fid 15.7; Eccl 38.4 and the Refrain; Nis 11.3.

122 Nat 17.7; Azym 20.18. In Sog 1.29, the verb 'to carry' (ܛܥܢ) is used.

123 Fid 5.19. Nis 1.7 refers to Jonah.

124 Azym 20.19.

125 Eccl 25:8.

126 Fid 15.7; Azym 20.18-19; Eccl 52.6; Nis 1.7; 38.4.

127 CDiat 16.8; Sog 1.29.

128 Nat 22.1.

129 Parad 5.13.

'thorns' (ܟܘ̈ܒܐ)[130] are occasionally linked with the term ܟܐܒܐ. Although ܟܐܒܐ has the literal meaning of a particular 'pain or disease', Ephrem uses it in the sense of ܟܘܪܗܢܐ too, referring to the general state of sickness or being sick. Therefore, it is often difficult to differentiate strictly between the way Ephrem uses ܟܐܒܐ and ܟܘܪܗܢܐ.

Furthermore, Ephrem mentions a variety of ܟܐ̈ܒܐ. He speaks of 'souls' pains' (ܟܐ̈ܒܐ ܕܢܦ̈ܫܬܐ),[131] 'the body's pain' (ܟܐܒܐ ܕܦܓܪܐ),[132] 'hidden pain' (ܟܐܒܐ ܟܣܝܐ),[133] 'first pain' (ܟܐܒܐ ܩܕܡܝܐ),[134] 'creation's pains' (ܟܐ̈ܒܝܗ ܕܒܪܝܬܐ),[135] 'women's pains' (ܟܐ̈ܒܐ ܕܢܩ̈ܒܬܐ),[136] 'freedom's pain' ( ܟܐܒܐ ܕܚܐܪܘܬܐ)[137] and 'Sheol's pain' (ܟܐܒܐ ܕܫܝܘܠ).[138] Beyond these, mainly in the hymns On Nisibis, Ephrem uses phrases such as 'it is a real pain' (ܟܐܒܐ ܗܘ ܫܪܝܪܬܐ ),[139] 'the pain that is customary among us' (ܟܐܒܐ ܕܐܟܝܕ ܒܟܘܢ),[140] 'the pain that the physician renewed' (ܟܐܒܐ ܕܚܕܬ ܐܣܝܐ)[141] and 'it is a great pain for us' (ܟܐܒܐ ܗܘ ܠܢ ܪܒܐ).[142]

Obviously ܟܐܒܐ refers not just to the body, but also to the soul and all of nature. In Virginity 7.9, the body (ܦܓܪܐ) is described as 'the source of pains' (ܡܒܘܥ ܟܐ̈ܒܐ). Likewise, Virg 4.4 speaks of 'bodies' (ܦܓܪ̈ܐ) as the 'vessels of pains' (ܡܐܢ̈ܝ ܟܐ̈ܒܐ). Morally, in Eccl 25.8 'pride' (ܫܘܒܗܪܐ) is

130 Eccl 48.11.
131 Nis 34.10; Iei 4.1; 10.6.
132 Iei 10.6.
133 Fid 38.7; Dom 19; Iei 4.1.
134 CDiat 11.5.
135 Sog 1.29.
136 Virg 24.11
137 Eccl 2.11.
138 Nis 37.2.
139 Nis 10.16.
140 Nis 21.6.
141 Nis 27.5.
142 Eccl 1.5.

considered as the 'cause of pain' (ܥܠܬ ܟܐܒܐ); and because of sin 'nature came to pains' (ܠܟܝܢܐ ܕܐܬܐ ܠܟܐ̈ܒܐ).[143]

The ܟܐܒܐ needs to be healed. While terms such as 'health' (ܚܘܠܡܢܐ),[144] 'medicines' (ܣܡ̈ܡܢܐ)[145] and 'physician' (ܐܣܝܐ)[146] are often linked closely with the term ܟܐܒܐ, the 'Medicine of Life' (ܣܡ ܚܝܐ) is only once directly linked with the term ܟܐܒܐ.[147] The ܣܡ̈ܡܢܐ and ܚܘܠܡ̈ܢܐ are contrasted with the ܟܐ̈ܒܐ and said to oppose them: ܠܘܩܒܠ ܟܐ̈ܒܐ.[148]

Beside the Lord Who is the main Healer[149] of the ܟܐ̈ܒܐ, we also find the 'remorse/compunction of soul' (ܬܘܬ ܢܦܫܐ),[150] 'oil' (ܡܫܝܚܐ),[151] 'fragrance' (ܪܝܚܐ),[152] 'fasting' (ܨܘܡܐ),[153] 'the hand of grace' (ܐܝܕܐ ܕܛܝܒܘܬܐ) and 'the hand of justice' ( ܐܝܕܐ ܕܟܐܢܘܬܐ),[154] 'His words' (ܦܬܓ̈ܡܘܗܝ)[155] and the words of the Apostles[156] as effecting their healing.

The passive participle ܡܟܐ̈ܒܐ is used in the Sermon On the Lord to describe the sick who are in need of a physician in general

---

[143] Fid 35.2; also see Nis 28.1 where Ephrem speaks of ܟܝ̈ܢܐ in plural.

[144] Dom 14; Virg 26.4; Nis 19.11; 26.5.

[145] Dom 19; 21; Virg 30.10; Fid 56.11; Iei 10.6; Eccl 38.4; 52.6.

[146] Dom 19; Fid 5.19; 56.11; Parad 11.9; Eccl 25.8. Nis 11.3.

[147] Epiph 5.14, which may not be by Ephrem.

[148] Dom 21; Virg 4.13; Nis 16.21.

[149] CDiat 16.8; Dom 14; 19; 21; Nat 17.7; 22.1-4; Sog 1.29; Fid 5.19; 15.7; Eccl 25.8 38.4 and the refrain; Nis 16.21; 34.10. Epiph 5.14 has ܦܘܪ̈ܣܗ ܕܡܫܝܚܐ as ܡܒܘܥܐ ܕܣܡ ܚܝܐ for ܟܐ̈ܒܐ; Virg 26.4 has ܡܚܠܬܐ; and Virg 30.10 ܫܘ̈ܚܐ.

[150] Virg 3.10.

[151] Virg 4.13; see also Virg 7.9.

[152] Parad 11.9.

[153] Iei 4.1.

[154] Azym 20.18; Nis 11.3.

[155] Eccl 52.6.

[156] Virg 4.4.

terms.[157] It seems that Ephrem refers to Mt 9:12 (with parallels in Mk 2:17; Lk 5:31-32), substituting this term for ܐܝܠܝܢ ܕܒܝܫ ܒܝܫ ܥܒܝܕܝܢ (S).[158] At the end of CDiat 16.24 ܟܐܒܐ is used once, instead of the more frequent ܡܚܝܚܐ, for the man assisted by the Good Samaritan.

### 3.1.3 ܡܚܐ and Related Terms

The verb ܡܚܐ means 'to strike, smite, beat or wound', whether literally or metaphorically; while the noun (ܡܚܘܬܐ) ranges in meaning from 'a blow, wound, sore or stripe' to 'sickness, disease; slaughter; affliction; scourge or plague'.[159] Ephrem uses the root as a verb (ܡܚܐ), passive participle (ܡܚܝܚܐ) or noun (ܡܚܘܬܐ) in several different contexts of healing. Attention is drawn here primarily to passages where Ephrem employs the terms in the sense of moral and/or spiritual wounding.

In CDiat 6.11b-15, Ephrem makes use of the double meaning of ܦܟܐ, 'blow, slap' and 'cheek', to contrast the Mosaic 'a blow for a blow' (ܦܟܐ ܚܠܦ ܦܟܐ, Ex 21:25) in response to someone striking (ܡܚܐ) one, with Christ's words 'Whoever strikes (ܡܚܐ) you, provide[160] him with the other [cheek]' (Lk 6:29). Whereas the Mosaic law raised people from the level of wickedness to that of justice (ܟܐܢܘܬܐ), Christ's command goes further and raises to the level of grace (ܛܝܒܘܬܐ).[161] In this way the sense of ܦܟܐ

---

[157] Dom 42: ܗܘ ܕܝܢ ܕܠܒܫܬ ܐܢܫܘܬܐ ܡܚܒܠ ܘܫܠܡܘܬܐ ܟܣܝܬ ܟܐܒܐ.

[158] Mt 9:2: P has ܐܝܠܝܢ ܕܒܝܫܐܝܬ ܥܒܝܕܝܢ.

[159] J. P. Smith, *A Compendious Syriac Dictionary*, 263; R. P. Smith, *Thesaurus Syriacus* II, 2065-68.

[160] CDiat 6.12; 6.14. ܦܢܝ is found in Mt 5:39 (S and C) and Lk 6:29 (S and P), whereas ܐܦܢܐ in Mt 5:39 (P H) and Lk 6:29 (H). Ephrem regularly uses ܐܬܩܡ, against ܦܢܝ in Mt 5:39 (S and C), Lk 6:29 (S and P), and ܐܦܢܐ in Mt 5:39 (P and H), Lk 6:29 (H).

[161] CDiat 6.14: ܡܘܫܐ ܓܝܪ ܐܣܩ ܡܢ ܕܪܓ ܒܝܫܘܬܐ. ܘܐܘܒܠ ܠܕܪܓ ܟܐܢܘܬܐ. ܕܠܐ ܬܡܚܐ ܠܚܒܪܟ ܒܡܠܐܬܟ. ܐܢ ܕܝܢ ܡܚܐ ܠܟ ܬܗܒ ܢܦܫܟ ܡܟܐܢܘܬܟ. ܡܪܢ ܕܝܢ ܐܣܩ ܡܢ ܕܪܓ ܟܐܢܘܬܐ. ܘܐܘܒܠ

☞

ܣܠܩ ܦܟܐ is 'reversed',[162] and in this way 'the person who provides the [other] cheek[163] in place of the cheek/blow [that has been struck] will prove victorious'.[164]

In the course of his discussion Ephrem points out[165] that Christ exemplified his own command when He Himself was struck on the cheek (Jn 18:22). This passage implicitly provides the answer to Ephrem's rhetorical question in hymn 15 On Unleavened Bread where he wonders why the hand that struck Jesus did not wither, whereas the fig tree did dry up (Mt 21:19).[166]

In some other passages Ephrem uses the term ܡܚܝܐ in a moral and spiritual sense. The subject of ܡܚܝܐ is no longer a man or a part of the body, but the Serpent and Satan. In CDiat 16.15, Ephrem brings together the Serpent of Genesis 3:1-18 with the serpents which bit the Israelites (Num 21:6). 'The Serpent wounded Adam in Paradise and killed him, and Israel in the camp and destroyed them.'[167] In hymn 37 On Virginity the Serpent is the subject and Eve the object: 'the Serpent wounded Eve' ( ܚܘܝܐ ܡܚܝܐ ܠܚܘܐ).[168] The participle ܡܡܚܝܐ also appears once with Satan as the subject. Here Satan's wounding is contrasted with the

---

ܒܪ̈ܢܫܐ ܕܚܘܒܬܐ. ܕܠܐ ܬܬܬܒܥ ܡܢ ܗܘ ܕܡܚܝܟ ܥܠ ܦܟܟ. ܐܠܐ ܐܬܠܘܗܝ ܠܗ ܐܚܪܢܐ. Cf. Ex 21:12-14; Mt 5:39; Lk 6:29.

162 CDiat 6.12.

163 So correctly Leloir's Latin translation; McCarthy's English translation wrongly renders ܦܟܐ by 'blow' here.

164 CDiat 6.15.

165 CDiat 6.13.

166 Azym 15.22-23: ܬܬܐ ܕܝܒܫܬܗ ܡܒܥܬ ܡܢ ܥܠ ܘܐܝܕܐ ܕܡܚܝܬܗ ܠܐ ܒܗ ܡܒܥܬ.

167 CDiat 16.15: ܡܚܝܐ ܚܘܝܐ ܠܐܕܡ ܒܦܪܕܝܣܐ ܘܩܛܠܗ. ܘܠܐܝܣܪܐܝܠ ܒܡܫܪܝܬܐ ܘܐܘܒܕ ܐܢܘܢ (Gen 3:1-18; Num 21:4-9). The term ܡܚܝܐ is used only once in the Paradise narrative. The enmity of the Serpent towards man is to 'wound him in his heel' (Gen 3:15: ܘܐܢܬ ܬܡܚܝܘܗܝ, ܒܥܩܒܗ). The Hebrew does not have the equivalent term מחה, but תשופנו; the Greek is quite different: τηρήσεις, 'watch out for'.

168 Virg 37.1.

possibility of healing: While 'Satan wounds' (ܣܛܢܐ ܡܡܚܐ), Scripture and Nature 'heal us' (ܡܐܣܝܢ ܠܢ).[169]

Unlike the Serpent and Satan, God strikes in order to heal. When God strikes,[170] He 'strikes in order to help' ( ܕܡܚܐ ܠܡܥܕܪܢܐ). To bring this out the verb 'to have mercy' (ܡܪܚܡ) is used along with 'to strike' (ܡܚܐ) as belonging to the same act. To strike is a part of education and discipline.[171] The 'rod' (ܫܒܛܐ) is the medium through which God performs His deeds and the benefit from it is the 'help' (ܡܥܕܪܢܐ). Those whom God 'strikes' are 'us' (ܠܢ), i.e. humanity.

In hymn 11 On Nisibis, it is God's justice which 'strikes'. Divine justice is the one who is the binder (ܚܒܟܗ ܠܬܒܪܗ) and who strikes (ܕܡܚܝܬ), and through both of them the Lord restores health (ܚܘܠܡܢܐ).[172]

---

[169] Virg 1.3:

ܣܛܢܐ ܡܡܚܐ ܘܗܢܘܢ ܡܐܣܝܢ ܠܢ
ܒܡܒܥܗ ܕܒܘܠܐ ܒܟܠܐ ܬܘܬ ܢܒܥܐ.

[170] God is frequently described as 'striking' in the OT, eg. Gen 12:17: ܘܡܚܐ ܡܪܝܐ ܠܦܪܥܘܢ ܡܚܘ̈ܬܐ ܪ̈ܘܪܒܬܐ; Dt 32:39: ܚܘ ܗܫܐ ܕܐܢܐ ܐܢܐ: ܘܠܝܬ ܐܠܗ ܠܒܪ ܡܢܝ: ܐܢܐ ܡܡܝܬ ܘܐܢܐ ܡܚܐ ܐܢܐ: ܐܢܐ ܡܚܐ ܐܢܐ ܘܐܢܐ ܡܐܣܐ ܐܢܐ: ܘܠܝܬ ܕܡܦܠܛ ܡܢ ܐܝ̈ܕܝ.

[171] Eccl 28.15:

ܪܒܘ ܕܦܘܪ̈ܥܢܐ ܠܡܚܢܝܘ ܒܟܠ ܥܒܕܘܗܝ
ܕܡܚܐ ܠܡܥܕܪܢܐ ܘܡܟܐܒܐ ܠܡܘܬܪܢܐ
ܕܫܒܛܐ ܡܢܗ [ܡܚܘܬܐ] ܠܗ ܠܒܢܝ ܡܚܝܢ ܠܗ
ܒܣܘܟܐ ܗܘ ܡܬܚܙܐ ܒܟܠܗܝܢ
ܡܪܚܡ ܘܡܚܐ ܠܢ ܕܢܗܦܘܟ ܟܠ ܡܘܬܪܐ
ܚܐܣ ܘܦܠܓ ܬܘܒ ܕܢܐܠ ܒܪܝܢ ܣܘܟ̈ܐ.

[172] Nis 11.7-8:

ܦܬܚ ܬܪܥ ܠܗ ܚܒܟܗ ܠܬܒܪܗ.
ܡܐ ܕܡܚܬ ܚܠܬ ܕܝܢ ܒܚܕ ܬܪ̈ܬܝܗܝܢ
ܬܘܠܕ ܚܘܠܡܢܐ .
ܦܬܚ ܦܐܐ ܪܘܓܙܗ ܘܚܬܡܗ̇ ܒܚܫܚܐ
ܘܠܐ ܡܘܪܡܪܗ̇ ܡܚܠܐ ܠܡܪ̈ܝܪܐ
ܕܢܫܘܘܢ ܒܚܫ̈ܚܐ .

Ephrem uses the passive of ܡܚܝܐ twice in connection with doctrinal error. In hymn 15 On Faith, Ephrem considers any Arian who pries into the Son as 'a limb that is wounded' ( ܗܕܡܐ ܗܘ ܕܐܬܡܚܝ), and he fears that this will harm the whole body if it is not healed immediately.[173] Furthermore, since this limb has been wounded (ܒܠܥ), 'He who heals all our ills will cut it off and throw it out from the flock'.[174] Here the 'limb' (ܗܕܡܐ) that is wounded through prying into the Son, is in danger of spreading infection and so 'harming the whole body' (ܢܒܐ ܠܟܠܗ ܠܦܓܪܐ). The verb ܬܐܣܐ which is used immediately after ܕܐܬܡܚܝ expresses the urgent need to heal the wounded limb. In hymn 10 On Fasting, the erring Israelites are 'smitten' (ܐܬܡܚܝܘ) by the Golden Calf, and 'fasts' (ܨܘܡܐ) are prescribed as the 'medicine' which will heal.[175] The verb was suggested by the Exodus narrative about the Golden Calf (Ex 32) where, however, the term ܡܚܝܐ is used with God as the subject: 'And the Lord struck the people because they worshipped the calf Aaron had made' (Ex 32:35).[176]

There are several significant verbs which are used together with ܡܚܝܐ. Firstly, the verb 'to heal' (ܐܣܝ) counteracts the effect of the 'striking'. This applies in two passages already quoted.[177] When the subject of ܡܚܝܐ is God, His grace or His justice, the verbs ܡܪܥܣ, ܚܒܫ and ܣܡ point to the positive aspect of

---

173 Fid 15.1.

174 Fid 15.7:

ܐܝܟ ܕܡܥܩܒ ܗܕܡܐ ܗܘ ܕܐܬܡܚܝ
ܬܐܣܐ ܕܠܡܐ ܢܒܐ ܠܟܠܗ ܠܦܓܪܐ
ܘܡܛܠ ܕܒܠܥ ܢܓܙܘܪ ܢܫܕܝܘܗܝ ܡܢ ܡܪܥܝܬܐ
ܡܐܣܝܐ ܕܟܠ ܟܐܒܝܢ.

175 Iei 10.4:

ܗܘܘ ܨܘܡܐ ܣܡܡܢܐ ܠܡܚܘܬܐ ܕܒܥܓܠܐ ܐܬܡܚܝܘ.

176 Ex 32:35: ܘܡܚܝܐ ܡܪܝܐ ܠܥܡܐ ܥܠ ܕܦܠܚܘ ܠܥܓܠܐ ܕܥܒܕ ܐܗܪܘܢ.

177 Virg 1.3; Fid 15.7.

ܡܚܝܐ.[178] If the term ܡܚܝܐ is negative and its subject is the Serpent or Satan, the verbs ܡܚܠ and ܟܠܒ emphasise the serious and dire effect of wounding.[179] But the verb ܟܠܒ is also used in connection with Jesus, when it describes Him as the victim.[180]

The noun 'wound' appears frequently in both the singular (ܡܚܘܬܐ) and plural form (ܡܚ̈ܘܬܐ). In the *Commentary on the Diatessaron*, Ephrem describes the issuing of blood as the 'hidden wound of that wounded woman' ( ܒܡܚܘܬܐ ܟܣܝܬܐ ܕܗ̇ܝ ܡܚܝܬܐ).[181] Ephrem also speaks of 'visible wounds' ( ܡܚ̈ܘܬܐ ܓܠܝ̈ܬܐ) and a 'bodily wound' (ܡܚܘܬܗ ܕܦܓܪܐ) which are the object of healing by Jesus. The singular ܡܚܘܬܐ usually describes a particular wound, such as the wound of the woman with the haemorrhage (ܡܚܘܬܗ̇), whereas the plural ܡܚ̈ܘܬܐ is used in a general sense.[182]

Ephrem uses the term 'wounds' in connection with Adam (ܡܚ̈ܘܬܐ ܕܐܕܡ), where Adam is the victim and not the agent.[183] 'We' are also the victims when the term ܡܚ̈ܘܬܢ or ܡܚܘܬܢ is used.[184] Likewise, Jesus is the victim of the wound (ܒܡܚܘܬܗ).[185] But people can be the agent too: 'the wounds that those before effected' (ܡܚ̈ܘܬܐ ܕܥܒܕܘ ܩܕܡܝܐ).[186] By contrast, the Serpent is the agent in the phrase: 'the wound of the first Serpent' (ܡܚܘܬܗ ܕܚܘܝܐ ܩܕܡܝܐ).[187] The same is the case in the phrase

---

178 Nis 11.7; Eccl 28.15. For the verb ܚܒܪ see below, chapter III, 2.4.

179 CDiat 16.15.

180 Nat 3.18: ܢܘܪܐ ܠܟܡ ܕܟܠܒ ܘܐܣܝ ܒܡܚܘܬܗ; CDiat 6.13: ܟܠܒ ܠܗ ܦܓܪܗ.

181 CDiat 7.1.

182 CDiat 7.9; 7.16; 7.20; Nis 74.14.

183 CDiat 16.10.

184 Nis 19.11; Nis 34.10; 34.12; Nat 22.3.

185 Nat 3.18; Mt 27:14.

186 CDiat 6.13.

187 Nat 1.28; Num 21:8f.

'the wound of death' (ܠܡܚܘܬܐ ܕܡܘܬܐ) where death causes the wound.[188]

In two passages it is a city which suffers from a 'wound', Edessa and Harran. Ephrem describes Edessa as speaking of 'my wound', referring to the time when the church in Edessa suffered badly under the Emperor Valens who assisted the Arians (ca. AD 365). Ephrem compares the city's suffering with that of the woman with the haemorrhage.[189] Harran's wound (ܡܚܘܬܗ), however, is considered along with that of Egypt and Babel as a 'gangrene of idolatry' (ܠܫܚܬܐ ܕܦܬܟܪܘܬܐ).[190]

The passive participle of the Pa'el has a nominal function on several occasions, often referring to specific people. Thus the masculine singular ܡܚܝܐ is used of the man who fell among thieves in the parable of the Good Samaritan (based on Lk 10:30 ܘܡܚܝܘܗܝ).[191] The feminine ܡܚܝܬܐ is employed to refer to either the woman with the haemorrhage (Lk 8:43-48; Mk 5:25-34),[192] or the sinful woman[193] in Luke 7:36-50. Ephrem uses the plural ܡ̈ܚܝܐ to refer to those in general who are in need of healing by Jesus the Physician.[194]

The passive participle is also occasionally used adjectivally. Thus, in connection with the episode of the Golden Calf, Ephrem speaks of 'the wounded [Israelite] camp' ( ܡܫܪܝܬܐ

---

188 Nis 74.14.

189 Nis 27.5:

ܐܦ ܠܐ ܦܫܚ ܢܠܒܪܐ ܕܡܚܘܬܝ ܠܗܘ ܢܠܒܪܐ
ܒܪܬ ܥܡ ܥܡܡ ܐܢܬܬܗ ܦܠܓܘܬ ܥܡܡܗ ܕܗܝ
ܒܐܒܐ ܕܫܪܬ ܐܣܝܐ ܕܐܣܝܬ ܒܠܘܬܟܐ.

190 Nis 34.5:

ܚܘ ܠܡܚܪܢ ܒܢܣܝܘܬܐ ܕܐܦ ܐܬܠܚܡܬ ܒܡܐܣܝܐ ܠܟ
ܘܫܠܬܐ ܕܦܬܟܪܘܬܐ ܒܚܪܢ ܫܠܚܬ.

191 CDiat 16.24; Eccl 33.3.

192 CDiat 7.1; 7.6.

193 Dom 42: ܐܝܟ ܕܐܦ ܐܣܝܐ ܕܠܐ ܠܡܟܐ̈ܒܐ ܢܬܐܘܬ ܠܘܬܗ ܐܘ ܦܓܪܐ ܒܡܪܐ ܕܝܗܒܬ ܒܠ ܐܣܝܐ ܕܠܟܐܒܐ ܡܪܒܬ ܠܗ ܡܚܝܬܐ. ܗܝ ܕܒܕܡ̈ܥܝܗ ܐܬܐܣܝ ܣܘܪܚܢܗ.

194 Dom 13; Nat 4.24; Nis 34.12.

ܡܡܚܝܘܬܐ).[195] Elsewhere Jesus is described as healing 'wounded minds' (ܪ̈ܥܝܢܐ ܡܡܚܝ̈ܢܐ).[196]

### 3.1.4 The Verb ܒܠܥ

The verb ܒܠܥ is often used in the Syriac Bible either with the sense of 'to swallow up, devour', or 'to be struck, smitten, beaten or wounded'. For the first time in the Peshitta Old Testament, ܒܠܥ appears in the narrative about Sodom and Gomorrah (Gen 19:1-29), where the two angels 'struck the men who were at the door of the house'.[197] Even though the word ܒܠܥ appears in the sense of 'to strike' physically, the reason is sin (cf. Gen 19:15). In certain other passages too sin is the reason people are 'struck' or 'wounded'.[198] The one who 'strikes, wounds or swallows' can be Satan (ܣܛܢܐ; 1 Pet 5:8) or Sheol (ܫܝܘܠ; Pr 1:12), the earth (ܐܪܥܐ; Ex 15:12; Num 16:30-40; Dtn 11:6) or the fish (ܢܘܢܐ) as in the case of Jonah and the whale (Jon 1:17; 2:1). Surprisingly, in the Bible, death appears as an object of ܒܠܥ, and not as a subject (Is 25:8; 1 Cor 15:54). Therefore, in particular at baptism, the ܡܝܘܬܘܬܐ of every single person 'will be swallowed up' (2 Cor 5:4: ܬܬܒܠܥ). However, ܒܠܥ is also used in the sense of a physical 'wounding', as in battles and war (cf. Ex 15:9; 22:2; 1 Sam 26:10).

Ephrem uses ܒܠܥ in his hymns,[199] as well as in the Commentary on the Diatessaron[200] and Sermo on the Lord.[201] Dom 3 is the most significant passage in which the verb ܒܠܥ is developed in the context of the mystery of salvation through Christ's descent to Sheol from where He freed Adam and all those who were 'swallowed' by death. Christ's incarnation is explained in the context of becoming an object for death: Since death was

---

195 Iei 10.4.

196 Dom 42: ܠܗܘ ܕܝܢ ܐܣܝ ܪ̈ܥܝܢܐ ܡܡܚܝ̈ܢܐ.

197 Gen 19:11: ܘܠܓܒܪ̈ܐ ܕܒܬܪܥܐ ܕܒܝܬܐ ܒܠܥܘ.

198 Ex 15:16; Num 16:26; Jos 22:20; Jer 51:6.

199 Nat 3.18; Fid 15.7; 28.11; Parad 3.14; Eccl 17.2; Nis 1.7.

200 CDiat 6.13-14.

201 Dom 3-5; 7.

unable to consume Him without a body or Sheol to swallow Him without flesh, He came to a virgin to provide Himself with a means to Sheol'.[202] Sheol is the subject of ܒܠܥ as well as death of ܐܟܠ. Both verbs are used in parallel and have a very close association, as do Sheol and death. Primarily, Sheol or death 'devour' mankind, but Ephrem plays with the term ܒܠܥ; particularly when death 'swallowed' the Life which is Christ, for in turn, death became the object of ܒܠܥ. While death is called the 'devourer' (ܒܠܘܥܐ),[203] Sheol is the 'devourer of all' (ܒܠܘܥܬ ܟܠ).[204] Sheol is never mentioned as an object of ܒܠܥ, only death (ܡܘܬܐ) and enemity (ܒܥܠܕܒܒܘܬܐ),[205] the former based on Paul (1 Cor 15:54).

Jesus also appears as the victim. In CDiat 6.13, Ephrem refers ܒܠܥ to Jesus in a physical sense: ܒܠܥ ܥܠ ܦܘܡܗ.[206] This phrase is in the context of commenting on Luke 6:29 (par Mt 5:39).[207] The verb ܒܠܥ is interchanged with ܡܚܝܐ. While the subject of ܡܚܝܐ is the agent, that of ܒܠܥ is the victim. In Nat 3.18, Ephrem praises the Lord for He 'was wounded and revived us by being struck'.[208]

In Parad 3.14, Adam appears as the victim, as he is compared with King Uzziah.[209] The cause of his being wounded is sin as he disobeyed the Lord's commandment. Likewise, the Arians are considered 'wounded' because of their sin. Consequently, Ephrem

---

202 Dom 3: ܘܡܛܠ ܕܠܐ ܡܨܝܐ ܗܘܐ ܡܘܬܐ ܕܢܐܟܠܝܘܗܝ ܕܠܐ ܦܓܪܐ ܘܐܦܠܐ ܫܝܘܠ ܕܬܒܠܥܝܘܗܝ ܕܠܐ ܒܣܪܐ. ܐܬܐ ܠܘܬ ܒܬܘܠܬܐ ܕܡܢ ܬܡܢ ܪܟܘܒܐ ܠܫܝܘܠ ܢܛܝܒ ܠܗ.

203 Dom 3: ܗܘ ܦܐܪܐ ܕܡܪܐ ܠܡܘܬܐ ܒܠܘܥܗ.

204 Dom 4: ܫܝܘܠ ܒܠܘܥܬ ܟܠ.

205 Dom 7: ܡܘܕܝܢ ܠܟ ܒܡܘܬܐ ܕܒܥܝܢܟ ܐܬܒܠܥܬ ܒܥܠܕܒܒܘܬܐ ܕܒܡܨܥܬܐ.

206 CDiat 6.13.

207 See also CDiat 6.14: ܠܐ ܗܘܐ ܦܘܪܥܢ ܦܓܥܐ ܡܕܡܝܐ ܢܛܪ ܗܘ ܠܗ ܡܢ ܐܝܟܢܐ ܡܛܠ ܕܒܠܥ. ܘܦܘܪܥܢ ܦܓܥܐ ܐܚܪܢܐ ܐܘܬܒܗ ܠܗ. ܐܦ ܟܕ ܠܐ ܢܒܠܥ ܡܛܠ ܕܐܬܗܡ.

208 Nat 3.18: ܢܘܕܐ ܠܡܢ ܕܒܠܥ ܘܐܚܝܢ ܒܡܚܘܬܗ.

209 Parad 3.14: ܘܕܒܠܥ ܐܝܟ ܒܥܘܙܝܐ ܐܬܪܗܒ ܕܢܦܘܩ ܠܗ.

wants to expel the Arian who has 'been wounded' from the community.[210]

The verb ܒܠܥ is also used in the sense of 'to swallow'. In Fid 28.11, ܡܬܒܠܥܝܢ refers to ܕܪ̈ܫܐ ܘܫܘܪ̈ܝܐ which will be 'swallowed up'.[211] In this sense ܒܠܥ is also used in hymn 1 On Nisibis where Nisibis during its third occupation by the Persians is compared with Noah's ark. As God sent a physician through the dove to the people in the ark and they were comforted, so also the '[physician's] joy swallowed their grief/sorrow'.[212]

The noun ܒܠܥܬܐ is used only once. The context is 'swallowed' in the sense of drinking: ܘܫܪܘ ܒܪܙ ܒܟܣܐ ܠܒܣܡܘ ܡܢ̈ܐ ܠܒܠܥܬܐ.[213] A similar idea is found in Isaiah 28:27 where ܒܠܥ is used as a verb: ܐܬܒܠܥܘ ܡܢ ܚܡܪܐ.

### 3.1.5 The Term ܬܒܪ

The basic meaning of the verb ܬܒܪ is 'to break, bruise, fracture'.[214] In the Old Testament ܬܒܪ appears in a variety of contexts. In Isaiah 42:3, the verb ܬܒܪ has ܩܢܝܐ as the subject ( ܩܢܝܐ ܪܥܝܥܐ ܠܐ ܢܬܒܪ), whereas Isaiah 61:1-2 uses the noun ܬܒܝܪ̈ܝ ܠܒܐ as the object of the verb 'to heal' (ܐܣܐ). In Proverbs 6:15 and 29:1 it is clear that ܬܒܪ contrasts with healing (ܐܣܝܘܬܐ).[215] Job 5:18, as well as Isaiah 30:26, contrast ܬܒܪ with ܚܒܫ.[216] Jeremiah 30:12 associates ܬܒܪܐ with ܟܐܒܐ and therefore he uses the verb

---

[210] Fid 15.7: ܘܡܛܠ ܕܒܠܥ ܢܓܘܪ ܠܚܘܠܡܗ, ܡܢ ܡܪܥܝܬܐ.

[211] Fid 28.11: ܘܕܪ̈ܫܐ ܘܫܘܪ̈ܝܐ ܐܝܟ ܒܘܪܐ ܘܐܝܟ ܒܢܪܐ ܡܬܒܠܥܝܢ. A similar sentence is found in Pr 21:20: ܣܝܡܬܐ ܘܡܣܟܠܐ ܕܒ̈ܢܝܢܫܐ ܢܒܠܥܝܗ̇.

[212] Nis 1.7: ܚܠ ܘܪܕܩ ܠܗ ܠܐܒܝ̈ܠܘܗܝ ܕܫܘܚܬܗ ܒܠܥܬ ܒܣܝܡܘܬܐ.

[213] Eccl 17.2.

[214] Cf. J. P. Smith, *A Compendious Syriac Dictionary*, 604.

[215] Pr 6:15: ܘܡܢ ܥܠܝܐ ܢܬܬܒܪ ܘܠܐ ܢܗܘܐ ܠܗ ܐܣܝܘܬܐ. Pr 29:1: ܒܫܠܝ ܢܬܬܒܪ ܘܠܐ ܬܗܘܐ ܠܗ ܐܣܝܘܬܐ.

[216] Jb 5:18: ܡܛܠ ܕܗܘ ܬܒܪ ܘܚܒܫ. Is 30:26: ܒܝܘܡܐ ܕܢܚܒܘܫ ܡܪܝܐ ܬܒܪܐ ܕܥܡܗ.

ܐܣܝ (Jer 6:14; 8:11) to make it clear that ܬܒܪܐ needs to be healed as a sickness.

In the New Testament, ܬܒܪ is rarely used in the context of healing. It appears in Mt 12:20 (ܩܢܝܐ ܪܥܝܥܐ ܠܐ ܢܬܒܪ) as a quotation from Isaiah 42:3, and in Lk 4:18 ( ܘܫܠܚܢܝ ܠܡܐܣܝܘ ܠܬܒܝܪ̈ܝ, ܠܒܐ) as a quotation from Isaiah 61:1-2.[217]

In Ephrem, ܬܒܪ usually appears together with terms based on the root ܚܒܫ,[218] whereas it is used only a few times in the context of healing without ܚܒܫ.[219] In Eccl 43, Ephrem plays with ܬܒܪ while he refers to the stone tablets that were broken (Ex 32:19). The breaking of the stone tablets indicates heart and mind (i.e. the inner man's tablets) that were fractured through idolatry. The latter were healed and bound up through the former (ܕܚܒܫܢܘܢ, ܠܗܘ ܚܘܒܐ ܠܘܚ̈ܐ ܬܒܝܪ̈ܬܐ).[220] Ephrem makes use of both meanings of the verb ܬܒܪ: 'to break' and 'to fracture'. The Law is described as a physician who does both ܬܒܪ and ܟܐܒܐ. Later the ܚܘܒܐ, who 'bound it up for it was fractured through idolatry',[221] is the subject of ܚܒܫ. However the 'broken tablets' (ܠܘܚ̈ܐ ܬܒܝܪ̈ܬܐ) are the binder up of the inner tablets ( ܘܗܢܝ ܐܬܚܒܫ ܠܠܘܚ̈ܐ ܒܠܘܚ̈ܐ ܬܒܝܪ̈ܬܐ).[222]

---

[217] Lk 4:18: ܘܫܠܚܢܝ ܠܡܐܣܝܘ ܠܬܒܝܪ̈ܝ, ܠܒܐ. ܘܠܡܟܪܙܘ ܠܫܒ̈ܝܐ ܫܘܒܩܢܐ. ܘܠܥܘܝܪ̈ܐ ܚܙܝܐ. ܘܠܡܫܪܐ ܠܬܒܝܪ̈ܐ ܒܫܘܒܩܢܐ. Furthermore, Mk 5:4 provides ܫܫܠܬܐ as the object in the context of healing the demon-possesed man (ܫܫܠܬܐ ܡܬܒܪ ܗܘܐ). John 19:31-36 (cf. Ex 12:46; Num 9:12; Ps 34:20) uses ܓܪܡܐ and ܫܩܐ as the object of ܬܒܪ.

[218] Cf. Nat 17.7; Iei 4.1; Crucif 2.30; Nis 2.17; 10.16; 14.2; 19.4; Eccl 43.5-8.

[219] Cf. Fid 5.19; Eccl 43.20; CDiat 2.25.

[220] Eccl 43.6.

[221] Eccl 43.7: ܕܚܫܘ ܕܐܬܬܒܪ ܠܘܚ̈ܐ ܥܒܘܫ̈ܬܐ ܚܘܒܐ ܚܒܫ ܢܦܫܗ ܕܐܬܬܒܪ ܒܚܢܦܘܬܐ.

[222] Eccl 43.8.

In Nat 17.7, ܬܒܪܐ is used as a synonym to ܟܐܒܐ whose 'binder up' (ܚܒܘܫܗ) is the Lord. In Iei 4, ܬܒܪܐ refers to the mind which needs to be bound up (ܚܒܫܗ) through fasting.[223]

Also hymn 2 On the Crucifixion, Ephrem plays with the term ܬܒܪ while he uses it as a verb (ܬܒܪ) in a physical sense and as a noun (ܬܒܝܪܐ) in a metaphorical sense. The physical meaning is based on the Bible (Jn 19:36; Ex 12:46; Num 9:12) where a bone of the lamb should not be broken. However, according to John 19:36 the phrase ܕܕܓܡܠܐ ܠܒܪܐ ܢܬܬܒܪ ܒܗ refers to Jesus on the cross who 'binds up the fractured' (ܕܗܘܝܘ ܚܒܫ ܠܬܒܝܪܐ).[224]

In the hymns on Nisibis, ܬܒܪ appears four times along with ܚܒܫ. As a verb it is used in Nis 2.17 with the connotation of 'to fracture', in contrast to ܚܒܫ; the noun ܫܠܐ is the subject of both. The contrast betwen ܬܒܪܐ and ܚܒܫܐ, both as nouns, is provided in Nis 10.16 where the adjective ܡܪܝܪܐ expresses the bitter suffering of the city Nisibis. Likewise in Nis 14.2, ܬܒܪܐ refers to the wounds and grief at the city during the war. The one who binds up is Bishop Babu of Nisibis. Here, however, ܬܒܪܐ could also mean 'the state of being defeated'. In Nis 19.4, Ephrem challenges Bishop Babu to 'bind up the fractured sheep' ( ܘܚܒܘܫ ܠܥܢܐ ܕܬܒܝܪܐ), based on Ez 34:4.[225] The responsibility of a bishop is not just to heal a physical fracture, but rather a spiritual one.

From the CDiat 2.25 and Fid 5.19, it is again clear that the term ܬܒܪ refers to spiritual fractures too, and not just a physical fracture, such as of bones. The term ܬܒܪ is also not limited to individuals. It can be used in a general sense, as when Ephrem speaks of 'our fractured state' (ܬܒܪܢ, i.e. mankind's),[226] or 'Adam's

---

223 Iei 4.1: ܬܒܪܐ ܪܒܐ ܕܪܥܝܢܐ.

224 Crucif 2.3.

225 Nis 19.4.

226 CDiat 2.25.

fractured state' (ܬܒܪܗ ܕܐܕܡ) that signifies the fractured state of all humanity.[227]

### 3.1.6 Some other Terms

#### *3.1.6.1 The Term* ܚܒܪܬܐ

The term ܚܒܪܬܐ, meaning 'bruise, sore',[228] is in its sense very close to ܫܘܡܬܐ; but ܚܒܪܬܐ differs, somewhat in that it is the immediate consequence of being beaten or struck.[229] ܚܒܪܬܐ does not occur in the Bible at all. In the Old Testament the etymologically related is חבורה rendered with ܫܘܩܦܐ (Gen 4:23) or ܦܠܐ (Ex 21:25) in the Peshitta. Isaiah 1:6 uses ܡܚ̈ܘܬܐ along with ܟܘܠܦ̈ܬܐ and ܫܘ̈ܡܬܐ referring to physical wounds.

In the context of healing, Ephrem uses only the plural ܚܒ̈ܪܬܐ.[230] The verb ܐܣܝ that describes the act of healing is used four times in connection with ܚܒ̈ܪܬܐ.[231] Through the 'tears' (ܕܡ̈ܥܐ) and kisses (ܢܘܫ̈ܩܬܐ) of the sinful woman 'her bruises were healed'.[232] The term ܚܒ̈ܪܬܗ̇ describes the sinful state of this woman; it does not refer to the corporal wounds, but rather to her moral and spiritual situation. Viginity 3.10 clarifies that ܚܒ̈ܪܬܗ̇ can be used for inner spiritual and psychological wounds: 'penitence heals through its constancy our bruises'.[233] In this context ܚܒ̈ܪܬܐ is equivalent to 'pains' (ܟܐ̈ܒܐ). Hymn 22 On the Nativity accounts ܚܒ̈ܪܬܐ among ܚܫ̈ܐ and ܟܐ̈ܒܐ.[234] In Fid

---

227 Fid 5.19.

228 Cf. J. P. Smith, *A Compendious Syriac Dictionary*, 125.

229 Cf. R. P. Smith, *Thesaurus Syriacus* I, 1185. The Hebrew has the same term חבורה; the Greek term is ελκος, 'wound, sore, ulcer'.

230 Dom 42; 44; Nat 3.20; 22.1; Virg 3.10; Fid 5.19; Eccl 5.6.

231 Dom 42; 44; Nat 3.20; Virg 3.10.

232 Dom 42: ܗܝ ܕܒܕܡ̈ܥܐ ܐܬܐܣܝ ܚܒ̈ܪܬܗ̇; Dom 44: ܘܒܢܘܫ̈ܩܬܗ̇ ܐܣܐ ܚܒ̈ܪܬܗ̇.

233 Virg 3.10: ܬܝܒܘܬܐ ܡܐܣܝܐ ܒܐܡܝܢܘܬܗ̇ ܠܚܒ̈ܪܬܢ.

234 Nat 22.1.

5.19, the terms ܫܘܡ̈ܬܐ and ܟܘܬܡ̈ܬܐ[235] are also mentioned to emphasise the moral wounds and pains of ܫܚܩ̈ܬܐ.[236] Even though ܫܚܩ̈ܬܐ is related to ܠܘܫܒܐ in Fid 5.19 and to ܦܓܪܐ in Eccl 5.6, it does not lose its spiritual sense. The 'Physician' (ܐܣܝܐ) Who came down from heaven 'healed the bruises' (ܘܐܣܝ ܫܚܩ̈ܬܐ)[237] which implies wounds caused by sin, death or Satan.

### *3.1.6.2 The Term* ܬܡܣܘܬܐ

The word ܬܡܣܘܬܐ, which means 'putrefaction, decay, rottenness, stink, pus and matter'[238] is not found in the Syriac biblical concordances,though the verb ܡܣܐ is often used.[239] This usually refers to flesh, body or physical limbs, in the sense 'to putrefy, melt and waste'.[240] The heart (ܠܒܐ)[241] and eyes (ܥܝ̈ܢܐ)[242] appear as the object of ܡܣܐ. Ezekiel uses ܡܣܐ twice together with [243] ܥܘܠܐ which implies that sin is the reason for ܡܣܐ.

Ephrem uses ܬܡܣܘܬܐ in the context of healing on several occasions. Epiph 8 uses examples from the Bible that symbolise baptism: Epiph 8.22 reminds us of Joshua, the son of Nun, who cursed the water of Jericho (cf. Jos 6:26); in turn, as a symbol of Jesus the water was blessed and healed, as the 'salt tears'[244] from

---

[235] The term ܟܘܬܡ̈ܬܐ which refers to the physical as well as spiritual 'stains' or 'marks' is often used with the verb ܚܘܪ; for example in Dom 44: ܕܚܘ̈ܒܘܗܝ ܚܘܪ ܟܘܬܡ̈ܬܐ ܘܒܘܫܚ̈ܬܗ ܐܝܟ ܐܣܝܐ ܫܚܩ̈ܬܗ. Further see Dom 2; Fid 5.19; Eccl 26.1; 31.7; CDiat 10.8; Epiph 5.7-8; Parad 4.5.

[236] Fid 5.19.

[237] Nat 3.20.

[238] Cf. J. P. Smith, *A Compendious Syriac Dictionary*, 615.

[239] Cf. 2 Sam 17:10; Sa 14:12; Jb 7:5; 10:10; Is 13:7; 19:3; 34:3-4; Ez 4:17; 17:9; 21:7; 24:11; 24:23; 33:10; Act 28:6.

[240] Sa 14:12: ܬܬܡܣܐ ܒܣܪܗܘܢ ܘܠܫܢܗܘܢ ܬܬܡܣܐ ܒܦܘܡܗܘܢ.

[241] Is 13:7; 19:1; Ez 21:7.

[242] Sa 14:12.

[243] Ez 17:9; 24:3.

[244] For 'salt' as 'dissolving' (ܡܕܝܒܬ) pus, see Aphr 23.49.

Mary 'were mixed with the water, and so the pus of our wickness flowed away (cf. 2 Kgs 2:20-22).[245] The abstract term ܡܚܝܠܘܬܢ implies the metaphorical sense of ܬܡܣܘܬܢ, so that the pus here is not physical, but spiritual. This is also the case in Nis 11, where Ephrem presents divine justice as a physician: 'its sharp medicine consumed the pus with its strong love.'[246] Likewise, in Eccl 52.4 the Lord is described as 'a pure Physician Who descends towards the ulcer so that His purity will heal the pus.'[247] Here the ܬܡܣܘܬܐ which needs a physician to heal it is linked with ܫܘܚܢܐ.[248] The term ܢܟܦܘܬܗ contrasts with ܛܢܦܘܬܐ, which is compared to ܬܡܣܘܬܐ. Thus, the healing of ܬܡܣܘܬܐ is similar to the act of purification. Ephrem emphasises the purity of God in contrast to the impurity of man, as he also does in Haer 33. The word ܬܡܣܘܬܐ, along with ܟܪܝܗܘܬܐ, ܟܐܒܐ, ܟܘܪ̈ܗܢܐ, ܫܒ̈ܪܬܐ and ܟܐ̈ܒܐ, describes the impurity of man (i.e in the sense of ܣܪܝܘܬܐ) that God wants to heal and purify. This action of healing and cleansing is related to the 'pure Physician' (ܐܣܝܐ ܢܟܦܐ), 'glorious Physician' (ܐܣܝܐ ܓܐܝܐ), and to the 'Medicine of Life' (ܣܡ ܚܝ̈ܐ). It is always this Physician Who approaches the ܬܡܣܘܬܐ to heal it.[249]

### *3.1.6.3 The Term* ܢܟ̈ܝܢܐ

The word ܢܟܝܢܐ is worth mentioning as Ephrem uses it in the context of healing, even though it is not a technical term for sickness, illness, or disease. The term ܢܟܝܢܐ can mean 'harm, hurt, damage, injury, pain and destruction'.[250] There is no particular biblical passage that links ܢܟܝܢܐ immediately with healing imagery.

---

245 Epiph 8.22.

246 Nis 11.5: ܣܡܗ ܚܪܝܦܐ ܒܚܘܒܗ ܥܫܝܢܐ ܐܟܠ ܬܡܣܘܬܐ.

247 Eccl 52.4: ܐܣܝܐ ܢܟܦܐ ܕܡܬܬܚܬܐ ܠܘܬ ܫܘܚܢܐ ܕܬܐܣܐ ܬܡܣܘܬܐ ܢܟܦܘܬܗ.

248 The term ܫܘܚܢܐ is only here (Eccl 52.4) to be found in the context of healing.

249 Cf. Haer 33.9-11.

250 Cf. J. P. Smith, *A Compendious Syriac Dictionary*, 339.

The Peshitta provides the verb ܢܟܐ with subjects, such as ܐܝܠܝܢ ܕܚܛܝܢ (Pr 8:36), ܚܠܐ (Pr 10:26), ܡܛܠܢܐ (Sa 3:1), ܒܝܫܐ (Act 10:38) and ܫܘܒܐ ܘܫܡܫܐ (Is 49:10). Apart from ܫܘܒܐ ܘܫܡܫܐ (Is 49:10) all the other passages imply spiritual harm through sinful deeds through the influence of evil. In Gal 5:17, ܒܣܪܐ and ܪܘܚܐ are contrasted as two rivals who 'harm' each other.[251]

Without referring to the biblical passages mentioned above or other verses using the verb ܢܟܐ, Ephrem uses the term ܢܟܝܢܐ; mainly in the plural to mean spiritual harm. In Virg 4.5, he speaks of 'healing of all hurts' (ܠܐܣܝܘܬܐ ܕܟܠ ܢܟܝ̈ܢܝܢ). This hymn compares 'oil' (ܡܫܚܐ) with 'Christ' (ܡܫܝܚܐ). The former naturally signifies the invisibility of the latter. As the oil naturally heals many kinds of physical 'hurts' (ܢܟܝ̈ܢܐ), and the people are 'healed' through it, so Jesus too was healing while He 'was driving out all hurts'.[252] ܟܠ ܢܟܝ̈ܢܐ is the object that needs to be 'driven out' and 'healed'. In Fid 15.7 the verb ܢܟܐ (in af'el) clearly contrasts with ܐܣܝ: the sick limb (i.e. the Arian) either 'will be healed' (ܬܬܐܣܐ) or 'will harm the whole body ( ܢܟܐ ܠܟܠܗ ܠܦܓܪܐ). In Eccl 25.8 ܢܟܝ̈ܢܐ and ܟܐܒܐ refer to the same thing: if the physician heals the ܟܐܒܐ, the hurt goes immediately. The source of the ܢܟܝ̈ܢܐ is nothing other than 'our evilness' (ܒܝܫܘܬܢ) which causes the ܢܟܝ̈ܢܐ, as well as the visible and invisible ܟܐ̈ܒܐ.[253] Finally, also Nis 11, uses ܢܟܝ̈ܢܐ in parallel to ܟܐ̈ܒܐ that can be healed by divine justice and mercy.[254]

---

251 Gal 5:17: ܒܣܪܐ ܓܝܪ ܪܓܐ ܡܕܡ ܕܢܟܐ ܠܪܘܚܐ. ܘܪܘܚܐ ܪܓܐ ܡܕܡ ܕܢܟܐ ܠܒܣܪܐ.

252 Virg 4.7: ܘܪܕܦ ܗܘܐ ܟܠ ܢܟܝ̈ܢܝܢ.

253 Eccl 32.1.

254 Nis 11.3-4.

#### *3.1.6.4 Some Important Terms that are seldom used*

There are a few terms left which Ephrem uses occasionally. Firstly, the word ܫܘܚܢܐ appears only once in Ecclesia 52.4 in the context of healing. It is used as the object towards which the 'pure Physician' (ܐܣܝܐ ܕܟܝܐ) descends. The term ܫܘܚܢܐ has the sense of the 'ulcer' that has ܬܡܣܘܬܐ and so needs to be cleansed.[255]

Secondly, the term ܫܘ̈ܡܬܐ[256] is found in hymn 46 On Virginity and 5 On Faith. The former hymn speaks of the 'imprint of scars' (ܪܘܫܡ ܫܘ̈ܡܬܐ)[257] in the sense that the sins committed before baptism are easily forgiven, but those after need greater effort. Even though sins committed after being baptised can be forgiven and the wounds healed, a mark of the wounded place will stay like an 'imprint of scars'.[258] On Faith 5.19 refers ܫܘ̈ܡܬܐ to ܢܦܫܐ when Ephrem speaks of ܫܘ̈ܡܬܐ ܕܢܦܫܢ in parallel to ܡܚ̈ܘܬܐ ܕܒܠܒܘܫܢ and ܫܘ̈ܡܬܬܐ ܒܪܘܫܢ.[259]

Finally, the term ܣܠܪܝܬܐ is used once in Nis 34.5 where Ephrem describes Egypt as a sick land and Harran as afflicted with a 'gangrene' (ܣܠܪܝܬܐ) that can not be healed; for even though its wound is healed, it will return again.[260]

## 3.2 Terms Related to Healing

Concerning healing the most significant terms are those based on the following roots: ܐܣܐ, 'to heal', ܣܡܡ, 'to give medicine', ܐܬܚܠܡ, 'to be restored', ܚܒܫ, 'to bind up', and ܣܥܪ, 'to visit'.

---

[255] Eccl 52.4.

[256] Lev 13:2-43 and 14:56 are typical passages where ܫܘܡܬܐ, in singular and not plural, is frequently used. Also Is 1:6; 53:5 and 1 Pet 2:24 employ the term ܫܘܡܬܐ.

[257] Virg 46.25; 46.27.

[258] Virg 46.21-27.

[259] Fid 5.19.

[260] Nis 34.5.

### 3.2.1 ܐܣܝ and Related Terms

#### *3.2.1.1 In the Syriac Bible*

The verb 'to heal' (ܐܣܝ) appears often in the Bible. The *paʿʿel* ܐܣܝ is mainly used in the context of the Lord's action.[261] Already in Gen 20:17, God (ܐܠܗܐ) occurs as the subject of ܐܣܝ, and humankind as object, such as the healing of Abimelech, the prophetess Miriam and the People. The Lord heals as a result of prayer.[262] In 2 Kgs 20:5, the Lord heard Hezekiah's prayer and promised to heal him from his sickness.[263] Prayer, as well as repentance and the whole way of life,[264] has a significant role in the context of healing and wounding. The subject of ܐܣܝ can also be the 'hands' of the Lord (ܐܝܕܘܗܝ), as in Job 5:18: where the verb ܟܐܒܐ is contrasted with ܐܣܝ, as ܬܒܪ with ܚܒܫ.[265]

---

[261] Gen 20:17; Num 12:13; Dt 32:39; 2 Kgs 2:21; 20:5; 20:8; 2 Chr 7:14; 30:20; Pr 14:23; Job 5:18; Is 19:22; 30:26; 57:18-19; Jer 3:22; 17:14; 30:13; 30:16(17); 33:6; Hos 6:1; 7:1; 11:3; 14:4(5).

[262] Gen 20:17: 'And Abraham prayed in the presence of God, and God healed Abimelech, his wife and his slave girls' ( ܘܨܠܝ ܐܒܪܗܡ ܩܕܡ ܐܠܗܐ: ܘܐܣܝ ܐܠܗܐ ܠܐܒܝܡܠܟ ܘܠܐܢܬܬܗ ܘܠܐܡܗܬܗ). In Num 12:13, Moses asked God to heal his sister Miriam from her leprosy, and she was healed: ܘܐܡܪ ܒܥܘ ܐܠܗܐ ܐܣܝܗ̇. In 2 Chr 30:20, the Lord heard Hezekiah, and 'He healed the People' (ܘܐܣܝܗ ܠܥܡܐ).

[263] 2 Kgs 20:5: ܫܡܥܬ ܨܠܘܬܟ ܘܚܙܝܬ ܕܡܥܝܟ ܗܐ ܡܐܣܐ ܐܢܐ ܠܟ; cf. 2 Kgs 20:8: ܡܢܐ ܗܝ ܐܬܐ ܕܡܐܣܐ ܠܝ ܡܪܝܐ.

[264] Is 57:18-19: ܐܘܪܚܬܗ ܚܙܝܬ: ܘܐܣܝܬܗ ܘܐܒܝܬܗ. ܘܦܪܥܬ ܒܘܝܐܐ ܠܗ ܘܠܐܒܝܠܘܗܝ. ܒܪܬ ܡܡܠܠܐ ܕܣܦܘܬܐ. ܫܠܡܐ. ܫܠܡܐ: ܠܪܚܝܩܐ ܘܠܩܪܝܒܐ ܐܡܪ ܡܪܝܐ. ܘܐܐܣܐ ܐܢܘܢ. In Hos 6:1, the prophet appeals to the Israelites: 'Come, let us return to the Lord; He has torn us to pieces but He will heal us' ( ܘܐܡܪܘܢ ܢܗܦܘܟ ܠܘܬ ܡܪܝܐ ܕܚܛܦ: ܘܗܘ ܢܐܣܝܢ: ܘܡܚܢ: ܘܗܘ ܢܚܒܫܢ ), and later in, Hos 14:4(5), the Lord says: 'I will heal their backsliding' (ܐܐܣܐ ܬܘܬܒܘܬܗܘܢ), as in Jer 3:22: ܬܘܒܘ ܒܢܝܐ ܬܘܒܢܐ ܘܐܐܣܐ ܬܘܬܒܘܬܗܘܢ.

[265] Job 5:18.

The object of healing can be the nation Israel,[266] Zion,[267] 'their land' (ܐܪܥܗܘܢ)[268] the 'water' (ܡ̈ܝܐ)[269] or 'me'.[270] The object of ܐܣܝ can also be 'every pain' (ܟܠ ܟܐܒ),[271] or even the pain of the wound inflicted by the Lord (ܘܟܐܒܐ ܕܡܚܘܬܗ ܢܐܣܐ).[272] Thus, the Lord is not just the agent of ܐܣܝ, but also of ܡܚܐ, 'to strike/wound'. In Dt 32:39, the Lord says: 'I am He Who wounds, and I am He Who heals.'[273] In Is 19:22, ܐܣܝ refers to the Egyptians whom the Lord will 'strike and heal'; in contrast to the Israelites, 'they will turn to the Lord, and He will respond to them and heal them'.[274] Nevertheless, the Lord promises to heal His People.[275]

Beside the Lord, certain people also appear as the agent of ܐܣܝ; for example, the prophet Elisha healed Naaman from his leprosy,[276] or Sheerah who 'healed the sick', among whom was Ladan the son of Ammihud.[277] Likewise, the shepherds may be the

---

[266] Hos 7:1: ܟܕ ܐܣܝܬ ܠܐܝܣܪܝܠ.

[267] Jer 30:13: ܘܠܝܬ ܕܕܐܢ ܕܝܢܟܝ ܠܟܘܪܗܢܝܟܝ ܘܐܣܝܘܬܟܝ ; Jer 30:16(17): ܘܡܢ ܡܚܘܬܟܝ ܐܣܝܟܝ ܐܡܪ ܡܪܝܐ.

[268] 2 Chr 7:14: ܘܐܫܒܘܩ ܠܚܛܗܝܗܘܢ ܘܐܐܣܐ ܐܪܥܗܘܢ.

[269] 2 Kgs 2:21: ܐܣܝܬ ܠܡ̈ܝܐ ܗܠܝܢ.

[270] Jer 17:14: ܐܣܝܢܝ ܡܪܝܐ ܘܐܬܐܣܐ.

[271] Pr 14:23.

[272] Is 30:26.

[273] Dt 32:39: ܐܢܐ ܡܚܐ ܘܐܢܐ ܡܐܣܐ ܐܢܐ. In Hos 11:3, even though God heals with love, yet the Israelites 'did not realise that I had healed them' (ܘܠܐ ܝܕܥܘ ܕܐܣܝܬ ܐܢܘܢ).

[274] Is 19:22: ܘܢܡܚܐ ܡܪܝܐ ܠܡܨܪ̈ܝܐ ܒܡܚܘܬܐ: ܘܢܐܣܐ ܐܢܘܢ. ܘܢܬܦܢܘܢ ܠܘܬ ܡܪܝܐ: ܘܢܥܢܐ ܐܢܘܢ: ܘܢܐܣܐ ܐܢܘܢ.

[275] Jer 33:6: ܘܐܣܐ ܐܢܘܢ ܘܐܓܠܐ ܠܗܘܢ.

[276] 2 Kgs 5:3-7.

[277] 1 Chr 7:24-26: ܘܒܪܬܗ ܕܐܬܚܫܒܬ ܥܡ ܣܘܪܢ ܬܚܬܝܬܐ ܘܥܠܝܬܐ: ܘܚܠܡܗܘܢ ܗܠܝܢ ܕܐܬܚܫܒܬ: ܐܣܝܬ ܒܪܬܗ. ܟܠܗܘܢ ܕܐܣܝܘܬܐ ܗܘܬ ܘܒܐܣܝܘܬ ܒܪ̈ܝܗܘܢ. ܘܐܣܝܬ ܠܠܥܕܢ ܒܪ ܥܡܝܗܘܕ (there is nothing about healing in the Hebrew original). In turn, in Jer 6:14 and 8:11, the prophets and priests, who should be able to heal, ignore their duties; Jer 6:14: ܘܡܐܣܝܢ ܠܬܒܪܐ ܕܒܪܬ ܥܡܝ ܒܒܨܝܪܐ.

subject of ܐܣܐ if they take their responsibility seriously, but often they do not.[278] In the same way, because of the Lord's judgment against Israel, a king 'is not able to heal' the sickness and sores of Ephraim,[279] and the people cannot heal Babylon.[280] Job calls his friends Zophar, Bildad and Eliphaz those 'who heal without anything' (ܘܡܐܣܝܢ ܒܠܐ ܡܕܡ ܐܢܬܘܢ)[281] for they blame him without a real reason.

As wisdom is supreme in the book of the Proverbs, its words are able 'to heal the whole flesh/body';[282] and the 'tongue of the wise heals'[283] too.

While the *ethpaʿʿal* ܐܬܐܣܝ appears more often in the context of humankind, it is only used once in the context of 'water' that has been healed/cured,[284] It is used four times in Leviticus, in the context of the regulations about infectious skin diseases, such as 'ulcer' (ܫܘܚܢܐ),[285] 'wound' (ܡܚܘܬܐ)[286] or 'leprosy's wound' (ܡܚܘܬܐ ܕܓܪܒܐ).[287] It appears in the context of individual people being healed from their sickness, such as 'Naaman from his leprosy'[288] and 'Joram from the wound'[289] - even though he was not healed. It can also apply to a whole nation, such as those who were

---

278 Ez 34:4: ܠܟܪ̈ܝܗܐ ܠܐ ܚܠܡܬܘܢ ܘܠܬܒ̈ܝܪܐ ܠܐ ܐܣܝܬܘܢ; cf. Sa 11:16: ܘܠܬܒ̈ܝܪܗܝܢ ܠܐ ܢܐܣܐ.

279 Hos 5:13: ܘܗܘ ܠܐ ܡܫܟܚ ܠܡܐܣܝܘܬܟܘܢ.

280 Jer 51:9: ܐܣܝܢܢ ܠܒܒܠ ܘܠܐ ܐܬܐܣܝܬ ܫܒܘܩܝܗ ܘܢܐܙܠ ܓܒܪ ܠܐܪܥܗ.

281 Job 13:4.

282 Pr 4:22: ܘܒܣܪܗ ܟܠܗ ܡܐܣܝܐ.

283 Pr 12:18: ܐܝܬ ܕܐܡܪܝܢ ܣܝܦܐ ܕܓܙܐ: ܠܫܢܐ ܕܝܢ ܕܚܟܝܡܐ ܡܐܣܝܐ.

284 2 Kgs 2:2: ܘܐܬܐܣܝܘ ܡܝ̈ܐ ܗܠܝܢ ܥܕܡܐ ܠܝܘܡܢܐ.

285 Lv 13:18: ܘܒܣܪܐ ܐܢ ܢܗܘܐ ܫܘܚܢܐ ܒܡܫܟܗ ܘܢܬܐܣܐ.

286 Lv 13:37: ܘܡܣܒܪܐ ܐܘܒܕܢܐ ܠܝܬ ܒܗ ܡܬܐܣܝܐ ܡܚܘܬܐ; cf Lv 14:48: ܡܛܠ ܕܐܬܐܣܝܬ ܠܗ ܡܚܘܬܗ.

287 Lv 14:3: ܐܢ ܐܬܐܣܝܬ ܡܚܘܬܐ ܕܓܪܒܐ ܡܢ ܓܒܪܐ.

288 2 Kgs 5:11: ܘܐܬܐܣܐ ܡܢ ܓܪܒܐ.

289 2 Kgs 8:29: ܠܡܬܐܣܝܘ ܒܐܝܙܪܥܠ ܡܢ ܡܚܘܬܐ; cf. 2 Kgs 9:15; 2 Chr 22:6.

circumcised at Gilgal,[290] or those who returned the ark to Israel.[291] However, healing cannot be achieved against the Lord's will. For example, when the Lord had afflicted man with tumours and festering sores because of disobedience, those who were afflicted could not be healed;[292] or if the Lord afflicts the knees and legs, then neither can they be healed.[293] Likewise, Babylon could not be healed because the Lord had proclaimed His judgement about her.[294] Anything that is in disagreement with the Lord is unable to be healed,[295] but if it is in accordance with the Lord's will then it can be healed, as in Jer 17:14: 'Heal me, o Lord, and I shall be healed.'[296] Likewise, man can be healed through the Lord, as in Is 53:5: 'and by His wounds/sores we will be healed'.[297] But, as Jer 15:18 emphasises, the wound would not be healed if it does not want to be healed: 'my wound is grievous and does not want to be healed'.[298]

The term ܐܣܝܐ, singular, is used twice in Exodus (Ex 15:26; 21:19), Proverbs (Pr 13:17; 14:30), Jeremiah (Jer 8:22; 33:6) and once in 1 Chr 7:25. In the latter, Sheerah is the only woman who is called 'physician' (ܐܣܝܬܐ)[299] Her function is described as healing sick people (ܘܡܐܣܝܬ ܟܪ̈ܝܗܝܢ). While Ex 21:19 speaks of an ordinary physician and his reward in the context of personal injuries,[300] Ex 15:26 presents the Lord as 'your Physician'

---

[290] Is 5:8: 'were in camp until they were healed' ( ܒܡܫܪܝܬܐ ܥܕܡܐ ܕܐܬܐܣܝܘ).

[291] 1 Sm 6:3: ܘܗܝܕܝܢ ܬܬܐܣܘܢ ܘܢܬܝܕܥ ܠܟܘܢ.

[292] Dt 28:27: ܘܒܛܘܪ̈ܐ ܘܒܓܪ̈ܒܐ ܘܒܫܚܢܐ ܕܠܐ ܬܫܟܚ ܠܡܬܐܣܝܘ.

[293] Dt 28:35: ܕܠܐ ܬܫܟܚ ܠܡܬܐܣܝܘ.

[294] Jer 51:8-9: ܐܝܠܠܘ ܥܠܝܗ̇ ܣܒܘ ܣܡ̈ܡܢܐ ܠܟܐܒܝܗ̇ ܕܠܡ ܬܬܐܣܐ ܐܣܝܢܗ̇ ܠܒܒܠ ܘܠܐ ܐܬܐܣܝܬ.

[295] Jer 19:11: ܕܬܘܒ ܠܐ ܡܫܟܚ ܠܡܬܐܣܝܘ.

[296] Jer 17:14: ܐܣܝܢܝ ܡܪܝܐ ܘܐܬܐܣܐ.

[297] Is 53:5: ܘܒܫܘ̈ܡܒܬܗ ܢܬܐܣܐ.

[298] Jer 15:18: ܘܡܚܘܬܝ ܚܒܝܫܐ ܘܠܐ ܨܒܝܐ ܠܡܬܐܣܝܘ.

[299] 1 Chr 7:25: ܡܛܠ ܕܐܣܝܬܐ ܗܘܬ ܘܡܐܣܝܬ ܟܪ̈ܝܗܝܢ.

[300] Ex 21:19: ܐܢ ܢܩܘܡ ܘܢܗܠܟ ܒܫܘܩܐ ܥܠ ܚܘܛܪܗ: ܙܟܐ ܡܢ ܕܡܚܝܗܝ. ܒܠܚܘܕ ܒܛܠܢܗ ܘܐܓܪ ܐܣܝܐ ܢܬܠ.

(ܐܣܝܟ)[301] Who will heal mankind if they are obedient, follow His commands and decrees, and do what is right in the eyes of the Lord. In Jer 8:22, the Lord asks the question: is there no 'physician' in Gilead to heal the 'wound of My People'?[302] Here the Lord does not describe Himself as the 'Physician', but wants to call someone to act as a physician on His behalf, as in Jer 33:6: 'I will bring health and healing to [Babylon]'.[303] The book of Proverbs calls a physician a 'trustworthy messenger' (ܘܐܝܙܓܕܐ ܡܗܝܡܢܐ),[304] and he who 'calms his wrath is the physician of his heart'.[305]

The plural ܐܣܘ̈ܬܐ, 'physicians', is used only twice; in Gen 50:2, in the context of the death of Joseph's father Jacob/Israel, 'Joseph directed the physicians in his service to embalm his father Israel; so the physicians embalmed him'.[306] The function of these ordinary physicians in Egypt is described as 'embalming' (ܚܢܛ) the dead person.

In the Old Testament, the derived noun ܐܣܝܘܬܐ appears in different contexts, often in a negative sense, such as in 2 Chr 36:16: 'the wrath of the Lord rose up against His People until they did not have any (source of) healing (ܐܣܝܘ) more'.[307] Jehoram was badly afflicted with disease so that there would not be any (further possibility of) 'healing' (ܐܣܝܘܬܐ)[308] The reason is the sin and the 'wound' (ܡܚܘܬܐ), as Lam 4:3 speaks of a 'wound

301 Ex 15:26: ܡܛܠ ܕܐܢܐ ܐܢܐ ܡܪܝܐ ܐܣܝܟ.

302 Jer 8:22: ܐܘ ܐܣܝܐ ܠܝܬ ܬܡܢ.

303 Jer 33:6: ܗܐ ܡܣܩ ܐܢܐ ܠܗ̇ ܠܘܠܟܪܐ ܐܣܝܐ ܘܐܣܐ ܐܢܘܢ.

304 Pr 13:17: ܘܐܝܙܓܕܐ ܡܗܝܡܢܐ ܐܣܝܐ ܗܘ.

305 Pr 14:30: ܕܡܟܝܟ ܚܡܬܗ ܐܣܝܐ ܗܘ ܕܠܒܗ ܘܣܘܣܐ ܕܓܪ̈ܡܐ ܛܢܢܐ ܗܘ.

306 Gen 50:2: ܘܦܩܕ ܝܘܣܦ ܠܥܒܕܘ̈ܗܝ ܐܣܘ̈ܬܐ ܠܡܚܢܛ ܠܐܒܘܗܝ ܘܚܢܛܘܗܝ ܐܣܘ̈ܬܐ ܠܐܝܣܪܝܠ.

307 2 Chr 36:16: ܘܗܘܘ ܡܒܙܚܝܢ ܥܠ ܡܠܐܟܘ̈ܗܝ ܕܡܪܝܐ ܘܡܒܣܪܝܢ ܥܠ ܡܠܘ̈ܗܝ. ܘܡܒܙܚܝܢ ܥܠ ܢܒܝܘ̈ܗܝ. ܥܕܡܐ ܕܣܠܩܬ ܚܡܬܗ ܕܡܪܝܐ ܒܥܡܗ: ܥܕܡܐ ܠܐܝܟܐ ܕܠܐ ܗܘܬ ܠܗܘܢ ܐܣܝܘ; cf. Lam 4:3; Pr 6:15; 29:1; Is 13:9; Jer 8:15; 8:22; 14:19; 46:11; Ez 30:21.

308 2 Chr 21:18: ܡܢ ܒܬܪ ܟܠܗܝܢ ܗܠܝܢ ܡܚܘܬܐ ܬܗܘܐ ܒܟܪܣܗ. ܘܒܟܘܪܗܢܐ ܡܣܟܢܐ ܢܒܠܬ. ܘܐܣܝܘܬܐ ܠܐ ܬܗܘܐ ܠܗ.

that does not have (the possibility of) healing' ( ܠܡܚܘܬܐ ܕܠܝܬ ܠܗ ܐܣܝܘܬܐ).[309] The reason for no longer being curable can be sin,[310] as well as the way of life,[311] being foolish[312] and stiff-necked.[313]

The term ܐܣܝܘܬܐ that contrasts with the verb ܬܒܪ[314] or the terms 'wound' (ܡܚܘܬܐ)[315] 'sickness' (ܟܘܪܗܢܐ)[316] 'grief' (ܟܘܬܐ)[317] and 'fear' (ܕܚܠܬܐ),[318] can also refer to individual people, such as to Jehoram;[319] as well as to a nation[320] and time, such as the 'day of the Lord' (ܝܘܡܗ ܕܡܪܝܐ).[321] It can also refer to different limbs of the body, such as 'your flesh/body' (ܒܣܪܟ),[322] 'tongue' (ܠܫܢܐ),[323] 'his bones' (ܠܓܪ̈ܡܘܗܝ)[324] and 'his arm' (ܕܪܥܗ).[325]

Nevertheless, it is the Lord Who promises and is able to cause ܐܣܝܘܬܐ 'to ascend' for Zion,[326] for on His day 'the sun of

---

309 Lam 4:3: ܟܠ ܐܝܟ ܬܢܝܢܐ ܬܕܡܝܢ: ܘܐܝܟ ܠܒ̈ܢܝܗܘܢ. ܗܘܬ ܒܪܬ ܥܡܝ ܠܡܚܘܬܐ ܕܠܝܬ ܠܗ ܐܣܝܘܬܐ: ܘܐܝܟ ܢܥܡܐ ܒܡܕܒܪܐ.

310 2 Chr 21:18; Is 13:9; Jer 8:15; 8:22; 14:19.

311 Pr 3:8.

312 Pr 6:15.

313 Pr 29:1.

314 Pr 6:15: Pr 29:1; Ez 30:21.

315 2 Chr 21:18; Lam 4:3; Jer 30:16(17); Jer 14:19 has the verb ܡܚܝܬܢ.

316 2 Chr 21:18.

317 Jer 8:15.

318 Jer 14:19.

319 2 Chr 21:18; see further Pr 6:15; Pr 29:1; Ez 30:21.

320 2 Chr 36:16; Lam 4:3; Jer 8:22; 14:19; 30:16(17); 46:11.

321 Is 13:9; Jer 8:15 and 14:19 speak of ܙܒܢܐ ܕܐܣܝܘܬܐ.

322 Pr 3:8.

323 Pr 15:4. In Ml 4:2: ܘܐܣܝܘܬܐ ܥܠ ܠܫܢܗ refers to the ܫܡܫܐ ܕܙܕܝܩܘܬܐ; see page 232, n.2.

324 Pr 16:24.

325 Ez 30:21.

326 Jer 30:16(17).

righteousness will rise, and healing on its tongue'.[327] In turn, Is 13:9 emphasises the lack of healing on the day of the Lord when He will destroy Babylon and its sinners.[328] However, ܐܣܝܘܬܐ is able to forgive many sins.[329] Pr 3:8 employs the fear of God as a way to result in 'healing for your flesh' (ܐܣܝܘܬܐ ܠܒܣܪܟ);[330] whereas Pr 15:4 describes the 'healing of the tongue' (ܐܣܝܘܬܐ ܕܠܫܢܐ) as a tree of life,[331] and Pr 16:24 compares the 'words of a wise person' to a honeycomb that is 'healing for his bones' ( ܐܣܝܘܬܐ ܗܝ ܠܓܪ̈ܡܘܗܝ).[332] Ez 47:12 speaks of a river from the temple and fruits and leaves; while the fruits will serve for food and 'their leaves for the process of healing' (ܘܛܪ̈ܦܝܗܘܢ ܠܐܣܝܘܬܐ); this image is taken over in Rev 22:2.[333]

In the New Testament (apart from Rev 22:2), the singular ܐܣܝܘܬܐ is used three times in 1 Cor (12:9; 12:28; 12:30) and once each in Acts 4:22 and Lk 9:11. In the latter passage Jesus heals those in need of ܐܣܝܘܬܐ, while talking to the crowds about the kingdom of God. Jesus combines teaching with healing.[334] In Acts 4:22, ܐܣܝܘܬܐ appears in the passage of the healing of the

---

[327] Ml 4:2: ܘܬܕܢܚ ܠܟܘܢ ܠܕܚܠܝ ܫܡܝ ܫܡܫܐ ܕܙܕܝܩܘܬܐ: ܘܐܣܝܘܬܐ ܥܠ ܠܫܢܗ: ܘܬܦܩܘܢ ܘܬܕܝܫܘܢ ܐܝܟ ܥܓ̈ܠܐ ܕܒܩܪܐ.

[328] Is 13:9: ܗܐ ܝܘܡܗ ܕܡܪܝܐ ܐܬܐ: ܕܐܣܝܘ ܠܝܬ ܠܗ. ܐܬܐ ܘܚܡܬܐ ܘܪܘܓܙܗ. ܕܢܚܪܒܝܗ̇ ܠܐܪܥܐ ܠܚܘܪܒܐ: ܘܚܛܝ̈ܗ̇ ܢܘܒܕ ܡܢܗ̇.

[329] Ec 10:4: ܐܢ ܪܘܚܐ ܕܫܠܝܛܐ ܬܣܩ ܥܠܝܟ: ܐܬܪܟ ܠܐ ܬܫܒܘܩ. ܡܛܠ ܕܐܣܝܘܬܐ ܫܒܩܐ ܣܟܠ̈ܘܬܐ ܣܓܝ̈ܐܬܐ.

[330] pr 3:8: ܠܐ ܬܗܘܐ ܚܟܝܡ ܒܥܝ̈ܢܝ ܢܦܫܟ. ܐܠܐ ܕܚܠ ܡܢ ܡܪܝܐ ܘܣܛܝ ܡܢ ܒܝܫܬܐ. ܕܬܗܘܐ ܐܣܝܘܬܐ ܠܒܣܪܟ.

[331] Pr 15:4: ܐܣܝܘܬܐ ܕܠܫܢܐ: ܐܝܠܢܐ ܗܝ ܕܚܝ̈ܐ ܘܐܟܠ ܡܢ ܦܐܪ̈ܘܗܝ: ܢܣܒܥ ܡܢܗ.

[332] Pr 16:24: ܟܘܪ̈ܬܐ ܕܕܒܫܐ ܡܐܡܪ̈ܘܗܝ ܕܚܟܝܡܐ: ܘܚܠܝܐ ܗܝ ܠܢܦܫܗ: ܘܐܣܝܘܬܐ ܗܝ ܠܓܪ̈ܡܘܗܝ.

[333] Ez 47:12: ܢܗܘܘܢ ܦܐܪ̈ܝܗܘܢ ܠܡܐܟܠܐ ܘܛܪ̈ܦܝܗܘܢ ܠܐܣܝܘܬܐ; cf. Rev 22:2: ܘܛܪ̈ܦܘܗܝ ܠܐܣܝܘܬܐ ܕܥܡ̈ܡܐ.

[334] Lk 9:11: ܟܢ̈ܫܐ ܕܝܢ ܟܕ ܝܕܥܘ: ܐܙܠܘ ܒܬܪܗ. ܘܩܒܠ ܐܢܘܢ ܘܡܡܠܠ ܗܘܐ ܥܡܗܘܢ ܥܠ ܡܠܟܘܬܐ ܕܐܠܗܐ. ܘܠܐܝܠܝܢ ܕܣܢܝܩܝܢ ܗܘܘ ܠܐܣܝܘܬܐ ܡܐܣܐ ܗܘܐ.

crippled beggar (Act 3:1ff). The fact that he was healed by Peter is called a 'sign of healing' (ܐܬܐ ܕܐܣܝܘܬܐ).[335] The ܐܣܝܘܬܐ is from God, and His chosen disciples, like Peter, receive power to restore people to perfect health (Act 3:16; Act 4:9-30). Therefore, Paul speaks of the 'gifts of perfect healing' ( ܡܘܗ̈ܒܬܐ ܕܐܣܝܘܬܐ) that some believers receive from the Holy Spirit.[336]

The plural ܐܣܘ̈ܬܐ - not to be confused with ܐܣ̈ܘܬܐ, 'physicians', - is used twice in the Peshitta New Testament. In Lk 13:32, when some Pharisees warned Jesus to leave Jerusalem because Herod wanted to kill Him, Jesus replies: 'Go tell that fox, see I will drive out demons and perform healing-miracles (ܐܣܘ̈ܬܐ).[337] The terms 'healing' (ܐܣܝܘܬܐ) and 'healing-miracles' (ܐܣܘ̈ܬܐ) describe the essential work of Jesus who provides 'healing' or fulfils with His 'healing-miracles' what is lacking in human beings. Likewise, the Apostles performed 'healing-miracles' as signs and wonders in the name of the Lord, as Peter and John pray: 'and You [God] stretch out your hand for healing-miracles (ܐܣܘ̈ܬܐ) and mighty acts and signs to take place in the name of your holy Son Jesus'.[338]

The term ܐܣܝܐ, 'physician', is rarely used. In Mt 9:12 (par Mk 2:17), ܐܣܝܐ appears in in a proverbial saying: 'the healthy do

---

[335] Act 4:22: ܕܗܘܬ ܒܗ ܗܕܐ ܐܬܐ ܕܐܣܝܘܬܐ.

[336] 1 Cor 12:9: ܠܐܚܪܢܐ ܡܘܗ̈ܒܬܐ ܕܐܣܝܘܬܐ ܒܗ ܒܪܘܚܐ. Those who receive the 'gifts of healing' are appointed in the church by God, like the apostles, prophets, teachers and workers of miracles and signs (1 Cor 12:28-30). The function of those who have the gifts of healing is not explicitly defined, but probably is nothing other than being able to heal individual sick from their suffering in the name of the Lord.

[337] Lk 13:32: ܐܡܪ ܠܗܘܢ ܙܠܘ. ܐܡܪܘ ܠܗ ܠܬܥܠܐ ܗܢܐ ܕܗܐ ܡܦܩ ܐܢܐ ܫܐ̈ܕܐ. ܘܐܣܘ̈ܬܐ ܥܒܕ ܐܢܐ. This is the Peshitta version, whereas the Codex Sinaiticus and the Codex Curetonianus use the singular 'my healing' (ܐܣܝܘܬܝ) along with the verb 'to fulfill' ( ܡܫܠܡ ܐܢܐ ܐܣܝܘܬܝ).

[338] Act 4:30: ܘܐܝܕܟ ܦܫܘܛ ܐܢܬ ܠܐܣܘ̈ܬܐ ܘܠܚܝ̈ܠܘܬܐ ܘܠܐܬ̈ܘܬܐ: ܕܢܗܘܝܢ ܒܫܡܗ ܕܒܪܟ ܩܕܝܫܐ ܝܫܘܥ.

not need a physician'.[339] However, the need of a physician is mentioned in the second half of the verse: 'those who are suffering badly'.[340] The other passage, where ܐܣܝܐ is used, Jesus says: 'probably you will tell me this proverb, "physician heal yourself"'.[341] This seems imposible for an ordinary physician. Finally, in Col 4:14 Luke is called physician.[342]

The plural ܐܣܘ̈ܬܐ, 'physicians', is used in the context of the woman with the haemorrhage, in Mk 5:26 ( ܐܝܕܐ ܕܣܓܝ ܣܒܠܬ ܡܢ ܐܣܘ̈ܬܐ ܣܓܝܐܐ) and Lk 8:43 ( ܗܝ ܕܒܝܬ ܐܣܘ̈ܬܐ ܟܠܗ ܩܢܝܢܗ ܐܦܩܬ). The ordinary physicians on whom she spent all her money were not able to heal her. According to Mt 5:26, she actually suffered more because of them. These physicians contrast with Jesus who healed her, but He is not called Physician in the Gospel, apart from in the metaphorical phrase in Mt 9:12 and parallels (see above).

The verb ܐܣܝ, in *pa``el*, appears both in the Gospel and in the Acts is often used having as subject Jesus[343] or his apostles.[344] In Lk 5:17, the 'power of the Lord' (ܚܝܠܐ ܕܡܪܝܐ) is the agent of the infinitive of 'to heal' (ܠܡܐܣܝܘ).[345] Furthermore, the infinitive is used in the question about healing on the Sabbath: 'is it allowed to heal on the Sabbath'?[346] The subject of ܐܣܝ may also be the noun ܐܣܝܐ, 'physician', as in the phrase: 'physician heal yourself'.[347] The way of healing might be through the laying on of the hand, as

---

[339] Mt 9:12: ܠܐ ܣܢܝܩܝܢ ܚܠܝܡ̈ܐ ܥܠ ܐܣܝܐ; cf. Mk 2:17 and Lk 5:31: ܠܐ ܡܬܒܥܐ ܐܣܝܐ ܠܚܠܝܡ̈ܐ.

[340] Lk 5:31: ܐܠܐ ܠܐܝܠܝܢ ܕܒܝܫ ܒܝܫ ܥܒܝܕܝܢ; cf. Mt 9:12; Mk 2:17.

[341] Lk 4:23: ܒܪܡ ܬܐܡܪܘܢ ܠܝ ܡܬܠܐ ܗܢܐ: ܐܣܝܐ ܐܣܐ ܢܦܫܟ.

[342] Col 4:14: ܫܐܠ ܒܫܠܡܟܘܢ ܠܘܩܐ ܐܣܝܐ ܚܒܝܒܢ ܘܕܝܡܐ.

[343] Mt 4:24; 8:7: 8:16; 12:15; 12:22; 13:15; 14:14; 15:30; 19:2; 21:14; Mk 1:34; 3:2; 3:10; 6:5; Lk 4:18; 4:40; 6:7; 6:19; 7:21; 9:11; 9:34; 9:42; 13:14; 14:4; 22:51; Jn 4:47; 12:40.

[344] Mt 10:1; 10:8; 17:16; 17:19; Mk 3:15; 6:13; LK 9:1-2; 9:6; 10:9.

[345] Lk 5:17: ܘܚܝܠܐ ܕܡܪܝܐ ܐܝܬܘܗܝ ܗܘܐ ܠܡܐܣܝܘܬܗܘܢ.

[346] Lk 14:3; Mt 12:10: ܕܐܢ ܫܠܝܛ ܒܫܒܬܐ ܠܡܐܣܝܘ.

[347] Lk 4:23: ܐܣܝܐ ܐܣܐ ܢܦܫܟ.

Jesus did;[348] or through oil, like the apostles.[349] In the case of Jesus, the object of healing could be either general and not defined, or it refers to individual people He has healed: Aeneas,[350] the demon-possessed man,[351] the centurion's son[352] or the official's son,[353] the man with a shrivelled hand,[354] the boy with an evil spirit,[355] a leper,[356] and the ear of a servant of the high priest.[357] The following undefined objects could refer to any kind of healing that Jesus performed: 'them' (ܐܢܘܢ),[358] 'all of them' (ܠܟܠܗܘܢ),[359] 'many' (ܣܓܝܐܐ),[360] 'sick' (ܟܪܝܗܐ)[361] or 'their sick' (ܟܪܝܗܝܗܘܢ),[362] those of 'broken heart' (ܬܒܝܪܝ ܠܒܐ),[363] 'all those who were in need of healing' (ܠܐܝܠܝܢ ܕܣܢܝܩܝܢ ܗܘܘ ܠܐܣܝܘܬܐ)[364] and 'those who have been harmed by Evil' ( ܗܢܘܢ ܕܐܬܢܟܝܘ ܡܢ

---

348 Lk 4:40: ܐܝܕܗ ܣܐܡ ܗܘܐ ܘܡܐܣܐ; cf. Mk 6:5.

349 Mk 6:13: ܘܡܫܚܝܢ ܗܘܘ ܒܡܫܚܐ ܟܪܝܗܐ ܣܓܝܐܐ ܘܡܐܣܝܢ ܗܘܘ.

350 Act 9:34: ܘܐܡܪ ܠܗ ܫܡܥܘܢ: ܐܢܝܐ: ܡܐܣܐ ܠܟ ܝܫܘܥ ܡܫܝܚܐ.

351 Mt 12:22: ܗܝܕܝܢ ܩܪܒܘ ܠܗ ܕܝܘܐ ܚܕ ܕܚܪܫ ܘܣܡܐ ܘܐܣܝܗ.

352 Mt 8:7: ܐܡܪ ܠܗ ܝܫܘܥ: ܐܢܐ ܐܬܐ ܘܐܣܝܘܗܝ.

353 Jn 4:47: ܘܐܙܠ ܠܘܬܗ ܘܒܥܐ ܗܘܐ ܡܢܗ: ܕܢܚܘܬ ܘܢܐܣܐ ܠܒܪܗ.

354 Mk 3:2: ܘܢܛܪܝܢ ܗܘܘ ܠܗ ܕܐܢ ܡܐܣܐ ܠܗ ܒܫܒܬܐ.

355 Lk 9:42: ܘܟܐܐ ܝܫܘܥ ܒܪܘܚܐ ܗܝ ܛܢܦܬܐ: ܘܐܣܝܗ ܠܛܠܝܐ.

356 Lk 14:4: ܗܢܘܢ ܕܝܢ ܫܬܩܘ: ܘܐܚܕܗ ܗܘ ܘܐܣܝܗ ܘܫܪܝܗ.

357 Lk 22:51: ܘܩܪܒ ܠܐܕܢܗ ܕܗܘ ܕܐܬܚܒܠ ܘܐܣܝܗ.

358 Mt 4:24; 8:16; 13:15; 15:30; 19:2; 21:14; Jn 12:40.

359 Mt 12:15; Lk 6:19.

360 Mk 1:34; 3:10; Lk 7:21.

361 Mk 6:5: ܘܠܐ ܡܫܟܚ ܗܘܐ ܕܢܥܒܕ ܬܡܢ ܐܦ ܠܐ ܚܕ ܚܝܠܐ: ܐܠܐ ܐܢ ܕܥܠ ܟܪܝܗܐ ܩܠܝܠ ܣܡ ܐܝܕܗ ܘܐܣܝ.

362 Mt 14:14: ܘܢܦܩ ܝܫܘܥ ܚܙܐ ܟܢܫܐ ܣܓܝܐܐ ܘܐܬܪܚܡ ܥܠܝܗܘܢ ܘܐܣܝ ܟܪܝܗܝܗܘܢ.

363 Lk 4:18: ܘܫܠܚܢܝ ܠܡܐܣܝܘ ܠܬܒܝܪܝ ܠܒܐ.

364 Lk 9:11: ܘܠܐܝܠܝܢ ܕܣܢܝܩܝܢ ܗܘܘ ܠܐܣܝܘܬܐ ܡܐܣܐ ܗܘܐ.

ܒܝܫܐ).[365] In the case of the disciples, we have only one particular person as object, namely the crippled beggar.[366] In the other passages the object is the 'sick' (ܟܪ̈ܝܗܐ),[367] or 'those who are sick' (ܠܐܝܠܝܢ ܕܟܪ̈ܝܗܝܢ).[368] Finally, the 'sicknesses' (ܟܘܪ̈ܗܢܐ)[369] and 'every pain and sicknesses' (ܟܠ ܟܐܒ ܘܟܘܪ̈ܗܢ)[370] occur as the object of healing. The disciples were not able to heal every kind of sicknesses for, as in Mt 17:16-19, they were not able to heal the boy with a demon who was suffering greatly; in turn Jesus healed him.[371]

The *ethpa"al* ܐܬܐܣܝ occurs in the four Gospels,[372] as well as in the Acts[373] and Epistles.[374] Mainly it is used in the context of Jesus through Whom many people have been healed, like the centurion's son,[375] the boy with a demon,[376] the woman with the haemorrhage,[377] the daughter of the Canaanite woman,[378] the

---

365 Act 10:38: ܥܠ ܝܫܘܥ ܕܡܢ ܢܨܪܬ: ܕܐܠܗܐ ܡܫܚܗ ܒܪܘܚܐ ܕܩܘܕܫܐ ܘܒܚܝܠܐ. ܘܗܘܝܘ ܕܡܬܟܪܟ ܗܘܐ ܘܡܐܣܐ ܠܗܘܢ ܕܐܬܢܟܝܘ ܡܢ ܒܝܫܐ.

366 Act 3:16: ܘܒܗܝܡܢܘܬܐ ܕܫܡܗ ܠܗܢܐ ܕܚܙܝܢ ܐܢܬܘܢ ܘܝܕܥܝܢ ܐܢܬܘܢ: ܗܘ ܐܫܪ ܘܐܣܝܗ.

367 Mt 10:10; Lk 9:2; Mk 3:15; 6:13.

368 Lk 10:9: ܘܐܣܘ ܠܐܝܠܝܢ ܕܟܪ̈ܝܗܝܢ ܒܗ̇. ܘܐܡܪܘ ܠܗܘܢ: ܩܪܒܬ ܠܟܘܢ ܡܠܟܘܬܗ ܕܐܠܗܐ.

369 Lk 9:1-2: ܘܩܪܐ ܝܫܘܥ ܠܬܪ̈ܥܣܪܬܗ: ܘܝܗܒ ܠܗܘܢ ܚܝܠܐ ܘܫܘܠܛܢܐ: ܥܠ ܟܠܗܘܢ ܫܐ̈ܕܐ ܘܟܘܪ̈ܗܢܐ ܠܡܐܣܝܘ. ܘܫܕܪ ܐܢܘܢ ܠܡܟܪܙܘ ܡܠܟܘܬܗ ܕܐܠܗܐ ܘܠܡܐܣܝܘ ܟܪ̈ܝܗܐ.

370 Mt 10:1: ܘܩܪܐ ܠܬܪ̈ܥܣܪ ܬܠܡܝ̈ܕܘܗܝ ܘܝܗܒ ܠܗܘܢ ܫܘܠܛܢܐ ܥܠ ܪܘܚܐ ܛܢ̈ܦܬܐ ܕܢܦܩܘܢ: ܘܠܡܐܣܝܘ ܟܠ ܟܐܒ ܘܟܘܪ̈ܗܢ.

371 Mt 17:16-18: ܘܩܪܒܬܗ ܠܬܠܡܝ̈ܕܝܟ: ܘܠܐ ܐܫܟܚܘ ܠܡܐܣܝܘܬܗ. .... ܘܟܐܐ ܒܗ ܝܫܘܥ: ܘܢܦܩ ܡܢܗ ܫܐܕܐ. ܘܐܬܐܣܝ ܡܢ ܗܝ ܫܥܬܐ

372 Mt 8:8; 8:13; 9:21-22; 14:36; 15:28; 17;18; Mk 5:29; 6:56; Lk 5:15; 6:18; 7:7; 8:2; 8:36; 8:43; 8:47; 13:14; Jn 5:10; 5:13; 9:36.

373 Act 4:14; 8:7; 28:9.

374 1 Pet 2:24; Hebr 12:13; Jas 5:16.

375 Mt 8:8; 8:13; Lk 7:7.

376 Mt 17:18: ܘܐܬܐܣܝ ܛܠܝܐ ܡܢ ܗܝ ܫܥܬܐ.

377 Mt 9:21-22; Mk 5:29; Lk 8:43; 8:47.

378 Mt 15:28: ܘܐܬܐܣܝܬ ܒܪܬܗ̇ ܡܢ ܗܝ ܫܥܬܐ.

demon-possessed man,[379] the man who has been thirty-eight years invalid[380] and the man born blind.[381] Beyond the individual people who have been healed, ܐܬܐܣܝܘ is also attributed to groups such as the 'women' (ܢܫ̈ܐ)[382] or 'those who' (ܐܝܠܝܢ ܕ....).[383] Sometimes the verb ܐܬܐܣܝܘ qualifies particular persons who have been healed, such as the man who has been sick for thirty-eight years,[384] the man born blind,[385] the 'women who have been healed'[386] and the crippled beggar.[387] The healing of the individual could be physical as well as spiritual, from different kinds of diseases. Generally, the healing could be from 'their sicknesses' (ܟܘܪ̈ܗܢܝܗܘܢ),[388] or 'from sicknesses and from evil spirits'( ܡܢ ܟܘܪ̈ܗܢܐ ܘܡܢ ܪ̈ܘܚܐ ܒܝ̈ܫܬܐ)[389] and 'defiled spirits' ( ܡܢ ܪ̈ܘܚܐ ܛܢ̈ܦܬܐ).[390] Approaching Jesus is a significant way of being healed;[391] likewise approaching some of the disciples, such as Paul

---

379 Lk 8:36: ܘܐܫܬܥܝܘ ܠܗܘܢ ܐܝܠܝܢ ܕܚܙܘ: ܐܝܟܢܐ ܐܬܐܣܝ ܓܒܪܐ ܗܘ ܕܕܝܘܢܐ.

380 Jn 5:10; 5:13: ܗܘ ܕܝܢ ܕܐܬܐܣܝ.

381 Jn 9:36: ܗܢܐ ܗܘ ܕܐܬܐܣܝ.

382 Lk 8:2: ܘܢܫ̈ܐ ܗܠܝܢ ܕܐܬܐܣܝ ܡܢ ܟܘܪ̈ܗܢܐ ܘܡܢ ܪ̈ܘܚܐ ܒܝܫܬܐ.

383 Mt 14:36; Mk 6:18; 6:56.

384 Jn 5:10: ܘܐܡܪܝܢ ܠܗ ܝܗܘ̈ܕܝܐ ܠܗܘ ܕܐܬܐܣܝ ܫܒܬܐ ܗܝ ܠܐ ܫܠܝܛ ܠܟ ܕܬܫܩܘܠ ܥܪܣܟ; cf. Jn 5:13.

385 Jn 9:36: ܗܢܐ ܗܘ ܕܐܬܐܣܝ ܘܐܡܪ ܡܢܘ ܡܪܝ ܕܐܗܝܡܢ ܒܗ.

386 Lk 8:2: ܘܢܫ̈ܐ ܗܠܝܢ ܕܐܬܐܣܝ ܡܢ ܟܘܪ̈ܗܢܐ ܘܡܢ ܪ̈ܘܚܐ ܒܝ̈ܫܬܐ.

387 Act 4:14: ܘܚܙܝܢ ܗܘܘ ܕܩܐܡ ܗܘܐ ܥܡܗܘܢ ܚܓܝܪܐ ܗܘ ܕܐܬܐܣܝ.

388 Lk 5:15: ܘܡܬܟܢܫ ܗܘܐ ܟܢܫܐ ܣܓܝܐܐ ܠܡܫܡܥ ܡܢܗ: ܘܠܡܬܐܣܝܘ ܡܢ ܟܘܪ̈ܗܢܝܗܘܢ; cf. Lk 6:18.

389 Lk 8:2.

390 Lk 6:18: ܕܐܬܘ ܕܢܫܡܥܘܢ ܡܠܬܗ: ܘܕܢܬܐܣܘܢ ܡܢ ܟܘܪ̈ܗܢܝܗܘܢ. ܘܐܝܠܝܢ ܕܡܬܐܠܨܝܢ ܡܢ ܪ̈ܘܚܐ ܛܢ̈ܦܬܐ. ܘܡܬܐܣܝܢ ܗܘܘ.

391 Mt 14:36; Mk 6:56.

on the island Malta.[392] Beside Paul, the crippled beggar was healed through Peter and John,[393] whereas in Samaria the 'paralytics and cripples' were healed through Philip.[394]

### *3.2.1.2 In Ephrem*

Ephrem uses the *pa''el* ܐܣܝ[395] more often than the *ethpa''el* ܐܬܐܣܝ.[396] The subject of ܐܣܝ can be the Lord, the prophets and disciples, as well as ordinary physicians[397] and other people. Also some natural products appear as the subject such as ordinary 'medicine' (ܣܡܐ)[398] and 'iron' (ܦܪܙܠܐ).[399]

When the Lord is the agent of ܐܣܝ, He may appear under different titles, such as 'Medicine of Life' (ܣܡ ܚܝܐ)[400] and

---

[392] Act 28:9.

[393] Act 4:14: ܘܚܙܝܢ ܗܘܘ ܕܩܐܡ ܗܘܐ ܥܡܗܘܢ ܚܓܝܪܐ ܗܘ ܕܐܬܐܣܝ.

[394] Act 8:7: ܘܐܚܪܢܐ ܡܫܪܝܐ ܘܡܚܓܪܐ ܐܬܐܣܝܘ. 1 Pet 2:24, based on Is 53, refers the fact of being healed to the 'wounds' of Jesus: ܕܒܡܚܘܬܐ ܕܝܠܗ ܚܝܢ. ܒܡܚܘܬܗ ܓܝܪ ܐܬܐܣܝܬܘܢ. Jas 5:16 emphasises the power of prayer through which 'you will be healed': ܘܗܘܝܬܘܢ ܡܨܠܝܢ ܚܕ ܥܠ ܚܕ܆ ܕܬܬܐܣܘܢ. ܪܒ ܗܘ ܓܝܪ ܚܝܠܗ ܕܨܠܘܬܐ ܐܝܢܐ ܕܙܕܝܩܐ ܡܨܠܝܐ ܠܗ. Finally, in Hebr 12:13, the term 'lame limb' (ܗܕܡܐ ܕܡܚܓܪ) is related to ܐܬܐܣܝ too: ܘܫܒܝܠܐ ܬܪܝܨܐ ܥܒܕܘ ܠܪܓܠܝܟܘܢ܆ ܗܕܡܐ ܕܡܚܓܪ ܠܐ ܢܬܥܒܕ܆ ܐܠܐ ܢܬܐܣܐ.

[395] CDiat 2.23; 5.19; 7.2; 7.6-7; 7.9; 7.12-13; 7.15; 7.21; 7.23; 7.27b; 10.7a; 11.7; 13.1; 13.3; 16.8; 16.10; 16.24; 16.32; Dom 21; 42; 44; Nat 1.28; 3.20; 21.12; 22.1; 23.11; Epiph 11.7; Virg 1.3-4; 3.10; 4.7-8; 14.11; 25.14; 26.6; 26.9; 34.3; 42.5-6; 46.15; 46.27; 49.15; Fid 2.15; 2.19; 8.12; 9.11; 10.6; 12.9; 36.1; 56.11; 75.18; Iei 4.1; 10.6; Crucif 3.18; Eccl 5.6; 26.1; 28.16; 38 Ref; 38.4 41.3-4; 43.6; 44.14; 52.4; Nis 6.1 27.2-3; 27.5; 34.1; 34.5; 34.7-12; 39.10; 46.8; 51.16; 74.14.

[396] CDiat 7.6-7; 7.10; 7.21; 7.22b; 7.24; 7.27b; 11.5; 11.7; 16.32; Dom 42; Nat 2.7; Epiph 8.22; Fid 15.7; Eccl 8.3; Nis 11.4; 34.9; 34.11.

[397] Nis 27.2; 34.12; 36.1; 51.16.

[398] Virg 49.15; Eccl 26.1: ܐܣܪܝ ܠܐ ܐܦ ܣܡܐ ܕܒܐܣܝܐ ܠܐ.

[399] Fid 56.11: ܘܠܦܪܙܠܐ ܡܪܐ ܒܪܗ ܠܡܐܣܝܘ.

[400] Nis 34.10; 74.14: ܠܡܣܝܒܘܬܐ ܐܣܝ ܒܡܣܒܪܢܘܬܐ ܕܐܒܝܫ ܘܠܡܣܝܒܘܬܐ ܕܒܣܡܐ ܣܡܐ ܠܐ ܢܦܠ ܠܐܣܝܘܬܗ، ܣܡ ܚܝܐ.

'Physician' (ܐܣܝܐ).[401] Some other titles used in this context point to His Sonship and co-existence with the Father. These are 'the Son of the Father' (ܒܪܗ ܕܐܒܐ),[402] 'the Son Who has been sent' (ܠܒܪܐ ܕܐܫܬܠܚ),[403] 'God's Word' (ܡܠܬܗ),[404] 'our Lord' (ܡܪܢ),[405] 'our Redeemer' (ܦܪܘܩܢ),[406] 'our Creator/Fashioner' (ܠܓܒܘܠܢ)[407] and 'the Lord of the prophets' (ܡܪܗܘܢ ܕܢܒܝܐ).[408] The spiritual healing aspect, especially healing in connection with forgiveness, is expressed, rather, with the following attributes: the 'Kind One' (ܒܣܝܡܐ)[409] and 'Merciful One' (ܚܢܢܐ),[410] 'Fervour of compassion/ mercy' (ܪܬܚܐ ܕܪ̈ܚܡܐ)[411] and 'Stream of compassion/mercy' (ܪܕܝܐ ܕܪ̈ܚܡܐ).[412] Several other terms used as subject are clearly related to Jesus, such as the 'providence of our Lord' (ܒܛܝܠܘܬܗ ܕܡܪܢ),[413] 'compassion/mercifulness' (ܡܪܚܡܢܘܬܐ), 'His Gospel/message' (ܣܒܪܬܗ),[414] 'not prying

---

401 Dom 44; Nat 3.20; Nis 6.1; Eccl 12.9; 28.16: ܐܝܟ ܐܣܝܐ ܡܐܣܐ ܠܟܠ ܟܠ; cf CDiat 10.7a; 16.8; Nis 39.10. Sometimes the personal pronoun 'You' (ܐܢܬ) is used for Jesus: Nis 27.3-5; Virg 34.3; cf. Mt 9:20; Mk 5:27; Lk 8:44.

402 Eccl 38 Ref; cf. Eccl 38.4.

403 Nat 22.1: ܕܝܠܕ ܐܢܐ ܒܫܘܬܐ ܐܝܟ ܠܒܪܐ ܕܐܫܬܠܚ.

404 CDiat 11.7.

405 CDiat 16.10; Dom 21.

406 CDiat 16.32; Eccl 41.4.

407 Nat 21.12: ܗܐ ܒܗܢܐ ܠܚܠܠܐ ܠܓܒܘܠܢ ܐܣܝܢ.

408 Dom 42: ܠܝܬ ܠܗܘܢ ܡܪܗܘܢ ܕܢܒܝܐ ܕܢܐܣܐ ܠܐܝܠܝܢ ܕܒܝܫ ܒܝܫ ܒܝܫܝܢ.

409 Fid 75.18: ܟܠ ܕܢܩ̈ܦܢ ܗܘ ܐܬܦܪܥ ܠܗ ܗܘ ܒܣܝܡܐ ܠܦܪܘܫܘܬܢ ܐܝܟ ܐܢܐܣܝܗ.

410 Crucif 3.18: ܐܕܢܐ ܕܝܢ ܚܢܢܐ ܘܐܣܝܗ̇ (the ear of the soldier).

411 Virg 25.14: ܕܪܬܚܐ ܕܪ̈ܚܡܐ ܥܠ ܦܘܪܪ ܘܐܣܝܗ̇; cf Mt 8:14.

412 Virg 26.6: ܠܦܘܠܚܢ ܐܬܬܐ ܪܕܝܐ ܕܪ̈ܚܡܐ ܦܠܓ ܒܟܢ ܘܐܣܐ ܪܕܝܐ ܕܕܡܟܢ.

413 Nis 46.8: ܐܢ ܕܝܢ ܒܛܝܠܘܬܗ ܕܡܪܢ ܡܬܩܝܡܐ ܠܝ ܕܐܣܝܗ ܠܒܪܝܬܐ ܠܟܠܗ ܟܠ ܡܕܡ.

414 Fid 8.12.

into Him … [but] the sight of Him' (ܠܐ ܒܚܙܬܗ...ܚܙܬܗ)[415] and 'His purity' (ܢܟܦܘܬܗ).[416]

Among the prophets, Abraham, Moses, Joseph,[417] Elisha[418] and Jonah[419] appear as subjects of ܐܣܐ; whereas none of the disciples is mentioned by name - only in Virg 4.8 does Ephrem use 'the shadow [of the disciples]' (ܛܠܠܝ̈ܗܘܢ)[420] as an agent of healing.

Furthermore, healing capability is not only limited to God and His people, but it can also be attributed to the 'Law' (ܢܡܘܣܐ),[421] 'Scripture' (ܟܬܒܐ) and 'Nature' (ܟܝܢܐ)[422] which all come from God; the same applies to the actions of the individual, such as 'faith' (ܗܝܡܢܘܬܟܝ),[423] 'fasting' (ܨܘܡܐ),[424] 'repentance' (ܬܝܒܘܬܐ)[425] and 'labours and compassion' (ܥܡ̈ܠܐ ܘܪ̈ܚܡܐ);[426] thus the agent of healing can be just 'we'.[427] In contrast to the

---

415 Fid 9.11: ܠܐ ܗܘܐ ܒܚܙܬܗ ܐܣܝܬ ܚܙܬܗ ܒܠܒܘܫܗ܆ ܐܣܝܬ.

416 Eccl 52.4:

ܐܝܟ ܐܣܝܐ ܢܟܦܐ   ܕܬܐܣܐ ܢܟܦܘܬܗ ܬܡܣܘܬܐ.

417 Nis 34.1-8.

418 Epiph 11.7; cf. 2 Kgs 2:19.

419 Virg 42.5-6.

420 Virg 4.8: ܕܛܠܠܝ̈ܗܘܢ ܒܬܪ ܕܐܣܝܐ.

421 Eccl 43.6: ܘܐܦ ܟܕ ܬܒܪ ܠܘܚ̈ܐ ܒܠܘܚ̈ܐ ܡܐܣܝܐ ܗܘܐ; Eccl 44.14: ܘܚܣܬ ܒܢܡܘܣܗ ܐܣܝ ܠܚܛ̈ܝܬܐ.

422 Virg 1.3-4:

ܩܛܠܐ ܡܡܚܝܐ ܘܗܘܝܢ ܡܐܣܝܢ ܠܟ
ܠܡܪ̈ܘܕܐ ܬܘܒ ܡܡܟܟ̈ܝܢ ܘܡܐܣܝܢ ܠܬܐܒ.

423 Virg 26.9; cf. Mt 15:28; Mk 7:29.

424 Iei 4.1:

ܗܘ ܨܘܡܐ ܡܐܣܝܢܐ   ܘܐܣܝ ܟܐܒ̈ܐ ܒܝ̈ܫܐ ܕܢܦܫܐ.

425 Virg 3.10: ܬܝܒܘܬܐ ܚܙܝ ܡܐܣܝܢܐ ܒܡܐܣܝܢܘܬܗ ܠܡܚܒ̈ܠܬܐ.

426 Virg 46.27:

ܘܡܢܐ ܕܠܒܘ ܐܣܝܘ ܥܡ̈ܠܐ ܘܪ̈ܚܡܐ
ܘܪܘܫܡ ܥܘܩܬܐ ܚܠܝܐ ܗܘ ܡܪܐ.

427 Virg 46.15:

ܡܢ ܢܦܫܢ ܠܢ ܕܢܒܕܚܬܝܢ   ܢܐܣܐ ܡܚܘܬܐ ܕܠܐ ܡܬܚܝܐ.

Also the good Samaritan (CDiat 16.24.), the 'fastened serpent' ( ܚܘܝܐ ܡܩܒܥܐ, Nat 1.28; cf. Num 21:8f), 'voices' (ܩ̈ܠܐ) and 'His word' ☞

Lord, the healing ability of the 'physicians of the world' ( ܐܣܘ̈ܬܐ ܕܥܠܡܐ )[428] is limited.

As the object of ܐܣܝ, the term ܡܚܘܬܐ refers to the general wound of humanity through death; only the Medicine of Life is able to heal the 'wound of death' (ܠܡܚܘܬܐ ܕܡܘܬܐ).[429] 'Adam's wounds' (ܡܚܘ̈ܬܗ ܕܐܕܡ)[430] are the object of ܐܣܝ, as well as those whom Jesus healed: 'the wounded person' (ܠܡܚܝܐ),[431] 'crippled' (ܚܓܝܪܐ),[432] 'paralytic' (ܕܡܫܪܝ),[433] the blind and possessed man,[434] the man born blind,[435] the man who had been sick for 38-years,[436] 'Peter's mother-in-law' (ܠܚܡܝ),[437] the 'bruises' (ܫܘ̈ܚܩܝܗ̇)[438] of the sinful woman and the woman with haemorrhage (ܪ̈ܕܝܐ ܕܕܡܗ̇)[439] are all explicitly mentioned.

The object of ܐܣܝ generally refers to people, such as the Israelites,[440] the 'living' (ܚܝܐ),[441] 'whole man' (ܠܒܪܢܫܐ ܟܠܗ),[442]

---

(ܦܬܓܡܗ, Fid 2.15; 2.19.), 'free medicine' (ܣܡܐ ܕܡܓܢ, Eccl 5.6) and 'spiritual medicinal herbs' (ܥܩܪ̈ܐ ܪܘܚܢ̈ܝܐ, Iei 10.6.) are used as subject of ܐܣܝ.

428 Nis 27.2; 34.12; Fid 36.1.

429 Nis 74.14.

430 CDiat 16.10; cf. Nat 22.1.

431 CDiat 16.24; cf. Lk 10:36-37.

432 Eccl 41.3: ܚܓܝܪܐ ܕܐܣܝ ܗܘܐ ܠܗ ܐܠܗܐ.

433 Nis 39.10: ܣܘܟ ܕܝܢ ܠܗܘ ܕܡܫܪܝ ܐܣܝ.

434 CDiat 10.7a: ܘܐܣܝܗ ܘܚܪܫܐ ܘܫܡܥ (Mt 12:22).

435 CDiat 16.32: ܟܕ... ܐܣܝ ܒܡܟܢܬܐ (Jn 9:5-8).

436 CDiat 13.1: ܐܣܝܬ ܡܪܥܝܢܘܬܐ ܠܗ̇ܘ; CDiat 13.3; 16.32 (cf. Jn 5:5-12).

437 Virg 25.14: ܕܪܬܚܐ ܕܐܣܘ̈ܬܐ ܥܠ ܡܘܪܪ ܘܐܣܝܗ (Mt 8:14).

438 Dom 44: ܘܒܬܝܒܘܬܗ̇ ܠܐܣܝܐ ܫܘ̈ܚܩܝܗ̇; see further chapter IV, 2.1.2.

439 Virg 26.6: ܠܦܘܩܕܢܗ ܐܬܬܐ ܕܪ̈ܕܝܐ ܕܐܣܘ̈ܬܐ ܦܠܓܬ ܟܠܗ ܘܐܣܝ ܪ̈ܕܝܐ ܕܕܡܗ̇ (Mt 9:20; Mk 5:25; Lk 8:44); cf. Nis 27.3.

440 CDiat 11.7: ܫܕܪ ܠܡܠܬܗ ܘܐܣܝ ܐܢܘܢ (cf. Ps 107:20).

441 Eccl 41.4: ܐܘ ܦܘܡ ܚܝܐ ܕܐܣܝܬ.

'all' (ܟܠ )[443] or just 'us' (ܐܣܝܢ);[444] but it is also used for a particular object, such as 'my lacerations' (ܒܘܣܡ̈ܣܝ)[445] or 'my perturbation' (ܪܗܝܒܘܬܝ).[446] More often, terms from the sphere of sickness and medicine are used as object: 'suffering of everyone' (ܚܫ̈ܐ ܕܟܠ ܐܢܫ),[447] 'pain' (ܟܐܒܐ),[448] 'pains' (ܟܐܒ̈ܐ)[449] or 'our pains' (ܟܐܒ̈ܝܢ),[450] 'the pains of souls' (ܟܐܒ̈ܐ ܕܢܦ̈ܫܬܐ),[451] 'pains and sickness' (ܟܐܒ̈ܐ ܘܟܘܪ̈ܗܢܐ),[452] 'our state of sickness' (ܠܟܪܝܗܘܬܢ)[453] or 'all those who are badly effected' ( ܠܟܠܗܘܢ ܕܒܝܫ ܒܝܫ ܒܒܝܫܝܢ).[454]

Some terms also distinguish between spiritual and corporal sickness, such as 'visible limbs' (ܗܕ̈ܡܐ ܕܡܬܚܙܝܢ)[455] - for instance 'eye' (ܥܝܢܐ)[456] and 'ear' (ܐܕܢܐ),[457] -, 'wounded minds'

---

[442] Nis 46.8: ܐܦ ܕܝܢ ܒܬܠܡܝܕܘܗܝ ܕܒܪܟ ܡܫܝܚܐ ܠܟ ܕܐܣܝܘܗܝ ܠܒܪܢܫܐ ܠܟܠܗ ܒܟܠ ܡܕܡ.

[443] Fid 12.9: ܐܣܝܐ ܕܐܣܝ ܟܠ; Eccl 28.16: ܐܝܟ ܐܣܝܐ ܡܐܣܝܐ ܠܟܠ ܒܟܠ.

[444] Nat 21.12: ܒܒܘܠܝ ܐܣܝܢ.

[445] Nis 6.1: ܐܪܗܛ ܒܐܘܠܨܢܝ ܠܘܬ ܐܣܝܐ ܕܒܟܠ ܕܐܣܝ ܠܒܘܣ̈ܡܣܝ ܡܪ̈ܕܐ ܘܬܢ̈ܝܢܐ, i.e. Nisibis.

[446] Fid 10.6: ܐܣܝܐ ܪܗܝܒܘܬܝ ܡܢ ܡܠܝܐ, i.e. the author.

[447] CDiat 16.8: ܚܫ̈ܐ ܒܪ ܕܟܠ ܐܢܫ ܐܣܝ ܗܘܐ.

[448] Nis 27.5: ܟܐܒܐ ܕܚܙܬ ܐܣܝܐ ܕܐܣܝܬ ܒܬܘܬܐ.

[449] Eccl 38.4: ܕܒܐܣܝܐ ܗܘܐ ܟܐܒ̈ܐ ܒܪ̈ܫܝܐ ܕܠܐ ܡܣܬܟܒ̈ܢܐ.

[450] Eccl 38 Ref.: ܟܐܒ̈ܝܢ ܘܐܣܝ ܠܒܪܗ ܕܫܕܪ ܠܐܒܐ ܫܘܒܚܐ.

[451] Nis 34.10: ܘܐܣܝ ܟܐܒ̈ܐ ܕܢܦ̈ܫܬܐ ܒܝܘܠܦܢܗ.

[452] CDiat 16.8: ܟܐܒ̈ܐ ܘܟܘܪ̈ܗܢܐ ܐܣܝ.

[453] Fid 75.18: ܒܟܠ ܕܩܒ̈ܠܢ ܗܘ ܐܬܦܪܥ ܠܗ ܗܘ ܒܡܫܝܚܐ ܠܟܪܝܗܘܬܢ ܐܝܟ ܕܐܣܝܗ.

[454] Dom 42: ܢܣܒ ܠܗ ܪܫܘܡܐ ܕܐܣ̈ܝܐ ܕܐܣܝܐ ܠܟܠܗܘܢ ܕܒܝܫ ܒܝܫ ܒܒܝܫܝܢ (Mt 9:12; Mk 2:17; Lk 5:31-32).

[455] Dom 21: ܦܪܗܣ ܕܝܢ ܐܣܝ ܗܕ̈ܡܐ ܕܡܬܚܙܝܢ; cf. the sinful woman (Lk 7:36-50).

[456] CDiat 16.32; Fid 45.1-2; Iei 6.4-8 (Mk 10:46); Nis 51.16; see the man born blind (Jn 9:5-8).

[457] Crucif 3.18; Eccl 29.2-3; Nis 46.8-9 (Lk 22:51).

(ܪ̈ܓܫܐ ܡܫܬܚܢܐ),[458] 'gluttony' (ܐܣܘܛܘܬܐ),[459] 'pus' (ܬܡܣܘܬܐ)[460] and 'bruises' (ܫܒ̈ܪܬܐ).[461] Finally Ephrem also uses geographical places, such as 'Zion' (ܨܗܝܘܢ) and the 'land of Egypt' (ܐܪܥܐ ܕܡܨܪ̈ܝܢ), as the object of ܐܣܐ.

The subject of the *ethpa``el* ܐܬܐܣܝ is mainly general, such as 'all' (ܟܠ),[462] 'thousands' (ܐܠܦ̈ܐ)[463] and 'man' (ܐܢܫܐ);[464] or not specified such as 'who ever' (ܕܐܝܠܐ).[465] In CDiat 7, the author uses the personal pronouns as the subject of the passive verb.[466] From the medical sphere only the terms 'her bruises' (ܫܒ̈ܪܬܗ̇)[467] and 'the wounded' woman (ܡܚܝܬܐ)[468] are used as a direct subject of ܐܬܐܣܝ. Only a few sicknesses are explicitly mentioned from which people were healed: those are an 'evil spirit' (ܪܘܚܐ ܒܝܫܬܐ),[469] 'pain' (ܟܐܒܐ)[470] and the 'hidden sickness of the soul' (ܟܘܪܗܢܐ ܟܣܝܐ ܕܢܦܫܐ).[471] The terms 'voice' (ܩܠܐ)[472]

---

458 Dom 42: ܠܟܘ ܕܝܢ ܐܣܐ ܪ̈ܓܫܐ ܡܫܬܚܢܐ.

459 Virg 14.11: ܕܐܣܐ ܒܝܘܡܗ ܐܣܘܛܘܬܐ.

460 Eccl 52.4; (cf. Haer 33.10-11).

461 Nat 3.20: ܒܪܝܟ ܐܣܝܐ ܕܢܣܬ ... ܘܐܣܐ ܫܒ̈ܪܬܐ ܡܣܟܢܬܐ ܕܠܐ ܒܕܡܝ; cf. Dom 44, the sinful woman (Lk 7:36-50).

462 Nat 2.7: ܡܢ ܟܠ ܕܐܬܐܣܝܘ ܚܝܠ ܕܐܝܠܐ ܒܠܒܘܫܗ.

463 Eccl 8.3: ܘܐܬܐܣܝܘ ܐܠܦ̈ܐ ܕܠܐ ܣܟ.

464 CDiat 7.6: ܘܐܦ ܠܕ̈ܘܟܝܐ ܒܬܪ ܩܪܒܝܢ ܗܘܘ ܠܗܘܢ ܐܢܫܐ ܘܡܬܐܣܝܢ ܗܘܘ.

465 Nis 11.4: ܡܢ ܪ̈ܚܡܐ ܝܗܒܬ ܕܒܐܝܬܘܬܟ ܒܣܘܒܐ ܘܐܘܣܝܐ ܠܟܠ ܢ̈ܦܫܬܗܘܢ ܕܐܝܠܐ ܕܡܬܐܣܝܐ. Cf. Fid 15.7: ܐܝܠܐ ܕܡܟܡܟ ܗܘ ܕܐܬܡܟܝܢ ܒܐܣܝܐ ܕܠܒܐ ܠܗ ܠܗ ܠܚܠܝܘܬܐ ܠܥܡܝܩܬܐ.

466 For ܐܢܬܘܢ see CDiat 11.5; ܗܢܘܢ CDiat 7.27b; ܗ̇ܝ CDiat 7.6; 7.24; 7.27a. In CDiat 11.7, the plural ܐܬܐܣܝܘ refers to the Israelites.

467 Dom 42.

468 CDiat 7.1; 7.6.

469 CDiat 11.7: ܒܪܘܚܐ ܠܗ ܡܢܗܘܢ ܪܘܚܐ ܒܝܫܬܐ ܘܐܬܐܣܝܘ.

470 CDiat 11.5: ܕܡܢܐ ܬܐܪܥܘܢ ܐܢ ܬܬܐܣܝܘܢ ܕܒܥܬܐ. ܟܕ ܠܐ ܡܗܝܡܢܝܢ ܐܢܬܘܢ. ܒܬܪ ܕܡܬܐܣܝܬܘܢ ܐܢ ܬܬܦܠܓܘܢ ܕܥܒܕ ܡܢ ܟܐܒܐ ܘܡܢܐ ܗܘܐ ܠܟܘܢ.

471 Nis 34.9: ܕܐܣܝܬ ܡܢ ܟܘܪܗܢܐ ܟܣܝܐ ܕܢܦܫܐ.

and 'His hand' (ܐܝܕܗ)[473] occur as the medium through which healing was performed. 'Approaching' Jesus (ܩܪܒ)[474] and 'tears' (ܕܡ̈ܥܐ)[475] cause man to be healed, as well.

The term ܐܣܝܬܐ (feminine), 'physician',[476] is only three times attested in Ephrem's work, whereas the masculine ܐܣܝܐ is often used, either as a title for Jesus,[477] the patriarchs and prophets,[478] or when the author speaks of an ordinary physician[479] or compares the function and use of other things to a physician.[480] The feminine term ܐܣܝܬܐ describes either the Lord's justice[481] or Egypt's reputation in medicine.[482]

The term 'physician' (ܐܣܝܐ) is especially used for Jesus. Commenting on the healing miracles Jesus had performed, Ephrem describes Jesus as the Physician, par excellence; he calls Him the

---

[472] CDiat 16.32: ܠܘܗ ܕܚܒܝܫ ܗܘܐ ܒܢ̈ܝܐ ܕܒܥܠܐ ܐܬܐܣܝ.

[473] Nis 34.11: ܗܒܡ ܒܐܝܕܗ ܐܬܐܣܝܘ.

[474] CDiat 7.6; 7.24: ܩܪܒܬ ܗܝ ܠܐܠܘܬܗ ܘܐܬܐܣܝܬ ܒܠܗ.

[475] Com 42: ܗܝ ܕܒܕܡ̈ܥܐ ܐܬܐܣ̈ܝ ܚܛ̈ܗܝܗ. In Epiph 8.22, it is through the 'salt' (ܡܠܚܐ) that water was healed.

[476] Azym 20.19; Nis 11.3; 34.8.

[477] CDiat 10.10; 17.3; Dom 14; 24; 42; 44; 48; Nat 3.20; 22.3; Virg 25.13-14; 26.10; 30.11; 35.3; Fid 5.19; 12.9; C.Jul 1.9; Eccl 25.8; 28.16; 52.4; Nis 1.7; 6.1; 26.3; 27.3; 34.9-10; 40.2. In some of these it is not obvious to which person of the Trinity ܐܣܝܐ refers; for instance the praise in Nat 3.19 (ܫܘܒܚܐ ܠܐܠܗܐ ܐܣܝܗܿ ܕܐܢܫܘܬܐ) links ܐܣܝܐ clearly with the term 'God' (ܐܠܗܐ), but the rest of the stanza and almost all the hymn praises Jesus as the Son of God for His economy.

[478] Virg 49.1; 49.13-14; Nis 34.1-2; 34.7.

[479] CDiat 17.1; Dom 19; Nat 22.3; Nis 51.16; Eccl 7.5; 8.3; 28.17; Fid 56.12.

[480] Eccl 43.6; Parad 11.9.

[481] Nis 11.3: ܕܗܝܡܢ ܐܣܝܬܐ ܒܣܝܘܬܐ ܕܟܐ̈ܒܝܗܘܢ ܘܡܟܒܫ ܣ̈ܢܝܗܘܢ; i.e. ܟܐܢܘܬܟ. In Azym 20.19, it is the 'hand of the Lord's justice' that functions as a physician: ܐܝܕܐ ܕܟܐܢܘܬܐ ܠܟܠ ܚܒܝܐ ܠܟܪܝܐ ܠܗ ܒܟ̈ܪܝܗ ܐܝܟ ܐܣܝܬܐ.

[482] Nis 34.8: ܡܨܪܝܢ ܐܣܝܬܐ ....

'heavenly Physician' (ܐܣܝܐ ܕܪܘܡܐ),[483] 'wise Physician' ( ܐܣܝܐ ܚܟܝܡܐ),[484] 'great Physician' (ܐܣܝܐ ܪܒܐ),[485] 'good Physician' (ܐܣܝܐ ܛܒܐ)[486] and 'pure Physician' (ܐܣܝܐ ܢܩܕܐ).[487] He is the Physician of those whom He had healed either from their spiritual or their physical afflictions. Thus, He is called the Physician of the sinful woman (ܚܛܝܬܐ),[488] Lazarus,[489] Peter's mother-in-law,[490] 'widow' (ܐܪܡܠܬܐ)[491] and the 'blind' (ܣܡܝܐ).[492] Since the function of this Physician, par excellence, is not just the healing of the individual, but of the whole of mankind, Ephrem presents Him as the Physician of 'all' (ܟܠ),[493] of 'us' (ܐܣܝܢ),[494] of 'humanity' (ܐܢܫܘܬܐ),[495] and of all 'sinners' (ܚܛ̈ܝܐ)[496] and wounded (ܡܚ̈ܝܢܐ).[497] His function is to heal all 'bruises' (ܚܒ̈ܪܬܐ)[498] and 'pains' (ܟܐ̈ܒܐ)[499] of man, and cut away

---

483 Virg 25.13: ܕܐܣܝܐ ܕܪܘܡܐ ܠܘܬ ܡܥܒܪ ܗܘܐ.

484 Eccl 25.8: ܗܘ ܕܐܝܟ ܐܣܝܐ ܚܟܝܡܐ.

485 Nis 34.6: ܛܒܐ ܟܕ ܒܒܘ̈ܣܡܘܗܝ ܡܬܬܣܝܡ ܠܦܘܪܥܢܐ ܐܝܟ ܐܣܝܐ ܪܒܐ ܠܟܠ ܦܢܝܢ.

486 Dom 48: ܗܢܐ ܗܘ ܐܣܝܐ ܛܒܐ ܕܢܦܩ ܕܢܐܙܠ ܠܘܬ ܚܛܝܬܐ.

487 Eccl 52.4: ܡܥܒܪ ܢܟܝܢܘܬܐ ܐܝܟ ܐܣܝܐ ܢܩܕܐ.

488 CDiat 10.10; Dom 14; 44; 48.

489 CDiat 17.3: ܐܣܝܗ ܕܝܢ ܕܠܥܙܪ ܕܒܥܘܬܗ ܗܘ ܢܗܪ ܗܘܐ.

490 Virg 25.14: ܒܚܡܬܗ ܕܐܣܝܢ ܢܘܪܐ ܕܪܘܡܐ; Virg 25.13.

491 Nat 26.10: ܠܐ ܒܟܘܬܢ ܦܬܪܗ ܗܘܬ ܠܐܣܝܐ.

492 Virg 35.3: ܐܘ ܐܣܝܐ ܕܠܡܣܡܝܐ ܒܟܘܪܐ ܡܟܬܫ ܗܘܐ.

493 Fid 12.9: ܘܚܝܡ ܡܛܠܬܐ ܐܣܝܐ ܕܐܣܐ ܟܠ; Eccl 28.16: ܐܝܟ ܐܣܝܐ ܡܐܣܐ ܠܟܠ ܒܟܠ.

494 Dom 42: ܕܒܥܘܬ ܟܠ ܐܣܝܢ ܕܠܟܪ̈ܝܗܐ ܦܬܚ ܠܗ ܡܟܣܝܢܘܬܐ.

495 Nat 3.19: ܥܘܩܒܐ ܠܐܠܗܐ ܐܣܝܗ̇ ܕܐܢܫܘܬܐ.

496 Virg 30.11: ܬܠܠܬܐ ܕܐܣܝܢ ܗ̇ܘ ܠܗܘܢ ܠܚܛ̈ܝܐ ܡܚܝ̈ܢܐ ܕܒܘܕ̈ܪܐ.

497 Dom 42.

498 Nat 3.20: ܒܪܝܟ ܐܣܝܐ ܕܢܚܬ ܘܓܙܪ ܕܠܐ ܣܟܝܢܐ ܘܐܣܐ ܚܒ̈ܪܬܐ ܒܡܣܡܐ ܕܠܐ ܚܘܫ.

the 'source of harm' (ܡܒܘܥܐ ܕܢܟܝ̈ܢܐ) and the 'cause of pain' (ܥܠܬ ܟܐܒܐ).[500]

The verb 'to become' (ܗܘܐ)[501] draws attention to the relationship of Jesus with those to whom He 'became' a Physician. Many other verbs emphasise His action as a Physician: 'to heal' (ܐܣܝ),[502] 'to visit' (ܣܥܪ),[503] 'to open' (ܦܬܚ),[504] 'went out to go' (ܢܦܩ ܕܢܐܙܠ),[505] 'to cut' (ܓܙܪ),[506] 'to cut off' (ܦܣܩ),[507] 'to dry up' (ܢܓܒ),[508] 'to drive away' (ܪܕܦ),[509] 'to propound' (ܡܦܪܫ),[510] 'to show' (ܚܘܝ).[511] In particular, the verbs 'to have pity' (ܚܣ)[512] and 'to have mercy upon' (ܐܬܪܚܡ)[513] signify the spiritual side of the divine Physician.

The term ܐܣܝܐ is also attributed to some prophets. In Nis 34, Abraham, Daniel, Moses and Jacob are explicitly mentioned.

---

[499] Fid 5.19: ܕܐܣܝܐ ܕܪܕܦ ܠܟܐܒ̈ܝܢ; C.Jul 1.9. Jesus is also described as the Physician of ܬܫܡܫܬܐ (Eccl 52.4), ܢܦ̈ܫܬܐ (Nis 1.7) and ܒܘܣܡ̈ܝܢ (Nis 6.1).

[500] Eccl 25.8: ܦܣܩ ܐܣܝܐ ܥܠܬ ܟܐܒܐ ܘܢܓܒܬ ܡܒܘܥܐ ܕܢܟܝ̈ܢܐ.

[501] CDiat 10.10: ܘܗܘܐ ܐܣܝܐ ܠܗ̇ܝ ܕܡܚܒܠܬ ܗܘܘ ܡܟܐܒܐ ܟܠ; cf. Virg 30.11; Nis 27.3.

[502] Dom 44, Nat 3.19; Fid 12.9; Eccl 28.16; 52.4.

[503] Virg 25.13: ܕܐܣܝܐ ܕܪܘܚܐ ܢܣܬ ܡܣܥܪܢ ܗܘܐ.

[504] Virg 35.3: ܐܘ ܐܣܝܐ ܕܠܡܣܟ̈ܢܐ ܒܒܘܪܐ ܡܦܬܚ ܗܘܐ.

[505] Dom 48: ܗܢܐ ܗܘ ܐܣܝܐ ܠܟܠܐ ܕܢܦܩ ܕܢܐܙܠ ܠܘܬ ܚܛܝܬܐ.

[506] Nat 3.20: ܒܪܝܟ ܐܣܝܐ ܕܢܚܬ ܘܓܙܪ ܕܠܐ ܚܫܐ ܘܐܣܝ ܚܒܘ̈ܪܬܐ ܒܣܡܐ ܕܠܐ ܚܪܝܦ; Azym 20.19.

[507] Eccl 25.8; cf. Nis 27.1: ܠܐܣܝܐ ܦܣܝܩܐ ܗܢܘ ܕܦܣܩܘܗ ܠܡܪܕܐ.

[508] Eccl 25.8: ܦܣܩ ܐܣܝܐ ܥܠܬ ܟܐܒܐ ܘܢܓܒܬ ܡܒܘܥܐ ܕܢܟܝ̈ܢܐ.

[509] Fid 5.19: ܐܘ ܡܢ ܡܒܝܪ ܛܒܝܢ ܕܐܣܝܐ ܕܪܕܦ ܠܟܐܒܝܢ ܚܝܢ ܒܗ ܡܚܝܢ ܠܘܡܝܢ.

[510] Dom 24: ܗܘܐ ܐܣܝܐ ܕܠܡܟܠ ܡܡܟ̈ܠܝܢ ܒܕܘܪ̈ܫܘܗܝ ܡܦܪܫ ܗܘܐ.

[511] CDiat 17.3: ܐܣܝܗ ܕܝܢ ܕܠܒܪ ܕܢܒܘܬ ܗܘ ܚܙܪ ܗܘܐ ܕܢܒܘܬܗ ܚܘܝܐ ܐܣܝܐ ܠܚܝܠܗ; cf. Nis 26.3.

[512] Nis 34.9: ܘܢܣܝܒ ܢܕܪܐ ܠܐܣܝܐ ܕܚܣܗ.

[513] Nis 34.10: ܚܣܗܝ ܘܐܬܪܚܡ ܐܣܝܐ ܕܠܟܠ ܣܦܩ.

Attention is drawn to how they acted as physicians to heal Harran, Babel and Egypt from their spiritual sickness.[514] Virg 49 deals with Jonah as the 'circumcised physician' (ܐܣܝܐ ܓܙܝܪܐ)[515] who was sent to Nineveh. He and his medicines are compared to Moses and his medicines on Sinai.[516] Surprisingly, in Eccl 43.5-6 the term ܐܣܝܐ is not used for Moses, but for the Law that acts as a physician, whereas in Parad 11.9, the fragrance of Paradise serves as a physician to Earth.[517]

In some other passages, Ephrem also speaks of an ordinary physician whose function is to go 'where suffering exists'[518] and to reveal the hidden pain with his medicines.[519] There is no physician who stops the wounded from coming to him.[520] Even though every one trusts the 'book of medicines in which a physician reads',[521] nevertheless, Ephrem warns people to be critical concerning the deeds and results of the physician's work: it is not his medicines that count, but rather his assistance.[522] Likewise, it is important to pay attention to the reputation of each individual physician, before trusting him.[523] Ephrem puts the ironical question: can a physician who is blind in himself increase light for others?[524] The aspect of light or the eye is also incorporated in Nis 51.16 where Ephrem says: 'and a physician does not heal an eye with the hated sting of a

---

514 Nis 34.1-9.

515 Virg 49.1.

516 Virg 49.13-14.

517 Parad 11.9.

518 CDiat 17.1: ܐܝܟ ܒܪ ܕܐܝܬ ܗܘ ܠܟ ܚܫܐ ܪܗܛ ܐܣܝܐ.

519 Dom 19: ܐܣܝܐ ܕܝܢ ܐܝܟܐ ܕܒܣܡ̈ܡܢܘܗܝ ܠܟܐܒܐ ܟܣܝܐ ܠܓܠܝܐ ܡܚܘܬܐ.... .

520 Dom 42: ܐܝܟܘ ܕܝܢ ܐܣܝܐ ܕܟܠܐ ܠܡܚ̈ܝܫܐ ܕܠܐ ܢܐܬܘܢ ܠܘܬܗ.

521 Fid 56.12: ܠܣܦܪܐ ܕܣܡ̈ܡܢܐ ܕܒܗ ܐܣܝܐ ܩܪܐ.

522 Eccl 28.17: ܠܐ ܗܘܐ ܒܣܡ̈ܡܢܘܗܝ ܕܐܣܝܐ ܚܘܪ ܣܟܠܐ ܐܠܐ ܒܥܘܕܪ̈ܢܘܗܝ.

523 Nat 22.3: ܐܝܟܢ ܒܝ ܡܢ̈ܝܢܐ ܐܢܫ ܬܗܪ ܒܗ ܒܐܣܝܐ ܐܠܐ ܥܒܕ ܘܠܟ

524 Eccl 7.5: ܕܗܐ ܐܣܝܐ ܥܘܝܪ ܠܡܘܣܦܗ ܢܘܗܪܐ ܡܫܟܚܐ ܠܐܚܪ̈ܢܐ.

scorpion'.[525] While an ordinary physician is able to amputate a limb, in contrast, the Lord can cut off a limb and replace it again in the same place.[526]

The plural ܐܣܘ̈ܬܐ is either used for ordinary physicians or for the prophets. It occurs mainly in the hymns On Nisibis.[527] In Nis 27.2, Ephrem speaks of ordinary 'physicians' (ܐܣܘ̈ܬܐ) in the context of the woman with the haemorrhage whom they could not heal;[528] whereas in Nis 34, Ephrem describes the patriarchs as 'great physicians' (ܕܐܣܘ̈ܬܐ ܪ̈ܘܪܒܐ)[529] and 'His famous visitors, physicians' (ܣܥܘܪ̈ܘܗܝ ܡܫܡ̈ܗܐ ܐܣܘ̈ܬܐ).[530] The patriarchs (i.e. Abraham, Daniel, Moses and Jacob) are called the 'physicians of the world' (ܐܣܘ̈ܬܐ ܕܥܠܡܐ)[531] or the physician of the world as a sick man (ܠܟܪܝܗܐ ܕܐܣܘ̈ܬܗ)[532] and as the body (ܠܦܓܪܐ) of the statue in Dan 2:31.[533] The function of those physicians was to heal, even though when they performed healing it involved pain (ܚܫܐ).[534] However, the world's physicians were not capable of performing perfect healing with their medicines.[535] In CDiat 10.7a, the author admits that the medicines of the ordinary physicians possess various powers,[536] but what they healed was

---

525 Nis 51.16: ܘܠܐ ܐܣܝܐ ܒܐܣܐ ܚܝܐ ܒܡܣܘܣܐ ܣܡܝܐ ܕܥܩܪܒܐ.

526 Nis 27.1: ܠܐܣܝܐ ܦܫܝܛܐ ܡܨܝ ܕܢܦܣܘܩ ܠܗܕܡܐ

527 Nis 27.2; 34.6-12.

528 Nis 27.2: ܥܢܝܐ ܬܬܒܪܬ ܘܣܓܝ ܦܪܣܘܗ̇ ܐܣܘ̈ܬܐ ܠܗ̇ ܐܬܬܐ ܕܕܡܗ̇ ܦܪܣܘ ܘܠܐ ܣܟܪܘ.

529 Nis 34.6: ܠܦܓܪܐ ܗܘ ܪܒܐ ܕܐܣܘ̈ܬܐ ܪ̈ܘܪܒܐ ܒܟܠܗ ܒܗ.

530 Nis 34.9: ܬܒܒܘ ܗܘܘ ܣܥܘܪ̈ܘܗܝ ܡܫܡ̈ܗܐ ܐܣܘ̈ܬܐ.

531 Nis 34.10; 34.12: ܒܝܫܐ ܗܘ ܚܝܒܝܢ ܠܡܐܣܝܘ ܐܣܘ̈ܬܐ ܕܥܠܡܐ.

532 Nis 34.7: ܐܘ ܠܟܪܝܗܐ ܕܐܣܘ̈ܬܗ ܡܢ ܟܠ ܥܡܘ̈ܗܝ.

533 Nis 34.6: ܠܦܓܪܐ ܗܘ ܪܒܐ ܕܐܣܘ̈ܬܐ ܪ̈ܘܪܒܐ ܒܟܠܗ ܒܗ; cf. Nis 34.9.

534 Nis 34.12.

535 Nis 34.10: ܠܐ ܣܦܩܘ ܠܗ ܕܝܢ ܠܥܠܡܐ ܐܣܘ̈ܬܐ ܒܡܣܡ̈ܢܝܗܘܢ.

536 CDiat 10.7: ܒܣܡ̈ܡܢܐ ܕܐܣܘ̈ܬܐ ܚܝ̈ܠܐ ܡܫܚܠܦܐ ܐܝܬ ܒܗܘܢ.

little compared to what they left.[537] Ephrem often includes the function of human physicians in his texts, in order to contrast it with that of Jesus; for instance, about Lazurus he comments: 'all physicians work on man before he dies, but Lazarus' Physician was waiting for him to die, so that through his death the Physician would show His victory/success.'[538]

The term ܡܐܣܐ ܟܠ, 'Healer of all',[539] is used for the Lord, such as in Nis 34.5: Egypt 'was healed through the Healer of all',[540] or in the context of the 'sinful woman' who believed that 'He was the Healer of all'.[541] Likewise, Jesus' medicine is called the healer of all'.[542]

The term ܡܐܣܝܢܐ, Healer, is not often used. In CDiat 14.22, as well as in Eccl 25:8-9 ܡܐܣܝܢܐ refers to Jesus; for instance, Ephrem speaks of 'the Healer of Zebedee's sons' (ܡܐܣܝܢܗܘܢ ܕܒܢ̈ܝ ܙܒܕܝ).[543] It is also used once each in connection with the spirit that is given to the disciples ( ܕܪܘܚܐ ܡܐܣܝܢܝܬܐ),[544] and with fasting (ܨܘܡܐ ܡܐܣܝܢܐ).[545]

The term ܐܣܝܘܬܐ, 'healing', is mainly related to Jesus himself.[546] In CDiat 13.6, the author uses Jesus' ܐܣܝܘܬܐ as a sign to identify Him with the Lord of Law ( ܘܐܦ ܕܢܡܘܣܐ ܐܣܝܘܬܗ ܕܡܪܐ ܢܡܘܣܐ ܗܘ), i.e. God. The way that Jesus grants ܐܣܝܘܬܐ to man, and only to man, is something that identifies Him as the Lord of Law. Jesus granted healing to man

---

537 Fid 36.1: ܘܐܬܐ ܐܣܝܘ̈ܬܐ ܘܒܛܠܗ ܘܠܐܝܘ ܐܡܪ ܩܠܝܠ ܘܫܒܩܘ ܣܓܝ.

538 CDiat 17.3: ܟܠ ܐܣܘ̈ܬܐ ܩܕܡ ܕܢܡܘܬ ܠܐܢܫ ܒܗ ܒܐܢܫ ܐܣܝܗ ܕܝܢ ܕܠܥܙܪ ܕܢܡܘܬ ܗܘ ܣܟܪ ܗܘܐ ܕܒܡܘܬܗ ܢܚܘܐ ܐܣܝܐ ܢܨܚܢܗ.

539 CDiat 10.10; Fid 15.7; Eccl 31.1; 4.16; 34.5.

540 Nis 34.5: ܕܐܦ ܐܬܐܣܝܬ ܒܡܐܣܐ ܟܠ.

541 CDiat 10.10: ܘܗܘܐ ܐܣܝܐ ܠܗ̇ ܕܗܝܡܢܬ ܕܗܘܝܘ ܡܐܣܐ ܟܠ.

542 Nis 4.20: ܢܟܬܗ ܐܝܟ ܕܚܘܝܐ ܣܡܐ ܡܐܣܐ ܟܠ.

543 Eccl 25.8-9.

544 Virg 4.4: ܕܪܘܚܐ ܡܐܣܝܢܝܬܐ ܦܪܚܘ ܥܠ ܡܪ̈ܥܐ.

545 Iei 4.1: ܗܢܐ ܗܘ ܨܘܡܐ ܡܐܣܝܢܐ.

546 CDiat 12.24; 13.6; 16.31; Dom 13-14; Fid 4.4.

through His 'word' (ܡܠܬܐ),[547] 'His clothes' (ܠܒܘܫܘܗܝ)[548] and the 'edge of His garment' (ܟܢܦܗ).[549] Since oil signifies Christ, it also possesses ܐܣܝܘܬܐ against all harms.[550] Along with oil, ܐܣܝܘܬܐ can be found at baptism too. While the pool of Shiloah could not grant healing to the man who had been an invalid for 38 years, the Church's baptismal font provides healing all the time.[551]

### 3.2.2 ܣܡܐ and Related Terms

The term ܣܡܐ means 'medicine, drug', as well as 'pigment' and with ܡܘܬܐ 'poison'. It is only used four times in the Bible: while in the New Testament the singular ܣܡܐ appears twice (Mk 16:4; Jas 3:8), in the Old Testament the plural ܣܡܡ̈ܢܐ is used twice too (Jr 51:8; Ez 23:14). Neither the term 'Medicine of Life' (ܣܡ ܚܝ̈ܐ), that contrasts with the 'poison of death' (ܣܡ ܡܘܬܐ), nor the verb ܣܡܡ or ܣܡܣܡ occur in the Bible.

In Jer 51:8, in the message about destroying and devastating Babylon, the term ܣܡܡ̈ܢܐ refers to Babylon's pains (ܟܐ̈ܒܝܗ̇): 'Wail over her; take medicines for her pains, perhaps she will be healed'.[552] Even though the term ܣܡܡ̈ܢܐ contrasts with ܟܐ̈ܒܐ, the ܣܡܡ̈ܢܐ are not powerful enough for Babylon's moral and spiritual ܟܐ̈ܒܐ that is sin. The ܣܡܡ̈ܢܐ are not defined here, but since the people are those who are challenged to get ܣܡܡ̈ܢܐ for Babylon's pains, ܣܡܡ̈ܢܐ belong to man and

---

[547] CDiat 12.24: ܘܒܡܠܬܐ ܝܗܒ ܐܣܝܘܬܐ; cf. Dom 13-14.

[548] Dom 13: ܒܗ̇ ܕܝܢ ܕܡܫܠܛ ܐܣܝܘܬܐ ܡܢ ܠܒܘܫܘܗܝ ܐܬܟܐܪܘ ܗܘܘ̈ ܕܠܐ ܡܛܠ ܐܣܝܘܬܐ ܡܢ ܡܠܘܗ̈ܝ.

[549] Dom 14: ܐܦ ܚܢܢ ܡܢ ܟܢܦܗ ܐܣܝܘܬܐ ܕܐܝܟ ܗܕܐ ܒܛܠܝܘܬܐ ܐܬܟܢܫܬ. ܡܟܝܠ ܢܣܒܘ ܗܘܐ ܠܐܣܝܘܬܐ ܕܡܠܬܗ ܒܦܘܪܣܝܐ ܕܗܟܢܐ ܬܘܗ; cf. Fid 4.4.

[550] Virg 4.5: ܐܦ ܡܥܡܕܢܐ ܒܪ ܗܘ ܚܕ ܗܘ ܥܡܕܗ̈ܐ ܕܡܟܠ ܣܓܝܐ̈ܐ ܕܡܕܒܚܝܢ ܒܟܠ ܥܕܢ ܠܐܣܝܘܬܐ ܕܟܠ ܢܟܝܢܝܢ.

[551] Epiph 11.6: ܠܘܒܝܟܝ ܕܐܣܝܘܬܟܝ ܒܟܝ ܗܝ ܠܥܠܡ.

[552] Jr 51:8: ܐܝܠܠܝ ܥܠܝܗ̇ ܣܒܘ ܣܡܡ̈ܢܐ ܠܟܐ̈ܒܝܗ̇ ܕܠܡܐ ܬܬܐܣܐ.

not to God. Man, with his ܣܡ̈ܡܢܐ, cannot heal the pains, because the Lord has already decided to act in vengeance against Babylon to destroy it (cf. Jr 51.1-14). Ez 23:14 uses ܣܡ̈ܡܢܐ in the sense of pigments: 'they saw men portrayed on a wall, figures of Chaldeans portrayed with pigments'.[553] The subject of ܚܙܘ are the two adulterous sisters, Samaria and Jerusalem.

In the New Testament, Mk 16:18 and Jas 3:8, ܣܡܐ is used in the sense of 'poison'. Both texts, precisely, speak of 'poison of death' (ܣܡܐ ܕܡܘܬܐ). Mk 16:18 is at the end of Mark's Gospel where Jesus sends His disciples into the world to proclaim the Gospel to the people. Those who believe in Jesus Christ will be immune against poison of death: 'even though they drink poison of death, it will not harm them.'[554]

### *3.2.2.1 The Term* ܣܡܐ

In Ephrem, usually the singular ܣܡܐ, in the sense of 'medicine', refers to the Lord Who is called, for example, the 'Binder up, Physician and Medicine' (ܚܒܘܫܐ ܗܘ ܘܐܣܝܐ ܘܣܡܐ).[555] The Son of God became Medicine for men (ܠܒܪܗ ܗܘܐ ܣܡܐ).[556] In Nis 4.20, the Lord's medicine is defined as 'medicine of Your salvation' (ܣܡܐ ܕܦܘܪܩܢܟ). Ephrem also speaks of the 'sharp

---

[553] Ez 23:14: ܘܚܙܬ ܠܓܒܪ̈ܐ ܕܨܝܪܝܢ ܒܐܣܛܘܐ: ܨܠܡ̈ܐ ܕܟܠܕܝ̈ܐ ܕܨܝܪܝܢ ܒܣܡ̈ܡܢܐ.

[554] Mk 16:18: ܘܐܢ ܣܡܐ ܕܡܘܬܐ ܢܫܬܘܢ ܠܐ ܢܗܪ ܐܢܘܢ. Jas 3:8, emphasises the impossibility of taming the tongue. The tongue is compared to 'fire' (ܢܘܪܐ, Jas 3:6) that can set a great forest on fire. Although man is able to tame all kinds of creatures, he is not able to tame the tongue for 'it is full of poison of death' (Jas 3:8: ܡܠܝܐ ܗܘ ܣܡܐ ܕܡܘܬܐ).

[555] Nis 34.11: ܘܐܢܬ ܐܠܗܐ ܒܢܝܐ ܘܟܐܒܐ ܕܢܘܓܪܐ ܢܒܥ ܕܐܦ ܥܘܕܪܐ ܗܘ ܐܦ ܚܒܘܫܐ ܗܘ ܘܐܣܝܐ ܘܣܡܐ.

[556] Nat 3.20: ܒܪܝܟ ܐܣܝܐ ܕܢܚܬ ܘܥܒܪ ܕܠܐ ܚܫܐ ܘܐܣܝ ܡܚ̈ܘܬܐ ܒܣܡܐ ܕܠܐ ܚܪܝܦ ܠܒܪܗ ܗܘܐ ܣܡܐ ܕܚܝܐ ܠܚܛܝ̈ܐ.

medicine' of the Lord's justice (ܣܡܗ̇ ܟܐܢܘܬܐ)[557] and of the 'medicine that is not overpowering' (ܣܡܐ ܕܠܐ ܟܒܝܫ).[558] However, ܣܡܐ can also have a negative sense, particularly when it refers to something evil, such as 'poison in food' ( ܣܡܐ ܒܡܐܟܘܠܬܐ);[559] or the disappointment of Nisibis was in the 'medicine' (ܣܡܐ) for which she was waiting, but suddenly it was revealed as a 'real pain'.[560]

The heavenly Medicine, as 'the Healer of all' (ܐܣܝܐ ܟܠ), was beneficial, for example, for the 'wound' of the woman with a haemorrhage (ܠܡܚܣܘܬܗ̇),[561] and is useful for the 'wound' (ܠܡܚܣܘܬܗ) of every sinner.[562] It can be also used for 'us' (ܠܢ),[563] for 'my laceration' (ܠܡܫܚܩܘܬܝ);[564] as well as, for 'sinners' (ܚܛܝ̈ܐ),[565] 'ill' (ܟܪ̈ܝܗܐ),[566] 'sick' (ܟܪܝܗܐ);[567] 'pain' (ܠܟܐܒܐ)[568] and 'wounds' (ܡܚ̈ܘܬܐ).[569]

Different verbs are used along with ܣܡܐ: while medicine can be the agent, as well as, the medium of the verb 'to heal'

---

557 Nis 11.5: ܗܟܢ ܚܝܐ ܘܪܚܡ ܟܪܘܗ̇ ܠܕܚܝܠܝܢ ܣܡܗ̇ ܟܐܢܘܬܐ ܒܚܘܒܗ ܟܒܝܫܐ.

558 Nat 3.20: ܒܪܡ ܐܣܝܐ ܕܚܣܬ ܘܓܒܪ ܕܠܐ ܚܛܐ ܘܐܣܝ ܚܛ̈ܗܬܐ ܒܣܡܐ ܕܠܐ ܟܒܝܫ ܠܗܘ ܗܘܐ ܣܡܐ ܕܚܛܐ ܠܚܛܝ̈ܐ.

559 Nat 26.9: ܐܝܟ ܕܣܡܐ ܒܠܐ ܐܦܝܣ ܘܐܘܟܠܗ ܠܗ ܣܡܐ ܒܡܐܟܘܠܬܐ.

560 Nis 10.16: ܣܡܐ ܕܠܗ ܣܟܝܬ ܟܐܒܐ ܗܘ ܫܪܝܪܬܐ.

561 Fid 12.11: ܚܒܠܬ ܓܠܝܬ ܣܡܐ ܠܡܚܣܘܬܗ̇.

562 Fid 15.1: ܘܐܝܢܐ ܕܬܒ ܚܛܝܐ ܗܘ ܠܟܠܗ ܣܡܐ ܕܢܣܒ ܠܡܚܣܘܬܗ.

563 Fid 5.19: ܫܠܘ ܗܡܝܠ ܕܠܒܝܫ ܕܐܝܢܐ ܣܡܐ ܢܣܒ ܠܢ ܗܡܫܡܫܝܢ ܠܢ ܒܐܣܝܢ ܕܠܒܝܫ ܒܗܢܐ ܘܠܗܘ.

564 Nis 4.20: ܐܣܝܪ ܠܡܫܚܩܘܬܝ ܣܡܐ ܕܡܒܪܘܪܝܢ.

565 Nat 3.20; Fid 15.1.

566 Virg 49.15: ܣܡܐ ܕܐܝܢܐ ܡܢ ܐܣܩܝܢ ܐܣܝܪ ܠܡܣܪ ܕܒܩܝܢ ܟܪ̈ܝܗܐ.

567 Nis 19.11: ܠܗ ܐܣܝܪ ܣܡܐ ܠܟܪܝܗܗ.

568 Nis 19.11: ܠܐ ܚܕ ܣܡܐ ܐܣܝܬ ܠܗ ܠܟܐܒܐ ܕܠܐܒܐ ܠܐ ܒܗܘܢ.

569 Nat 3.20; Eccl 5.6.

(ܐܣܝ);[570] the term ܣܡܐ appears always as the object in the context of the verb 'to propound' (ܐܣܪܚ).[571] The verbs 'to be useful' (ܥܕܪ)[572] and 'to be victorious' (ܙܟܐ)[573] have ܣܡܐ as agent and signify the power of medicine. The verb 'to have pity on' (ܚܣ)[574] is used along with 'sinners' (ܚܛܝ̈ܐ) and portrays the spiritual effect, i.e. the forgiveness of sin. The phrase 'she stole and took' (ܘܓܢܒܬ ܘܫܩܠܬ)[575] refers to the way in which the woman with the haemorrhage managed to receive medicine from Jesus by touching His garment. Both verbs have ܣܡܐ as object and emphasise her longing for it. In turn, the verbs 'to hold out/stretch' (ܐܘܫܛ)[576] and 'to taste' (ܐܛܥܡ)[577] are used for the act of the Evil One and indicate his enmity towards mankind; ܣܡܐ is here the object in the sense of 'poison'.

### *3.2.2.2 The Term ܣܡ̈ܡܢܐ*

The term ܣܡ̈ܡܢܐ, in the plural, is used more often, either in the sense of 'pigments'[578] or 'medicines'.[579] Even though ܣܡ̈ܡܢܐ is sometimes used in the sense of pigments, the pigments can be associated with the new spiritual image of Adam/man. For

---

570 Nat 3.20; Eccl 5.6; Nis 74.14; Virg 49.15.

571 Nis 4.20; 19.11.

572 Fid 5.19: ܕܐܝܟܢܐ ܣܡܐ ܥܕܪ ܠܗ; Fid 15.1: ܘܐܝܟܢܐ ܬܘܒ ܕܚܛܝܐ ܗܘ ܒܟܐ ܣܡܐ ܕܥܕܪ ܠܚܘܣܬܗ.

573 Virg 49.14: ܚܣܘܐ ܬܒܬ ܠܘܩܡ ܡܪܬ ܐܬܚܫܒ ܐܣܝܘܬܐ ܕܙܟܝ ܣܡܗ.

574 Nat 3.20.

575 Fid 12.11.

576 Nat 26.9: ܐܝܟ ܪܫܐ ܢܚܠܐ ܐܘܫܛ ܘܐܘܫܛ ܠܗ ܣܡܐ ܒܐܟܘܠܬܐ.

577 Virg 24.4.

578 Nat 16.7; Virg 7.5; 28.2-3; Fid 5.12; 31.5; 33.4-14; 85.2; Parad 4.9; 11.7; Azym 15.9-11; Eccl 10.6; 20.6; Nis 17.12; 48.7; 68.9.

579 CDiat 5.23; 7.1; 7.20-21; 10.7a; Dom 19; 44; Nat 4.24; 8.2; Virg 30.10; 37.3; 49.17; Fid 2.16; 10.7; 19.11; 28.2; 41.3; 53.6-7; 56.11-12; Iei 4.1; 10.4; 10.6; Azym 20.16; Eccl 1.7; 28.17; 38.4; 52.6; Nis 4.16;-17; 11.6; 16.21; 18.10; 19.11; 34.8; 34.10; 74.14.

Christians, baptism is the place where the new image, the image of the kingdom, is portrayed through the 'visible pigments' (ܣܡ̈ܡܢܐ ܡܬܚܙ̈ܝܢܐ), i.e. oil. This new image contrasts with the corruptible image of Adam.[580] The verb 'to paint/portray' (ܨܳܪ)[581] appears always with the term ܣܡ̈ܡܢܐ when it is used in the sense of pigments, and signifies the act of painting. The term ܣܡ̈ܡܢܐ can also be attributed to 'our free will' (ܚܐܪܘܬܢ),[582] 'faith' (ܗܝܡܢܘܬܐ)[583] and to the mixing (ܡܙܓ) together of the divine and human natures (ܟܝ̈ܢܐ) which produces the God-Man (ܐܠܗ ܒܪ ܐܢܫ), i.e Jesus Christ.[584]

The term ܣܡ̈ܡܢܐ, in the sense of medicines, may belong to the ordinary 'physicians' (ܐܣܘ̈ܬܐ)[585] or 'physician' (ܐܣܝܐ),[586] as well as to the Lord,[587] or to individual people.[588] Even though the medicines of the physicians have different powers so that they can cleanse, consume, cause to grow etc;[589] they were not sufficient for the world.[590] The ordinary physician, along with his medicines, is sometimes used as a metaphor for the Lord and His medicines.[591] A good physician uses the ܣܡ̈ܡܢܐ as an element through which he 'reveals' (ܠܓܠܝܐ ܟܣܝܬܐ) the hidden pains that

---

580 Virg 7.5.

581 Fid 31.5; 33.4-14; 85.2; Parad 4.9; 11.7; Azym 15.9-11; Eccl 10.6; 20.6; Nis 17.12.

582 Fid 31.5.

583 Nat 16.7.

584 Nat 8.2: ܟܝ̈ܢܐ ܡܙܓ ܐܝܟ ܣܡ̈ܡܢܐ ܘܗܘܐ ܐܠܗ ܒܪ ܐܢܫ.

585 CDiat 10.7; Virg 49.14; Nis 34.16.

586 Dom 19; Eccl 28.17.

587 Nat 4.24; Virg 30.10; 37.3; Fid 10.7; 10.11; Azym 20.16; Eccl 38.4; 52.6; Nis 4.16-17; 11.6; 16.21.

588 Dom 44; Virg 49.17; Nis 17.12; 19.11; Nis 34.8.

589 CDiat 10.7: ܒܣܡ̈ܡܢܐ ܕܐܣܘ̈ܬܐ ܚܝ̈ܠܐ ܡܫܚ̈ܠܦܐ ܐܝܬ ܒܗܘܢ.

590 Nis 34.10: ܠܐ ܣܦܩܘ ܠܗ ܕܝܢ ܠܥܠܡܐ ܐܣܘ̈ܬܐ ܒܣܡ̈ܡܢܝܗܘܢ.

591 Dom 19; 44; Eccl 28.17.

can be 'uprooted' (ܡܬܥܩܪ).[592] For Ephrem, the physician's medicines are valued if they possess any power and help.[593] The power of ܣܡ̈ܡܢܐ is a significant aspect for their definition. Even though the nature of their power cannot be defined,[594] one has to be careful how to use ܣܡ̈ܡܢܐ; their power can be 'victorious', but also it can 'kill' (ܩܛܠ).[595] Usually, every one trusts medicines and, in particular, people believe the book of medicines (ܠܣܦܪܐ ܕܣܡ̈ܡܢܐ), such as a blind person will trust medicines.[596] Nevertheless, those who use ܣܡ̈ܡܢܐ have to consider the effect of medicines and not just their visible element.[597]

Although the medicines of Egypt were famous, Moses rejected 'the treasury of medicines' (ܣܝܡܬܐ ܕܣܡ̈ܡܢܐ),[598] for those medicines affected only the body, but not the soul; i.e. at best ordinary medicines might be useful just for physical pains and sickness. The function of ܣܡ̈ܡܢܐ is often to heal the 'pains' (ܟܐ̈ܒܐ),[599] but sometimes they are attributed to 'sickness' (ܟܘܪܗܢܐ), 'wounds' (ܡܚ̈ܘܬܐ)[600] and 'sick' (ܟܪ̈ܝܗܐ)[601] too. If medicines do not have the power of healing anymore, they are

[592] Dom 19: ܐܣܝܐ ܕܝܢ ܐܝܟܐ ܕܒܣܡ̈ܡܢܘܗܝ، ܠܟܐܒܐ ܒܣܝܡܐ ܠܟܠܝܐ ܡܫܬܐܠܐ ܠܗ: ܠܐ ܗܘܐ ܡܒܪܢܫܗ ܗܘ ܕܟܐܒܐ ܐܠܐ ܡܬܠܡܝܕܘܗܝ. ܒܐܒܐ ܓܝܪ ܡܢ ܕܒܣܝܐ ܡܬܠܡܝܢ ܗܘ ܒܫܪ̈ܒܐ. ܐܡܬܝ ܕܝܢ ܕܢܬܟܠ ܒܣܡ̈ܡܢܐ ܡܬܥܩܪ.

[593] Eccl 28.17: ܠܐ ܗܘܐ ܒܣܡ̈ܡܢܘܗܝ، ܕܐܣܝܐ ܚܣܝܪ ܚܝܠܐ ܐܠܐ ܒܥܘܕܪ̈ܢܘܗܝ.

[594] Fid 42.3.

[595] Fid 53.6-7.

[596] Fid 56.11-12.

[597] Eccl 28.17.

[598] Iei 10.6.

[599] Dom 19; Virg 30.10; Fid 56.11; Iei 10.6; Eccl 1.7; 38.4; 52.6; Nis 16.21; 18.10; 34.8.

[600] Nis 74.14.

[601] Fid 19.11.

considered as useless: 'if medicines lose their [power], then no pains can be healed/restored'.[602]

In contrast, the Lord is able to heal 'without medicines' ( ܕܠܐ ܣܡܡ̈ܢܐ)[603] for His words became medicines, useful for every kind of pain.[604] The Lord's medicines cannot be compared to any others; they are gratis and their reward (ܐܓܪܐ ܕܣܡܡ̈ܢܘܗܝ)[605] cannot be paid for by any one.

Ephrem links ܣܡܡ̈ܢܐ to different things that are related to the Lord: the [Birth]day of the Lord is the 'treasure of medicines' (ܣܝܡܬ ܣܡܡ̈ܢܐ);[606] His garment is the 'fountain of medicines' (ܡܒܘܥܐ ܕܣܡܡ̈ܢܐ);[607] His words are like ܣܡܡ̈ܢܐ;[608] His grace carries ܣܡܡ̈ܢܐ;[609] His 'nails' (ܣ̈ܟܐ) became as ܣܡܡ̈ܢܐ.[610] In Virg 37.3, Ephrem speaks of three ܣܡܡ̈ܢܐ through which the Lord 'bound up our sickness' ( ܒܣܡܡ̈ܢܐ ܬܠܬܐ ܚܒܫܗ̇ ܠܟܘܪܗܢܢ): 'wheat, the olive and grapes' (ܚܛܬܐ ܙܝܬܐ ܘܥܢ̈ܒܐ).[611]

The ܣܡܡ̈ܢܐ through which the Lord performs healing do not necessarily come directly from God. Such as in the case of the sinful woman, ܣܡܡ̈ܢܐ can be provided by man. The oil of the sinful woman is considered as 'medicines' that she brought with her and poured over the Lord; the Lord healed her through medicines that she brought.[612] Likewise, 'fasting' (ܨܘܡܐ) can be

602 Nis 18.10: ܕܐܢ ܣܡܡ̈ܢܐ ܦܟܝܗܝܢ ܐܦܠܐ ܟܐ̈ܒܐ ܡܬܐܣܝܢ.

603 Eccl 38.4: ܕܐܣܝܐ ܗܘܐ ܟܐ̈ܒܐ ܒܪ̈ܢܫܐ ܕܠܐ ܣܡܡ̈ܢܐ.

604 Eccl 52.6.

605 Nis 4.16-17.

606 Nat 4.24.

607 Fid 10.7.

608 Eccl 52.6: ܦܬܓܡܘܗܝ ܕܡܝܢ ܠܣܡܡ̈ܢܐ. Cf. Fid 53.6: ܡ̈ܠܐ ܕܦܘܪܫܢܐ ܕܡܝܢ ܠܣܡܡ̈ܢܐ.

609 Azym 20.16: ܛܝܒܘܬܗ ܛܥܝܢܐ ܣܡܡ̈ܢܐ.

610 Virg 30.10.

611 Virg 37.3.

612 Dom 44.

medicines that perform healing.[613] Ephrem also attributes ܡܐܣܝܢܘܬܐ to some people, so that they can perform spiritual healing; such as Jonah possessed ܡܐܣܝܢܘܬܐ,[614] Ephrem challenges the spiritual shepherds to take ܡܐܣܝܢܘܬܐ for their work.[615]

### *3.2.2.3 The Title 'Medicine of Life' (ܣܡ ܚܝܐ)*

The title 'Medicine of Life' (ܣܡ ܚܝܐ) is used for Jesus, Paradise's fragrance, the Tree of Life and for other terms that represent and symbolize the Son of God. In hymn 9 On Paradise, the fragrance of Paradise is not just the air that we breathe, but it has rather a metaphorical character that symbolises the 'Medicine of life' ( ܣܡ ܚܝܐ).[616] Paradise serves as a fountain of well-being (ܚܘܠܡܢܐ) for life on earth as well: the fragrance proclaims the sending of the Medicine of Life.[617]

The function of the fragrant breath which symbolises the Physician and the Medicine of Life is described as follows: Paradise 'cures our sickness' (ܡܐܣܝܐ ܟܘܪܗܢܢ) that entered into the world through the Serpent; the breath 'gives sweetness to the bitterness of this region' (ܡܒܣܡܐ ܠܗ̇ ܠܡܪܝܪܘܬܗ̇ ܕܗܢܐ ܐܬܪܐ); it 'tempers the curse of this earth of ours' ( ܡܟܦܦܗ̇ ܠܗ̇ ܠܗ̇,

613 Iei 4.1; 10.4.

614 Virg 49.17.

615 Nis 19.11.

616 For the background of the phrase in ancient Mesopotamian religion see Widengren, *Mesopotamian Elements in Manichaeism*, 129-38. A comprehensive treatment of the title in a sacramental setting may be found in P. Yousif, *L'Eucharistie chez Saint Ephrem de Nisibe*, OCA 224 (Rome 1984), 317ff.

617 In Parad 11.9-12, Ephrem uses three terms for the fragrance and breath of Paradise. These are ܪܝܚܐ (fragrance), ܢܫܒܐ (breeze, light wind) and ܢܦܘܚܐ (breath, puff of air). In stanza 13 there also appears ܦܝܪܡܐ (censer), ܬܢܢܐ (smoke), ܡܘܫܐ (whiff) and ܗܘܪܡܐ (aroma). While the aspect of the 'fountain' and 'river' refers to Gen 2:6 and 2:10-14, that of 'fragrance breath' has no basis in the Biblical narrative of Paradise. In Parad 11.10, Ephrem gives the reasons for the coming of the Medicine of Life as follows: it is the 'diseased world' (ܥܠܡܐ ܟܪܝܗܐ), its 'sickness' (ܟܘܪܗܢܗ) and 'our mortality' (ܡܝܘܬܘܬܢ).

ܠܘܛܬܐ ܕܐܕܡ); the blessing should 'make clean the fountains of it [the world] that had become polluted by curses' ( ܬܕܟܐ ܠܡܒ̈ܘܥܘܗܝ، ܕܡܪ̈ܝܢ ܒܠܘ̈ܛܬܐ).[618]

In Ephrem's texts, the term 'Medicine of Life' (ܣܡ ܚܝ̈ܐ) frequently characterises Jesus as the Physician. If we have here the same meaning, it is not obvious. The use of the verb 'send' (ܫܕܪ) for the 'Medicine of Life', reminds us of the sending of the Son. Even though in other hymns Ephrem uses other verbs, the role and the function of the Medicine of Life is the same. In Nat 13.2, Ephrem speaks of the Medicine of Life Who 'descended to revive the mother of his mother'.[619] Also in Nat 26.9, Ephrem characterises Jesus as the Medicine of Life who was incarnate in order to grant Adam 'immortality' and to destroy the 'devourer'.[620] Jesus was incarnate because of the mortality and corruptibility of man. The 'medicine' of the economy of Christ should restore the corruptible Adam.[621]

In Eccl 19.7, the term 'Medicine of Life' (ܣܡ ܚܝ̈ܐ) appears contrasted with the 'poison of death' (ܣܡ ܡܘܬܐ). Both terms are described as fruit which the 'free will' of man can pluck (ܩܛܦ). Through the different tenses used the contrast between the Medicine of Life and the poison of death is emphasised. Just as free will plucked the poison of death before, so too she can pluck the Medicine of Life now. The different tenses help us to relate the poison of death to the Tree of Knowledge, and the Medicine of

618 Cf. Parad 11.9-10.

619 Nat 13.2:

ܚܕ̈ܝ ܚܘܐ ܘܐܡܪ̈ܝ ܬܫܒܘܚܬܐ ܘܡܚܝܢ ܗܘܐ ܒܥܘܕܠ
ܕܗܘܐ ܒܪ ܒܪܬܗ̇ ܐܬܐ ܣܡ ܚܝ̈ܐ ܢܚܬ ܕܢܚܐ ܐܡܐ ܕܐܡܗ
ܒܥܠ ܒܪܢܟܐ ܢܪܦܣ ܪܫܗ ܕܚܘܝܐ ܕܚܒܠܗ̇.

620 Nat 26.9:

ܣܡ ܚܝ̈ܐ ܐܬܦܓܪ ܠܡܝܘܬܘܬܗܘܢ ܠܓܙ ܦܓܪܐ ܘܐܬܦܪܣ ܠܡܝܘܬܘܬܗܘܢ
ܠܐܡܝܘܬܐ ܠܐܕܡ ܘܝܗܒ ܠܗ ܠܐܟܘܠܐ ܕܐܟܠܗ ܐܣܬܪܩ.

621 Cf. Eccl 20.6. The word ܣܡ̈ܡܢܐ can have two meanings here: 'medicine' as well as 'pigments'. The verb ܨܪܗ which Beck put in brackets goes with meaning of 'pigments' for painting the image of Adam.

Life to Christ Who is the Tree of Life.[622] In Parad 15.12, the 'Tree of Paradise' has been considered as the 'poison of death' ( ܣܡ ܡܘܬܐ) in contrast to the 'censer of the inner sanctuary'.[623]

'Medicine of Life' (ܣܡ ܚܝܐ) contrasts with the 'poison of death' (ܣܡ ܡܘܬܐ),[624] as the Tree of Life with the Tree of Knowledge.[625] Since the Tree of Knowledge produces the 'poison of death' (ܣܡ ܡܘܬܐ)[626] and caused man's death, in turn, the 'Medicine of Life' (ܣܡ ܚܝܐ) serves as food to nourish every one for life. Thus, Ephrem often uses the title 'Medicine of Life' in connection with 'bread' (ܠܚܡܐ),[627] 'unleavened bread' (ܦܛܝܪܐ),[628] 'lamb' (ܐܡܪܐ),[629] 'fruit' (ܦܐܪܐ),[630] 'cluster' (ܣܓܘܠܐ) or 'bunch' (ܥܛܘܦܬܐ)[631] and 'body' (ܦܓܪܐ).[632]

Furthermore, the aspect of knowledge plays a significant role in the narrative about Paradise, for it is strictly linked with the poison of death. In turn, Ephrem speaks of Jesus 'teaching'

---

622 Eccl 19.7:

ܚܘܪ [ܒܗ̇] ܒܚܐܪܘܬܐ ܕܐܝܟ ܐܢܫܐ [ܗܝ]
ܕܡܚܝܐ ܕܠܟܠ ܦܐܪܝܢ ܬܬܥܘܬܥܛ
ܘܐܝܟ ܕܐܬܡܚܝܬ ܡܢ ܠܘܩܕܡ
ܕܬܬܘܠܦ ܘܬܣܒ ܠܗ̇ ܣܡ ܡܘܬܐ
ܡܚܝܐ ܗܝ ܕܬܬܘܠܦ ܠܗ̇ ܣܡ ܚܝܐ.

623 Parad 15.12: ܐܝܠܢܐ ܕܦܪܕܝܣܐ ܐܣܬܒܪ ܕܣܡ ܡܘܬܐ ܗܘ.

624 Azym 18.15-17; 19.22-24; fide 5.16; Eccl 19.7.

625 See the exegetical section on The Tree of Knowledge and Its Fruit.

626 Eccl 19.7.

627 Nat 4.99; 19.16; Epiph 8.23; Azym 14.14-16.

628 Azym 18.16: ܐܝܟ ܠܦܛܝܪܐ ܡܢ ܣܡ ܚܝܐ ܢܗܒܗ ܠܢܘܗܪܐ ܐܝܟ ܣܡ ܡܘܬܐ.

629 Crucif 2.4: ܕܗܘܐ ܗܘܐ ܐܝܟ ܣܡ ܚܝܐ ܒܪܝܟ ܐܡܪܐ ܕܙܢܗܝ ܐܪܙܗ.

630 Fid 5.16.

631 Fid 12.8; Nat 3.15.

632 Epiph 7.6; Fid 54.10. See also Dom 15; Nat 4.33; Nat 26.9; Epiph 7.23.

(ܘܦܘܠܚܢܗ)[633] and 'His word' (ܦܬܓܡܗ)[634] as the Medicine of Life.

In all other passages, apart from two,[635] Ephrem uses the title 'Medicine of Life' only for Jesus Christ whose presence Ruth had already recognised in Boaz[636] and Tamar in Judah.[637] Likewise, for Moses its symbol was hidden in the unleavened bread (ܦܛܝܪܐ),[638] and in the lamb (ܐܡܪܐ).[639] Moreover, the spiritual bread of the Eucharist does not just symbolise Jesus Christ as the Medicine of Life, but it is 'the Living Bread of the Son'[640] as well.

There are various verbs used in connection with ܣܡ ܚܝܐ. First of all, the verbs 'to descend' (ܢܚܬ),[641] 'to appear/shine' (ܕܢܚ)[642] and 'put on body' (ܠܒܫ ܦܓܪܐ)[643] describe the

---

[633] Dom 15: ܠܐ ܗܘܐ ܒܪ ܡܛܠ ܒܡܘܫܐ ܣܠܩ ܗܘܐ ܡܪ̈ܝܐ ܒܡ ܐܒܝ̈ܠܐ ܘܥܬܝܪ̈ܐ ܐܝܟ ܕܗܘܝ ܦܓܪ̈ܐ. ܐܠܐ ܕܒܡܐܒܠܘܬܗܘܢ ܕܠܗܘܢ ܕܡܚܒ̈ܠܬܐ: ܢܫܠܘܛ ܗܘܐ ܠܗܘܢ ܘܦܘܠܚܢܗ ܐܝܟ ܣܡ ܚܝܐ.

[634] Fid 2.19: ܛܘܒܗܝ، ܠܐܢܫܐ ܕܗܘܐ ܠܗ ܦܬܓܡܗ ܐܝܟ ܣܡ ܚܝܐ ܘܐܣܝܗ̇ ܡܢ̈ܘܬܐ ܟ̈ܠܠܐ

[635] In Virg 49.18 ܣܡ ܚܝܐ is used for Jonah's voice: ܩܠܗ ܕܝܘܢܢ ܗܘܐ ܣܡ ܚܝܐ; and Iei 1.7 refers ܣܡ ܚܝܐ to prayer: ܐܝܬ ܨܠܘܬܐ ܕܚܢܢܬܐ ܗܝ، ܘܐܝܬ ܬܘܒ ܕܣܡ ܚܝܐ.

[636] Nat 1.13: ܪܥܘܬ ܕܝܢ ܒܟܝ ܢܦܠܬ ܗܘܬ ܕܣܡ ܚܝܐ ܚܙܬ ܕܟܣܐ ܒܗ (see chapter IV, 1.3.3).

[637] Eccl 11.10: ܬܡܪ ܕܝܢ ܒܝܬ ܐܘܪܚܬܐ ܥܠ ܝܗܘܕܐ ܢܦܠܬ ܗܘܬ ܘܓܢܒܬ ܡܢܗ ܣܡ ܚܝܐ ܕܟܣܐ ܗܘܐ ܒܗ (see chapter IV, 1.3.1).

[638] Azym 18.15: ܪܙܗ ܗܘ ܕܒܪܐ ܠܦܛܝܪ ܗܘܐ ܡܫܘܕܥ ܟܠܗ ܗܘ ܦܛܝܪܐ ܐܝܟ ܣܡ ܚܝܐ.

[639] Crucif 2.4: ܗܢܐ ܚܫܡܐ ܘܡܒܪܘܢܐ ܕܗܘܐ ܐܝܟ ܣܡ ܚܝܐ ܒܪܝܟ ܐܡܪܐ ܕܪܙܗ ܐܘܪܚܗ.

[640] Azym 17.8-12. See further Nat 4.99; 19.16; Epiph 8.23; Azym 14.14-16.

[641] Dom 3: ܦܢܐ ܒܪ ܣܡ ܚܝܐ ܢܚܬ ܡܢ ܪܘܡܐ ܘܐܬܚܒܠ ܒܟܠܗ ܦܓܪܐ ܒܐܪܥܐ ܡܝܘܬܬܐ; Fid 5.16.

[642] Nat 4.24: ܡܫܝܚܬ ܡܫܒܚܬܐ ܗܘ ܢܡܘܣܐ ܪܒܐ ܕܒܗ ܕܢܚ ܣܡ ܚܝܐ ܠܡܟܪ̈ܝܗܐ.

[643] Nat 26.9: ܣܡ ܚܝܐ ܐܬܦܪܣ ܠܬܪ̈ܝܗܘܢ ܠܒܫ ܦܓܪܐ ܘܐܬܦܪܣ ܠܬܪ̈ܝܗܘܢ.

descending of the Son as the Medicine of Life for the world; furthermore, the verb 'to descend' (ܢܚܬ)[644] along with 'to enter' (ܥܠ)[645] refers to the Lord's descending to Sheol to rend it asunder (ܨܪܝܗܝ).[646] The verb 'to be' (ܐܝܬܘܗܝ)[647] confesses the essentiality of the Son as the Medicine of Life, to whom Mary gave birth (ܝܠܕܬ).[648] While the verb 'to be concealed' (ܟܣܐ, passive)[649] and 'to hide/cover' (ܛܡܪ)[650] is used for His invisibility either as a symbol, such as in the 'lamb' (ܐܡܪܐ), or as real in a human body; the verbs 'to mix' (ܚܠܛ), 'to mingle' (ܡܙܓ) and 'to put on' (ܠܒܫ) describe His act as presenting Himself in the visible elements, such as bread, for man to benefit from Him as the Medicine of Life. Responding to this divine offer, man is allowed 'to eat' (ܐܟܠ)[651] and 'to receive' (ܩܒܠ)[652] it literally in the eucharistic bread and to be 'His consumers' (ܐܟ̈ܘܠܘܗܝ),[653] and man's 'mind' (ܗܘܢܐ) may 'take' (ܢܣܒ)[654] Him. Since 'free will' (ܚܐܪܘܬܐ) enabled man to take the fruit of death, so too, man's free will is free to act and 'pluck' (ܬܩܛܘܦ)[655] the Medicine of Life. Sin, like man's disputation, can 'cut' (ܚܠܐ) man off from the Medicine of Life.[656]

---

644 Nat 13.2: ܕܗܐ ܒܪ ܒܪܬܗ̇ ܐܝܟ ܣܡ ܚܝ̈ܐ ܢܚܬ ܕܢܚܘܣ ܐܒܐ ܕܐܒܘܗ̇; cf. Virg 49.16: ܣܡ ܬܢܝ̈ܢܐ.

645 Nis 36.14.

646 Nat 4.33: ܢܚܬܗ̇ ܐܦ ܐܠܗܗ̇ ܒܡܘܬܐ ܒܫܝܘܠ ܘܨܪܝܗܝ ܣܡ ܚܝ̈ܐ ܕܟܣܝܐ ܗܘܐ ܒܗ.

647 Nat 1.52; Nat 19.16; Azym 14.16.

648 Epiph 8.23.

649 Nat 1.13; 4.33.

650 Azym 18.15: ܪܙܗ ܗܘ ܕܐܡܪܐ ܛܡܪ ܗܘܐ ܒܦܨܚܐ ܒܟܠܗ ܗܘ ܦܛܝܪܐ ܐܝܟ ܣܡ ܚܝ̈ܐ.

651 Azym 19.22; Epiph 7.6; Nat 26.9.

652 Azym 18.17; 19.24.

653 Epiph 7.23:

ܟܘܠܗ ܘܗܘܘ ܡܢ ܐܟ̈ܘܠܘܗܝ ܕܗܘ̇ ܣܡ ܚܝ̈ܐ ܕܐܚܝ ܟܠ.

654 Nat 4.99:

ܠܣܡܐ ܗܘ ܕܚܝ̈ܐ ܦܘܪܫܐܝܬ ܢܣܒ ܠܗ ܗܘܢܐ ܐܝܟ ܣܡ ܚܝ̈ܐ.

655 Eccl 19.7.

656 Fid 54.10:

☞

### *3.2.2.4 The 'Poison of Death' (ܣܡ ܡܘܬܐ)*

The word ܣܡܐ can mean 'poison' as well as 'medicine'. As we saw above in Fid 5.16, Ephrem uses the term ܣܡܐ in both senses: the 'poison of death' and the 'Medicine' of Life.[657] In this context, 'death' and 'life' define the meaning of ܣܡ: the Fruit Which descended can be both Medicine of Life and the poison of death.

The ܣܡ ܡܘܬܐ can be 'Paradise's tree' ( ܐܝܠܢܐ ܕܦܪܕܝܣܐ),[658] the fruit of Paradise or the heavenly Fruit (ܦܐܪܐ), the Son of God,[659] the 'Unleavened Bread' (ܦܛܝܪܐ),[660] 'greed' (ܥܠܘܒܘܬܐ)[661] or hidden in the worldly 'care' (ܟܪܝܘܬܐ).[662]

Ephrem frequently links poison with food. In hymn 26 On the Birth, he speaks of 'poison in food'.[663] The 'poison of death' (ܣܡ ܡܘܬܐ) has its root in the poisonous fruit of Paradise. As a

---

ܕܪܫܡܘܢ ܥܠ ܐܦܘܢ ܒܠܗ ܕܣܡ ܚܝܐ
ܠܐ ܢܐܟܠܘܢ ܐܦ ܠܡ ܕܪܫܝܡ ܕܠܐ ܢܬܐ.

The Son of God descended from heaven as the Fruit which can be either the 'Medicine of Life' (ܣܡ ܚܝܐ) or the 'Medicine of Death' ( ܣܡ ܡܘܬܐ). In On Faith 5.16, the heavenly Fruit is the Medicine of Life for those who are faithful and possess good deeds, such as fasting, praying and being generous towards fellow human beings; or the same Fruit can be the 'poison of death' (ܣܡ ܡܘܬܐ):

ܥܡ ܘܢܝܚܬ ܠܬܗܘܢ ܦܐܪܐ ܒܫܘܒܚܐ ܠܓܢܣܗܘܢ
ܫܠܡܘܬܗ ܬܗܕܝܢ ܠܐ ܬܗܘܝܢ ܒܓܘܬܗ
ܣܡ ܚܝܐ ܗܘ ܕܡܟܫܝܢ ܐܦ ܣܡ ܡܘܬܐ ܠܡܫܘܐ.

[657] Fid 5.16. For ܣܡ ܡܘܬܐ see Fid 5.16; Parad 15.12; Iei 1.6; Azym 18.11-17; 19.22-24; Eccl 11.6; 19.7.

[658] Parad 15.12: ܐܝܠܢܐ ܕܦܪܕܝܣܐ ܐܣܬܒܪ ܕܣܡ ܡܘܬܐ ܗܘ.

[659] Eccl 19.7; Fid 5.16.

[660] Azym 18.11; 18.16-17; 19.22; 19.24.

[661] Eccl 11.6: ܚܙܐ ܟܢܫܝܢ ܠܟܣܐ ܡܛܠ ܕܢܦܩ ܦܣܝܪ ܡܚܠܠܘܬܗ ܘܓܠܬ ܦܣܝܪ ܒܥܘܡܪܗ ܕܡܘܬ ܠܗ ܦܣܐ ܕܡܘܬܐ.

[662] Iei 1.6: ܠܐ ܢܗܘܐ ܠܫܡܐ ܘܢܪܐ ܒܟܪܝܘܬܐ ܕܥܠܡܐ ܒܗ ܣܡܐ ܕܡܘܬܐ ܟܣܝܐ.

[663] Cf. Nat 26.9: ܣܡܐ ܒܡܐܟܘܠܬܐ.

contrast to this poison Ephrem often refers to and portrays the Medicine of Life.[664]

The 'tree of Paradise' (ܐܝܠܢܐ ܕܦܪܕܝܣܐ) offered the 'poison of death' to Adam whose free will (ܚܐܪܘܬܐ) allowed him to pick fruit from it, so too everyone has the free will to pluck either the 'poison of death' or the 'Medicine of Life'.[665] While Ephrem identifies the holy bread of the Eucharist with the Medicine of Life; in turn, he portrays the 'Unleavened Bread' (ܦܛܝܪܐ) as the poison of death, even though in the Old Covenent the Unleavened Bread of the Passover symbolised the Medicine of Life and Bread of Life.[666] In Azym 18 and 19, Ephrem illustrates what happened during the Last Supper to the Unleavened Bread in which the symbol of the Medicine of Life was hidden. In Azym 19.22-24, Ephrem speaks of 'Unleavened Bread of the [Jewish] People' (ܦܛܝܪܗ ܕܥܡܐ), that contrasts with 'our offering' (ܩܘܪܒܢܢ), i.e. the holy Eucharist.[667] The symbol of the Medicine of Life in the Unleavened Bread is taken away from the Passover so that the Unleavened Bread became the poison of death. In turn, the bread of the Eucharist became the real Medicine of Life, no longer only a symbol. For Judas Iscariot, the Medicine of Life was

---

[664] Cf. Fid 5.16; Eccl 19.7; Azym 18.16-17; Azym 19.22-24. As has been discussed in the previous section, in Eccl 19.7, Ephrem presents the 'poison of death' or 'poison in food' and the 'Medicine of Life' in chronological order. The 'poison of death' or 'poison in food' proclaims the victory of the Evil One and Death at the beginning, while the 'Medicine of Life' caused the debts of the Evil One and Death, and He brought man's salvation at the end.

[665] Eccl 19.7; Fid 5.16.

[666] Azym 17.5.

[667] Azym 19.22-24:

ܠܐ ܢܐܟܘܠ ܐܚܝ̈ ܒܗ ܣܡ ܚܝ̈ܐ
ܦܛܝܪܗ ܕܥܡܐ ܐܝܟ ܣܡ ܡܘܬܐ.
ܕܒܗ ܪܐܙ ܕܡܫܝܚܐ ܡܛܫܐ ܘܫܪܐ
ܒܦܛܝܪܗ ܕܥܡܐ ܘܒܩܘܪܒܢܢ.
ܕܫܩܠܗ ܒܩܘܪܒܢܐ ܫܩܠ ܣܡ ܚܝ̈ܐ
ܕܐܟܠܗ ܥܡ ܥܡܐ ܫܩܠ ܣܡ ܡܘܬܐ.

washed from the Unleavened Bread so it became the poison of death for him.[668]

### *3.2.2.5 Excursus: The Term 'Bitterness' (ܡܪܪܬܐ)*

The word ܡܪܪܬܐ, from the root ܡܪ, 'to be bitter, sour, acid', has the meaning of 'bitterness, gall, bile'.[669] In the context of healing, Ephrem also uses it in the sense of poison or venom.[670]

Ephrem considers the advice of the Serpent as an act of 'pouring venom into [Eve's] ears'.[671] While here ܡܪܪܬܐ is related to the Serpent, in hymn 9 On Paradise it refers to the Evil One who 'mixed his cup, proffering its venom to all'.[672] Ephrem links this venom directly to the eating of the fruit. Ordinary fruit gives forth its sweetness in due season but 'a fruit that is out of season, proves bitter to him who plucks it.'[673] The bitterness of the Evil One is so strong that Ephrem compares it with the sea:

> How strong is his bitterness, upsetting the whole
> world.
> Who can hold back the sea of that bitter one?
> Everyone contains drops of it that can harm you.
> Judas was the treasurer (Jn 12:6) of his bitterness,
> and although Satan's form is hidden, in Judas he is
> totally visible;
> though Satan's history is a long one, it is summed up in
> the Iscariot.[674]

---

668 Azym 18.16-17:

ܐܫܝܓܗ ܠܦܛܝܪܐ ܡܢ ܗܘܐ ܣܡܐ
ܢܣܒܗ ܠܝܗܘܕܐ ܐܝܟ ܗܘܐ ܕܡܘܬܐ.
ܗܘܐ ܕܡܘܬܗ ܣܡܝܠ ܕܐܣܟܪܝܘܛܐ
ܥܠܠ ܐܝܟ ܕܒܗ ܕܗܘ ܦܛܝܪܐ.

669 Cf. Azym 30.4; Eccl 8.3; 11.6; Nis 14.2.

670 Parad 7.6; 9.2; 12.3; 15.15.

671 Parad 7.6:

ܬܡܢ ܒܬܘܠܬܐ ܕܫܝܢܐ ܕܐܬܛܠܡ
ܚܘܝܐ ܕܒܫܡܥܝܗ̇ ܡܪܪܬܐ ܙܪܩ ܒܐܕܢ̈ܝܗ̇.

672 Parad 9.2: ܟܣܗ ܡܙܓ ܒܫܝܢܐ ܡܪܪܬܗ ܠܟܠ ܢܫ.

673 Parad 12.3: ܦܐܪܐ ܕܠܐ ܒܙܒܢܗ ܡܪܪܬܐ ܗܘ ܠܡܠܩܛܗ.

674 Parad 15.15:

ܗܐ ܡܪܪܬܗ ܪܒܐ ܗܝ ܕܠܥܠܡܐ ܕܠܚܫܬ

☞

Here for instance 'Judas was the treasurer of his bitterness', but this is not independent of man's free will and thought. As Ephrem shows in hymn 7 On Paradise, man has the freedom and ability to quell the 'bitterness of his thoughts' so that 'springs of sweetness' may well up in his limbs. Here the term ܡܪܝܪܬܐ refers more to the speech and moral life of man.[675]

In hymn 11 On Paradise, in parallel to the 'curse' (ܠܘܛܬܐ),[676] ܡܪܝܪܬܐ has the meaning of bitterness which becomes sweet by the breath of Paradise. Because of the curse, all life on earth would have been bitter, if there had not been the fragrance of Paradise. The source of bitterness may be the 'Serpent' (ܚܘܝܐ)[677] and 'Evil One' (ܒܝܫܐ) on the one hand, or man's 'free will' (ܚܐܪܘܬܐ)[678] and 'greed' (ܥܠܘܒܘܬܐ)[679] on the other.

### *3.2.2.6 The Verb ܣܡܣܡ*

The denominative verb ܣܡܣܡ derives from ܣܡܐ, 'drug, medicine', as well as 'poison' and 'pigment'. While the Pael conjugation ܣܡܡ has a negative meaning, such as 'to poison'; the Palpel ܣܡܣܡ has only a positive sense, such as 'to give medicine, to heal, to cure'.

The verb ܣܡܣܡ is rarely used by Ephrem,[680] whereas ܣܡܡ does not not occur at all. In the hymns On Paradise, the participle ܣܡܣܡ is found twice, in Parad 9.14 and 11.9. In the

---

675 Parad 7.14:

ܘܡܢܘ ܚܙܐ ܕܐܟܠܐ ܢܟܗ ܗܘܐ ܕܒܪ̈ܢܝܐ
ܥܠ ܐܝܟ ܢ̈ܛܘܪܬܐ ܗܘ ܒܟܒܫܐ ܕܠܫܕܪ ܠܗ
ܫܘܕܪܐ ܗܘ ܠܒܪܐ ܕܡܪܝܪܘܬܗ
ܕܗܝ ܓܘܪܬܗ ܒܫܠܝܐ ܗܝ ܒܫܘ ܡܬܝܚܐ ܥܠܗ
ܕܪܒܐ ܗܝ ܠܫܬܥܝܘܬܗ ܡܡܢܗ ܡܡܪܘܛܐ ܗܘ.

ܐܝܟܐ ܕܒܟܘܗ ܗܘܐ ܡܪܝܪܘܬܐ ܕܚܘܫ̈ܒܘܗܝ
ܬܡܢ ܕܚܠܝܘܬܐ ܕܬܠܝܢ ܒܗܕ̈ܡܘܗܝ.

676 Cf. Parad 11.10.

677 Parad 7.6.

678 Eccl 8.3.

679 Eccl 11.6; further more see Parad 7.14; Nis 14.2.

680 Parad 9.14; 11.9; Nis 5.21; Virg 45.22.

latter ܒܡܣܡܣܡ is linked with the term ܟܪܝܗܘܬܐ, 'state of sickness'. It has the meaning of 'curing with medicine, putting a balm on the wound', i.e 'giving medicine to the state of sickness'.[681] The healing of the sickness of earth refers to the breath and fragrance of Paradise. In Parad 9.14, Ephrem portrays this in the 'air' (ܐܐܪ) that is essential for all life on earth. In the context of fire, Ephrem says: 'If fire is confined in a place without air, its flame starts to flicker whereas when it has a breath [of air] this revives it (ܒܡܣܡܣܡ ܠܗ).[682]

In Nis 5.21, ܡܣܡܣܡ is used along with the verb 'to grow' (ܪܒܐ) and refers to the sick 'fruits' (ܦܐܪ̈ܐ) that have survived the wrath.[683] The metaphor of the sick fruits is used for the inhabitants of Nisibis. Nisibis addresses its supplication to the Lord 'to give medicine' and let its fruits grow. While here the agent of ܡܣܡܣܡ is the Lord, in Virg 45.22, the Ninivites are employed as the subject of ܡܣܡܣܡ and they, as sinners, 'gave medicine to [Jonah]'.[684]

### 3.2.3 ܐܬܚܠܡ and Related Terms

While the verb ܐܬܚܠܡ[685] appears six times and ܐܚܠܡ[686] twice in the Old Testament, the terms ܚܘܠܡܢܐ, ܚܠܝܡܐ and ܚܠܝܡܘܬܐ do not occur at all. The concordance for the Syriac Pentateuch does not provide any references for the verb, while in the whole Mautbe it is used only three times, in 2 Kgs 1:2; 8:8 and 20:7. At

---

681 Parad 11.9:
ܒܪܝܚܐ ܕܚܘܠܡܢܗܘܢ ܒܡܣܡܣܡ ܟܪܝܗܘܬܐ ܕܒܠܬ ܒܝܬ ܢܘܚܐ.

682 Parad 9.14:
ܕܐܠܘ ܕܐܬܚܒܫܬ ܐܫܬܐ ܐܬܪܐ ܕܠܝܬ ܐܐܪ
ܕܠܗܒܗ̇ ܡܬܠܦܠܦ ܠܗ ܘܣܘܣܗ̇ ܒܡܣܡܣܡ ܠܗ.

683 Nis 5.21:
ܡܣܡܣܡ ܘܪܒܐ ܒܪܝ܂ ܦܐܪ̈ܐ ܕܐܬܘܬܪ ܪܘܓܙܐ
ܕܗܒ ܠܝ ܐܝܟ ܠܟܪ̈ܝܗܐ ܕܦܠܛܘ ܒܚܡܬܐ.

684 Virg 45.22:
ܒܐܠܦܐ ܡܬܪܘܗܝ ܥܠ ܚ̈ܠܝܢܐ
ܒܚܘܒܐ ܡܣܡܣܡܘܗܝ ܥܠ ܚܛܝ̈ܐ.

685 1 Kgs 20:7; 2 Kgs 1:2; 8:8; Is 38:21; 39:1; Ez 30:21.

686 Is 38:16; Hs 5:13.

the begining of 2 Kings, ܐܬܐܣܝ appears along with ܟܘܪܗܢܐ: after Ahaziah fell and became sick (ܐܬܟܪܗ) he asks Baal-Zebub if he would be 'restored' (ܡܬܐܣܐ) from his sickness (ܟܘܪܗܢܝ)[687] The same phrase, as a question, is also found in 2 Kgs 8:8 where Ben Hadad king of Aram was sick and, therefore, asked Elisha: 'Will I be restored from this sickness'?[688] In Kgs 20:7, the verb ܐܬܐܣܝ refers to ܫܘܚܢܐ instead of ܟܘܪܗܢܐ; the ܫܘܚܢܐ was 'restored' through a 'poultice of figs'.[689]

In the prophets, the verb ܐܣܝ occurs in Is 38:12 and Hs 5:13, whereas ܐܬܐܣܝ is used in Is 38:21; 39:1 and Ez 30:21. In Is 38:21 (= 1 Kgs 20:7), ܐܬܐܣܝ is used again in the context of Hezekiah's sickness; Is 38:16 uses ܚܝ[690] and Is 39:1 ܚܠܡ[691] along with ܐܬܐܣܝ/ܐܣܝ.

In Ez 30:21, ܐܬܐܣܝ refers to the Pharaoh's arm which the Lord has 'broken' (ܬܒܪܬ) and would 'not be bound up and restored to hold a sword'.[692] While in the context of Hezekiah ܐܬܐܣܝ contrasts with ܐܬܟܪܗ, in Ez 30:21 it contrasts with ܬܒܪ. Hosea 5:13 uses ܐܣܝ and ܐܣܐ together in the context of

---

687 2 Kgs 1:2: ܘܢܦܠ ܐܚܙܝܐ ܡܢ ܟܘܫܟܬܐ ܕܥܠܝܬܗ ܕܒܫܡܪܝܢ: ܘܐܬܟܪܗ ܘܫܕܪ ܐܝܙܓܕܐ ܘܐܡܪ ܠܗܘܢ: ܙܠ ܫܐܠܘ ܡܢ ܒܥܠܙܒܘܒ ܐܠܗܐ ܕܥܩܪܘܢ: ܐܢ ܡܬܐܣܐ ܐܢܐ ܡܢ ܟܘܪܗܢܝ ܗܢܐ.

688 2 Kgs 8:8: ܘܐܡܪ ܡܠܟܐ ܠܚܙܐܝܠ: ܣܒ ܒܐܝܕܝܟ ܩܘܪܒܢܐ: ܘܙܠ ܠܐܘܪܥܐ ܕܢܒܝܗ ܕܐܠܗܐ. ܘܫܐܠ ܡܛܠܬܗ ܕܡܪܝܐ ܒܝܕܗ. ܘܐܡܪ ܠܗ: ܐܢ ܡܬܐܣܐ ܐܢܐ ܡܢ ܟܘܪܗܢܝ ܗܢܐ.

689 1 Kgs 20:7: ܘܐܡܪ ܐܫܥܝܐ: ܢܣܒܘܢ ܕܒܠܬܐ ܕܬܐܢܐ ܘܢܣܝܡܘܢ ܥܠ ܫܘܚܢܐ ܘܡܬܐܣܐ.

690 Is 38:16: ܡܛܠ ܗܠܝܢ ܚܝܐ ܕܪܘܚܝ ܐܚܠܡܬܢܝ ܘܐܚܝܢܝ.

691 Is 39:1: ܡܛܠ ܕܫܡܥ ܕܐܬܟܪܗ ܘܚܠܡ ܘܐܬܐܣܝ.

692 Ez 30:21: ܒܪܢܫܐ: ܕܪܥܗ ܕܦܪܥܘܢ ܡܠܟܐ ܕܡܨܪܝܢ ܬܒܪܬ: ܘܠܐ ܡܬܚܒܫ ܕܬܗܘܐ ܠܗ ܐܣܝܘܬܐ: ܘܠܐ ܢܬܬܣܝܡ ܒܠܘܗܝ ܡܠܦܦܐ: ܘܠܐ ܢܬܚܒܫ ܘܠܐ ܢܬܐܣܐ: ܕܢܐܚܘܕ ܣܝܦܐ.

Ephraim's ܟܘܪ̈ܗܢܐ and Judah's ܟܐ̈ܒܐ. Both verbs ܐܚܠܡ and ܐܣܝ refer to 'their pains' (ܟܐ̈ܒܝܗܘܢ).[693]

In the New Testament, ܚܠܝܡܘܬܐ is used only in Acts 3:13, whereas the verb ܐܬܚܠܡ[694] and adjective ܚܠܝܡܐ[695] appear more often. As a verb, ܐܚܠܡ usually appears in the Gospel in the context of Jesus' healing miracles: It is used for the healing of the official's son (Jn 4:52), the man sick for 38 years at the pool-Bethesda (Jn 5:4-15), the daughter of one of the synagogue rulers (Mk 5:23), and for healing on the Sabbath (Jn 7:23). Summarising Jesus' healing miracles, Mt 15:31 refers ܐܬܚܠܡ to the 'crippled' (ܚܓܝ̈ܪܐ), whereas in Acts 5:16 ܐܬܚܠܡ refers to the 'sick and those who have had impure spirits' ( ܟܪ̈ܝܗܐ ܘܐܝܠܝܢ ܕܗ̈ܘܝܢ ܗܘܘ ܠܗܘܢ ܪ̈ܘܚܐ ܛܢ̈ܦܬܐ). Concerning Lazarus, ܐܬܚܠܡ is used along with the verb 'to sleep' (ܕܡܟ) where the disciples say: 'if [Lazarus] is sleeping he will recover' (Jn 11:12: ܐܢ ܕܡܟ ܡܬܚܠܡ).[696]

---

693 Hs 5:13: ܘܚܙܐ ܐܦܪܝܡ ܟܘܪܗܢܗ܆ ܘܝܗܘܕܐ ܟܐܒܗ܆ ܘܐܙܠ ܐܦܪܝܡ ܠܐܬܘܪ܆ ܘܫܕܪ ܠܘܬ ܡܠܟܐ ܕܢܝܪܒ܆ ܘܗܘ ܠܐ ܢܫܟܚ ܠܡܐܣܝܘܬܟܘܢ܆ ܘܠܐ ܢܚܠܡ ܡܢܟܘܢ ܟܐ̈ܒܝܟܘܢ.

694 Mt 15:31 P ܡܬܚܠܡܝܢ, [H ܕܚܠܡܝܢ]; Mk 5:23 P ܬܬܚܠܡ, S ܬܚܝܐ, [H ܕܐܬܦܨܐ ܘܬܚܝܐ]; Mk 16:18 C P ܢܬܚܠܡܘܢ, [H ܘܠܛܒܐܝܬ ܢܗܘܘܢ]; Jn 4:52 C ܗܘܐ ܥܪܝܪ, P ܐܬܚܠܡ, [H ܗܘܐ ܒܛܐܝܬ]; Jn 5:4 P ܡܬܚܠܡ ܗܘܐ, [H ܚܠܝܡܐ ܗܘܐ], not in C; Jn 5:6 S C ܥܪܝܪ, P ܕܬܬܚܠܡ, [H ܚܠܝܡܐ ܠܡܗܘܐ]; Jn 5:9 S C ܐܬܚܠܡ, [H ܚܠܝܡܐ]; Jn 5:15 C ܕܐܚܠܡܢܝ, S P ܕܐܚܠܡܗ, [H ܕܥܒܕܗ ܚܠܝܡܐ]; Jn 7:23 S C P ܐܚܠܡܬ, [H ܚܠܝܡܐ ܥܒܕܬ]; Jn 11:12 S ܚܝܐ, P ܡܬܚܠܡ, [H ܡܬܦܨܐ]; Act 5:16; 28:8; Jas 5:15.

695 Mt 9:12; Mk 2:17; 5:34; Lk 5:31 P [H] ܠܚܠܝ̈ܡܐ; Lk 7:10; 15:27; Jn 5:4 P ܡܬܚܠܡ ܗܘܐ, [H ܚܠܝܡܐ ܗܘܐ], not in C; Jn 5:11 S C ܕܐܚܠܡܢܝ, P [H] ܕܥܒܕܢܝ ܚܠܝܡܐ; Act 4:10; 23:30; Tit 1:9; 1:13; 2:1; 2:7; 2:9; 1 Tim 1:10; 6:3; 2 Tim 1:13; 4:3; 3 Jn 1:2ph.

696 In Rev 13:12 the object of ܐܚܠܡ is ܡܚܘܬܐ ܕܡܘܬܗ. Once, the phrase 'faithful prayer' (ܨܠܘܬܐ ܕܗܝܡܢܘܬܐ) occurs as the subject of ܐܚܠܡ: 'the faithful prayer will restore the sick person' (Jas 5:15: ܘܨܠܘܬܐ ܕܗܝܡܢܘܬܐ ܡܚܠܡܐ ܠܗ ܠܗܘ ܕܟܪܝܗ).

The laying on of hands is a way by which the sick were restored. The sick were restored to health either through Jesus laying on His hand, or through His disciples' hands as they received power to restore sick people (Mk 16:18), for example Paul (Act 28:8).

The term ܚܠܝܡܘܬܐ appears only once in Act 3:13 where the sick person received ܚܠܝܡܘܬܐ through faith (ܗܝܡܢܘܬܐ): 'and the faith in him granted him this health in front of everyone' (Act 3:16: ܘܗܝܡܢܘܬܐ ܕܒܗ ܝܗܒܬ ܠܗ ܗܕܐ ܚܠܝܡܘܬܐ ܩܕܡ ܟܠ).

The term ܚܠܝܡ or ܚܠܝܡܐ is used in four different contexts. First of all, the best known phrase is found in Mt 9:12: ܠܐ ܣܢܝܩܝܢ ܚܠܝ̈ܡܐ ܠܐܣܝܐ. While Mk 2:17 uses the same phrase, Lk 5:31 uses ܡܬܒܥܐ instead of ܣܢܝܩܝܢ and, therefore, the order of the sentence is changed as follows: ܠܐ ܡܬܒܥܐ ܐܣܝܐ ܠܚܠܝ̈ܡܐ.[697] This is the only passage where the plural ܚܠܝ̈ܡܐ is used. Secondly, ܚܠܝܡ refers to individuals who were restored from their physical and/or spiritual sickness; thus the centurion's servant (Lk 7:10), the prodigal son who came back safe and 'sound' (ܚܠܝܡ) to his father (Lk 15:27); the woman who had been subject to bleeding for twelve years (Mk 5:4); the healing at the pool of the one who had been an invalid for 38 years (Jn 5:4; 5:11); the healing of the crippled beggar (Act 4:10) and the healing of many by the apostles, especially of those who were tormented 'by evil spirits' (Act 23:30).[698] Thirdly, in Tit 1:3 ܚܠܝܡܝܢ refers to faith, and in Tit 2:2, furthermore, to faith, love and endurance. Finally, in the epistles to Timothy and Titus, ܚܠܝܡܐ is attributed to 'teaching' (ܝܘܠܦܢܐ)[699] and 'the word' (ܡܠܬܐ).[700]

697 Ephrem quotes this verse in CDiat 5:21.

698 In 3 Jn 1:2, the author prays that Gaius may be ܚܠܝܡ.

699 1 Tim 1:10; 2 Tim 4:3; Tit 1:9; 2:1.

700 1 Tim 6:3; 2 Tim 1:13; Tit 2:7.

In Parad 3.11, Ephrem employs ܚܠܝܡܘܬܐ to denote the perfect state of man, contrasted with ܟܪܝܗܘܬܐ, his fallen state.[701] Being in the state of sickness, ܚܠܝܡܘܬܐ remains a theoretical and almost unrealistic idea that man cannot reach on his own. However, the Lord is never explicitly mentioned in connection with the term ܚܠܝܡܘܬܐ, but instead, the 'oil' (ܡܫܚܐ) 'gives medicine to the state of sickness' (ܡܣܡܡ ܠܟܪܝܗܘܬܐ) and functions as 'the wall of good health' (ܫܘܪܐ ܕܚܠܝܡܘܬܐ).[702] In Eccl 28.10, Ephrem speaks of ܕܘܪܫܐ ܕܚܠܝܡܘܬܐ and considers it as a 'weapon for the body'.[703] By ܕܘܪܫܐ ܕܚܠܝܡܘܬܐ Ephrem means self-discipline in fasting and ascetical training, 'so that [his body] might be restored' (ܕܢܬܚܠܡ),[704] and also be spiritually strong against 'desires' (ܪ̈ܓܝܓܬܐ) and 'our debts' (ܚܘ̈ܒܝܢ).[705]

In contrast to the pain in the world, Paradise is the 'company of restoratives' (ܠܘܝܬܐ ܕܚܘܠܡ̈ܢܐ).[706] While man is not able to reach either ܚܘܠܡܢܐ or the perfect state of ܚܠܝܡܘܬܐ on his own (this would have been granted to him if Adam had been obedient to the Lord's commandment), the Lord alone remains as the 'Treasure of Restoratives' (ܓܙܐ ܕܚܘܠܡ̈ܢܐ),[707] and

701 Parad 3.11: ܕܐܕܡ ܠܒܪ ܒܡܘܣܡܗ ܢܦܩܐ ܠܚܠܝܡܘܬܐ ܘܢܦܩ ܒܪܝܫܗ ܒܗܢܐ ܗܝ ܟܪܝܗܘܬܐ.

702 Virg 4.10: ܗܘ ܡܣܡܡܢ ܠܟܪܝܗܘܬܐ ܘܗܘܘ ܫܘܪܐ ܕܚܠܝܡܘܬܐ.

703 Eccl 28.10: ܠܦܓܪܐ ܐܝܟ ܙܝܢܐ ܗܘ ܠܗ ܕܘܪܫܐ ܕܚܠܝܡܘܬܐ.

704 Eccl 28.9: ܕܬܠܐ ܘܡܟܠܐ ܠܗ ܠܦܓܪܗ ܐܢ ܣܢܝܩܐ ܗܘ ܒܨ̈ܘܡܐ ܘܒܥܡ̈ܠܐ ܕܢܬܚܠܡ ܒܕܘܪܫܐ.

705 Eccl 28.10: ܠܦܓܪܐ ܐܝܟ ܙܝܢܐ ܗܘ ܠܗ ܕܘܪܫܐ ܕܚܠܝܡܘܬܐ ܕܐܦ ܠܢܦܫܬܐ ܠܒܫܐ ܐܦ ܢܦܫܐ ܚܛ̈ܗܐ ܕܚܘܒܬܐ ܘܕܝܢܐ ܪ̈ܓܝܓܬܐ.

706 Parad 5.13: ܬܗܡܬ ܕܒܪ ܒܚܙܬ ܬܘܣܡܗ ܕܦܪܕܝܣܐ ܦܫܛ ܘܦܫܛܬ ܗܘܬ ܠܘܝܬܐ ܕܚܘܠܡ̈ܢܐ.

707 Dom 13: ܠܐ ܗܘܐ ܠܒܪ ܦܓܪܐ ܒܠܚܘܕ ܠܒܪ ܡܢܐ. ܐܠܐ ܐܦ ܗܕ̈ܡܐ ܡܢ ܫܘܬܐ ܐܬܒܠܥ. ܕܒܪ ܗܕ̈ܡܘܗܝ ܘܫܘܬܗܘܢ ܢܬܠܒܒܘܢ ܡܒܣܡܢܐ ܠܡܣܪ ܠܓܙܐ ܕܚܘܠܡ̈ܢܐ.

descended to the world to be the 'Fountain of Restoratives among the sick' (ܡܒܘܥ ܚܘܠܡܢ̈ܐ ܒܝܬ ܟܪ̈ܝܗܐ).[708] For example, the Lord 'brought a treasure of restoratives for the sinful woman's pain',[709] and everyone who accepted Jesus as the Lord received 'the treasure of restoratives for his pains';[710] or 'His right [hand] was full of restoratives'.[711] The term ܚܘܠܡܢܐ is used for the restored health that the Lord granted to the individual,[712] as well as to mankind in general.[713]

In connection with ܚܘܠܡܢܐ different verbs are used, such as: 'He fought with His restoratives against their pains';[714] 'He stretched out and gave restoratives as well as promises'[715] and 'He raised him in (restored) health'.[716] Likewise, people 'have put on health';[717] 'the children ran towards His restoratives';[718] or the sinful

---

708 Dom 42: ܗܘ ܕܡܢ ܕܢܚܬ ܕܢܗܘܐ ܡܒܘܥ ܚܘܠܡܢ̈ܐ ܒܝܬ ܟܪ̈ܝܗܐ. ܗܘܐ ܡܟܪܙ ܗܘܐ ܕܟܠ ܕܨܗܐ ܢܐܬܐ ܘܢܫܬܐ (Jn 7:37).

709 Dom 14: ܡܫܝܚܐ ܗܘܬ ܠܗܝܢ ܟܢ ܠܬܠܬ ܐܣܘܬܗ ܒܡܫܝܚܐ ܕܒܣܡܝܢ. ܕܒܣܡܝܢ ܐܝܬܝ ܠܗ ܣܝܡܬ ܚܘܠܡܢ̈ܐ ܠܟܐܒ̈ܝܗ; cf. Lk 7:36-50.

710 CDiat 7.5: ܘܕܗܘܒ ܗܘܐ ܠܗ ܐܠܗܘܬܐ ܣܝܡܬ ܚܘܠܡܢ̈ܐ ܠܟܐܒܘ̈ܗܝ، ܡܫܡܫ ܗܘܐ.

711 CDiat 13.6: ܐܠܐ ܝܡܝܢܗ ܗܘ ܡܠܝܐ ܚܘܠܡܢܐ.

712 CDiat 6.22b: ܘܗܕܐ ܗܝ ܬܘܕܝܬܐ ܕܐܦ ܩܕܡ ܚܘܠܡܢܗ ܕܛܠܝܐ ܬܪ̈ܝܢ ܢܦܫܗ ܘܩܕܡܗ ܠܒܪܐ ܒܡܗܝܡܢܘܬܗ (Mt 8:8; Lk 7:6); or ܚܘܠܡܢܐ of the woman with the haemorrhage, CDiat 7.2: ܐܪܡܝܬ ܟܢ ܥܠܘܗܝ ܣܘܟܠܐ ܡܗܝܡܢܘܬܐ. ܘܝܗܒ ܠܗ ܗܘ ܦܘܪܥܢ ܣܘܟܠܗ ܚܘܠܡܢܐ (cf Lk 8:45f); cf. CDiat 7.9; 7.20.

713 Such as ܚܘܠܡܢܐ ܕܦܓܪܐ; cf. CDiat 6.21b: ܝܗܒ ܟܢ ܠܟܠܢ ܐܢܫܐ ܚܘܠܡܢܐ ܕܦܓܪܐ. ܘܐܣܝܘܬܐ ܕܢܦ̈ܫܬܐ.

714 Dom 21: ܥܠ ܕܐܘܪܒܘ ܥܡ ܟܐܒܐ ܗܘ ܕܐܘܪܒ ܒܚܘܠܡܢܘ̈ܗܝ، ܠܘܩܒܠ ܟܐܒ̈ܝܗܘܢ.

715 Resurr 1.10:

ܗܘ ܥܠ ܟܐܒ̈ܝ ܐܘܫܛ ܘܝܗܒ ܐܦ ܚܘܠܡܢ̈ܐ ܥܡ ܡܘܠܟ̈ܢܐ.

716 Fide 54.4:

ܟܕܐ ܚܙܐ ܕܐܪܟܐ ܐܩܝܡܗ ܒܚܘܠܡܢܐ.

717 Fide 86.4:

ܘܕܢܚܐ ܥܠܝܐ ܒܟܠܗܐ ܪܘܚܐ ܠܒܫܘ ܚܘܠܡܢܐ.

718 Resurr 1.10: ܪܗܛܘ ܥܒܕܗ ܥܡ ܚܘܠܡܢܘ̈ܗܝ.

woman 'stole health from the edge of His garment'.[719] In contrast, instead of 'coming towards' the health[720] that the Lord can create,[721] man is able to reject it too.[722] Therefore, in Nis 26.5, Ephrem warns man to stay in his final (restored) health lest he perish.[723] Beside the Lord, also those chosen by God are able to provide healing and restore the sick to health.[724] The oil offers restoration and symbolises the restored health that the Lord grants.[725]

Obviously, according to the Gospel, Ephrem refers to the Lord as the agent of ܐܚܠܡ, but he quotes only once from the Gospel where Jesus is the subject of ܐܚܠܡ: 'He who restored me is the one who said to me take up your bed.'[726] Based on this, Ephrem speaks of restoring the limbs: 'see He has restored the

---

[719] Dom 49: ܗ̇ܝ ܕܬܪܒ ܗܘܐ ܕܟܒܗ̇ ܚܘܠܡܢܐ ܡܢ ܩܪܢܐ ܕܟܪܦܘܬܗ ܓܢܒܬ.

[720] Nis 5.22:

ܒܟܝܗ̇ ܕܟܠܬܝ ܡܪܝ ܒܟܢܪܬ ܕܐܝܟ ܢܘܚܐ ܗܘ
ܕܡܫܒܪ̈ܐ ܡܪܕ ܠܗ ܘܢܦܠ ܒܒܘܪܗܢܐ
ܢܐܬܐ ܠܚܘܠܡܢܐ ܕܢܦܘܐ ܠܒܘܝܐܐ.

[721] Nis 11.7: ܬܘܠܕ ܚܘܠܡܢܐ.

[722] C.Jul 1.9:

ܘܩܛ̈ܠܐ ܕܐܬܟܡܫܘ ܠܐ ܚܙܘ ܒܟܐܒ̈ܝܗܘܢ
ܘܟܕ ܐܣܝܐ ܩܪܒ ܢܓܕܘܗܝ ܠܚܘܠܡܢܐ.

[723] Nis 26.5:

ܢܠܦܪ ܒܢܝܫܗ ܣܟܐ ܕܠܐ ܢܬܢܫܘܗܝ
ܠܝ ܟܐܒ ܕܐܬܒܪܬ ܘܕܐܬܦܩܣܘ ܗܘܠܝ
ܢܛܘܪ ܒܚܘܠܡܢܐ ܐܚܪܝܐ ܕܠܐ ܢܐܒܕ.

[724] Nis 19.11:

ܠܕܪܫܗ ܫܡܥܐ ܐܣܝܪ ܠܗ ܘܠܐܝܢܐ ܕܚܠܝܡ ܢܦܩܪܐ
ܐܫܟܚܐ ܡܪܒ ܒܡܕ̈ܪܢܐ ܕܒܐܒܐ ܢܦܫܐ ܚܘܠܡܢܐ.

[725] Virg 4.4:

ܡܫܝܚܐ ܟܪ ܕܡܗܬ ܡܟܐ ܘܒܗ ܗܘ ܙܕܩ ܒܡܕ̈ܪܢܐ
ܠܡܕ̈ܒܪܐ ܐܝܟ ܠܠܒܐܢܐ ܠܟܠܠ ܬܘܒ ܚܘܠܡ̈ܢܐ...
ܘܟܠܗ ܡܫܚܐ ܚܘܠܡ̈ܢܝܗܘܢ ܒܟܗ ܦܓ̈ܪܐ ܠܟܐܒ̈ܐ ܒܐ̈ܒܐ.

[726] CDiat 13.3: ܗܘ ܠܝ ܕܐܚܠܡܢܝ ܗܘ ܐܡܪ ܠܝ ܕܫܩܘܠ ܥܪܣܟ; Jn 5:11 C.

limbs' (ܕܗܐ ܐܣܠܡ ܗܕܡ̈ܐ).[727] The Lord is the agent here, as in CDiat 16.12: 'He restored [Nicodemus's] sickness through His gentle voice'.[728] The Lord does not only restore individual limbs, but also 'sick bodies' (ܐܣܠܡ ܦܓܪ̈ܐ ܟܪ̈ܝܗܐ);[729] and 'He restored ill and sick people' (ܠܡܪ̈ܥܐ ܘܠܟܪ̈ܝܗܐ ܐܣܠܡ).[730] Just as in the case of Lazarus, Ephrem goes beyond the physical sense of ܐܣܠܡ and attributed ܐܣܠܡ to 'our wounds' (ܟܐ̈ܒܝܢ),[731] and in an abstract sense to 'the heart's mouth' (ܦܘܡܐ ܕܠܒܐ),[732] 'our sickness' (ܒܘܪܗܢܢ)[733] and 'our souls' (ܢܦܫ̈ܬܢ).[734]

Individual people are restored or can be restored through the Lord; as 'Simon's mother-in-law was restored'[735] and the one who

---

[727] Dom 21: ܠܐ ܕܝܢ ܡܬܕܠܚܠܐ ܗܘܬ ܕܠܐ ܥܒܕ ܣܘܠܚܐ ܡܛܠ ܕܗܐ ܐܣܠܡ ܗܕܡ̈ܐ.

[728] CDiat 16.12: ܘܐܣܠܡ ܟܘܪܗܢܗ ܒܝܕ ܩܠܗ ܡܟܝܟܐ; cf. Virg 29.5. Jn 3:1-21 does not speak of restoring/healing Nicodemus.

[729] Dom 42: ܒܥܘܩܐ ܠܟܢ ܐܣܠܡ ܦܓܪ̈ܐ ܟܪ̈ܝܗܐ.

[730] Nis 39.3:
ܗܢܐ ܥܢܘܝܐ ܘܡܟܝܟܐ ܕܟܣܝܬ ܒܠܗܘܢ، ܠܡܪ̈ܥܐ ܘܠܟܪ̈ܝܗܐ ܐܣܠܡ.

[731] Nis 34.10:
ܘܐܦ ܣܡ ܒܦܓܪܗ ܘܐܕܡܗ ܐܣܠܡܗ ܟܐ̈ܒܝܢ.

[732] Eccl App a:
ܠܦܘܡܐ ܕܠܒܐ ܡܪܝ ܐܣܠܡ ܢܗܐ ܒܘܪܐ ܠܡܚܫ̈ܬܐ.

[733] Fide 35.4:
ܡܪܝ ܐܣܠܡ ܒܘܪܗܢܢ ܕܐܣܠܡܬ ܢܟܒ̈ܐ ܥܒܕܝ.

Nis 6.1:
ܐܪܗܛ ܒܐܘܠܨ̈ܢ ܠܘܬ ܐܣܝܐ ܕܡܟܝܠ
ܕܐܣܝ ܠܒܘܣ̈ܡܣ ܡܕ̈ܝܢܬܐ ܘܬܫ̈ܢܝܩܐ
ܕܐܣܠܡ ܬܠܝܬ̈ܝܐ ܢܐܣܐ ܐܪ̈ܒܥܝܢ.

[734] CDiat 7.27b:
ܗܕܐ [ ] ܣܡܟܬܐ ܕܐܠܗܘܬܐ
ܕܒܗ ܡܐܣܐ ܗܘܐ ܦܓܪܐ
[ ] ܣܠܡ ܐܦ ܢܦܫ̈ܬܐ.

[735] Nis 39.15: ܚܡܬܗ ܕܫܡܥܘܢ ܐܬܐܣܠܡܬ; Mk 1:30 and Lk 4:38 do not use ܐܬܐܣܠܡܬ/ܐܣܠܡ.

was sick for 38 years;[736] or the sinful woman[737] and her 'pains' (ܟܐ̈ܒܐ);[738] also the 'crippled' (ܚܓܝܖ̈ܐ),[739] and those who were 'sick' (ܟܪ̈ܝܗܝܢ).[740] Referring to the healing of the demon-possessed man in the region of the Gerasenes, Ephrem plays with the verbs ܐܣܝ/ܐܬܐܣܝ and ܐܠܦ/ܝܠܦ; while the Lord is the agent of restoring and teaching, the demon-possessed man is the one who 'has been restored' first and then 'learned'.[741]

The use of the verb ܐܣܝ/ܐܬܐܣܝ occurs in the context of the prophet Elisha too who 'restored the illness/sickness of the barren land'.[742] While here ܐܣܝ is attributed to the ܟܘܪܗܢܗ ܕܐܪܥܐ ܥܩܪܬܐ, in Parad 11.11 ܐܬܐܣܝ refers to the element water that was 'restored through the salt'.[743] This is taken as a metaphor for the spiritual restoration of the world.[744] In particular, 'our breath' (ܦܘܚܢ) can be 'restored through the restored fragrance of Paradise'.[745] Furthermore, the verb ܐܬܐܣܝ is used

---

[736] CDiat 13.3: ܗܘ ܠܡ ܕܐܣܝܢܝ ܗܘ ܐܡܪ ܠܝ ܕܫܩܘܠ ܥܪܣܟ ... ܒܬܪ ܗܠܝܢ ܚܙܝܗܝ ܘܐܡܪ ܠܗ. ܗܐ ܚܠܝܡ ܐܢܬ ܬܘܒ ܠܐ ܬܚܛܐ; Jn 5:11-15.

[737] Fide 10.6: ܘܐܝܟ ܗܝ ܕܬܗܪܬ ܘܐܬܠܒܒܬ ܕܐܬܐܣܝܬ; Lk 7:36-50.

[738] Virg 26.4: ܛܘܒ ܠܟܐ̈ܒܝܗ ܕܐܬܐܣܝܘ ܒܡܠܬܐ; Lk 7:36-50.

[739] Virg 19.2: ܚܓܝܖ̈ܐ ܕܐܬܐܣܝܘ ܕܪܓܘ ܘܪܗܛܘ ܒܗܝܢ; for ܚܓܝܖ̈ܐ see Mt 11:5; 15:30-31; Lk 7:22.

[740] Virg 4.8: ܛܠܠ ܫܡܥܘܢ ܟܕ ܢܦܠ ܗܘܐ ܥܠ ܟܪ̈ܝܗܝܢ ܘܡܬܐܣܝܢ ܗܘܘ; for ܛܠܠܐ cf. Act 5:15.

[741] Azym 1.3:

ܠܡܪܢ ܗܘ ܒܠܒܘܬܗ ܕܐܡܪܐ ܢܣܒ ܘܐܠܦ
ܠܫܐܕܐ ܕܐܣܝ ܐܣܝܗ ܘܗܘ ܝܠܦ
ܐܡܪܐ ܢܣܒ ܕܝܠܦ ܕܟܕ ܐܬܐܣܝ ܝܠܦ

(Mt 8:29; Mk 5:7; Lk 8:28).

[742] Epiph 11.7: ܡܢܐ ܟܪ̈ܝܗܐ ܐܣܝ ܢܒܝܐ ܘܐܣܝ ܗܘܐ ܟܘܪܗܢܗ ܕܐܪܥܐ ܥܩܪܬܐ; 2 Kgs 2:19-22.

[743] Parad 11.11: ܐܝܟ ܕܐܬܐܣܝܘ ܡܝ̈ܐ ܟܪ̈ܝܗܐ ܒܝܕ ܡܠܚܐ; 2 Kgs 2:19-22.

[744] Parad 11.11: ܘܬܐܣܝ ܠܡܥܡܘܕܗ ܡܕܝ̈ܢܬܐ ܒܠܘܛܬܐ.

[745] Parad 11.12:

☞

for geographical places: the sick land[746] was restored through the Lord's sweat; Egypt was restored through the Healer of All;[747] and Babel as the head that went mad in the desert was restored through the prophet Daniel.[748]

In some general contexts, Ephrem portrays the characteristics of medicine: 'if medicine becomes powerless, no pains can be restored'.[749] Two other sayings are based on Scripture and Nature. The former is based on Mt 9:12 (Mk 2:17; Lk 5:31-32): 'when this man's fellow Pharisees took exception to the healing of sinners, the Physician explained this about His art, that the door was open to the sick, not to the healthy: »the healthy have no need of a physician, but those who have engaged in all kinds of evil«'.[750] The second proverbial saying is based on Nature: 'the nature of sweetness is sweet for the one who is restored, [but] bitter for the one who is sick; likewise the free will is sick for the sinners, but restored for the just.'[751]

---

ܘܒܗ ܠܒܗܐ ܢܦܫ    ܟܕ ܡܬܐܣܝܢ ܗܘܘ
ܒܡܟܒܗ ܚܠܝܡܐ    ܕܦܪܕܝܣܐ.

746 Crucif 8.1:

ܛܘܒ ܠܐܪܥܐ ܕܒܕܘܥܬܗ ܒܣܡܗ̇
ܘܕܟܪܝܗܐ ܐܬܐܣܝܬ ܕܒܗ̇ ܕܥܠܬ
ܡܠܘ ܚܝܐ ܡܬܘܡ ܠܟܪܝܗܐ
ܕܐܬܐܣܝܬ ܒܕܘܥܬܐ ܕܠܐ ܕܝܠܗ.

747 Nis 34.5:
ܚܘ ܠܡܨܪܝܢ ܟܪܝܗܬܐ ܕܐܦ ܐܬܐܣܝܬ ܒܡܐܣܝܐ ܟܠ
ܘܟܡܐ ܕܐܬܐܣܝܬ ܠܝܬ ܬܘܕܝܬܐ ܟܠ ܚܘܠܡܢܗ̇.

748 Nis 34.8: ܐܦ ܕܫܐܛ ܠܒܒܠ ܕܡܝܐ ܐܝܟ ܕܪܫܐ ܕܫܢܐ ܒܡܕܒܪܐ ܘܐܬܐܣܝܬ ܘܐܘܕܝ.

749 Nis 18.10: ܕܐܢ ܣܡ̈ܡܢܐ ܦܣܝܩܝܢ ܐܦܠܐ ܟܐܒ̈ܐ ܡܬܐܣܝܢ.

750 Dom 42: ܟܕ ܕܝܢ ܪܛܢܘ ܗܘܘ ܦܪ̈ܝܫܐ ܚܒܪ̈ܘܗܝ ܕܗܢܐ ܥܠ ܚܘܠܡܢܗܘܢ ܕܚܛܝ̈ܐ. ܐܦܩ ܐܣܝܐ ܥܠ ܐܘܡܢܘܬܗ ܕܬܪܥܐ ܠܡܟܐܒ̈ܐ ܗܘ ܦܬܝܚ ܘܠܐ ܠܚܠܝܡ̈ܐ. ܠܐ ܠܡ ܚܪ ܣܢܝܩܝܢ ܚܠܝ̈ܡܐ ܥܠ ܐܣܝܐ ܐܠܐ ܐܝܠܝܢ ܕܒܫܫܝܢ ܒܟܠ ܒܝܫܢ. ܡܟܝܠ ܐܣܝܐ ܡܠܘܫܗ ܚܘܠܡܢܐ ܗܘ ܕܡܟܐܒ̈ܐ. Mt 9:12; Mk 2:17; Lk 5:31-32.

751 Eccl 2.19: ܟܝܢܗ̇ ܕܚܠܝܘܬܐ ܚܠܝܐ ܠܗ̇ ܠܡܢ ܕܚܠܝܡ ܡܪܝܪܐ ܠܗ̇ ܠܡܢ ܕܟܪܝܗ ܗܟܢ ܐܦ ܚܐܪܘܬܐ ܟܪܝܗܐ ܠܚܛ̈ܝܐ ܘܚܠܝܡܐ ܠܙܕܝ̈ܩܐ.

From all this it is obvious that ܚܘܠܡܢܐ belong to the Lord, especially when Ephrem uses the term ܚܘܠܡܢ̈ܘܗܝ, 'His restoratives'[752] or ܚܘܠܡܢܟ, 'Your restorative (power)'.[753] But because man is the receiver of ܚܘܠܡܢܐ, Ephrem can also attribute ܚܘܠܡܢܐ to individuals,[754] peoples[755] and places, such as Egypt.[756]

The adjective ܚܠܝܡܬܐ/ܚܠܝܡܐ can also refer to individual limbs, such as 'ear' (ܐܕܢܐ),[757] 'mouth' (ܦܘܡܐ)[758] and 'hands' (ܐܝ̈ܕܝܐ);[759] as well as to the 'senses' (ܪ̈ܓܫܐ),[760] 'voice' (ܩܠܐ),[761] the world as 'body' (ܦܓܪܐ),[762] or the sheep as a metaphor for man (ܢܩܝܐ);[763] it can also refer to the fragrance of Paradise (ܡܥܛܪܗ).[764]

---

752 Dom 21: ܗܘ ܕܐܘܪܒ ܒܚܘܠܡܢ̈ܘܗܝ ܠܗܘܒܠ ܒܐܣܝ̈ܘܬܗܘܢ; Resurr 1.10: ܪܗܛܘ ܥܒ̈ܕܗ ܓܝܪ ܚܘܠܡܢ̈ܘܗܝ.

753 Nat 18.27: ܒܪܢܟ ܚܘܠܡܢܟ.

754 In Nis 39.15, ܚܘܠܡܢܗ̇, 'her health', is used for Simon's mother-in-law: ܚܡܬܗ ܕܫܡܥܘܢ ܐܬܚܠܡܬ ܠܚܘܒܠ ܕܝܢ ܐܚܪܬܗ ܠܟܐܒܐ ܕܚܘܠܡܢܗ̇; in CDiat 7.9, for the woman with the haemorrhage: ܡܛܠ ܕܒܥܬܗ̇ ܗܘܐ ܚܘܠܡܢܗ̇; cf. CDiat 7.2; 7.18; 7.20.

755 In Dom 42, ܚܘܠܡܢܝ̈ܗܘܢ refers to sinners: ܒܗ ܕܝܢ ܪܓܠܘ ܦܬ̈ܟܪܐ ܚܒ̈ܪܘܗܝ ܕܗܢܐ ܥܠ ܚܘܠܡܢܝ̈ܗܘܢ ܕܚܛܝ̈ܐ.

756 Nis 34.5: ܬܠܬ ܬܘܠܕܬܐ ܥܠ ܚܘܠܡܢܗ̇ ܘܒܡܐ ܕܐܬܚܠܡܬ.

757 Virg 30.3:

[ܐܕܢܐ] ܚܠܝܡܬܐ [ܒܡܐ ܫܡܥܬ] ܠܗ̇ ܩܠܐ ܚܠܝ̈ܡܐ ܠܗ̇.

758 Eccl 2.20: ܦܘܡܐ ܗܘ ܚܠܝܡܐ ܒܢ̈ܝ ܟܘܪܐ ܕܬܠܡܝܕܘܬܐ; cf. Eccl 43.20: ܗܐ ܬܒܪܝܗܝ ܦܘܡܗ ܕܒܟܪ ܚܠܝ̈ܡܬܐ.

759 Nis 43.9: ܬܘܒ ܗܘ ܐܠܝܥܙܪ ܐܝܕ̈ܘܗܝ ܒܪ̈ܝܫܘܬܐ ܥܠ ܐܝ̈ܕܐ ܚܠܝ̈ܡܬܐ ܕܡܠܟܐ ܢܣܒ ܗܒܪܗ.

760 Fide 42.1: ܟܠܗ ܡܢܐ ܪ̈ܓܫܐ ܚܠܝ̈ܡܬܐ ܕܢܦܩܘ ܠܗ

761 Virg 30.3; Fide 22.3.

762 Nis 34.13: ܠܟܠܐ ܕܠܐ، ܒܟܠܡܐ ܕܢܗܘܐ ܟܠܗ ܠܦܓܪܐ ܚܠܝܡܐ.

763 Nis 19.4: ܢܩܝܐ ܚܠܝܡܐ ܢܛܪ; 19.11: ܘܠܝܢܐ ܕܚܠܝܡ ܢܛܪܐ.

764 Parad 11.12: ܒܗ ܕܡܬܚܠܡ ܗܘܐ ܒܡܥܛܪܗ ܚܠܝܡܐ ܕܦܪܕܝܣܐ.

### 3.2.4 ܚܒܫ and Related Terms

The verb ܚܒܫ means 'to bind up or bandage', such as a wound.[765] In the Peshitta Old Testament, the object is normally 'that which is broken',[766] though in Ps 147:3 it is the ܟܐܒ̈ܝܗܘܢ of the 'broken hearted'. The only occurrence of the verb in the Syriac New Testament is in Luke 10:34, in the parable of the Good Samaritan.

Ephrem uses ܚܒܫ in several hymns.[767] In the context of healing, the verb appears only in the active. Although the subject of ܚܒܫ is often related to God, such as 'the hand of Your grace' (ܐܝܕܐ ܕܛܝܒܘܬܟ),[768] Nevertheless, people can also act as the subject.[769] As in the Old Testament, the main words used to denote the object of the verb are based on the root ܬܒܪ.[770] However, the terms ܟܠ ܟܐܒ̈ܝܢ, ܟܘܪ̈ܗܢܝܢ and ܬܒ̈ܪܐ also appear as the object of ܚܒܫ.[771]

The noun ܚܒܫܐ, 'binding' or 'bandage', appears only four times in the context of spiritual healing.[772] The form ܚܒܘܫܐ, along with 'guard' (ܢܛܘܪܐ), 'pardoner' (ܫܒܘܩܐ) and 'pursuer' (ܪܕܘܦܐ), appears as a title for the Lord Who is the 'Binder up of their wounds'.[773] Likewise, in Crucif 2.3 where Ephrem speaks about the Passover, the term ܚܒܫ ܟܠ is used once for Jesus the 'New Lamb' (ܐܡܪܐ ܚܕܬܐ): 'for He is the One Who binds up

---

765 Cf. J. P. Smith, A Compendious Syriac Dictionary, 423.

766 Eg. Ezek 34:4 ܠܕܬܒܝܪܐ; Is 30:26 ܬܒܪܐ ܕܥܡܗ; Is 61:1 ܬܒܝܪ̈ܝ ܠܒܐ.

767 Cf. Azym 20.18; Crucif 2.3; Eccl 5.2; 33.3; 43.6-7; Iei 4.1; Nis 2.17; 14.2; 19.4; 34.1; Virg 4.9; 37.3.

768 Azym 20.16; Crucif 2.3; Eccl 5.2; 33.3; Nis 11.7.

769 Cf. Virg 49.13; Nis 14.2; 34.1.

770 Cf. Nat 17.7; Iei 4.1; Crucif 2.3; Eccl 43.6-7; Nis 2.17; 10.16; 14.2; 19.4.

771 Cf. Virg 37.3; Azym 20.18; Eccl 5.2.

772 Cf. Nat 17.7; Nis 10.16; 11.7; Virg 49.13.

773 Nat 17.7: ܘܕܟܐܒ̈ܝܗܘܢ ܗܘ ܚܒܘܫܐ ܠܬܒܝܪ̈ܝܗܘܢ.

the wounded; thanks to the Lord Who binds up all' ( ܕܗܘܝܘ ܚܒܫ ܠܬܒܝܪܐ܆ ܬܘܕܝ ܠܡܪܐ ܚܒܫ ܟܠ).[774]

In Virg 4.9, the oil which signifies Jesus is used as the subject: 'in vexation it bandaged their heads' ( ܒܡܥܝܩܘܬܐ ܚܒܫ ܪ̈ܝܫܝܗܘܢ),[775] the 'bandaging' referring to the healing effect of the anointing of the forehead (ܪܘܫܡܐ) in baptism. In order to describe the function of the oil which is the treasure of symbols, Ephrem uses other verbs too, such as ܐܠܒܫ, ܐܣܒܥ, ܐܪܘܝ and ܟܒܫ.[776] While the oil is the subject, in Virg 37.3, the 'wheat' (ܚܛܬܐ), 'olive' (ܙܝܬܐ) and 'grapes' (ܘܥܢ̈ܒܐ) are the medium through which the 'binding' is performed: 'with three medicines You bound up our sickness'.[777] The object, 'our sickness' (ܠܟܘܪܗܢܢ), is not further defined. But from the context it is obvious that Ephrem means the sickness that was caused by the Serpent and Satan.

In Azym 20.18, it is 'the hand of His grace' ( ܐܝܕܐ ܕܛܝܒܘܬܗ) which 'binds up all ills' (ܚܒܫܐ ܟܠ ܟܐܒ̈ܝܢ).[778] The hymn compares God's grace with His justice. While the verb ܚܒܫ is associated with the Lord's grace, 'cut away' (ܓܙܪ) is linked to the Lord's justice. The contrast is also pointed out by means of the adjectives ܪܟܝܟܐ and ܚܪܝܦܐ. The softness of bandaging is compared with the action of a woman who gives birth ( ܐܝܟ ܝܠܕܬܐ). Surprisingly, the softness of ܝܠܕܬܐ contrasts with the fear of ܐܣܝܘܬܐ.[779] In Eccl 5.2, where Ephrem again speaks about the Lord's justice and His mercy, it is His grace which 'binds up' - not so much the pains and wounds, but the 'penitents' (ܬܝ̈ܒܐ). The term ܚܒܫ is used here in the context of disciplining and education. Therefore, the Lord's grace which 'binds up the

---

774 Crucif 2.3.

775 Virg 4.9.

776 Cf. Virg 4.9-10.

777 Virg 37.3: ܒܣܡ̈ܡܢܐ ܬܠܬܐ ܚܒܫܬܗ ܠܟܘܪܗܢܢ.

778 Azym 20.18.

779 Azym 20.16-19.

penitents' (ܚܒܫܐ ܠܬܝ̈ܒܐ) is called 'the mother of the teachers' (ܐܡܐ ܕܪ̈ܒܢܐ).[780] In view of this, it is not surprising that in Nis 11, it is no longer God's mercy, but His justice which 'binds up'. Ephrem emphasises the benefit of the Lord's punishment that is performed by His justice: 'Justice's binding up presses hard upon her surgery; when she has smitten, she has pity, so that from the two actions she may give birth to healing'.[781]

Based on the parable of the Good Samaritan (Lk 10:34f.), Ephrem uses the verb ܚܒܫ twice in Eccl 33.3. In order to describe what happened in the parable briefly, Ephrem uses three verbs, ܚܒܫ together with ܛܥܢ and ܝܗܒ ܐܓܪܐ. In the following lines the suffix of ܪ̈ܚܡܘܗܝ, 'his/His mercies', which 'bound up the wounded man with wine and oil', is ambiguous and could refer either to the Good Samaritan, or to Christ.

In Iei 4.2, Ephrem speaks about the healing aspect of fasting. Here he uses the verb ܚܒܫ along with ܐܣܝ, with 'fasting' (ܨܘܡܐ) as subject. Fasting, which 'descended from Sinai to the smitten Israelite camp, bound up the 'great fracture of mind' (ܬܒܪܐ ܪܒܐ ܕܪ̈ܥܝܢܐ). Parallel with this is the phrase 'and He healed the soul's hidden pains'.[782]

Three human beings are also described as 'binding up'. In Virg 49.13-14, Ephrem contrast the behaviour of Jonah with that of some other biblical figures. He speaks of Moses' binding up (ܚܒܫܗ). Both Moses and Jonah are called physicians, but the results of their actions contrast with each other. In the case of Moses, 'he was upset because his binding up did not profit', whereas in Jonah's case, even though his medicine (ܣܡܗ) was victorious (ܢܨܚ), he became upset (ܐܬܬܥܝܩ).[783] In Nis 34.1, the verbs ܚܒܫ and ܐܣܝ are used together. The subject is Abraham, the medium is ܡܠܬܐ ܕܩܘܫܬܐ and the object is Harran, Canaan and Egypt. These three cities are described as a sick body,

---

780 Eccl 5.2.

781 Nis 11.7; cf. Nis 11.2-8.

782 Iei 4.1: ܘܐܣܝ ܠܟܐ̈ܒܐ ܟܣ̈ܝܐ ܕܢܦܫܐ.

783 Virg 49.13-14.

which he 'visited' (ܣܥܪܗ).[784] In Nis 14.2, Ephrem allots a line to each of the three famous bishops of Nisibis: the labour of bishop Jacob 'bound up the land [during] its affliction' ( ܚܒܫܗ ܠܐܪܥܐ ܒܐܘܠܨܢܗ), and the 'speech' (ܡܡܠܠܗ) of bishop Vologeses 'made sweet our bitterness in affliction ' (ܚܠܐ ܡܪܬܢ ܒܐܘܠܨܢܐ). Between them comes bishop Babu, whose 'bread and wine' bound up the town in its fractured state (ܠܩܪܝܬܐ ܚܒܫܗ ܒܬܒܪܗ).[785]

In Nis 2.17, Ephrem speaks of the defeat of the Persians and the saving of the city of Nisibis. He describes the 'breach' (ܬܘܪܥܬܐ) as a mirror through which both the enemies and the inhabitants of the city saw the 'power that wounded and bound up' (ܚܝܠܐ ܕܬܒܪ ܘܚܒܫ).[786] The object of the verbs is not explicitly mentioned: it seems both verbs ܬܒܪ and ܚܒܫ refer to the same people, namely, the inhabitants of the city Nisibis. Alternatively, ܬܒܪ could refer to the enemies and ܚܒܫ to the inhabitants. But as we saw above, God's mercy and His justice wound and bind up at the same time. Thus, it is likely that 'the power' (ܚܝܠܐ), which is God's power, is acting in a similar way here too.

In Nis 10, Ephrem expresses his disappointment at the hopelessness of the situation of the city. Probably he speaks about the war in AD 359. Waiting in hope for rescue took longer than expected. Ephrem uses the noun ܚܒܫܐ in parallel with ܣܡܟܐ to describe the help he was waiting for. But, instead of theܣܡܟܐ he expected, there was ܟܐܒܐ, and instead of ܚܒܫܐ there was ܬܒܪܐ ܡܪܝܪܐ.[787]

The imperative ܚܒܘܫ is used once when Ephrem advises the bishop of Nisibis to act as a shepherd. The hymn reflects the language of Ezekiel when he speaks about the shepherds and sheep (Ez 34).[788] The bishop is to 'bind up that which is fractured'.[789]

---

784 Nis 34.1; Gen 11:31.

785 Nis 14.2.

786 Nis 2.17.

787 Nis 10.16.

788 On Ezekiel, see chapter II, 3.1.8.

789 Nis 19.4: ܚܒܘܫ ܠܐܝܕܐ ܕܬܒܝܪܐ.

Finally, in Eccl 43, the verb ܚܒܫ is used twice. Ephrem speaks about the breaking of the Law's tablets in which reposes healing power; these, even after they were broken, 'bound up that people', since 'on seeing that the glorious tablets were broken', the people 'who had been broken by paganism' came to their senses and so 'bound themselves up' ( ܥܡܐ ܚܒܫ ܢܦܫܗ ܕܐܬܬܒܪ ܒܚܢܦܘܬܐ).[790]

### 3.2.5 ܣܥܪ and Related Terms

The verb ܣܥܪ has a wide range of meaning: it can be translated 'to visit, inspect, look after, care for, provide', as well as 'to do, deal, commit, act, effect, perform; to treat or to exact'. In some dictionaries, ܣܥܪ is also rendered with 'to heal',[791] because ܣܥܪ is often used in the context of healing as long as 'healing' can be the result of visiting. However, ܣܥܪ does not actually mean 'to heal'. Ephrem uses ܣܥܪ in the sense of 'to visit' only in the active, with the second and third person singular. Often terms based on the root ܟܪܗ are the object that needs to be visited. Mainly it is the Lord or something related to Him that performs this action.

In the Syriac Gospel the action and salvation of God is occasionally described using the verb ܣܥܪ. Those who have been 'visited' or 'healed' are 'His People' (ܥܡܗ). Notable examples are Lk 1:68: 'Blessed be the Lord God of Israel, for He visited His People and effected their redemption';[792] and Lk 7:16: 'And God visited His People' (ܘܣܥܪ ܡܪܝܐ ܐܠܗܐ ܠܥܡܗ). While God (i.e. the Father) is the subject of ܣܥܪ here, Ephrem often specifies Jesus, the Son of God, as the One Who 'visits'.[793] In Nat 3.1, the term ܟܪܝܗܘܬܢ applies to the 'state of sickness' of humanity (i.e.

---

[790] Eccl 43.6-7.

[791] J. P. Smith, *A Compendious Syriac Dictionary* (1902), 384; C. Brockelmann, *Lexicon Syriacum* (1928), 488.

[792] Lk 1:68: ܡܒܪܟ ܗܘ ܡܪܝܐ ܐܠܗܗ ܕܐܝܣܪܝܠ ܕܣܥܪ ܥܡܗ ܘܥܒܕ ܠܗ ܦܘܪܩܢܐ.

[793] Cf. CDiat 6.13; Nat 3.1; Virg 25.13; Fid 36.1.

the result of the Fall).[794] The Son is the agent of healing the state of sickness. In Fid 36.1, Ephrem compares the Physician Who 'descended' with the other physicians before Him: while the other physicians healed a little and left much, 'the Son descended to visit the servants because their sickness continued and was long'.[795] While these objects, ܥܒ̈ܕܐ ܕܐܓܪܘ ܘܐܘܪܟܘ ܟܘܪ̈ܗܢܝܗܘܢ and ܟܘܪܗܢܘܬܢ, as mentioned above, have a general sense, in Virg 25.13 the verb ܣܥܪ is connected with a particular figure, namely Simon's mother-in-law (Mk 1:29-31 and parallel). Her Healer is called the 'Physician of the height' (ܐܣܝܐ ܕܪܘܡܐ) Who 'descended to visit you' (ܢܚܬ ܡܣܥܪܟܝ ܗܘܐ).[796]

'Visiting' does not only refer to human sickness but also to the suffering of the cities. Nis 4.16 illustrates the hope of the Church in Nisibis. The church addresses its prayer to the Lord Who is the Healer: 'You, the Healer of all, have visited/looked after me in my sickness'.[797] The verb ܣܥܪ describes the actions of ܒܐܣܝܐ ܕܟܠ.

The imperative ܣܥܘܪ appears three times in the context of healing. In Nis 19.4, Ephrem advises bishop Abraham to act as a shepherd and serve the church of Nisibis: 'visit the one that is sick'.[798] The 'sick sheep' need to be 'visited', and the visitor is the bishop here - no longer the Lord. The parable of the Lost Sheep in the Syriac Gospel (Lk 15:1-7; Mt 18:10-14) does not use the verb ܣܥܪ, but it does appear in Ezekiel's advice to the Shepherds (Ez 34:12). Nevertheless, ܣܥܪ is used along with ܟܪܝܗܐ in the

---

794 Nat 3.1: ܒܪܝܟ ܕܐܪ̈ܟܢܘܗܝ ܪ̈ܚܡܘܗܝ ܕܢܣܥܘܪ ܟܘܪܗܢܘܬܢ.

795 Fid 36.1:

ܒܪܐ ܢܚܬ ܗܘܐ ܕܢܣܥܘܪ ܥܒ̈ܕܐ
ܕܐܓܪܘ ܘܐܘܪܟܘ ܟܘܪ̈ܗܢܝܗܘܢ
ܕܒܬܘ ܘܐܬܘ ܐܣܘ̈ܬܐ ܘܒܛܠܘ ܘܠܐܝܘ
ܐܣܝܘ ܩܠܝܠ ܘܫܒܩܘ ܣܓܝ.

796 Virg 25.13.

797 Nis 4.16: ܐܢܬ ܗܘ ܒܐܣܝܐ ܕܟܠ ܣܥܪܬܢܝ ܒܟܘܪ̈ܗܢܝ.

798 Nis 19.4: ܢܦܫܐ ܕܫܠܝܛܐ ܢܛܪ ܘܣܥܘܪ ܠܐܡܪܐ ܕܟܪܝܗܐ.

episode about the Sheep and the Goats (Mt 26:31-46): 'I was sick and you have visited me'.[799]

In Nis 55.31 and 58.23, the imperative ܣܥܘܪ has a negative connotation, since death is the agent and subject of ܣܥܘܪ. In both hymns Ephrem lets Satan and death argue. As result of the dialogue, Satan advises death: 'you shall go and effect sickness, and I [will place] snares'.[800] Here ܣܥܘܪ means 'to effect sickness', or 'to place, put' along with ܦܚ̈ܐ. This becomes clear in Nis 58.23, where Satan reminds death about the snares which he had placed, and tels him to 'visit all those who are sick'.[801] The 'sick' are those who have to be visited, and the visitor is death.

The verb ܣܥܪ is also used in the sense of 'to effect' or 'to perform' in connection with Jesus. Using the verb ܣܥܪ with ܠܐ in the CDiat 6.13, Ephrem says: '[Jesus] has not effected any of the wounds that those before did towards the people'.[802] Here ܣܥܪ has the same meaning as ܥܒܕ, used in the same line. In turn, ܣܥܪ in the sense of 'to effect' or 'to perform' has a positive aspect in the CDiat 16.29 where it is used in the context of giving sight to the man born blind (Jn 9:1-38) when Naaman's healing from his leprosy (2 Kgs 5:1-27) is mentioned: here it is 'the commandment' which is said to have effected (ܐܠܐ ܦܘܩܕܢܐ ܣܥܪ) this (and not the clay or the water, the immediate agents).[803]

The subject of ܣܥܪ can also be the 'hand of the Lord's justice' or just 'His justice'. In Nis 11.3, Ephrem says: 'My Lord, the hand [of your justice] has visited the sick a great deal'.[804] This hymn emphasises the benefit of the Lord's punishment. The hand

799 Mt 26:36: ܟܪܝܗܐ ܗܘܝܬ ܘܣܥܪܬܘܢܝ. [H has ܐܬܟܪܗܬ instead of ܟܪܝܗܐ ܗܘܝܬ (Mt 26:36; cf. 25:43)].

800 Nis 55.31: ܙܠ ܐܢܬ ܘܣܥܘܪ ܟܘܪ̈ܗܢܐ ܘܐܢܐ ܦܚ̈ܐ.

801 Nis 58.23: ܐܙܠ ܐܕܘܒ ܥܠ ܦܚ̈ܐ ܕܛܫܝܬ ܘܐܦ ܐܢܬ ܒܥܘܬܐ ܦܪܘܫ ܘܣܥܘܪ ܟܠ ܕܟܪ̈ܝܗܝܢ.

802 CDiat 6.13: ܘܐܢܫ ܡܢ ܡܚ̈ܘܬܐ ܕܥܒܕܘ ܩܕ̈ܡܝܐ ܠܘܬ ܥܡܐ ܠܐ ܣܥܪ.

803 CDiat 16.29; Jn 9:1-38 does not use the verb ܣܥܪ.

804 Nis 11.3: ܣܓܝ ܗܘ ܣܥܪܬ ܡܪܝ ܐܝܕܗ ܠܟܪ̈ܝܗܐ.

of the Lord's justice is described as the 'hidden physician (fem.) of their pains and the source of their life'.[805] Therefore, Nis 21.18, Ephrem 'praises the hand that visited [the world]'.[806] The object is ܥܠܡܐ which include all human beings, and no longer ܥܡܗ as in the Gospel (Lk1:68; 7:16). In the refrain of Nis 34, the Lord is praised for caring for humanity 'since He increased those who visited it in all generations'.[807] The 'visitors' are the patriarchs and prophets who were sent by God. In this context only Abraham is explicitly mentioned in connection with the verb ܣܥܪ: '[Abraham] visited the whole body' (ܟܠܗ ܠܓܘܫܡܐ ܣܥܪܗ).[808] Here the verbs ܚܒܫ and ܐܣܝ are used along with ܣܥܪ. With the term 'body' (ܓܘܫܡܐ) Ephrem primarily means Harran, Canaan and Egypt, but it also applies to the whole world (ܬܒܝܠ) and Nature (ܟܝܢܐ). The terms and phrases such as 'gangrene of idolatry' (ܐܟܠܬܐ ܕܦܬܟܪܘܬܐ),[809] 'wound' (ܡܚܘܬܐ)[810] and 'sick heel' (ܥܩܒܐ ܟܪܝܗܬܐ),[811] describe the sickness of the whole world that is the object of visiting. In order to emphasise this, Ephrem uses the term ܟܘܪܗܢܐ, and ܟܐܒܐ too.[812] Ephrem uses the term ܣܘܥܪܢܐ once to describe the actions of the 'great physicians'

---

[805] Nis 11.3: ܐܣܝܬܐ ܟܣܝܬܐ ܕܟܐܒܝ̈ܗܘܢ ܘܡܒܘܥ ܚܝ̈ܝܗܘܢ.

[806] Nis 21.18: ܫܘܒܚܐ ܠܐܝܕܐ ܕܣܥܪܬܗ.

[807] Nis 34: ܒܛܝܒܘܬܐ: ܒܪܝܟ ܗܘ ܕܠܐ ܟܡ ܡܬܘܡ ܫܒܩܗ̇ ܠܐܢܫܘܬܐ ܕܐܣܓܝ ܒܟܠ ܕܪ̈ܝܢ ܣܥܘܪ̈ܝܗ̇. In this hymn, the world (ܥܠܡܐ) is described as a 'body' (ܓܘܫܡܐ) that was sick with the 'fever of paganism' (ܒܐܫܬܗ̇ ܕܚܢܦܘܬܐ), the source of sickness (ܟܘܪܗܢܐ). Here ܓܘܫܡܐ refers to Harran, Canaan and Egypt.

[808] Nis 34.1.

[809] Nis 34.5.

[810] Nis 34.5; 34.10; 34.12.

[811] Nis 34.8.

[812] In Nis 34.9, Ephrem speaks of ܟܘܪ̈ܗܢܘܗܝ ܠܟܠܢܫ, ܟܘܪܗܢܐ ܟܣܝܐ ܕܢܦܫܐ, ܬܒܝܠ ܟܪܝܗܬܐ. In Nis 34.10 the phrase ܟܐܒܐ ܕܢܦ̈ܫܬܐ, and in Nis 34.11 ܚܝܠܐ ܘܟܐܒܐ ܕܢܦܫܐ appear.

(ܐܣܘ̈ܬܐ ܪܘܪ̈ܒܐ)[813] who are called 'visitors' (ܣܥܘܪ̈ܐ) sent by God to 'visit' (ܠܡܣܥܘܪ) the world.[814]

Finally, in hymn 43 On Nisibis where Ephrem speaks about the benefits through the chosen and righteous people, he plays on the word ܣܥܪ in connection with the sick Elisha (2 Kgs 13:14-19): 'It is a matter of wonder that the sickness of diligent people is a source of visiting for the body of those who visits him/it. Make me worthy, You Who visit those who visit You (ܣܥܪ ܠܡܣܥܪ̈ܘܗܝ), of their actions (ܠܡܣܥܪܢܘܗܘܢ)'.[815] With the phrase ܣܥܪ ܠܡܣܥܪ̈ܘܗܝ Ephrem addresses the Lord, whereas ܡܣܥܪܢܘܗܘܢ describes the actions of God's chosen people.

---

813 Nis 34.6.

814 Nis 34.9.

815 Nis 43.9-10:

ܬܘܒ ܗܘ ܐܠܝܫܥ ܐܬܟܪܗ ܒܟܪܝܗܘܬܐ
ܥܠ ܐܚܪܐ ܚܠܝܫܘ̈ܬܐ ܕܡܠܟܐ ܕܚܫܬ ܡܣܥܪܗ
ܚܝܠܐ ܗܘ ܘܚܙܝ ܟܪܝܐ ܕܡܣܥܪܢܐ
ܠܒܝܬܗܘܢ ܒܡܣܥܪܢܘܬܐ ܕܒܪ̈ܝܐ
ܕܒܟܐ ܗܘ ܕܫܘܠܚܢܐ ܠܦܓܪܐ ܕܡܣܥܪ̈ܘܗܝ
ܠܡܣܥܪܢܘܗܘܢ ܐܫܘܝܢ ܣܥܪ ܠܡܣܥܪ̈ܘܗܝ.

# 4 EPHREM'S BIBLICAL EXEGESIS

ܡܛܠ ܕܐܟܬܒ ܕܝܢ ܡ̈ܠܐ ܕܦܘܪܫܢܐ ܕܕܡܝܢ
ܠܣܡ̈ܡܢܐ
ܕܟܕ ܠܐ ܫܘܝܢ ܫܘܝܢ ܒܗܕܐ ܕܟܠ ܣܒܪܐ
ܟܠܗܘܢ ܕܚܘܠܡܢܐ ܡܬܟܢܫܝܢ ܘܐܬܝܢ
ܘܐܝܢܐ ܕܠܐ ܝܕܥ ܚܝܠܗܘܢ ܒܗܘܢ ܩܛܠ
ܘܐܝܢܐ ܕܝܕܥ ܬܘܒ ܚܝܠܗܘܢ ܒܗܘܢ ܙܟܐ.

ܡܢܗ̇ ܕܬܚܘܝܬܐ ܗܕܐ ܕܣܡ̈ܡܢܐ ܐܬܩܪܒ
ܠܟܬ̈ܒܐ
ܐܝܬ ܓܒܪ ܕܗܕܝܘܛ̈ܝܢ ܣܓܝ ܠܥܩ̈ܪܐ
ܘܐܝܬ ܬܘܒ ܕܢܘܟܪ̈ܝܢ ܣܓܝ ܠܩܪ̈ܝܢܐ
ܘܠܝܢ ܠܗܘܢ ܡ̈ܠܐ ܒܦܘܡ ܣܦܪ̈ܐ ܣܟ̈ܠܐ
ܟܬ̈ܒܐ ܡܠܝܢ ܫܝܢܐ ܘܣܦܪ̈ܐ ܫܓܝܫܘܬܐ.

Because he caused discerning sayings to be written
which were like medicines,
which, although they are not all the same, in that they
all concerned hope
of health, are collected and come.
Whoever does not know their powers might kill with
them,
and whoever does know their powers
will win victory [over sicknesses] with them.

From this example of the medicines approach the
Scriptures.
There are people who are very ignorant about
medicinal herbs
and there are also those who are real strangers
to the reading [of Scripture].
Words are contentious in the mouths of learned fools.
The Scriptures are full of peace
but the learned [are filled] with disturbance.

*Fid 53.6-7*

These stanzas emerge in a context where Ephrem has accused the Arians of misunderstanding the Scripture and thereby the Son of God. All the contentious divisions which resulted in various factions forming within the church, are based on the misunderstanding of Holy Scripture. As in the above hymn, and in Fid 35.2 and 64.12, as well as in Virg 1.3-4, Ephrem understands Scripture as a healer and as an assistance for man, provided it is approached in the right way. In Fid 35.2, Ephrem rebukes the Arians for their misunderstanding of Scripture, in a similar way to the rebuke given to readers by Moses and John. This was intended to remind the reader that the correct interpretation of the Scriptures would enable them to avoid becoming unhealthy, and to proclaim that Nature suffered because of Adam's sin and that the Lord had also suffered.[1] False interpretations of Scripture causes disturbance, like someone using medicine and drugs without knowing their effects.[2] Therefore, in this chapter a few themes and figures of Scripture are presented in order to illustrate Ephrem's biblical exegesis concerning sickness and healing.

The first part of this chapter includes certain healing aspects related to the Old Testament, whereas the second part presents healing imagery based on the New Testament.

## 4.1 Old Testament

This part deals first of all with the health of Adam and Eve in Paradise and on the earth of thorns. Ephrem frequently refers to the immortal life of Adam and Eve in Paradise before the expulsion, and to their mortality after the fall. Here, I focus on Ephrem's perspective on the health of the inhabitants of Eden at the time they were created. Obeying or disobeying the Lord's commandment and the structure of Paradise were important influences concerning their well-being. The shift from immortality to mortality is caused through the persuasion of the Evil One and Serpent, whom they obeyed by their free will. The punishment is a consequence of their action, though even here there is a positive side in that death provides a limitation to pains and pangs. Although life on the earth includes sickness, pain and grief, the

---

1 Fid 35.2.

2 Fid 53.7.

fragrance of Paradise appears as a Medicine and Physician for the earth, and so minimises its illness.

I then go on to illustrate Ephrem's use of medical imagery in connection with four biblical figures of the Old Testament to whom he often refers. As the fall of man was the consequence of sin, so too was the leprosy of Miriam, Gehazi and King Uzziah, which was caused by their evil will, speech or acts. While the Syrian Naaman and Miriam, the sister of Moses, were healed because they followed the commandments of the prophets, King Uzziah and Gehazi suffered from leprosy the rest of their life.

Finally, Ephrem draws attention to some women in the Old Testament. According to the genealogy of Jesus, Ephrem emphasises the acts of Tamar, Rahab and Ruth who risked their lives and transgressed the Law in order to participate in the Medicine of Life, whom Ephrem identifies with Jesus Christ.

### 4.1.1 The Health of Adam and Eve in Paradise and on the Earth of Thorns

In the hymns On Paradise Ephrem delineates his concept of Paradise where he considers it as an abode for its inhabitants. Starting in hymn 1 On Paradise, by reading the Genesis narrative of the creation, Ephrem is spiritually transported in his inner vision to the splendour of Paradise which is beyond comprehension. Here he describes, on the basis of the biblical narrative and his own vision of it, the creation of Adam and Eve, the position of the Tree of Knowledge and of the Tree of Life, as well as the seduction of Adam and Eve by the Evil One. In hymn 5 onwards, where Ephrem reaches the narrative of the Fall of Adam and Eve, he is transported back into the world of thorns, pains and griefs.

Since the hymns On Paradise above all discuss the life of Paradise, its inhabitants and their 'health', they will be used as the main source for this section. We find some other related passages in the Commentary on Genesis, the Commentary on the Diatessaron, the Hymns On Faith, On the Church, On Nisibis, On the Nativity and in some other places.[3]

---

[3] For instance CDiat 16.5; Fid 6.10-16; Nat 49.16; 8.4; Eccl 13.25; 20.6; 50.7-8; Haer 21.6; Nis 57.1-3; 69.4; Nat 1.27-27; 13.2; 26.9; etc.

In the following, Ephrem's picture of the health of the created Adam and Eve in the well-being of Eden is presented. Attention is drawn to their primordial good health, to the transgression of the Lord's commandment and its consequences. An important role is played by the structure of Paradise and by the Tree of Knowledge and the Tree of Life within it. Finally, this section deals with the function of Paradise as a Medicine and Physician for life on earth.

#### 4.1.1.1 *The Creation of Adam and Eve in an Intermediate State*

ܘܒܪܐ ܐܠܗܐ ܠܐܕܡ ܒܨܠܡܗ.
ܒܨܠܡ ܐܠܗܐ ܒܪܝܗܝ.
ܕܟܪ ܘܢܩܒܐ ܒܪܐ ܐܢܘܢ.
ܘܚܙܐ ܐܠܗܐ ܟܠ ܕܥܒܕ ܘܗܐ ܛܒ ܫܦܝܪ.

So God created Adam in His own image,
in the image of God He created him;
male and female He created them (Gen 1:27).
God saw all that he had made, and it was very good (Gen 1:31)

According to Ephrem, Adam and Eve were created in an intermediate state, neither mortal (ܡܝܘܬܐ) nor immortal (ܠܐܡܝܘܬܐ). Through their free will they were enabled to decide. 'For, when God created Adam, He did not make him mortal, nor did He fashion him immortal, so that Adam, by either keeping or transgressing the commandments, might acquire from one of the trees the [life] that he preferred.'[4] Does this intermediate state apply to the health of Adam and Eve too? In Ephrem's view, Adam was created pure in Paradise, in the Garden which is a 'companion of well-being' (ܠܘܝܬܐ ܕܒܘܣܡܪܐ).[5] In Parad 3.10, where Ephrem discusses the consequences of obeying or disobeying the commandment, he says:

ܗܟܢܐ ܐܝܟ ܕܢܒܝܐ ܕܐܢ ܗܘ ܕܐܟܠ ܡܢܗ
ܚܘܒܗܝ ܗܘ ܕܪܓܐ ܕܐܘܣܦ ܒܪܘܡܘܬܗ
ܚܘܒܗܝ ܬܘܒ ܫܘܦܠܐ ܕܐܫܬܟܚ ܠܥܘܠܗ

---

4 CGen 2.17: ܡܛܠ ܓܝܪ ܕܟܕ ܒܪܐ ܠܗ: ܠܐ ܡܝܘܬܐ ܥܒܕܗ ܕܗܘ ܐܕܡ ܒܢܛܪ ܦܘܩܕܢܐ ܐܘ ܗܘܐ. ܘܠܐ ܕܠܐ ܡܝܘܬܐ ܓܒܠܗ ܗܘܐ ܒܥܒܪ ܦܘܩܕܢܐ. ܢܣܒ ܡܢ ܚܕ ܡܢ ܐܝܠܢܐ ܐܝܢܐ ܕܨܒܐ ܗܘܐ.

5 Parad 5.13.

ܘܐܢ ܗܘ ܕܙܟܐ ܘܢܨܚ ܠܡܠܒܫܘܗܝ
ܫܘܒܚܐ ܘܢܓܠܐ ܠܗ ܐܦ ܒܗܬܬܐ ܟܝܢܐ ܗܝ
ܕܢܩܢܐ ܒܗ ܚܘܠܡܢܐ ܝܕܥܬܐ ܕܟܘܪܗܢܐ

God established the Tree as judge, so that if Adam
should eat from it,
it might show him that rank which he had lost through
his pride,
and show him, as well, that low estate he had acquired,
to his torment.
Whereas, if he should overcome and conquer, it would
robe him
in glory and reveal to him also the nature of shame,
so that he might acquire, in his good health, an
understanding of sickness.

*Parad 3.10*

Ephrem has the idea that Adam was created healthy, but in his intermediate state he lacked the knowledge both of his health and of sickness. Apparently, the 'understanding of sickness' (ܝܕܥܬܐ ܕܟܘܪܗܢܐ) cannot be separated from ܚܘܠܡܢܐ, i.e. the state of good health. Adam was in 'good health' (ܚܠܝܡܘܬܐ) but he did not know this for he had not yet gained the understanding of sickness. Adam would have acquired the understanding of sickness, if he had obeyed the commandment of the Lord. In Parad 3.11-12, Ephrem explains the significance of knowledge of 'good health' (ܚܠܝܡܘܬܐ) and 'state of sickness' (ܟܪܝܗܘܬܐ) and applies it to Adam:

ܕܐܝܟ ܠܒܪ ܒܡܘܠܡܗ ܢܩܢܐ ܚܠܝܡܘܬܐ
ܘܢܕܥ ܒܪܟܝܢܗ ܡܟܐ ܗܝ ܟܪܝܗܘܬܐ
ܕܢܩܢܐ ܠܒܘܕܪܢܐ ܕܢܕܥ ܠܝܘܬܪܢܐ
ܕܐܝܟ ܕܐܦ ܒܟܘܪܗܢܐ ܗܘܐ ܪܒܐ
ܘܢܕܥ ܒܪܟܝܢܗ ܡܟܐ ܗܝ ܚܠܝܡܘܬܐ
ܡܪܗ ܡܠܦ ܠܗ ܡܕܒܪ ܡܟܝܠ ܠܗ.

ܐܠܘ ܕܝܢ ܐܕܡ ܗܘܐ ܡܟܐ ܗܘܐ ܠܗ
ܠܫܘܒܚܐ ܒܗ̈ܕܡܘܗܝ، ܠܚܝܐ ܒܦܘܩܕܢܘܗܝ،
ܕܢܦܪܩ ܒܗ̈ܕܡܘܗܝ، ܘܢܐܪܒ ܒܦܘܩܕܢܘܗܝ،
ܚܘܝܐ ܗܦܟ ܐܠܨ ܘܐܬܠܒܟܗ
ܫܩܠ ܒܡܘܒܠܢܐ ܘܫܘܒܚܐ ܒܒܗܘܕܪܐ
ܕܒܚܫܘܬܗ ܢܒܗܬ ܘܟܠ ܐܒܕܬܗ ܢܠܠ.

A man, indeed, who has acquired good health in
himself,
and is aware in his mind of what the state of sickness is,
has gained something beneficial and he knows
something profitable;
but a man who lies in sickness,
and knows in his mind what good health is,
is vexed by his sickness and tormented in his mind.

Had Adam conquered, he would have acquired
glory upon his limbs, and discernment of what
suffering is,
so that he might be radiant in his limbs and grow in his
discernment.
But the serpent reversed all this and made him taste
abasement in reality, and glory in recollection only,
so that he might feel shame at what he had found
and weep at what he had lost.

*Parad 3.11-12*

Before the transgression, Adam and Eve were not fully aware either of suffering or of the good health in which they were created. Though God had granted manifest knowledge to Adam, 'whereby he gave names to Eve and to the animals',[6] He had not yet revealed the 'hidden knowledge' (ܐܝܕܥܬܐ ܟܣܝܬܐ) to him. In their good health Adam and Eve did not possess the 'discernment of what suffering is' (ܠܝܫܐ ܒܘܪ̈ܫܢܘܗܝ), and they did not have the knowledge of 'what the state of sickness is' ( ܡܢܐ ܗܝ ܟܪܝܗܘܬܐ), neither did they know 'what good health is' (ܡܢܐ ܗܝ ܚܠܝܡܘܬܐ). In CGen 2.34 also Ephrem draws attention to this matter where he emphasises the knowledge and

---

6 Parad 12.16:

ܗܿܝ ܓܝܪ ܐܝܕܥܬܐ ܓܠܝܬܐ ܕܝܗܒ ܗܘܐ ܠܗ
ܕܒܗܿ ܗ̣ܘ ܩܪܐ ܫܡܗ̈ܐ ܠܚܘܐ ܘܚܝܘ̈ܬܐ
ܠܐ ܗ̣ܘܐ ܫܚܝ̈ܬܐ ܟܠܐ ܠܗ ܕܡܫܡ̈ܫܬܐ
ܗܝ ܕܝܢ ܐܝܕܥܬܐ ܟܣܝܬܐ
ܡܢ ܩܕܡܝ̈ܐ ܘܠܚܘܐ ܟܣܝܐ ܗܘܐ ܕܢܕܪܟܘܢ ܗܘܐ
ܟܣܝܬܐ ܕܟܠ ܡܕܡ ܕܐܝܬܘܗܝ ܟܠܗ ܬܟܝܠ.

awareness of Evil things through the Good. Even if Adam and Eve had been aware of pains, suffering and illness, their knowledge would have been just through the good things. In so far as they did not suffer before eating from the fruit, they just thought positively about griefs and pains, but yet they did not taste them in reality.[7] Their disobedience caused them to be stripped of the glory and to incur the curse. The knowledge and real discernment was hidden in the Tree of Knowledge (ܐܝܠܢ ܐܝܕܥܬܐ).

### *4.1.1.2 The Tree of Knowledge and Its Fruit*

Ephrem calls the Tree of Knowledge (ܐܝܠܢ ܐܝܕܥܬܐ) the 'tree of wisdom'[8] and the 'wood/cross of knowledge'.[9] The Tree of Knowledge was established as 'judge' (ܕܝܢܐ) and is strictly linked with the commandment of the Lord.[10] Both the transgression and the keeping of the commandment had consequences and they would change the state of Adam and Eve. Therefore, the primordial state of Adam and Eve was not an eternal one, but a temporary one. The Tree of Knowledge, which is planted in the midst of Paradise in order to separate off 'above from below, the sanctuary from the Holy of Holies',[11] plays the same role as the sanctuary veil: Adam and Eve were not allowed to penetrate inside it yet. 'The Tree was to him like a gate; its fruit was the veil

---

7 CGen 2.34: ܒܪܡ ܕܝܢ ܘܐܦܢ ܐܝܕܥܘ ܗܘܘ ܠܗܘܢ ܕܟܐܒܬ ܐܕܡ ܬܪ̈ܬܝܗܘܢ. ܗ̇ܘ ܒܠܚܘܕ ܙ̈ܒܢܝܢ ܗܘܘ. ܘܥܠ ܒܝܫܬܐ ܒܛܒܬܐ ܫܡܥܝܢ ܗܘܘ. ܒܬܪ ܕܝܢ ܕܐܟܠܘ ܗܘܐ ܫܘܠܡܐ. ܕܒ̈ܝܫܬܐ ܢܣܒܘܢ ܟܠ ܫܘܕܥܬܐ. ܒܡܒܕܐ ܕܝܢ ܢܛܥܡܘܢܗ̇ ܠܗ̇ ܠܒܝܫܬܐ. ܒܬܪ ܟܢ ܛܥܡܘܢ ܫܘܒܚܐ ܕܐܠܒܫܝܢ ܗܘܘ. ܘܫܩܠܬܗ ܒܗܘܢ ܠܘ̈ܛܐ ܕܡܛܠܬܗܘܢ ܡܒܪܢܫ ܗܘܘ.

8 Parad 12.15: ܕܚܟ̈ܡܬܐ [ܐܝܠܢܐ]

9 Parad 3.3: ܩܝܣܐ ܕܐܝܕܥܬܐ or ܩܝܣܐ ܕܝܕܥܬܐ; Parad 15.5: ܩܝܣܐ ܕܐܝܬܘܬܗ ܕܝܕܥܬܐ.

10 Parad 3.10; CGen 2.17.

11 Parad 3.14:

ܒܡܨܥ ܘܠܝܨܒܗ ܗܘܐ ܠܐܝܠܢ ܐܝܕܥܬܐ
ܕܢܦܪܘܫ ܠܥܠ ܘܠܬܚܬ ܘܩܘܕܫܐ ܘܩܘܕܫ ܩܘܕ̈ܫܐ.

covering the hidden Tabernacle. Adam snatched the fruit, casting aside the commandment.'[12]

The Tree of Knowledge and its 'excellent fruit' ( ܦܐܪܐ ܛܒܐ) are not to be considered as poisonous, but when its fruit is picked out of season it has a bad effect.[13] Ephrem illustrates this by using the example of an ordinary, natural tree and its fruit. The fruit gives forth its sweetness if it is plucked in due season, but out of season it proves sour if it is plucked prematurely.[14] Adam died 'for taking the fruit prematurely'.[15] Adam did not wait for the season of the fruit for he did not obey the commandment of the Lord. If Adam and Eve had obeyed the divine commandment then their eyes would have been opened to the glory which the Creator had destined for them, and they would have been raised to a higher state so that they would have entered the Holy of Holies, the Tree of Life.[16]

### *4.1.1.3 The Tree of Life*

In Ephrem's view, the position of the Paradisiacal trees plays an important role. While the Tree of Knowledge is planted in the middle of Paradise and serves as a borderline between the lower/outer part of Paradise proper and its highest/innermost section, the Tree of Life is placed in the upper/inner circle of Paradise proper, in the Holy of Holies.[17] Both the Tree of Knowledge and that of Life were a 'source of every good', and they would lead Adam to become the likeness of God through life without death and error.

---

[12] Parad 3.13:

ܗܘ ܕܝܢ ܐܝܠܢܐ ܗܘܐ ܠܗ ܒܐܕܪ ܐܪܥܐ [ܬܪܥܐ]
ܘܦܐܪܗ ܐܦ ܬܪܥܐ ܕܗܘܐ ܡܟܣܝܢܐ ܟܣܝܐ
ܐܕܡ ܚܛܦ ܦܐܪܐ ܘܫܒܩܗ ܠܦܘܩܕܢܐ.

N. Séd explains this symbolism quite fully in his important article 'Les Hymnes sur le paradis de Saint Éphrem et les traditons juives', *Le Muséon* 81 (1968), 455-501.

[13] Parad 15.12.

[14] Parad 12.3: ܦܐܪܐ ܕܠܐ ܒܙܒܢܗ ܡܚܪܬܐ ܗܘ ܠܛܥܘܡܗ.

[15] Parad 15.8: ܒܛܥܡܬܐ ܕܚܛܦ ܐܕܡ ܒܦܐܪܐ ܕܠܐ ܒܙܒܢܗ.

[16] Parad 3.2-8.

[17] Parad 3; 12.

ܬܪ̈ܝܢ ܓܒܪ ܐܝܠܢ̈ܝܢ ܣܡ ܒܗ ܒܦܪܕܝܣܐ
ܐܝܠܢ ܚܝܘܬܐ ܐܚܪܢܐ ܕܝܕܥܬܐ
ܙܘܓܐ ܕܡܒܪ̈ܟܐ ܡ̈ܒܘܥܐ ܕܟܠ ܛܒ̈ܢ
ܒܗܠܝܢ ܬܪ̈ܬܝܢ ܙܘ̈ܓܐ ܡܫܒ̈ܚܝܢ
ܡܫܬܘܐ ܕܢܗܘܐ ܐܢܫ ܕܡܘܬܗ ܕܐܠܗܐ
ܒܚܝܐ ܕܠܐ ܡܘܬܐ ܘܚܟܡܬܐ ܕܠܐ ܛܘܥܝܢ.

Two Trees did God place in Paradise,
the Tree of Life and that of Wisdom,
a pair of blessed fountains, source of every good,
by means of this glorious pair
the human person can become the likeness of God,
endowed with immortal life and wisdom that does not err.

*Parad 12.15*

The absolute image of God is the Son of God, Jesus Christ, who is represented by the invisible Tree of Life in Paradise. In hymn 6 On Faith, where Ephrem emphasises the participation of the Son in the creation of the world, he draws attention to the divine commandment in the plural form 'Let us make Man in our image'. The 'likeness' of the Lord is represented in 'one tree of life'.[18] After the fall, the way to the Tree of Life in Paradise was closed by the sword until Jesus opened it on the cross.[19] In hymn 49 and 50 On the Church, Ephrem describes the Tree of Life as the symbol (ܪܐܙܐ) of the Son of God[20] who gives life to all with it fruits.[21]

---

18 Fid 6.10-16. Fid 6.14: ܚܕ ܐܝܠܢ ܚܝ̈ܐ ܗܘ ܠܝܘܒܐ ܕܡܘܬܗ.

19 Nat 8.4:

ܒܪܝܟ ܚܠܠܐ ܕܚܙܐ ܪܘܡܚܐ ܣܟܪ ܦܪܕܝܣܐ
ܕܬܠܬ ܐܘܪܚܐ ܕܐܝܠܢ ܚܝ̈ܐ
ܘܐܬܐ ܢܣܒ ܠܗ ܦܓܪܐ ܕܒܠܒ
ܕܬܪܒ ܣܝܦܗ ܢܬܘܒ ܐܘܪܚܐ ܠܓܘ ܦܪܕܝܣܐ.

20 Eccl 49.16:

ܒܡܬ̈ܠܐ ܕܡܟܣܝܢ ܠܗ̇ ܠܗܝ ܒܐܬܐ ܕܫܝܢܐ
ܕܒܗ̇ ܗܘ ܐܝܠܢ ܚܝܐ ܪܐܙܗ ܕܒܪ ܚܝܐ
ܕܠܐ ܣܦܩܐ ܐܝܟ ܗܘ ܐܘܪܫܠܡ ܕܝܕܥܬ.

21 Eccl 50.7-8:

ܒܪ ܟܠ ܣܘܦ ܗܒܠ ܠܟܘܠܗ ܕܦܪܕܝܣܐ
ܦܐܪ̈ܘܗܝ ܬܪ̈ܬܝܗܘܢ ܠܘܬ ܗܘ ܐܝܠܢ ܚܝ̈ܐ

☞

### *4.1.1.4 The Serpent*

Ephrem describes the Serpent as being 'subtle',[22] 'false',[23] 'lying',[24] 'deceitful'[25] and 'cunning'.[26] He also calls it a 'reptile/dragon',[27] a 'viper'[28] and a 'basilisk'.[29] The Serpent originally had a good nature; whereas evil is a matter of evil will. According to Ephrem, the Serpent belongs to the species of animals that God created on the fifth day at the beginning. Apart from the Evil One's use of it the Serpent was 'healthy'.[30] As Ephrem says in hymn 4 On Paradise, Adam was pure in Eden until 'the Serpent had breathed on him'.[31] Adam and Eve were created and formed by the mercy of God:

> ܓܒܝܠ ܦܓܪܐ ܒܚܟܡܬܐ ܢܦܫܐ ܢܦܝܚܐ ܒܛܝܒܘܬܗ
> ܡܙܝܓ ܚܘܒܐ ܒܫܠܡܘܬܗ ܦܪܫܗ ܚܘܝܐ ܒܒܝܫܘܬܗ.
>
> The body was formed by wisdom, the soul was
> breathed by grace,
> the love was mixed in harmony, the Serpent divided it
> by evil.
>
> *Nis 69.4*

In hymn 8 On Paradise, Ephrem discusses the relationship of the soul to the body. When Adam and Eve were created, they were 'pure and perfect' (ܕܟܝܢ ܫܠܡܝܢ) with body and soul before entering the 'perfect place' (ܫܠܡܐ). When they became 'impure'

---

ܕܢܝܚܐ ܒܡܟܝܢܘܬܐ ܘܢܛܪ ܒܠܒܝܒܘܬܐ.
ܘܐܦ ܕܝܢ ܚܘܝܐ ܕܒܝܫܐ ܠܐ ܐܬܒܣܝܡ ܕܢܝܚܐ
ܕܠܐ ܗܘ ܐܝܟ ܣܢܐ ܒܗܘ ܡܓܪܐ ܕܢܝܚܐ
ܟܠܗ̇ ܒܪܐ ܚܝܐ ܦܐܪܗ ܕܢܝ̈ܚܐ ܒܗܠ.

22 E.g. Parad 12,6: ܥܪܝܡܐ.

23 E.g. Parad 12.2: ܕܓܠܐ.

24 E.g. Eccl 48,9: ܟܕܒܐ.

25 E.g. Iei 3.1: ܢܟܠܐ.

26 E.g. Eccl 48.1: ܨܢܝܥܐ.

27 E.g. CNis 62,3; Nat 1.28: ܬܢܝܢܐ; cf. Ex 7:11f.

28 E.g. Crucif 8.14: ܟܪܣܐ.

29 E.g. Iei 3.4: ܚܪܡܢܐ.

30 Haer 21.6: ܟܠܗ ܒܢܝܐ ܓܒܪ ܗܘ ܗܘܐ ܚܠܝܡ ܗܘܐ.

31 Parad 4.4:

ܐܕܡ ܕܟܐ ܗܘܐ ܠܗ ܒܗ̇ ܓܢܬܐ ܦܐܝܬܐ
ܥܕ ܕܝܢ ܘܐܬܡܣܬܒ ܕܚܘܝܐ ܢܦܚ ܗܘܐ ܒܗ.

(ܛܥ̈ܐܡ), they left Paradise.[32] This happened because the Serpent served as an instrument of the Evil One and seduced Adam and Eve. Ephrem uses the verb 'steal' in connection with the term 'cunning/crafty thief':

ܐܕܡ ܢܛܘܪܗ ܒܡܠܬܐ ܕܦܪܕܝܣܐ
ܐܬܐ ܓܝܪ ܓܢܒܐ ܚܪܝܡܐ ܕܒܓܢܒܘ ܥܠ ܗܘܐ
ܐܪܦܝ ܥܒܡ ܦܐܪܐ ܕܟܠ ܐܢܫ ܠܗܘܢ ܪܗܛ
ܓܢܒܗ ܠܢܛܘܪܗ ܕܓܢܬܐ.

Adam was heedless as guardian of Paradise,
for the crafty thief stealthily entered;
leaving aside the fruit - which most men would covet –
he stole instead the Garden's inhabitant!

*Parad 8.10*

The 'crafty thief' (ܓܢܒܐ ܚܪܝܡܐ) seduced Adam and Eve by the poison of the forbidden fruit. Hymn 26 On the Nativity links the biblical account of the seven days of creation with the incarnation of Jesus Christ. On the sixth day, Ephrem considers the poison of the forbidden fruit in contrast to the Medicine of Life:

ܝܘܡܐ ܫܬܝܬܝܐ ܢܫܒܚ ܠܗܘ ܕܒܪܐ
ܒܥܪܘܒܬܐ ܠܐܕܡ ܕܒܝܫܐ ܚܣܡ ܗܘܐ ܒܗ
ܐܝܟ ܪܚܡܐ ܢܟܠܐ ܐܦܝܣܗ ܘܐܘܫܛ ܠܗ
ܣܡܐ ܒܡܐܟܘܠܬܐ
ܣܡ ܚܝܐ ܐܬܦܪܣ ܠܬܪ̈ܝܗܘܢ
ܠܒܫ ܦܓܪܐ ܘܐܬܩܪܒ ܠܬܪ̈ܝܗܘܢ
ܡܝܘܬܐ ܛܥܡܗ ܘܚܝܐ ܒܗ
ܐܟܘܠܐ ܕܐܟܠܗ ܐܣܬܪܩ.

Let the sixth day praise him who created
on Friday Adam whom the Evil One envied.
As a false friend he pleased him [by] offering him
poison in [his] food.
The medicine of life diffused himself to them both.
He put on a body and was offered to them both.
The mortal tasted him and lived by him.
The devourer who ate him was destroyed.

*Nat 26.9*

---

32 Parad 8.9.

The Evil One 'envied' (ܚܣܡ) Adam and offered them 'poison in food' (ܣܡܐ ܒܡܐܟܘܠܬܐ). The reptile who is used by the Devil 'deceived' (ܛܥܬܗ̇) Eve and caused Adam to sin (ܐܚܛܝ).[33] Adam and Eve were wounded by the Serpent (ܒܢܟܬܗ ܕܚܘܝܐ), and they were 'swallowed' by the Reptile.[34] Their wounds were healed by the Medicine of Life who came to 'crush the head of the Serpent'.[35] Through the 'impurity of the Serpent' (ܛܐܬܗ ܕܚܘܝܐ)[36] Adam and Eve were harmed for they had been corrupted by sin.[37] In the Commentary on the Diatessaron Ephrem goes further and speaks of the Serpent killing Adam: 'The Serpent struck Adam in Paradise and killed him.'[38]

Through the Serpent Adam and Eve were seduced; they transgressed the divine commandment and so sinned. Therefore, they were expelled from Paradise to the land of thorns, while with them through the Serpent's agency sickness entered the land that is under a curse.[39]

### 4.1.1.5 *The Transgression of the Divine Commandment*

The Fall of Adam and Eve was initiated by the poisonous advice of the Evil One, suggesting they would receive divinity, by eating from the Tree of Knowledge. Ephrem points out the twofold error of Satan, as well as his jealousy and envy of Adam and Eve. According to Ephrem, as also in the later Syriac Fathers, the

33 Nis 57.1-3.

34 Nat 1.27-28: ܬܢܝܢܐ ܕܒܠܥ ܠܐܕܡ ܘܠܚܘܐ.

35 Nat 13.2:

ܚܙܝ ܠܟܝ ܘܐܡܪܝ ܬܘܕܝܬܐ ܘܩܘܡ ܚܘܐ ܒܚܝܘܠ
ܕܗܐ ܒܪ ܒܪܬܗ̇ ܐܬܐ ܣܡ ܫܦܝܐ
ܠܡܚܐ ܕܢܟܬܗ ܐܡܐ ܕܐܡܗ
ܘܟܠܐ ܒܪܢܫܐ ܕܪܥ ܪܫܗ ܕܚܘܝܐ ܕܢܟܬܗ̇.

36 Eccl 13.25: ܘܩܘܡܟ ܒܦܪ ܗܘܐ ܛܐܬܗ ܕܚܘܝܐ ܘܡܕܒܪܢܐ.

37 Eccl 20.6:
[ܚܪܗ] ܒܡܫܡܠܝܐ [ܕܠܝܬܘܗܝ] ܠܐܕܡ ܕܐܬܚܒܠ ܒܚܛܗܘܗܝ.

38 CDiat 16.15: ܢܟܬܗ ܚܘܝܐ ܠܐܕܡ ܒܦܪܕܝܣܐ ܘܩܛܠܗ.

39 Parad 11.9: ܒܪܝܬܐ ܕܠܛܬ ܒܝܕ ܚܘܝܐ.

etymology of the name of Satan is based of its similarity to the verb ܣܛܐ, which means 'turn aside, go astray, go wrong':

ܟܡܐ ܕܫܡܐ ܠܟ [ܠܟ] ܣܛܢܐ ܕܡܐ ܐܘ ܣܛܝܐ
ܕܗܐ ܐܘܪܚܐ ܣܛܝܬ ܐܦ ܐܣܛܝܬ ܠܐܕܡ ܫܒܪܐ.

How this name of yours, O Satan, resembles you
for You have gone astray from the [right] way,
and you have led infantile Adam astray.

*Nis 54.9*

Satan fell from his rank and led astray Adam and Eve from Paradise.[40] The Evil One was jealous and greatly envious, because Adam and Eve had received so much, in that they had been created in the image of the Lord. The Evil One 'profferred poison in food' to Adam.[41]

The fruit was profferred through the Serpent to Eve and then to Adam. The Serpent persuaded Eve and deceived her into eating from the fruit. As we saw above, though the Serpent was 'more crafty than any of the wild animals' (Gen 3:1), in its nature it was originally good like the rest of the creation. While the Serpent led the inhabitants of Paradise to sin, it was used as an instrument of the Evil One.

The 'Serpent' became a symbol of all evil seduction; for instance Ephrem describes Amnon as a serpent/snake because of his desire and deceitful plan. In order to destroy the treasure of Tamar's virginity, he clothed himself in the 'attire of illness'.

ܠܒܘ̈ܫܬܐ ܟܪܝܗ̇ ܗܘܐ
ܐܘ ܟܡ̈ܝܢܘܬܐ ܕܠܒܘ̈ܫܬܐ ܠܐܡܢܘܢ ܠܟܐ ܐܟܠܬ
ܚܘܝܐ ܗܘܐ ܓܒܪ ܕܒܢܟܠܘܬܗ
ܐܬܚܦܝ ܗܘܐ ܐܣܟܡܐ ܒܟܘܪܗܢܐ
ܕܚܠܘܗܝ ܬܓܡܐ ܐܝܟ ܘܢܟܣܝܗ̇

[40] Haer 26.4. For further information about the etymology of 'Satan' see T. Kronholm, *Motifs from Genesis 1-11 in the Genuine Hymns of Ephrem the Syrian with particular Reference to the Influence of Jewish Exegetical Tradition* (Lund 1978), 90-94.

[41] Eccl 48.11; Nat 26.9:

ܘܟܡܐ ܥܬܝܬܐ ܢܟܝܠ ܠܗܘ ܕܒܪܐ
ܒܦܐܪܬܐ ܠܐܕܡ ܕܒܝܫܐ ܣܡܡ ܗܘܐ ܒܗ
ܐܝܟ ܪܚܡܐ ܢܟܠܐ ܐܦܝܣ ܘܐܘܟܠ ܠܗ
ܣܡܐ ܒܡܐܟܘܠܬܐ.

ܕܪ̈ܓܬܐ ܠܒܬܘܠܘܬܐ ܢܟܠܬ ܘܛܢܦܬܗ̇
ܠܪ̈ܓܬܐ ܢܟܠܬ ܚܡܬܐ ܘܚܒܠܬܗ̇.

Hearts he was seeking –
O the rational one who made hearts for the heartless
one!
For he was a snake who in his cunning
clothed himself in the attire of illness,
so that she would fail to notice him, and he would
wound her.
Since desire deceived and defiled virginity,
rage deceived and destroyed desire.

*Virg 2.3*

Eve obeyed the advice of the Serpent and gave the fruit to Adam. Therefore, Ephrem calls her ironically the 'diligent wife' who made for Adam a garment of spots'.[42] As in Nis 54.9, Adam is called 'infantile' (ܫܒܪܐ), so too in Nat 26.8, Ephrem calls Eve 'infantile' (ܫܒܪܬܐ),[43] and they were weak (ܐܠܝ̈ܠܐ).[44] Both Adam and Eve desired the excellent fruit, but disobeyed the divine commandment. Man's free will was divided. Ephrem compares man's free will with the uprightness of the Lord. Man's free will in its craftiness approaches divine uprightness.[45] The free will with which man was created led Adam and Eve astray in error that is the cause of sickness.[46] Free will enables man to decide between good and evil matters. By free will the inhabitants of Paradise stretched their hands out to the fruit which was the 'poison of death', and they did not choose the fruit of the 'Medicine of Life'.[47] So the

---

42 Parad 4.5:

ܐܕܡ ܥܛܝܦ ܘܦܐܐ ܘܐܢܬܬܗ ܕܟܫܝܪܬܐ
ܟܡܠܬ ܘܥܒܕܬ ܠܗ ܠܒܘܫܐ ܕܟܘ̈ܬܡܬܐ.

43 Nis 54.9; Nat 26.8.

44 Eccl 11.10:

ܘܠܟ ܥܠܝܐ ܪܒܐ ܕܒ̣ܗ ܥܒܕܗ ܕܐܕܡ ܐܬܚܫܠ
ܕܫܠܝܬܐ ܒܟܝܢܐ ܢܦܫܬ ܘܣܘܟܐ ܘܦܐܪܐ ܗܘܘ ܐܠܝ̈ܠܐ.

45 Eccl 2.11: ܚܐܪܘܬ̱ ܒܢܟܠܘܬܗ̇ ܩܪܒܐ ܠܟܐܢܘܬܟ.

46 Eccl 8.3:

ܪܚܡܬܐ ܕܢܦܫܟ [ܗܕܐ] ܚܐܪܘܬܐ ܠܟܠܢ ܐܢܫܐ
ܐܪܬܝ ܘܛܥܝܐ ܥܠ ܛܘܥܝܢ ܗ̇ܝ ܕܗܘܬ [ܥܠܬ] ܟܘܪܗܢܐ.

47 Eccl 19.7:

☞

transgression of the divine commandment and the eating of the forbidden fruit was the first wrong decision of human free will, but not the last one. Ephrem describes the way of taking the fruit as stealing, for man's free will was divided against the Lord.[48] Adam did not trust the Lord by preferring to steal and so eat the fruit, when he wished to become divinised.[49] Therefore, Ephrem goes further and considers free will as a spring of all visible and invisible diseases:

ܚܘܣܝܗ̇ ܛܒܐ ܠܚܐܪܘܬܢ
ܕܐܝܬܝܗ̇ ܡܒܘܥܐ ܕܟܠ ܢܟܝ̈ܢ
ܚܘܫ̈ܒܝܗ̇ ܟܐܒ̈ܐ ܟܣܝ̈ܐ
ܐܦ ܣܘܥܪ̈ܢܝܗ̇ ܟܐܒ̈ܐ ܓܠܝ̈ܐ
ܡܢܗ̇ ܓܝܪ ܫܪܐ ܦܘܩܕܢܐ ܩܕܡܝܐ ܕܟܠ ܚܘ̈ܒܝܢ
ܕܡܨ̈ܥܝܐ ܐܦ ܐܚܪ̈ܝܐ
ܫܦܝܐ ܫܦܝ ܚܐܪܘܬܢ
ܡܒܘܥܐ ܕܗܘ ܠܢܦܫܗ ܡܬܕܠܚܐ.

O Good One have pity on our wickedness
which is the spring of all kinds of harm.
Its thoughts [are] hidden diseases,
also its deeds [are] visible diseases.
For it is from it that the first transgression of all debt
comes:
of the middle as well as of the last [debts].
You who are serene make serene our free will,
the spring which muddied itself.

*Eccl 32.1*

Free will is a spring that muddied itself and acts against its creator. Ephrem illustrates this in connection with another biblical figure. In hymn 38 On Faith Ephrem compares Adam with king

---

ܚܘܪ [ܒܗ̇] ܒܚܐܪܘܬܐ ܕܐܝܟ ܐܢܫܐ [ܗܝ]
ܕܡܬܝܕܥܐ ܕܠܟܠ ܦܐܪ̈ܝܢ ܬܫܬܘܬܦ
ܘܐܝܟܢ ܕܐܬܡܬܝܕܥܬ ܡܢ ܠܘܩܕܡ
ܕܬܦܠܘܓ ܘܬܗܘܐ ܠܗ̇ ܗܘܐ ܡܬܘܬܐ
ܡܪܝܐ ܗܘ ܕܬܦܠܘܓ ܠܗ̇ ܗܘܐ ܣܢܝܐ.

48 Crucif 8.2:

ܒܗ̇ ܓܝܪ [ܒܓܢܬܐ] ܦܠܓܬ ܗܘܬ ܩܕܡ ܐܕܡ
ܥܠ ܒܪܘܝܗ ܕܓܢܒ ܘܐܟܠ.

49 Nis 69.12: ܢܟܠ ܪܒܐ ܕܐܕܡ ܐܠܗܐ ܒܥܐ ܕܢܗܘܐ.

Uzziah who ministered in the holy sanctuary as a priest without being one (cf. 2 Chr 26:16-21). His will incited him to enter the Holy of Holies against the divine commandment.[50] Both Adam and King Uzziah lost their glory and kingship for their boldness. They were expelled because of their status as the lepers outside the Israelite camp.[51] So Adam lost the glory of Paradise and inherited the earth of thorns.

### 4.1.1.6 *The Expulsion from Paradise to the Earth of Thorns*

ܬܗܪܬ ܕܟܕ ܥܒܪܬ ܬܚܘܡܗ ܕܦܪܕܝܣܐ
ܫܝܢܬ ܘܗܦܟܬ ܗܘܬ ܠܘܬܐ ܕܫܘܠܦܢܐ
ܘܟܕ ܡܛܝܬ ܠܣܦܪܐ ܕܐܪܥܐ ܐܡܐ ܕܟܘ̈ܒܐ
ܦܓܥܘ ܒܝ ܟܐ̈ܒܐ ܘܫܢ̈ܩܐ ܕܟܠ ܓܢܣ
ܝܠܦܬ ܕܒܝܬܢ ܐܣܝܪ̈ܐ ܗܘ ܐܬܪ̈ܐ ܒܒܢ̈ܝܢ ܗܘ
ܚܒܝ̈ܫܐ ܕܒܗ ܒܟܝܢ ܡܐ ܕܢܦܩܝܢ ܡܢܗ.

I was in wonder as I crossed the border of Paradise at how
well-being, as though a companion, turned round and remained behind.
And when I reached the shore of earth, the mother of thorns (Gn 3:18),
I encountered all kinds of pain and suffering.
I learned how, compared to Paradise, our abode is but a dungeon;
yet the prisoners within it weep when they leave it!

*Parad 5.13*

In contrast to hymn 1 On Paradise where Ephrem was transported spiritually to Paradise while he joyfully started to read the narrative of Paradise in Genesis, here in hymn 5 he is transported back to the world of pain and suffering, when he began reading the narrative concerning the earth, the mother of thorns (Gen 3:18). As Ephrem explains his feeling further in the following two stanzas,

---

[50] Fid 38.17: (it is quoted below with the translation in English)

ܘܢܐ ܥܒܕܐ ܠܡܐܪܬ ܐܪܕܡ
ܘܗܘܐ ܠܗ ܗܘ ܦܪܘܬ ܐܪܒܐ
ܥܒܕܐ ܒܘܝܢܐ ܕܢܘܣܦ ܗܘܐ ܠܗ ܐܦ ܒܡܠܟܘܬܐ
ܘܐܬܬܘܣܦ ܠܗ ܓܪܒܐ ܢܚܫܐ.

[51] Parad 4.3-5.

he understands the earth as a prison, darkness and death in comparison with the well-being of Paradise.[52] Adam and Eve lost Paradise and their glory for they had sinned and did not confess.[53] The loss of the garment of Paradise (glory) is considered as the cause of their nakedness (Gen 3:7): 'It was also said that, when Adam sinned and was deprived of that glory with which he was clothed, he hid his nakedness with the leaves of the fig tree (cf. Gen 3:7)'.[54] The consequence of transgression of the divine commandment was not the divinisation that Adam and Eve had expected, but their 'humiliation in reality' (ܫܘܦܠܐ ܒܣܘܥܪܢܐ), with corporeal 'shame' (ܒܗܬܬܐ), 'sickness' (ܟܘܪܗܢܐ) and 'suffering' (ܚܫܐ). The Tree of Knowledge granted to them twofold knowledge: the knowledge that they had lost their glory and the realisation of their nakedness.[55] After his disobedience Adam became mortal,[56] leprous, repulsive[57] and subject to corruption.[58] Adam sinned and he gained all kinds of sickness and shame.[59] He caused death and sin to enter into the world,[60] so that the earth grew old (ܐܬܒܠܝܬ) and it was accursed (ܐܬܬܠܝܛܬ).[61] Therefore, not only humanity suffered, became weak and ill,[62] but also the whole of nature.[63]

---

52 Parad 5.13-15.

53 CGen 2.27-29.

54 CDiat 16.10: ܬܘܒ ܡܬܐܡܪܐ ܕܟܕ ܚܛܐ ܠܗ ܐܕܡ. ܘܐܫܬܠܚ ܡܢ ܬܫܒܘܚܬܐ ܗܝ ܕܠܒܝܫ ܗܘܐ. ܘܒܛܪ̈ܦܐ ܕܬܬܐ ܥܪܛܠܝܘܬܗ ܟܣܐ ܗܘܐ.

55 Parad 3.6-12.

56 Parad 15.8; Crucif 8.14: ܕܗܘ ܠܡܘܬܐ ܕܢܦܠ ܠܐܕܡ.

57 Parad 4.4: ܠܒܪ ܕܝܢ ܘܐܣܬܠܒ.

58 Eccl 20.6.

59 Epiph 10.1; Nis 57.2; 60.29.

60 Epiph 7.15; Nat 1.62:

ܕܐܥܠ ܐܕܡ ܠܬܪܒܝܬܐ
ܥܢܬ ܡܘܬܐ ܒܫܠܝܛܘܬܐ [ܒܫܠܝܛܘܬܐ]

61 Nat 17.12; Nachträge, Serm II,154; Virg 26.10.

62 Virg 37.3.

63 Fid 35.2.

The main punishment of Eve consists in the birth-pangs and pains.[64] Eve succumbed (ܣܚܒܬ) in Paradise and she was cursed (ܐܬܬܠܛܬ).[65] Through her ear the poison of the Evil One (ܡܪ̈ܬܗ ܕܒܝܫܐ) entered into the world.[66] In hymn 2 On the Crucifixion, Ephrem speaks of the leaven of Eve that grew old and made all old.[67] Her individual punishment was the bringing forth of children in pains.[68] The pains of birth-giving entered through the Serpent to Eve and to all women.[69]

In the Commentary on Genesis, Ephrem draws attention to the cursing of the earth because of Adam's transgression. By the curse of the earth Adam was also cursed for he had to eat from it amidst thorns, thistles and painful toil. While in Paradise he ate from the fresh fruits without pain and grief, here on earth he will eat from the fruit of the field by his sweat.[70] Because of his disobedience, Adam was ordered to eat the bread of grief and thorns by his sweat on the cursed earth. All these, the thorns and the pains, as well as the sweat, labour and the fig leaves were the gift of the Evil One.[71] Adam caused the thorns to grow up through his transgression of God's commandment by his free will.[72] Death and Satan enslaved and humbled Adam.[73] Ephrem goes further, saying that Death had authority over Adam and his children.[74]

---

64 CGen 2.30: ܒܬܪ ܕܝܢ ܥܠ ܚܘܐ ܘܐܡܪ: ܕܡܣܓܝܘ ܐܣܓܐ ܟܐ̈ܒܝܟܝ ܘܒܥܘܠ̈ܝܟܝ. ܘܒܚ̈ܒܠܐ ܬܐܠܕܝܢ ܒܢ̈ܝܐ (Gen 3:16).

65 Nat 2.7; Nat Sog 1.11, 26.

66 Nat 21.15; Eccl 48.2; 49.7; Nachträge, Serm II, 159-160.

67 Crucif 2.5.

68 Fid 6.14; Virg 24.11; Parad 7.8.

69 Virg 24.11: ܟܐ̈ܒܐ ܕܡܘܠܕܬܐ; CGen 2.32: ܚ̈ܒܠܐ ܥܠ ܚܘܐ ܘܒ̈ܢܬܗ.

70 CGen 2.31.

71 Eccl 48.11; Virg 31.14:

ܕܐܟܠ ܗܘܐ ܒܙܘܥܬܐ ܠܚܡ ܟܐ̈ܒܐ ܘܟܘ̈ܒܐ.

72 Nis 33.2.

73 Nat Sog 1.11:

ܘܫܠܛܗ ܠܡܘܬܐ ܘܣܛܢܐ ܕܢܫܥܒܕܘܢ ܗܘܘ ܠܐܕܡ ܘܢܫܦܠܘܗܝ.

74 CGen 2.32: ܘܐܦܢ ܕܐܫܬܠܛܘ ܟܐ̈ܒܐ ܘܡܘܬܐ ܥܠ ܐܕܡ ܘܒܢ̈ܘܗܝ.

Adam was killed by the Evil One and he died.[75] Ephrem understands the death of Adam as liberty from the curse of pains. Otherwise Adam would suffer all the time on the earth of thorns.[76]

### 4.1.1.7 *The Relationship of Paradise to the Earth*

While pain and suffering exist outside Paradise, from within Paradise fragrance wafts like a 'physician to heal the ills of a land that is under a curse'.[77] In contrast to the land of thorns, the 'blossoms' (ܦܘܩܚܝܗ̇) and 'fragrance' (ܪܝܚܐ) of Paradise are like a 'physician' (ܐܣܝܐ) for this world. Ephrem contrasts the 'Physician' (ܐܣܝܐ) with 'pains' (ܟܐܒܐ), and the 'restorative' (ܣܘܠܒܢܐ) with the 'state of sickness' (ܟܪܝܗܘܬܐ), just as Paradise is contrasted with the earth.[78] Paradise is described as ܠܘܝܬܐ ܕܣܘܠܒܢܐ in contrast to the 'earth as the mother of pains' (ܐܪܥܐ ܐܡܐ ܕܟܘܐܒܐ) related to 'pains and suffering' (ܟܐܒܐ ܘܫܢܩܐ).[79]

Before the transgression the earth was not cursed, and therefore, in Paradise neither illness nor pains existed. Likewise, after the disobedience of Adam and Eve, Paradise was not cursed; instead the land of 'this diseased world that has been so long in sickness'[80] was cursed. The land of Paradise was created in a

---

75 Crucif 8.14; Parad 15.8.

76 CGen 2.35.

77 Parad 11.9:

ܡܢ ܡܘܩܒܝܗ̇ ܕܗܕܪܐ ܥܒܝܐ ܕܡܬܢܝܚܐ
ܦܘܩܚܝܗ̇ ܕܗܝ ܐܪܥܐ ܡܫܬܡܥܝܢ ܘܠܝܬܝܢ
ܘܡܢܗ ܕܗܘ ܪܝܚܐ ܕܦܐܫ ܒܠܒܛܬܐ
ܐܝܟ ܐܣܝܐ ܠܟܐܒܝܗ̇ ܡܥܬܠܢ
ܕܐܪܥܐ ܕܠܛܝܬܐ ܒܪܝܚܐ ܕܣܘܠܒܢܘܗܝ
ܡܣܡܣܡ ܟܪܝܗܘܬܐ ܕܥܠܬ ܒܢ ܚܘܝܐ.

78 Parad 11.9. It should also be noticed that Ephrem refers to the sickness of the earth which is under the curse of the Serpent. The sickness entered the land through the Serpent.

79 Parad 5.13.

80 Parad 11.10:

ܗܘܦܐ ܕܡܢ ܓܢܬܗ ܒܪܝܟܐ ܕܦܪܕܝܣܐ
ܢܦܫ ܡܚܝܠܐ ܠܗ̇ ܠܡܪܬܗ ܕܗܢܐ ܐܬܪܐ

☞

healthy state and remained so after the fall of Adam and Eve. The earth still benefits from Paradise which is the 'life-breath' (ܢܫܡܬܗ) of our earth.

Furthermore, a river flows forth out of Paradise into the world and divides up (cf. Gen 2:10). By the river 'the blessing of Paradise should be mingled by means of water as it issues forth to irrigate the world, making clean its fountains that had become polluted by curses - just as that »sickly water« had been made wholesome by the salt (cf. 2 Kgs 2:21)'.[81] As there is a river of water, so there is also a fountain of 'perfumes' which penetrates our souls through breathing: 'Our inhalation is healed by this healing breath from Paradise; springs receive a blessing from that blessed spring which issues forth from there.'[82]

The fragrance of Paradise is not just the air that we breathe because Ephrem does not mean this literally. It has, rather, a metaphorical sense that symbolises the 'Medicine of Life' ( ܣܡ ܚܝ̈ܐ). Even Paradise serves as a fountain of 'restoratives'

---

ܗܘܝܘ ܡܫܡܫܗ̇ ܠܗ̇ ܠܗ̇ܝ ܠܛܠܬܐ ܕܐܪܥܢ
ܗ̇ܝ ܠܥܠܬܐ ܐܝܬܝܗ̇ ܢܫܡܬܗ
ܕܗܘ̱ ܚܠܛܐ ܡܪܥܐ ܕܐܟܪ ܒܒܘܪܗܢܐ
ܐܒܪ ܕܣܡ ܚܝ̈ܐ ܐܫܬܠܚ ܠܡܚܘܬܗ̱.

81 Parad 11.11:

ܡܒܥܐ ܗܘܝܐ ܗܘܬ ܐܪܥܐ ܕܡܢ ܬܡܢ
ܢܙ ܘܢܦܩܘ ܠܗ̇ ܢܗܪܐ ܕܡܬܦܠܓ
ܐܠܐ ܕܬܬܡܙܓ ܒܘܪܟܬܐ ܒܝܕ ܡܝ̈ܐ
ܘܬܦܘܩ ܠܡܫܩܝܘܬܗ ܕܥܠܡܐ
ܘܬܚܠܡ ܠܡܒܘ̈ܥܘܗܝ ܡܬܝ̈ܒܢ ܒܠܘ̈ܛܬܐ
ܐܝܟ ܕܐܬܚܠܡܘ ܡܝ̈ܐ ܟܪ̈ܝܗܐ ܒܝܕ ܡܠܚܐ.

In hymn 4 On Virg Ephrem compares the oil and the sacraments of the church with Eden's four rivers (cf. Virg 4.14).

82 Parad 11.12:

ܗܟܢ ܒܡܒܘܥܐ ܐܚܪܢܐ ܕܪ̈ܘܚܢܐ
ܕܡܢ ܠܗ ܒܝ̱ ܢܦܩ ܘܛܥܢ ܟܠܗ ܐܐܪ
ܗܘܦܐ ܕܒܪ̈ܘܚܢܐ ܘܒܗ ܢܒܗܐ ܢܦܫܢ
ܒܝܕ ܡܬܚܠܡ ܫܘܡܢ ܒܡܫܒܘܗ
ܣܠܝܚܐ ܕܦܪ̈ܕܝܣܐ ܘܡܬܒܪܟܝܢ ܢ̈ܒܥܐ
ܒܝܕ ܗܘ ܡܒܘܥܐ ܒܪܝܟܐ ܕܡܢ ܬܡܢ.

(ܚܘܠܡܢܐ) for life on earth, the fragrance/breath proclaims metaphorically the sending of the Medicine of Life.[83] The reason for the coming of the Medicine of Life is the 'diseased world' (ܥܠܡܐ ܟܪܝܗܐ), its 'sickness' (ܟܘܪܗܢܐ) and 'our mortality' (ܡܝܘܬܘܬܢ).[84]The function of the fragrant breath which symbolises the Physician and the Medicine of Life is described as follows: the Paradise 'cures our sickness' (ܡܣܡܣ ܟܘܪܗܢܘܬܢ) that entered into the world through the Serpent; the breath 'gives sweetness to the bitterness of this region' (ܡܚܠܐ ܠܗ ܠܡܪܝܪܘܬܗ ܕܗܢܐ ܐܬܪܐ); it 'tempers that curse of our earth' ( ܡܡܙܓ ܠܗ ܠܗܝ ܠܘܛܬܐ ܕܐܪܥܢ); the blessing should 'make clean the fountains of it [the world] that had become polluted by curses' ( ܬܚܠܡ ܠܡܒܘܥܘܗܝ ܕܣܪܝܘ ܒܠܘܛܬܐ).[85]

It will have been seen that, in his descriptions of the biblical narrative of Paradise and the Fall, Ephrem frequently introduces imagery from the sphere of medicine. In Paradise, Adam and Eve enjoy 'good health' (ܚܘܠܡܢܐ), and once the Fall has occurred the fragrant breath of Paradise is as a 'physician' (ܐܣܝܐ), since it can help heal the 'pains' (ܟܐܒܐ) that have resulted from the Fall. In the same way the health of Paradise is in contrast to the sickness, pains and griefs of the earth.[86] The verb ܡܣܡܣ describes the curing and dressing of the wound. Frequently Ephrem also uses the verb ܐܚܠܡ in parallel to ܡܣܡܣ.[87] The 'curse' (ܠܘܛܬܐ) is often related to the earth with its pains, thorns, and griefs, although man was not directly cursed in the biblical narrative.[88] While sickness entered the world throught the Serpent, Ephrem links it also with free will (ܚܐܪܘܬܐ).[89] In the case of Eve the 'pains' (ܟܐܒܐ) refer to

---

83 For the different terms used for the fragrance and breath of Paradise in Parad 11.9-13 see Chapter Two under 'Medicine of Life'.

84 Parad 11.10.

85 Parad 11.9-10.

86 Parad 5.13; 11.9-12.

87 Parad 11.11-12.

88 Gen 3:14; 3:17.

89 Parad 11.9; Virg 2.3; Eccl 32.1.

birth-giving and in Adam's case, that he shall eat in pain, which is in contrast to the 'pleasing fruits' of Paradise. The pains and pangs of birth-giving have been multiplied for Eve and she became mortal, since she had sinned.[90] The pains, pangs and death do not belong to the primordial state of Adam and Eve, but to the mortal life which is a consequence of the fall and the punishment. All these belong to the limited curse which is in contrast to 'glory' and ends with 'death' (ܡܘܬܐ).[91] In Genesis 3:16-19, in the description of the punishment after the transgression, death was not explicitly mentioned as being decreed against Eve or Adam (cf. Gen 3:16-19). Before the expulsion, the possibility of immortality proclaims an eternal life without death. In Ephrem's view, while the pains and pangs are the prime consequence of the disobedience, death was invented in order to make the pains and pangs temporal.[92] Now that the humans have chosen to know evil as well as good, the gift of mortality is an act of mercy complementary to the aspect of punishment. In the Commentray on Genesis death as well as the pains refer to Adam and his posterity, whereas the pangs are reserved to Eve and her daughters.[93] Eventually mortal Adam tasted the Medicine of Life and was revived.[94] In the eschatological Paradise, Satan laments for there is no death and no growing old.[95] By contrast, in the eschatological Paradise the crippled, deformed, blind and deaf will be restored to good health, so that they will 'rejoice to behold the beauty of Paradise'.[96]

---

90 Gen 3:17; CGen 2.30-31.

91 CGen 2.32; 2.35.

92 CGen 2.30; 2.35.

93 CGen 2.32.

94 Nat 26.9.

95 Parad 7.22; 14.11.

96 Parad 7.13:

ܕܢܚܝܢ ܒܦܪܕܝܣܐ ܚܓܝܪ̈ܐ ܕܠܐ ܗܠܟܘ
ܕܗ̇ ܦܪܚܝܢ ܒܐܐܪ ܦܫܝ̈ܓܐ ܕܠܐ ܫܦܦܘ
ܘܡܚ̈ܝܠܐ ܐܦ ܕܗ̈ܘܠܐ ܕܡܢ ܡܪܒܥܐ ܒܡܘܡ
ܕܚܒܠܘ ܠܫܘܦܪܐ ܘܠܐ ܚܙܘ
ܫܘܦܪܗ ܕܦܪܕܝܣܐ ܡܚܙܐ ܠܚܝ̈ܢܝܗܘܢ
ܘܢܒܥܐ ܕܚܢ̈ܘܗܝ ܡܒܥܐ ܠܐܕ̈ܢܝܗܘܢ.

### 4.1.2 Leprosy

In the biblical tradition, healing is perceived as the work of Yahweh. It is God Who cures human ills and grants or restores health to the faithful people. God is also the One Who sends sickness to the erring and disobedient. One of the most notable biblical diseases which Ephrem deals with in his poetry is leprosy (ܓܪܒܐ). Ephrem frequently refers to the lepers Miriam, Naaman, Gehazi and King Uzziah. The Lord struck Miriam with leprosy for her audacity in claiming a role equal to that of Moses, as God's instrument (Num 12:13-15). While the Syrian army commander Naaman received a cure for his leprosy through the prophet Elisha, Gehazi was punished with leprosy for his deceitfulness and greediness (2 Kgs 7). Similarly, King Uzziah was cursed with leprosy for having presumed to enter the sanctuary of the Jerusalem temple and burn incense to the Lord as a priest without being one (2 Chr 26).

These instances of leprosy as punishment for presumption are brought together notably in hymn 28 of the cycle On Faith. Here Ephrem accuses the Arians of 'prying into' and 'seeking/demanding to know' about the Divinity. The Creator is unlimited while creation is limited, and there is a chasm between them that can only be crossed by the Creator. Therefore, in Ephrem's view, created beings should not pry into God, Who is incomprehensible. If they do this, it will be harmful. Ephrem illustrates the consequences with examples from Nature and Scripture. From Nature, he illustrates the power of thunder, lightning, earthquakes, storm and floods which are fearsome to man if they appear in their strength against the weakness of man.[97] Likewise, medicine, wine, and spices, as well as eating and sleeping, are harmful without proper order and moderation.[98] Using created things in an orderly way helps man, who can benefit from them.[99] The Creator put order, structure and limits on every thing, and also on man. While the limits of Nature are fixed, the freedom and mind of man has the Law.[100] Even though human nature is

---

97 Fid 28.1, 15.

98 Fid 28.2, 15.

99 Fid 28.3.

100 Fid 28.4-5.

bounded well by Divine grace, the will of man can be disturbed by freedom and by his way of life.[101] Furthermore, prying into God disturbs human nature. The Scripture as a 'pure mirror of the mind' reflects human willfulness and the result of the wrong use of free will[102] which results in leprosy. Since hymn 28 On Faith brings together three of the four biblical figures, it can conveniently serve as an introduction to a more detailed discussion of each individual in turn:

28.9

ܗܐ ܓܪܒܐ ܕܐܟܣܗ ܠܡ̈ܠܠܐ
ܟܟܣܗ ܠܗ ܠܚܘܨܦܐ ܕܒܨܘ̈ܝܐ
ܕܐܢ ܡܪܝܡ ܕܡܠܠܬ ܒܡܟܝܟܐ
ܣܦܘ̈ܬܗ̇ ܙܩܪ ܠܗ̇ ܢܚܬܐ ܕܓܪܒܐ
ܚܘܒܗ ܡܠܘܐ ܗܘܐ ܠܥܘܠܐ ܒܓܘ ܡ̈ܝܐ
ܐܛܝܦܬ ܒܓܘ ܝܒܫܐ ܠܒܗ̇ ܕܒܪܬ ܦܪܥܘܢ
ܕܗܘ ܛܠܝܐ ܕܛܐܦ ܗܘܐ
ܒܡ ܐܓܪܗ ܐܦ ܠܐܡܗ ܬܪܣܝ ܗܘܐ

Behold, leprosy, which reproved the talkative,
reproves the boldness of those who pry.
If, in the case of Miriam, who spoke against the humble one [Moses],
her lips wove for herself a robe of leprosy (Num 12:1-10),
[yet] her love of him had accompanied the baby in the water (Ex 2:1-10):
she had made the heart of Pharaoh's daughter swim on dry land,
for the child that had been floating
also supported his own mother with the wage [paid for] him.

28.10

ܗܐ ܬܡܝܗܐ ܘܬܗܪܐ ܘܪܗܒܘܬܐ
ܕܐܢ ܡܪܝܡ ܕܡܠܠܬ ܒܡܟܝܟܘܬܐ
ܕܛܥܝܢܬܐ ܚܒ ܠܗ ܒܓܘ ܡ̈ܝܐ
ܘܐܦ ܡܠܟܗ ܕܡܘܫܐ ܡܫܝܚܐ ܗܘܬ
ܘܒܐܠܐ ܕܟܦܪ ܗܘܐ ܕܬܫܦܪܘܢ ܡܫ̈ܚܐ
ܠܗ̇ ܡܫܚܬܐ ܢܫܝܬܐ ܓܒܪ ܕܠܐ ܚܘܫܡ

[101] Fid 28.7.
[102] Fid 28.14.

ܡܢ ܙܟܐ ܐܢ ܢܒܨܐ
ܠܝܚܝܕܝܗ ܕܗܘ ܬܒܥ ܡ̈ܠܠܐ

Behold, amazement, wonder and perturbation!
If Miriam, who spoke against the mortal one,
who was indebted to her for [her] kindness in the water,
and she was also older than Moses,
yet the righteous man, who had commanded that the elders
should be honored (Lev 19:32), dishonored the old prophetess pitilessly,
who will be blameless if he pries
into the Only-Begotten One of Him Who exacts revenge from the talkative?

28.11

ܐܢ ܗܟܝܠ ܠܥܒܕܐ ܬܒܥ ܪܡܐ
ܡܢ ܚܬܗ ܢܒܝܬܐ ܕܡܟܣܬ ܒܗ
ܡܢ ܢܡܟܣ ܒܒܪܗ ܕܪܒܘܬܐ
ܕܒܪ ܥܘܒܐ ܗܘ ܕܢܘܪܐ ܗܝ ܐܟܠܬܐ
ܘܒܪܩܐ ܘܫܠ̈ܗܒܐ ܡܫܬܠܗܒܝܢ ܡܢܗ
ܒܥܬܐ ܕܡܪ̈ܚܐ ܐܝܟ ܚܫܬܐ ܗܝ ܩܕܡܘܗܝ
ܘܕܪܫܐ ܘܚܪܝܢܐ
ܐܝܟ ܥܘܪܐ ܘܐܝܟ ܣܢܪܐ ܡܬܒܠܥܝܢ

If the Lofty thus exacts revenge on behalf of [his] servant
from the prophetess sister who assailed him,
who would assail the Son of Greatness
who is the Son of the bosom which is devouring fire,
and lightning and flames glow from Him.
The inquiry of the insolent is like stubble before it,
and disputation and strife
are swallowed up [in it] like chaff and briars.

28.12

ܘܐܦ ܓܚܙܝ ܕܒܙܚ ܘܐܬܒܙܚ
ܟܕ ܠܒܐ ܕܪܒܗ ܘܐܬܦܪܣ
ܡܪ̈ܥܐ ܟܠܗܝܢ ܠܐܢܫܘܬܐ
ܕܒܫ̈ܡܗܐ ܡܒܕܩܝܢ ܬܠܝ̈ܬܐ
ܥܠ ܦܘܡ ܬܠܬܐ ܕܝܢ ܡܩܝܡܝܢ ܕܝ̈ܢܐ
ܗܐ ܣܗ̈ܕܐ ܬܠܬܐ ܕܫܪܝܢ ܠܥܠ ܚܙܝܢ
ܡܢ ܡܨܐ ܢܦܠܓ
ܥܠ ܣܗ̈ܕܐ ܡܫܪ̈ܪܐ ܕܒܪܗ

As Gehazi, who scorned and was scorned,

eluded the observation of his master and was exposed
(2 Kgs 5:20-27),
so the insolent deceive humanity,
for they baptise in the three names.
Judges confirm according to the speech of three (cf.
Dtn 19:15; 2 Cor 13:1).
Behold, here are three witnesses who dissolve all strife.
Who, then, would disagree
with the holy witnesses of his baptism?

28.13

ܐܢ ܒܝܬܐ ܐܬܬܒܥ ܕܐܬܒܣܪ
ܡܢ ܢܒܨܐ ܢܒܣܪ ܠܡܪܐ ܟܠ
ܠܐ ܬܩܪܘܒ ܠܫܪܒܗ ܕܠܐ ܬܐܒܕ
ܕܥܘܙܝܐ ܠܒܣܡܐ ܩܪܒ ܘܐܬܡܚܝ
ܘܕܠܐ ܒܗܬ ܕܢܒܘܛ ܠܒܘܣܝܗ ܕܩܕܝܫܐ
ܒܗܬ ܟܠܗܘܢ ܝܘܡܘܗܝ ܕܓܪܒܗ ܡܛܫܐ ܗܘܐ
ܘܕܒܙܚ ܒܝܬ ܩܘܕܫܐ
ܚܒܫ ܢܦܫܗ ܒܒܝܬܗ ܐܝܟ ܛܡܐܐ

If the Temple was avenged because it was scorned,
who would pry into, and scorn the Lord of All?
Do not approach his story lest you perish.
For Uzziah offered incense and was chastised,
For he was not ashamed to treat with contempt
the glory of the Holy One,
he was shamed into hiding his leprosy all his days.
And because he had mocked the holy House,
he confined himself in his own house as unclean (2 Chr
26:16-21).

28.14

ܗܐ ܨܝܪܝܢ ܬܪ̈ܝܗܘܢ ܠܝܕ̈ܘܥܐ
ܒܡܚܙܝܬܐ ܕܕܟܝܬܐ ܕܡܚܫܒܬܐ
ܕܚܕ ܨܠܡܐ ܠܒܫܘ ܗܘܘ ܕܨܒܝܢܐ
ܘܚܕ ܛܒܥܐ ܕܚܡܬܐ ܡܢ ܚܐܪܘܬܐ
ܬܪ̈ܝܗܘܢ ܠܐܠܗܐ ܒܡܪ̈ܕܐ ܨܒܘ ܕܢܗܘܘܢ
ܒܦܘܪܫܢܗܘܢ ܟܠܐ ܨܒܪ ܠܒܗܘܢ ܒܚܫܐ
ܕܒܥܠܬ ܦܘܪ̈ܥܢܐ
ܒܡ̈ܚܘܬܗܘܢ ܟܠܝܠܬ ܐܬܦܪܣܝ

Behold, they are both depicted for those with
understanding
in the pure mirror of thought,
because they had put on a single image of willfulness
and a single seal of wrath as a result of free will.

They both wanted to be priests of God.
Their hidden heart is represented in their open
offering.
On account of their offerings
their hidden [thoughts] were openly laid bare.
28.15

ܒܝܬ ܩܘܕܫܐ ܕܐܝܬܘܗܝ ܡܩܕܫ ܟܠ
ܢܦܩ ܡܢܗ ܓܪܒܐ ܡܛܢܦܐ ܟܘܠ
ܘܝܘܠܦܢܐ ܕܐܝܬܘܗܝ ܡܬܪܨ ܟܠ
ܐܘܠܕ ܠܢ ܕܪܫܐ ܡܕܘܕ ܟܠ
ܡܛܪܐ ܡܥܕܪ ܟܠ ܒܣܘܓܐܗ ܡܣܟܠ ܠܢ
ܘܫܡܫܐ ܡܗܕܪ ܟܠ ܒܚܝܠܗ ܡܥܘܪ ܠܢ
ܘܐܦ ܠܚܡܐ ܡܚܝܐ ܟܠ
ܠܕܐܟܠ ܠܒܥܐܬ ܩܛܘܠܐ ܗܘ

From the Temple which makes all holy
the leper who makes all unclean came out.
And the doctrine which directs all
has brought forth for us disputation which disturbs all.
Rain, which helps everything, in excess harms us.
And the sun, which adorns everything, blinds us with
its power.
Even bread, which gives life to all,
is a killer for someone who eats [too] greedily.
28.16

ܛܟܣܗ ܡܟܣ ܠܡܪ̈ܚܐ
ܕܒܢܘܪܐ ܚܕܪܗ ܠܒܝܬ ܩܘܕܫܐ
ܘܠܡܐܬܝܢ ܕܐܡܪܚܘ ܘܟܗܢܘ ܗܘܘ
ܒܗܘܢ ܦܩܥܬ ܢܘܪܐ ܪܚܡܬ ܩܘܕܫܐ
ܐܟܠܬ ܒܢܘ̈ܗܝ ܕܐܗܪܘܢ
ܕܢܘܟܪܝܬܐ ܢܘܪܐ ܐܥܠܘ ܐܝܟ ܙܢܝܬܐ
ܘܛܢܬ ܡܩܕܫܬܐ ܘܝܕܥܬܐ ܕܫܪܪܐ
ܛܢܬ ܠܗ ܒܒܢܬܐ ܡܩܕܫܬܐ

His arrangement rebukes the impudent
because he has hedged the Temple around with fire.
And in the case of the 200 [sons of Aaron],
who dared and served as priests,
the fire, the lover of the holy, burst them out.
It devoured the sons of Aaron,
because they brought strange fire in like a harlot (Num
16:1-35).
The holy [fire] was jealous, and knowledge of truth

was zealous against profane inquiry.

*Fid 28.9-16*

### *4.1.2.1 The Leprosy of Miriam (Num 12:1-16)*

Miriam is mentioned by name in seven passages of the Old Testament.[103] She is presented as the sister of Moses and Aaron[104] and identified with the sister of Moses who watched from a distance what would happen to Moses in the ark of bullrushes (cf. Ex 2:1-10). As a 'prophetess', Miriam took a leading role in the wilderness community with Moses and Aaron (cf. Ex 15:20-21). According to Numbers 12, Miriam and Aaron had an argument with Moses during the exodus because of his Cushite wife and his authority in rendering God's word. They claimed to have the power of prophecy equal to that of Moses. Thus, they were rebuked, but the chief punishment fell upon Miriam (Num 12:9-10). When Aaron saw Miriam's leprosy, he regretted what he had said and prayed with Moses for her healing (cf. Num 12:10-15).

Ephrem uses the illustration of the punishment of Miriam (Num 12:1-10) as an admonition to the Arians. Because Miriam criticised Moses for his Cushite wife and reproved the humble man, the Lord punished her skin with leprosy. Ephrem is amazed, perturbed and full of wonder that the skin of Moses' older sister was diseased, when she had saved his life by approaching Pharaoh's daughter and advising her to find a wet-nurse for Moses (Ex 2:1-10). If this happened to Miriam because she spoke against the prophet, how much more severe would the disease be of those who pryingly seek to know the Lord of the prophets?[105]

In the Second discourse on Admonition, Ephrem deals extensively with Miriam as an example from the Scripture. He frames the biblical passage with the significance of speech or word.[106] The word granted life to the robber on the cross (cf. Lk 23:42), but the mocking speech of Miriam afflicted her with

---

[103] Ex 15:20-21; Num 12:1-16; 20:1; 26:59; Dtn 24:9; 1 Chr 5:29 (6:3); Mic 6:4.

[104] Ex 15:20-21; Num 20:1; 26:59; 1 Chr 5:29 (6:3); Mic 6:4.

[105] Fid 28.10; I Serm 2.1213-16.

[106] I Serm 2.1203-1380.

leprosy.[107] As a prophetess, Miriam had the right to ask that God talk to her, but it was not right to be proud and arrogant, to rebuke and mock her brother in argument. Miriam spoke to God, she was near to him and she had the gift of prophecy, but because she thought that she was privileged, she became distant from the Lord.[108] Words of mocking and rebuking are evil in the eye of the Lord, and man has to give account on the day of the judgment for every careless word he has spoken.[109] Furthermore, all 'uprightness' (ܟܐܢܘܬܐ), 'holiness' (ܩܕܝܫܘܬܐ), 'purity' (ܕܟܝܘܬܐ), 'faith' (ܗܝܡܢܘܬܐ), 'concord' (ܐܘܝܘܬܐ), 'gift/charism' (ܡܘܗܒܬܐ), 'prayer' (ܨܠܘܬܐ), 'fasting' (ܨܘܡܐ) and 'pure love' ( ܚܘܒܐ ܕܟܝܐ) are not 'true' and will be rejected and refused if they are mixed with 'iniquity' (ܥܘܠܐ), 'impurity' (ܛܡܐܘܬܐ), 'magical ablutions' (ܣܘܚܝܐ; variant: 'defilement/abomination'=ܣܘܝܒܐ), 'augury/divination' (ܢܚܫܐ), 'division' (ܦܘܠܓܐ), 'pride' (ܫܘܒܗܪܐ), 'haughtiness' (ܪܡܘܬܐ), 'hatred of heart' ( ܣܢܐܬ ܠܒܐ) or 'jealousy' (ܛܢܢܐ).[110] The same is true with natural substances. If poison is mixed with food then death will follow.[111] So it is with truth for Ephrem. Also, since what is visible is true and clear, because the mind and soul are invisible, the body serves as their mirror which reflects their role. The visible disease of the body reflects the invisible illness of mind. The leprosy of the body is equivalent to the rebuke of the mind. Moreover, the visible disease shows how hateful mocking and scorn is, and how impure as a result of it the mind and soul are.[112]

For Ephrem man is healthy if the relationship of the body, mind and soul is full of harmony and the 'limbs' are not acting against each other. Therefore, he includes another form of argument for the cause of the leprosy of Miriam's body. The 'division' of the 'limbs' (body) against a person through diseases is a sign of impurity and defilement, and it is an evil. As a man rejects

[107] I Serm 2.1207-16.

[108] I Serm 2.1333-42.

[109] I Serm 2.1377-80; Mt 12:36.

[110] I Serm 2.1225-42.

[111] I Serm 2.1247-59.

[112] I Serm 2.1257-77.

the defiled part of himself, so God too rejects a man if he doubts, sins and is unclean; and as one part of a person worries about another part, so God also worries about his chosen people.[113]

While in Fid 28, Ephrem does not mention the healing of Miriam, he does so in the Second Admonition[114] and in Haer 43 where he presents God as the Creator of the body and Jesus as the healer of the body. Both are the same God who loves human nature. Among many other images of healing, Ephrem refers to the healing of Miriam and Naaman:

ܪܚܡ ܦܓܪܐ ܠܡܪܝܡ ܕܟܐ ܐܦ ܠܢܥܡܢ
ܣܢܐ ܦܓܪܐ ܠܥܣܪܐ ܕܓܪ̈ܒܝ
ܠܒܪ̈ܐ ܕܢܟܣܘܢ ܠܐܟܠܝ ܕܩܪ̈ܨܘ
ܕܐܝܟ ܡܠܬܗܘܢ ܠܗܘ ܡܢ ܕܐܣܓܝ ܘܠܐ ܠܡܥܕܠ

'The one who loves the body' cured Miriam [and] also Naaman.
'The one who hates the body' cured the ten lepers (Lk 17:12),
so that they might reprove those who accused falsely;
for, according to their word, the one who has increased should be blamed.

*Haer 43.16*

This text is in the context of hymns 42 - 44 of Against Heresies where Ephrem offers various arguments against the Marcionites and Bardaisanites who dared to separate the Son from the Father. For Marcion (ca. 70-150 C.E.) the Demiurge, as Creator of the body, 'loves the body', whereas Jesus represents the supreme good God, and so is seen as 'hating the body'. Ephrem points out ironically the illogicality of Marcion's separation between the Good God and the Creator. Therefore, unlike the heretics (Marcionites and Bardaisanites), Ephrem emphasises the love of Jesus for the human body which is the creation of the Father. Jesus loved the body of man and therefore He cured human bodies, just as His Father, the Creator of the body, did. Neither Jesus nor His Father hates the body. While in this hymn God is proclaimed as the Healer of man, and so also as the Healer of the leprosy of Miriam, in the Second Admonition Ephrem emphasises the method of

---

[113] I Serm 2.1277-92:

[114] I Serm 2.1315-44.

healing, which is man's purification from sin. Just as through sin and mocking speech disease afflicts the body, so through 'holiness' (ܩܕܝܫܘܬܐ) God granted Miriam health and made her pure from her leprosy. Both 'holiness' and sin have to do with the will of man and his use of free will, and at the same time with his relationship with God. The cursing of disease, or the healing or restoring of man is dependent on the relationship between man's body, mind and soul, as well as on a proper relationship to the Creator of human nature. The healing of leprosy is a symbol of the new birth; disease becomes cleansed from the body, just as sin from man at baptism.[115]

Therefore, the mind of man should be holy, and any investigation of the Lord implies a division of the mind. The tenor of the whole of hymn 28 On Faith is provided in the refrain which praises the Son Who cannot be known.[116] The Son of God is described as the 'Son of the bosom of devouring fire' which swallowed up the disputers and inquirers.[117] In the Second Admonition, Ephrem says:

ܐܢ [ܐܢ] ܡܪܝܡ ܕܢܒܝܬܐ ܗܘܬ ܒܡܘܝܩܘܬܐ ܗܘܝ
ܒܪܘܬ

ܐܚܪܬܐ ܐܢܫܘ ܕܬܒܙܚ ܘܓܗܢܐ ܗܝ ܠܗ̇ ܙܥܘܪܐ.

If Miriam who was a prophetess was cursed with
leprosy because of mocking,
if another one mocks, for her even Gehenna is too
small.

*I Serm 1213-16*

### 4.1.2.2 *The Cure of Naaman's Leprosy and Gehazi's Greed and Punishment (2 Kgs 5:1-27)*

Diseased with leprosy, Naaman visited the prophet Elisha in Samaria in the hope of being cured (cf. 2 Kgs 5:1-27). On his arrival Naaman was ordered to bathe himself seven times in the Jordan (2 Kgs 5:8-12). Obeying the word of the prophet, Naaman dipped himself seven times in the River Jordan and he was cured (2 Kgs 5:13-14).

---

115 CDiat 16.13; I Serm 2.1257-.1335.

116 Fid 28.Refrain: ܒܪܝܟ ܛܠܝܐ ܕܠܐ ܡܫܟܚ ܠܡܬܒܨܝܘ.

117 Fid 28.11.

In a passage which was quoted above it was stated that 'the One Who loves the body cleansed Miriam and Naaman from their leprosy and the One Who hates the body cured ten'.[118] Ephrem here refers to the biblical narrative concerning Naaman to illustrate the unity of Jesus with his Father. As Jesus restored human bodies, so the Father cured people like Naaman, who believed that there is only one God, the God of Israel.[119] Furthermore, the body of man is the dwelling place of the body and blood of Christ and not the dwelling place of demons, as they dwelt in swine and the sea.[120] God loves the human body, He restores it, cures and purifies it. Jesus also loves it.

A further point is made in the CDiat 12.21, where attention is drawn to the fact that Jesus touched (Mt 8:3) the leper even though this was against the Law. Elisha followed the Law and did not touch Naaman while the Lord did 'in order to show that the Law was not an obstacle to Him Who had constituted the Law'.[121] In CDiat 16.31, where Jesus tries to explain rebirth to Nicodemus, Ephrem refers to Naaman. Without a womb, Naaman was renewed through the words of Elisha: 'He went and washed himself and was cleansed, and his flesh became like that of a little child.'[122]

The cleansing of the body of Naaman from leprosy through the few words of Elisha and through the water reminds us of baptism. According to Ephrem, it was not the water of the River Jordan which cured Naaman, but it was the 'command' (ܦܘܩܕܢܐ). The prophet of the Lord commanded Naaman to wash in the river as the Lord commanded the man born blind to wash in Siloam (cf. Jn 9). Therefore, it is not the element of water which effected the purification of Naaman, as it is not the 'water of atonement' (ܡܝ̈ܐ ܕܚܘܣܝܐ) which gives atonement to human beings, but the names pronounced over the water.[123]

---

118 Haer 43.16.

119 2 Kgs 5:15; cf. Haer 43.16.

120 Haer 43.3.

121 CDiat 12.21; Mt 8:3.

122 CDiat 16.13; 2 Kgs 5:14.

123 CDiat 16.29. By the 'water of atonement' Ephrem means baptism.

Faith is certainly important. Commenting on the verses 'physician, heal yourself' (Lk 4:23) and 'a prophet is not accepted in his own town' (Lk 4:24), Ephrem refers to Elisha as an example. Likewise, Jesus refers to Elisha when He is rejected at Nazareth.[124] To those who believed in Jesus, He was like a 'fountain' (ܡܒܘܥܐ) for them. Elisha was a fountain in the thirsty land for thirsty people, but because they did not have faith in him, they could not drink from it. It sprang forth for the leper Naaman and granted him healing, because he believed.[125] Ephrem uses this as a part of his polemic against the Jews. Particular allusion is made to Judas Iscariot in Eccl 31.9: the majesty of Jesus is much more exalted than that of Elisha who healed Naaman, since the Lord healed many.[126] Therefore, Judas Iscariot should have had much more faith in the Lord than Naaman had in Elisha: Naaman trusted the prophet by obeying him and honouring him, while Gehazi reproached the prophet of the Lord.

In hymn 28 On Faith quoted above, Ephrem also uses Gehazi as an example in order to demonstrate the boldness of the Arians who 'pry into' God. The narrative of the cure of Naaman's leprosy (2 Kgs 5:1-27) described Gehazi as greedy and deceitful. Because Gehazi lied to Elisha over his having taken two talents of silver and two changes of clothing from Naaman, his skin became diseased with leprosy (2 Kgs 5:20-27). His leprosy was the result of his free will and wilfulness, for he had scorned his master freely, of his will.[127] The scorning of the servant of the Lord is like scorning God and lying to Him. Because of this Ephrem accounts Gehazi along with Cain, Pharaoh, Saul, Herod and Judas Iscariot. Their hatred precipitated the doing of iniquity and they thought to deceive God.[128] Like Achar (cf. Josh 7:1-26) and the Israelites in the desert during the Exodus (cf. Ex 32:1-35), Gehazi loved gold (2 Kgs 5:22-23) which clothed him with leprosy. The lying of Gehazi

---

[124] Lk 4:27; CDiat 11.23-27.

[125] Nis 42.5.

[126] Eccl 31.9.

[127] Fid 28.12, 14.

[128] CDiat 3.5.

over the gold is given as a parallel to the reproach of Moses by Miriam.[129]

The visible leprosy serves as a mirror of the inner mind of Gehazi. In hymn 31 On the Church, Ephrem uses the same argument as in the case of Miriam. The leprosy of his body 'heralded' and mirrored 'the darkness of his mind'.[130] Also the light of day does not enlighten the inner darkness. Gehazi pretends in the presence of the prophet to be light and pure while his mind was dark and defiled, like Iscariot in front of Jesus, the powerful Son. Likewise, Miriam thought herself to be near to God while she was far from him because of her inner mind.

### *4.1.2.3 The Leprosy of King Uzziah (2 Chr 26:16-21)*

Another example of leprosy that Ephrem frequently uses is that of King Uzziah. During the early years of his reign, King Uzziah was instructed in the fear of God by a certain Zechariah (cf. 2 Chr 26:5), and he did what was right in the eyes of the Lord (cf. 2 Kgs 15:3). But, because he had entered the holy sanctuary to burn incense as a priest unfaithfully and without obeying the commandments of the Lord, he was afflicted with leprosy (cf. 2 Chr. 26:16-21).

Ephrem refers to King Uzziah in three hymns On Faith and in three On Paradise.[131] In hymn 8, 28 and 38 On Faith, Ephrem

---

[129] CDiat 8.1c has gold (ܕܗܒܐ). In Eccl 31.7, Ephrem uses the term silver (ܣܐܡܐ) instead of gold (ܕܗܒܐ), while Peshitta has ܟܣܦܐ (cf. 2 Kgs 5:22-23; see M. Weitzman, *The Syriac Version of the Old Testament* (Cambridge 1999), 174). The greed and deceitful deeds of Gehazi are also reflected in the story of the woman of Shunem (2 Kgs 4:8-37). The woman of Shunem became afraid while Gehazi approached her son and touched him with the staff. Since he turned back with the staff without healing the child, Ephrem describes him as a thief (cf. Nis 39.2; 2 Kgs 4:31). Gehazi's greed could not revive the child of the Shunamite woman, and his theft, which is the influence of the Evil One (cf. Nis. 57.22), accused him and reproved him so that he might escape from leprosy (cf Nis 37.1; 42.6; Eccl 31.10):

ܥܡܠ ܠܓܚܙܝ ܦܓܥ ܗܘܐ ܗܘܐ ܠܟܣܝ ܕܐܦ ܕܠܗ ܠܐܠܝܫܥ ܛܠܡ ܗܘܐ
ܐܟܣܗ ܗܘܐ ܣܘܓܪܐ ܕܢܥܪܘܩ ܡܢ ܓܪܒܐ.

[130] Eccl 31.7; I Serm 2.1269-78.

[131] Cf. Fid 8.11; 28.13-15; 38.17; Parad 3.13-15; 12.4; 15.9-12.

discusses King Uzziah's leprosy as an example of those who pry into God. The biblical narrative of Uzziah is one among many others. According to Ephrem, it points to the reproach of those who pry into the Lord by their wilfulness and free will, and do not obey the commandments of the Lord.[132] His argument is mainly against the Arians.[133] Disobeying the commandments of the Lord, King Uzziah entered the holy temple by his own wilfulness, just as Gehazi freely lied to the prophet Elijah. His wilfulness led him to act against the Law, just as Miriam had scorned the prophet. He was free to do this and had the freedom which enabled him to use deceit and to do whatever he likes, even if it is against God.[134] Ephrem draws a parallel with Adam who expected to be divinised by the eating of fruit. However, quite the opposite occurred and he lost his glory and was expelled from Paradise:

ܙܝܘܐ ܨܒܐ ܠܡܐܪܬ ܐܕܡ
ܘܗܘܐ ܠܗ ܗܘ ܝܘܪܬܗ ܐܪܥܐ
ܨܒܐ ܥܘܙܝܐ ܕܢܘܣܦ ܗܘܐ ܠܗ ܐܦ ܟܗܢܘܬܐ
ܘܐܬܬܘܣܦ ܠܗ ܠܓܪܒܐ ܢܕܝܕܐ

Adam wanted to inherit the brightness,
but the earth became his inheritance.
Uzziah wanted to add priesthood for himself,
but he was given in addition an abominable leprosy.
*Fid 38.17*

For Ephrem, Adam's and Uzziah's wills manifestly contradict the will of God. Nevertheless, God had once granted free will to man who therefore is enabled to act freely. While it is the Evil One who is the prime rebel against God, man sins because he is persuaded by the Devil. The Devil deceived Adam and made him eat from the Tree of Knowledge and led Uzziah to enter the holy temple.[135] The Tree of Knowledge serves as a parallel to the holy sanctuary, as does Adam to King Uzziah. Adam dared to touch the fruit and Uzziah to enter the holy sanctuary. Both of them were

---

132 Fid 8.8-16: the 250 priests and Korah (Num 16:1-50), the priest Uzzah (2 Sam 6:1-8), the River Jordan (Josh 3:7-4:9), Daniel (Dan 8:15-27).

133 Fid 28.13-15; 38.13.

134 Fid 28.14; 38.17; Parad 12.4.

135 Parad 12.4; 15.9.

disobedient and acted in boldness.[136] Adam and Uzziah demanded much more than what God had granted to them. Adam was in possession of the luxury of Paradise and Uzziah of that of kingship. Because of their boldness, they lost their rank.[137] However, if Adam and Uzziah had followed the commandments of the Lord they would not have sinned. As we have seen in the context of Gehazi, the free will of man is not limited in the way that nature is bounded, but it has the Law. Following the commandments of the Lord will save man from all harm, and prevent him from being influenced by the Evil One.

Furthermore, Ephrem contrasts the holiness of the sanctuary with the disease of leprosy. The expectations from the holy sanctuary are obvious: the king expected holiness and purification from it, but he received leprosy. 'The leper who makes all unclean came out of the temple which makes all holy'.[138] It is clear that the inner mind and thought of man are influential here, and that the 'holiness' or 'sinfulness' of man is dependent on the invisible mind. Man can sin even in the holy sanctuary which makes all holy if he is not pure in his mind. King Uzziah scorned and mocked the temple of the Lord while he was offering the incense, and 'he was not ashamed to treat with contempt the glory of the Holy One …'.[139] To clarify his argument further, Ephrem refers to some examples from nature. Man benefits from rain and sun, but if they are too strong they become harmful. Although bread gives life to all, yet to the greedy it gives death.[140]

In all this, Ephrem warns against prying into the Lord. Man is liable to be persuaded by the Evil One, and so it is necessary to follow the Lord's commandments and to obey the Law. Otherwise, the consequences of disobedience are harmful. The disease of leprosy is a visible disease of the invisible human mind. Ephrem describes it as a punishment which is a consequence of man's own fault, seeing that he is free.

---

136 Parad 3.14.

137 Parad 15.9-10; Fid 38.17.

138 Fid 28.15; Parad 15.12.

139 Fid 28.13.

140 Fid 28.15.

### 4.1.3 Jesus Christ as the Hidden Medicine in the Seed of Abraham/David

The evangelist Matthew mentions explicitly three biblical women in the genealogy of Jesus, apart from Mary the Mother of Jesus: Tamar (Mt 1.3), Rahab and Ruth (Mt 1.5). They are not Jews, but they became a part of the genealogy of Jesus in a significant way: they had recognised the 'hidden messianic seed' in their husbands; they risked their own lives and wanted to participate in the new life, even if their actions were against the Law. In the cases of Tamar and Ruth, Ephrem specifically identifies this messianic seed as 'the Medicine of Life'.

By way of introduction I take Nat 9.7-16, where Ephrem brings together these three women who, out of their love, hoped for Jesus and wanted to partake in his ancestry. By bringing these three women of the genealogy together Ephrem implicitly identifies Rahab of Matthew 1:5 with the Rahab of Joshua 2 (see below):

9.7

ܡܛܠܬܟ ܢܫ̈ܐ ܪܗ̣ܛ ܗܘ̈ܝ ܒܬܪ ܓܒܪ̈ܐ
ܬܡܪ ܪܓܬ ܠܓܒܪܐ ܕܐܪܡܠ
ܘܪܥܘܬ ܪܚܡܬ ܠܓܒܪܐ ܕܣܐܒ
ܐܦ ܗܝ ܪܚܒ ܕܨܝܕܬ ܓܒܪ̈ܐ ܒܟ ܐܬܨܝܕܬ

Because of You, women pursued men:
Tamar desired a man who was widowed,
and Ruth loved a man who was old.
Even Rahab, who captivated men, by You was taken captive.

9.8

ܢܦܩܬ ܬܡܪ ܘܒܚܫܘܟܐ ܓܢܒܬ ܢܘܗܪܐ
ܘܒܛܢܦܘܬܐ ܓܢܒܬ ܩܘܕܫܐ
ܘܒܦܪܗܣܝܐ ܓܢܒܬ ܥܠܬ
ܠܟ ܝܩܝܪܐ ܕܥܒܕ ܢܟ̈ܦܐ ܡܢ ܙܠܝ̈ܠܐ

Tamar went out and in darkness she stole the light,
and by impurity she stole chastity,
and by nakedness she entered furtively to You,
the Honorable One, Who produces chaste people from the licentious.

9.9

ܚܣܝܗ̇ ܡܗܠܟܐ ܘܡܢܛ ܘܪܗܛ ܐܝܟ ܕܠܒܥܙ
ܐܕܒܪ ܕܢܒܐ ܘܠܐ ܕܢܒܠܬ ܗܘܬ
ܪܓܫܐ ܘܡܣܒܐ ܘܠܐ ܡܢܛܠܬ ܗܘܬ
ܢܓܠܘ ܠܓܘܪܐ ܓܠܐ ܗܘܐ ܕܠܟ ܢܓܠܐ ܗܘܐ

Satan saw her and was afraid and ran as if to hinder [her];
He reminded [her] of judgment, but she feared not,
of stoning and the sword, but she was not afraid.
The teacher of adultery was hindering adultery to hinder You.

9.10

ܙܘܢܝܐ ܗܘܐ ܢܟܦ ܠܒܘܪܗ ܕܬܡܪ ܡܛܠܬܟ
ܠܟ ܨܗܝܐ ܗܘܬ ܡܒܘܥܐ ܕܟܝܐ
ܝܗܘܕܐ ܓܢܒܗ ܡܢ ܫܩܝܘܬܟ
ܡܒܘܥܐ ܨܗܝܬܐ ܓܢܒܬ ܫܩܝܟ ܡܢ ܡܒܘܥܗ

For the adultery of Tamar became chaste because of You.
For You she thirsted, O pure Fountain.
Judah cheated her of drinking You.
A thirsty fount stole Your drink from its source.

9.11

ܗܘܬ ܐܪܡܠܬܐ ܡܛܠܬܟ ܠܟ ܗܘ ܪܓܬ
ܪܗܛܬ ܘܗܘܬ ܐܦ ܙܢܝܬܐ
ܡܛܠܬܟ ܠܟ ܗܘ ܣܘܝܬ
ܢܛܪܬ ܘܗܘܬ ܡܩܕܫܬܐ ܠܟ ܗܘ ܪܚܡܬ

She was a widow. For Your sake she desired You.
She pursued You, and even became a harlot.
For Your sake she longed for You.
She kept [pure] and became a holy woman, [for] she loved You.

9.12

ܪܥܘܬ ܬܣܬܒܪ ܕܒܥܬ ܥܘܬܪܟ ܥܠ ܠܗ ܡܘܐܒ
ܬܚܕܐ ܬܡܪ ܕܐܬܐ ܡܪܗ
ܕܫܡܗ ܐܟܪܙ ܥܠ ܒܪ ܡܪܗ
ܐܦ ܟܘܢܝܗ ܠܟ ܩܪܐ ܗܘܐ ܕܬܐܬܐ ܨܐܕܝܗ

May Ruth receive good tidings, for she sought Your wealth; Moab entered into it.
Let Tamar rejoice that her Lord has come,
for her name announced the Son of her Lord
and her appellation called You to come to her.

9.13

ܡܢ ܐܪܙܠܠ ܢܨܒ̈ܬܐ ܫܒܝܒ ܒܘܠܐ
ܠܟ ܗܘ ܓܢܒܬ ܒܝܬ ܐܘܪ̈ܚܬܐ
ܕܪ̈ܫ ܐܘܪܚܐ ܠܒܝܬ ܡܠܟܘܬܐ
ܕܢ̈ܫܐ ܓܢܒܬ ܠܗ ܣܦܩ ܣܦܩܐ ܕܢܚܬܗ ܗܘܐ

By You honorable women made themselves
contemptible, [You] the One Who makes all
chaste.
She stole You at the crossroads,
[You] Who prepared the road to the house of the
kingdom.
Since she stole life, the sword was insufficient to kill
her.

9.14

ܪܥܘܬ ܥܡ ܓܒܪܐ ܒܐܕܪܐ ܢܦܠܬ ܡܛܠܬܟ
ܐܚܨܦ ܚܘܒܗ̇ ܡܛܠܬܟ
ܡܠܦ ܚܘܨܦܐ ܠܟܠ ܬ̈ܝܒܐ
ܐܣܠܝ ܐܕ̈ܢܝܗ̇ ܠܟܠ ܩܠܝܢ ܡܛܠ ܩܠܟ

Ruth lay down with a man on the threshing floor for
Your sake.
Her love was bold for Your sake.
She teaches boldness to all penitents.
Her ears held in contempt all [other] voices for the sake
of Your voice.

9.15

ܓܡܘܪܬܐ ܕܪܚܫܬ ܒܥܪܣܗ ܕܒܥܙ ܣܠܩܬ ܢܦܠܬ
ܚܙܬ ܪܒ ܟܘܡܪܐ ܕܛܫܐ ܒܚ̈ܨܘܗ
ܢܘܪܐ ܠܦܝܪܡܗ ܪܗܛܬ ܘܗܘܬ
ܥܓܠܬܗ ܕܒܥܙ ܠܟ ܗܘ ܝܠܕܬ ܬܘܪܐ ܕܦܛܡܐ

The fiery coal that crept into the bed of Boaz went up
and lay down.
She saw the Chief Priest hidden in his loins,
she ran and became the fire for his censer.
The heifer of Boaz brought forth the fatted ox for You.

9.16

ܠܩܛܐ ܠܩܛܬ ܡܛܠ ܚܘܒܟ ܬ̈ܒܢܐ ܓܒܬ
ܦܪܥܬܗ̇ ܒܥܓܠ ܐܓܪܐ ܕܡܘܟܟܗ̇
ܚܠܦ ܫ̈ܒܠܐ ܫܪܫܐ ܕܡ̈ܠܟܐ
ܘܚܠܦ ܬ̈ܒܢܐ ܥܡܪܐ ܕܚܝܐ ܕܢܒܥܬ ܡܢܗ̇

She went gleaning; for Your love she gathered straw.
You repaid her quickly the wage of her humiliation:
instead of ears [of wheat], the Root of kings,
and instead of straw, the Sheaf of Life that descends
from her.

*Nat 9.7-16*

### *4.1.3.1 Tamar (Gen 38)*

According to the biblical account (Gen 38), Tamar was the wife of Er, the firstborn of Judah who was in the fourth generation in the genealogy of Jesus from Abraham onwards (cf Mt 1.3). God let Er die for his wickedness. When Onan the second son of Judah also died, Judah tried to save his youngest son Shelah by delaying giving Tamar to him as a wife. Tamar, however, took the matter into her own hands after Judah's wife died. Disguised as a harlot, she had relations with Judah and she became pregnant. The pledge, the seal and its cord, and the staff, which she took from him, bore witness that he was the father of her children. She gave birth to twin sons, Perez and Zerah, and Perez was an ancestor of David.

In the Commentary on Genesis Ephrem draws attention to the aim of Tamar. She was yearning for the blessing (ܒܘܪܟܬܐ)[141] and treasure (ܣܝܡܬܐ)[142] which were hidden in the Hebrew man. In order to fill her hunger and to make her poverty rich from the hidden treasure she dared to act against the Law. 'She who had been cheated out of marriage was held innocent in her fornication …'[143]

In CGen 34.3, Ephrem does not specify further the 'blessing' and the 'treasure' which were hidden in the circumcised man.[144] From the context we may suppose that Ephrem implies a messianic interpretation. Ephrem expresses this clearly in his hymns.[145] In Virg 22.19-20, where Ephrem comments on the Samaritan woman, he says:

---

141 CGen 34.2.

142 CGen 34.3-4.

143 CGen 34.6: ܕܐܬܛܠܡܬ ܒܙܘܘܓܘܬܐ ܐܙܕܕܩܬ ܒܙܢܝܘܬܗ; cf. Nat 15.8.

144 CGen 34.3.

145 Nat 9.7-16; Virg 22.20. In his article 'Holy Adultery', Tryggve Kronholm draws attention to Ephrem's interpretation of Genesis 38. He says that 'Ephrem explicitly advocates the idea that Tamar's adultery in reality was something holy, since the measures she was taking were performed solely with an end to the coming of the Messiah' (Kronholm, 150). Cf. T. Kronholm, 'Holy Adultery. The Interpretation of the Story of Judah and Tamar (Gen 38) in the Genuine Hymns of Ephraem Syrus (ca. 306-373)', *OS* 40 (1991), 149-63. H. Urs von Balthasar, 'Casta Meretix' in

☞

22.19

ܬܡܪ ܚܙܬ ܗܘܬ ܕܡܝܬܘ ܫܘܬܦܝ̈ܗ̇
ܘܝܬܒܬ ܗܘܬ ܠܚܣܕܐ ܪܒܐ
ܝܗܘܕܐ ܕܚܠ ܕܠܐ ܢܡܘܬ ܐܦ ܫܠܐ
... ܛܘܦܣܐ ܕܚܠܘ ܫܡܪ̈ܝܐ
ܬܡܪ ܓܢܒܬ ܘܠܚܣܕܗ̇ ܐܥܒܪܬ
ܫܡܪܝܬܐ ܐܦ ܚܣܕܗ̇ ܛܫܝܬ
ܕܬܡܪ ܐܬܓܠܝ ܢܟܠܗ̇ ܠܥܘܕܪܢ
ܘܕܗ̇ܝ [ܠܝܘܬܪܢ].

Tamar saw that her consorts were dead
and she sat down to great reproach.
Judah feared that Shelah also would die
… type, the Samaritans feared.
Tamar stole and made her reproach pass away,
and the Samaritan woman concealed her reproach.
Tamar's deceit was revealed for our benefit,
and hers for our advantage.

22.20

ܬܡܪ ܗܝܡܢܬ ܕܡܢ ܝܗܘܕܐ
ܕܢܚ ܡܠܟܐ ܕܓܢܒܬ ܪܐܙܗ
ܐܦ ܗ̇ܝ ܣ̇ܟܝܬ ܒܝܬ ܫܡܪ̈ܝܐ
ܕܟܒܪ ܡܢܗ̇ ܡܫܝܚܐ ܢܕܢܚ
ܕܬܡܪ ܗܘ ܣܒܪܗ̇ ܠܐ ܕܥܟ
ܐܦ ܗ̇ܝ ܣܘܟܝܗ̇ ܠܐ ܒܛܠ
ܐܝܟ ܡܢܗ̇ ܓܝܪ ܕܢܚ ܡܪܢ ܒܗ̇ܘ ܩܘܪܝܐ
ܕܒܗ̇ ܐܬܓܠܝ ܬܡܢ.

Tamar trusted that from Judah
would arise the king whose symbol she stole.
This woman, too, among the Samaritans expected
that perhaps the Messiah would arise from her.
Tamar's hope was not extinguished,
nor was this woman's expectation in vain,
as from her, therefore, our Lord arose in this town,
for by her He was revealed there.

*Virg 22.19-20*

---

his collection *Sponsa Verbi* (Einsiedeln 1961), 203-305, in the course of a long patristic study of Rahab and other biblical types, has a section on 'Thamar, die Dirnengestalt der Kirche' (pp. 280-89), but he did not know Ephrem's poetry and misses his much greater symbolic richness.

In CDiat 12.19, Ephrem also links the story of Tamar with that of the Samaritan woman. After Ephrem has discussed some of the faithful and righteous people in hymn 11 On the Church, he contrasts Tamar with Eve. Love of the 'new life' (ܚܝܐ ܚܕ̈ܬܐ) caused the prophets and the faithful to bear and suffer much in order to receive life. It is only in this context that Ephrem introduces the image of 'Medicine of Life' (ܣܡ ܚܝܐ). This 'Medicine of Life' was hidden in Judah. Tamar stole the Medicine of Life from Judah, for she recognised it hidden in Judah:

ܒܓܘ ܫܝܢܐ ܪܒܐ ܕܥܕܢ ܫܘܒܚܗ ܕܐܕܡ ܐܬܓܢܒ
ܕܚܛܝܬܐ ܒܓܝܣܐ ܢܦܩܬ ܘܚܘܝܐ ܘܚܘܐ ܗܘܘ ܐܠ̈ܦܐ
ܬܡܪ ܕܝܢ ܒܝܬ ܐܘܪ̈ܚܬܐ ܥܠ ܬܓܪܐ ܢܦܠܬ ܗܘܬ
ܘܓܢܒܬ ܡܢܗ ܣܡ ܚܝܐ ܕܟܣܐ ܗܘܐ ܒܗ
ܚܛܝܬܐ ܕܓܢܒܬ ܐܬܓܢܒܬ ܒܕܝܢܐ ܕܙܟܬ ܐܙܕܟܝܬ
ܡܘܬܐ ܟܕ ܥܝܪ ܐܬܓܢܒ ܕܡܪܢ ܣܪܩ ܣܝܡܬܗ.

Amid the great tranquillity of Eden the glory of Adam
was robbed.
For sin came out with a band of robbers
and the snake and Eve became the instigators.
Tamar, however, fell upon the merchant in the
crossroads,
and she stole from him the medicine of life that was
hidden in him.
The sin that stole, itself was stolen, and in the judgment
in which it was victorious, it has been defeated.
Death was robbed while it was awake,
because our Lord had emptied out its treasures.

*Eccl 11.10*

According to Ephrem, Jesus as the 'Medicine of Life' was hidden in the descendants of Abraham. Tamar realised this in Judah and she wanted to 'steal' it from him.[146] We find the same idea concerning the role of Ruth,[147] but the case of Rahab is more complicated (Josh 2; 6).

---

146 Nat 1.12; 16.14: Ephrem often uses the verb 'steal' (ܓܢܒ).

147 Nat 1.12-13; 9.7-16

### *4.1.3.2 Rahab (Jos 2; 6)*

As is mentioned above, the name of Rahab is included in the genealogy of Jesus (Mt 1.5). Rahab is related to the 'Medicine of Life' only in as far as she appears in the context of Tamar and Ruth.[148] The story of Rahab is embedded in the account of the Israelite conquest of Jericho (Josh 2; 6). She is introduced as a harlot (ܙܢܝܬܐ) (Josh; 2:1; 6:17, 25). Rahab hides the two spies of Joshua from the ruler of Jericho. Rahab acknowledges the power of the Lord of Israel, and the spies promise her that she and her family will be saved when the Israelites overwhelm Jericho. The spies kept their promise and her household survived and 'she dwelt in Israel to this day' (Josh 6:25).

In the Christian tradition Matthew accords a certain Rahab a prominent position in the genealogy of Jesus. She is identified as the wife of Salmon who is in the 10th generation of the genealogy from Abraham onwards. She gave birth to Boaz, the husband of Ruth. Two other references in the New Testament to the Rahab of Joshua may have encouraged the identification of Rahab the harlot with Rahab the wife of Salmon.[149] It seems that by associating Rahab with Tamar and Ruth in Nat 1.33, Ephrem follows the Christian tradition. He counts Rahab among the significant figures of the Old Testament and links her to the prophecies concerning Jesus' birth. The tying of a scarlet cord in the window was the sign for saving her household:

ܪܚܒ ܠܗ ܗܘ ܚܙܬ ܗܘܬ ܕܐܢ ܚܘܛܐ ܙܚܘܪܝܬܐ
ܒܐܪܙܐ ܦܪܩܗ ܡܢ ܪܘܓܙܐ ܒܐܪܙܐ ܛܥܡܬܗ
ܠܫܪܪܐ.

Rahab beheld Him; for if the scarlet thread
saved her by a symbol from [divine] wrath,
by a symbol she tasted the truth.

*Nat 1.33*

Rahab symbolised the hope of salvation, because she and her family were saved through the Jews. Ephrem does not associate Rahab with Salmon as the evangelist Matthew does, but he

---

[148] Nat 9.7-16.

[149] Heb 11:31; Jas 2:25. This is not a tradition known to any Jewish sources: see H. L. Strack & P. Billerbeck, *Kommentar zum Neuen Testament aus Talmud und Midrash* I (München 1922), 20-23.

emphasises her attitude to the two spies. Even if Ephrem does not say explicitly that she had any relationship to them or later to another Jew, he gives her the same status as Tamar and Ruth: 'Because of You, women pursued men... Even Rahab who captivated men, by You, was taken captive.'[150]

### *4.1.3.3 Ruth (Ruth 3)*

In Ephrem's poetry Ruth is mentioned mainly in the hymns on the Nativity as a woman who saw the 'Medicine of Life' in Boaz. The Moabite woman Ruth returned as a widow with her mother-in-law Naomi from Moab to Bethlehem. Here her mother-in-law conceived a plan for securing Ruth a home. Obeying Naomi, Ruth went to Boaz at night and asked him to marry her. He married her and she bore a son Obed who was the father of Jesse (cf. Mt 1:5-6).

Ephrem draws a parallel between Tamar and Ruth. Tamar saw in Judah the coming Messiah; likewise Ruth was aware of the hidden 'Medicine of Life' in Boaz:

> 1.12
> Since the King was hidden in Judah, Tamar stole Him
> today shone forth the splendour of the beauty whose
> hidden form she loved.
> 1.13
> Ruth lay down with Boaz because she saw hidden in
> him the medicine of life;
> today her vow is fulfilled since from her seed arose the
> Giver of all Life.[151]
>
> *Nat 1.12-13*

Ephrem used some other terms instead of 'Medicine of Life' as we saw above: treasure and blessing.[152] In Nat 9, he deals extensively with Tamar, Rahab and Ruth; and he emphasises the risks in their lives and their love for the coming Messiah who is

---

150 Nat 9.7.

151 Nat 1.12-13:

ܕܡܠܟܐ ܟܣܝܐ ܗܘܐ ܒܝܗܘܕܐ ܓܢܒܬܗ ܬܡܪ ܡܢ ܚܨܗ
ܝܘܡܢܐ ܕܢܚ ܠܫܘܦܪܗ ܕܫܘܦܪܐ ܕܪܚܡܬ ܟܣܝܘܬܗ.
ܪܥܘܬ ܡܢ ܒܥܙ ܠܥܠܬ ܗܘܬ ܕܣܡܐ ܚܝܐ ܚܙܬ ܕܟܣܐ ܒܗ
ܝܘܡܢ ܐܫܬܠܡ ܢܕܪܗ ܕܡܢ ܙܪܥܗ ܕܢܚ ܡܚܝܢܐ ܟܠ.

152 CGen 34.2-4.

described as 'light' (ܢܘܗܪܐ), 'holiness' (ܩܘܕܫܐ), 'pure fountain' (ܢܒܥܐ ܕܟܝܐ), etc.[153]

## 4.2 New Testament

Ephrem refers to or comments on most of the healing miracles that Jesus and the Apostles performed during their ministry. Only the healing of two women, the sinful woman (Lk 7:36-50) and the woman with a haemorrhage (Lk 8:43-48), is extensively discussed here. As a third aspect, the miracles of giving sight to the blind are studied and presented.

### 4.2.1 The Healing of the Sinful Woman in the House of Simon the Pharisee (Lk 7:36-50)

The episode of the sinful woman who anointed and washed Jesus' feet in the house of Simon the Pharisee is the most developed theme in Ephrem's poetry. In the Commentary on the Diatessaron, Ephrem highlights her in sections 7.18 and 10.8-10 as a person who openly acted cleverly and, therefore, Jesus as the Physician Who heals everyone became her personal Healer.[154] The sinful woman appears as the central focus of the mimro On Our Lord where Ephrem contrasts her markedly with Simon the Pharisee.[155] II Serm 4 delineates the inner thoughts of the sinful woman in a dialogue between her and the seller of unguents, Satan and Simon.[156] The first three subsections deal with these three works, while the last subsection takes in all the other relevant references.[157]

The various biblical narratives of the four Gospels[158] cause a problem. A considerable difference is to be seen between Luke and the other three Gospels, so that one can perhaps speak of two different women anointing Jesus' feet. First of all, according to

---

[153] Nat 9.7-16.

[154] Cf. CDiat 7.18; 10.8-10. Briefly, Ephrem also refers to the sinful woman in CDiat 8.15; 15.1; 22.5.

[155] The main chapters are in Dom 14-24; 42-44 and 48-49.

[156] See the whole II Serm 4, including App I.A and I.B.

[157] See Virg 4.11; 26.4; 35.5-8; Fid 10.5; Nat 4.40; Epiph 3.2-3; Nis 60.1-8; Eccl 9.19; Azym 14.1-4; Haer 47.8; Hebd 2.1-265; I Serm 8.196-97; I Serm 7.229; III Serm 4.636.

[158] Mt 26:6-13; Mk 14:3-9; Lk 7:36-50; Jn 12:1-8.

Luke, this drama is located in the house of Simon the Pharisee (Lk 7:36), and not, as Matthew and Mark state, in Bethany in the house of Simon the leper (Mt 26:6; Mk 14:3), or as John, who links it with the resurrection of Lazarus in Bethany (John 12:1-2). Secondly, Luke speaks of a 'sinful woman'; Matthew and Mark of 'a woman' (Mt 27:7; Mk 14:3); whereas John calls her 'Mary' the sister of Martha (Jn 12:3). Thirdly, according to Luke and John Jesus' feet are anointed (Lk 7:38; Jn 12:3) and not His head as Matthew and Mark say (Mt 26:7; Mk 14:3). And finally, a major difference concerns the reaction of the audience: according to Luke, the sinful woman is in the house of Simon the Pharisee, and Simon doubted Jesus' 'prophethood'; therefore Jesus told him the parable of the two debtors in order to explain to him the forgiveness of her sins (Lk 7:41-49). The biblical texts do not provide any healing imagery. The forgiveness of her sins provides Ephrem with the starting point for his healing theology, and it is only in Luke that this sentence occurs: 'Your sins have been forgiven' (Lk 7:48: ܫܒܝܩܝܢ ܠܟܝ ܚܛܗܝܟܝ). In contrast, the other three Gospels present 'the costly oil' which could help the poor as the reason for the reaction (in Mt 26:8 they are the 'disciples' who are confused; Mk 14:4 does not define them ('some'); whereas Jn 12:4 attributes it to Judas Iscariot). In response, Jesus explains the importance of this anointing as signifying His burial, and referring to His death.

Since Ephrem mainly associates this episode with Simon the Pharisee and he uses the term 'sinful woman' (ܚܛܝܬܐ) as a common name, it is obvious that Luke's narrative is dominant. Certain passages, such as CDiat 8.17; Virg 4.11 and 35.8, may cause us to assume that Ephrem includes some elements from the other Gospels, i.e. he intermingled the different texts and identifies the four different biblical narratives as one historical event without differentiating between them. In the case of identifying them, Mary and the sinful woman would be the same person, otherwise Luke's narrative would be a different one from that of Matthew, Mark and John. However, studying the healing of the sinful woman, it is unlikely that Ephrem identifies them, rather he separates them.

#### *4.2.1.1 The Sinful Woman in the Commentary on the Diatessaron*

In the Commentary on the Diatessaron, Ephrem mentions the sinful woman in five different passages. In CDiat 8.15, 15.1 and

22.5 the sinful woman is just mentioned, whereas in sections 7.18 and 10.8-10 Ephrem comments widely on her. In CDiat 8.15, Ephrem compares Mary, the sister of Martha, with the sinful woman, who sat at the feet of Jesus (Lk 10:39) 'that had granted forgiveness of sins to the sinful woman'.[159] Here the forgiveness of sins is specifically referred to the feet of Jesus. The same idea occurs in the mimro On Our Lord where Ephrem says: 'With her kisses the sinful woman received the grace/favour of the blessed feet that had laboured to bring her the forgiveness of sins.'[160] In CDiat 15.1, Ephrem contrasts the way in which the rich man (Lk 10:17-24) draws near to Jesus with the humble way in which the sinful woman approached Christ.[161] She drew near to Jesus, because she accepted Him as the 'One Who forgives sins' (ܫܒܘܩܐ), whereas, the rich man considered Him as the 'One Who establishes the law' (ܣܐܡ ܢܡܘܣܐ).

The other passages where Ephrem deals with the sinful woman are more concerned with healing. In the entire section of CDiat 7.18, Ephrem emphasises the faithful approach of the sinful woman to the body of Jesus, in contrast to Simon the Pharisee. Referring to the Old Testament, Ephrem illustrates the negative influence of gentile women on Solomon, and contrasts this with Jesus' positive miraculous healing of gentile women, such as the sinful woman.[162]

Healing is illustrated primarily in CDiat 10.8-10. The tears, the washing of the feet and all the visible deeds of the sinful woman brought her invisible healing. Her faith contrasts with the faith of Simon the Pharisee. So because of her faith, Jesus was her

---

159 CDiat 8.15: ܐܬܬ ܠܡ ܡܪܝܡ ܝܬܒܬ ܠܗ ܠܘܬ ܪ̈ܓܠܘܗܝ. ܗܘܐ ܕܝܢ ܐܝܟ ܕܗܠ ܐܘܪܚܐ ܪܚܝܩܬܐ ܠܘܬ ܪ̈ܓܠܘܗܝ، ܝܬܒܐ ܗܘܬ. ܗܠܝܢ ܕܐܬܒ ܠܚܛܝܬܐ ܫܘܒܩܢ ܚܛ̈ܗܝܗ ܝܗܒ ܗܘܝ (cf. Lk 10:39; Lk 7:38). Here the sinful woman and Mary are mentioned as being two different figures.

160 Dom 14: ܚܛܝܬܐ ܒܢܫܝܩܬܐ ܟܪܬ ܠܛܝܒܘܬܗܝܢ ܕܪ̈ܓܠܐ ܡܒܪ̈ܟܬܐ. ܕܠܐܝ ܗܘܝ. ܕܢܗܠܟ ܘܢܐܬܐ ܕܫܘܒܩܢ ܚܛ̈ܗܝܗ ܢܘܒܠ ܠܗ̇.

161 CDiat 15.1: ܠܘܬ ܚܛܝܬܐ ܕܝܢ ܐܝܟ ܠܐܠܗܐ ܗܘܐ. ܗ̇ܝ، ܓܝܪ ܐܝܟ ܕܠܘܬ ܫܒܘܩܐ ܐܬܬ. ܗܢܐ ܕܝܢ ܐܝܟ ܕܠܘܬ ܣܐܡ ܢܡܘܣܐ. ܗܘ ܕܢܣܒ ܙ̈ܕܩܘܗܝ، ܒܫܒܚܬܐ ܕܣܐܡ ܢܡܘܣܐ

162 Cf. CDiat 7.18.

Physician, as Ephrem says: 'He became a Physician to her that believed, for it is He Who heals everyone.'[163] Her faith caused her healing, which is not physical, but spiritual. It is the healing from sin, and forgiveness of debts, because 'she had come to Him as to One Who forgives'.[164] Because she was healed through her 'remedies/unguents' (ܣܡܡ̈ܢܐ), Ephrem calls her a 'physician' (ܐܣܝܬܐ):

> [This was] like that sinful woman who was a physician to her wounds, because of the remedies/unguents she had taken, and went to Him for Whom it was easy to mix into everything His forgiveness, which restores/heals all sorts of pains.[165]

This is the final paragraph where the sinful woman is mentioned, this time together with Zacchaeus the tax collector (Lk 19:1-10) and the blind son of Timaeus (Mk 10:46-52). In comparison, Jesus Himself is not called the 'Physician' (ܐܣܝܐ) in this passage, but instead Ephrem connects the healing with 'His forgiveness which heals/restores all sorts of pains' ( ܫܘܒܩܢܗ ܡܫܠܡ ܠܟܠ ܟܐܒ̈ܝܢ). Jesus is able to 'mix' (ܢܚܠܛ) His forgiveness with everything.

For Ephrem, faith in particular is important. He compares the faith of the sinful woman with that of Simon the Pharisee. The parable of the two debtors, one of five hundred denarii and the other of fifty, explains the relationship of Jesus to the sinful woman and Simon (Lk 7:41). Jesus forgave both, as a creditor annuls the debt of his debtors. Ephrem emphasises the meaning of the deeds of the sinful woman, how she dared to enter the house of Simon,

---

[163] CDiat 10.10: ܘܗܘܐ ܐܣܝܐ ܠܗ̇ ܕܗܝܡܢܬ ܕܗܘܝܘ ܡܐܣܐ ܠܟܠ.

[164] CDiat 15.1: ܠܘܬ ܚܛܝܬܐ ܕܝܢ ܟܐܢܐ ܠܒܥܠ ܚܘܒܐ ܗܘܐ. ܗ̇ܝ ܓܝܪ ܐܝܟ ܕܠܘܬ ܫܒܘܩܐ ܐܬܬ. CDiat 8.15: ܐܬܬ ܠܗ ܡܚܝܪ ܬܒܬ ܠܗ̇ ܠܘܬ ܪ̈ܓܠܘܗܝ. ܗܘܐ ܕܝܢ ܐܝܟ ܕܟܠ ܐܢܫܐ ܥܢܝܪܬܐ ܠܘܬ ܪ̈ܓܠܘܗܝ ܬܒܥܐ ܗܘܬ. ܡܠܝܡ ܕܐܦ ܠܚܛܝܬܐ ܫܘܒܩܢ ܚܛܗ̈ܐ ܝܗܒ ܗܘܐ.

[165] CDiat 22.5: ܐܝܟ ܗ̇ܝ ܚܛܝܬܐ ܕܗܘܬ ܐܣܝܬܐ ܠܡܚ̈ܘܬܗ̇ ܒܣܡܡ̈ܢܐ ܕܢܣܒܬ ܘܐܙܠܬ ܠܘܬ ܗܘ ܕܦܫܝܩ ܠܗ ܕܒܟܠ ܡܕܡ ܢܚܠܛ ܫܘܒܩܢܗ ܡܫܠܡ ܠܟܠ ܟܐܒ̈ܝܢ. The term ܣܡܡ̈ܢܐ refers to her penitence represented by her decision to go to Jesus, and replaces the biblical term 'fragrant oil' (ܡܫܚܐ ܕܒܣܡܐ; Lk 7:37-38, 46).

how she moistened, dried and anointed Jesus' feet. As a consequence of her deeds, Ephrem explains what happened in a hidden way while she was acting openly:

> Through her tears she washed the dust which was on His feet, while He, through His words, cleansed the scars which were on her flesh. She cleansed Him with her impure tears, while He cleansed her with His holy words. He was cleansed of dust, and in return He cleansed her of iniquity. His feet were washed with tears, while His word granted forgiveness of sins.[166]

Here Ephrem draws attention to the invisible effect of Jesus' 'holy words' (ܒܡ̈ܠܘܗܝ ܩܕ̈ܝܫܬܐ) which 'whitened' (ܚܘܪ) her scars, 'washed' (ܐܣܚܬܗ) her and 'granted forgiveness of sins' (ܘܝܗܒ ܫܘܒܩܢ ܚܛܗ̈ܐ). In this chapter, Ephrem strictly distinguishes between Jesus' divinity and humanity. While the sinful woman was only able to approach His humanity and wash it with her tears, His divinity was capable of forgiving her hidden sins. His humanity was refreshed, whereas His divinity granted her redemption.[167] A parallel text can be found in CDiat 7.18, where Ephrem illustrates Jesus as a Mediator between the sinful woman and Simon the Pharisee. Since her hands were stretched out to Jesus' body, for He 'showed His humanity' to her, she believed in His divinity. In contrast, Simon accepted Jesus just as a human being, as a prophet, whereas she accepted Him as God.[168] Simon's doubt and suspicion contrast with the faith and humility of the

---

[166] CDiat 10.8: ܗܝ ܒܕܡ̈ܥܝܗ̇ ܐܣܚܬ ܚܠܐ ܕܥܠ ܪ̈ܓܠܘܗܝ. ܘܗܘ ܒܡ̈ܠܘܗܝ ܚܘܪ ܠܡܚ̈ܘܬܐ ܕܥܠ ܒܣܪ̈ܗ̇. ܐܣܚܬܗ ܗܝ ܒܕܡ̈ܥܝܗ̇ ܛܢ̈ܦܬܐ. ܘܐܣܚܗ̇ ܗܘ ܒܡ̈ܠܘܗܝ ܩܕ̈ܝܫܬܐ. ܣܚܐ ܗܘ ܡܢ ܚܠܐ. ܘܗܦܟ ܐܣܚܗ̇ ܠܗ̇ ܕܠܫܗ̇ ܡܢ ܥܘܠܐ. ܣܚܝ ܒܢ ܪ̈ܓܠܘܗܝ ܒܕܡ̈ܥܐ. ܘܝܗܒ ܡ̈ܠܘܗܝ ܫܘܒܩܢ ܚܛܗ̈ܐ.

[167] CDiat 10.8: ܐܢܫܘܬܗ ܡܫܚܬ ܗܘܬ ܒܕܡ̈ܥܝܗ̇ ܘܐܬܬܢܝܚܬ. ܘܐܠܗܘܬܗ ܝܗܒܬ ܠܗ̇ ܐܓܪܐ ܦܘܪܩܢ. ܕܬܡܣܟܢܐ ܓܝܪ ܐܢܫܘܬܗ ܗܘ ܠܒܫܗ ܩܪܝܒܐ ܗܘܬ. ܕܬܚܣܢܐ ܕܝܢ ܚܛܗ̈ܐ ܕܠܐ ܡܬܚܙܝܢ. ܐܠܗܘܬܗ ܗܘ ܡܫܒܩܢܐ ܗܘܬ.

[168] CDiat 7.18: ܕܫܠܛܬܐ ܐܝܟ ܐܠܗܐ ܫܒܩܬܗ ܗܘܬ. ܗܝܡܢܘܬܗ. ܣܒܪܐ ܗܘܬ. ܘܫܡܥܘܢ ܕܐܝܟ ܒܪ ܐܢܫܐ ܫܒܩܗ. ܟܢܫܐ ܒܢܒܝܐ ܥܒܕܗ ܗܘܐ.

sinful woman whose actions are an acknowledgement of Christ as the Son of God. Simon was in the middle - as Solomon was in the middle - and had to decide who Jesus was. In reference to 1 Kgs 11:1-40, Ephrem contrasts the faith and role of the women healed by Jesus, including the sinful woman, to the gentile women by whom Solomon was 'wounded'. Ephrem goes further and puts the reader ('us') in the middle, addressing him/her to make decision.

> But now, how is it, we are in the middle; and like Solomon we have fallen between women. But, even if we have fallen between women like Solomon, we are not, like Solomon, wounded by women. For these gentile women were turning Solomon aside from the fear of God to their idols by means of their allurements. But here we place the faith of the gentile women above the heroic exploits of the Hebrew women. Those rendered Solomon's healthy faith sick through the wholeness of their bodies, while these restore our ailing faith to health through their being healed. Therefore, who should not be healed?[169]

In the biblical text of 1 Kings 11:1-40, to which Ephrem refers here, no reference is made to healing or sickness. Instead, the Lord's commandment and faith are emphasised. Ephrem draws attention to Solomon's healthy faith which has become sick because of the gentile women. While those women through the 'wholeness of their bodies' caused Solomon to worship their idols and to sin, the faith of the gentile women of the New Testament, i.e. the sinful woman, restores the faith of the believers. As the gentile women have been healed through their faith by Christ, every one can be healed. Therefore, Ephrem ends the paragraph with the rhetorical question: 'for who should not be healed?' The healing of the women in the Gospel encourages the faith of

---

[169] CDiat 7.18: ܐܠܐ ܐܝܟܢܐ ܗܫܐ ܐܬܡܨܥܢܢ. ܘܐܝܟ ܫܠܝܡܘܢ ܒܝܢܬ ܢܫ̈ܐ ܢܦܠܢ. ܐܠܐ ܐܦ ܐܝܟ ܫܠܝܡܘܢ ܒܝܢܬ ܢܫ̈ܐ ܢܦܠܢ. ܐܠܐ ܠܐ ܗܘܐ ܐܝܟ ܫܠܝܡܘܢ ܡܢ ܢܫ̈ܐ ܐܬܡܚܝܢ. ܗܠܝܢ ܓܝܪ ܒܢ̈ܬ ܥܡܡ̈ܐ. ܠܫܠܝܡܘܢ ܡܢ ܕܚܠܬ ܐܠܗܐ ܠܘܬ ܦܬܟܪ̈ܝܗܝܢ ܒܪ̈ܓܝܓܬܗܝܢ ܡܨܠܝܢ ܗܘܝ ܠܗ. ܘܗܪܟܐ ܠܗܝܡܢܘܬܐ ܕܒܢ̈ܬ ܥܡܡ̈ܐ ܡܢ ܓܢܒܪ̈ܘܬܗܝܢ ܕܥܒܪ̈ܝܬܐ ܗܐ ܡܪܝܡܝܢܢ. ܗܠܝܢ ܒܚܘܠܡܗܝܢ ܦܓܪ̈ܝܗܝܢ ܠܗܝܡܢܘܬܗ ܚܠܝܡܬܐ ܕܫܠܝܡܘܢ ܐܟܪܗܝܗ̇ ܗܘܝ. ܗܠܝܢ ܕܝܢ ܒܐܣܝܘܬܗܝܢ ܠܗܝܡܢܘܬܢ ܟܪܝܗܬܐ ܗܐ ܡܚܠܡܢ. ܡܢܘ ܓܝܪ ܠܐ ܢܬܚܠܡ.

believers. And this is in contrast to the deeds of the gentile women at the time of Solomon. Ephrem emphasises their wickedness; even though he speaks of the 'wholeness of their bodies' ( ܚܘܠܡ ܦܓܪ̈ܝܗܝܢ), they made the faith of Solomon 'sick' (ܐܟܪܗ). The idea of the good reputation and healthy effect of the sinful woman because of her repentance goes back to Matthew and Mark where Jesus says: 'Truly I tell you, wherever this good news is proclaimed in the whole world, what she has done will be told in remembrance of her.'[170]

### 4.2.1.2 *The Sinful Woman in the Mimro On Our Lord*

The interpretation of the biblical narrative of the sinful woman in the house of Simon the Pharisee appears as the central focus of the mimro On Our Lord (14-24). After dealing at length with Paul's blinding which shows the mildness of Christ's speech in comparison to that of Simon the Pharisee (25-33), Ephrem again returns to the case of the sinful woman (41-49). Throughout the homily, in contrast to the sinful woman, the theme of Israel's turning away from God recurs (cf. 6, 18-19). Thus, Simon the Pharisee exemplifies the 'idolatry' (ܦܬܟܪܘܬܐ) and 'paganism' (ܚܢܦܘܬܐ) of Israel, whereas the sinful woman illustrates the gentiles' faith in Jesus, just as CDiat 7.18 does.[171]

Ephrem, in his extensive treatment of the theme of the sinful woman, frequently uses healing imagery, such as 'healing' (ܐܣܝܘܬܐ), 'restorative' (ܚܘܠܡܢܐ), 'physician' (ܐܣܝܐ), 'medicines' (ܣܡܡ̈ܢܐ), 'pains' (ܟܐ̈ܒܐ), 'stricken/afflicted people' (ܟܪ̈ܝܗܐ) and the verb 'to heal' (ܐܣܝ). At the beginning of paragraph fourteen, he emphasises the healing through Christ's 'healing word' (ܐܣܝܘܬܐ ܕܡܠܬܗ), which is more powerful than healing through His garments:

> If, however, such healing as this was snatched from His hem in secret, who would have been sufficient for the

---

170 Mt 26:13: ܘܐܡܝܢ ܐܡܪ ܐܢܐ ܠܟܘܢ. ܕܐܝܟܐ ܕܬܬܟܪܙ ܣܒܪܬܝ ܗܕܐ ܒܟܠܗ ܥܠܡܐ. ܢܬܡܠܠ ܐܦ ܡܕܡ ܕܥܒܕܬ ܗܕܐ (cf. Mk 14:9).

171 Finally, in Dom 50-58, there are discussions about the transfer of priesthood and prophecy to Christ and through him to Simon the disciple.

> healing that His word has granted in public? And if impure lips became holy by kissing His feet, how much holier would pure lips become by kissing His mouth.[172]

With the comparison of healing through approaching His garment and His body, and through the kissing of His feet and lips, Ephrem draws attention to healing through Jesus' word, as he does in the Commentary on the Diatessaron. The term 'healing' (ܐܣܝܘܬܐ) in its abstract form appears four times in the mimro On Our Lord: twice it is related to the healing of the woman who had an issue of blood for twelve years (Mt 9:20; Lk 8:43), and the other two times refers to the public audience who heard the speech and words of Jesus. By comparison, healing through Jesus' words is more potent than being healed by touching His clothes or body: 'Through the fact that she received healing from His clothes, those who had not been healed by His words were rebuked.'[173] This sentence parallels the sentence quoted above. While in Dom 13 healing refers to Jesus' clothes (ܐܣܝܘܬܐ ܡܢ ܠܒܘܫܘ̈ܗܝ) and His words (plural: ܐܣܝܘܬܐ ܡܢ ܡ̈ܠܘܗܝ), in Dom 14 it refers to His hem (ܡܢ ܟܢܦܗ ܐܣܝܘܬܐ) and His word (singular: ܐܣܝܘܬܐ ܕܡܠܬܗ). The healing of the woman with the haemorrhage who touched His hem is paralleled with the healing of the sinful woman who cleansed and kissed Jesus' feet. But, Ephrem does not use the term ܐܣܝܘܬܐ in relation to the sinful woman; instead, the term ܩܕܫ (to make holy) occurs. The effect of kissing His feet is contrasted with the kissing of His lips, just as healing through His hem/clothes was contrasted with the healing through His word/words.

---

[172] Dom 14: ܐܢ ܓܝܪ ܡܢ ܟܢܦܗ ܐܣܝܘܬܐ ܕܐܓܢܒ ܗܘܐ ܒܛܘܫܝܐ ܐܬܓܠܝܬ. ܡܢ ܟܕ ܢܓܢܘܒ ܗܘܐ ܠܐܣܝܘܬܐ ܕܡܠܬܗ ܒܦܪܗܣܝܐ ܝܗܒܐ ܗܘܬ. ܘܐܢ ܒܢܘܫܩܬܐ ܕܪ̈ܓܠܘܗܝ ܣܦ̈ܘܬܐ ܛܢ̈ܦܬܐ ܐܬܩܕܫ ܗܘ̈ܝ. ܚܕ ܟܡܐ ܢܬܩܕܫܢ ܗܘ̈ܝ ܒܢܘܫܩܬ ܦܘܡܗ ܣܦ̈ܘܬܐ ܕܟ̈ܝܬܐ. Healing (ܐܣܝܘܬܐ) was performed through touching Jesus' garment. The stealing of healing reminds the reader of Tamar and Ruth who stole the medicine of life from the Hebrew men.

[173] Dom 13:

ܒܗܿܝ ܕܝܢ ܕܩܒܠܬ ܐܣܝܘܬܐ ܡܢ ܠܒܘܫܘ̈ܗܝ،
ܐܬܟܐܪܘ ܗܢܘܢ ܕܠܐ ܩܒܠܘ ܐܣܝܘܬܐ ܡܢ ܡ̈ܠܘܗܝ.

The other term for healing that Ephrem employs frequently is ܣܘܠܡܢܐ, 'restorative'. In Dom 13, it illustrates the limbs and body of Christ which serve as an intermediary to the 'treasure of restoratives' (ܓܙܐ ܕܣܘܠܡܢ̈ܐ):

> Our Lord did not only put on a body, but He also arrayed Himself with limbs and clothes, so that by reason of His limbs and clothes, the stricken would be encouraged to approach the treasure of restoratives.[174]

The treasure of restoratives alludes to the invisible divinity of Christ, which those who had been stricken (ܡܚܝ̈ܢܐ) will reach through His humanity, namely His limbs and body.[175] As a parallel to the term ܓܙܐ ܕܣܘܠܡܢ̈ܐ, there occurs in Dom 14 the term 'Treasury of Restoratives' (ܣܝܡܬ ܣܘܠܡܢ̈ܐ), and in Dom 42 'Fountain of Restoratives' (ܡܒܘܥ ܣܘܠܡܢ̈ܐ) with the same implied sense: both terms are employed in connection with the invisible power of Christ's Divinity Which the sinful woman approached: 'She was freely comforting with oil the feet of her Physician Who had freely brought the Treasury of Restoratives to her suffering'.[176] Here, the Treasury of Restoratives has been brought by Jesus to the suffering of the sinful woman, whereas in

---

[174] Dom 13:
ܠܐ ܗܘܐ ܓܝܪ ܦܓܪܐ ܒܠܚܘܕ ܠܒܫ ܡܪܢ܆ ܐܠܐ ܐܦ ܗܕ̈ܡܐ ܘܢܚ̈ܬܐ ܐܬܥܛܦ. ܕܒܝܕ ܗܕ̈ܡܘܗܝ ܘܢܚ̈ܬܘܗܝ، ܢܬܠܒܒܘܢ ܡܚܝ̈ܢܐ ܠܡܩܪܒ ܠܓܙܐ ܕܣܘܠܡܢ̈ܐ.

[175] Dom 1-13 is devoted mainly to the incarnation of Christ, His descent to Sheol and the redemption of Adam and man. To emphasise the reality of His incarnation, Ephrem draws attention to the humanity of Christ and emphasises its function as intermediary: 'That unreachable power came down and put on limbs that could be touched so that the needy could approach Him and, embracing His humanity, become aware of His Divinity. By means of the fingers of [Jesus'] body, the deaf-mute sensed that He came near his ears and touched his tongue' (Dom 10; cf. Mk 7:32-33). Thus, the humanity of Christ was visible for man in order to touch His invisible Divinity (cf. Dom 9-11).

[176] Dom 14:
ܡܒܣܡܐ ܗܘܬ ܠܗܝܢ ܡܓܢ ܠܪ̈ܓܠܐ ܐܣܝܗ̇ ܒܡܫܚܐ ܕܡܓܢ
ܐܝܬܝ ܠܗ̇ ܣܝܡܬ ܣܘܠܡܢ̈ܐ ܠܟܐܒ̈ܝܗ̇.

Dom 42, the Lord Himself 'descended to be a Fountain of Restoratives among the sick'.[177]

Furthermore, the term ܚܘܠܡܢܐ also occurs as a single word with reference to Jesus' property. Just as He has forgiven sins, so He has restored limbs in order to display the testimony of His Divinity against those who did not believe in Him:

> Nor could it be denied that He had not forgiven sins, for, behold, He had [in fact] restored limbs. So our Lord linked His hidden testimonies to visible testimonies, so that their own testimony would choke the infidels. Thus, our Lord caused their own thoughts to fight against them, for they had fought against the Good One, Who fought against their sicknesses with His restoratives.[178]

The phrase 'restored limbs' (ܐܚܠܡ ܗܕ̈ܡܐ) implies physical sickness, and not spiritual sickness. Even in Dom 42, where Ephrem does not use the term limbs (ܗܕ̈ܡܐ), he connects the verb 'to restore' (ܐܚܠܡ) with physical sickness: 'in the streets, He had restored sick bodies'.[179] Ephrem contrasts 'His restoratives' (ܚܘܠܡ̈ܢܘܗܝ) with man's sickness. The healing of men from their sickness includes the forgiveness of sins and the whole of redemption. In Dom 42, Ephrem speaks of the 'restoration of sinners' (ܚܘܠܡܢܗܘܢ ܕܚܛܝ̈ܐ).[180] Nevertheless, the term ܚܘܠܡܢܐ also occurs in the context of the sick who are contrasted with those who are restored, as Ephrem says: 'the door of a

---

[177] Dom 43: ܗܘ ܕܐܦ ܕܢܚܬ ܕܢܗܘܐ ܡܒܘܥ ܚܘܠܡ̈ܢܐ ܒܝܢܬ ܟܪ̈ܝܗܐ.

[178] Dom 21: ܠܐ ܕܝܢ ܡܬܕܓܠܐ ܗܘܬ ܕܠܐ ܫܒܩ ܚܛܗ̈ܐ ܡܛܠ ܕܗܐ ܐܚܠܡ ܗܕ̈ܡܐ ܐܣܪ [ܐܝܢ] ܟܢ ܡܪܢ ܠܣܗ̈ܕܘܬܗ ܟܣ̈ܝܬܐ ܒܓܠܝ̈ܬܐ ܐܝܟ ܕܬܚܢܩ ܐܢܘܢ ܠܟܦܘܪ̈ܐ ܣܗܕܘܬܐ ܕܕܝܠܗܘܢ. ܠܚܘܫ̈ܒܝܗܘܢ ܗܟܝܠ ܟܕܢ ܡܪܢ ܕܢܩܪܒܘܢ ܠܘܩܒܠܗܘܢ ܥܠ ܕܐܬܩܪܒܘ ܥܡ ܛܒܐ ܗܘ ܕܐܬܩܪܒ ܒܚܘܠܡ̈ܢܘܗܝ ܠܘܩܒܠ ܟܐܒ̈ܝܗܘܢ.

[179] Dom 42: ܒܫܘܩ̈ܐ ܟܢ ܐܚܠܡ ܦܓܪ̈ܐ ܟܪ̈ܝܗܐ. In Dom 21, where the visible healing of the body is compared to the invisible forgiveness of sins, the verbs ܐܣܝ and ܐܚܝ occur together with ܗܕ̈ܡܐ.

[180] Cf. Dom 42; here Ephrem combines the term ܚܘܠܡܢܐ (singular) with sinners.

physician is open to the sick, not to the restored' (Mt 9:12), and 'restoring the sick is the physician's glory'.[181] In Dom 49, Ephrem uses the term ܚܘܠܡܢܐ in connection with the woman with the haemorrhage, but ܫܘܒܩܢܐ, 'forgiveness', with the sinful woman. Thus, the woman with the haemorrhage drew near to the Physician and she stole 'restoration' from the edge of His cloak, whereas the sinful woman gained 'the forgiveness of debts'.[182]

In order to explain to Simon the action of the sinful woman, as well as her treatment by Jesus as the Physician Who healed her from sin, Ephrem refers to the behaviour of an ordinary physician, saying:

> The physician who brings a hidden pain out into the open is not a supporter of the pain but its destroyer. So long as pain remains hidden, it reigns in the limbs, but once it is revealed, it can be uprooted by medicines.[183]

The revelation of a pain implies making it known: once it has been diagnosed, then it can be extirpated through medicine. Although this passage explicitly speaks of the physical pain, it can also refer to that of the mind. Ephrem indicates that Jesus did not only offer His medicine and remedies to the sinful woman, but also to Simon the Pharisee. While Ephrem compares the faith and attitude of Simon with that of the sinful woman, he described him in his 'error' (ܛܘܥܝܬܐ) as someone with 'feeble love' ( ܒܣܝܪܘܬ ܚܘܒܗ), 'without faith' (ܕܠܐ ܗܝܡܢܘ), with 'doubt of mind' (ܦܘܠܓ ܪܥܝܢܐ) and speaks of 'his blind mind' ( ܬܪܥܝܬܗ ܥܘܝܪܬܐ).[184] Because of Simon's weak faith, the Lord reproached him (ܟܐܪ) in order to help him (ܡܛܠ ܚܘܠܡܗ، ܥܒܕ ܡܥܕܪܢܘܬܐ).

---

[181] Dom 42: ܠܡܟܐܒ̈ܐ ܗܘ ܦܬܝܚ ܘܠܐ ܠܚܠܝܡ̈ܐ. ..... ܡܚܝܠ ܐܣܝܐ ܘܫܘܒܚܗ ܚܘܠܡܢܐ ܗܘ ܕܡܟܐܒ̈ܐ.

[182] Dom 49: ܗܝ ܕܓܢܒܬ ܗܘܐ ܕܡܢܗ ܚܘܠܡܢܐ ܡܢ ܩܪܢܐ ܕܡܪ̈ܛܘܛܗ ܓܢܒܬ.

[183] Dom 19: ܐܣܝܐ ܕܝܢ ܐܝܢܐ ܕܒܣܡ̈ܢܘܗܝ ܠܟܐܒܐ ܟܣܝܐ ܠܓܠܝܐ ܡܦܩ ܠܗ. ܠܐ ܗ̇ܘܐ ܡܣܝܥܢܗ ܗ̇ܘ ܕܟܐܒܐ ܐܠܐ ܡܘܒܕܢܗ. ܟܐܒܐ ܓܝܪ ܟܡܐ ܕܟܣܐ ܡܫܠܛ ܗ̇ܘ ܒܗܕ̈ܡܐ. ܐܡܬܝ ܕܝܢ ܕܐܬܓܠܝ ܒܣܡܡ̈ܢܐ ܡܬܥܩܪ.

[184] Cf. Dom 16-17.

Evidently, 'reproaching' (ܟܘܐܪܐ) is seen as a way of restoring the mind, the inner man, the attitude and the feeble faith of a person. After Jesus had reproached Simon, He told him the parable of the two debtors, and let Simon be the judge. By this parable Simon was reminded (ܒܡܘܕܥܢܐ) of his mistake.

He is reminded after being reproached.[185] As we saw above, the visible signs point to hidden acts and deeds.[186] Ephrem compares Simon's situation with that of Israel at the time of Moses.[187] It was necessary for Simon to realise his mistake in order for it to be dispelled: knowledge of the Lord was first revealed over the error, and then dispelled it (ܒܕܪܬܗ̇).[188] Jesus granted 'His assistance' (ܒܥܘܕܪ̈ܢܘܗܝ) to Simon the Pharisee, using the parable of the two debtors (Lk 7:41) as a persuasive lesson in humility.[189] Such a lesson can be either provoking, in that it evokes anger and so injures the one to whom it is addressed, or it can be persuasive, by means of love and admonition, and helpful.[190] The hidden sickness of Simon was his divided mind and his erroneous understanding. The skill of Jesus' words which, as a Physician, He had prepared as medicine, lay in the fact that they were beneficial, not just for Simon, but for every one.

> And so, at the very outset of His parable, our Lord put a word of conciliation, so that through His conciliation He might bring peace to the Pharisee, for whom doubt had caused division in his mind. This is the Physician Who prepared His help for our adversities.[191]

---

185 Dom 17: ܗܝܕܝܢ ܐܬܟܣܝ ܒܠܒܘܬܗ ܘܗܘ ܕܐܟܣܐ ܒܠܒܘܬܗ ܪܚܡ ܗܘܐ. ܠܒܘܬܗ ܓܝܪ ܗܕܐ ܠܠܒܘܫܐ ܕܠܒܫ ܕܡܠܒܫܐ ܠܠܒܫܐ ܗܘܐ. ܡܟܠ ܕܝܢ ܒܡܘܕܥܢܐ ܡܢ ܗܘ ܕܐܬܐ ܕܐܒܕܗ ܠܕܠܒܝܢ.

186 Cf. Dom 21.

187 Cf. Dom 16-17.

188 Dom 19: ܟܕ ܕܝܢ ܒܥܬ ܒܗ ܒܛܘܥܝܐ ܠܒܘܬܗ. ܗܝܕܝܢ ܐܬܓܠܝܬ ܥܠܝܗ̇ ܐܝܕܥܬܗ ܕܡܪܢ ܘܒܕܪܬܗ̇..

189 Cf. Dom 22.

190 Cf. Dom 22-23.

191 Dom 24: ܗܟ ܗܟܝܠ ܡܪܢ ܒܪܫ ܡܬܠܗ ܡܠܬܐ ܕܐܫܘܝܘܬܐ. ܕܒܐܫܘܝܘܬܗ ܢܫܝܢ ܠܦܪܝܫܐ ܗܘ ܕܦܠܓܘܬܐ [ܘ]ܣܘܕܩܐ ܒܪܥܝܢܗ ܥܒܕܬ. ܗܢܘ ܐܣܝܐ ܕܠܘܩܒܠ ܣܘܩ̈ܒܠܝܢ ܒܥܘܕܪ̈ܢܘܗܝ ܡܛܝܒ ܗܘܐ.

In Dom 42, Ephrem extends the discussion of Jesus as the Physician. Addressing Simon the Pharisee, Ephrem asks him rhetorically:

> Because prophets were unable to give sinners life, the Lord of the prophets Himself descended to heal those who were badly affected. Which physician prevents the stricken from coming to him, you blind Pharisee who blasphemed against our Physician? Why did the stricken woman, whose wounds were healed by her tears, approach Him? He Who descended to be a Fountain of Restoratives among the sick was announcing this: »Whoever is thirsty, let him come and drink« (Jn 7:37). When this man's fellow Pharisees took exception to the restoration of sinners, the Physician explained this about His art, that the door was open to those with pains, not to the healthy: »It is not the healthy who are in need of a physician, but those who are badly affected« (cf Mt 9:12; Mk 2:17; Lk 5:31-32). Therefore, restoring the sick is the physician's glory. But to increase the disgrace of the Pharisee, who had disparaged the glory of our Physician, our Lord Who worked signs in the streets, worked even greater signs once He entered the Pharisee's house than those that He had worked outside. In the streets, He had healed sick bodies, but inside, He healed stricken minds. Outside, He had given life to the dead state of Lazarus; inside, He gave life to the dead state of the sinful woman. He returned the living soul to the dead body that it had left, and He drove off the deadly sin from a sinful woman in whom it had dwelt.[192]

---

192 Dom 42: ܒܗ̇ ܓܝܪ ܕܠܐ ܡܫܟܚܘ ܢܒ̈ܝܐ ܠܡܚܝܘ ܠܚ̈ܛܝܐ. ܢܚܬ ܠܗ ܡܪܗܘܢ ܕܢܒ̈ܝܐ ܕܢܐܣܐ ܠܐܝܠܝܢ ܕܒܝܫ ܒܝܫ ܚܒܝܫܝܢ. ܐܝܢܘ ܕܝܢ ܐܣܝܐ ܕܟܠܐ ܠܡ̈ܚܘܫܐ ܕܠܐ ܢܐܬܘܢ ܠܘܬܗ ܐܘ ܦܪܝܫܐ ܥܘܝܪܐ. ܕܓܕܦܬ ܥܠ ܐܣܝܢ ܕܠܡܢܐ ܩܪܒܬ ܠܗ ܡܚܝܫܬܐ. ܗ̇ܝ ܕܒܕܡ̈ܥܝܗ̇ ܐܬܐܣ̈ܝ ܡܚܘ̈ܬܗ̇. ܗܘ ܕܝܢ ܕܢܚܬ ܕܢܗܘܐ ܡܒܘܥ ܚܘܠܡ̈ܢܐ ܒܝܢܬ ܡܟܐ̈ܒܐ. ܗܕܐ ܗܘܐ ܡܟܪܙ ܕܟܠ ܕܨܗܐ ܢܐܬܐ ܘܢܫܬܐ. ܟܕ ܕܝܢ ܪ̈ܛܢܘ ܗܘܘ ܦܪ̈ܝܫܐ ܚܒܪ̈ܘܗܝ ܕܗܢܐ ܥܠ ܚܘܠܡܢܗܘܢ ܕܚ̈ܛܝܐ. ܐܦܫܩ ܐܣܝܐ ܥܠ ܐܘܡܢܘܬܗ ܕܬܪܥܐ ܠܡܟܐ̈ܒܐ ܗܘ ܦܬܝܚ ܘܠܐ ܠܚܠܝ̈ܡܐ. ܠܐ ܠܗ ܓܝܪ ܣܢܝܩܝܢ ܚܠܝ̈ܡܐ ܥܠ ܐܣܝܐ ܐܠܐ ܐܝܠܝܢ ܕܒܝܫ ܒܝܫ ܚܒܝܫܝܢ. ܡܟܝܠ ܐܣܝܐ ܫܘܒܚܗ ܚܘܠܡܢܐ ܗܘ ܕܡܟܐ̈ܒܐ. ܐܝܟ ܕܢܣܓܐ ܒܗܬܬܗ

☞

The term physician is used 6 times - thrice it refers to Jesus and the other three times to an ordinary physician. Obviously the term 'Our Physician' (ܐܣܝܢ) describes Jesus Who treats the stricken person as would an ordinary physician. For just as the door of an ordinary physician is not closed to the 'afflicted/stricken' (ܡܟܐ̈ܒܐ), so too Jesus as a Physician did not prevent the sinful woman, who is also 'stricken' (ܡܟܐܒܬܐ), from coming to Him. The description of an ordinary physician is not contrasted here with Jesus' behaviour, but helps the reader to understand how He treats the sick.[193] Ephrem relates this to Mark 2:17 (par Mt 9:12; Lk 5:31), which he quotes exactly. The same idea, that the physician is there for those who need him, is expressed by reference to John 7:37: 'whoever is thirsty, let him come and drink'. Consequently, Ephrem says that 'restoring the sick is the physician's glory' ( ܐܣܝܐ ܫܘܒܚܗ ܚܘܠܡܢܗܘܢ ܕܡܟ̈ܐܒܐ). Thus, the Lord as a Physician was ready to grant His help to the needy. With her tears the sinful woman was longing to be healed by Jesus: 'Her wounds' (ܫܘ̈ܡܬܗ) were healed by her tears, when she drew near to Him. At the end of the passage quoted above, Ephrem gives the impression, that she was dead because of her sin which was dwelling within her. Healing her is comparable to the return of a living soul to Lazarus when the Lord revived him.

Having twice referred to Christ as 'Our Physician' (ܐܣܝܢ), Ephrem also calls Him 'her Physician' (ܐܣܝܗ): 'She was comforting the feet of her Physician with gracious oil, for He had

---

ܕܦܪ̈ܝܫܐ ܕܟܘܠܗܘܢ ܕܐܣܝܢ ܠܒܝܫ. ܡܪܢ̱ ܕܝܢ ܗܘ ܕܐܬ̈ܘܬܐ ܒܟܐ̈ܒܐ ܡܣܒܐ ܗܘܐ. ܐܦ ܒܪ̈ ܟܠ ܠܒܝܬܗ ܕܦܪܝܫܐ ܗܘ. ܐܬ̈ܘܬܐ ܕܪ̈ܘܚܡ ܡܢ ܗܠܝܢ ܕܠܒܪ ܡܣܒܐ ܗܘܐ. ܒܟܐ̈ܒܐ ܠܒܪ ܐܫܠܡ ܦܓܪ̈ܐ ܒܪ̈ܝܗܐ. ܠܟܘ ܕܝܢ ܐܣܐ ܪ̈ܒܝܬܐ ܡܬܟܣܝܐ. ܠܒܪ ܐܝܟ ܡܒܝܬܘܬܗ ܕܠܒܪ. ܠܟܘ ܕܝܢ ܐܝܟ ܡܒܝܬܘܬܗ ܕܚܛܝܬܐ. ܗܝ ܠܥܠܝܐ ܢܦܫܐ ܚܝܬܐ ܕܢܦܩܬ ܡܢܗ. ܘܪܕܦ ܡܢ ܒܟܠܗܘܢ ܗܘܬ ܕܟܪ̈ܝܐ ܦܠܘܠܬܐ ܚܛܝܬܐ ܐܝܬܘܬܐ.

[193] See the section about Jonah, where Jonah's behaviour as a good physician contrasts with the weak actions of an ordinary physician who acts for his own profit.

graciously brought the Treasury of Restoratives to her pains'.[194] The oil/medicine has a significant role here, as it does in Dom 44. While she was anointing His feet, He was her Physician. Ephrem describes the oil of the sinful woman as a 'bribe' (ܫܘܚܕܐ) provided by her repentance and as 'medicines' (ܣܡ̈ܡܢܐ) for her wounds. Thus, she was healed through her oil, tears and kisses. Ephrem concludes his portrayal of Jesus as the Physician 'Who heals a person with the medicine which that person brings to him' as follows:

> The precious oil of the sinful woman was proclaiming that it was a bribe provided by [her] for repentance. These medicines the sinful woman offered her Physician, so that He could whiten the stains [of her sin] with her tears, and heal her wounds with her kisses, and through oil make her bad name as sweet as the fragrance of her oil. This is the Physician Who heals a person with the medicine which that person brings to Him![195]

Together with oil the sinful woman also offered tears and kisses through which He healed her wounds ( ܒܢܘܫ̈ܩܬܗ̇ ܐܣܝܐ ܚܒܪ̈ܬܗ̇). While here the tears are related to the stains of her sin (ܟܘܬܡ̈ܬܗ̇) which had been 'whitened' (ܚܘܪ), in Dom 42 the tears have the function of healing 'her wounds' (ܚܒܪ̈ܬܗ̇). The three verbs ܐܣܝ, ܐܚܠܡ and ܐܚܝ are used in parallel.[196] The term ܐܣܝ, together with ܐܚܠܡ, is also used with reference to healing the limbs.[197] In Dom 49, her tears caused the forgiveness of sins,

---

[194] Dom 14: ܡܚܝܢܐ ܗܘܬ ܠܗܝܢ ܚܢܢ ܠܬ̈ܟܠܢ ܐܣܘܬܗ̇ ܒܡܚܝܢܐ ܕܡܟܝܟ. ܕܡܟܝܟ. ܐܘܒܠ ܠܗ̇ ܣܝܡܬ ܚܘܠܡ̈ܢܐ ܠܟܐ̈ܒܝܗ̇.

[195] Dom 44: ܡܫܚܗ̇ ܠܦܐ ܕܢܦܠܬܐ ܡܟܪܙ ܗ̤ܘܐ ܕܫܘܚܕܐ ܗܘܐ ܕܬܝܒܘܬܐ. ܗܠܝܢ ܣܡ̈ܡܢܐ ܩܪܒܬ ܢܦܠܬܐ ܠܐܣܝܗ̇. ܕܒܕ̈ܡܥܝܗ̇ ܢܚܘܪ ܟܘܬܡ̈ܬܗ̇ ܘܒܢܘܫ̈ܩܬܗ̇ ܢܐܣܐ ܚܒܪ̈ܬܗ̇. ܘܒܡܫܚܗ̇ ܒܣܡܐ ܢܒܣܡ ܫܡܗ̇ ܒܝܫܐ ܐܝܟ ܪܝܚ ܡܫܚܗ̇. ܗܢܐ ܗܘ ܐܣܝܐ ܕܒܣܡ̈ܡܢܐ ܕܡܝܬܐ ܠܗ ܐܢܫ. ܒܗܘܢ ܗ̇ܘ ܡܐܣܐ ܠܗ.

[196] Cf. Dom 42.

[197] Cf. Dom 21.

issuing from Jesus' feet.[198] However, the deeds of the sinful woman were a witness to her faith. Therefore, seeing that there was not any verbal communication between Jesus and herself, there was also no need for her to ask verbally for forgiveness.[199] Since she was searching after Him in her inner mind and thoughts, He went out to meet her. This refers to His invisible action: He knew what she needed, and therefore He drew near to her: 'This is the Good Physician Who set out to go to the sinful woman who sought Him out in her mind'.[200] This is the only passage in the mimro where Jesus is described as the 'Good Physician' (ܐܣܝܐ ܛܒܐ).

Finally, the term 'medicine of life' (ܣܡ ܚܝܐ) deserves mention: in Dom 15, where Ephrem comments on Simon's invitation to Jesus, the author emphasises that Jesus was not hungry for the Pharisee's refreshments that perish, but for the tears of the sinful woman. Jesus accepted the invitation in order to show that He had been invited to help the 'mind' (ܪܥܝܢܐ), and 'to mix His teaching in the food of mortals as the Medicine of Life'.[201] This is the only place in the mimro where Jesus' teaching is described as the 'medicine of life'. Ephrem illustrates two different ways of teaching; teaching by words and by deeds. The teaching of Simon and Paul, however, was only by words, whereas the teaching of the disciples was by words and deeds. While the light struck the weak eyes of Saul, injured them and blinded them, the voice passed through his ears and opened them, because through the word our

---

[198] Cf. Dom 49: ܚܛܝܬܐ ܗܟܝܠ ܒܡܠܘܐܐ ܕܕ̈ܡܥܐ ܥܘܒܕܝܗ ܚܘ̈ܝܐ ܡܢ ܠܘܬ ܪ̈ܓܠܘܗܝ ܒܦܪܗܣܝܐ ܐܬܬܟܪܬ. ܘܗ̇ܝ ܕܬܪܥܐ ܗܘܐ ܕܒܗ̇ ܚܘܠܡܢܐ ܡܢ ܦܘܪܐ ܕܡܛܪ̈ܦܬܗ ܒܥܒܬ.

[199] Dom 44: ܠܐ ܕܝܢ ܫܘܒܩܢܐ ܗܘܬ ܚܛܝܬܐ ܕܒܫܬ̈ܩܘܬܗ ܬܫܐܠܝܘܗܝ ܗܘܬ ܠܡܪܢ. ܡܛܠ ܕܗܝܡܢܘܬܗ̇ ܕܝܕܥ ܗܘܐ ܐܝܟ ܐܠܗܐ ܫ̈ܐܠܬܐ ܕܒܠܒܗ̇ ܒܕ̈ܘܟܝܢܗ̇. ܐܦܠܐ ܡܪܢ ܫܐܠܗ̇ ܕܢܒܥܐ ܒܒܥܘܬܗ̇. ܡܛܠ ܕܝܕܥ ܗܘܐ ܕܒܠܒܘܫܬܗ̇ ܕܒܥܝܬܐ ܫܘܥܬܗ̇ ܠܬܐ̈ܒܘܬܐ ܦܪܥܐ ܗܘܬ. ܗܝ ܗܟܝܠ ܒܗܝܡܢܘܬ ܕܝܕܥ ܒܩܢܝܬܐ ܗܘ. ܠܫܐܠܬܗ̇ ܒܠܒܗ̇ ܗܘ ܡܦܪܥܐ ܗܘܬ ܠܗ. ܕܝܕܥ ܒܩܢܝܬܐ ܒܪܢܫ ܟܠ ܫܩܘ̈ܬܐ ܒܥܘ̈ܬܐ ܠܐ ܫܐܠܐ.

[200] Dom 48: ܗܘ ܐܣܝܐ ܛܒܐ ܕܢܦܩ ܕܢܐܙܠ ܠܘܬ ܚܛܝܬܐ. ܗ̇ܝ ܕܒܥܬܗ ܪ̈ܥܝܢܗ̇ ܒܡܟܣܝܐ ܗܘܬ ܒܠܒܗ̇.

[201] Cf. Dom 15.

Lord was able to show that He was persecuted by Saul.[202] In Dom 36, Ephrem says:

> Any master who intends to teach a person something teaches either by deeds or by words. If he does not teach by words or deeds, a person could not be instructed in his craft. And so, although it was not with deeds that our Lord taught Paul humility, He taught him with the voice about that persecution of which He was unable to teach him with deeds. Before He was crucified, when He taught the persecution of humility to His disciples, He taught them by deeds. After He completed [His] persecution by the crucifixion, as He said, «behold, everything is completed» (Jn 19:30), He could not go back again and foolishly begin something that once and for all had been finished wisely.[203]

To the sinful woman Jesus also acted by words, saying 'your sins have been forgiven' (Lk 7:49). Thus, she was healed and revived to a new life.

### *4.2.1.3 The Sinful Woman in II Serm 4*

There is healing imagery in the narrative mimro on the sinful woman that is addressed to the listeners/readers. As the sinful

---

[202] Cf. Dom 32. In Dom 31, Ephrem explains the influence of the humble speech in the example of Saul's conversion. He contrasts the pride of Saul with the humility of our Lord. Ephrem also compares God's revelation to Moses with the one to Saul. The brilliant light became for Saul a blinding light, because his inner eyes were blind, while the eyes of Moses radiated with the glory he saw, because another power lovingly reinforced the eyes of Moses beyond their natural power.

[203] Dom 36: ܚܕ ܡܢ ܪ̈ܒܢܐ ܕܡܢ ܕܨܒܐ ܕܢܠܦ ܡܕܡ ܠܐܢܫ. ܒܥܒ̈ܕܐ ܐܘ ܒܡ̈ܠܐ ܡܠܦ ܠܗ. ܐܢ ܕܝܢ ܠܐ ܒܡ̈ܠܐ ܘܠܐ ܒܥܒ̈ܕܐ ܡܠܦ ܠܗ. ܐܦ ܐܢܫ ܠܐܘܡܢܘܬܗ ܕܢܬܬܠܡܕ ܠܐ ܡܫܟܚ. ܐܡܬܝ ܕܐܦ ܡܪܢ ܐܦܢ ܠܐ ܗܘܐ ܒܥܒ̈ܕܐ ܐܠܦܗ ܡܟܝܟܘܬܐ ܠܦܘܠܘܣ. ܐܠܐ ܒܩܠܐ ܐܠܦܗ ܗ̇ܘܐ ܪ̈ܕܘܦܝܐ ܗ̇ܘ ܕܒܥܒ̈ܕܐ ܕܢܠܦܗ ܠܐ ܡܫܟܚ ܗܘܐ. ܩܕܡ ܓܝܪ ܕܢܙܕܩܦ ܗܘܐ ܡܪܢ ܪ̈ܕܘܦܝܐ ܕܡܟܝܟܘܬܐ ܗ̇ܘ ܕܐܠܦ ܗ̇ܘܐ ܠܬܠܡ̈ܝܕܘܗܝ ܒܥܒ̈ܕܐ ܠܗܘܢ ܐܠܦ ܗܘܐ. ܡܢ ܒܬܪ ܕܝܢ ܕܫܠܡܗ̇ ܠܪ̈ܕܘܦܝܐ ܒܙܩܝܦܘܬܐ. ܐܝܟܢܐ ܕܐܡ̇ܪ ܕܗܐ ܡܫܠܡ ܟܠ ܡܕܡ. ܠܐ ܬܘܒ ܡܫܟܚ ܗ̇ܘܐ ܕܢܗܦܘܟ ܢܫܪܐ ܣܟܠܐܝܬ ܡܕܡ ܕܚܕܐ ܙܒܢ ܐܫܬܠܡ ܚܟܝܡܐܝܬ.

woman heard that Jesus heals all through His medicine, she regretted her prostitution and decided to go to see Him in Simon's house (1-58). First, she goes to the unguent-seller[204] with her gold to fill her jar with oil (59-74). The seller is astonished by her appearance. By putting the words into the seller's mouth, and later in her speech, the author compares her former life with her current thoughts (75-134). Then Satan[205] intervenes in a dialogue between them. He tries to persuade her not to visit Jesus (135-223). When he fails, Satan thinks about telling Jesus about her sins and past life, so that He might reject her (224-61). Instead, Satan goes off to Simon to urge him to keep the sinful woman out of his house (262-75). Finally, after she appears and Jesus calls her to enter the house (276-323), He explains her situation to Simon by referring to the episode of the two debtors (324-65).

Healing imagery occurs at a number of points in the mimro: at the beginning of this mimro, by wondering how merciful the Lord is, the author refers to the sinful woman who is also called a 'prostitute' (ܙܢܝܬܐ) and 'lustful person' (ܙܠܝܠܬܐ).[206] In a similar way, the blind man whose eyes have been opened (Jn 9:6) and the paralytic are mentioned together with the sinful woman as a witness to the mercy and medical assistance of the Lord:

ܥܒܕܘ ܘܐܬܠܒܒܘ ܚܛ̈ܝܐ
ܕܚܙܐ ܡܪܚܡܢ ܐܠܗܐ
ܠܙܢܝܬܐ ܥܒܕ ܠܗ̇ ܚܘܣܝܗ̇
ܐܦ ܣܡܟܗ̇ ܕܡܚܡܐ [ܕܡܚܝܠܐ] ܗܘܬ
ܠܣܡܝܐ ܒܓܠܝܐ ܦܬܚ ܥܝ̈ܢܘܗܝ
ܘܚܙܝ ܢܘܗܪܐ ܒܒ̈ܬܗ

[204] The common name for the seller of unguent is ܒܣܡܐ; cf. II Serm 4.72; 4.113; 4.116; 4.134; 4.137.

[205] After the first third of the *mimro*, the name of Satan occurses frequently; cf. II Serm 4.135; 4.155; 4.182; 4.186; 4.195; 4.204; 4.222; 4.228; 4.252; 4.272.

[206] Cf. II Serm 4.52; 4.56; 4.78-88; 4.112-14; 4.133; 4.221-22; 4.242-43; 4.249; 4.295-99; 4.319; 4.333. Throughout the *mimro*, the terms ܙܠܝܠܬܐ, ܙܠܝܠܐ and ܙܠܝܠܘܬܐ are used; together with ܙܢܝܬܐ and ܙܢܝܘܬܐ denote the idea of the sinful woman as a prostitute. But frequently she is also called 'the sinful woman' (ܚܛܝܬܐ); cf. II Serm 4.3; 4.17; 4.180; 4.187; 4.276; 4.307; 4.314.

ܘܠܡܫܪܝܐ ܝܗܒ ܚܘܠܡܢܐ
ܩܡ ܗܠܟ ܘܫܩܠ ܥܪܣܗ
ܘܠܢ ܝܗܒ ܠܢ ܡܪ̈ܓܢܝܬܐ
ܦܓܪܗ ܘܕܡܗ ܩܕܝܫܐ [ܠܚܘܣܝܐ]
ܫܩܠ ܗܘܐ ܣܡ̈ܡܢܘܗܝ ܒܛܘܫܝܐܝܬ
ܘܡܐܣܐ ܗܘܐ ܒܗܘܢ ܓܠܝܐܝܬ
ܘܡܬܟܪܟ ܗܘܐ ܒܐܪܥܐ ܕܝܗܘܕ:
ܐܝܟ ܐܣܝܐ ܫܩܠ ܣܡ̈ܡܢܘܗܝ

1 Hear and be comforted, my beloved,
how merciful is God:
3 To the sinful woman He forgave her debts;
as well as, He upheld her for she was sad [weak].
5 In the case of the blind man, He opened his eyes
with clay,
and the pupils of his eyes beheld the light (Jn 9:6).
7 Also to the paralytic He granted restoration,
he arose up to walk and carried his bed (Mt 9:2).
9 And to us He granted the pearls:
His holy body and blood [for reconciliation].
11 He carried His medicines secretly,
and He was healing with them openly.
13 And He was wandering round in the land of
Judea
as a physician carrying his medicines.[207]

The term 'medicines' (ܣܡ̈ܡܢܐ) occurs twice in this passage, but is not found again in the mimro; both times it is linked to the verb 'to carry/bear' (ܫܩܠ), the verb that is used for the paralytic carrying his bed. The miracle of forgiving the sinful woman her debts, together with that of opening the eyes of the blind man and granting 'restoration' (ܚܘܠܡܢܐ) to the paralytic, provide evidence for the medicine that Jesus bore with Him secretly. Since Jesus had visited the city of Judea, He took 'His medicines' (ܣܡ̈ܡܢܘܗܝ) with Him as a 'physician' (ܐܣܝܐ). The term physician is not used again, but it appears in the additional material after line 298,[208] where Jesus is described as the One Who is able to fulfill the needs of everyone. Since Jesus is described as the 'Table of Life' ( ܦܬܘܪ

207 II Serm 4.1-14.

208 The Appendix II.B is taken from Br. M. add. 17266.

ܚܝ̈ܐ), 'Blessed Fountain' (ܡܒܘܥܐ ܒܪܝܟܐ) and 'Great Physician' (ܐܣܝܐ ܪܒܐ), He tells Simon to let the sinful woman enter his house, saying:

ܬܐ ܠܟܐ ܫܡܥܘܢ ܐܡܿܪ ܠܟ
ܠܐ ܐܢܫ ܩܐܡ ܗܘܐ ܒܬܪܥܐ
ܡܢ ܕܐܝܬܘܗܝ ܦܬܚ ܠܗ ܢܥܘܠ
ܢܣܒ ܘܢܐܙܠ ܣܘܢܩܢܗ
ܘܐܢ ܟܦܢܐ ܗܘ ܕܟܦܢ ܠܠܚܡܐ
ܗܐ ܦܬܘܪ ܚܝ̈ܐ ܒܒܝܬܟ
ܘܐܢ ܨܗܝܐ ܗܘ ܕܨܗܐ ܠܡܝ̈ܐ
ܗܐ ܡܒܘܥܐ ܒܪܝܟܐ ܒܒܝܬܟ
ܘܐܢ ܟܪܝܗܐ ܗܘ ܘܫܐܠ ܚܘܠܡܢܐ
ܗܐ ܐܣܝܐ ܪܒܐ ܒܒܝܬܟ
ܢܚܙܘܢ ܚܛܝ̈ܐ ܢܘܢ ܠܝ
ܕܡܛܠܬܗܘܢ ܐܬܬܚܬܬ

29 Come here, Simon, I will tell you;
is not someone standing at the door?
31 Whoever he is, open to him that he may come in
to receive his need and go.
33 If he is hungry and hungers for bread,
behold, the Table of Life is in your house.
35 If he is thirsty, and thirsts for water,
behold, the Blessed Fountain is in your house.
37 If he is sick and asks for restoration,
behold, the Great Physician is in your house.
39 Let the sinners see me,
because for their sakes I came down [from heaven].[209]

While in the previous quotation, Jesus' wandering around is compared to that of a physician bearing his medicines,[210] here He is called 'Great Physician' (ܐܣܝܐ ܪܒܐ). Only in this passage is this particular phrase used. This passage, opening the door to the people who are hungry, thirsty, sick and sinners, reminds us of Dom 42, where Ephrem says that 'the door of an ordinary physician is open to the sick' ( ܠܟܐܒ̈ܐ ܗܘ ܦܬܝܚ ܘܠܐ ܠܚܠܝ̈ܡܐ). In this passage, Jesus does not rebuke Simon, but He

[209] II Serm App II.B.29-40.

[210] Cf. II Serm 4.14.

tells him just to open the door, indicating to him at the same time that He is the 'Table of Life' (ܦܬܘܪ ܚܝ̈ܐ), 'Blessed Fountain' (ܠܡܒܘܥܐ ܒܪܝܟܐ) and 'Great Physician' (ܐܣܝܐ ܪܒܐ) Who came down from heaven for the needy. Surprisingly, in an earlier additional passage in B when Satan tried to persuade Simon not to let the women in, Simon speaks out positively for Jesus. He explains Jesus' good deeds to Satan:

ܡܐܣܐ ܟܪ̈ܝܗܐ ܕܠܐ ܐܓܪܐ
ܘܡܐܣܐ ܡܓܢ ܚܒܘ̈ܪ ܗܘܐ
ܩܪܒ ܩܐܡ ܥܠ ܩܒܪܐ
ܘܩܪܐ ܘܩܝܡܝܢ ܡܝ̈ܬܐ
ܩܪܝܗܝ ܝܘܐܪܫ ܕܢܐܚܐ ܠܒܪܬܗ
ܘܬܟܝܠ ܗܘܐ ܕܡܐܚܐ ܗܘܐ ܠܗ̇
ܘܟܕ ܐܙܠ ܥܡܗ ܒܐܘܪܚܐ
ܝܗܒ ܚܘܠܡܢܐ ܠܡܚܒܬܐ
ܕܠܒܟܬ ܒܟܢܦܐ ܕܡܪܛܘܛܗ
ܘܓܢܒܬ ܡܢܗ ܚܘܠܡܢܐ
ܘܟܐܒܗ̇ ܩܫܝܐ ܘܡܪܝܪܐ
ܡܚܕܐ ܥܒܪ ܡܢ ܓܐܕܝܗ̇

7 He heals the sick without payment,
He binds up wounds for no charge.
9 He approaches and stands by the grave,
and calls, and the dead arise.
11 Jairus called Him to raise his daughter to life (Mk 5:22),
trusting that He could revive her.
13 And as He went with him in the way,
He gave restoration to the stricken woman (Mt 9:20)
15 who laid hold of the hem of His garment
and stole restoration from Him
17 and her pain which was hard and bitter
at once departed from her.[211]

Simon presents Jesus as the One who 'heals the sick' (ܡܐܣܐ ܟܪ̈ܝܗܐ) and 'binds up wounds' (ܘܡܐܣܐ ܚܒܘ̈ܪ) graciously. Simon refers to some miracles that Jesus performed as a witness. Among them is the healing of the woman with the

---

[211] II Serm 4.App.I.B.7-18.

haemorrhage who 'stole restoration from Him' ( ܘܓܢܒܬ ܡܢܗ ܚܘܠܡܢܐ), and 'He granted restoration to the stricken woman' (ܝܗܒ ܚܘܠܡܢܐ ܠܡܟܒܒܬܐ), so that 'her strong pain' ( ܟܐܒܗ̇ ܡܥܝܢܐ) ceased. Here, she is called 'the stricken woman' (ܡܟܐܒܬܐ). Later on, Simon mentions further healing miracles: Jesus granted 'restoration' (ܚܘܠܡܢܐ) to the debtor, He 'cleansed' (ܕܟܝ) lepers, 'made firm' (ܚܝܠ) the limbs of the 'paralytic' (ܡܫܪܝܐ) and 'opened' (ܦܬܚ) the eyes of the blind.[212] The way of her repentance and healing is alluded to in the dialogue between her and Satan. When Satan tried to persuade her and described her sadness and appearance as that of someone whose friend had died, she takes the idea of death literally and transforms it to her sin:

ܛܒܐܝܬ ܚܝܪ ܕܡܝܬ ܠܝ
ܠܐܢܫ ܕܐܙܠ ܠܡܩܒܪ ܡܝܬܐ
ܚܛܝܬܐ ܕܚܘܫ̈ܒܝ ܡܝܬܬ܆
ܘܐܙܠܐ ܐܢܐ ܕܐܩܒܪܝܗ̇

Well, rightly you have compared me
[183] with someone who is going to bury a dead person:
the sin of my thoughts has died,
[185] and I am going to bury it.[213]

The sin which will be buried is that of her 'thoughts' (ܚܛܝܬܐ ܕܚܘܫ̈ܒܝ). In the mimro On our Lord, Ephrem illustrates the healing of the sinful woman as reviving her with a living spirit, while 'he drove off the deadly sin' from her.[214] Because of her sinful deeds, in the dialogue with Satan, she presents herself as someone who 'was blind' (ܣܡܝܐ ܗܘܝܬ) and 'bound' ( ܦܟܝܪܐ ܗܘܝܬ).

ܚܘܪ ܠܝ [ܣܡܟ] ܥ̈ܝܢܐ [ܘܚܙܪ] ܚܝ̈ܠ

---

[212] II Serm 4.App I.B.31-38:

ܠܗ̇ ܚܒܪܐ ܕܚܝܒ ܘܫܒܩ ܟܠܗ ܐܘܦܝܗ ܚܘܠܡܢܐ
ܘܠܓܪ̈ܒܐ ܕܟܝ ܒܡܠܬܗ ܘܠܡܫܪܝܐ ܚܝܠ ܗܕ̈ܡܘܗܝ
ܠܣܡܝܐ ܣܟܝܪܐ ܘܡܦܬܚܐ ܦܬܚ ܥܝ̈ܢܘܗܝ ܘܚܙܐ ܢܘܗܪܐ
ܘܠܐܢܫܐ ܬܪܝܢ ܕܐܦܣܩܘܗܝ ܡܚܙܐ ܦܬܚ ܥܝ̈ܢܘܗܝ.

[213] II Serm 4.182-85.

[214] Cf. Dom 42.

ܘܒܥܘܪܝ ܥܘܪܬ ܣܓܝ̈ܐܐ
ܣܡܝܐ ܗܘܝܬ ܘܠܐ ܝܕܥܐ ܗܘܝܬ
ܕܐܝܬ ܗܘ ܕܡܢܗܪ ܠܣܡܝܐ
ܘܗܐ ܐܙܠܐ ܐܢܐ ܕܐܢܗܪ ܥܝܢ̈ܝ
ܘܒܢܘܗܪܝ ܐܢܗܪ ܣܓܝ̈ܐܐ
ܦܟܝܪܐ ܗܘܝܬ ܘܠܐ ܝܕܥܐ ܗܘܝܬ
ܕܐܝܬ ܗܘ ܕܫܪܐ ܠܦܟܝܪ̈ܐ
ܘܗܐ ܐܙܠܐ ܐܢܐ ܐܫܪܐ ܦܟ̈ܪܝ
ܘܦܫܪ̈ܝ [ܘܒܫܪܝܢ] ܐܫܪܐ ܣܓܝ̈ܐܐ

The eye-paint blinded my eyes,[215]
209 and with my blindness I blinded many.
I was blind and knew not
211 that there is One Who gives light to the blind.
Behold, I am going to enlighten my eyes,
213 and with my light I will give light to many.
I was bound fast, and knew not
215 that there is One Who releases those who are bound.
Behold, I am going to untie my bonds,
217 and with my untying I will untie many.[216]

In order to explain her goal to Satan, she argues that through Jesus Who 'binds up those who are broken/shattered' ( ܚܒܫ ܠܬܒܝܪ̈ܐ) she is able to bind up her wounds; through Him Who 'gives light to the blind' (ܡܢܗܪ ܠܣܡܝܐ) she will give light to her eyes; and through Him Who can 'loose the bonds' (ܫܪܐ ܠܦܟܝܪ̈ܐ) she will loose her own bonds. These three points have the same form and structure, so that their texts are parallel. If she has been able to receive healing from Jesus with her actions, then she will also be able to bind up the broken, enlighten the eyes and untie the bonds of many.

---

[215] The term ܨܒܥܐ, together with ܟܘܚܠܐ, appears also in II Serm 4.45-48: ܐܬܚܫܟܬ ܘܥܘܪܬ ܡܢ ܟܘܚ̈ܠܝܗ ܨܒܥܐ ܕܟܘܪ ܫ̈ܘܦܝܗ ܘܦܘ̈ܩܕܝܗ ܕܫ̈ܡܫܐ ܕܟܒܟ̈ܒܬܗ ܥܠ ܟܘܚܠܐ ܗܘ ܡܬܠܐ. Manuscript B has ܣܡ ܨܒܥܐ, which can be translated as 'pigment of eye-paint.

[216] Cf. II Serm 4.208-17; in 217 A's ܘܦܫܪ̈ܝ must be a corruption of B's ܘܒܫܪܝ[ܢ].

The verb 'to heal' (ܡܐܣܐ) appears twice: here, with the object 'sick', (ܟܪ̈ܝܗܐ) Jesus intervenes as the Healer, whereas in the first passage quoted above it illustrates the general effect of Jesus' medicine. Jesus acts as a Physician.[217] Both sentences 'healing the sick' and 'binding sickness' have a chiastic structure. The verb 'to bind up' (ܚܒܫ) is used another three times. Here it is connected with the term 'pains' (ܟܐ̈ܒܐ), whereas in the middle of the mimro it occurs together with shattered people' (ܬܒܝܪ̈ܐ).[218] The sinful woman rejects Satan's advice and feels very sad and depressed because of her past life. Since she knows that Jesus is the One Who 'binds up the shattered people' (ܚܒܫ ܠܬܒܝܪ̈ܐ), she decides to go to Jesus:

ܬܒܝܪܐ ܗܘܝܬ ܘܠܐ ܝܕܥܐ ܗܘܝܬ
ܕܐܝܬ ܗܘ ܕܚܒܫ ܠܬܒܝܪ̈ܐ
ܘܗܐ ܐܙܠܐ ܐܢܐ ܐܚܒܘܫ ܠܬܒܝܪ[ܘܬ]ܝ
ܘܒܚܒܫܝ ܐܚܒܘܫ ܣܓܝ̈ܐܐ

I was shattered and knew not
219 that there is One Who binds up those who are shattered.
Behold, I go to bind up my shattered state.
221 and through my binding I will bind up many.

The idea of the 'binding up' of the sinful woman as an example for the healing of others is found in the Commentary on the Diatessaron where Ephrem compares the gentile women of the New Testament with the gentile women at the time of Solomon.[219] In the Commentary on the Diatessaron the sinful woman was called 'a physician to her own wounds' (ܐܣܝܬܐ ܠܡܚܘ̈ܬܗ̇),[220] whereas here she has the function 'of binding up' (ܐܚܒܘܫ) her own broken state, and through this, providing an example for the 'binding up' of many other broken people. Her healing will heal many who are shattered (ܬܒܝܪ̈ܐ), when they believe in Jesus. With the form of the first person singular in line 220, specific attention is

---

217 Cf. II Serm 4.11-14; II Serm 4.App.I.B.7-8.

218 Cf. II Serm 4.218-21.

219 Cf. CDiat 7.18 (on the sinful woman, see chapter IV, 2.1.1).

220 Cf. CDiat 22.5.

drawn to her motivation, in that she took the initiative to go to Jesus and so cured herself.

It is important to keep in mind that the healing of the sinful woman consists in the forgiveness of her sins, as stated at the beginning of the mimro: 'to the sinful woman He forgave her debts'.[221] Whereas she is a sinner full of debts ( ܚܛܝܬܐ ܡܠܝܬ ܚܘ̈ܒܐ),[222] Jesus, as the one who forgave the two debtors,[223] is the One Who forgives sins and debts (ܕܫܒܩ ܚܘ̈ܒܐ ܘܚܛ̈ܗܐ).[224] In her dialogue with the perfumer, she tells him that the new person that she has met was a rich Merchant:

ܗܘ ܓܢܒܢ ܘܐܢܐ ܓܢܒܬܗ
ܗܘ ܓܢܒ ܚܘ̈ܒܝ ܘܚܛ̈ܗܝ
ܘܐܢܐ ܓܢܒܬ ܠܥܘܬܪܗ [ܬܐ ܠܥܘܬܪܗ]

He has robbed me and I have robbed Him;
[131] He has robbed me of my debts and sins
and I have robbed Him of His wealth.[225]

The wealth of the Lord is capable to forgive, 'to rob/steal away', sins. She received forgiveness by His mercy[226] and put on the garment of reconciliation.[227] Finally, because of her deeds Jesus asks Simon rhetorically:

ܦܠܐ ܠܗ̇ ܕܬܦܘܩ ܫܡܥܘܢ
ܟܕ ܠܐ ܢܣܒܬ ܫܘܒܩܢܐ

Simon, is it appropriate for her to leave
361 before receiving forgiveness?[228]

Jesus grants her forgiveness of her debts and transgressions because of His mercy and her repentance. Her words with the

---

[221] II Serm 4.3. The term ܚܘ̈ܒܐ is also used in II Serm 4.131; 4.276; 4.307; 4.321; 4.340.

[222] Cf. II Serm 4.276; 4.307.

[223] Cf. II Serm 4.342: Here the term 'debt' is in singular and feminine (ܘܫܒܩ ܚܘܒܬܐ ܕܬܪ̈ܝܗܘܢ) instead of masculine plural (ܚܘ̈ܒܐ).

[224] Cf. II Serm 4.321.

[225] II Serm 4.130-32.

[226] Cf. II Serm 4.1-4.

[227] II Serm 4.53-54: ܘܐܬܚܫܒܬ ܕܬܐܙܠ ܬܠܒܫ ܟܘܬܝܢ ܡܐ̈ܢܐ ܕܫܘܝܢܐ [ܚܫܐ].

[228] II Serm 4.360-61.

perfumer, as well as with Satan and Simon, and her deeds, are all witnesses of her repentance and faith.

#### 4.2.1.4 *The Sinful Woman in some other Texts*

There are several hymns and memre where the episode of the anointing of Jesus' feet features.[229] Only the most important references will be discussed here

In hymn 4 On Virginity which is about oil, olives and the symbol of the Lord, Ephrem uses various types of symbols. The oil, as the treasure of symbols, symbolises Christ the Physician. Ephrem plays on the name Christ, the 'Anointed One' (ܡܫܝܚܐ) and the 'oil' (ܡܫܚܐ) as a healing and restorative substance. Sinners use oil as their currency, so that their sins might be forgiven. In Virg 4.4, Ephrem draws attention to the sinful woman where he links Luke's with John's narrative:[230]

ܡܠܘܐܐ ܗܘ ܡܫܝܚܐ ܕܐܬܬܓܪܘ ܒܗ̣ ܚܛܝ̈ܬܐ ܫܘܒܩܢ
ܚܘ̈ܒܐ

---

[229] See Virg 4.11; 26.4; 35.5-8; Fid 10.5; Nat 4.40; [Epiph 3.2-3]; Nis 60.1-8; Eccl 9.19; Azym 14.1-4; Haer 47.8; Hebd 2.1-265; I Serm 8.196-97; I Serm 7.229; [III Serm 4.636].

[230] Apparently, Ephrem brings the episodes of Lk 7:36-50 and Jn 12:1-8 (Mk 14:3-9) together. McVey, in her introduction to Virg 4, suggests that here Ephrem identifies the sinful woman with Mary of Jn 12:1-8 with the woman of Lk 7; cf. K. E. McVey, *Ephrem the Syrian Hymns* (New York 1989), 275. However, if Eccl 9.19 is taken into consideration, this points against their identification. The author attributes 'the kissing of His feet' to the sinful woman, whereas 'the anointing of His head' to Mary. Both sentences are connected with the conjuction ܐܦ which signifies a parallel action on the part of both women: ܚܛܝܬܐ ܐܡܛܠܪ ܗܘܟܢܐ ܢܫܩܘܗ̈ܝ [ܕܡܪܗ̇] ܠܡ ܠܒܪܐ --- ܕܫܦܠܬܐ ܢܫܩܬ ܪ̈ܓܠܘܗܝ ܐܦ ܡܪܝܡ ܪܫܗ ܡܫܚܬ ܗܘܬ. 'Mary' appears only in John, 'head' only in Mt and Lk, 'feet' only in Lk and Jn, 'sinner' only in Lk. John's narrative concerning Mary speaks of 'anointing of His feet (Jn 11:2; 12:3), whereas the parallel episode in Mk 14:3 says: ܐܬܬ ܐܢܬܬܐ ܕܐܝܬ ܠܘܬܗ̇ ܫܛܝܦܬܐ ܕܡܫܚܐ ܕܢܪܕܝܢ ܪܫܝܐ ܣܓܝ ܕܡܝ̈ܐ. ܘܦܬܚܬܗ̇ ܘܐܫܦܟܬܗ̇ ܥܠ ܪܫܗ ܕܝܫܘܥ. Also in other places, such as in Azym 14.1-4, Ephrem uses the name Mary in the context of anointing Jesus.

ܠܚܛܝܬܐ ܕܡܫܚܬ ܪ̈ܓܠܐ ܡܫܝܚܐ ܒܡܫܚܐ ܫܒܩ
ܚܘ̈ܒܝܗ̇
ܒܗ ܐܫܦܟܬ ܡܪܝܡ ܚܘܒܗ̇ ܥܠ ܪܝܫܗ ܕܡܪܐ ܚܘܒܗ̇
ܦܚ ܪܝܚܗ ܒܚܢ ܠܡܫ̈ܬܘܬܐ ܐܝܟ ܕܒܟܘܪܐ
ܗܘ ܦܪܣܗ̇ ܠܓܢܒܘܬܐ ܕܠܒܝܫܐ ܒܝܨܝܦܘܬ ܡܣ̈ܟܢܐ
ܗܘܐ ܓܫܪܐ ܠܥܘܗܕܢܗ̇ ܕܡܪܝܡ ܕܢܥܒܪ ܫܘܒܚܗ̇ ܡܢ ܕܪ
ܠܕܪ.

A commodity is oil with which sinners do business:
the forgiveness of debts.
To the sinful woman who anointed [His] feet
the Anointed One forgave her debts by oil (Lk 7.36-50).
With [oil] Mary poured out her debt
upon the head of the Lord of her debt (Mk 14:3-9; Jn 12:1-8).[231]
Its scent wafted; it tested the guests as in a furnace (cf. Jn 12:3):
it exposed the theft clothed in the care of the poor (Jn 12:6).
It became the bridge to the remembrance of Mary
to pass on her glory from generation to generation.

*Virg 4.11*

Oil as mediator signifies what happened secretly. Jesus forgave the sins of the sinful woman through the use of oil, as she poured out her sin upon the Lord with the visible oil. In this hymn, oil plays a significant role, with visible and invisible effects: oil gives life to the body and to the mind.[232] Another reference for the

[231] ܡܪܐ ܚܘܒܐ means creditor.

[232] Virg 4.4 illustrates the image of a ship on the ocean, which symbolises oil. All kinds of beneficial effects (ܥܘܕܪ̈ܢܐ) are in the ship. The healing spirit/wind (ܪܘܚܐ ܡܐܣܝܢܝܬܐ) draws the ship to the harbour of the sick (ܟܪ̈ܝܗܐ) in order to heal the sick. The term ܟܪ̈ܝܗܐ also occurs in Virg 4.5, where Ephrem especially plays on the words ܡܫܚܐ and ܡܫܝܚܐ: the 'oil' and the 'Anointed One' sacrifice themselves, so that the sick (ܟܪ̈ܝܗܐ) may obtain help (ܥܘܕܪ̈ܢܝܢ) and healing. The oil, which has many different names, is compounded with herbs for 'the healing of all hurts' (ܠܐܣܝܘܬܐ ܕܟܠ ܢܟܬ̈ܝܢ). Virg 4.6, emphasises the general benefits of oil and the Anointed One which are able to be 'all with all' (ܕܢܗܘܐ ܟܠ ܥܡ ܟܠ). The next two stanzas (Virg

☞

symbolic effect of oil occurs in hymn 3 On Epiphany - the authenticity is doubtful - which praises the sinful woman because she had anointed her Lord's feet. The oil served as an offering that gave pleasure to her Creditor. Thus, the forgiveness of her sins is achieved through oil. Because the sinful woman was in need of forgiveness, oil served as an offering, with which she pleased the Lord.

ܡܛܠ ܕܝܢ ܗ̇ܝ ܚܛܝܬܐ
ܥܠ ܫܘܒܩܢܐ ܣܢܝܩܐ ܗܘܬ
ܡܫܚܐ ܗܘܐ ܠܗ̇ ܩܘܪܒܢܐ
ܘܒܗ ܪܥܬ ܠܡܪܐ ܚܘܒ̈ܗ̇ [ܠܡܪܐ ܚܘܒ̈ܐ]

Because the sinful woman
was in need of forgiveness,
oil became for her an offering
and with it she reconciled the Lord of her debts [the Creditor].

*Epiph 3.3*

In hymn 26 On Virginity where Ephrem characterises a series of women from the Gospel as spiritual brides of Christ, the forgiveness of the sinful woman's debts is associated with her kissing His holy feet:

---

4.7-8) describe the 'symbol' (ܪܐܙܐ) of oil as the Anointed One, the Messiah. While oil is visible like a shadow, Christ is a secret, hidden mystery. Ephrem illustrates the effect of shadow with some examples from Scripture: the disciples were sent out in order to anoint and heal (ܘܒܗ ܕܡܫܝ̈ܚܝܢ ܗܘܘ ܘܡܐܣܝܢ) by oil (cf. Lk 10:9; Jas 5:14), and their shadow caused healing (ܕܛܠܠܗܘܢ ܥܒ̣ܕ ܕܐܣܝܐ). Likewise, the shadow of Jesus fell upon the sick and they were healed. Oil helps in all cases. It filled the place of lineage for strangers, it is the sceptre for old age, and the armour for youth (Virg 4.9-10). Particularly significant is the following sentence in Virg 4.10: 'It supports sickness and is the bulwark of health' (ܗܘ ܡܣܡܟܢ ܠܟܘܪܗܢܘܬܐ ܘܗܘܝܘ ܫܘܪܗ̇ ܕܚܠܝܡܘܬܐ). Stanza 13 stresses the power of oil against the diseases which are described as a 'second demon' (ܫܐܕܐ ܗܘ ܕܬܪܝܢ). As the Lord persecuted and punished the demon (cf. Mk 5:1-20 and parallels), so too, the power of oil acts against 'pains' (ܟܐ̈ܒܐ). According to stanza 14, this power is still available in the sacraments of the church, and it is flowing as Eden's four rivers in order to gladden the body and enlighten the holy church (Virg 4.13-14).

ܛܘܒܝܟܝ ܐܢܬܬܐ ܚܣܝܡܬ ܒܢܫ̈ܐ
ܕܢܫܩܬܝ ܪ̈ܓܠܐ ܩܕܝ̈ܫܬܐ
ܐܝܕ̈ܝܟܝ ܡܫܚܘ̈ܗܝ ܠܡܫܝܚ ܩܘܕܫܐ
ܕܩܪܢܗ ܡܫܚܬ ܟܗ̈ܢܐ ܘܡ̈ܠܟܐ
ܛܘܒ ܠܟܐܒ̈ܝܟܝ ܕܐܬܐܣܝܘ ܒܡܠܬܐ
ܘܠܚܘ̈ܒܝܟܝ ܕܐܫܬܒܩܘ ܒܢܘܫܩܬܐ
ܐܠܦ ܠܥܕܬܗ ܕܬܢܫܘܩ ܒܕܟܝܘܬܗ
ܠܦܓܪܐ ܡܩܕܫ ܟܠ.

Blessed are you, woman, most enviable of women,
who kissed the holy feet (Lk 7:38,39)!
Your hands anointed the Anointed One of the
Sanctuary
Whose horn had anointed priests and kings.
Blessed are your sufferings that were healed by the
word
and your sins that were forgiven by a kiss (Lk 7:45-48).
He taught His church to kiss in purity
[His] all-sanctifying body.

*Virg 26.4*

Jesus' anointing by the sinful woman is put in the context of priestly and royal messiahship, and of the forgiveness of sins. While the sins of the sinful woman were forgiven by kissing His holy feet, her 'pains' (ܟܐܒ̈ܝܟܝ) were 'healed' (ܐܬܐܣܝܘ) by His word (ܡܠܬܐ). Ephrem draws attention to the holiness of Jesus, when he speaks of His 'holy feet' (ܪ̈ܓܠܐ ܩܕܝ̈ܫܬܐ) and His 'all-sanctifying body' (ܠܦܓܪܐ ܡܩܕܫ ܟܠ), and Jesus as the 'Anointed One of the Sanctuary' (ܠܡܫܝܚ ܩܘܕܫܐ).[233] In hymn 35 On Virginity, Jesus' holiness is contrasted with the impurity of the sinful woman. Since the sinful woman, as the 'impure one' (ܛܡܐܬܐ), drew near to the Holy One, Ephrem encourages sinners to draw near to the Lord so that their sins will be forgiven and they will be cleansed.[234] Likewise, he considers himself as a

---

233 In Haer 47.8, Ephrem emphasises that the sinful woman touched the real body of Jesus in contrast to those heretics who defined his humanity as a 'shadow': ܦܓܪܐ ܗܘ ܫܪܝܪܐ ܓܫܬ ܚܛܝܬܐ ܕܠܡܣܝܢ ܩܪܒܬ.

234 Virg 35.5-7:

☞

---

[5] ܚܛܝܬܐ ܬܘܕܐ ܠܡܫܐܬܐ ܕܠܐ ܒܗܬܬ ܕܠܡܫܬܘܝܐ ܥܠܬ ܕܕܟܝܐ
ܘܩܕܝܫܐ

ܒܐܝܠܐ ܕܝ ܚܘܝܦܐ ܒܥܠܝܐ ܝܪܬ ܥܠܬ ܚܛܗܐ ܚܠܦ ܚܛܗܐ
ܚܘܒܐ ܗܘ ܐܪܘܚܗ

ܕܥܠ ܕܠܒܫ ܪܓܫܬ ܡܪܢܝܐ ܚܦܬ ܗܘ ܠܗ ܡܫܝܚܐ ܕܐܬܚܝܠ ܕܚܝܠܐ
ܡܚܝܡ ܕܠܐ ܚܝܠ.

[6] ܒܡܣܪܩܗ ܥܡܠܬ ܗܘܬ ܟܕ ܕܘܥܬܗ ܒܘܪܟܬܐ ܨܐܬܐ ܕܦܓܪ
ܦܓܪܟ ܡܪܩܬܗ ܠܬܪܥܝܬܗ

ܘܥܠܬ ܡܘܬܐ ܠܟܠܢܫ ܒܚܝܐ ܗܘܬ ܥܠܬ ܬܝܒܘܬܐ ܠܣܓܝܐܐ ܗܘܬ
ܗܘܬ

ܠܟܐܐ ܕܣܐܘܪܗ ܥܒܕܘܟ ܘܣܛܝܢܐ ܣܐܘܪܗ ܘܦܠܫܘܟ ܘܩܕܝܫܐ
ܬܘܪܘ ܒܗ ܘܚܠܠܘܟ.

[7] ܨܒܬܗ ܘܟܕܘܠܗ ܕܐܣܛܝܘ ܠܣܪܝܐ ܡܕܘܟܐ ܗܘܘ ܠܟ ܕܕܟܠܝܟ
ܘܪܦܐ ܗܘܘ

ܡܪܘܠܬܐ ܕܐܬܥܒܕܬ ܠܓܠܟܗ ܠܡܪܘܝܟ ܒܗܘ ܡܪܩ ܕܐܬܒܕܬ ܒܗ
ܐܬܚܒܠܬ ܕܡܫܚܬܗ

ܕܒܝܫ ܗܘܐ ܡܫܝܚܐ ܕܢܫܩܗ ܘܐܬܡܪܩ ܦܘܡܗ ܕܠܟܐܗ ܘܐܬܦܪܥ
ܥܦܪܗ ܕܐܪܥܗ.

In the context of Simon the Pharisee (Lk 7:36-50), Ephrem would not describe Simon's 'banquet of the pure and holy', because Ephrem identifies Simon as an unfaithful person like his ancestors. The sinful woman received 'blessing' (ܒܘܪܟܬܐ) from His 'sweat' (ܕܘܥܬܐ) by cleansing His feet with her hair. The invisible effect of the visible deed is, furthermore, emphasised by contrasting the 'dirt' (ܨܐܬܐ) of Jesus' body with the sinful woman's mind: since she cleansed the dust from His body, He cleansed her mind. Thus, her 'repentance' (ܬܝܒܘܬܐ) and her blessing changed her position. While in her previous life she caused many people to die, now she causes many to repent. Before she was 'an occasion of death' (ܥܠܬ ܡܘܬܐ), now she serves as 'an occasion of repentance' (ܥܠܬ ܬܝܒܘܬܐ; (Virg 35.6). The same idea appears in Nat 4.40, where Ephrem contrasts paradoxically many things that have been changed in Jesus' new era. Since the sinful woman has changed the way of her life, she has become an example for all penitents that they can be encouraged by her spirit: 'The sinful woman who had been a snare for men, He made her a mirror for penitents' (Nat 4.40: ܚܛܝܬܐ ܕܗܘܬ ܦܚܐ ܠܓܒܪܐ ܥܒܕܗ ܡܚܙܝܬܐ ܠܬܝܒܐ). In the next stanza, Virg 35.8, Ephrem speaks about Mary (Jn 12:1-8); and then about Martha (Virg 35.9) and the Mount

☞

sinner who fears to approach the Eucharist of bread and wine, but prays for his fear to be healed as the the sinful woman and the woman with haemorrhage were healed.[235]

---

of Olives (Virg 35.10). Lk 7:36-50 and Jn 12:1-8 are not conflated, and so the sinful woman is not identified with Mary.

[235] Cf. Fid 10.1-5. Fid 10.5-7 (Lk 7:37ff; cf. Mk 5:25ff; Lk 8:43ff):

ܕܐܦ ܗܘ ܕܢܘܣܒ ܗܘ ܪܒܐ ܡܚܐ ܗܘܐ ܕܠܐ ܠܡ ܥܘܐ ܐܢܐ ܠܒܪܘܟܐ
ܡܪܝ، ܕܡܩܣܝܢܝ

ܐܝܟ ܚܛܝܬܐ ܒܗܘ ܛܠܠܗ ܕܢܫܬܟܚ ܐܠܦܘܗ ܕܟܠܗ ܐܪܙܐ.
ܘܐܝܟ ܗ̇ܝ، ܕܐܬܪܗܒܬ ܘܐܬܠܒܒܬ ܕܐܬܚܠܡܬ ܐܟܙܐ ܪܗܒܘܬܝ
ܡܢ ܩܠܝܠܐ ܘܒܝ ܐܬܠܒܒ

ܡܢ ܝܬܪ. ܢܣܬܝ ܐܬܚܒܠ ܝܬܪ. ܗܘ ܦܓܪܝ ܕܐܝܟ ܣܡ ܐܬܥܒܕܘܗܝ.
ܢܣܬܝ ܡܪܝ، ܐܬܘܗܝ، ܡܒܘܥܐ ܕܐܣܘ̈ܬܐ ܠܟܠܢ ܟܠܗ ܥܙܐ
ܒܗ ܣܠܝܬ ܒܣܡܐ

ܪܘܡܐ ܘܢܘܗܪܐ ܕܝܢ ܦܘܡܝ ܬܘܒ ܢܘܗܪܐ ܗܘ ܪܒܐ ܕܢܘܗܪܐ ܒܟܠܗ
ܛܝܒܗ.

While the repentance of the sinful woman reconciled the Lord and pleased the faithful people, the changing of her life caused the Evil One to worry, for he saw her repentance as betrayal. This theme of the Evil One becoming despondent and full of despair is developed in Nis 60.1-8. With the repentance of the sinful woman who was the 'head of the impure' (ܪܫ ܠܛܡ̈ܐܬܐ) and of Zachaeus the 'head of the greedy people' (ܪܫ ܥܠܘ̈ܒܐ), Ephrem dramatically illustrates the fall of the Evil One whose two wings have been broken (Nis 60.9, see below). However, this hymn does not include any healing imagery. It is worth mentioning that Ephrem emphasises the influence of teaching. Since the sinful woman received Jesus' leaven (ܚܡܝܪܐ), she dispelled the evil knowledge (ܝܘܠܦ), teaching (ܬܘܠܡܕܢ) and love (ܚܘܒܐ) from her mind, so that she renounced her relationship with the Evil One and rejected his image from her thoughts.

Nis 60.1-10:

[1] ܐܘ ܬܗܪܐ ܕܟܒܝܫܗ ܠܒܝܫܐ ܡܢ ܥܠ ܐܝܟ ܕܚܛܝܬܐ ܐܬܬܘܒܬ
ܗܘܬ ܘܩܡܬ ܠܒܝܫܐ.

ܒܬܝܒܘܬܐ: ܬܫܒܘܚܬܐ ܠܚܝ ܒܠܒܘܫܘܗܝ، ܕܪܟܐ ܠܒܝܫܐ ܘܠܗ ܟܕ ܠܗ
ܐܦ ܬܘܕܝܬܐ ܕܢܣܘܚܗ ܠܟܘܡܬܐ.

[2] ܗܘܬ ܒܝܫܐ ܕܐܝܟܘ ܠܚܣܡܗ̇ ܘܐܝܟܘ ܒܣܡܡܗ̇ ܘܐܝܟܘ ܪܥܝܗ̇
ܘܚܒܬܗ̇ ܟܠܗ ܘܪܥܝܢܗ̇ ܒܣܡܐ.

☞

### 4.2.2 The Healing of the Woman with a Haemorrhage (Lk 8:43-48)

Although Ephrem comments in detail on the woman with a haemorrhage (Lk 8:43-48) in the Commentary on the Diatessaron, he also mentions her in the hymns On Virginity and On Nisibis.[236] The healing imagery of this woman is unique, and it provides a wide spectrum of Ephrem's healing theology by means of illustrating Jesus' divinity among humankind that heals men

---

[3]ܕܚܠܦ ܒܘܣܡܗ̇ ܗ̇ܘ ܐܝܠܐ ܕܒܒܝܬܐ ܒܝܬܐ ܗܒܪܗ̇ ܢܫܪܬ ܒܐܬܪܗ ܕܢܚܘܒ ܠܡܟܦܪܘ.

[4]ܠܐ ܡܢܥ ܒܗ̇ ܡܢ ܢܘܠܦܝ ܐܦ ܠܐ ܦܪ ܒܗ̇ ܡܢ ܬܘܠܥܬܐ ܦܠܛܬ ܘܫܕܬ ܥܠ ܕܐܠܦܬܗ̇.

[5]ܒܦܪܬ ܐܦ ܡܢ ܘܒܒܝܫܡ ܘܐܝܟ ܗ̇ܘ ܕܐܦ ܠܐ ܚܛܬ ܡܒܠܒܬܐ ܒܛܠܬܗ ܠܚܠܡܝ ܡܢ ܪܚܫܗ̇.

[6]ܚܒܝܪܗ ܕܢܚܘܒ ܚܝܐ ܦܪܫ ܒܗ̇ ܕܢܚܘܒ ܥܠܐ ܗܘܝ ܡܬܚܝܦܐ ܚܝܦܬ ܚܠܬ ܒܪ ܠܐ ܡܪܐܘܗ̇.

[7]ܠܛܠܬܗ ܠܫܘܒܡ ܗ̇ܘ ܕܥܬܝܕܐ ܘܒܪܦܦ ܒܝܬܐ ܒܝܬ ܠܝ ܐܦ ܠܗ̇ ܥܠܬ ܗܘܬ ܡܒܘܬܐ ܡܫܒܬ.

[8]ܚܠܦ ܚܢܪ ܒܘܣܡܐ ܒܒܝܬܐ ܒܣܡ ܠܗ̇ ܘܚܠܦ ܒܘܣܡܐ ܡܛܪܐ ܕܕܒܒܐ ܘܚܠܦ ܡܡܠܐ ܚܘܐ ܒܒܢܪܐ.

[9]ܠܒܪ ܒܒܝܬ ܪܥܐ ܒܠܘܒܐ ܠܡܪܐ ܒܒܝܬ ܪܥܐ ܠܛܒܐܬܐ ܠܛܪܡ ܒܩ̈ ܬܪܝ ܢܘܚܒ.

[10]ܐܝܟ ܗ̇ܘ ܕܪܒ ܐܬܬܠܒܕ ܠܗ ܘܐܟ ܗ̇ܘ ܕܗܪܐ ܐܬܬܡܒܬܐ ܠܗ ܡܒܡܗ ܡܒܝܠ ܐܘܡܒܘܬܐ.

Finally, mimro 2 On the Holy Week (certainly not genuine) deals at great length with the sinful woman anointing Jesus (Hebd 2.1-265). This treatment is mainly based on John's narrative. The memro speaks of Mary who is the sinful woman, Simon (in Hebd 2.5 Ephrem says that Jesus was in the 'house of Simon whose name is Leper', ܒܝܬ ܫܡܥܘܢ ܕܫܡܗ ܓܪܒܐ; cf. also Hebd 2.25) and of Judas Iscariot (Hebd 2.186; 2.208; 2.212f.) according to John's Gospel (Jn 12:1-12). The text does not include any healing imagery about the sinful woman, except that she repented and found reconciliation and forgiveness and mercy because of her faith. The verb ܐܬܬܘܝܬ is used in Hebd 2.30f. Her 'faith' (ܗܝܡܢܘܬܐ) is expressed for instance in Hebd 2.28 and the 'forgiveness' (ܫܘܒܩܢܐ) of her 'sins' (ܚܛܗ̈ܐ) and 'debts' (ܚܘ̈ܒܬܐ) in Hebd 2.35f; 2.48f; 2.11f).

236 Cf. CDiat 7.1-27; Virg 26; 31.3; 34.1; Nis 27.1-5.

because of their faith. In his interpretation and analysis of the episode of the woman with a haemorrhage, Ephrem delineates the healing's character and the power of the 'Healer of all' ( ܡܐܣܝܐ ܟܠ).

The biblical narrative of the woman with an issue of blood occurs in all three synoptic Gospels. Matthew's shorter version provides the essence of this healing miracle,[237] whereas Mark and Luke include more information. Since Ephrem comments in his Commentary on the Diatessaron on elements which only appear in Luke or Mark, one can assume that they will have been combined in the Diatessaron. Because Luke and Mark are very similar, the discussion will be mainly based on Luke.[238] The following phrases from Luke, absent from Matthew, are given attention in Ephrem's commentary:

'She who had spent all her living upon physicians, and could not be healed by anyone, …'[239] Ephrem contrasts Jesus' healing power with that of ordinary physicians and their remedies/medicines.[240] The woman showed her affliction to many physicians, to whom she gave payment, but neither their medical skill nor their medicines could cure her. In contrast, the stretching of her empty hand to Jesus restored her to health.[241]

'And Jesus said, who is it that touched me?'[242] By repeating this question twelve times, Ephrem illustrates his healing theology on the basis of this sentence that serves as a guideline to prove

---

237 Mt 9:20-22: ܘܗܐ ܐܢܬܬܐ ܕܕܘܒܐ ܗܘܐ ܕܡܗ ܫܢܝܢ ܬܪܬܥܣܪܐ܇ ܐܬܬ ܡܢ ܒܣܬܪܗ܇ ܘܩܪܒܬ ܠܟܢܦܐ ܕܠܒܘܫܗ. ܐܡܪܐ ܗܘܬ ܓܝܪ ܒܢܦܫܗ܇ ܐܦܢ ܒܠܚܘܕ ܠܡܐܢܘܗܝ ܩܪܒܐ ܐܢܐ ܡܬܐܣܝܐ ܐܢܐ. ܝܫܘܥ ܕܝܢ ܐܬܦܢܝ ܚܙܝܗ ܘܐܡܪ ܠܗ܇ ܐܬܠܒܒܝ ܒܪܬܝ܇ ܗܝܡܢܘܬܟܝ ܐܚܝܬܟܝ. ܘܐܬܐܣܝܬ ܐܢܬܬܐ ܡܢ ܗܝ ܫܥܬܐ.

238 Cf. CDiat 7.1-27. For instance the name Simon is mentioned only in Lk 8:45.

239 Lk 8:43: ܗܝ ܕܒܝܬ ܐܣܘ̈ܬܐ ܟܠܗ ܩܢܝܢܗ ܐܘܒܕܬ: ܘܠܐ ܐܫܟܚܬ ܕܡܢ ܐܢܫ ܬܬܐܣܐ.

240 Cf. CDiat 7.2; 7.7; 7.12.

241 Cf. CDiat 7.1-23.

242 Lk 8:45: ܘܐܡܪ ܝܫܘܥ. ܡܢܘ ܩܪܒ ܠܝ.

Jesus' divinity and hidden knowledge, as well as, the way that He treats people for the sake of their health.[243]

'I perceived that power had gone forth from me.'[244] Since Jesus is aware of everything, His hidden power contrasts with the physicians' visible remedies.[245] The divine power is like fire capable of purifying everything, whereas it cannot be polluted. This invisible power performs its actions for the sake of humanity.[246]

'And when the woman saw that she was not hidden, she came trembling ...'[247] For Ephrem, this sentence refers to Jesus' divinity that nothing can be hidden from it. When she saw that she had not escaped Jesus' attention, she realised that He, as the 'Healer of visible wounds' (ܐܣܝܐ ܡܚ̈ܘܬܐ ܓܠܝ̈ܬܐ) and as the 'Searcher of the mind's hidden things' (ܒܨܝܐ ܟܣܝ̈ܬܐ ܕܪ̈ܥܝܢܐ), is the 'Lord of the body' (ܡܪܗ ܕܦܓܪܐ) and the 'Judge of the mind' (ܘܕܝܢܐ ܕܪ̈ܥܝܢܐ).[248]

Finally, Jesus' encouraging words: 'My daughter, be encouraged, your faith has saved you, go in peace.'[249] With these words that caused her healing by means of her faith, Jesus, as the Lord of the crown, granted to her the 'crown' (ܟܠܝܠܐ) of victory.[250]

The opening paragraph of section 7 of the Commentary on the Diatessaron introduces the reader to the theme of the healing of the woman with the haemorrhage, together with the next paragraph, and goes on to mention the most important aspects and terms that are extended and commented on later. It starts by praising the 'hidden Offspring of Being' (ܠܝܠܕܗ ܟܣܝܐ ܕܐܝܬܘܬܐ) Who granted health to the hidden suffering/affliction.

---

243 Cf. CDiat 7.2-3; 7.6-7; 7.9-12; 7.15-16; 7.21.

244 Lk 8:46: ܐܢܐ ܓܝܪ ܝܕܥܬ ܕܚܝܠܐ ܢܦܩ ܡܢܝ.

245 Cf. CDiat 7.2.

246 Cf. CDiat 7.7-9; 7.12-13; 7.15-16; 7.20; 7.24-25.

247 Lk 8:47: ܗܝ ܕܝܢ ܐܢܬܬܐ ܟܕ ܚܙܬ ܕܠܐ ܛܥܬܗ: ܐܬܬ ܟܕ ܪܬܝܬ. It should be noticed that the verb ܛܥܬܗ can also be translated 'to escape the attention of'.

248 Cf. CDiat 7.9.

249 Lk 8:48: ܐܬܠܒܒܝ ܒܪܬܝ ܗܝܡܢܘܬܟܝ ܐܚܝܬܟܝ: ܙܠܝ ܒܫܠܡܐ.

250 Cf. CDiat 7.10-12.

[1] Glory to you, hidden Offspring of Being, because Your healing was proclaimed through the hidden suffering of her that was afflicted (Lk 8:43-48; et par). By means of a woman whom they could see, they were enabled to see the divinity which cannot be seen. Through the Son's Own healing His divinity became known, and through the afflicted woman's being healed her faith was made manifest. She caused Him to be proclaimed, and indeed she was proclaimed with Him, for it is true that His heralds will be proclaimed together with Him. Although she was a witness to His divinity, He in turn was a witness to her faith.[251]

[2] She poured faith on Him by way of remuneration, and He bestowed healing on her as the reward for her remuneration. Since the woman's faith had become public, her healing too was being proclaimed in public. Because His power had become resplendent, and had magnified the Son, the physicians were put to shame with regard to their remedies. It became manifest how much faith surpasses the [healing] art, and how much hidden power surpasses visible remedies. Beforehand, however He already knew her thoughts, even though they were imagining that He did not know her appearance. Nor did our Lord allow to be harmed those who were seeking a reason to harm, in that He had asked [who touched me]. Although He may have given the impression of not knowing, through asking who touched Him (Lk 8:45), but He was aware nonetheless of the hidden [realities], since He only healed the one whom He knew believed in Him. First of all, He saw the woman's hidden faith, and then He gave her a visible healing. If He could thus see a faith

---

[251] CDiat 7.1: ܠܟ ܫܘܒܚܐ ܝܠܕܗ ܟܣܝܐ ܕܐܝܬܘܬܐ. ܕܒܚܫܝܫܘܬܗ̇ ܟܣܝܬܐ ܕܗ̇ܝ ܡܚܫܫܬܐ. ܐܣܝܘܬܟ ܡܬܟܪܙܐ ܗܘܬ. ܘܒܐܢܬܬܐ ܕܚܙܝܢ ܗܘܘ. ܠܐܠܗܘܬܐ ܕܠܐ ܡܬܚܙܝܐ ܚܙܝܢ ܗܘܘ. ܒܐܣܝܘܬܗ ܕܝܠܗ ܕܒܪܐ. ܐܠܗܘܬܗ ܡܬܝܕܥܐ ܗܘܬ. ܘܒܡܬܐܣܝܢܘܬܗ̇ ܕܝܠܗ̇ ܕܡܚܫܫܬܐ ܗܝܡܢܘܬܗ̇ ܡܬܒܕܩܐ ܗܘܬ. ܐܟܪܙܬܗ̇ ܕܝܢ ܗ̇ܝ، ܘܐܬܟܪܙܬ ܥܡܗ. ܡܛܠ ܕܫܪܝܪܐ ܗܘ ܕܥܡܗ ܡܬܟܪܙܝܢ ܐܦ ܟܪ̈ܘܙܘܗܝ. ܐܦܢ ܒܢ ܗ̇ܝ ܠܐܠܗܘܬܗ ܣܗܕܐ ܗܘܬ. ܐܠܐ ܐܦ ܗܘ ܠܗܝܡܢܘܬܗ̇ ܣܗܕܐ ܗܘܐ ܗܘܐ.

that was not visible, how much more was He capable of seeing humanity that was visible.[252]

### 4.2.2.1 *The Affliction of the Woman with a Haemorrhage*

Ephrem calls the woman with the haemorrhage ܡܟܬܫܬܐ, 'afflicted' woman,[253] the term by which she is regularly known in later Syriac tradition. The word does not appear in the New Testament. Nevertheless, Mark provides a related term ܡܟܬܘܫܬܗ̇, when he writes: 'and she felt in her body that she was healed of her affliction'.[254] Thus, because of her affliction, she is called the 'stricken', or 'afflicted one' (ܡܟܬܫܬܐ).The woman was afflicted for twelve years, while she was haemorrhaging, and she suffered because of the physicians (Mk 5:25-26). Her wound was hidden, just as Jesus' divinity was invisible ( ܕܡܟܬܘܫܬܐ ܟܣܝܬܐ ܕܝܠܗ̇ ܡܟܬܫܬܐ).[255] Her 'wound' (ܡܟܬܘܫܬܐ) was unique for she encountered many physicians who were all unable to cure her. The ordinary 'medical skill of healing' (ܐܘܡܢܘܬܐ ܕܐܣܝܘܬܐ) actually increased her suffering and disease instead of restoring her

---

[252] CDiat 7.2: ܐܪܓܫܬ ܒܪ ܟܠܗܘܢ܆ ܣܘܟܠܐ ܡܟܬܘܫܬܐ. ܘܟܕ ܠܗ̇ ܗܘ ܦܘܪܫܢ ܣܘܟܠܗ̇ ܣܘܟܠܢܐ. ܟܕ ܕܝܢ ܡܟܬܘܫܬܗ̇ ܕܠܗ̇ ܕܐܢܬܬܐ ܠܟܠܢܫܐ ܐܬܬ ܗܘܬ. ܗܢܝܢ ܐܦ ܐܣܝܘܬܗ̇ ܕܟܠܢܫ ܡܬܕܒܪܢܐ ܗܘܬ. ܘܟܕ ܣܠܗ ܕܠܗ̇ ܐܬܠܝܛ ܘܐܬܒܪܗ ܠܒܪܐ. ܡܢ ܐܣܝ̈ܘܬܐ ܒܡܟܬ̈ܫܢܘܬܗܘܢ ܒܗܬܝܢ ܗܘܘ. ܐܬܚܝܠܬ ܠܒܪ ܒܢܐ ܡܬܪܐ ܡܟܬܘܫܬܐ ܡܢ ܐܘܡܢܘܬܐ. ܘܒܟܢܐ ܡܛܪ ܣܠܩܐ ܒܟܣܝܐ ܡܢ ܡܣܟ̈ܢܐ ܡܬܚܣܢܐ. ܠܗܘܕ ܕܝܢ ܬܪܥܘܬܗ. ܢܕܒ ܗܘܐ. ܕܗ̇ܝ ܕܐܦܠܐ ܠܦܘܪܥܢܗ̇ ܡܟܢܫ ܕܢܕܒ ܗܘܐ. ܘܐܦܠܐ ܕܝܢ ܒܗ̇ ܒܗ̇ܝ ܕܢܟܠ ܥܒܡ ܗܘܐ ܐܠܘ ܡܢܝ ܠܗ̇ܘܢ ܕܚܠܬܐ ܠܗܘܢ ܠܒܝܫܘܢ ܒܗܝܢ ܗܘܘ. ܐܦ ܠܒܪ ܕܢܣܒܬ ܠܒܘܫܗ ܗܘܐ ܐܢܫ ܠܐ ܢܕܥܐ. ܒܗ̇ ܕܢܟܠ ܕܟܢ ܩܪܒ ܠܗ. ܐܠܐ ܗܘܐ ܠܗ ܢܕܒ ܒܫܬ̈ܘܬܐ ܒܗ̇. ܕܠܐ ܐܫ ܐܠܐ ܠܟܠܢܐ ܕܢܕܒ ܕܗܘܡܢ ܒܗ. ܠܗܘܕ ܠܒܪ ܡܟܬܘܫܬܗ̇ ܗܘ ܒܫܘܬܐ ܕܐܢܬܬܐ ܚܝܐ ܗܘܐ. ܘܡܢ ܢܗܒ ܠܗ̇ ܐܣܝܘܬܐ ܠܟܠܬܐ. ܐܢ ܗܟܝܠ ܡܟܬܘܫܬܐ ܕܠܐ ܡܬܚܙܝܐ ܚܙܐ ܗܘܐ. ܚܝ ܟܡܐ ܐܢܫܘܬܐ ܡܬܚܙܝܢܝܬܐ ܚܙܐ ܗܘܐ.

[253] Cf. CDiat 7.1; 7.6.

[254] Mk 5:29: ܘܐܪܓܫܬ ܒܦܓܪܗ̇ ܕܐܬܐܣܝܬ ܡܢ ܡܟܬܘܫܬܗ̇. Ephrem quotes this in the CDiat 7.16.

[255] Cf. CDiat 7.1.

to health: 'it added pain to pain' ( ܟܐܒܐ ܥܠ ܟܐܒܐ ܐܘܣܦܬ ܠܗ).[256] In order to be healed, this suffering had to be uprooted from its root. But unfortunately during the twelve years, the physicians caused the opposite. The sickness of the woman with the haemorrhage was not just physical, but gradually also became mental. Because of the many physicians her thoughts were scattered and not gathered together. The 'scattering of her thoughts' (ܬܪܥܝܬܗ ܒܡܒܕܪܘܬܐ) parallels the flow of her blood and faith that had flowed for twelve years.[257] In CDiat 7.20, Ephrem compares her treatment by the physicians to treating a wild beast, because of her affliction. The physicians hastened to run away from her wound, even though she paid them well to heal her affliction.[258] And in CDiat 7.21, Ephrem says: 'These physicians were adding pain after pain, so that she could not be healed. [These] physicians were deceiving the minds of every one by cunning persuasion, lest [their] healing art be reproached by anyone.'[259]

The term ܡܪܕܝܬܐ of Luke 8:44 (and Mk 5:25) which Ephrem also uses,[260] describes the kind of illness she had. Blood flowed out of her, and therefore in contrast to the virgin's womb her womb was 'unclean' (ܡܪܒܥܐ ܛܡܐܐ) according to the Law.[261] The impurity according to the Law can be varied and changed by means of faith. Thus, because of her faith the Lord sent His power to her impure womb, and it was not polluted by touching the womb.[262]

---

[256] Cf. CDiat 7.16.

[257] Cf. CDiat 19: ܒܥܠܬܗ ܕܝܢ ܚܕܐ ܕܐܣܝܢ. ܬܪܥܝܬܗ ܒܡܒܕܪܘܬܐ ܠܫܢܝ̈ܐ ܗܘܣܦܘ ܐܟܙܢ ܗܘܝ.

[258] CDiat 7.20.

[259] CDiat 7.21: ܐܣܘ̈ܬܐ ܗܠܝܢ ܟܕ ܟܐܒܐ ܥܠ ܟܐܒܐ ܡܘܣܦܝܢ ܗܘܘ ܠܗ ܕܠܐ ܬܬܐܣܐ. ܐܣܘ̈ܬܐ ܕܝܢ ܒܡܦܝ̈ܣܐ ܢܟܝ̈ܠܬܐ ܪ̈ܥܝܢܐ ܕܟܠ ܐܟܙ ܠܟܠܢܫ ܗܘܘ. ܕܐܘܡܢܘܬܐ ܡܢ ܐܢܫ ܠܐ ܬܬܟܐܪ. Cf. CDiat 7.16 too. The term ܟܐܒܘ̈ܗܝ is used in CDiat 7.5.

[260] Cf. CDiat 7.7; 7.19; 7.24.

[261] Cf. CDiat 7.13; CDiat 7.7: ܐܫܬܕܪ ܗܘܐ ܚܝܠܐ ܕܢܦܩ ܡܢܗ ܠܡܪܒܥܐ ܛܡܐܐ. Cf. Lev 12:1-8.

[262] Cf. CDiat 7.7; 7.13; 7.15.

The womb is also called 'afflicted' (ܡܪܒܥܐ ܟܐܒܐ),[263] and impure blood flowed out of it for twelve years, in contrast to the rock in the desert from which purifying waters for the twelve tribes flowed.[264] The diseased 'flow' (ܡܪܕܝܬܐ ܕܒܝܫܘܬܐ) of her blood, which polluted her whole body,[265] identifies 'her being polluted by her blood' (ܕܒܟܣܝܐ ܕܕܡܗ̇ ܡܛܢܦܐ ܗܘܬ)[266] with the 'impurity in the Law' (ܠܛܢܦܘܬܐ ܕܢܡܘܣܐ).[267]

*4.2.2.2 'Your Faith has saved you' (Lk 8:48 and parallels)*

The phrase 'your faith has saved you' always appears in the last verse of the synoptic narratives that Ephrem quotes in his commentary.[268] While the term 'faith' (ܗܝܡܢܘܬܐ) is often used, the verb 'to believe' (ܗܝܡܢ) rarely occurs.[269] The faith and healing are strictly linked to each other. In CDiat 7.1, quoted above, Ephrem presents the fact that the woman was healed as a witness to her faith: 'and through the healing of the afflicted woman her faith was made manifest.'[270] Since it is Jesus Who healed her, because of her faith, He became a witness to her faith as she was a witness to His divinity.[271] Although Jesus explicitly asked about the person who approached Him, He knew her hidden faith before He made public the healing He granted to her visible humanity. Many approached Him because of neccesity, but 'He only healed the one

---

263 CDiat 7.8.

264 Cf. CDiat 7.24; Exod 17:5-6. See R. Murray, *Symbols of Church and Kingdom* (Cambridge 1975), 211-212.

265 Cf. Diat 7.24: ܡܪܕܝܬܐ ܕܒܝܫܘܬܐ. ܡܛܢܦܐ ܕܕܡܐ.

266 Cf. CDiat 7.7.

267 CDiat 7.8; 7.13; 7.15.

268 Mt 9:22; Mk 5:34; Lk 8:48: ܗܝܡܢܘܬܟܝ ܐܚܝܬܟܝ. Cf. CDiat 7.10.

269 For ܗܝܡܢܘܬܐ see CDiat 7.2-3; 7.9-13; 7.17-21; 7.27; and for ܗܝܡܢ see CDiat 7.1-2; 7.6; 7.9; 7.17; 7.17.

270 CDiat 7.1: ܘܒܐܣܝܘܬܗ̇ ܕܗ̇ܝ ܕܡܚܝܢܬܐ ܗܝܡܢܘܬܗ̇ ܡܬܒܕܩܐ ܗܘܬ.

271 CDiat 7.1: ܐܝܟ ܚܝܪ ܗ̇ܝ ܠܐܠܗܘܬܗ ܣܗܕܐ ܗܘܬ. ܐܠܐ ܐܦ ܗܘ ܠܗܝܡܢܘܬܗ̇ ܣܗܕܐ ܗܘܐ ܗܘܐ.

whom He knew believed in Him'.[272] With His question, Jesus wanted to reveal her 'faith that had touched Him' and not the identity of the person who had touched Him. Physically He was touched by many, but faithfully just by her.[273] Revealing her faith did not just happen because of the Lord's glory, but mainly because of the perfection of her healing. Ephrem distinguished between 'physical healing' ( ܐܣܝܘܬܐ ܕܦܓܪܐ - ܐܬܐܣܝܬ ܦܓܪܢܐܝܬ) and 'spiritual' or 'mental healing' ( ܐܣܝܘܬܐ ܕܪܥܝܢܐ - ܪܘܚܢܐܝܬ). Because of her faith, she was healed physically, and by showing her faith through Jesus' words, she was enabled to be spiritually or mentally cured:

> [6] If the afflicted woman had been healed and had gone away secretly, apart from the fact that the miracle would have been hidden from many people, she too would have become spiritually sick, although bodily healed. Even if she believed that He was a Righteous man because He had healed her, she would have doubted that He was God, because He would not have been aware [of her]. In fact, there were people who were touching the righteous and they were being healed, but these righteous did not know which among those who had touched them were healed. So that the mind of the one who had been healed in her body might not be sick, He took care also with regard to the healing of her mind, since it was for the sake of the healing of minds that He also drew near to the healing of bodies. This is why [He asked], »Who touched my garments?« (Mk 5:30). He revealed that someone had definitely touched Him, but He did not wish to reveal

---

272 CDiat 7.2: ܐܦ ܠܒܪ ܗܘܐ ܐܝܟ ܠܐ ܝܕܘܥܐ. ܒܗ̇ ܕܫܐܠ ܕܡܢ ܩܪܒ ܠܗ̇. ܐܠܐ ܗܘܐ ܠܗ ܝܕܥ ܒܡܫܬܐ ܒܗ̇ ܕܠܐ ܐܢܫ ܐܠܐ ܠܐܝܠܝܢ ܕܝܕܥ ܕܗܝܡܢܘ ܒܗ. ܠܡܦܪܣ ܠܒܪ ܗܝܡܢܘܬܗ̇ ܗܘ ܒܥܝܬܐ ܕܐܢܬܬܐ ܚܙܐ ܗܘܐ. ܘܟܡ ܢܣܒ ܠܗ̇ ܐܣܝܘܬܐ ܓܠܝܬܐ. ܐܢ ܡܚܝܠ ܗܝܡܢܘܬܐ ܕܠܐ ܡܬܚܙܝܢܐ ܚܙܐ ܗܘܐ. ܚܕ ܒܟܠܐ ܐܣܝܘܬܐ ܡܬܚܙܝܢܝܬܐ ܚܙܐ ܗܘܐ.

273 CDiat 7:3: ܒܙܒܢܗ ܡܚܝܠ ܗܝܡܢܘܬܐ ܗܘ ܕܒ ܩܪܒܐ ܠܗ ܠܡܪܢ ܝܕܥ ܕܢܫܘܐ ܠܡܪܢ. ܡܪܢ ܕܝܢ ܡܫܒܚܘܬܐ ܗܘ ܕܩܪܒܬ ܠܗ ܝܕܥ ܕܢܫܘܗܝ ܠܫܡܥܘܢ. The name of Simon is only mentioned in Lk 8:45.

> who it was that had touched Him. It was not that He wished to deceive, He Who, by means of this very [word], was seeking to denounce deceitfulness. Nor was it that He might avoid professing the truth. Indeed, it was [precisely] that people might profess the truth that He did this.[274]

Thus, physical healing results in mental and spiritual healing. The healing of bodies happens because of the healing of the mind and spirit. The term 'became sick' (ܡܬܟܪܗܐ ܗܘܬ) contrasts with the verb 'became healed' (ܐܬܐܣܝܬ ܗܘܬ). Likewise, 'the healing of bodies' (ܐܣܝܘܬܐ ܕܦܓܪ̈ܐ) contrasts with the 'healing of minds' (ܐܣܝܘܬܐ ܕܪ̈ܥܝܢܐ). If Jesus had not manifested her faith, although she was healed physically, she would have become spiritually or mentally sick. Ephrem discusses this against the background of healing through the 'righteous' (ܙܕܝ̈ܩܐ). The righteous healed the sick because of their faith, but they were not aware about the inner spirit and mind of those who approached them, neither who they were. If Jesus had not showed her faith, she would then have accepted Him just as a righteous person. Since Jesus is much more than these righteous people, He, as the divine Being, knew her faith, thoughts and mind. In order to cause her faith to be perfected, and with it her healing, He

---

[274] Diat 7.6: ܐܠܐ ܕܝܢ ܐܬܐܣܝܬ ܗܘܬ ܡܟܣܝܬܐ. ܘܐܙܠܬ ܐܙܠܗ̇ ܠܛܥܝܐ. ܟܕ ܗ̇ܝ ܕܒܗ̇ ܡܫܒ̈ܚܐ ܠܕܡܘܪܬܐ ܕܡܛܥܝܢܐ ܗܘܬ. ܐܠܐ ܐܦ ܗܝ ܗ̇ܝ ܕܐܬܐܣܝܬ ܦܓܪܢܐܝܬ. ܡܬܟܪܗܐ ܗܘܬ ܠܗ̇ ܪܘܚܢܐܝܬ. ܘܐܦܢ ܚܢܢ ܡܛܠ ܕܐܣܝܘܬܗ̇ ܒܗܝܡܢܘܬܐ ܗܘܬ ܒܗ ܕܙܕܝ̈ܩܐ ܗܘ. ܐܠܐ ܡܛܠ ܕܠܐ ܐܪܓܫ ܡܬܦܠܓܐ ܗܘܬ ܠܗ̇ ܕܠܘ ܐܠܗܐ ܗܘ. ܘܐܦ ܠܙܕ̈ܝܩܐ ܚܢܢ ܡܩܪܒܝܢ ܗܘܘ ܠܗܘܢ ܐܝܟܐ ܘܡܬܐܣܝܢ ܗܘܘ. ܐܠܐ ܠܐ ܠܙܕ̈ܝܩܐ. ܐܝܠܝܢ ܕܡܢ ܗ̇ܢܘܢ ܕܩܪܒܘ ܠܗܘܢ ܐܬܐܣܝܘ. ܝܕܥܝܢ ܗܘܘ ܗ̇ܢܘܢ ܕܠܐ ܡܚܝܠ ܢܛܪܗ̇ ܗܘܐ ܠܗ ܪ̈ܚܡܝܗ̇ ܕܗ̇ܝ ܕܐܬܐܣܝܬ ܒܦܓܪܗ̇. ܐܬܒܛܠܬ ܠܗ ܟܠ ܐܣܝܘܬܐ ܕܪ̈ܚܡܝܗ̇. ܠܗ̇ܘ ܕܡܛܠ ܐܣܝܘܬܐ ܕܪ̈ܥܝܢܐ ܡܢܟ ܗܘܐ. ܘܐܦ ܠܐܣܝܘܬܐ ܕܦܓܪ̈ܐ. ܡܛܠ ܗܢܐ ܡܢ ܡܢܟ ܠܢܫܘܬ, ܕܡܗܡܢܟ ܡܢܟ ܠܗ ܐܝܟ ܟܠܐ ܗܘܐ. ܕܟܕ ܕܝܢ ܡܢܟ ܠܗ ܠܐ ܨܒܐ ܕܢܓܠܐ. ܠܘ ܕܝܢ ܕܢܓܠܐ ܨܒܐ ܗܘܐ. ܗ̇ܘ ܕܓܠܝܢ ܒܗ̇ ܗܘ ܒܗܕܐ ܕܢܓܠܐ ܨܒܐ ܗܘܐ. ܘܠܘ ܡܛܠ ܕܠܐ ܢܘܕܐ ܒܫܪܪܬܐ. ܗܐ ܚܢܢ ܡܛܠ ܕܢܘܕܘܢ ܗܘܘ ܐܢܫܐ ܒܫܪܪܬܐ ܗܝ ܗܕܐ ܥܒܕ ܗܘܐ.

manifested and confirmed her faith so that she could stay mentally healthy, by believing in Jesus' divinity.

Furthermore, at the end of this paragraph, Ephrem plays on the terms 'to forget/deceive' (ܛܥܐ) and 'error/deceitfulness' (ܛܘܥܝܬܐ). The same idea is continued further in CDiat 7.9, where the verb 'to reveal' (ܓܠܐ) contrasts with the term 'to forget/go astray' (ܛܥܐ) that is used in Luke.[275] Since Jesus is the divine Being, nothing can be hidden from Him. His divine plan denounces 'error/deceitfulness' (ܛܘܥܝܬܐ) which most probably means the denouncement of Satan's leading in error. Therefore, the revealing of her faith, instead of its being forgotten, manifests her healing and makes His divine knowledge known.

> [9] Why then did our Lord say, »Who touched me?« (Lk 8:45). [It was] so that she who had become aware of her healing might know that He too was aware of her faith. By means of her restored health she knew that He was the Healer of everyone, and by His question she knew that He was the One Who searches everyone, »when she saw that even this was not hidden from Him« (Lk 8:47). In that she saw that even this was not hidden from Him, - she had indeed thought to herself that she would be able to hide it from Him - consequently, our Lord showed her that nothing was hidden from Him, lest she go away from Him deceived. She learned through this therefore that he healed visible afflictions. Moreover, she learned that He was also aware of hidden realities. She believed that He, Who healed bodily afflictions and probed the hidden realities of the mind, is the Lord of the body and Judge of the mind.
>
> Wherefore, [as though] for the Lord of the body, she subdued the body with its passions, and [as though] for the Judge of the mind, she refined the mind and its reflections. For she was afraid to commit any offence, since she believed that He could see her, He Who saw her when «she touched His cloak from behind Him» (Mk 5:27). And she was afraid to transgress, even in thought, for she knew that nothing was hidden from

---

[275] Lk 8:47: ܗܝ ܕܝܢ ܐܢܬܬܐ ܟܕ ܚܙܬ ܕܠܐ ܛܥܬܗ ....

> Him concerning whom she had testified: »For this too is not hidden from Him« (cf. Lk 8:47).[276]

The woman with the haemorrhage believed in Jesus being 'the Healer of everyone' (ܡܐܣܝܐ ܟܠ). Because of her faith, Jesus enabled her to know who He was for the sake of her 'restoration' (ܣܘܠܚܢܐ).[277] Through His words she learned, that He is not just able to 'heal the visible afflictions' (ܕܡܐܣܝܐ ܟܘܝܬܐ ܓܠܝܬܐ) of the body, but also, as He knows and searches out everything, that He is the Lord of the invisible mind. To have faith in Jesus being the Lord of the mind is infinitely more than just believing that He is the Healer of the visible body. The ability to heal the body and to know a person's thoughts illustrates His supernatural knowledge. Because the woman with the haemorrhage believed in Jesus, He crowned her faith:

> [10] If [the woman] then, once cured, had withdrawn from Him in secret, our Lord would have deprived [her] of a crown of victory. For it was fitting that the faith, which had shone forth brightly in this agony which was hidden, be publicly crowned. Consequently, He wove an eloquent crown for her, in that He said to her, »Go in peace« (Mk 5:34). The peace He gave therefore was

---

[276] CDiat 7.9: ܠܢܫܐ ܕܝܢ ܐܡܪ ܡܪܢ ܕܡܢܘ ܩܪܒ ܠܝ. ܐܠܐ ܡܛܠ ܕܬܕܥ ܗܘܬ. ܗܝ ܕܐܬܓܠܝܬ ܒܐܣܘܬܗ. ܕܐܦ ܗܘ ܐܪܓܫ ܒܡܫܡܠܝܘܬܗ̇. ܡܛܠ ܣܘܠܚܢܗ̇ ܗܘܝܠ ܝܕܥܬܗ̇. ܕܐܝܬܘܗܝ ܡܐܣܝܐ ܕܟܠ. ܘܡܛܠ ܥܘܐܠܗ̇ ܝܕܥܬܗ̇ ܕܐܝܬܘܗܝ ܒܨܐ ܟܠ. ܟܕ ܚܙܬ ܠܗ̇ ܕܝܢ ܕܐܦ ܗܕܐ ܠܐ ܛܥܬܗ. ܒܗܕܐ ܓܝܪ ܕܚܙܬ ܕܐܦܠܐ ܗܕܐ ܛܥܬܗ. ܘܡܣܒܪ ܣܒܪܐ ܗܘܬ. ܕܡܬܛܫܝܐ ܗܘܬ ܗܝ, ܗܕܐ ܕܐܬܛܠܡܬܗ̇, ܣܘܥܪܢܗ̇ ܗܟܝܠ ܗܘ ܡܪܢ ܕܠܐ ܛܠܡܐ ܠܗ ܟܕܡ. ܕܠܐ ܬܐܙܠ ܠܗ̇ ܗܝ, ܟܕ ܛܠܝܡܐ ܡܢ ܨܐܕܘܗܝ. ܥܡ ܗܝ, ܗܟܝܠ ܕܠܘܬ ܕܡܐܣܝܐ ܟܘܝܬܐ ܓܠܝܬܐ. ܠܘܬ ܬܘܒ ܕܐܦ ܝܕܥ ܒܟܣܝܬܐ ܗܘ ܘܡܢ ܕܡܐܣܐ ܒܓܠܝܬܐ ܕܦܓܪܐ. ܘܒܨܐ ܒܟܣܝܬܗ ܕܪܥܝܢܐ. ܗܝܡܢܘܬ ܕܗܘܐ ܡܪܗ ܕܦܓܪܐ ܘܕܝܠܗ ܕܪܥܝܢܐ. ܡܛܠ ܗܢܐ ܐܝܟ ܕܠܡܪܗ ܕܦܓܪܐ. ܦܓܪܐ ܡܢ ܙ̈ܟܝܘܬܗ ܥܒܕܬ. ܘܐܝܟ ܠܕܝܠܗ ܕܪܥܝܢܐ ܪ̈ܥܝܢܐ ܡܢ ܣܘܥܪܢܘܗܝ ܝܠܠܬ. ܕܣܠܩܬ ܟܢ ܠܡܫܟܠܘ ܒܟܒܝܪܐ. ܡܛܠ ܕܡܫܬܡܥܬ ܕܐܣܝܐ ܠܗ̇. ܗܘ ܕܡܢ ܕܣܝܗ̇ ܟܕ ܡܢ ܒܡܣܬܪܗ ܠܡܬܛܠܛܠܗ ܡܪܟܐ ܗܘܬ. ܘܕܚܠܬ ܠܡܫܟܠܘ ܘܠܡܫܐܠܐ ܐܦ ܒܫܘܥܒܕܐ. ܕܝܕܥܬ ܕܠܐ ܛܠܡܐ ܠܗ ܠܗ̇ ܕܝܢ, ܡܫܘܕܐ ܠܗ. ܕܐܦ ܗܕܐ ܠܡ ܠܐ ܛܥܬܗ.

[277] The term ܣܘܠܚܢܐ is also used in CDiat 7.2; 7.9; 7.18; 7.20.

the crown of her victory. But, so that it be known who the Lord of this crown was, when He said, »Go in peace« (Mk 5:34), He did not end here, but also added, »Your faith has saved you« (Mt 9:22), so that it would be known thus that the peace which His mouth wove was the crown with which He crowned her faith, »Your faith has saved you« (Mt 5:30). For, if it was faith that restored her to life, it is clear that it was also her faith that He crowned with a crown. …[278] Because of Jesus' words addressed to this woman, Ephrem speaks of an 'eloquent crown' (ܟܠܝܠܐ ܡܡܠܠܐ) that He granted to her. Her faith was victorious in the hidden agony of her life; and because of its perfection it was necessary to crown her faith publicly. Here for the first time, Ephrem quotes the sentence 'your faith has saved you'. As she was saved, she was also crowned because of her great faith. Faith is capable of bringing life as well as victory. Although her faith approached Jesus in a hidden way that is called 'stealing' (ܓܢܒܘܬܐ), because of the good will of faith, Ephrem gives a positive aspect to the negative association of stealing:

[11] »I know that someone has touched me« (Lk 8:48). Why did He not bring into the middle by force the one who had touched Him? Because he wished to teach concerning freedom of speech in relation to faith, for faith was stealing in secret and boasting its theft in public. Because He let go of His treasure in the presence of faith He was teaching faith to steal. Because He praised it after its theft He was enticing it to boast over its theft. For it stole and grew rich. It got

---

[278] CDiat 7.10: ܐܠܐ ܡܛܠ ܕܝܢ ܐܬܐܡܪܬ ܫܠܡܬ ܗܘܬ ܡܢ ܐܘܪܚܗ̇ ܒܠܘܚܝܐ. ܟܠܝܠܐ ܡܢ ܕܩܢܐ ܡܪܢ ܠܗ̇ [ܠܗ̇] ܗܘܐ. ܗܝܡܢܘܬܐ ܓܝܪ ܕܐܚܝܬ ܒܐܓܘܢܐ ܒܟܣܝܘܬ. ܘܙܕܩ ܗܘܐ ܕܬܬܟܠܠ ܒܓܠܝܘܬ. ܡܛܠ ܗܢܐ ܟܠܝܠܐ ܡܡܠܠܐ ܝܗܒ ܠܗ̇. ܒܗ̇ܝ ܕܐܡܪ ܠܗ̇ ܙܠܝ ܒܫܠܡܐ. ܫܠܡܗ ܓܝܪ ܕܦܘܡܗ ܟܠܝܠܐ ܗܘ ܠܗܝܡܢܘܬܗ̇ ܕܠܗ̇. ܐܠܐ ܕܢܬܝܕܥ ܕܡܢܘ ܡܪܗ ܕܟܠܝܠܐ ܗܢܐ. ܟܕ ܐܡܪ ܙܠܝ ܒܫܠܡܐ. ܠܐ ܫܠܝ. ܐܠܐ ܐܘܣܦ ܘܐܡܪ ܕܗܝܡܢܘܬܟܝ ܐܚܝܬܟܝ. ܐܝܟ ܕܢܬܝܕܥ ܕܫܠܡܐ ܕܓܕܠ ܦܘܡܗ ܟܠܝܠܐ ܗܘ ܕܠܗܝܡܢܘܬܗ̇ ܟܠܠ. ܗܝܡܢܘܬܟܝ ܠܟܝ ܓܝܪ ܐܚܝܬܟܝ. ܐܢ ܓܝܪ ܒܗܢܐ ܗܝܡܢܘܬܐ ܗܝ ܐܚܝܬܗ̇ ܝܕܝܥܐ ܕܐܦ ܒܟܠܝܠܐ ܗܝܡܢܘܬܗ̇ ܗܘ ܟܠܠܬܗ̇ …

caught out and was praised. This was in order to show how impoverished and abased faith can become when it does not steal, and how it is thrown into confusion when it is not taken in the act. Thus, Rachel was praised on account of the idol she stole, and was crowned on account of the falsehood which she devised (cf. Gen 31:19-35). Michal too, by means of her falsehood, sheltered David, and because of her deceit was invited to the reward of his kingship (cf. 1 Sam 19:11-17). A marvel to hear about then! That while all robberies bring robbers into shame, the theft of faith is praised in front of everyone![279]

The Lord taught faith how to steal from His treasure. The term (ܦܪܗܣܝܐ ܠܗ) explains the freedom, confidence and liberty of faith concerning any kind of deeds done by faith. Even though stealing is forbidden according to the Law, the Lord was teaching faith how to steal:

[12] »Who touched me?« The Lord of the treasure was seeking the one who had stolen His treasure, so that He might reproach and confound through her those who were unwilling to steal His treasure, even though His treasure was given over to all humanity. Those who were lazy in their faith were tormented by poverty, while those whose faith was diligent were hastening to seek it out openly, and were in a hurry to steal it in secret. »Who touched me, for power has gone forth

---

[279] CDiat 7.11: ܐܢܐ ܠܡ ܚܙܐ ܐܢܐ ܕܐܢܫ ܩܪܒ ܠܝ. ܘܠܡܢܐ ܠܐ ܐܬܝܗ ܒܦܠܛܪܐ ܠܡܬܓܠܝܘܬܐ ܠܗܘ ܡܢ ܕܩܪܒ ܠܗ. ܐܠܐ ܡܛܠ ܕܦܪܗܣܝܐ ܠܡܗܝܡܢܘܬܐ. ܕܐܠܦ ܗܟܢܐ ܗܘܐ. ܕܗܘܬ ܗܝܡܢܘܬܐ ܓܢܒܐ ܒܚܘܫܐ. ܘܗܘܬ ܡܫܬܒܗܪܐ ܒܓܢܒܘܬܗ ܒܓܠܝܐ. ܒܗ، ܓܒܪ ܕܐܪܥܠ ܠܗ ܡܢ ܡܗܝܡܢܘܬܐ. ܓܢܒܘܬܐ ܠܡܗܝܡܢܘܬܐ ܡܠܦ ܗܘܐ. ܘܒܗ، ܕܠܘܩܒܠܗ ܡܢ ܒܬܪ ܕܓܢܒܬ. ܒܓܢܒܘܬܗ ܕܬܫܬܒܗܪ ܡܬܓܪ ܗܘܐ ܠܗ. ܓܢܒܬ ܓܝܪ ܘܒܗܬܬ. ܘܐܬܓܠܝܬ ܘܐܫܬܒܚܬ. ܕܢܚܘܐ ܕܡܗܝܡܢܘܬܐ ܥܛܠܬܐ. ܕܠܐ ܓܢܒܬ ܒܗܝܢܐ ܐܬܡܣܟܢܬ. ܘܒܗ، ܕܠܐ ܐܬܬܚܕܬ ܒܗܝܢܐ ܐܬܒܗܬܬ. ܗܟܢܐ ܐܦ ܪܚܝܠ ܒܨܠܡܐ ܕܓܢܒܬ ܐܫܬܒܚܬ. ܘܒܕܓܠܘܬܐ ܕܪܟܒܬ ܐܬܟܠܠܬ. ܘܡܝܟܠ ܬܘܒ ܒܕܓܠܘܬܗ ܠܕܘܝܕ ܣܬܪܬ. ܘܒܢܟܠܗ ܠܦܘܪܥܢ ܡܠܟܘܬܗ ܐܙܕܡܢܬ. ܬܗܪܐ ܕܝܢ ܠܡܫܡܥ. ܕܟܕ ܟܠ ܓܘܢܒܝܢ ܠܓܢܒܝܢ ܡܒܗܬܝܢ. ܓܢܒܘܬܗ ܕܡܗܝܡܢܘܬܐ ܠܗ ܕܝܠܗ ܩܕܡ ܟܠ ܐܢܫ ܡܫܬܒܚܐ.

from me?« (Lk 8:45-46). Would not He, who knew that power had gone forth from Him, know upon whom the power which had gone forth from Him had rested? Or why would His power have been divided against Him? Or his healing stolen without His [consent]? But, because there are roots which give helpful [remedies] without being aware of this, our Lord wished to show the one receiving [healing] that He was aware of what He was giving. He showed that it was not like a medicine, which by its nature heals all who take it, but rather He was healing with discernment and willingly all those who love Him.[280]

The effect of faith's stealing contrasts with ordinary stealing which when found out brings blame and reproof on robbers. In contrast, faith steals and as a result becomes rich and can boast. Ephrem concludes this viewpoint by saying that faith has to steal in order to get rich and should be revealed to be honoured; otherwise it will become poor and abashed. To illustrate this, Ephrem refers to the Scriptures. He uses the example of Rachel who stole the idols of her father (cf. Gen 31:19-35), and of Michal saving David by lying (cf. 1 Sam 19:11-17). Stealing and lying can have a positive aspect if they occur because of faith.

God opens His treasure for the faithful to come and steal whatever they need from it. Ephrem contrasts 'those who are lazy in [their] faith' (ܐܝܠܝܢ ܕܡܒܛ̈ܠܝܢ ܗܘܘ ܒܗܝܡܢܘܬܐ) with 'those whose faith is diligent' (ܐܝܠܝܢ ܕܗܝܡܢܘܬܗܘܢ ܚܦܝܛܐ ܗܘܐ).

[280] CDiat 7.12: ܡܢܘ ܠܡ ܩܪܒ ܠܝ. ܡܕܪܐ ܝܕܥ ܠܚܝܠܐ ܝܕܥ ܗܘܐ ܒܟܐ ܗܘܐ. ܕܢܦܩ. ܘܠܐܝܢܐ ܒܗ ܐܝܠܝܢ ܕܝܕܥ ܠܚܝܠܘܗܝ ܠܐ ܝܕܥܗ. ܟܕ ܝܕܥ ܗܘ ܩܕܡ ܥܠ ܐܝܢ ܡܕܥܠ ܗܘܐ. ܐܝܠܝܢ ܕܡܒܛ̈ܠܝܢ ܗܘܘ ܒܗܝܡܢܘܬܐ. ܒܡܗܝܡܢܘܬܐ ܡܬܥܬܪܝܢ ܗܘܘ. ܘܐܝܠܝܢ ܕܗܝܡܢܘܬܗܘܢ ܚܦܝܛܐ ܗܘܐ. ܒܓܠܝܐ ܠܡܬܐܠ ܙܗܝܪܐ ܗܘܐ. ܘܒܡܟܣܝܐ ܠܡܬܓܢܒ ܡܫܬܪܗܒܐ ܗܘܬ. ܐܦ ܠܡ ܩܪܒ ܠܝ. ܚܝܠܐ ܠܡ ܓܢܒ ܢܦܩ ܡܢܝ. ܗܘ ܡܫܐܠ ܕܝܕܥ ܕܢܦܩ ܡܢܗ ܚܝܠܐ. ܠܐ ܟܕ ܝܕܥ ܟܠ ܐܦ ܡܢܟ ܚܝܠܐ ܕܢܦܩ ܡܢܗ. ܐܘ ܕܠܡܐ ܚܝܠܗ ܥܠܘܗܝ ܦܠܝܓ ܗܘܐ. ܘܐܣܝܘܬܗ ܒܠܥܕܘܗܝ ܡܬܓܢܒܐ ܗܘܐ. ܐܠܐ ܡܛܠ ܕܐܝܬ ܗܘ ܥܩܪܐ ܕܝܗܒܝܢ ܥܘܕܪܢܐ. ܟܕ ܗܢܘܢ ܠܐ ܡܪܓܫܝܢ. ܨܒܐ ܡܪܢ ܕܢܚܘܐ ܠܡܩܒܠܢܐ ܕܪܓܫ ܗܘ ܒܗ ܡܘܗܒܐ. ܘܚܘܝ ܕܠܘ ܐܝܟ ܣܡܐ ܕܒܟܝܢܗ ܡܐܣܐ ܠܟܠ ܕܢܣܒ ܠܗ. ܐܠܐ ܐܝܟ ܦܪܘܫܐ ܡܐܣܐ ܒܨܒܝܢܗ ܠܟܠ ܕܡܚܒ ܠܗ.

While the former will be tormented by poverty, the latter will search out so as to steal. The Lord is aware of those who steal from His treasure; and nothing can be stolen without His knowledge. Of course, the healing of the woman with the haemorrhage was stolen with His consent. The healing from the Lord's treasure, does not take place automatically as 'a medicine which by its nature heals all who take it'; nor is it like some 'roots which give helpful remedies without being aware of this'. Because the Lord knows everything, He is aware of the 'power' (ܚܝܠܐ) going from Him; and He also cures with 'discernment and willingly all those who love Him'.[281]

Although the woman with the haemorrhage was impure, the divine power touched her womb because of faith. Faith is described as 'a tree upon which divine gifts rest':

> [13] This power then went forth from the glorious divinity. He healed the unclean womb of her who was impure according to the Law, that He might show that the divinity does not abhor anything with which faith is associated. Indeed faith is a tree upon which divine gifts rest. For, [in the case of] uncleanness which comes from the Law, when faith of the will is associated with it, even if uncleanness sets apart and renders impure, nevertheless faith sanctifies and unites. Even if the Law selects and rejects, nevertheless the will renders equal and reconciles. Even if the Law commands and separates, nevertheless Elijah believed and sanctified, not in contention with the Law, but by making peace with the Law. Elijah was not rebuking the Law, that it be necessary that food be declared clean, but the Law taught Elijah that it was not necessary that food be defiled.[282]

---

[281] Cf. CDiat 7.12. For ܚܝܠܐ also see CDiat 7.2; 7.7-9; 7.13; 7.15-16; 7.20-21.

[282] CDiat 7.13: ܚܝܠܐ ܕܝܢ ܗܢܐ ܢܦܩ ܡܢ ܐܠܗܘܬܐ ܡܫܒܚܬܐ. ܘܗܘ ܐܣܝ ܠܡܪܒܥܐ ܠܛܢܦܐ. ܕܗܝ ܡܣܝܒܬ ܒܢܡܘܣܐ. ܕܢܚܘܐ ܕܠܐ ܡܣܠܝܐ ܐܠܗܘܬܐ ܡܢ ܡܕܡ ܕܡܫܘܬܦܐ ܥܡܗ ܗܝܡܢܘܬܐ. ܗܝܡܢܘܬܐ ܓܝܪ ܐܝܠܢܐ ܗܘ ܕܥܠܘܗܝ ܫܪܝܢ ܡܘܗܒܬܐ ܐܠܗܝܬܐ. ܠܛܢܦܘܬܐ ܓܝܪ ܕܒܢܡܘܣܐ ܟܕ ܡܫܬܘܬܦܐ ܠܗ ܗܝܡܢܘܬܐ ܕܨܒܝܢܐ. ܐܦ ܠܛܢܦܘܬܐ ܡܦܪܫܐ ܘܡܛܢܦܐ. ܐܠܐ ܗܝܡܢܘܬܐ ܡܩܕܫܐ ܘܡܚܠܛܐ. ܘܐܦ ܢܡܘܣܐ ܓܒܐ ܘܡܣܠܐ. ܐܠܐ ܨܒܝܢܐ ܡܫܘܐ ☞

Ephrem speaks of the 'faith of the will' ( ܗܝܡܢܘܬܐ ܕܨܒܝܢܐ). As the tree is rooted in the earth and upon it the divine gifts rest, so too faith is dependent on the free will of man. It means that faith is an action, deed or decision that has to be made by human beings of their own free will. If this faith grows up, its fruits are supernatural; holiness, purity and divine gifts. Even though the faith of free will acts in disagreement to the Law, as Elijah did by eating food brought by impure crows (1 Kgs 17:4-6), the divine power does not abhor faith's fruits. Neither does the faith abhor the Law and the will of Him Who had established the Law. Because Elijah's faithful deeds were against the Law, but not against the Law's will, he was blessed; whereas the Hebrews 'received to drink in the desert from the mouth of the pure rock' (cf. Num 20:7-11), but they did not fulfil the Law's will which is God's will.[283] Therefore, Jesus' power touched the impure womb and healed it for she believed in Him. At the same time He alludes to His miraculous birth from the virgin's womb, so that those who were unfaithful might believe in His divinity.

> [15] … Our Lord knew indeed that He had come forth from a womb, and He also knew those who did not believe that He had come forth from the womb. Consequently, He sent forth His power into an unclean womb, that perhaps by means of an unclean [womb] they might believe in His Own coming forth from a pure womb.[284]

The incarnation fulfilled the revelation of Jesus' divinity through His humanity. The miracles which happened as a result of

---

ܘܡܟܝܢ. ܐܦ ܠܒܪ ܢܡܘܣܐ ܦܩܕ ܘܦܩܕ. ܐܠܐ ܐܠܗܐ ܗܝܡܢܝܢ ܘܦܩܕ. ܠܐ ܕܝܢ ܗܘ ܡܬܚܪܐ ܥܡ ܢܡܘܣܐ. ܐܠܐ ܗܘ ܡܫܝܢ ܥܡ ܨܒܝܢܗ ܥܡ ܢܡܘܣܐ. ܠܐ ܗܘܐ ܒܪ ܐܠܗܐ ܡܒܣܐ ܗܘܐ ܠܢܡܘܣܐ. ܘܦܐܐ ܕܬܬܛܢܦܢ ܡܟܐܢ̈ܬܐ. ܐܠܐ ܢܡܘܣܐ ܡܠܦ ܗܘܐ ܠܐܠܗܐ ܕܠܐ ܘܠܐ ܕܬܬܛܢܦܢ ܡܟܐܢ̈ܬܐ.

[283] Cf. CDiat 7.13. For the terms ܢܡܘܣܐ or ܛܟܐܬܐ ܕܒܢܡܘܣܐ see further CDiat 7.7-8; 7.13; 7.15.

[284] CDiat 7.15: ܡܪܢ ܗܟܝܠ ܗܘ ܠܗ ܝܕܥ ܗܘܐ ܕܡܢ ܡܪܒܥܐ ܢܦܩ. ܐܠܐ ܐܦ ܠܐܝܠܝܢ ܕܠܐ ܡܗܝܡܢܝܢ ܒܡܦܩܬܗ ܕܡܢ ܡܪܒܥܐ ܝܕܥ ܗܘܐ. ܡܛܠ ܗܢܐ ܫܕܪ ܚܝܠܗ ܠܡܪܒܥܐ ܛܡܐܐ. ܕܐܦ ܒܗ ܒܛܡܐܐ ܢܗܝܡܢܘܢ ܒܡܦܩܬܗ ܕܝܠܗ ܕܡܢ ܡܪܒܥܐ ܕܕܟܝܐ.

faith are a witness to show His divinity to man that he should believe in Him. Since He took flesh, He invited man to cross over to divinity by means of His humanity.

> [17] Whereas the art [of healing] clothed with all kinds of [practical] wisdom was reduced to silence, the divinty clothed with garments was proclaimed. He clothed Himself in the body and came down to humanity, so that humanity might despoil Him. He revealed His divinity through signs, so that faith in His humanity alone could not be explained. He revealed His humanity that the higher beings might believe that He was a lower being, and He revealed His divinity so that the lower beings would accept that He was a higher being. He assumed a human body so that humanity might be able to accede to divinity, and He revealed His divinity so that His humanity might not be trampled under foot.[285]

In order to teach how to approach Jesus' divinity by His humanity, Ephrem refers to the faith of the sinful woman (Lk 9:36-50) and to that of Solomon and the Hebrew women. Ephrem speaks of the sinful woman's faith bearing witness to Jesus' divinity.[286] Thus, our ailing faith can be healed by the strong faith of the gentile women who have been healed because they believed in Jesus' divinity, such as the woman with the haemorrhage and the sinful woman. But the faith of the former was not healthy at the beginning, as it was scattered for twelve years, just as the flow of her blood. When she met the 'heavenly Physician' ( ܐܣܝܐ ܫܡܝܢܐ), she approached Him with 'heavenly faith' ( ܗܝܡܢܘܬܐ ܫܡܝܢܝܬܐ), and so her thoughts were collected and as result her

---

[285] CDiat 7.17: ܟܕ ܗܟܝܠ ܐܫܬܬܩܬ ܐܘܡܢܘܬܐ ܡܠܒܫܬ ܟܠ ܚܟܡܢ. ܗܝ ܐܬܟܪܙܬ ܐܠܗܘܬܐ ܡܠܒܫܬ ܠܒܘܫ̈ܐ. ܠܒܫ ܕܝܢ ܦܓܪܐ ܘܢܚܬ ܠܘܬ ܐܢܫܘܬܐ. ܕܐܢܫܘܬܐ ܩܢܝܗ ܬܗܘܐ. ܗܘ ܕܝܢ ܐܠܗܘܬܗ ܒܐܬ̈ܘܬܐ ܕܗܝܡܢܘܬܐ ܒܐܢܫܘܬܗ ܒܠܚܘܕ ܠܐ ܬܬܦܫܩ. ܗܘ ܐܢܫܘܬܗ ܕܢܗܝܡܢܘܢ ܥܠܝ̈ܐ. ܕܬܚܬܝܐ ܗܘ. ܘܗܘ ܐܠܗܘܬܗ ܕܢܩܒܠܘܢ ܬܚܬ̈ܝܐ. ܕܥܠܝܐ ܗܘ. ܢܣܒ ܦܓܪܐ ܡܢ ܐܢܫܘܬܐ. ܕܐܢܫܘܬܐ ܠܘܬ ܐܠܗܘܬܐ ܬܬܡܛܐ ܠܡܥܒܪ. ܘܗܘ ܐܠܗܘܬܗ ܕܠܐ ܬܬܕܝܫ ܐܢܫܘܬܗ.

[286] Cf. CDiat 7.18.

blood stopped flowing.[287] Heavenly faith is 'hidden faith' (ܗܝܡܢܘܬܐ ܕܠܐ ܡܬܚܙܝܢܐ - ܗܝܡܢܘܬܐ ܟܣܝܬܐ) and results in spiritual heavenly gifts. The woman with the haemorrhage could not be cured as long as she offered visible fees instead of invisible faith. She was healed when she showed her heavenly faith by stretching out her empty hand. The hidden faith contrasts with the 'visible fees' (ܐܓܪܐ ܡܬܚܙܝܢܐ); as well as ܗܝܡܢܘܬܐ ܕܠܐ ܡܬܚܙܝܢܐ with ܐܓܪܐ ܕܡܬܚܙܝܢܐ. The consequence of 'public faith' (ܗܝܡܢܘܬܐ ܓܠܝܬܐ) is the 'secret health' (ܐܣܝܘܬܐ ܡܛܫܝܬܐ). What she offered is also called 'stolen fees' (ܐܓܪܐ ܓܢܝܒܐ) that contrasts with 'hidden healing' (ܫܘܠܡܢܐ ܡܛܫܝܐ).[288] Here her faith was revealed publically for it is worthy to be highly esteemed by every one,[289] whereas in other miracles Jesus told those who He healed to remain silent, so as to teach the disciples that they should not boast or become exalted.[290] He taught them to remain silent for He 'was drawing them towards faith' (ܘܠܗܝܡܢܘܬܐ ܢܓܕ ܗܘܐ ܠܗܘܢ), 'so that the darkness of error might be driven away by the light of His miracles'.[291]

---

[287] CDiat 7.19: ܗܝܡܢܘܬܗ̇ ܒܡܪܕܝܬܐ. ܕܬܬܒܣܪܐ ܥܠܝܗ̇ ܪܗܛܐ ܗܘܬ. ܘܚܙܐ ܟܠܐ ܐܝܟ ܕܦܩܕ ܚܝܠܐ ܐܙܕܠܓܬ. ܒܥܝ̈ܢܐ ܕܝܢ ܡܚܙܝܢܘܬܐ ܐܣܝܘܬܐ ܡܚܙܝܢܐ ܡܬܒܥܝܢ ܗܘܘ. ܒܥܝ̈ܢܝܗܘܢ ܡܚܙܝܢܘܬܐ ܕܐܣܝܘܬܐ ܡܚܙܝܢܘܬܗ ܢܣܩܘܬܗ ܡܚܙܝܢܘܬܐ. ܕܗܝ ܡܬܒܥܝܢ ܗܘܘ. ܒܥܒܕܗ ܕܝܢ ܚܙܐ ܕܐܣܝܢ. ܬܘܒ ܚܙܝܬܗ ܡܒܕܪܬܐ ܠܚܙܐ ܡܢܗ ܘܠܟܠܗ ܐܬܒܥܝ ܗܘܐ. ܟܕ ܐܣܝܘܬܐ ܠܐ ܐܬܒܥܝ ܡܬܐܣܝܢ ܗܘܘ ܠܗ̇ ܢܣܩܘܬܐ ܕܒܗ ܐܓܪܐ ܡܫܟܚ ܗܘܬ ܠܗܘܢ. ܟܕ ܕܝܢ ܐܣܝܐ ܥܒܝܕܐ ܐܬܚܙܝ ܠܗ̇. ܗܝܡܢܘܬܐ ܥܒܝܕܬܐ ܩܪܒܬ ܠܗ. ܘܒܗܘܬܐ ܒܥܬ ܐܓܪܐ ܒܠܐ ܐܓܪܐ ܒܐܓܪܐ ܐܫܬܟܚ ܗܘܘ ܘܒܡܘܗܒܬܐ ܪܘܚܢܝܬܐ ܒܗ ܪܘܚܢܐ ܠܢܘܚܐ ܐܬܒܠܝܬ.

[288] CDiat 7.20.

[289] Cf. CDiat 7.21: ܕܗܝܡܢܘܬܗ̇ ܒܓܠܝܐ ܡܢ ܟܠ ܐܢܫ ܬܬܩܠܣ.

[290] Cf. Mt 6:1; 6:5; 6:16; 23:5; Mk 1:44; 5:19; 5:45; 7:36.

[291] CDiat 7.27b:
ܠܚܢܢܐ ܕܝܢ ܡܟܣܣ ܗܘܐ ܠܗ ܡܢ ܠܗܠܝܢ ܕܡܬܐܣܝܢ ܕܢܫܬܩܘܢ ܘܠܐ ܢܟܪܙܘܢ. ܘܒܗܕܐ ܐܠܦ ܐܢܘܢ ܦܩܕ ܗܘܐ ܠܗܘܢ ܕܡܬܐܣܝܐ ܕܠܚܪܘܗܝ ܠܐܣܝܘܬܗ. ܗܕܐ ܕܝܢ ܕܐܡܪ ܗܘܐ ܕܢܫܠܘܢ. ܕܠܬܠܡܝ̈ܕܘܗܝ ܢܠܦ ܕܠܐ ܢܬܚܪܘܢ ܒܐܣܝܘܬܐ ܕܥܒܕܝܢ ܘܠܐ ܢܬܒܗܪܘܢ ܘܢܬܬܪܝܡܘܢ ܕܠܒܢ̈ܝ ܐܢܫܐ ܢܣܘܢ. ܗܘ ܕܝܢ ܡܛܠ ܕܐܠܗܐ. ܘܠܗܝܡܢܘܬܐ ܢܓܕ ܗܘܐ

☞

[16] »Who touched Me? For a power has gone forth from Me« (Lk 8:45-46). In no [other] place is there a detail such as this reported about our Physician. This is because in no other place did our Physician encounter an affliction such as this. For this affliction had been presented to many physicians, yet only one Physician encountered this affliction [to heal it]. For many [physicians] had encountered and wearied her. But only One encountered her, Who was able to give her rest from the toil of many [physicians]. The art of healing encountered a shameful affliction, but added pain after pain to it. The more they came, the worse [the affliction] got (cf. Mk 5:26). The fringe of [the Lord's] cloak touched her (cf. Mt 9:20) and uprooted this suffering from its root. »She perceived within herself that she was healed of her affliction« (Mk 5:29).[292]

*4.2.2.3 The Woman with the Haemorrhage in other Texts*

Hymn 26 and 34 On Virginity and 27 On Nisibis illustrate the healing of the woman with the haemorrhage briefly. The latter

ܠܗܘܢ. ܡܕܡ ܒܢ̈ܝܐ ܕܟܠ ܐܢܫ ܒܒܪ ܗܘܐ. ܕܒܠܘܣܪܐ ܕܬܡܪ̈ܬܗ ܠܫܘܒܚܐ ܕܐܠܗܘܬܗ [ܕ]ܪܘܪܒ [ ] ܠܬܠܡ[ ] ܕܝܢ [ ] ܒ̈ܢܝ ܐܢܫ[ܐ] ܐܝܟܢ [ ] ܒܪܗܡܐ [ܕ]ܝܢ ܘܢܦܫܐ ܕܒܠܝܐ [ ] ܦܪ̈ܐ ܡܦܣܩ ܗܘܐ [ ] ܡܠܝܢ ܠܐ ܬܕܥ ܡܢ[ ] ܒܒܕܐ ܡܣܝܢ. [ܕ]ܕܠܟܠܐ ܗܘ ܡܕܡ ܕܡܠܠ ܐܠܗܐ ܗܘܐ. ܫܘܒܚܐ ܦܪܘܩܐ ܠܣܟܠܘܗܝ، ܘܐܣܝܪܬܐ ܬܘܒ ܕܠܠܐ ܗܝܡܢܘܬܐ ܕܗܘܕܪ̈ܐ ܠܟܘ. ܕܠܗܘܢ ܕܡܬܐܣܝܢ ܒܗ ܡܟܝܠ ܠܗܘܢ ܕܢܬܠܘܢ ܠܐ ܡܬܦܠܣܝܢ. ܐܠܐ ܡܒܕܪܝܢ ܠܗ. ܕܠܐ ܬܬܚܫܐ ܠܦܠܚܘܬܐ ܕܗܘܬ ܒܗܘܢ. ܡܗܘܕܪ̈ܐ ܕܝܢ ܒܪ ܚܕ ܐܬܘ̈ܬܐ ܡܬܦܠܓܝܢ ܘܠܐ ܡܗܡܡܝܢ.

[292] CDiat 7.16: ܡܢܘ ܠܡ ܩܪܒ ܠܝ. ܚܝܠܐ ܠܡ ܓܝܪ ܢܦܩ ܡܢܝ. ܒܚܕܐ ܡܢ ܕܘܟ̈ܝܢ ܠܐ ܐܫܬܪܝܐ ܠܗ ܠܐܣܝܢ ܡܠܬܐ ܕܐܝܟ ܗܕܐ. ܐܠܐ ܐܦ ܒܚܕܐ ܡܢ ܕܘܟ̈ܝܢ ܠܐ ܦܓܥܬ ܒܗ ܒܐܣܝܢ ܟܘܪܗܢܐ ܕܐܝܟ ܗܕܐ. ܗ̇ܝ ܕܝܢ ܟܘܪܗܢܐ ܕܐܣ̈ܘܬܐ ܣܓܝ̈ܐܐ ܦܓܥܬ ܗܘܬ.. ܒܗ̇ ܕܝܢ ܒܟܘܪܗܢܐ ܚܕ ܗܘ ܐܣܝܐ ܦܓܥ ܗܘܐ ܒܗ̇. ܟܠ ܕܦܓܥܘ ܒܗ̇ ܓܝܪ ܣܓܝ̈ܐܐ ܘܐܠܐܝܘܗ̇. ܦܓܥ ܒܗ̇ ܚܕ ܕܝܢ ܒܥܡܠܐ ܕܣܓܝ̈ܐܐ ܠܢܝܚܗ̇. ܐܘܡܢܘܬܐ ܕܐܣܝܘܬܐ ܦܓܥܬ ܒܟܘܪܗܢܐ ܢܟܦܬܐ. ܘܟܐܒܐ ܥܠ ܟܐܒܐ ܐܘܣܦܬ ܠܗ̇. ܟܡܐ ܠܡ ܓܝܪ ܕܐܬܝܐ ܗܘܬ ܡܒܐܫܐ ܗܘܬ. ܟܢܦܐ ܕܝܢ ܕܠܒܘܫܐ ܦܓܥ ܒܗ̇ ܘܥܩܪܗ ܠܚܫܐ ܡܢ ܥܩܪܗ̇. ܐܪܓܫܬ ܠܡ ܒܢܦܫܗ̇ ܕܐܬܐܣܝܬ ܡܢ ܡܚܘܬܗ̇.

speaks about the physicians' helplessness in contrast to the Lord's being ready to heal this woman. For twelve years she suffered among the physicians who 'stripped her naked' (ܦܪܣܝܘܗ̇). Ephrem plays on two senses of the verb ܦܪܣܝ: 'stripping' her of clothes, and put to shame. Therefore, at this point Ephrem emphasises the negative effect the physicians had. If they had healed her physically, it would have been ignominious - how much more so since they could not heal her. In order to heal her, the physicians stripped her naked and failed, whereas she was healed just as she touched Jesus' garment instead of His body. Consequently, Ephrem describes Jesus' garment as a 'physician' (ܐܣܝܐ):

ܥܣܪܐ ܬܪ̈ܬܝܢ ܘܫܢܝܢ ܦܪܣܝܘܗ̇ ܐܣܘ̈ܬܐ
ܠܗ̇ܝ ܐܢܬܬܐ ܕܕܡܗ̇ ܦܪܣܝܘܗ̇ ܘܠܐ ܥܕܪܘ
ܐܠܘ ܐܣܝܘ ܓܢܝܐ ܗܘ ܟܡܐ ܚܝܬ ܕܠܐ ܐܣܝܘ.
ܟܡܐ ܕܦܪܣܝܘܗ̇ ܗ̣ܘܘ ܢܟܦܬ ܘܐܣܝܬܗ̇
ܕܐܬܟܣܝܬ ܩܪܒܬ ܠܠܒܫܟ ܘܠܐ ܠܦܓܪܟ
ܠܒܘܫܐ ܡ̇ܢܟܦ ܟܠ ܐܣܝܐ ܗܘ̣ܐ ܗܘܐ ܠܗ̇.

For twelve years the physicians stripped [of clothes]
the woman with the blood; they stripped her, but they
did not help.
Although if they had healed her, [it would [have been a
matter of shame]; but how much more the fact
that they did not heal her?

Whereas they stripped her [of clothes],
You acted in modesty and healed her.
While she was covered,
she touched Your garment, but not Your body.
The garment that makes all chaste, became a physician
to her.

*Nis 27.2-3*

With the insult and disgrace to this woman, Ephrem illustrates the historical situation of the church in Edessa. The church, naked and insulted, is looking forward to be covered and healed by the Lord. The six years of the 'new pain' (ܟܐܒܐ ܕܚܕܬܐ) of Edessa is compared to the twelve years of the 'old' (ܥܬܝܩܐ) pain of the woman with the haemorrhage.[293]

In Virg 26, Ephrem speaks of the blood's flow ( ܪ̈ܕܝܐ ܕܕ̈ܡܟܝ) of the woman with the haemorrhage who met the 'flow of mercy' (ܪ̈ܕܝܐ ܕܪ̈ܚܡܐ). While Jesus is described as the Sun Which dissolves the frost with its rays, for she tasted the 'healing of the source of the sea of help' ( ܫܘܠܡ ܡܒ̈ܘܥܘܗܝ ܕܝܡܐ ܕܥܘܕܪ̈ܢܐ); the wound of the woman with the haemorrhage is compared to the 'fresh anger of the opened fountain' ( ܪܘܓܙܐ ܪܛܝܒܐ ܕܡܒܘܥܐ ܦܬܝܚܬܐ) that has been dried out by touching Jesus. Here Ephrem uses the term 'your finger' (ܨܒܥܟܝ) instead of hand.

ܛܘܒܝܟܝ ܐܢ̱ܬܬܐ ܕܪ̈ܕܝܐ ܕܪ̈ܚܡܐ
ܦܓܥ ܒܟܝ ܘܐܣܝ [ܘܐܣܪ] ܪ̈ܕܝܐ ܕܕ̈ܡܟܝ
ܫܡܫܐ ܗܘ̇ ܕܗܘ̣ ܫܪܐ ܩܪܝܪܘܬܗ
ܕܡܘܬܐ ܟܣܝܐ ܡܢ ܢܦ̈ܫܬܐ
ܕܙܠܝܩܘܗ̇ ܡܚܬܗ̇ ܟܣܝܐ ܘܝܒܫܗ̇
ܠܗܘ ܪܘܓܙܐ ܪܛܝܒܐ ܕܡܒܘܥܐ ܦܬܝܚܬܐ
ܒܪܝܫ ܨܒܥܟܝ ܛܥܡܬܝ، ܫܘܠܡ ܡܒ̈ܘܥܘܗܝ
ܕܝܡܐ ܕܥܘܕܪ̈ܢܐ.

Blessed are you, woman, for the Flow of Mercy
met you and healed the flow of your blood.
That Sun Who dispelled from souls
the frost of the hidden death
its hidden flash radiated and dried up
every fresh anger of the open fountain.
With the tip of your finger, you tasted the healing of
the springs

---

293 Nis 27.4-5:

ܒܗܬܐ ܚܙܬ ܬܠܡܝܕ ܡܪܢ، ܠܡܕܝܢܬܟ ܕܗܘܐ ܐܠܝܬ
ܕܐܦ ܒܒ̈ܢܝ، ܐܢܫܝܐ ܐܫܬܠܡ ܗܘ ܨܒܥܗ ܠܡܕܝܢܬܐ ܢܚܘܬ
ܘܠܡܕܝܢܬܟ ܦܪܘܫܬ.
ܐܦ ܠܐ ܦܣܩ ܢܘܟܪܝܐ ܕܡܘܬܗ، ܠܗܘ ܢܘܟܪܝܐ
ܒܪܬ ܬܪ̈ܬ ܥܣܪ̈ܐ ܐܬܐܝܗ ܦܠܚܘܬ ܥܣܪ̈ܝܢ ܕܗ̇ܝ، ܒܐܟܐ ܕܣܡܬ ܐܣܝܐ
ܕܐܣܝܬ ܟܐܒܐ ܥܬܝܩܐ.

of the Sea of benefits.

*Virg 26.6*

In Virg 34.1, Ephrem presents the fear, faith, will and love of the woman with the haemorrhage. Likewise, Ephrem speaks about Jesus as being willing to meet her in order to dry up her wound.

ܕܕܡܗ̇ ܕܚܠܬ ܗܘܬ ܕܬܩܪܘܒ ܠܡܪܐ ܟܠ
ܐܬܠܒܒܬ ܡܢ ܗܘ̇ ܡܠܒܒ ܠܚܛܝ̈ܐ
ܒܨܒܝܢܗ̇ ܐܪܓܫ ܕܨܒܝܐ ܗ̱ܝ ܕܬܬܒܣܡ ܒܗ
ܠܗܝܡܢܘܬܗ̇ ܐܣܬܩܒܠ ܐܬܐ ܕܗܘ̣ܐ ܨܒܐ
ܕܡܗ̇ ܪܕܐ ܘܚܘܒܗ̇ ܟܒܝܫ ܗܘܐ
ܒܕܡܗ̇ ܚܕܝܬ ܗܘܬ ܕܐܘܒܫܗ
ܘܒܡܒܘܥܐ ܕܚܘܒܗ̇ ܕܐܪܕܝܗ.

The woman with the haemorrhage feared to approach
the Lord of all.
She was encouraged by the One Who encourages
sinners.
In her wish He perceived that she wanted to delight in
Him
He happened upon her faith [but] He was present since
He willed it.
Her blood flowed, but her love was restrained.
As to her blood, she rejoiced that He dried it up,
but as to the fount of her love, [she rejoiced] that He
made it flow.

*Virg 34.1*

In hymn 10 On Faith, Ephrem honours Jesus as the Incarnate-Divine-Logos, Who is present as fire and spirit in the church's sacraments. Ephrem shows the right attitude and way of approaching the Divinity: he asks in humility for the help and will of God in order to be enabled to start in the lowest rank. He wonders about the many explanations of the one divine nature.[294] Ephrem wants to start as John did undoing the straps of the Lord's sandals, and as the woman did approaching (touching) His robe, so that the Eucharist of bread and wine can be wondered at.[295] Ephrem dares to go further, from the robe to the body of Christ. But he prays for his fear to be healed in the same way as the curing

---

[294] Cf. Fid 10.1-3.

[295] Fid 10.4-5.

of the sinful woman and the woman with the haemorrhage.[296] Thus, the power of the Lord dwells in the sacraments of the church as it did in Jesus' robe, body and spittle. Therefore, man should draw near to the Church's sacraments, as people drew near to Jesus and were healed.

### 4.2.3 The Blind Receive Sight

The opening of the eyes of the blind is considered as a great miracle that Jesus performed on several occasions. In his texts, Ephrem refers to this act of giving sight to the blind to demonstrate the co-existence of Jesus with the Father from the beginning of the World. In the context of the man born blind (Jn 9:1-41), Ephrem illustrates the deficency of human nature and its perfection through Jesus. Also attention is drawn to the power of the divine names which are invoked when the miracles take place.[297] Commenting on the blind Bartimaeus of Jericho (Mk 10:46-52),[298] Ephrem distinguishes strictly between the corporeal eye and that of the mind. Faith and trust play an essential role. The

---

[296] Fid 10.5-7 (Lk 7:37ff; cf. Mk 5:25ff; Lk 8:43ff):
ܕܐܦ ܗܘ ܕܢܘܣܚ ܗ̇ܘ ܪܟܐ ܡܟܐ ܗܘܐ ܕܠܐ ܠܡ ܥܘܐ ܐܢܐ ܠܒܪܘܟܐ
ܡܪܝ ܕܡܫ̈ܩܝܢ
ܐܝܟ ܣܝܡܬܐ ܒܗ̇ܘ ܛܠܠܗ ܕܢܣܒܬܟ ܐܠܦܗ ܕܒܢܝܗ ܐܨܪܐ.
ܘܐܝܟ ܗ̇ܝ ܕܐܬܗܪܒܬ ܘܐܬܠܒܒܬ ܕܐܬܠܚܡܬ ܐܣܐ ܪܗܒܘܬܗ̇
ܡܢ ܟܢܦܗ ܘܒܟ ܐܬܠܒܒ
ܡܢ ܚܕ ܢܣܒܬܟ ܐܬܚܒܠ ܚܕ ܗܘ ܦܓܪܟ ܕܐܝܟ ܣܠܩ ܐܣܬܚܝܗ.
ܢܣܒܬܟ ܡܪܝ ܐܣܝܬܗ̇ ܡܟܡܟܐ ܕܡܣܟܢ̈ܐ ܠܟܡܫܝܢ ܟܠܗ ܠܟܐ ܫܪܐ
ܒܗ ܣܠܝܟ ܚܡܫܐ
ܪܘܩܐ ܕܚܘܪܐ ܕܡܢ ܦܘܡܟ ܬܘܒ ܢܘܗܪܐ ܗܘ ܪܟܐ ܕܢܘܗܪܐ ܟܠܗ
ܠܒܝܫܗ.

[297] Cf. CDiat 16.28-32; Fid 41.7; Virg 35.3; Azym 13.12. - Jn 9:1-41 speaks of the man born blind to whom Jesus granted sight through spitting on the ground, putting mud on his eyes and telling him to wash in the pool of Siloam. The passage is not found in the other Gospels, though Mt 8:22-26 tells of the healing of a blind man at Bethsaida, to whom Jesus gave sight through spitting on his eyes and putting his hand on them.

[298] The name Bartimaeus is only mentioned in Mk 10:46-52. The parallel passages are slightly diferent. While Mt 20: 29-34 (so too Mt 9:27-34) speaks of two blind men in Jericho, Lk 18:35-43 has just one.

metaphor of the sun is used to clarify the sense of the spiritual interior eye.[299] Ephrem develops the idea of the inner eye which is blinded by free will and evil thought. Its existence and healthy situation is highly relevant to everyone at all times. Therefore, he asks the Lord to enlighten 'our' interior eye for our own benefit.[300]

### *4.2.3.1 The Healing of the Man Born Blind (Jn 9:1-41)*

Ephrem attributes the creation of the world not only to the first person of the Trinity, namely to the Father, but also to the Son. When drawing attention to the clay/mud (ܛܝܢܐ) from which Jesus formed eyeballs for the man born blind (Jn 9:1-41), Ephrem emphasises Jesus' divinity and His role as the One Who fulfilled 'what was lacking in the fashioning' (ܚܣܝܪܘܬܗ ܕܓܒܝܠܬܐ). Immediately after the quotation from John's Gospel, Ephrem comments:

> »After He had said this, He spat on the ground, and fashioned clay from His spittle« (Jn 9:6), and made the eyes with His clay. He caused the light to spring forth from the dust, just as He did in the beginning, when the shadow of the heavens was spread out as darkness over everything (cf. Gen 1:2-3). He commanded the light, and it was born from the darkness.[301]

The spitting on the ground and making clay from the spittle in order to fashion eyes with the clay, is compared to the creation of the world. Here, Ephrem alludes to the equality of the Son with His Father in divinity, for the world was created by the Father through the Son. Ephrem illustrates the Son's action as perfection of the Father's creation:

> Likewise here too, He fashioned clay from His spittle, and brought to fullness what was lacking in the fashioning, which was from the beginning, to show that He by Whose hand that which was lacking in [human]

---

299 Cf. CDiat 15.22; Eccl 9.8; Iei 6.4-8.

300 Cf. Fid 45.1-2; 65.10-13; Eccl 13.7-15; Iei 6.4-8; CDiat 13.13.

301 CDiat 16.28: ܘܟܕ ܐܡܪ ܗܠܝܢ. ܪܩ ܥܠ ܐܪܥܐ ܘܓܒܠ ܛܝܢܐ ܡܢ ܪܘܩܗ. ܘܓܒܠ ܥܝ̈ܢܐ ܡܢ ܛܝܢܗ ܘܐܕܢܚ ܢܘܗܪܐ ܡܢ ܥܦܪܐ. ܐܝܟ ܕܥܒܕ ܒܪܫܝܬ. ܟܕ ܛܠܠܗ ܕܫܡܝܐ. ܚܫܘܟܐ ܥܠ ܟܠ ܦܪܝܣ ܗܘܐ. ܘܦܩܕ ܠܢܘܗܪܐ. ܘܡܢ ܚܫܘܟܐ ܐܬܝܠܕ.

> nature was brought to fullness, was the One by Whose hand the fashioning had been established from the beginning.[302]

While Ephrem draws attention to the deficiency of nature, he does not explain here the imperfect situation of fashioning and nature. Questions arise, such as: does Ephrem understand the creation of the world as imperfect? Or does the imperfect situation go back to the fall from Paradise? It seems later that Ephrem refers what was lacking in the fashioning (ܫܘܡܠܝܘܬܗ ܕܓܒܝܠܬܐ) or human nature (ܫܘܡܠܝܘܬܗ ܕܟܝܢܐ) to Adam himself, and finally to the human body lacking limbs (ܚܘܣܪܢ ܗܕܡܐ). The Son Who co-exists with His Father from the beginning fulfilled what was lacking in Adam through the 'body' (ܦܓܪܐ ) which means through His own body by being incarnated:

> Because they were unwilling to believe that He was before Abraham, the action persuaded them that He was the Son of Him Whose hand had formed the First Adam from the earth (cf. Gen 2:7). Thus, by means of the body, He restored to fullness what was lacking.[303]

In Jesus' healing miracle the mystery that He is the Son of the Creator was hidden: 'and a symbol of the Son of the Creator of life was delineated in His work of Healing'.[304] Healing is taken as a general good deed that indicates God. The light was born from clay by the order, that means, by the command and words of God, as at the creation of the earth and the springing forth of light from the darkness (cf. Gen 1:2-3). Man came to exist by the commandment of the Lord. The existence of man cannot be described by the schema of the four traditional elements. Ephrem illustrates how

---

302 CDiat 16.28: ܗܟܢܐ ܐܦ ܗܪܟܐ ܒܟܠ ܠܢܫܐ ܗܘ ܪܘܫܡܗ. ܘܟܠ ܫܘܡܠܝܘܬܗ ܕܓܒܝܠܬܐ. ܗܝ ܕܡܢ ܒܪܝܬ. ܕܢܘܕܥ ܕܗܘܝܘ ܕܒܐܝܕܗ ܐܬܟܠܠܬ ܫܘܡܠܝܘܬܗ ܕܟܝܢܐ. ܒܐܝܕܗ ܗܘ ܐܬܬܩܢܬ ܓܒܝܠܬܐ ܕܡܢ ܒܪܝܬ.

303 CDiat 16.28; ܘܕܠܐ ܨܒܘ ܕܢܗܝܡܢܘܢ. ܕܩܕܡ ܐܒܪܗܡ ܐܝܬܘܗܝ، ܗܘܐ. ܐܦܝܣ ܐܢܘܢ ܥܒܕܐ ܕܒܪܗ ܗܘ ܕܗܘܝܘ ܕܒܐܝܕܗ ܓܒܠܗ ܡܢ ܐܪܥܐ ܠܐܕܡ ܩܕܡܝܐ. ܕܗܐ ܫܘܡܠܝܘܬܗ ܒܝܕ ܦܓܪܐ ܡܠܐ ܗܘܐ.

304 CDiat 16.31: ܘܐܪܫܡ ܗܘܐ ܒܥܒܕ ܐܣܝܘܬܗ ܐܪܙܐ ܕܒܪܗ ܗܘ ܕܥܒܘܕܐ.

earth and Jesus' spittle, or water, are sufficient as elements for the creation of the body's missing limbs.

> In order to put to shame once more those who were saying that human beings were formed from the four elements, behold, He restored the deficiency of the members/limbs [of the body] from the earth and from spittle.[305]

Here, even though Ephrem does not explicitly speak of 'creatio ex nihilo', he draws attention to the power of the divine names spoken over the action, so that it is easy to assume that God's word alone performs the deed. The mud, spittle and water in the case of the man born blind are not essential elements for forming the eyeballs and giving him sight. But they are elements which indicate the miracle to the beholders in order to increase their faith and so that they should be healed spiritually.

> [He did] these things for their benefit, since miracles [were effective] in inciting them to believe. »The Jews ask for miracles« (1 Cor 1:22). It was not [the pool of] Siloam that opened [the eyes of] the blind man, just as it was not the waters of the Jordan that purified Naaman (cf. 2 Kgs 5:14). It was [the Lord's] command which effected it. So too, it is not the water of our atonement that cleanses, rather, it is the names pronounced over it which give us atonement.[306]

Although this healing miracle causes people to think that the healing of the man born blind was a skill effected through the clay/mud, spittle and water, it was not, for Jesus was sure and without any doubts that He is capable to give him sight. The

---

[305] CDiat 16.29: ܘܕܢܒܗܬ ܬܘܒ ܠܐܝܠܝܢ ܕܐܡܪܝܢ ܕܡܢ ܐܪܒܥܐ ܐܣܛܘܟܣܝܢ ܐܬܓܒܠ ܒܪ ܐܢܫܐ. ܗܐ ܒܪ ܡܢ ܐܪܥܐ ܘܪܘܩܐ ܬܘܡ ܚܘܣܪܢ ܗܕ̈ܡܐ. Cf. CDiat 16.32: ܘܡܢ ܚܝܠ ܡܝ̈ܐ ܠܫܝܠܘܚܐ ܡܛܪ ܡܫܠܡܐ ܠܣܘܟܠܗ.

[306] CDiat 16.29: ܘܗܠܝܢ ܠܡܘܬܪܢܗܘܢ ܡܛܠ ܕܐܬ̈ܘܬܐ ܗܘ ܡܥܝܪܢ ܗܘܝ ܠܗܘܢ ܕܢܗܝܡܢܘܢ. ܝܗܘܕ̈ܝܐ ܠܡ ܓܝܪ ܐܬ̈ܘܬܐ ܗܘ ܫܐܠܝܢ. ܠܘ ܓܝܪ ܫܝܠܘܚܐ ܦܬܚ ܣܡܝܐ. ܐܝܟ ܕܠܘ ܡܝ̈ܐ ܕܝܘܪܕܢܢ ܕܟܝܘ ܠܢܥܡܢ. ܐܠܐ ܦܘܩܕܢܐ ܗܘ ܣܥܪ. ܘܐܦ ܡܝ̈ܐ ܕܚܘܣܝܢ ܠܘ ܗܢܘܢ ܡܕܟܝܢ. ܐܠܐ ܫܡ̈ܗܐ ܕܥܠܝܗܘܢ ܡܬܩܪܝܢ. ܗܢܘܢ ܗܘܝܢ ܠܢ ܡܚܣܝܢܐ. The atonement water (ܡܝ̈ܐ ܕܚܘܣܝܢ) is the water of the baptism.

healing power was hidden in Jesus' words as 'glorious treasures' (ܣܝ̈ܡܬܐ ܡܫܒܚܬܐ).

> There were indeed glorious treasures hidden in [the Lord's] few words, and a symbol was delineated in His word of healing, that He is the Son of the Creator of life. [He said], »Go, wash your face« (Jn 9:7), as though someone might think that this healing was closer to a [medical] skill than to a miracle. For He sent him to wash, in order to show, that the man was not in doubt that He would heal him. Thus, in making inquiries as he went about, he would be proclaiming the event and his faith would be seen.[307]

Jesus performed this healing miracle to increase the faith of the observers, 'since miracles [were effective] in inciting them to believe'.[308] When Jesus healed the man born blind, physically by giving him sight, many others were healed spiritually. For instance, in contrast to the sinful woman who was sick because of her sinful way of life, this man was born blind physically, not because of his sin or that of his parents, but because of the glory of God (cf. Jn 9:2-3). Even though he was physically blind, spiritually he was guiding the others to see Jesus Christ as the Son of God. His blindness is indicated in the visible clay/mud (ܛܝܢܐ), whereas their blindness is described as invisible blindness of the heart (ܥܘܝܪܘܬ ܠܒܐ). Therefore, the healing of the man born blind initiated the enlightenment of the hearts of many:

> Those whose [eyes] were exteriorly open were led by the blind man publically who was able to see interiorly; and the blind man was led in a hidden way by those whose [eyes] were opened, but who were interiorly blind. The [blind man] washed the clay from his eyes, and he could see. These others washed their blindness from their hearts, and were approved. When our Lord

---

[307] CDiat 16.31: ܠܡ̈ܠܐ ܐܝܟ ܓܝܪ ܒܒܨܝܪ̈ܬܐ ܡ̈ܠܘܗܝ ܙܥܘܪ̈ܬܐ ܣܝ̈ܡܬܐ ܡܫܒܚܬܐ. ܘܐܪܫܡ ܗܘܐ ܒܡܠܬ ܐܣܝܘܬܗ ܐܪܙܐ ܕܒܪܗ ܗܘ ܕܒܪܘܝܐ. ܕܚܝ ܠܡ ܙܠ ܐܫܝܓ ܐܦ̈ܝܟ ܐܝܟ ܕܢܣܒܪ ܐܢܫ ܕܠܐܘܡܢܘܬܐ ܗܘ ܩܪܝܒܐ ܗܕܐ ܐܣܝܘܬܐ. ܡܛܠ ܗܢ ܕܠܡܣܚܐ ܫܕܪܗ ܠܒܪ ܕܢܫܓ. ܕܢܚܘܐ ܕܠܐ ܡܦܠܓ ܗܘܐ ܥܠܘܗܝ ܕܡܐܣܐ ܠܗ. ܘܟܕ ܡܫܐܠ ܘܐܙܠ ܡܟܪܙ ܗܘܐ ܠܣܘܥܪܢܐ. ܘܐܦ ܬܬܚܙܐ ܗܝܡܢܘܬܗ ܕܝܠܗ.

[308] CDiat 16.29.

> opened [the eyes of] one blind man publicly at that time, He opened [the eyes of] many blind people secretly. That blind man who was [indeed] blind was like a capital sum for our Lord, since He made gains of many blind people through him from blindness of heart.[309]

To clarify this idea, Ephrem refers to Jesus' word: 'those who do not see will see, and those who do see will become blind' (Jn 9:39). Ephrem interprets this as the paradox of the spiritual and physical sight.

> »<Those who do not see will see;> those who see will become blind« (Jn 9:39). [He said] this with regard to the blind, that they would see him physically, and with regard to those with open [eyes], for He was not perceived by them spiritually.[310]

There is a significant difference between the sight of the physical eyes and the sight of faith and mind. According to John's Gospel, Ephrem rebukes the Pharisees for ignoring Jesus' healing miracles and reproaching Him for healing on the Sabbath. Provocatively Ephrem asks: 'Well then, who in fact has broken [the Sabbath] more? Our Saviour, Who healed [on it], or those who spoke with envy about their benefactor?'[311]

The wonder of the healing of the blind man is neglected by the Pharisees. They are not aware of the jealousy in their hearts which is invisible and against the divine Law, but they draw

---

[309] CDiat 16.30: ܦܬܝܚܝܢ ܗܘܘ ܓܠܝܐܝܬ ܦܬܘܚܝܐ ܠܣܡܝܐ ܕܚܕܐ ܗܘܐ ܡܢ ܠܒܪ. ܘܦܬܚ ܗܘܐ ܒܟܣܝܐܝܬ ܣܡ̈ܝܐ ܠܦܬܚܝܐ ܕܒܥܘܪܝܢ ܒܠܒܗܘܢ. ܘܐܬܚܙܝ ܠܗ. ܐܝܟܢܐ ܗܘܐ ܡܢ ܠܒܪ. ܐܝܟܢܐ ܗܘ ܠܥܘܝܪܐ ܡܢ ܗܠܝܢ ܒܡܪܘܬܐ ܡܢ ܠܒܘܗܝ ܘܐܬܒܣܪ ܠܗܘܢ. ܘܒܗ ܚܕ ܣܡܝܐ ܦܬܚ ܗܘܐ ܡܪܢ ܗܘ ܒܗ ܓܠܝܐܝܬ. ܣܡ̈ܝܐ ܣܓܝ̈ܐܐ ܦܬܚ ܗܘܐ ܒܟܣܝܐܝܬ. ܘܗܘ ܣܡܝܐ ܕܒܪܝܐ. ܗܘܐ ܗܘܐ ܠܗ ܠܡܪܢ ܐܝܟ ܪܫܡܠܐ. ܕܒܗ ܬܓܪ ܐܬܬܓܪ ܡܪܢ ܣܡ̈ܝܐ ܣܓܝ̈ܐܐ ܡܢ ܥܘܝܪܘܬ ܠܒܐ.

[310] CDiat 16.32: ܕܐܝܠܝܢ ܕܚܙܝܢ ܠܗ ܢܣܡܘܢ. ܗܠܝܢ ܕܝܢ ܠܣܡ̈ܝܐ ܕܢܚܙܘܢܝܗܝ ܦܓܪܢܐܝܬ. ܘܠܦܬܝ̈ܚܐ ܕܠܐ ܡܬܚܙܐ ܗܘܐ ܠܗܘܢ ܪܘܚܢܐܝܬ.

[311] CDiat 16.32: ܐܝܢ. ܡܢܘ ܟܕܝܢ ܐܣܓܝ ܫܪܝܗ. ܦܪܘܩܢ ܕܐܣܝ. ܐܘ ܗܢܘܢ ܕܡܠܠܘ ܚܣܡܐ ܥܠ ܡܪܐ ܛܒ̈ܬܗܘܢ.

attention to the Sabbath. In Fid 41.7, Ephrem compares the scribes with Balaam who ignored the miracle of the Lord:

ܟܕ ܡܠܠܬ ܡܢ ܥܠ ܗܝ ܗܝ ܐܬܢܐ
ܒܠܥܡ ܚܙܐ ܬܡܗܐ ܘܐܪܦܝ ܫܒܩ ܬܗܪܐ
ܘܐܟܝܢ ܗܘ ܕܡܠܠܐ ܗܘ ܦܘܡܗ ܕܐܬܢܐ
ܛܥܐ ܠܗ ܘܠܚܡܪܗ ܡܦܝܣ ܗܘܐ
ܣܦܪܐ ܫܒܩܘ ܬܗܪܐ ܣܡܝ̈ܐ ܕܐܬܦܬܚܘ
ܘܥܠ ܫܒܬܐ ܘܛܝܢܐ ܒܒܥܬܐ ܡܥܩܒܝܢ ܗܘܘ

When the ass spoke all of a sudden,
Balaam saw a wonder but neglected the miracle.
As though the mouth of the ass was capable of speaking,
he went astray, persuading his donkey (Num 22:15-35).
The scribes let a miracle go, the blind whose [eyes] were opened,
and they set forth on an inquiry into the Sabbath and mud.

*Fid 41.7*

In hymn 35 On Virginity, in contrast to the priests' jealousy, Ephrem expresses his wonder about Jesus as a Physician Who heals in unexpected ways. Through the elements which make the eyes blind, like 'the place where He spat' (ܕܘܟܬܐ ܕܪܩ ܗܘܐ ܒܗ̇), 'the clay/mud' (ܛܝܢܐ), 'dust' (ܥܦܪܐ) and 'speck' (ܟܘܪܐ), He granted sight to the man born blind.

ܕܘܟܬܐ ܕܪܩ ܗܘܐ ܒܗ̇ ܬܗܪܐ ܢܒܥ ܒܓܘܗ̇
ܕܡܢ ܛܝܢܐ ܫܝ̈ܦܐ ܥܒܕ ܗܘܐ ܠܥܝ̈ܢܬܐ
ܫܩܠ ܘܫܕܐ ܥܦܪܐ ܒܥܝ̈ܢܐ ܘܐܬܦܬܚ
ܐܘ ܐܣܝܐ ܕܠܣܡܝܐ ܒܟܘܪܐ ܡܦܬܚ ܗܘܐ
ܚܣܡܘ ܒܗ ܟܗ̈ܢܐ ܕܫܪܗ̇ ܠܫܒܬܐ
ܕܫܪܝܐ ܕܝܠܗ̇ ܠܗܘܢ ܐܣܪ
ܕܫܪܝܘ ܐܬܦܫܪܘ ܘܐܬܒܝܫܘ

A wonder sprouted in the place where He spat
that from clay He made salves for the eyes (cf. Jn 9:6-7).
He took and cast dust on the eyes, and they were opened.
O Healer Who opened [the eyes of] the blind man with a speck!
The priests were jealous that He had broken the Sabbath,
for the breaking of it bound them (cf. Jn 9:16ff):

> because they disputed, they were bound and stifled.[312]
>
> *Virg 35.3*

Here again, Ephrem contrasts the healing miracle with the reaction of the priests who were bound because of their jealousy. Their behaviour is transferred to those who pry into the mystery of Jesus' divinity. Jesus is called the 'Physician' (ܐܣܝܐ) Who performed the miracle through the clay. In hymn 13 On Unleavened Bread, the term clay/mud (ܛܝܢܐ) is mentioned together in the context of accusing those who dishonoured Jesus:

> ܛܝܢܐ ܕܪܩܗ ܦܬܚ ܣܡܝܐ
> ܕܢܬܦܛܪ ܠܗ ܥܡܐ ܕܠܡܢ ܨܥܪ
>
> The clay from His spittle opened [the eyes of] the blind man,
> so that the People might be accused seeing whom it was
> they had treated shamefully.
>
> *Azym 13.12*

### *4.2.3.2 The Healing of the Blind Bartimaeus (Mk 10:46-52)*

The passage about the blind man of Jericho (Lk 18: 35-43)[313] called Bartimaeus (Mk 10:46-52) is introduced by Ephrem with a reference to Jesus as the Light Which came into the world: 'the Light came into the world to give sight to the blind and faith to those who lacked it.'[314] There is a parallel drawn between 'sight' (ܚܙܬܐ) and 'faith' (ܗܝܡܢܘܬܐ). As Jesus gave sight to the blind, so too he granted faith to those who lacked it. Faith is necessary, because sight involves not just corporeal sight, but also spiritual. Ephrem emphasises the role of faith when he quotes Lk 18:22: '»see, your faith has saved you« (Lk 18:22); He did not say to him, it is your faith that has caused you to see.'[315]

---

[312] Virg 35.3.

[313] Mt 20:29-34 speaks of two blind men in Jericho.

[314] CDiat 15.22: ܐܬܐ ܢܘܗܪܐ ܠܥܠܡܐ ܕܠܣܡܝܐ ܢܬܠ ܚܙܬܐ. ܘܠܚܣܝܪܐ ܗܝܡܢܘܬܐ.

[315] CDiat 15.22: ܚܙܝ ܠܟ ܗܝܡܢܘܬܟ ܐܚܝܬܟ. ܘܠܐ ܐܡܪ ܠܗ ܕܗܝܡܢܘܬܟ ܐܚܝܬܟ.

Faith gives life to people who trust Jesus. The priority is the inner circumstances of men. If men are saved, then the physical healing can follow, as with the blind man of Jericho: 'that [faith] had first given him life, and then corporeal sight' ( ܕܠܘܩܕܡ ܚܝܐ ܝܗܒܬ ܠܗ. ܘܗܡ ܦܘܬܚ ܥܝܢܐ). The healing miracle is strictly related to faith. Therefore, because of his faith the blind man called Jesus not just 'Jesus the Nazarene' as the others called Him without love, but 'Jesus the Son of David, have mercy on me'.[316] Because of this faith his inner eyes were more enlightened than those of the others:

> When our Lord saw that the eyes of his inner self were greatly enlightened and the eyes of the outer self did not see even a little, He enlightened the eyes of the outer self like those of the inner self, so that, when [the blind man] wanted to hasten towards Him again, he would be able to see Him.[317]

Although Bartimaeus could not see Jesus corporally, he saw more than the others were able to see; he saw in Him the invisible and incomprehensible God. More than the other people he believed and confessed that He is the incarnate God. In Eccl 9.8, Ephrem praises Bartimaeus for seeing the image of God. His example serves as a way how to approach God and benefit from Him:

> Again the teaching of love brought me in captivity, for
> it made me a disciple of its words.
> It commanded me to open my ears, so that its word
> will be planted in my mind.
> Watch him and imitate him, the blind man, who called
> out on the way.
> The people rebuked him to keep silent, but he went on
> to raise his voice still further.
> His persistence pleased his Saviour;

---

[316] CDiat 15.22: ܟܕ ܫܐܠ ܠܒܪ ܕܘܝܕ. ܐܫܬܘܝ ܠܗ ܕܢܫܡܥ ܩܠܗ. ܣܡܝܐ. ܢܕܥ ܕܠܘ ܒܢܘܗܪܐ ܐܫܬܘܝ ܠܗ. ܫܡܥܗ ܕܟܠܗܒܢܝܐ ܘܐܚܕ ܗ̇ܘ ܕܣܡܝ̈ܐ. ܕܒܪܗ ܕܕܘܝܕ ܐܬܪܚܡ ܥܠ. Here, Ephrem paradoxically contrasts Jesus' action with that of David (2 Sam 5:6-8).

[317] CDiat 15.22: ܟܕ ܚܙܐ ܡܪܢ ܕܥܝܢ̈ܐ ܕܠܓܘ ܣܓܝ ܢܗܝܪ̈ܢ. ܥܝܢ̈ܐ ܕܝܢ ܕܠܒܪ ܐܦ ܠܐ ܩܠܝܠ ܚܙܝ. ܐܢܗܪ ܥܝܢ̈ܐ ܕܠܒܪ ܐܝܟ ܥܝܢ̈ܐ ܕܠܓܘ. ܕܟܕ ܨܒܐ ܕܢܪܗܛ ܬܘܒ ܠܘܬܗ ܗܘܐ ܡܬܚܙܐ ܠܗ.

and He enlightened his quenched lamps, so that he saw
all the creation/world through them.
Blessed is he who saw the image of God Who became
a man.[318]

*Eccl 9.8*

Later in Eccl 27.8, Ephrem compares the effect of Lazarus' response with that of Jesus to the blind man; Jesus is asked to respond to our prayer as He did to that of Bartimaeus, and we should answer Him as Lazarus did:

ܥܢܝܟ ܡܝܬܐ ܘܗܘܐ ܐܪܙܐ
ܥܢܝܬ ܠܣܡܝܐ ܘܗܘܐ ܛܘܦܣܐ
ܥܢܝܟ ܡܝܬܐ ܘܙܟܐ ܠܡܘܬܐ
ܥܢܝܬ ܠܣܡܝܐ ܘܙܟܐ ܠܚܫܘܟܐ
ܥܢܝܟ ܡܝܬܐ ܥܢܝܢ ܡܝ̈ܬܐ ܒܢܘܚܡܐ
ܥܢܝܬ ܠܣܡܝܐ ܥܢܝ ܠܚܝ̈ܐ ܐܝܟ ܕܠܣܡܝܐ
ܥܢܝܢܝ ܡܪܝ ܐܝܟ ܕܠܛܝܡܝ
ܥܢܝܢ ܚܕ ܠܝ ܐܝܟ ܠܒܪ.

The dead person responded to You and he became a
mystery.
You responded to the blind man and he became an
example.
The dead person responded to You and he became
victorious over death.
You responded to the blind man and he became
victorious over the darkness.
The dead person responded to You;
- the dead will respond to You at the resurrection.
You responded to the blind man,
respond to the living as You did to the blind man.
Respond to me, my Lord, as [You responded to Bar]
Timaeus.

[318] Eccl 9.8:

ܛܘܒ ܥܒܕ ܢܘܠܩܡ ܣܘܟܐ ܘܚܒܝܒܝ ܠܗ ܬܠܡܝܕܘ ܬ̈ܒܠܐ
ܘܦܩܕ ܠܗ ܕܐܦܬܚ ܐܕ̈ܢܝ ܘܡܬܪ̈ܥܝܬܐ ܟܠܗ̈ܘܢ ܢܗ̈ܪܝܢ
ܚܙܐ ܒܗ ܠܟ ܐܝܟ ܕܚܙܐ ܒܗ ܒܥܘ ܡܣܡܝܐ ܕܡܒܐ ܒܐܘܪܚܐ
ܘܒܐܘ ܒܗ ܒܢ̈ܝܐ ܕܐܢܫܐ ܐܝܟ ܕܠܡܬܝܒܘ
ܘܗܘ ܛܘܒ ܐܘܣܦ ܥܠ ܩܠܗ ܘܒܣܡ ܢܘܗܪܗ ܠܦܪܘܣܗ
ܘܐܢܗܪ ܫܪ̈ܓܘܗܝ ܕܥܡ̈ܝܢ ܘܚܙܐ ܒܗܘܢ ܥܠ ܒܪܝܬܐ
ܛܘܒܘܗܝ ܕܚܙܐ ܨܘܪܬܗ ܕܐܠܗܐ ܕܗܘܐ ܒܪܢܫܐ.

We will answer You as did Lazarus.

*Eccl 27.8*

The example of Bartimaeus is significant for the glory of Jericho as were Zachaeus (Lk 9:1-10) and Rahab (Josh 2). Because of them Ephrem stimulates Jericho to praise the Lord:

ܐܪܝܚܘ ܬܣܓܘܕ܆ ܠܗ ܟܠܝܠܐ ܬܩܪܒ ܠܗ
ܒܦܘܡ ܙܟܝ ܙܥܘܪܐ ܬܘܪܒܗ̇ ܠܬܫܒܘܚܬܐ
ܘܒܩܠܐ ܕܒܪ ܛܝܡܝ ܬܡܬܚܝܗ̇ ܠܬܘܕܝܬܐ
ܘܒܚܘܛܐ ܙܗܝܐ ܕܪܚܒ ܠܟܠܝܠܗ ܬܚܘܦܝܘܗܝ
ܒܝܕ ܪܚܒ ܕܚܝܬ ܬܗܠܠܝܘܗܝ
ܒܒܪ ܛܝܡܝ ܕܚܙܐ ܬܫܒܚܝܘܗܝ
ܘܒܙܟܝ ܕܙܟܐ ܬܟܠܠܝܘܗܝ.

Let Jericho worship Him; offer Him a crown.
By the mouth of the short Zacchaeus (Lk 19:1-10),
let her extend praise,
and by the voice of Bartimaeus (Mk 10:46-52)
let her extend thanksgiving,
and with the splendid thread of Rahab (Josh 2)
let her gird on His crown.
By means of Rahab who was saved, let her sing His praise;
by Bar Timaeus, who saw, let her glorify Him,
and in Zacchaeus who conquered, let her crown Him.

*Virg 35.1*

Bartimaeus is a character who signifies faith and trust in God. Therefore, he became a figure to be imitated. In Iei 6.4-8, Ephrem goes further and prays to the Lord to open our inner eyes as He opened Bartimaeus' corporeal eyes.[319]

### *4.2.3.3 The Healing of the Interior and Exterior Blindness*

Apart from the miracles of giving sight to the man born blind and to Bartimaeus, Ephrem also uses the metaphor of the eye and blindness in the context of 'light' (ܢܘܗܪܐ), 'sun' (ܫܡܫܐ) and 'brightness' (ܙܗܪܐ) to illustrate the interior sight of man. In Fid 45.1-2, the mind (ܬܪܥܝܬܐ) is compared to the eye, and the light

319 Cf. Iei 6.4-8.

with truth. As the light is essential to the eye, so too, the truth, which is identified as Scripture, is to the mind:

ܥܝܢܐ ܘܬܪܥܝܬܐ ܢܠܦܘܢ ܚܕܐ ܠܚܕܐ
ܕܙܥܘܪ ܐܦܢ ܗܘ ܕܢܦܠ ܒܓܘ ܥܝܢܟ
ܥܟܪ ܘܕܠܚ ܠܗ ܘܗܟܢ ܠܬܪܥܝܬܟ
ܟܬܒܐ ܘܢܘܗܪܐ ܢܚܟܡܘܢܟ
ܢܘܗܪܐ ܦܐܐ ܠܥܝܢܐ ܘܩܘܫܬܐ ܠܬܪܥܝܬܐ
ܢܘܗܪܐ ܓܒܝ ܠܥܝܢܟ ܟܬܒ̈ܐ ܠܬܪܥܝܬܟ

Let the eye and the mind teach one another
because [even] a little thing, if it falls into your eye,
upsets and disturbs it, and likewise for your mind.
Scripture and light will make you wise:
light is fitting for the eye and truth for the mind.
Choose light for your eye and the Scriptures for your
mind.

ܟܡܐ ܣܢܝܐ ܥܝܢܐ ܠܡܕܡ ܕܢܦܠ ܒܗ
ܡܚܫܒܬܐ ܗܘ ܕܝܢ ܒܝܫܬܐ ܪܡܝܐ ܒܗ ܒܡܚܫܒܬܢ
ܢܬܪܐ ܩܫܐ ܠܥܝܢ̈ܐ ܟܡܐ ܕܝܢ ܩܫܐ ܠܢܦܫܐ
ܡܚܫܒܬܐ ܡܚܒܠ ܟܠ ܒܟܠܙܒܢ
ܠܐ ܥܕܪܐ ܠܥܝܢܐ ܨܒܥܐ ܕܬܒܚܘܫ ܒܗ
ܘܐܦ ܠܐ ܠܬܪܥܝܬܐ ܒܨܝܘܬܐ ܕܬܒܚܘܫܝܗ ܒܗ

How the eye hates something that falls in it!
It is [like] an evil thought cast into our mind;
a crumb is hard for [our] eyes. How hard, indeed, for
the soul
is a thought which corrupts everything all the time!
It does not benefit the eye [for] a finger to probe it,
and it is no help for the mind for inquiry to attack it.

*Fid 45.1-2*

The eye is sensitive to the smallest thing, likewise the mind to an evil thought. Because evil thoughts disturb the mind as a crumb injures the eye, thoughts should be held under control. To attack the Scripture, which means to inquire and 'pry into' the divinity which can not be comprehended, is like probing the eye with a finger and hurting it. In hymn 65 On Faith, the inquiry refers to 'prying into' the Son of God. The inquiry of the mind about the divinity of the Son, is like a blind person inquiring about the light and the sun. The blind one is just able to imagine the beauty and essence of light, if he believes those who tell him about it. Concerning the holy divinity, faith is requested to believe the 'utterance of God' (ܠܡܠܬܗ ܕܐܠܗܐ). If a blind man inquires and does not believe, he is considered as doubly blind: both physically and mentally:

65.10

ܡܛܠ ܐܢ ܣܡܝܐ ܒܨܐ ܠܢܘܗܪܐ
ܟܕ ܠܐ ܡܨܐ ܕܢܨܘܪ ܫܡܫܐ ܘܙܠܝܩܘܗܝ
ܒܠܒܐ ܕܡܚܫܒܬܗ ܕܠܡܐ ܡܨܐ ܗܘܐ
ܕܢܚܙܝܘܗܝ ܠܙܠܝܩܗ ܘܠܝܠܕܗ ܕܗܘ ܫܡܫܐ
ܐܠܐ ܐܢ ܗܘ ܕܗܝܡܢ ܒܠܚܘܕ ܡܗܝܡܢܘ
ܠܐܢܫܐ ܕܐܡܪ ܠܗ.

Therefore, if a blind man inquires into light,
although he is not able to depict the sun and its rays
in the heart of his thoughts, could he be capable
of seeing its ray and the generation of the sun
unless he only trustingly believed
someone who told him [about it].

65.11

ܡܛܠ ܐܢ ܨܒܐ ܥܘܝܪܐ ܕܢܬܟܬܫ
ܕܫܡܥ ܘܠܐ ܗܝܡܢ ܒܪܒܘ ܢܦܠ ܒܒܝܫܐ
ܕܒܨܐ ܘܠܐ ܡܣܬܟܠ ܘܨܒܐ ܕܐܦ ܣܡܝܐ
ܢܫܬܟܚ ܒܬܪܬܝܗܘܢ ܒܥܝܢܐ ܘܒܪܥܝܢܐ
ܕܐܠܘ ܨܒܐ ܘܗܝܡܢ ܐܢܗܪܗ ܠܣܡܝܘܬܗ
ܦܝܣܐ ܕܟܐܢܘܬܐ.

Therefore, if a blind man wants to resist what he hears
and not believe, he would fall into a multitude of evils
because he inquires but does not understand; and he was willing
to be found blind in two [respects]: in the eyes and in the mind.
But if he were willing and believed,
just persuasion would enlighten his blindness.

65.12

ܡܢܐ ܚܒܝܫܝܢ ܐܢܚܢ ܐܦ ܐܢܚܢ ܒܫܘ̈ܐܠܐ
ܡܢܐ ܫܓܝܫܝܢ ܐܢܚܢ ܐܦ ܚܢܢ ܒܒܘ̈ܨܝܐ
ܣܡܝܐ ܗܝ ܬܪܥܝܬܢ ܕܬܚܙܐ ܒܗܘ ܝܠܕܐ
ܘܬܨܝܪܝܘܗܝ ܕܐܝܟ ܗܘ ܕܠܐ ܐܝܬ ܦܘܪܣ ܐܚܪܝܢ
ܐܠܐ ܕܐܢܫ ܒܠܚܘܕ ܢܗܝܡܢ ܡܗܝܡܢܘ
ܠܡܠܬܗ ܕܫܪܝܪܐ.

Why are we harassed by questions?
Why are we upset by investigations?
Our mind is too blind to look at the Begotten

and to inquire into what sort [of being] He is, because
there is
no other way [for us to find Him]
except only for a person really to believe the voice of
the True One.

65.13

ܡܢܘ ܕܠܐ ܢܕܚܠ ܕܐܢ ܡܬܟܣܐ ܣܡܝܐ
ܕܫܡܥ ܘܠܐ ܡܟܝܪ ܠܡܠܬܗ ܕܒܪܢܫܐ
ܕܨܒܐ ܕܢܐܡܪ ܠܗ ܢܘܗܪܐ ܕܐܝܟܢ ܗܘ
ܟܡܐ ܢܬܕܝܢ ܐܢܫܐ ܕܫܡܥ ܘܠܐ ܗܝܡܢ
ܠܡܠܬܗ ܕܐܠܗܐ ܕܩܠܐ ܕܝܠܘܕܗ
ܐܟܪܙ ܕܗܢܘ ܒܪܝ.

Who would not be afraid because, if a blind man is
censured
because he hears and does not trust the word of a
human
who wants to tell him what light is like,
how much would someone be judged who heard and
did not believe
the utterance of God? For the voice of His Begetter
proclaimed:
'this is my Son' (Mt 3:17).

*Fid 65.10-13*

Consequently, Ephrem asks the reader to 'believe the voice of the True One', so that the mind should not be blind. Blindness of mind appears not just by inquiry, but also with any sin. In hymn 13 On the Church, Ephrem compares sin to darkness which only through the ray of God can be enlightened. The inner darkness is compared to a house with closed windows which can be illumined by the light of the Lord. Therefore, Ephrem prays to the Lord to open his interior blind eye as He opened the eyes of the blind man:

13.7

ܒܠܘܦܣܐ ܕܫܘܚܐ ܒܗ ܕܢܦܩ ܣܘܟܪ
ܒܝܬܐ ܣܬܝܡ ܟܘ̈ܘܗܝ ܟܝ ܢܢܗܪܘܢ ܙ̈ܠܝܩܘܗܝ.

13.8

ܦܬܚ ܒܝ ܙܗܪܗ ܫܡܫܐ ܒܡܐܬܝܬܗ
ܣܡܝܐ ܕܠܐ ܡܘܩܡ ܢܗ̈ܪܐ ܕܢܫܠܚܘܢܝ.

13.9

ܕܠܝ ܬܒܥܝܗܐ ܡܢܝ ܕܐܢܗܪܬ ܠܣܡ̈ܝܐ
ܟܘ̈ܐ ܬܪ̈ܬܝܢ ܕܝܗܒ ܠܡܫܡܫܐ ܕܢܦܩ ܠܣܡܝܐ.

13.10

ܗܟܢ ܡܚܝܠ ܕܐܦܠܐ ܐܢ ܛܦܐ ܬܪܥ ܥܝܢܐ
ܡܨܐ ܕܢܦܬܚܝܗ ܘܢܥܘܠ ܡܛܠ ܡܚܝܠܘܬܗ.

13.11

ܘܐܦ ܠܝܬ ܠܗ ܩܠܝܕܐ ܕܢܦܬܚ ܠܣܡܝܘܬܐ
ܕܢܟܣ ܠܣܓܘܕܘܗܝ ܕܚܙܐ ܟܥܘܝܪܝܢ ܗܘܘ.

13.12

ܙܗܪܟ ܦܬܚ ܐܢܝܢ ܠܥܝܢܐ ܕܣܟܝܪܢ ܗ̈ܘܝ
ܕܛܝܢܐ ܗܘ ܛܫܬ ܐܢܝܢ ܫܝܥܐ ܬܪ̈ܝܢ ܦܬܚܬ.

13.13

ܫܠܛ ܠܒܢ ܕܒܪܐ ܢܘܗܪܟ ܘܠܟܐ ܕܐܦ̈ܝ ܬܪ̈ܬܐ
ܕܗ̇ܘ ܫܘܫܡܢܬܐ ܒܒܪ̈ܬ ܒܫܘܒܐ.

13.14

ܛܒ ܕܝܢ ܒܫܠܘܚܐ ܠܝܢܐ ܕܐܫܝܓ ܥܝ̈ܢܐ
ܘܢܦܩ ܡܠܐ ܐܝܟ ܫܡ̈ܫܐ ܕܢܗܪܐ.

13.15

ܫܘܒ ܐܢܗܪ ܥܝܢܐ ܒܫܘܚܬܐ ܕܗܡܝܢܐ ܒܝ
[ܕܪܫܡ ܫܠܘܚܐ] ܢܦܩ ܡܠܐ ܢܘܗܪܐ ܗܘ.

13.7

Like darkness my debts dwell in me.
The house withheld
its windows; through you let its senses be enlightened.

13.8

With his single ray when the sun comes it overwhelms
the darkness that the seas are not able to wash away.

13.9

My Lord, Your [deed] is admirable for you have given light
to the blind with the two windows
which were victorious over the sun that overcome the darkness.

13.10

So [the sun] is weak, that if the door of the eye is closed
it cannot open it and enter because of its weakness.

13.11

Also it does not have a key to open the blindness
to rebuke its worshippers seeing how blind they were.

13.12

Your brightness opened the eyes that were stopped up.
You daubed them with clay (Jn 9:6)
[and] opened the double plastering.

13.13

Your light crept in and rent asunder the pair of the
door's curtains
of that ant which lives in darkness.
13.14
In Shiloah (Jn 9:6), the clay which cleansed the eyes
sank,
and poured and filled them (with) abundance of light.
13.15
Jesus, enlighten the hidden eye which is blind in me;
for Shiloah is far away, your cup is full of light.
*Eccl 13.7-15*

In hymn 6 On the Fast, Ephrem contrasts the opening of Bartimaeus' eyes with that of Adam who was hurt and injured when his eyes were opened. When Adam was created, he wore the garment of light and glory, although he did not recognize it as such as long as he was in Paradise. After the fall, Adam's eyes were opened to see the loss of his glorious garment, as he found himself naked. Although his eyes were opened, in actual fact they were closed and blinded. Adam was hurt and injured when his eyes were opened, and through him darkness and error entered into human life. Ephrem emphasises that man's physical eyes are not strong enough to see God's gift that is provided for us: because they are fixed on passing wealth, he calls them 'the blind who see just gold'. The free will is capable of giving sight or making blind.[320] In order to give sight to the inner eye, Ephrem invites God to spit on 'our face', and not on the ground, as He did for the man born blind. The reason for the blindness is not just the free will alone, but also the Evil One who opened Adam's eyes for his disaster.

6.4
ܪܒܐ ܗܝ ܡܘܗܒܬܐ ܕܫܕܝܐ ܩܕܡ ܣܡܝܘܬܢ
ܟܕ ܬܪ̈ܬܝܢ ܬܪ̈ܬܝܢ ܥܝ̈ܢܝܢ ܐܝܬ ܠܟܠܢ
ܕܠܦ̈ܐ ܐܝܟ ܕܚܙܐܘܗ̇ ܗܘܘ ܠܗ̇ ܠܡܘܗܒܬܐ
ܕܡܟܐ ܗܝ ܘܕܪ̈ܟܢ ܗܝ
ܣܘܦ ܡܢܝ ܠܡܘ̈ܢܐ ܕܕܗܒܐ ܗܘ ܒܠܚܘܕ ܚܙܝܢ.

The gift which is thrown in front of our blindness is
great.
Even though all of us have two eyes,

[320] Eccl 7.5: ܒܪ̈ܢܫ ܗܘ ܗ̇ܘ ܕܢܗܒ ܠܗ ܥܝ̈ܢܐ ܕܗܘ [ܚܙܐ] ܐܦ ܗܘ ܡܣܡܐ.

few are those who saw the gift,
what it is and to whom it belongs.
My Lord, have mercy on the blind who see just gold.

6.5

ܝܫܘܥ ܕܦܬܚ ܒܒ̈ܐܬܐ ܕܒܪ ܛܝܡܝ
ܦܬܚܬ ܐܢܝܢ ܕܐܬܥܘܪ ܗܘ̈ܝ ܟܕ ܠܐ ܨܒܐ
ܦܬܚ ܡܪܝ ܥܝ̈ܢܐ ܕܥܘܪܢ ܐܢܝܢ
ܟܕ ܨܒܝܢ ܚܢܢ ܕܬܐܪܒ ܛܝܒܘܬܟ
ܛܝܢܟ ܡܪܝ ܐܠܦ ܕܐܢܬ ܐܢܬ ܒܪ ܒܪܘܝܐ.

Jesus Who opened Bartimaeus' eyeballs (Mk 10:46) –
You opened them which were blind against his wish.
My Lord, open the eyes which are blind,
while we wish this, so that Your grace might increase.
My Lord, Your clay taught [us] that You are the Son of the Creator.

6.6

ܡܢܘ ܐܟܘܬܟ ܐܘ ܡܝܩܪ ܦܪ̈ܨܘܦܝܢ
ܒܐܪܥܐ ܗܘ ܪܩܬ ܘܠܐ ܗܘܐ ܒܐܦ̈ܐ ܕܬܪܘܒ ܨܠܡܢ
ܠܢ ܕܝܢ ܡܪܢ ܪܘܩ ܠܢ ܒܐܦ̈ܝܢ
ܘܦܬܚ ܥܝ̈ܢܐ ܕܐܚܕܬ ܚܐܪܘܬܢ
ܒܪܝܟ ܗܘ ܕܝܗܒ ܥܝܢܐ ܕܗܘܢܐ ܠܗ̇ ܕܥܘܪܢܗ̇.

Who is like You Who honour our face:
You spat on the ground,
and not on the face, to magnify our image.
In our case, our Lord, spit on our faces,
and open the eyes which our free will has closed.
Blessed
is He Who granted the eye of mind that we have made blind.

6.7

ܡܢܘ ܕܠܐ ܬܗܝ ܒܐܕܡ ܘܒܦܬܚܘܗܝ
ܠܐܕܡ ܓܝܪ ܣܓܝ ܣܓܦ ܦܬܚ ܥܝ̈ܢܘܗܝ
ܠܢ ܕܝܢ ܡܪܢ ܣܓܝ ܥܕܪ ܦܬܚ ܥܝ̈ܢܐ
ܕܛܠܡܐ ܐܢܝܢ ܒܝܫܐ
ܒܪܝܟ ܕܐܣܝ ܘܦܬܚ ܥܝ̈ܢܐ ܕܥܘܪ ܗܘܐ.

Who does not wonder about Adam and the opening [of his eyes].
The opening of his eyes hurt Adam a lot;
but with us, our Lord, the opening of the eyes helped a lot,
since the Evil One shut them.

Blessed is He Who closed and opened the eyes to help
us.

6.8

ܡܢܘ ܕܠܐ ܢܠܘܛܝܗ̇ ܠܥܘܣܐ ܕܡܥܠܝ ܠܢ
ܢܟܠ ܘܦܬܚ ܥܝܢ̈ܝ ܐܕܡ ܘܚܙܐ ܨܥܪܗ
ܠܢ ܕܝܢ ܐܛܥܝ ܘܗܐ ܐܚܕ ܥܝܢ̈ܝܢ
ܕܠܐ ܢܚܙܝܘܗ̇ ܠܥܪܛܠܝܢ ܪܒܐ
ܠܘܛܝܗ̇ ܡܪܝ ܡܢ ܟܠ ܕܐܢܬ ܡܢ ܟܠ ܬܬܒܪܟ.

Who will not curse the thorn who betrayed us.
He deceived and opened Adam's eyes, and he saw his
dishonour.
[The Evil One] seduced us and, behold, he has closed
our eyes,
so that we might see our great nakedness.
O Lord, curse him
from/above everyone, so that You might be blessed by
everyone.

*Iei 6.4-8*

Both the exterior and the interior eyes are essential for man, and both should be enlightened. Likewise faith and the sight of man should be perfect. In the context of the healing of the blind man at Bethsaida (Mk 8:22-26; cf. Jn 9:1-7), Ephrem brings the process of hidden eyes together clearly with the corporeal eyes:

> When a little light had arisen in his eyes, a great light arose in his mind. His faith was made perfect interiorly and his sight was crowned exteriorly.[321]

Herod is considered a blind man, because of his envy (ܚܣܡܐ). Even though he knew from the prophets who Jesus was, he did not recognise Him for his mind (ܡܕܥܗ) was drunk in his envy (ܪܘܐ ܒܚܣܡܗ).[322] Everyone who does not accept the Gospel of the Lord is considered blind. Those who saw the miracles of the Lord but did not believe, - even though they saw -

[321] CDiat 13.13: ܟܕ ܕܢܚ ܠܗ ܢܘܗܪܐ ܙܥܘܪܐ ܒܥܝܢ̈ܘܗܝ܆ ܕܢܚ ܠܗ ܢܘܗܪܐ ܪܒܐ ܒܡܕܥܗ. ܐܬܓܡܪܬ ܗܝܡܢܘܬܗ ܡܢ ܠܓܘ. ܐܬܟܠܠܬ ܐܦ ܚܙܬܗ ܡܢ ܠܒܪ.

[322] CDiat 3.4: ܠܐ ܝܕܥ ܗܪܘܕܣ ܐܝܟܢܐ ܢܒܚܢܗ̇ ܠܡܠܟܘܬܐ. ܡܛܠ ܕܥܘܝܪ ܗܘܐ ܒܚܣܡܐ. ܡܛܠ ܗܢܐ ܠܐ ܐܫܟܚ. ... ܘܟܕ ܒܗܠܝܢ ܟܠܗܝܢ ܝܕܝܥ ܗܘܐ. ܠܐ ܝܕܥ ܗ̇ܘ ܪܘܐ ܒܚܣܡܐ. ܠܡܕܥܗ.

are blind.[323] However, those who are physically blind will rejoice to see the beauty of Paradise.[324]

[323] Cf. CDiat 8.6.

[324] Cf. Parad 7.13.

# 5 SALVATION HISTORY AS A PROCESS OF HEALING

It is noticeable that Ephrem frequently uses imagery from the sphere of medicine in the context of salvation. In Paradise, Adam and Eve enjoy good health, but after the Fall they come under the curse and suffer pains because they had sinned. There are two agents that cause sin and sickness: one of them is external to human beings, namely Satan, also called the Evil One and the Devil; and the other is internal, namely, man's free will. Thus, sin is the result of the influence of the Evil One and the misuse of man's free will. Ephrem personifies sin and considers it to be the poison of death which the Evil One offered to the inhabitants of Eden. Sin caused man to fall from Paradise where neither sickness nor death, nor suffering, pains or grief exist. In turn, the fallen state, life on earth, introduced mortality and afflictions of different illnesses and pains. At the beginning of mankind's history, sin persuaded man through a particular action, namely through disobedience and eating from the fruit of the Tree of Knowledge; later sin continues its poisonous actions to wound man in many different ways. Disobedience to God, as well as desire, gluttony, idolatry, etc. can be ways in which mankind is affected spiritually, morally and physically.

Secondly, man needs to be healed and restored. Attention is drawn to the salvation of man as restoration from his diseased state into good health. The fragrance of Paradise appears as a Medicine and Physician for the earth, and so minimises its illness. During the Old Covenant, God provided medicine and physicians for His people. God sends chosen people, like the patriarchs and prophets, to act as physicians and to heal His people from their sickness. Finally, God sends His Son, Jesus Christ Who personifies the whole revelation of God, to save man from the wound of sin. Jesus Christ, as the best Physician, Healer of All and Medicine of Life, is capable not only of healing individual sicknesses, such as the prophets did, but He was able to heal Adam's wound and rescue humanity from its sick state to health.

This universal restorative process continues, as it has been made accessible to individual people through Jesus Christ's presence in the sacraments of the church. Everyone can be restored to health through faith in the Lord and following His divine commandments.

## 5.1 The Cause of Sickness

### 5.1.1 The Expulsion from Paradise into a State of Sickness

As we have seen in the exegetical chapter about the creation of Adam and Eve, Ephrem considers life in Paradise to be a companion of well-being (ܠܘܝܬܐ ܕܚܘܠܡ̈ܢܐ)[1] in which Adam and Eve were created healthy and pure. In Paradise, the inhabitants of Eden could not suffer any pain or experience the effect of sickness. Understandably, they could not know what it means to be cursed with pains and afflicted with sickness. The knowledge of the real meaning of sickness was missing, and therefore Ephrem speaks of 'hidden knowledge' (ܐܝܕܥܬܐ ܟܣܝܬܐ). In their good health Adam and Eve did not possess, as Ephrem says, the 'discernment of what suffering is' (ܚܫܐ ܟܘܪ̈ܗܢܘܗܝ), and they did not have the knowledge of 'what good health is' (ܡܢܐ ܗܝ ܚܠܝܡܘܬܐ);[2]

---

[1] Parad 5.13; cf. Parad 4.4: ܠܒܬܐ ܒܐܝܬܐ; Parad 5.14: ܠܒܬܐ ܕܐܠܗܘ̈ܬܐ; Parad 15.10: ܦܘܢ̈ܝܐ ܕܦܘܪܢܣܐ.

[2] Parad 3.11-12: A man, indeed, who has acquired good health in himself,

and is aware in his mind of what sickness is,

has gained something beneficial and he knows something profitable;

but a man who lies in sickness,

and knows in his mind what good health is,

is vexed by his sickness and tormented in his mind.

Had Adam conquered, he would have acquired

glory upon his limbs, and discernment of what suffering is,

so that he might be radiant in his limbs and grow in his discernment.

☞

i.e. in their intermediate state they lacked the knowledge both of their health and of sickness.[3]

The same could be said of the created intermediate state between mortality and immortality. The Lord's commandment played an essential role; both the keeping and the transgressing of the divine commandment would lead the inhabitants of Eden from their temporal intermediate state to another state.[4] Life was a 'contest' (ܐܓܘܢܐ) so that Adam might receive a crown that befitted his actions.[5] If the inhabitants of Eden had obeyed the Lord's commandment, they would have been led via the Tree of Knowledge to the Tree of Life and so to a permanent state. They would be totally in the presence of God where they would glorify and praise Him for ever. Sickness and pain do not exist in the created world of Paradise, or in the expected state of eternal life.

Now, we will focus on the fact that the inhabitants of Eden disobeyed their Creator. In Ephrem's view, the divine commandment was not too difficult to keep; it was very easy and simple. Even after failing to keep it, God was merciful and was waiting to hear Adam confess his sin and repent. Thus, because

---

But the serpent reversed all this and made him taste
abasement in reality, and glory in recollection only,
so that he might feel shame at what he had found and weep at what he had lost.

[3] Parad 3.10: God established the Tree as judge, so that if Adam should eat from it,
it might show him that rank which he had lost through his pride,
and show him, as well, that low estate he had acquired, to his torment.
Whereas, if he should overcome and conquer, it would robe him in glory
and reveal to him also the nature of shame,
so that he might acquire, in his good health, an understanding of sickness.

[4] Parad 3.10; CGen 2.17:
ܡܛܠ ܓܝܪ ܕܒܪ ܒܪܐ: ܠܐ ܡܝܘܬܐ ܒܒܪܝܗ ܗܘܐ. ܘܠܐ ܕܠܐ ܡܝܘܬܐ ܒܟܠܗ ܗܘܐ.
ܕܗܘ ܐܕܡ ܒܢܛܪ ܦܘܩܕܢܐ ܐܘ ܒܥܒܪ ܦܘܩܕܢܐ. ܢܣܒ ܡܢ ܚܕ ܡܢ ܐܝܠܢܐ ܐܝܢܐ ܕܨܒܐ ܗܘܐ.

[5] Parad 3.9: ܕܢܣܒ ܒܐܓܘܢܗ ܟܠܝܠܐ ܕܐܝܟ ܒܥܡܠܘܗܝ.

they did not acknowledge their sin they were expelled from their healthy Paradise into the cursed land of thorns and thistles that signifies the fallen state, the sick state of mankind.[6]

The transgression of the Lord's commandment took place because of man's wickedness that harms humanity both spiritually and physically. 'Our wickedness' (ܒܝܫܘܬܢ) is able to produce visible and invisible pains.[7] The transgression of the divine commandment was leading Adam and Eve to eternal death; not to the physical death that people experience in their life on earth, but to something similar to a (second) death at the final judgment, for if God had not expelled Adam and Eve from Paradise, they would have stretched their hand to the Tree of Life and would have eaten the cause of eternal death and pains that are irreversable. Thus, humanity would have been tortured eternally by pains.[8]

Explicitly, Eve and the Serpent are mentioned as the cause of death. In Parad 11.9, Ephrem speaks of the 'state of sickness that entered through the Serpent';[9] whereas it is said that Eve became the source of death,[10] and she has been the 'vine' (ܓܦܬܐ) of death and the 'vine-twigs' (ܫܘ̈ܛܬܐ) that brought the first pains.[11]

Both Adam and Eve also serve as representatives of all mankind. Death enslaved Eve and Adam,[12] but also their

---

6 CGen 2.19; 2.23.

7 Eccl 32.1 (cf. Nat 23.3):

ܘܚܫܗ̇ ܛܒܐ ܠܒܝܫܘܬܢ ܕܐܬܬܗ̇ ܡܟܐܒܐ ܕܟܠ ܢܟܝ̈ܢܝܢ
ܘܡܚ̈ܘܬܗ̇ ܟܐ̈ܒܐ ܟܣ̈ܝܐ ܐܦ ܡܘܕ̈ܥܢܝܬܗ̇ ܟܐ̈ܒܐ ܓܠ̈ܝܐ
ܡܢܗ̇ ܓܝܪ ܒܝܕ ܦܘܩܕܢܐ ܡܕܡܟܐ ܕܒܥܠ ܣܘܦ̈ܢܝܢ ...

8 Cf. Parad 4.1-2; CGen 2.35 (see Gen 3:22).

9 Parad 11.9: ܟܪܝܗܘܬܐ ܕܥܠܬ ܒܝܕ ܚܘܝܐ.

10 Dom 3: ܚܘܐ ... ܗܘܬ ܠܗ̇ ܡܒܘܥ ܡܘܬܐ ܠܟܠ ܕܚܝ. For ܡܒܘܥܘܬܐ see also Dom 42; Eccl 13.18.

11 Virg 23.9: ܚܘܐ ܗܘܬ ܗܘܬ ܓܦܬܐ ܕܡܘܬܐ ܫܘ̈ܛܬܐ ܕܡܢܗ̇ ܒܘܟܪ ܟܐ̈ܒܐ. In Virg 34.2, therefore, Ephrem speaks of 'Eve's death' (ܘܠܡܘܬܐ ܕܚܘܐ).

12 Sog 1.11: ܘܫܠܛܗ ܠܡܘܬܐ ܘܫܠܝܛܐ ܕܫܥܒܕܘ ܗܘܘ ܠܐܕܡ ܘܫܥܒܕܘܗܝ. Further about death see Dom 3; Nat 3.18; 4.33; 13.4; Epiph 11.7; Sog 1.11; 1.28; Virg 5.8; 5.11; 23.9; 26.6; 30.12; 34.2; 34.12; 35.6; ☞

descendants. Consequently, Ephrem refers the cause of death to all mankind who caused death, the curse and thistles to enter into the world and dwell in it.[13] For instance, before her repentance Ephrem considers the sinful woman as the cause of death for everyone.[14] Generally speaking, humanity is badly affected by death that 'swallows us up' (ܒܠܥܢ)[15] and 'absorbs us' (ܣܪܦ ܠܢ).[16] Sadly, 'we' often enjoy our death for we do not recognise it as such.[17] Thus, mankind became an object of death and can be described as ܡܝܘܬܐ,[18] particularly the body.[19] Because after the Fall God intervened and introduced physical death to limit Adam's pains and suffering,[20] physical death is seen as mercy and not as condemnation. Nevertheless, pains and suffering are the curse put upon man due to the fact he is living on earth and not any more in the Garden of Eden.

Here, on earth, on the cursed land, Adam and Eve tasted the reality of sickness and gained the knowledge about pain and suffering. Likewise they realised that they had lost the paradisiacal abode where they were pure and perfect. Instead they became impure, leprous and poisoned,[21] as well as wounded and stained.[22] In other words, Adam lost his garment of glory (Gen 3:21)[23] and in

---

43.11-12; 48.5; 51.8; Nis 35.1; 35.19; 42.8; 52-59; Fid 10.18; 46.1; 64.12; 67.14; Azym 14.1; Parad 5.14; 7.19; Eccl 1.6; 11.10; 17.2.

[13] Sog 1.28: ܬܠܝܢܗ ܕܐܪܥܐ ܐܣܟܘ ܠܗ ܠܘܛܬܐ ܘܟܘ̈ܒܐ ܕܫܘܠܛܗ ܘܐܟܠܘ ܐܪܥܘ ܒܗ ܡܘܬܐ ܕܚܪܒ ܠܗ.

[14] Virg 35.6: ܘܕܥܠܬ ܡܘܬܐ ܠܟܠܢܫ ܚܛܝܐ ܗܘܬ.

[15] Nat 3.18: ܒܡܘܬܐ ܕܒܠܥܢ ܗܘܐ.

[16] Fid 10.18: ܠܡܘܬܐ ܕܗܘܐ ܣܪܦ ܠܢ.

[17] Eccl 1.6: ܕܡܘܬܢ ܒܣܡ ܠܢ.

[18] Fid 15.1.

[19] Fid 80.2.

[20] Cf. CGen 3:25. The role of death is well illustrated in the dialogue between death and Satan in Nis 52-59; particularly see Nis 52.8; 52.13; 53.5; 54.7.

[21] Parad 4.4; 8.9; Nat 26.9.

[22] CDiat 16.15.

[23] CDiat 16.10; Nat 23.13; Virg 16.9. See further S. P. Brock, *The Luminous Eye. The Spiritual World Vision of St Ephrem* (Rome 1985), 65-76.

his nakedness became subject to sickness.[24] Along with his nakedness, Adam also realised his sick state. Through the Fall, the life of Adam, representative of all human beings, changed radically: on the earth he faced a totally different world, a world where man can be afflicted with any kind of sickness. Therefore, Ephrem also speaks of the fractured state of Adam/man (ܬܒܪܗ)[25] and of the darkness of error.[26] The fallen state set in motion a long life of pain and suffering that could affect not just individuals, but also larger groups within the nation or the nation as a whole. And the Fall affected not just human beings, but the earth and the whole world of nature as well.[27]

Ephrem describes this general human condition after the expulsion of Paradise with the term ܟܪܝܗܘܬܐ, state of sickness, that has been brought about by the Serpent.[28] Likewise Paul uses ܟܪܝܗܘܬܐ with the same sense when he denotes humanity's spiritual fallen state as a state of sickness.[29]

Because of this universal human condition of spiritual sickness, other sicknesses, diseases and pain can take place in human life and affect man spiritually as well as physically. Because of the 'state of sickness' (ܟܪܝܗܘܬܐ) error could grow strong in the world[30] and remain with people.[31] Thus with Simon the Pharisee, his thoughts concerning Jesus went astray because 'error had entered him'.[32] Likewise, the city of Nineveh as a whole fell into error,[33] and the Chaldaeans are called the 'heralds of error'.[34]

---

24 CDiat 16.10; Parad 3.13 (cf. Gen 3:7); 4.3-5; Iei 6.8.

25 CDiat 2.25.

26 CDiat 5.17; cf. CDiat 11.6.

27 Fid 35.2; Epiph 7.15; Nat 1.62; 17.12; Virg 26.10; Nachträge Serm 2.153-154.

28 Parad 11.9. See also Parad 3.11; Nat 3.1; Fid 60.13; 75.18; Virg 4.10; 11.13; 39.7.

29 Rom 5:6; 6:19; 8:18; 8:26; Gal 4.13; cf also Hebr 4:15.

30 Fid 60.13: ܠܛܘܥܝܢ ܕܬܬܥܫܢ ܡܛܠ ܟܪܝܗܘܬܢ.

31 CDiat 11.6.

32 Dom 16: ܕܡܢ ܒܪ ܕܥܠܬ ܠܗܘܢ ܛܥܝܘܬܐ ܡܢ ܬܡܢ; cf. Lk 7:39.

33 Virg 45.9: ܢܝܢܘܐ ܕܐܬܛܥܝܬ ܠܦܘܪܢܐ ܒܛܠܝܗܝܢ.

Thus, error 'blinded' (ܥܘܪܬ) humanity,[35] became the 'cause of sickness' ([ܥܠܬ] ܟܘܪܗܢܐ)[36] and spread its 'nets' (ܡܨܝܕ̈ܬܐ) everywhere.[37] Error is bitterness and provides the 'bitterness of death' (ܡܪܝܪܘܬ ܡܘܬܐ), the 'poison of death' (ܣܡ ܡܘܬܐ) and the 'dragon's gall' (ܡܪܬܗ ܕܬܢܝܢܐ).[38]

Paradise and Adam's health and 'glory' (ܫܘܒܚܐ) in it remain only in memory after he sinned, and he 'weeps at what he had lost'.[39] Likewise Adam/man and 'our soul' (ܢܦܫܢ) are considered as having become 'lost' and 'perished' (ܐܒܝܕܐ).[40] Humanity lost Paradise and became a prisoner on earth[41] which is a dungeon compared to Paradise.[42] People on earth are 'captives' (ܐܣܝ̈ܪܐ)[43] and in 'confinement' (ܚܒܝ̈ܫܐ).[44] Earth is the place of 'suffocation' (ܚܢܝܩܘܬܐ)[45] and humanity is drowned in it.[46] Earth is also described as ܒܝܬ ܚܫܘ̈ܟܐ,[47] for gloom, darkness and night have taken power over it.[48] Darkness affects humanity badly for it is full of suffering.[49]

---

[34] Nat 22.32: ܦܪ̈ܣܝܢ ܗܘܘ ܒܟܠܗܘܢ ܠܒ̈ܢܐ ܘܡܬܛܫܝܢ ܠܟܠܗܘܢ ܗܘܘ ܒܬܒܝܠ ܒܦܘܪ̈ܣܘܗܝ ܕܛܘܥܝܝ.

[35] Nat 22.15: ܛܘܥܝܝ ܥܘܪܬ ܠܐܢܫܐ ܕܠܒܪ̈ܝܬܐ ܢܣܒ̈ܪܘܢ.

[36] Eccl 8.3: ܛܘܥܝܝ ܗܝ ܕܗܘܬ [ܥܠܬ] ܟܘܪܗܢܐ. The reading ܥܠܬ is introduced by E. Beck.

[37] Nat 22.33.

[38] Nat 28.8. Further for ܛܘܥܝܝ see Nat 22.19; 22.27; Virg 5.2; 29.12; 31.7; 34.5; 40.8; Iei 10.4; Azym 4.11; 5.1.

[39] Parad 3.12: ܘܥܠ ܐܒܕܬܗ ܢܠܠ.

[40] Virg 30.12; Virg 32.6.

[41] Virg 30.11-12.

[42] Parad 5.13.

[43] Virg 30.11.

[44] Parad 5.13.

[45] Parad 5.14.

[46] Nat 3.19.

[47] Nat 6.8.

[48] Virg 51.8: ܥܡܛܢܐ ܘܚܫܘܟܐ ܘܠܠܝܐ.

[49] CDiat 17.2: ܚܫܘܟܐ ܡܠܐ ܚܫ̈ܐ. For ܚܫܘܟܐ see further Virg 5.2; 5.8; 52.1; Epiph 7.22; Eccl 13.7-9.

Because of the transgression Adam's eyes were opened to see 'his disgrace' (ܨ̈ܥܪܗ)[50] and 'his nakedness' (ܦܘܪܣܝܗ).[51] Even though the eyes of the inhabitants of Eden were opened before the Fall, they were closed to see their nakedness for they were covered with 'glory' (ܬܫܒܘܚܬܐ).[52] Adam was ashamed of his nakedness and tried to cover it with the 'leaves of figs' (ܒܛܪ̈ܦܐ ܕܬܬܐ).[53] The nakedness of Adam became 'our great nakedness' ( ܦܘܪܣܝܢ ܪܒܐ).[54]

Humanity, in its nakedness, became an object for sicknesses. Not just the physical naked 'body' (ܦܓܪܐ - ܓܘܫܡܐ) could be affected, but also the 'spirit' (ܪܘܚܐ), 'soul' (ܢܦܫܐ) and man's 'mind' or 'intellect' (ܗܘܢܐ - ܪܥܝܢܐ - ܬܪܥܝܬܐ). In Virg 32.6, Ephrem speaks of what has happened to our spirit, soul and body, namely that our spirit has fallen into error, our soul has utterly perished, and our body sinned.[55] In Fid 5.19, Ephrem uses medical terms in the context of these three parts[56] of man: 'bruises on our bodies, scars on our souls, marks on our spirits'.[57] Because the human body is 'weak' (ܡܚܝܠܐ)[58] and 'mortal' (ܡܝܘܬܐ),[59] it can

---

50 Iei 6.8: ܘܦܬܚ ܥܝ̈ܢܝ ܐܕܡ ܘܚܙܐ ܨ̈ܥܪܗ.

51 CDiat 16.10: ܬܘܒ ܡܬܐܡܪ ܕܟܕ ܚܙܐ ܠܗ ܐܕܡ. ܘܐܫܬܠܚ ܡܢ ܬܫܒܘܚܬܐ ܗܝ ܕܠܒܝܫ ܗܘܐ. ܘܒܛܪ̈ܦܐ ܕܬܬܐ ܦܘܪܣܝܗ ܚܦܐ ܗܘܐ. See also Nis 57.2.

52 CDiat 16.10; Parad 3.6; 3.13.

53 CDiat 16.10; Parad 3.13. For ܬܬܐ see CDiat 16.1-10; Parad 12.13-14; Virg 50.25; Azym 15.22.

54 Iei 6.8.

55 Virg 32.6: ܠܘ ܪܘܚܢ ܕܛܥܬ ܘܐܦܢܫܢ ܠܘ ܢܦܫ ܕܐܒܕܬ ܘܐܓܘܫܡܢ ܠܘ ܦܓܪ̈ ܕܚܛܐ ܘܣܡܗ̇.

56 In Parad 9.20 we find a gradation of ܦܓܪܐ - ܢܦܫܐ - ܬܪܥܝܬܐ.

57 Fid 5.19: ܕܫܘ̈ܡܬܐ ܒܓܘܫܡܝܢ ܥܘ̈ܒܬܐ ܒܢܦܫܝܢ ܘܡܬ̈ܒܬܐ ܒܪܘܚܝܢ.

58 Virg 24.13; 29.1.

59 Fid 80.1-2; Dom 3; 9.

be afflicted with 'bruises' (ܡܚܘ̈ܬܐ)[60] and 'pains' (ܟܐ̈ܒܐ),[61] and become 'sick' (ܟܪ̈ܝܗܐ),[62] 'dumb' (ܚܪ̈ܫܐ),[63] 'blind' (ܣܡܝ̈ܐ)[64] and 'leprous' (ܓܪ̈ܒܐ).[65] Likewise, the soul can be spiritually in pain and become dumb and blind.[66] As we saw above, the spirit and intellect of man are not saved either. While the spirit can go astray and be harmed with 'marks' (ܫܘܡ̈ܬܐ);[67] the 'intellect' (ܗܘܢܐ) can be disturbed,[68] the 'mind' (ܪܥܝܢܐ) can be fractured and become bitter and sick,[69] and ܬܪܥܝܬܐ be affected with blindness like the eye.[70]

Mankind can become physically and spiritually blind,[71] and be deficient in its nature. Ephrem speaks of 'our deficiency' (ܡܚܣܝܪܘܬܢ)[72] and 'what is lacking in our creation' ( ܡܚܣܝܪܘܬܐ ܕܒܪܝܬܢ).[73] Compared to the angels, man's nature is weak and is liable to produce 'pus' (ܬܒܣܘܬܐ).[74] Likewise, it can be afflicted with 'pains' (ܟܐ̈ܒܐ),[75] 'sicknesses' (ܟܘܪ̈ܗܢܐ),[76] 'suffering'

---

[60] Fid 5.19; 5.6. For ܡܚܘ̈ܬܐ see also Virg 3.10; Nat 3.20; 22.1; Dom 42.

[61] Iei 10.6.

[62] Fid 19.10; Dom 42.

[63] Parad 8.5.

[64] Parad 8.4

[65] Fid 28.9-13; 38.17 (on Leprosy, see chapter IV, 1.2).

[66] Iei 4.1; 10.6; Parad 8.4-5.

[67] Virg 32.6; Fid 5.19.

[68] Iei App 1.9.

[69] Iei 4.1 (cf. Dom 19; 42); Dom 24; Fid 2.16; 79.9.

[70] Dom 16; Fid 45.1-2; 65.12.

[71] Iei 6.4; 10.4; Nat 24.11-12.

[72] Nat 3.1. Cf. Fid 19.11-12.

[73] Dom 11-12; CDiat 16.28; Virg 5.1.

[74] Epiph 8.22. For ܡܚܝܠܘܬܐ see Dom 27-28; Virg 39.7; Fid 2.16; 11.22; 70.13.

[75] CDiat 6.27; 11.5; Dom 19; 21; Nat 17.7; 22.1-3; Epiph 5.14; Sog 1.29; Virg 3.10; 4.4; 23.9; 24.11; 31.14; Fid 6.14; 35.2; 38.7; Parad 5.13; 11.9; C.Jul 1.9; Iei 4.1; 10.6; Azym 20.16-19; Eccl 1.5-7; 2.11; 25.7; 32.1; 34.2.

[76] Parad 3.10-11; 8.5; 11.10; Eccl 8.3; 17.2; Virg 2.1-3; 4.4; 36.1; 39.7; 68.22; Fid 35.4; Sog 1.29; Iei 10.7.

(ܚܒ̈ܪܐ),[77] 'scars' (ܫܘܡ̈ܬܐ),[78] 'marks' (ܟܘܬܡ̈ܬܐ)[79] and 'harms' (ܬܘܟ̈ܐ).[80] Humanity is surrounded by 'iniquity' (ܥܘܠܐ),[81] 'dirt/foulness' (ܨܐܬܐ),[82] 'debts' (ܚܘܒ̈ܐ)[83] and the 'curse' (ܠܘܛܬܐ),[84] where moral and medical terminology are more or less used interchangeably. People such as 'lepers' (ܓܪ̈ܒܐ),[85] the 'deaf' (ܕܘ̈ܓܐ), 'crippled' (ܚܓܝ̈ܪܐ) and 'dumb' (ܚܪ̈ܫܐ),[86] or 'blind' (ܣܡ̈ܝܐ),[87] 'paralysed' (ܦܫܝ̈ܓܐ),[88] 'sick' (ܟܪ̈ܝܗܐ)[89] and 'wounded' (ܡܚܒ̈ܠܐ)[90] point to signify the weakness and deficiency of humanity after the Fall.

In this context, the question of theodicy can be understood: God created a good world, and planted human beings in it bearing His image. Mankind caused a gap between itself and its Creator. Thus, actually mankind must bear the responsibility for pain and suffering in the world, but God in His mercy offers medicine and healing to restore human beings. Ephrem does not understand all that happened to man after the Fall as a just God's punishment and curse, but rather as the consequence of sin, the effect of the Evil One, man's free Will and his actions. The presence of sickness and suffering in the fallen state of the human condition is the gift of the

---

77 CDiat 17.2; Nat 22.1; Virg 4.13; 38.4; Parad 5.13-14.

78 Virg 46.25-27; Fid 5.19.

79 Fid 5.19; Epiph 5.6-8.

80 CDiat 16.9; Parad 12.4.

81 Nat 3.19.

82 Virg 35.6; Eccl 13.25.

83 Virg 7.9; 49.16; Eccl 5.2-6; 5.16; 13.7-8; Epiph 5.6-8.

84 Nat 3.15; Epiph 8.2; Sog 15.8; Virg 24.11; 31.14; Parad 3.5; 6.8; 7.8; 7.14; 9.1; 9.12; 11.9-11; Iei 6.8; Eccl 28.16.

85 Nat 17.17-18; CDiat 8.1; Epiph 3.16-17; 5.6-8; 6.2; Fid 28.13; 38.17; Parad 4.3-5; 12.4; 12.9-14; 15.12; Eccl 5.22; 11.5.

86 Nat 17.13-18; Virg 19.2; Parad 6.8; 7.13; 8.5.

87 CDiat 10.7; 16.28-33; Virg 16.7; 35.3; Fid 41.7; 56.11-12; 65.10-13; Nat 6.8; 17.13-18; 26.7; Epiph 7.22; Parad 7.13; Azym 13.12; Eccl 1.5; 9.8; 13.7-15.

88 Parad 7.13.

89 Virg 5.11; 19.2; Fid 2.16; 19.10-12; 35.4; 47.1; Virg 52.3; Iei 10.7; Eccl 38 Refrain.

90 Nat 4.24; Dom 42; Virg 37.1; Iei 4.1.

Evil One,[91] Death and Satan who enslaved and humbled Adam.[92] The reason for the radical change in the early history of man is sin; and the main source of sin is fallen Satan and man's free will.

### 5.1.2 Satan, Evil One and the Devil

The reason for the radical change in the life of mankind is sin; and the main source of sin is the fallen Satan as an external power, and man's free will as an internal and essential part of human creation. In this section we will look closer at the former, namely Satan who fell from his rank and led Adam and Eve astray in Paradise and continues to affect man. Significantly, in the dialogue between Satan and death, in Nis 52-59, Ephrem emphasises that Satan did not only cause Adam and Eve to sin, but also caused all mankind to become sinners.[93] Ephrem plays with the name 'Satan' (ܣܛܢܐ) and associates it, through a popular etymology, with the verb ܣܛܐ, 'to turn aside, go astray'.[94] Satan turned himself aside from God and causes humanity to turn aside too.[95]

As a 'dragon' (ܬܢܝܢܐ),[96] Satan is 'cunning' (ܨܢܝܥܐ),[97] a 'liar' (ܟܕܒܐ)[98] and 'false' (ܪܐܦܐ).[99] As if in a 'contest' (ܐܓܘܢܐ),[100] Satan 'fights' (ܡܬܟܬܫ)[101] against humanity which he 'hates' (ܣܢܐ),[102] 'deceives' (ܢܟܠ)[103] and 'laughs at' (ܓܚܟ).[104] Furthermore, through 'jealousy' (ܚܣܡܐ),[105] 'deceit' (ܢܟܠܐ),[106]

---

91 Eccl 48.11; Virg 31.14.

92 Nat Sog 1.11.

93 Nis 52.2; 53.7; 53.9; 53.26; 57.1.

94 Cf. Haer 26.4. For information about this popular etymology of 'Satan' see chapter IV, 1.1.4.

95 Nis 54.9; 59.12.

96 Nis 57.3.

97 Nis 54.11; cf. Eccl 1.3.

98 Nis 55.5.

99 Nis 56.8. In Fid 38.7, ܪܐܦܐ is considered as ܟܐܒܐ ܒܣܝܡܐ.

100 Nis 56.1; cf. Parad 3.9.

101 Nis 55.24.

102 Nis 55.9; Virg 3.5.

103 Nis 57.3.

104 Nis 57.5.

105 Nis 57.15; Fid 50.5-6; Eccl 1.2.

'contention/controversy' (ܚܪܝܢܐ),[107] 'iniquity' (ܥܘܠܐ),[108] 'desires/lusts' (ܪ̈ܓܝܓܬܐ),[109] 'cupidity/greediness'(ܥܠܘܒܘܬܐ),[110] 'theft' (ܓܢܒܘܬܐ),[111] 'godlessness/impiety' (ܚܢܦܘܬܐ),[112] 'gluttony/debauchery' (ܐܣܘܛܘܬܐ),[113] as well as through 'oracle, augury and divination' ( ܩܨܡܐ ܘܢܚܫܐ ܘܥܘܪ̈ܦܢܐ),[114] Satan causes man 'to sin' (ܐܚܛܝ),[115] 'destroys man's hope' ( ܦܣܩ ܣܒܪܗ ܕܐܢܫܐ)[116] and 'becomes victorious' (ܙܟܐ).[117] Likewise, he wins over man by means of 'habit, ease, advantage and persistence' (ܥܝܕܐ ܢܝܚܐ ܘܝܘܬܪܢܐ ܘܐܡܝܢܘܬܐ).[118] Considering all these, Ephrem customarily describes Satan with the term ܒܝܫܐ, 'Evil One', and uses it as a name for Satan.[119]

Satan, the 'Evil One' (ܒܝܫܐ), is 'divided' (ܐܬܦܠܓ)[120] in himself, and his name is 'hated' (ܣܢܝܐ).[121] The Evil One acts in his free will and thus has authority over himself; but whatever he does and performs is hidden and invisible. In Virg 20.4, Ephrem says: 'the Evil One sang in them [using] hidden deceit' ( ܒܝܫܐ ܙܡܪ ܒܗܘܢ ܢܟܠܐ ܟܣܝܐ). The Evil One dwells in mankind and is invisible so that the ܢܦܫܐ is unable to perceive him. He cannot be

---

106 Nis 52.2; 57.3; Virg 20.4.

107 Nis 53.3; Virg 14.3.

108 Nis 56.10; 57.26.

109 Nis 52.20; Virg 1.6-8; 32.8.

110 Virg 14.11; Nat 22.17.

111 Nis 57.22.

112 Nis 57.18.

113 Virg 14.11.

114 Nis 55.11; 57.16.

115 Nis 53.9; 53.26; 55.11; 57.1-2.

116 Nis 52.23.

117 Nis 53.7; 53.15; 54.13; cf. Virg 52.1.

118 Nis 55.27. For ܥܝ̈ܕܐ see also Eccl 1.6.

119 Nis 35.8; 52.19; 53.6; 57.1; cf. Fid 38.7; 50.6-7; C.Jul 1.9; Nat 13.5; 21.11; 22.17; 22.30; 22.34; Virg 1.4-6; 10.4; 20.4; 30.7; 48.12; 52.1.

120 Nis 53.20; cf. Nis 56.18.

121 Nis 52.15; 52.19; 54.17; 55.9; 57.26; Fide 38.7.

seen or touched, neither can his bitterness be tasted.[122] Therefore, the Evil One is able to say: 'some of my breath was in them, the lump of dough of humans (cf. 1 Cor 5:6) is a companion of our leaven'.[123] The Evil One can dwell in man by means of 'devils and demons' (ܫܐ̈ܕܐ ܘܕܝ̈ܘܐ) which are described as the children of sin.[124]

The Evil One became victorious and thought never to be defeated.[125] He ruled in the world as a god,[126] 'swallowed the whole creation',[127] misled and harmed everyone.[128] In Virg 1.3, it is explicitly said that 'Satan wounds' (ܣܛܢܐ ܡܚܒܠܐ).[129] The Evil One does not have to do this, but he chooses to.[130] He knows how to 'harm' (ܠܚܡ), 'blind' (ܡܣܡܐ), or 'injure us' (ܡܣܠܡ), and to hold people as if in prison.[131] The Evil One 'intoxicated' (ܐܪܘܝ), 'perturbed/disturbed' (ܕܘܕ) and rent mankind in pieces (ܒܣܒܣ); but the foolish who have been torn in pieces did not realise their pains.[132] Furthermore, through his 'arrow' (ܓܐܪܐ) and poisoned food,[133] or through 'strangling' (ܚܢܘܩܝܬܐ),[134] and his 'snares and noose of subtlety' (ܦܚܐ ܘܚܒܠܐ ܕܢܟܝܠܘܬܐ),[135] Satan

122 Fide 50.6-7.

123 Nis 35.8: ܐܝܬ ܗܘܐ ܒܗܘܢ ܢܘܦܐ ܡܢ ܕܝܠܝ ܠܝܫܬܐ ܕܒܢ̈ܝ ܐܢܫܐ ܒܪܬ ܙܘܓܗ ܗܝ ܕܚܡܝܪܢ.

124 Nis 35.2: ܫܠܝܛܬܐ ܡܠܟܘܬ ܠܒܢ̈ܝܗ ܠܫܐ̈ܕܐ ܘܠܕܝ̈ܘܐ. Cf. Virg 4.13.

125 Virg 52.1: ܐܟܝ ܥܒܕܐ ܠܐܕܡ ܘܣܒܪ ܗܘܐ ܕܠܐ ܢܚܘܒ.

126 Nat 21.11: ܐܪܒܝ ܗܘܐ ܒܪܘܫܢܗ ܐܝܟ ܐܠܗܐ.

127 Nat 22.30: ܒܠܥܗ ܠܟܠܗ ܒܪܝܬܐ.

128 Virg 1.4-6.

129 Virg 1.3: ܣܛܢܐ ܡܚܒܠܐ ܘܗܘܠܢ ܡܣܐܡ.

130 Nat 22.34.

131 Nat 22.17.

132 C.Jul 1.9. For ܐܪܘܝ see further Virg 27.2. In Virg 37.5, sin is considered as a wild animal that has secretly torn man in pieces. Drawing attention to the invisibility of the Evil One, Ephrem says that the Evil One cannot be depicted with any pigments (Fid 33.7).

133 Virg 14.11; Virg 14.11-14.

134 Nis 53.17; cf. Nat 3.19; Parad 5.14.

135 Nis 52.4; 58.23; cf. Eccl 1.5.

'strikes' (ܡܚܝܢܐ)[136] and kills mankind,[137] as he killed Adam through the Serpent.[138] In contrast to death who kills physically, Satan kills spiritually as well.[139]

The Fall of Adam and Eve was initiated by the advice of the Evil One who is described as having 'proferred poison in food' to Adam.[140] The 'poison' (ܣܡܐ) was offered to Eve through the Serpent. The term ܣܡܐ is in itself a neutral word: only by response to it does it prove to be ܣܡ ܡܘܬܐ, 'poison of death', or, alternatively, ܣܡ ܚܝܐ, 'Medicine of Life'. The Serpent was used by the Devil and became a symbol of evil seduction,[141] for it, as a reptile, 'deceived' (ܛܠܡܬܗ) Eve and caused Adam 'to sin' (ܐܚܛܝܗ).[142] Apart from being an agent of the Evil One, the Serpent was 'healthy'.[143] Nevertheless, Adam and Eve were wounded by the Serpent (ܡܚܘܬܗ ܕܚܘܝܐ), and, as Ephrem says, they were 'swallowed' by the Reptile.[144] Adam was pure in Eden until 'the Serpent had breathed on him',[145] and it was through the Serpent that Adam's healthy state was changed into a 'state of sickness' (ܟܪܝܗܘܬܐ).[146] The Serpent did not only wound Adam (Gn 3:1-18), but also the Israelites in the camp (Num 21:4-9): 'the Serpent struck Adam in Paradise and killed him, and the Israelites in the

136 Virg 1.3.

137 Nis 53.9; 54.7; 54.16; 55.9.

138 CDiat 16.15: The Serpent struck Adam in Paradise and killed him.

139 Nis 54.7; 54.16; 55.11.

140 Cf. Eccl 48.11; Nat 26.9; Virg 10.4; 13-14.

141 For Amnon who is described as a serpent/snake (Virg 2.3) see chapter V, 1.4.1.

142 Cf. Nis 57.1-3.

143 Cf. Haer 21.6: although the Serpent was 'more crafty than any of the wild animals' (Gen 3:1), in its nature it was originally good like the rest of the creation and like the Tree of Knowledge.

144 Nat 1.27-28.

145 Parad 4.4.

146 Parad 11.9.

camp and disturbed them.'[147] Thus, the Serpent, as Satan, can be the agent of wounding humanity.[148]

In the context of sickness imagery, the idea of 'poison in food' is the most significant. The Evil One seduces Adam and Eve by the poison of the forbidden fruit: 'As a false friend he pleased him [by] offering him poison in [his] food'.[149] Poison appears mainly in the context of food, and since it is related to the Evil One, Ephrem often speaks of the 'poison of death' (ܣܡ ܕܡܘܬܐ).[150] Because of the Evil One, the fruit[151] and the paradisiacal tree[152] served as the poison of death for Adam and Eve. Along with Adam and Eve, the poison of death entered into the world and remains as a means for the Evil One by which he is still able to poison mankind. The advice of the Serpent is understood as 'pouring venom into [Eve's] ears'.[153] The 'venom' (ܡܪܪܬܐ), as the 'poison of death' (ܣܡ ܕܡܘܬܐ), affects the whole creation. 'The Evil One mixed his cup, showed his venom to every one',[154] so that, for example, the free will - or in particular 'greed' (ܝܥܢܘܬܐ) and worldly 'care' (ܡܪܢܝܬܐ), become a cause of poison and venom.[155] Furthermore, the Son of God can be both Medicine of Life and poison of death: approaching Him with Faith, He is the Medicine of Life; whereas having doubts and prying into Him will have an effect like the poison of death.[156] This is clearly illustrated both in the case of the eucharistic bread as the Medicine of Life and in that of the

---

[147] CDiat 16.15: ܒܚܝܐ ܚܘܝܐ ܠܐܕܡ ܒܦܪܕܝܣܐ ܘܦܠܛܗ ܘܠܐܣܛܪܛܝܐ ܒܡܪܪܬܐ ܘܫܓܫ ܐܢܘܢ.

[148] In Virg 3.1, it is explicitly said that 'the Serpent wounded Eve' (ܚܘܝܐ ܡܚܝܐ ܠܚܘܐ), and in Virg 1.3, that 'Satan wounds' (ܣܛܢܐ ܡܚܝܐ).

[149] Nat 26.9: ܐܝܟ ܪܚܡܐ ܢܟܠܐ ܐܗܢܝܗ ܘܐܘܫܛ ܠܗ ܣܡܐ ܒܡܐܟܘܠܬܐ.

[150] Cf. Parad 15.12; Azym 18.16-17; 19.22-24.

[151] Parad 12.3; cf. Eccl 19.7; Fid 5.16.

[152] Parad 15.12.

[153] Parad 7.6.

[154] Parad 9.2.

[155] Parad 7.6; 7.14; Iei 1.6; Eccl 8.3; Eccl 11.6; Nis 14.2.

[156] Eccl 19.7; Fid 5.16 (on prying and probing, see chapter V, 1.4.7).

unleavened bread as the poison of death.[157] The 'unleavened bread' (ܦܛܝܪܐ) as the poison of death refers to the Evil One: 'behold he gave us from his unleavened bread to be in us as the poison of death.'[158] Since the term ܡܪܬܐ can also mean bitterness, the Evil One is described as 'bitter' (ܡܪܝܪܐ),[159] and he is considered as the cause of bitterness in the world. In Dom 15, it is explicitly said that 'the Evil One gave his bitter counsel to the house of Adam through the food'.[160] Thus, the poison of death, as well as venom and bitterness, entered into human life through the mouth (i.e. eating the food that the Evil One offered)[161] and ear (i.e. listening to his deceptive advice).

Finally the wickedness of the Evil One becomes our wickedness and a part of us: 'our wickedness is the source of all harms: its thoughts are hidden pains, and its deeds are visible pains.'[162] Nevertheless, not everyone is so badly harmed. Even though Satan also affects some of the prophets and kings, he does not have power over the just and upright.[163] Ephrem's hymns 53 and 57 On Nisibis provide a list of significant biblical figures, like Aaron, David, Solomon, Samson, Ezekiel and Simon, who were affected by Satan; but Ephrem also gives a list of some of the just and upright, like Joseph, Moses, Elijah, Job and John, who were victorious over the Evil One.[164] Thus, the Evil One and Death can

---

157 Azym 18-19.

158 Azym 18.11.

159 Parad 15.15.

160 Dom 15: ܕܒܡܐܟܘܠܬܐ ܗܘ ܝܗܒ ܗܘܐ ܒܝܫܐ ܡܠܟܗ ܐܕܡ ܠܒܝܬ ܡܪܝܪܐ. In Parad 3.8, Ephrem says: ܣܡܗ ܕܚܘܝܐ ܐܟܠܘܢ ܕܬܐܟܠܘܢ.

161 Isa 6:5-7 is one of many biblical passages where the lips are identified as the locus of sin, perhaps because the lips are the visible and audible gateway of the human heart (cf. Prov 6:14) where evil originates (cf. Gen 6:5; 8:21: Jer 17:9; as well as Mt 15:8, Lk 6:45; Rom 3:13; 1 Pet 3:10).

162 Eccl 32.1: ܒܝܫܘܬܢ ܡܒܘܥܐ ܕܟܠ ܢܟܝܢܝܢ ܚܘܫܒܘܗܝ ܟܐܒܐ ܟܣܝܐ ܐܦ ܣܘܥܪܢܘܗܝ ܟܐܒܐ ܓܠܝܐ.

163 Nis 53.6; 53.24.

164 Nis 53.6-26; 57.3-32. Ephrem's 'lists' or sequences of examples relate to an older tradition is explored in R. Murray's article, 'Some

☞

be weak too, particularly in the fight against the just and upright and, above all, against Jesus.[165]

### 5.1.3 Free Will (ܚܐܪܘܬܐ)

Besides the influence of the Evil One, Ephrem emphasises man's free will as another reason for man's state of sickness and for sickness in the world. Like the Serpent, Fruit and the Tree of Knowledge the nature of free will is not evil. Being astonished at the natural beauty of Paradise, Ephrem considers the beauty of free will even more excellent: 'free will was envious of the Garden and from itself brought forth victorious fruits whose crowns vanquish the very splendours of Paradise.'[166] Thus, free will is beautiful and can act and perform deeds in a good manner. The Lord granted it to humanity as a gift par excellence, and it is the greatest divine gift through which humanity has been honoured.[167] It is compared to the sun, and its authority and power to God.[168] Therefore, the imago Dei is depicted in it,[169] and, even though He could, God does not force humanity to keep His commandments. Although God may act against nature,[170] He does not act against free will:

---

rhetorical patterns in early Syriac Literature', in R. H. Fischwer (ed.), *A Tribute to Arthur Vööbus* (Chicago 1977), 109-31.

[165] Nis 54.1-2; 56.2; 56.18.

[166] Parad 6.15: ܚܣܡܬ ܚܐܪܘܬܐ ܒܓܢܬܐ ܘܥܒܕܬ ܢܦܫܗ̇ ܡܢܗ̇ ܦܐܪ̈ܐ ܕܙܟܘܬܐ ܕܙܟܘ ܟܠܝܠܝܗܘܢ ܠܒܣܝܡܘܬܗ̇ ܕܦܪܕܝܣܐ.

[167] Haer 11.1:
ܐܝܟ ܐܝܟܢܐ ܚܐܪܘܬܢ ܒܢ ܘܒܢ ܬܬܐܡܪܐ ܬܬܫܒܚܢܐ ܠܐ ܬܬܫܡܥܐ
ܡܢ ܒܥܘܕܪ̈ܢܗ ܕܒܢ ܗܘ ܡܟܐܡ ܐܦ ܫܘܠܛܢܗ
ܘܒܗܬܐ ܪܒܬܐ ܕܒܗ ܗܘ ܐܘܪܒܬܗ ܡܢ ܡܒܥܝܐ ܕܐܫܟܝܡ
ܒܬܘܒܚܝܗܘܢ ܡܢ ܐܪܒܐ ܥܒܕܐ ܘܦܠܘܪܐ ܕܡܢ ܒܠܒܗ ܫܦܝܪ ܘܒܪܡ
ܒܚܝܠܬܐ: ܦܠܓܐ ܘܒܪܘܪܐ ܒܚܐܪܘܬܐ ܡܢ ܟܠ ܒܢܝܢ ܡܢܝ
ܐܘܪܒܬܗ܆.

[168] Haer 11.4: ܟܠܗ ܫܘܚܢܗ ܠܚܐܪܘܬܐ ܕܐܝܟ ܥܒܕܐ ܕܚܝܠܐ ܒܐܘܪܚܐ ܡܢܗ ܢܛܠܒ ܥܘܠܛܢܗ ܕܐܝܟ ܐܠܗܐ ܚܝܘ ܫܠܛ.

[169] Haer 49.7. See also N. El-Khoury, *Die Interpretation der Welt bei Ephrem dem Syrer* (Mainz 1976), 111-20.

[170] Virg 30.5-6.

'our Lord did not wish to force our will, nor our free will'.[171] Neither does free will act under compulsion from the Evil One and so choose the worst. Man is created with the gift of free will to enable him to be himself, creative and knowledgeable, to know good and bad, and to be able to make his own decisions. In Ephrem's words: 'free will is the treasure of humanity' ( ܠܚܐܪܘܬܐ ܣܝܡܬܐ ܕܐܢܫܘܬܐ).[172]

In Eccl 2.19, the nature of free will is compared to the nature of sweetness that 'is sweet for the one who is restored in good health, but bitter for the one who is sick; i.e. free will when it is sick produces sinners, but when healthy it produces upright people.'[173] Ephrem clarifies the effect of the action of free will better in Eccl 19.7 where he alludes to the Tree of Knowledge as the poison of death and the Son of God as the Medicine of Life: as at the beginning free will chose to pluck the poison of death, now it is also able to pluck the Medicine of Life.[174]

Thus, free will can be strong and become victorious against Satan,[175] but he fights against our free will;[176] and although it is strong it can be defeated by means of habit, ease, advantage and persistence.[177] Just as the Evil One is responsible for his actions because he possesses free will,[178] likewise, man is responsible for his actions because of his free will.

---

171 Virg 20.5: ܡܪܢ ܕܠܐ ܨܒܐ ܕܢܥܨܐ ܡܨܒܝܢܘܬܢ ܐܘ ܨܒܝܢܢ ܐܘ ܚܐܪܘܬܢ.

172 Eccl 2.23.

173 Eccl 2.19: ܚܠܝܘܬܗ ܕܚܠܝܘܬܐ ܚܠܝܐ ܠܗܘ ܕܚܠܝܡ ܡܪܐ ܠܗܘ ܕܟܪܝܗ. ܗܟܢ ܐܦ ܚܐܪܘܬܐ ܟܪܝܗܐ ܠܚܛܝ̈ܐ ܘܚܠܝܡܐ ܠܙ̈ܕܝܩܐ.

174 Eccl 19.7:

ܚܘܪ (ܒܗ̇) ܒܚܐܪܘܬܐ ܕܐܝܟ ܐܝܠܢܐ (ܗܝ) ܕܡܘܬܐ ܕܠܥܠ ܦܐܪܝܢ ܬܬܩܛܦ

ܘܐܝܟ ܕܐܬܡܨܝܬ ܡܢ ܠܘܩܕܡ ܕܬܩܛܘܦ ܘܬܐܟܘܠ ܠܗ̇ ܣܡ ܡܘܬܐ ܡܨܝܐ ܗܝ ܕܬܩܛܘܦ ܠܗ̇ ܣܡ ܚܝ̈ܐ.

175 Nis 55.29: ܐܢ ܗܘ ܕܢܨܚܬ ܚܐܪܘܬܐ ܐܬܓܒܪܬ.

176 Nis 56.1: ܥܡ ܚܐܪܘܬܐ ܐܬܟܬܫܐ ܐܝܬ ܠܗ ܒܟܢܫܐ.

177 Nis 55.27: ܒܥܝܕܐ ܢܝܚܐ ܘܬܘܪܬܐ ܘܐܡܝܢܘܬܐ ܒܗܘܢ ܡܬܕܒܪܐ ܚܐܪܘܬܐ ܥܫܝܢܬ ܡܢ ܟܠ.

178 Virg 30.7.

The state of 'free will' (ܚܐܪܘܬܐ) contrasts with the state of 'slavery' (ܥܒܕܘܬܐ). But since free will is misused, Ephrem says that people 'have sold their free will and bought slavery',[179] and have fallen under the yoke.[180] Free will becomes like a thief, and in its richness it robs a person of the divine gifts.[181] Furthermore, 'we subdue' our free will.[182] Therefore, Ephrem says that our free will, despised by the Evil One,[183] has 'closed' our eyes.[184] But since free will is wrongly used so that it makes wrong decisions and acts against the Lord, Ephrem can speak of 'free will as the source of sickness' and of the 'pain of free will' (ܟܐܒܐ ܕܚܐܪܘܬܐ).[185] He compares free will to a 'fountain that is disturbed by itself' (ܡܒܘܥܐ ܕܗܘ ܢܦܫܗ ܡܬܕܠܚܐ).[186]

At the beginning man's free will was divided, and in its craftiness it sought to approach divine righteousness.[187] In their free will, both Adam and Eve failed for they desired the excellent fruit and ignored God's commandment. They were 'infantile' (ܫܒܪܘܬܐ/ܫܒܪܐ)[188] and 'weak' (ܐܠܝܠܐ).[189] The free will with which man was created led Adam and Eve astray in error that is the cause of sickness.[190] By free will the inhabitants of Paradise stretched out their hands to the fruit which was the 'poison of death'.[191] Adam did not trust the Lord, preferring to steal[192] and so

---

179 Virg 31.1: ܙܒܢܘ ܚܐܪܘܬܗܘܢ ܘܙܒܢܘ ܥܒܕܘܬܗܘܢ.

180 Nat 26.10: ܕܢܦܠܬ ܠܗ ܚܐܪܘܬܐ ܬܚܝܬ ܢܝܪܐ.

181 Virg 34.10: ܡܥܬܪܬ ܚܐܪܘܬܐ ܓܢܒܐ ܗܝ ܠܡܘܗܒܬܐ ܘܐܢܐ ܕܡܣܟܢܐ ܠܥܬܝܪܐ ܕܛܝܒܘܬܐ.

182 Parad 7.31: ܠܟܐ ܕܚܐܪܘܬܐ ܝܗܒ ܠܗ ܘܫܥܒܕܢܝܗ.

183 C.Jul 1.9: ܒܝܫܐ ܚܙܐ ܕܐܪܘܝ ܘܕܘܕ ܟܕ ܐܢܫܐ ܘܚܙܝ ܘܫܬܩ ܐܣܝܪ ܘܟܣܝܗ ܠܚܐܪܘܬܐ.

184 Iei 6.6: ܘܩܦܠ ܥܝܢܐ ܕܐܢܫܘܬ ܚܐܪܘܬܢ.

185 Eccl 2.11.

186 Eccl 32.1.

187 Cf. Eccl 2.11.

188 Cf. Nis 54.9; Nat 26.8.

189 Eccl 11.10.

190 Eccl 8.3: ܚܐܪܘܬܐ ܥܠܬ ܟܘܪܗܢܐ.

191 Cf. Eccl 19.7.

192 Crucif 8.2.

eat the fruit, when he wished to become divine.[193] In consequence he became leprous.[194] Therefore, Ephrem goes further and considers free will as a spring of all visible and invisible diseases that 'muddied itself' and acts or thinks evil against its Creator.[195] As Adam, so too King Uzziah was misled by his free will that incited him to enter the Holy of Holies against the divine commandment.[196] The result was the loss of kingship and leprosy.[197]

Not only did Adam and King Uzziah undergo the testing of their free will, but so does everyone born on earth. Ephrem uses the Hebrews as an example in that they, as a nation, fell into idolatry and into the sickness of error because of their free will.[198] In the hymns On Faith, Ephrem often rebukes the Arians, who are considered as a sick limb, for trying to investigate the Son of God. They are able to do so because of their free will.[199] Mankind with its free will might also criticise God for bestowing free will upon humanity. Ephrem condemns those who rebuke Divinity through

---

193 Cf. Nis 69.12.

194 Parad 4.4.

195 Eccl 32.1: O Good One have pity on our wickedness
which is the spring of all kind of harm.
Its thoughts [are] hidden diseases,
also its deeds [are] visible diseases.
For it is from it that the first transgression of all wrongdoings comes,
of the middle as well as of the last ones.
You who are serene make serene our free will,
the spring which muddied itself.

196 Fide 38.17: Adam wanted to inherit the brightness
and the earth became his inheritance.
Uzziah wanted to add priesthood for himself
and he was given in addition an abominable leprosy (2 Chr 26:16-21).
The Syriac text is given in chapter IV, 1.2.3.

197 Fid 28.14: Behold they are both depicted for the knowing
in the pure mirror of thought,
for they had put on the same image of the will
and the same seal of anger coming from free will.

198 CDiat 11.6.

199 Fid 28.16 (for the effect of investigation see chapter V, 1.4.7).

their free will.[200] Free will, the gift of God, is misused by man through his evil actions and thoughts, and it became like a soul for the desires that live by it.[201]

In Virg 48.13-15, Ephrem contrasts free will with the grace of the Lord. He emphasises the responsibility of free will that repeatedly acts mistakenly, leads into error and sickness, and in this way caused Adam's beauty to become ugly; whereas divine grace continually corrects free will's mistakes and re-establishes man from his fallen ways.[202] Although Jesus, making us free from the slavery of sin, granted us true free will as the Father did at the beginning,[203] nevertheless people still sin because of their free will. In Parad 6, the Church corresponds to Paradise;[204] i.e. as Adam and Eve, everyone is required to obey the Lord's commandment and let his free will act in a proper way as the just do. In contrast to Adam and Eve, 'the effort of free will adorns the church with all manners of fruits'.[205]

### 5.1.4 Sin (ܚܛܝܬܐ)

In Ephrem's view, Sin is the result of the Evil One's deceit and of man's wrong use of free will. Sin, by means of disobedience, jealousy, lust, rebellion, crime, etc., causes a great gap, a chasm, between Creator and Creation and alienates human beings from God and their original created state. In many cases it does not matter whether sin is committed intentionally or unintentionally: the consequence can be the same, such as pain, grief, sickness and even death.

Ephrem personifies sin and considers it as something which kills (ܩܛܘܠܬܐ)[206] and swallows up people.[207] It tries to gain

---

200 Dom 30.

201 Virg 3.8.

202 Virg 48.13-16.

203 Virg 6.12.

204 Parad 6.7-8.

205 Parad 6.10: ܒܥܡܠܐ ܕܚܐܪܘܬܐ ܡܨܒܬܗ̇ ܒܟܠ ܦܐܪ̈ܝܢ.

206 Dom 21; 42; cf. Haer 18.3: ܒܪܬܗ ܕܚܘܝܐ ܒܩܛܝܪܐ ܗܘ ܩܛܠܐ ܚܛܗܐ ܕܒ̈ܢܝܐ ܗܘ...

207 Virg 43.15.

authority over everything[208] and spreads its snares everywhere.[209] At the beginning, Adam sinned while he ate from the forbidden fruit.[210] Consequently he fell into corruption and was wounded,[211] and as a result humanity was enslaved[212] because of sin.[213] Futhermore, sin has swallowed up humanity and torn mankind into pieces like a wild animal,[214] and it became universal so that there is no person who does not sin (cf. 1 Kgs 8:46; 2 Chr 6:36), but Jesus.

The spiritual 'pains, debts and sins' ( ܟܐ̈ܒܐ ܘܚܘ̈ܒܐ ܘܚܛ̈ܗܐ) belong together.[215] In the context of Nineveh, Ephrem explicitly attributes sickness to wilful sin: '[this] is the sickness of sin that [is caused] by the will and not by force'.[216] In the sermon On Repentance (ܬܝܒܘܬܐ), Ephrem considers 'laziness and listlessness' (ܡܐܢܘܬܐ ܘܦܫܠܐ) as a fruit of 'sickness' (ܟܘܪܗܢܐ) and speaks of the 'pains of sin' (ܟܐ̈ܒܐ ܕܚܛܝܬܐ).[217] Likewise in the hymns on Julian Saba, the author (Ephrem's authorship is doubtful) praises Julian Saba for not suffering the 'pains of sin' (ܒܟܐ̈ܒܐ ܕܚܛܝܬܐ),[218] because 'it is a pain to sin' (ܕܟܐܒܐ ܗܘ ܠܡܚܛܐ).[219] In Nachträge (most probably not genuine Ephrem), the author compares the pains caused by sin with those of fever: 'the pain of a sinner is more grievous than that

208 Nat 22.19.

209 Nat 22.33.

210 Parad 1.10; 3.8.

211 CDiat 16.10: ܬܒܪܗ ܕܐܕܡ; Eccl 20.6: ܠܐܕܡ ܕܐܬܚܒܠ ܒܚܛ̈ܗܘܗܝ.

212 Virg 6.12.

213 Eccl 20.6; cf. Parad 1.10; 7.8; 7.31. In Eccl 11.10 (cf. Virg 4.9), sin is also described as 'stealing' (ܓܢܒܬ).

214 Virg 37.5: ܘܚܛܝܬܐ ܒܡܣܟܢܐ ܚܘܣܬܐ ܗܝ ܕܡܣܟܢܘܬܗ. See further Virg 43.15.

215 I Serm 7.109.

216 II Serm 1.137: ܟܘܪܗܢܐ ܗܘ ܕܚܛܝܬܐ ܕܨܒܝܢܐ ܘܠܐ ܕܩܛܝܪܐ.

217 I Serm 7.249: ܠܐ ܢܦܘܩ ܒܝ ܟܘܪܗܢܐ ܕܡܐܢܘܬܐ ܘܦܫܠܐ ܕܐܝܢܐ ܟܐ̈ܒܐ ܕܚܛܝܬܐ ܚܘܠܡܢܐ ܒܬܝܒܘܬܐ.

218 Jul.Saba 23.6: ܒܟܐ̈ܒܐ ܕܚܛܝܬܐ ܠܐ ܐܬܢܬܘܢ.

219 Jul.Saba 23.9: ܕܟܐܒܐ ܗܘ ܠܡܚܛܐ ܘܡܚܠܐ ܠܬܒܥ.

of a person who lies in fever'.[220] Thus, human beings are considered as sick and as being immersed in sins,[221] so that our sin does not only injure us, but it also harms the whole of creation.[222]

Thus, Sin is present in man's life, in particular in vices that cause spiritual sickness and blindness.[223] Ephrem uses many terms in the context of sickness, such as 'greed' (ܥܠܘܒܘܬܐ), 'jealousy' (ܚܣܡܐ), 'deceit' (ܢܟܝܠܘܬܐ), 'hatred' (ܣܢܐܬܐ), 'haughtiness' (ܫܘܒܗܪܐ) and 'pride' (ܪܡܘܬܐ), 'wrath' (ܪܘܓܙܐ) and 'anger' (ܚܡܬܐ), 'lust' (ܪܓܬܐ) and 'fornication' (ܙܢܝܘܬܐ), as well as 'mocking' (ܒܙܚܐ), 'blasphemy' (ܓܘܕܦܐ) and 'abuse' (ܨܘܚܝܬܐ). Furthermore, investigation and prying into God, as well as 'paganism' (ܚܢܦܘܬܐ) and 'idolatry' (ܦܬܟܪܘܬܐ) are causes of spiritual sickness. Although Ephrem does not mention all of these explicitly as the cause of sickness, they are involved as ways of causing man to sin and become sick.[224] Later, a selection is made to illustrate those that are explicitly considered as a cause of sickness and suffering.

But first, let us look at another aspect, namely sin as the cause of spiritual blindness. According to Ephrem, spiritual blindness indicates the spiritual sickness of man, and so his sin. In other words, to sin means to become spiritually sick or blind.[225] Sin

---

220 Nachträge Auszug 2.184: ܢܦܝܫ ܗܘ ܟܐܒܐ ܕܫܟܝܒܐ ܒܗ ܗܘ̇ ܕܪܡܐ ܒܐܫܬܐ.

221 Nachträge Auszug 7.147: ܕܒܪ̈ܢܫܐ ܫܠܡ ܒܚܛܗ̈ܐ.

222 Fid 35.8: ܠܒܝܫܐ ܕܢܦܫܗ ܚܛܗܝܢ. Cf Fid 35.2: ܠܒܝܫܐ ܕܐܬܐ ܠܐܪ̈ܥܐ.

223 Ephrem does not know of specific cardinal virtues, or of the seven deadly sins, both of which represent later developments.

224 In Eccl 1.6, for example, Ephrem says: 'evil habits are much more bitter than the snares of wealth, haughtiness, lust and greed' ( ܡܪ̈ܝܪܝܢ ܐܦܢ ܠܚܕ ܛܒ ܥܝ̈ܕܐ ܒܝ̈ܫܐ ܡܢ ܦܚ̈ܐ ܕܥܘܬܪܐ ܘܕܫܘܒܗܪܐ ܘܕܪܓܬܐ ܘܕܥܠܘܒܘܬܐ).

225 Restoration is in contrast to sin. For example in CDiat 13.3, Ephrem says (cf. Jn 5:14): 'see you are restored, do not sin any more [again]' (ܗܐ ܚܠܝܡ ܐܢܬ ܬܘܒ ܠܐ ܬܚܛܐ ). To be healed means to repent and not to sin again: ܐܦܢ ܠܚܕ ܗܘܐ ܥܒܕܐ ܡܣܒܪ ܠܚܘܠܡܢܐ. ܒܕ

caused man to fall into darkness, described as spiritual blindness.[226] In the commentary on the call of Matthew (Mt 9:9), Ephrem makes it clear that being in darkness means being spiritually sick, and finding the doctor means coming to the light.[227] Elsewhere too, sickness is compared with darkness: 'a little radiance from [the Sun of Righteousness] is sufficient for me to remove sickness, as it [removes] darkness'.[228] Metaphorically speaking, darkness is full of pain,[229] and it causes weakness and doubt in the believers, and it blinds them from believing in the truth and in God. Thus, to be lacking in faith means being spiritually blind and sick. This is best illustrated by Nicodemus who was blind and sick, so unable to see the real truth of baptism,[230] and Simon the Pharisee who was

ܗܘ ܕܡܢ ܢܦܫܗ ܠܐ ܡܬܛܠܫ. ܚܙܐ ܓܒܪܐ ܗܘ ܐܣܝܐ ܕܠܟܐܒܬܐ. ܗܘ ܕܗܘܐ ܠܚܛܝ̈ܐ ܠܬܝܒܘܬܐ (CDiat 5.17a; cf. Lk 5:32).

226 For example, in CDiat 8.6, Ephrem says: 'the angels in Sodom, however, rendered blind even those who could see' (CDiat 8.6: ܗܢܘܢ ܕܝܢ ܚܙܘ ܐܬ̈ܘܬܐ. ܡܣܟ̈ܢܐ ܕܐܬܒܣܪܘ. ܡܠܐܟ̈ܐ ܕܝܢ ܒܣܕܘܡ ܐܦ ܠܐܝܠܝܢ ܕܚܙܝܢ ܗܘܘ ܣܡܝܘ; cf. Mt 11:5).

227 CDiat 5.17a: ܟܪ̈ܝܗܐ ܕܝܢ ܐܣܝܐ ܘܗܢܘܢ ܕܒܚܫܘܟܐ ܕܛܘܥܝܢ ܠܘܬ ܫܡܫܐ ܕܙܕܝܩܘܬܐ.

228 CDiat 6.22a-b: ܟܠ ܡܠܠ ܙܠܝܩܐ ܕܡܢܗ ܣܦܩ ܐܢܐ ܕܐܥܒܪܝܘܗܝ ܠܟܘܪܗܢܐ ܐܝܟ ܕܠܚܫܘܟܐ (cf. Lk 7.6ff). Blindness, in Ephrem, often means spiritual blindness that comes to exist because of lack of faith and sin. For example in CDiat 10.7, Ephrem refers to Jn 9:39 and quotes: 'the blind will see, and those who see will become blind' ( ܗܝ ܕܝܢ ܕܣܡܝ̈ܐ ܢܚܙܘܢ. ܘܕܚܙܝܢ ܢܣܡܘܢ; cf. Jn 9:39). Based on Isa 6:10, Ephrem attributes blindness to the Hebrews who are represented by the dumb and blind man who was possessed by a demon (Mt 13:15): ܐܝܟ ܕܐܡܪ ܐܫܥܝܐ ܕܐܬܥܒܝ ܠܗ ܠܒܗ ܕܥܡܐ ܗܢܐ. ܘܐܕܢܘ̈ܗܝ ܐܘܩܪ. ܘܥܝܢܘ̈ܗܝ ܥܡܨ. ܕܠܐ ܢܚܙܐ ܒܥܝܢܘ̈ܗܝ ܘܢܫܡܥ ܒܐܕܢܘ̈ܗܝ (CDiat 10.7). In turn, the blind man at Bethsaida (Mk 8:25) was healed not only exteriorly, but also interiorly: ܟܕ ܕܢܚ ܠܗ ܢܘܗܪܐ ܠܒܪ ܒܥܝܢܘ̈ܗܝ. ܕܢܚ ܠܗ ܢܘܗܪܐ ܓܘ ܒܓܘ ܬܪܥܝܬܗ. ܐܬܟܪܝܬ ܣܡܝܘܬܗ ܡܢ ܠܒܗ. ܐܫܬܠܠܬ ܐܦ ܚܫܘܟܗ ܡܢ ܠܒܪ (CDiat 13.13).

229 CDiat 17.2: ܚܫܘܟܐ ܡܠܐ ܚܫ̈ܐ.

230 CDiat 16.12.

likewise blind and sick as he was unable to recognize Jesus as the Son of God.[231]

### *5.1.4.1 Lust (ܪܓܬܐ)*

The term ܪܓܬܐ can mean both desire and lust, and Ephrem uses it in the context of sickness. He speaks of the 'breath of lust' (ܗܘܬܐ ܕܪܓܬܐ) that exists in the fallen world and is related to the naked state (ܦܘܪܣܝܐ) of man.[232] Lust (ܪܓܬܐ) is temptation leading man astray into sin and so into sickness. Lust causes man to strive for evil and can cause rebellion against divine commandments, such as desire for wealth or any forbidden object, like Eve's desire for the forbidden fruit in Eden (Gen 3:6). In this sense lust is generally considered to be sin, and it is on the same level as greed, jealousy and hatred, etc.[233]

Referring to Scripture, Ephrem attributes the sickness of ܪܓܬܐ to both the body and the mind. Lust is bitter and involves hatred,[234] and the result can be death. As Eve desired the fruit and plucked it, so too Adam and his descendants can be considered as subject to desire.[235] As individuals, Amnon and Gehazi were afflicted because of ܪܓܬܐ, whereas Moses underwent the same test and survived. Because of his lust, Amnon raped Tamar (2 Sam 13.1-22) and, therefore, is called 'sick' (ܟܪܝܗܐ), 'crafty' (ܚܢܝܟܐ) and a 'serpent' (ܚܘܝܐ); and 'he carried out the lust of the flesh' (ܓܡܪ ܪܓܬ ܒܣܪܐ) and 'clothed himself in the attire of sickness' (ܐܬܥܛܦ ܗܘܐ ܐܣܟܝܡ ܟܘܪܗܢܐ).[236] Gehazi desired gold (ܪܓ݂ܬ ܕܗܒܐ) and was afflicted with leprosy.[237] Likewise, a

---

[231] Dom 16-21.

[232] Virg 32.8; Parad 7.5. In Virg 7.9, it is explicitly said that the body is a 'fountain of pains' (ܠܦܓܪܐ ܡܒܘܥ ܟܐ̈ܒܐ).

[233] Nis 47.7: ܘܐܦ ܗܘ ܕܒܪ ܣܢܝܬܐ ܪܓܬܐ ܘܚܣܡܘܬܐ ܘܓܪܒܐ ܕܚܣܡ̈ܘܬܐ.

[234] Eccl 1.5; Virg 1.8.

[235] Virg 23.9: ܚܘܐ ܗܘܬ ܗܘܬ ܠܒܬܐ ܕܒܘܬܐ ܦ̈ܐܬܐ ܕܒܠܥܬܗ̇ ܒܪܘ ܟܐ̈ܒܐ ܩܛܠܬ ܒܪܓܬܐ ܦܐܪܐ ܕܐܟܠ ܗܘ ܓܘܪܒܐ ܗܘܐ.

[236] Virg 2.1-3.

[237] Eccl 11.5.

whole community could be afflicted because of lust: the contemporaries of Noah did not become victorious over their lust, and so they died. Ephrem contrasts those who are baptised with the contemporaries of Noah, and challenges the baptised not to sin because of lusts.[238] Ephrem looks to a future life in Paradise where lust, along with vile emotions and anger, will cease to exist.[239] However, as long as man is on earth, in the fallen state, he can be weak and sick because of his lust. In Haer 11.2, Ephrem explicitly speaks of the power of 'our mind' (ܪ̈ܥܝܢܬܢ) being sick because of its lust.[240] Likewise, he speaks of the gluttonous people who ate the manna in the desert as 'being sick because of lust'.[241] Man is supposed to be strong and to control his lust by his free will, so that he may not be badly harmed.[242]

---

[238] Virg 7.9: ܠܛܘܦܢܐ ܠܒܪ ܐܝܟ ܟܐܢܐ ܒܟܐܢܘܬ ܠܐ ܬܚܛܐ ܠܪ̈ܓܝܓܬܐ ܐܠܐ ܗܢܘ ܗܢܘܢ ܕܟܠܗܘܢ ܠܛܘܦ ܕܐܬܛܦܘ ܒܗ.

[239] Parad 7.5: Both men and women are clothed in raiment of light;
the garments provided to cover their nakedness are swallowed up in glory;
all the limbs' vile emotions are silenced, the fountains of lust are stopped up,
anger is removed and the soul purified
and, like wheat, it flourishes in Eden, unchoked by thorns.

[240] Haer 11.2: ܚܝܠ ܗܘܢܢ ܪ̈ܥܝܢܬܢ ܕܒܚܘܫܒܐ ܟܪܝܗ ܒ̈ܪܓܝܓܬܗ ܘܒܡܫ̈ܚܢܐ ܚܘ̈ܫܒܘܗܝ ܘܒ̈ܪܓܝܓܬܗ ܟܪܝܗ ܫܘܠܛܢܐ.

[241] Iei 10.10: ܒܡܣܡܣܐ ܗܘ ܐܠܗܘܗܝ ܒܐܪܙ ܡ̈ܪܒܝܐ ܐܣܛܘܡܟܐ ܒ̈ܢܘܗܝ ܒ̈ܢܝܫܬܐ ܡܪܝܪܐ ܘܦܛܝܪܐ ܐܟܠܘ ܗܘܘ ܕܢܬܒܪܘܢ ܣܘܠܕܐ ܒܪ ܐܪܟܐ ܠܚܝܘܬܐ ܥܒܝܫܐ ܒܘܪܟܡܐ ܐܟܠܘܗܝ ܗܘܘ ܕܒܟܪ̈ܝܗܐ ܡܪ̈ܥܐ ܡܟܪܗܝܢ ܗܘܘ

[242] Finally, it is worth mentioning that in Nachträge Auszug 5.89, the author uses the terms 'health' (ܚܘܠܡܢܐ) and 'sickness' (ܟܘܪܗܢܐ) in reverse connotation: physical health has a negative aspect for it 'inflames lust' (ܚܘܠܡܢܟ ܪܓܬܐ ܡܓܡܪ) and your 'massage bears fornication' (ܫܘܦܝܢܟ ܠܙܢܝܘܬܐ ܡܘܠܕ); whereas physical sickness 'stops iniquity' (ܟܘܪܗܢܟ ܟܠܐ ܥܘܠܐ) and 'pain cools lust': ܚܘܠܡܢܟ ܪܓܬܐ ܡܓܡܪ ܐܦ ܫܘܦܝܢܟ ܠܙܢܝܘܬܐ ܡܘܠܕ ܟܘܪܗܢܟ ܟܠܐ ܠܗ ܠܥܘܠܐ ܘܟܐܒܐ ܠܪܓܬܐ (Nachträge Auszug 5.89; cf. Eccl 17.2). The term ܫܘ̇ܦܝܢ which is metrically too long, has obscure sense and is difficult to translate. Brockelman gives ܫܘ̇ܦܝܐ, the meaning, however, is not suitable, 'broth',

### *5.1.4.2 Greed (ܥܠܘܒܘܬܐ)*

Greed, considered as 'gluttony' (ܐܣܘܛܘܬܐ),[243] is another drive within man which tempts him to make evil decisions. Greed destroys the right attitude, and the right approach towards worldly wealth. It is often related either to food or to worldly wealth as gold. Greed is never satisfied, and it will never be fulfilled. As Ephrem says: greed is always 'hungry for new things'.[244]

Because of his tempting, Satan, the enemy of humanity, is called the 'Greedy One' (ܥܠܘܒܐ) for whom we are made his bread,[245] and he leads people astray to follow his own example, making them greedy like him. Ephrem speaks of the greed of Satan's tool, the Serpent (ܚܘܝܐ ܘܠܥܠܘܒܘܬܗ), who offered food to Eve, a symbol for all mankind.[246] Satan also confronted Jesus and tried to tempt Him with bread that is a 'symbol of the greed of Adam' (ܪ̈ܐܙ ܥܠܘܒܘܬܐ ܕܠܘܬ ܐܕܡ).[247] It was his 'greedy mouth' (ܦܘܡܐ ܥܠܘܒܐ) that swallowed Niniveh.[248] Besides Satan, Ephrem also describes death as greedy so that through 'his greed' (ܥܠܘܒܘܬܗ) he defeats mankind. Death swallows people like a hungry person.[249] Moreover, greed is not only something external to man, but it can also exist inside everyone, as long as man is alive on earth. But once physical death approaches, and sickness falls

---

or (Audo) 'pig fat'. It might be corrected by altering ܝ to ܪ which results in the word ܫܘܦܪܟ, meaning 'beauty'.

[243] Virg 14.11; Iei 10.7.

[244] Iei 10.7: ܚܙܝܗ ܕܝܢ ܣܘܝܐ ܕܐܣܘܛܘܬܐ ܒܘܪܗܢܐ ܗܘ ܡܣܟܠ ܠܚܕ̈ܬܬܐ. ܗܘ ܚܙܐ ܡܣܟܠ ܟܠܗ ܦܘܡܗ ܒܪ̈ܘܢܐ ܥܣܩ̈ܬܐ.. ܕܠܚܘܬܐ. ܚܙܝܗ ܕܥܠܘܒܘܬܐ ܐܟܠ ܒܘܠܥܢܐ ܘܥܬܐ ܒܘܪܟܢܐ ܒܪܝܗܐ ܗܘ. ܕܡܬܟܣܐ ܠܐ ܡܥܒܕ ܡܬܬܠܐ ܦܘܠܣܗ ܕܟܡ ܗܘ ܠܫܪ̈ܬܬܐ. For example, for the venom of food see further Parad 9.23; Dom 15.

[245] Fid 10.18: ܠܣܟܐ ܡܛܠ ܠܗ ܠܒܟܝܐ ܕܒ̈ܒܝ ܠܣܟܗ.

[246] Iei 4.4: ܒܪܝܟ ܗܘ ܕܝܗܒ ܦܘܡܐ ܠܚܘܐ ܕܐܬܕܡܝܐ ܠܚܘܝܐ ܘܠܥܠܘܒܘܬܗ.

[247] Virg 14.11.

[248] Virg 45.17.

[249] Dom 3. In Azym 3.10-11, Ephrem speaks of ܥܠܘܒܘܬܗ ܕܡܨܪ̈ܝܢ and ܥܠܘܒܘܬܗ ܕܥܫܘ.

upon man causing him to suffer, the mouth of greed will be closed;[250] i.e. when man realises the end of his earthly life is at hand through his physical pains or sickness which indicate to him that he is going to die, then greed and longing for any wealth or other secular objects will not exist any longer in his heart.

Greed draws the attention of man towards wealth and earthly richness, and so it can blind and harm humanity with the result that the 'blind can only see gold'[251] and long for it. Greed's (ܥܠܘܒܘܬܐ) evil name has spread to every generation,[252] it enslaves mankind in every generation and can afflict individuals even with physical disease, like Gehazi whose leprosy proclaims his greed.[253] Gehazi is again a typical figure for Ephrem: '[gold] clothed Gehazi with leprosy'.[254] While Gehazi was afflicted physically, Achar (Josh 7:1-26) was deprived of life, and the Israelites (cf. Exod 32.1-35) were led into sin.[255] Furthermore, Esau (Gen 25.30ff) was affected by greed, so that greed became like the 'poison of death' ( ܣܡܐ ܕܡܘܬܐ) for him; it made him 'bitter' (ܐܡܪܬܗ) and 'slew' him (ܩܛܠܬܗ).[256] Likewise, Iscariot hanged himself because of greed. Furthermore, it also works in those who 'steal' (ܓܢ̈ܒܐ) and kill, like Cain.[257]

### 5.1.4.3 *Jealousy (ܚܣܡܐ), Deceit (ܢܟܝܠܘܬܐ) and Hatred (ܣܢܐܬܐ)*

'Jealousy' (ܚܣܡܐ), 'deceit' (ܢܟܝܠܘܬܐ) and 'hatred' (ܣܢܐܬܐ) all have a bad effect on mankind, too. The subject of these can be both the Evil One as well as man, but in both cases the object is man. Either the Evil One envies, deceives and hates mankind, or

---

[250] Eccl 17.2; cf. Nachträge Auszug 5.89.

[251] Iei 6.4: ܣܘ̄ ܡܚܙܝ ܠܥܘ̈ܝܪܐ ܕܕܗܒܐ ܒܠܚܘܕ ܚܙܝܢ.

[252] Eccl 11.7.

[253] Eccl 11.5.

[254] CDiat 8.1c: ܗܘ ܥܟܪ ܥܟܪ. ܐܦ ܠܥܟܪ ܕܡܢ ܣܢܐ. ܘܠܓܚܙܝ ܐܠܒܫ ܓܪܒܐ. ܘܠܟܠܗ ܥܡܐ ܐܚܛܝ ܒܡܕܒܪܐ. (2 Kgs 5:20-27). Cf. CDiat 3.5; Eccl 31.10.

[255] CDiat 8.1c.

[256] Eccl 11.6.

[257] Eccl 11.7.

humans themselves envy, deceive and hate each other. The effect can be a spiritual wound, blindness and also death.

In hymn 26 On Nativity, a meditation on the biblical account of the seven days of the creation, Ephrem refers to the poisoned food offered to Adam by the Evil One. Before offering the food, the Evil One 'envied' (ܚܣܡ) Adam as a 'deceitful friend' ( ܪܚܡܐ ܢܟܝܠܐ).[258] While here the subject of envy or jealousy is the Evil One, elsewhere it is man, particularly his 'free will' (ܚܐܪܘܬܐ).[259] In CDiat 3.4, Ephrem says that Herod 'was blinded by jealousy' (ܥܘܪ ܒܚܣܡܐ) and 'was intoxicated with jealousy' ( ܪܘܐ ܒܚܣܡܐ).[260] Jealousy brings not only blindness, but also murder, as in the case of the innocent children who were murdered because of Herod's jealousy.[261] In CDiat 16.32, the jealousy of the Pharisees is contrasted with the healing ministry of Jesus.[262]

The Evil One affects mankind through his deceit.[263] Since Eve was deceived by the Serpent, Ephrem uses the serpent as a symbol for all kinds of deceit. While Amnon (2 Sam 13:1-22) is described as a serpent who performed his evil action in deceit,[264] Nathanael, in contrast to Adam, became victorious over the serpent's deceit: Adam was put to shame by the Serpent, whereas Nathanael did not 'put on the Serpent's deceit'.[265] In a non-authentic text attributed to Ephrem, the wound of the deceitful one is contrasted with the pain of a scorpion: 'the pain of a scorpion [lasts for] one day, and its

---

[258] Nat 26.9: ܠܐܕܡ ܕܒܢܝܐ ܚܣܡ ܗܘܐ ܒܗ ܐܝܟ ܪܚܡܐ ܢܟܝܠܐ ܐܓܫ ܘܐܘܟܠ ܠܗ ܣܡܐ ܒܡܐܟܘܠܬܐ.

[259] Parad 6.15: ܚܣܡܬ ܚܐܪܘܬܐ ܒܟܝܢܬܐ ܘܠܒܫ ܫܘܚܐ ܒܥܒܕܗ̇ ܒܐܪܐ ܕܙܢܘܬܐ. Cf. CDiat 3.4; 16.32; Nat 26.2; Virg 35.3.

[260] CDiat 3.4.

[261] Nat 26.2: ܘܚܣܡܐ ܒܚܣܦܐ ܠܝ̈ܠܘܕܐ.

[262] CDiat 16.32: ܐܝܡ ܡܢܘ ܡܢܕܝܢ ܐܣܝܐ ܘܥܒܕ̈ܘܗܝ [ܠܥܒܕܬܐ] . ܦܪ̈ܘܣܡ ܕܐܣܐ ܐܘ ܗܘܝܘ ܕܒܠܠ ܚܣܡܐ ܠܐ ܚܒܪ ܠܦܠܚܘ̈ܬܗܘܢ. Cf. CDiat 11.8; Virg 35.3.

[263] Virg 20.4.

[264] Virg 2.3: ܚܘܝܐ ܗܘܐ ܟܕ ܕܒܢܟܠܘܬܗ ܐܬܚܠܦ ܗܘܐ ܒܗܘܪܐ] ܐܬܚܣܡ].

[265] Virg 16.8: ܫܪܝܬܐ ܕܠܐ ܠܒܫ ܢܟܠܗ ܕܚܘܝܐ ܥܒܝܐ ܕܐܕܡ ܒܗ ܐܬܚܣܕ.

wound will stop; the wound of the tongue of the deceitful one is permanent, day and night'.[266]

Like 'jealousy' (ܚܣܡܐ) and 'deceit' (ܢܟܝܠܘܬܐ), 'hatred' (ܣܢܐܬܐ) is also related to the Serpent and so to sickness. The Lord, Scripture and Nature give witness about the hatred of the Serpent.[267] Hatred persuaded free will to make Adam's beauty ugly.[268] Some actions and habits are described as hateful and, therefore, as sickness: 'the hateful habit of the prodigal is a sickness that disturbs the [sense of] taste'.[269]

### *5.1.4.4 Wrath (ܪܘܓܙܐ) and Anger (ܚܡܬܐ)*

In the context of sickness, both terms 'wrath' (ܪܘܓܙܐ) and 'anger' (ܚܡܬܐ) have a negative connotation and are attributed to mankind. Unlike the Old Testament, there are no references attested in Ephrem where he explicitly speaks of divine wrath that causes sickness or disease or causes harm to mankind (Num 11:33; cf. Ez 5:13-17; 1 Sam 6:4). Man's wrath and anger contrast with 'humility' (ܡܟܝܟܘܬܐ), and they are expressed mainly in the way humans treat their fellows, particularly how they communicate with each other. Generally, words, or speech, make human beings rational, and language is considered as a splendid gift God has given to humanity.[270] But when people speak in anger or wrath, they misuse the divine gift, and consequently it injures them. Human wrath and anger reflect the loss of self-control and result in irrational and irresponsible action, as Ephrem says: 'the ferocity of anger does not permit enemies to speak reasonably to each other'.[271] The bad effect is explained with the noun ܣܘܓܦܢ̈ܐ,

---

[266] Nachträge Auszug 3.81: ܟܐܒܗ̇ ܕܚܪܒܐ ܚܕ ܝܘܡ ܘܗܘ̣ ܡܚܘܬܗ̇ ܡܬܒܛܠܐ. ܡܚܘܬ ܠܫܢܗ ܕܢܟܝܠܐ ܐܡܝܢܐ ܗ̱ܝ ܠܠܝܐ ܘܐܝܡܡ.

[267] Virg 29.11.

[268] Virg 48.15: ܚܐܪܘܬܐ [ܐܣܢܝܬ] ܫܘܦܪܗ ܕܐܕܡ.

[269] Iei 10.7: ܥܝܕܗ ܕܝܢ ܣܢܝܐ ܕܐܣܘܛܐ ܟܘܪܗܢܐ ܗܘ ܕܡܚܒܠ ܠܛܥܡ̈ܬܐ.

[270] Fid 1.12; Dom 11.

[271] Dom 23: ܠܐ ܓܝܪ ܫܒܩܐ ܥܫܝܢܘܬܐ ܕܚܡܬܐ. ܕܐܝܟ ܕܒܗܘܢܐ ܢܡܠܠܘܢ ܒܥܠܕܒ̈ܒܐ ܚܕ ܥܡ ܚܕ.

'injuries',[272] and the verb ܚܒܠ, 'to injure', describes the effect of wrath. In contrast to mercy and forgiveness (cf. Lk 14.1-8), 'wrath' (ܪܘܓܙܐ) is a source of sin which injures both its friends and its enemies.

Wrath is compared to an evil storehouse from which all kinds of evil can blaze up.[273] Wrath and anger cause not only an irrational and irresponsible way of communication, but also produce evil actions and deeds, as the case of Adam and King Uzziah shows us: both of them put on 'the same seal of anger as a result of free will'.[274]

In Dom 22, Ephrem uses the symbolic metaphor of 'pounding rain' (ܡܛܪܐ ܕܡܚ ܚܒܝܛܐ) in contrast to 'gentle showers' (ܪܣܝܣܐ ܓܝܪ ܪܟܝܟܐ) to demonstrate the effect of wrath: while 'gentle showers soften the earth ....., a beating rain hardens and compresses the surface of the earth so that the rain will not be absorbed'.[275] Likewise a word spoken in anger can provoke more anger and so injure the person to whom it is addressed: '»a harsh statement provokes anger« (Prov 15:1) and with [a harsh statement] comes injury: whenever a harsh word opens a door, anger enters in, and on the heels of anger, injuries'.[276]

### *5.1.4.5 Pride (ܪܡܘܬܐ) and Haughtiness (ܫܘܒܗܪܐ)*

Ephrem considers ܪܡܘܬܐ, 'pride', as evil and often attributes it to Satan. It too contrasts with ܡܟܝܟܘܬܐ, 'humility', and is 'sick'

---

[272] CDiat 14.23; Eccl 25; Parad 9.23.

[273] CDiat 14.22: ܪܘܓܙܐ ܓܝܪ ܠܬܫܡܫܘܗܝ ܘܠܒܥܠܕܒܒܘܗܝ ܡܚܒܠ. ܘܡܢܗ ܡܕܠܩܢ ܟܠܗܝܢ ܒܝ̈ܫܬܐ ܐܝܟ ܕܡܢ ܐܘܨܪܐ ܒܝܫܐ.

[274] Fid 28.14: ܘܚܕ ܛܒܥܐ ܕܚܡܬܐ ܡܢ ܚܐܪܘܬܐ.

[275] Dom 22: ܪܣܝܣܐ ܗܘ ܓܝܪ ܪܟܝܟܐ ܪܟܐ ܠܗ ܠܐܪܥܐ ܘܦܬܚ ܠܗ ܒܟܠܗ. ܡܛܪܐ ܕܡܚ ܚܒܝܛܐ ܚܒܛ ܘܡܩܫܐ ܠܗܝܢ ܐܦ̈ܝܗ ܕܐܪܥܐ ܕܠܐ ܬܩܒܠܘܗܝ.

[276] Dom 22: ܡܠܬܐ ܠܡ ܓܝܪ ܩܫܝܬܐ ܡܥܝܪܐ ܪܘܓܙܐ ܘܥܡܗ ܐܝܬܝܗ ܚܘܒ̈ܠܐ. ܘܡܐ ܕܦܬܚܬ ܬܪܥܐ ܡܠܬܐ ܩܫܝܬܐ ܥܐܠ ܪܘܓܙܐ. ܘܒܥܩܒܗ ܕܪܘܓܙܐ ܥܐܠܝܢ ܒܥܩܒܗ ܚܘܒ̈ܠܐ.

(ܟܪܝܗܐ) so that it 'cannot look at the strength/power of humility'.[277]

In Eccl 1.6, ܫܘܒܗܪܐ, 'haughtiness', is considered as an evil that causes bitterness, along with wealth, lust and greed.[278] Ignorant questions asked cause 'venom' (ܡܐܪܬܐ).[279] Ephrem understands the request of the sons of Zebedee (James and John, Mk 10:35-39, cf. Mt 20:20-22) to be seated on the right and left of Jesus in His Kingdom, as a 'venom of haughtiness' (ܠܡܐܪܬܗ ܕܫܘܒܗܪܐ),[280] that puts humans under the pressure and burden of competition so as to gain the best rank.[281] Only the foolish person can believe in 'his pride' (ܪܒܘܬܗ) and ignore the evidence of his nature which is weak and sick, indicating that it is in an imperfect state as long as it experiences pain, hunger and thirst.[282] 'Haughtiness' (ܫܘܒܗܪܐ) accompanies error,[283] so that 'pride' (ܪܒܘܬܐ) can cause the fall of everything.[284] For example, ܫܘܒܗܪܐ can take part in the process of teaching and learning: 'there is no one among us who teaches with suffering, and there is no one who learns with pain; for he who teaches does so out of haughtiness, and he who learns

---

[277] Eccl 52.3: ܟܪܝܗܐ ܗܝ [ܪܒܘܬܐ] ܘܠܐ ܡܫܟܚܐ ܕܬܚܘܪ [ܒܘܙܪܐ] ܕܡܟܝܟܘܬܐ. Cf. Virg 14.8.

[278] Eccl 1.6: ܡܪ̈ܝܪܝܢ ܐܢܘܢ ܠܢ ܗܟܢ ܒ̈ܢܝܐ ܒܝ̈ܫܐ ܡܢ ܦܫ̈ܐ ܕܡܡܘܢܐ ܘܕܫܘܒܗܪܐ ܘܕܪܓܬܐ ܘܕܥܠܘܒܘܬܐ.

[279] Eccl 25.3: ܕܟܠ ܫܐܠܐ ܕܕܠܐ ܝܕܥܬܐ ܗܝ ܡܐܪܬܐ ܠܒܠܐ ܠܫܐܘ̈ܠܗ̇.

[280] Eccl 25.8: ܗܘ ܕܝܢ ܐܣܝܐ ܚܟܝܡܐ ܕܚܙܗ̇ ܠܡܐܪܬܗ ܕܫܘܒܗܪܐ ܕܦܪܚܬ ܠܗ̇ ܒܒ̈ܢܝ ܙܒܕܝ.

[281] Eccl 25.7: ܝܗܒܬ ܠܒܪ ܕܐܟܠܐ ܬܠ̈ܠܬܐ ܕܒܬܫܡ ܘܡܪܗܛܬ ܒܢ̈ܝ ܐܝܟܐ ܕܢܠܒܫܘܢ ܠܗܘܢ ܕܪ̈ܟܢ ܕܪ̈ܟܢ ܘܐܬܚܦܘܢ ܒܒܪܐ ܠܡܫܬܚܫܘܬܐ ܘܫܒܩܘܗܝ ܠܫܒܝܠܐ ܬܪܝܨܐ. In this hymn, Ephrem often uses the term ܦܘܠܓܐ to emphasise that an evil inquiry can injure.

[282] Eccl 26.8-9.

[283] Eccl 26.9: ܗܘ ܫܘܒܗܪܐ ܠܗ ܕܛܘܥܝܐ ܟܢܫܐ.

[284] Dom 22: ܕܡܫܝ̈ܚܘܬܐ ܕܒܟܠܐ ܒܠܥܗܘܢ ܪܒܘܬܐ ܠܟܠܗܘܢ ܒܫܘܒܗܪܐ ܕܪܢܐ ܠܗܘܢ.

does so out of honour.'[285] The best example is Adam: the loss of his state goes back to his pride.[286]

Thus, both ܪܘܪܒܘܬܐ and ܫܘܒܗܪܐ are basically the fruit of free will and, therefore, can harm and cause pain and sickness: the pain of pride can grow strong also because of man's free will. Ephrem explicitly speaks of the 'disease of pride' ( ܟܐܒܐ ܕܪܘܪܒܘܬܐ) along with the 'disease of blasphemy' ( ܟܐܒܐ ܕܓܘܕܦܐ) and the 'passion/suffering of haughtiness' ( ܚܫܐ ܕܫܘܒܗܪܐ).[287]

### *5.1.4.6 Paganism (ܚܢܦܘܬܐ) and Idolatry (ܦܬܟܪܘܬܐ)*

Ephrem often attributes 'paganism' (ܚܢܦܘܬܐ) to a nation or a group of people. Paganism existed in Egypt already when the people of God, following Joseph, went there. The Israelites came to know paganism in Egypt, and when they left Egypt they took it, as an evil spirit, with them the whole way through the sea and desert. Therefore, Ephrem speaks of the 'paganism of Egypt' (ܠܚܢܦܘܬܐ ܕܡܨܪܝܢ) as the origin of the paganism of the 'People' (ܥܡܐ), or of the 'evil spirit' (ܪܘܚܐ ܒܝܫܬܐ) that they acquired in Egypt.[288] Furthermore, Ephrem speaks of the whole world that

[285] I Serm 1.402: ܠܘܬ ܡܢ ܕܚܫܝܫܐ ܥܠܗ ܐܠܐ ܕܟܐܒܐ ܠܗ ܕܡܠܟ ܡܛܠ ܫܘܒܗܪܐ ܕܠܟ ܡܛܠ ܐܝܩܪܐ.

[286] Parad 3.10: ܕܐܘܒܕ ܒܪܘܪܒܘܬܗ.

[287] Haer 51.2: ܟܐܒܐ ܕܓܘܕܦܐ ܘܚܫܐ ܕܫܘܒܗܪܐ ... ܕܡܣܘܪ ܒܡܫܝܚܘܬܐ ܟܐ̈ܒܐ ܕܪܘܪܒܘܬܐ ܕܒܚܫܘ ܒܐܢܫܘܬܐ. Cf. Nis 2.2 where it is said that the Lord has taken away haughtiness from human beings.

[288] Dom 17: ܚܪ ܠܗ ܒܥܡܐ ܕܠܐ ܦܪܩ ܕܡܗܪܐ ܚܠܬܐ ܦܪܩܬܐ ܢܬܦܪܒ ܠܚܢܦܘܬܐ ܕܡܨܪܝܢ. Ephrem compares Israel to the man with the unclean spirit which left him and which brought back seven of his companions (CDiat 11.5; cf. Mt 12:43-45). In CDiat 11.7, Ephrem illustrates this with the historical events associated with Israel in Egypt and the Exodus: 'Morever, through the figure of a man, Christ was attributing the unclean spirit to Israel. When they were dwelling in Egypt, they had an evil spirit in them, while in service to Pharaoh. But, when [God] sent them a deliverer to lead them out, the evil spirit fled from them, and they were healed. »For he sent his word, and healed them and delivered them from destruction« (Ps 107:20). He led them across the sea ☞

'fell as a body into a great sickness for it became hot with the fever of paganism ... that is the cause of its sickness'.[289] God prolonged the Exodus through the desert so that Israel had time to leave its

---

so that they would be cleansed, but they were unwilling. He led them into fire, but they were not purified, as the apostle attests' (cf. 1 Cor 10:1-5). CDiat 11.7: ܬܘܒ ܕܝܢ ܪܘܚܐ ܛܢܦܬܐ ܣܐܡ ܠܐܝܣܪܐܝܠ ܒܥܡ ܐܢܫܐ. ܟܕ ܒܡܨܪ̈ܝܢ ܒܡܨܪܝܢ ܗܘܘ. ܘܪܘܚܐ ܒܝܫܬܐ ܒܗܘܢ ܐܝܬ ܗܘܐ ܟܕ ܠܦܪܥܘܢ ܡܫܥܒܕܝܢ ܗܘܘ. ܘܟܕ ܥܒܪ ܠܗܘܢ ܦܘܪܩܢܐ ܕܢܦܩ ܐܢܘܢ: ܚܪܘܬ ܠܗ ܒܓܘܗܘܢ ܪܘܚܐ ܒܝܫܬܐ ܘܐܬܐܡܢܘ. ܥܒܪ ܠܗ ܡܬܠܬܗ ܘܐܡܪ ܐܢܘܢ: ܘܦܩܕ ܐܢܘܢ ܡܢ ܚܝܠܐ. ܐܥܒܪ ܐܢܘܢ ܒܝܡܐ ܒܝܕ ܕܢܬܕܟܘܢ. ܘܠܐ ܨܒܘ. ܘܐܥܠ ܐܢܘܢ ܒܢܘܪܐ ܘܠܐ ܐܬܕܟܝܘ. ܐܝܟ ܕܫܠܝܚܐ ܡܣܗܕ. Ephrem goes on to say that the evil spirit departed from them (Israel) to find a resting (waterless) place among the Gentiles. But because it did not find such a place it returned to Israel. Even the Babylonian exile did not purify Israel from its sin. At the time of Jesus the evil spirit threw them down again (cf. ܫܕܐ in Lk 4.35 and Mk 1.26), for it found them full of envy toward Jesus. 'But this [time] their evil deed was worse than the former one. They routed the prophets with slaughter, and hung Christ on the cross. Consequently they were thrown away like a vessel for which there was no use' (CDiat 11.8: ܗܫܟܬ ܕܝܢ ܥܒܕܬ ܐܢܘܢ ܒܝܫܘ̈ܬ ܡܢ̈. ܘܐܫܟܚܬ ܐܢܘܢ ܕܡܠܝܢ ܚܣܡܐ ܥܠ ܦܘܪܩܢܗܘܢ. ܘܒܗܕܐ ܢܟܪܬ ܒܝܫܬܗܘܢ ܡܢ ܩܕܡܝܬܐ. ܠܢܒܝ̈ܐ ܒܪ ܩܛܠܐ ܦܪܩܘ ܗܘܐ. ܠܡܫܝܚܐ ܕܝܢ ܒܨܠܝܒܐ ܬܠܘ. ܡܛܠ ܗܢܐ ܐܫܬܕܝܘ ܐܝܟ ܡܐܢܐ ܕܠܝܬ ܒܗ ܚܫܚܘ). Ephrem also draws a parallel between the impure spirit of the Canaanite woman and the impure spirit of the Canaanites at the time of Joshua, son of Nun (cf. Num 14:1-38): 'This name [Joshua] destroyed the giants before them, and this [impure] spirit went off to the Canaanites, who came then to do battle against Joshua, son of Nun. But when the true Jesus came, it was by means of the faith of the Canaanites that he drove out the spirit from the young girl, who was a symbol of the race of Canaan' (CDiat 12.14: ܫܡܐ ܗܢܐ ܕܐܒܕ ܡܢ ܩܕܡܝܗܘܢ ܓܢܒܪ̈ܐ. ܘܐܙܠܬ ܠܗ ܗܝ ܪܘܚܐ ܠܘܬ ܟܢܥܢ̈ܝܐ. ܘܐܬܘ ܠܗܘܢ ܕܢܩܪܒܘܢ ܥܡ ܝܫܘܥ ܒܪ ܢܘܢ. ܟܕ ܐܬܐ ܠܗ ܕܝܢ ܝܫܘܥ ܫܪܝܪܐ: ܒܝܕ ܗܝܡܢܘܬܗܘܢ ܕܟܢܥܢ̈ܝܐ ܕܪܕܗ ܠܪܘܚܐ ܡܢ ܛܠܝܬܐ. ܕܐܝܬܝܗ ܐܪܙ ܫܪܒܬܗ ܕܟܢܥܢ).

[289] Nis 21.18: ܟܠܗ ܥܠܡܐ ܐܝܟ ܠܓܘܫܡܐ ܒܟܘܪܗܢܐ ܪܒܐ ܢܦܠ ܗܘܐ ܕܒܐܝܬܘܬܗ ܕܚܢܦܘܬܐ ܐܫܬܚܢ ܘܡܟܪܒ ܘܢܦܠ. ܡܚܝܠܐ ܟܝܢܐ ܕܐܢ̈ܫܐ ܠܡܐܬܝܬܗ ܘܒܟܣܬ ܢܦܫܗ ܒܚܝܠܐ. ܦܫܩܬ ܒܟܠܟܠ ܚܦܝܛܘܬܐ ܕܗܘ ܗܘ ܥܠܬ ܟܘܪܗܢܗ.

paganism in the desert, 'so that their paganism should not spread among the gentiles'.[290] Likewise, God took them through the water to wash it from them, but on the dry land 'they reverted to paganism' (ܐܚܢܦ).[291] The sickness of their paganism could not be healed through Moses' healing activity either.[292]

The sickness of paganism caused pain, and it could not be healed with the Egyptians' medicine, because it was a disease of the 'soul' (ܢܦܫܐ), not of the body.[293] Paganism was hidden in the mind of the People.[294] The People were blinded (ܥܡܐ ܥܘܝܪܐ) with the 'delight of idolatry' (ܒܣܡܐ) and wounded by the calf as they went astray (ܠܥ̈ܡܐ ܕܒܥܓܠܐ ܐܬܢܟܝܘ).[295] The engraved calf was dead and could not move, but as a wild animal with its horn, it wounded and killed by its paganism.[296] Therefore, Ephrem speaks of the Hebrew People who had become sick and were broken by paganism (ܐܬܬܒܪ ܒܚܢܦܘܬܐ), but they bandaged their wound

290 Dom 20: ܐܘܪܚܗ ܕܝܢ ܐܠܗܐ ܠܐܝܣܪܝܠ ܕܢܬܟܣܐ ܚܢܦܘܬܗ ܒܡܕܒܪܐ ܪܘܚܝܐ. ܕܢܚܒܝܗ ܐܠܗܐ ܒܡܫܦܩܐ ܠܥܡ̈ܡܐ. ܕܠܐ ܬܦܪܘܣ ܠܗ ܚܢܦܘܬܗܘܢ ܒܝܬ ܥܡ̈ܡܐ.

291 [Epiph 7.6: ܥܒܪ ܥܡܐ ܒܡ̈ܝܐ ܘܥܒܪ. ܗܠܟ ܥܡܐ ܠܝܒܫܐ ܘܐܚܢܦ. ܗܟܢ ܦܘܕܢܐ ܒܐܕܢ̈ܝܗܘܢ. ܥܪܝ، ܡܢ ܒܬܪ ܡܐܢ̈ܝܗܘܢ.]

292 Virg 49.13: ܡܘܫܐ ܐܠܦ ܥܡܐ ܐܚܢܦ ܐܬܬܚܠܡ ܐܣܘܬܐ ܕܠܐ ܐܗܝܠ ܚܝܠܗ.

293 Iei 10.6: ܕܠܘ ܟܐܒܐ ܗܘ ܕܦܓܪܐ ܐܠܐ ܕܢܦܫܐ.

294 Dom 43: ܚܢܦܘܬܐ ܓܝܪ ܟܣܝܐ ܗܘܬ ܒܪܥܝܢܗ ܕܥܡܐ.

295 Iei 10.4. In the context of paganism, Ephrem often uses the term ܦܬܟܪܘܬܐ, 'idolatry', that indicates the abandonment of the true God and the worship of dead idols. Again, Israelites learned this idolatry from Egypt: ܡܪܥܝܬܐ ܠܦܬܟܪ̈ܐ ܡܝ̈ܬܐ ܒܡܨܪܝܢ ܗܘܘ... ܦܬܟܪܘܬܐ ܓܝܪ ܗܝ، ܕܝܠܦܘ ܒܠܒܘܬܗܘܢ ܘܐܦܩܘܗ ܡܢ ܡܨܪܝܢ. ܟܕ ܢܦܩܬ ܠܓܠܝܐ ܘܡܠܠܬ ܐܝܟ ܠܓܠܝܬܐ (Dom 6). Likewise, Nineveh was sick because of idolatry (Virg 45.9). See further Dom 5; 17; 19; Virg 27.2.

296 Iei 10.5: ܗܐ ܥܓܠܐ ܢܩܫܐ ܕܠܐ ܙܘ̈ܥܐ ܦܬܟܪܬܐ ܥܒܕ. ܗܝ ܡܥܒܕܢܘܬܐ. ܒܩܪܢܐ ܓܝܪ ܟܚܝܘܬܐ ܕܚܢܦܘܬܐ ܠܡܥ̈ܠܘܗܝ، ܒܚܢܩܐ ܕܩܪ ܘܩܛܠ.

when they saw the broken tablets of stone.[297] Paganism was not only the cause of sickness for the People as a nation, but also for particular individuals, such as Simon the Pharisee[298] and Marcion who further increased his pains.[299]

The sickness and pain of the People were always present for they did not want to be healed. The People were led astray and they were leading others astray.[300] Referring to Isaiah, Ephrem says: 'they are the People whose sores break out each hour and the fountain of their sickness never fails'.[301] It is a serious bruise that can be injured any time and by any matter. For Ephrem a sickness that lasts for so long is an insidious pain ( ܕܟܐܒܐ ܗܘ ܕܓܢ̈ܝܒܬܐ).[302] The pain of the People was hidden (ܛܫܝܐ ܟܐܒܐ) and they were sick willingly (ܠܟܐܒܐ ܕܐܬܒܪܗ ܒܨܒܝܢܗ); therefore, the medicine that was offered increased their sickness instead of healing it.[303] In this context, Ephrem also speaks of 'feebleness among the Hebrew People' ( ܡܣܟܢܘܬܐ ܒܥܡܐ ܕܥܒܪ̈ܝܐ) and of the 'pains that cannot be bound up or compacted' (ܟܐܒܐ ܕܠܐ ܠܡܚܒܫ ܐܦܠܐ ܠܡܥܨܪ),[304]

### *5.1.4.7 Investigation (ܒܘܨܝܐ), Disputation (ܕܪ̈ܫܐ), Prying in (ܒܥܬܐ) and Probing (ܓܘܫܐ)*

Above all in the hymns On Faith, Ephrem strongly criticizes the Arians for 'prying into' (ܒܥܐ) God and 'investigating' (ܒܨܐ) the invisible and incomprehensible divine Nature. Human nature is too

---

[297] Eccl 43.7: ܥܡܐ ܚܝܒ ܢܦܫܗ ܕܐܬܬܒܪ ܒܣܩܘܒܠܘܬܐ; cf. Eccl 44.14: ܠܒܪܗ̇ ܠܣܩܘܒܠܘܬܐ ܘܣܝܗ̇ ܠܡܫܪܝܬܐ.

[298] Dom 17; cf Dom 18-20.

[299] Haer 32.1: ܥܡܐ ܕܥܒܪ̈ܝܐ ܕܐܬܒܪܗ ܒܣܩܘܒܠܘܬܐ ܠܦܘܪܣܐ ܘܡܠܠܬܐ ܕܪܒ ܡܐܣܐ ܥܠ ܡܪܘܥܗ̇ ܥܒܕ ܐܝܟ ܥܠܬܐ ܠܦܘܪܢܣܗ ܘܐܣܝܟ ܒܗܝܢ ܟܐܒܘ̈ܗܝ. Cf. Dom 5; 17.

[300] Haer 51.7.

[301] Haer 51.3: ܕܥܡܐ ܗܘ ܕܡܚܘܬ̈ܗ ܥܠ ܟܠ ܫܥܐ ܡܬܦܬܚܢ ܘܠܐ ܚܣܪܐ ܡܢ ܡܒܘܥܐ ܕܟܘܪܗܢܗ.

[302] Haer 51.9.

[303] Haer 51.7-8.

[304] Haer 51.5; 51.7.

weak to 'pry into' (ܒܨܐ) its Creator; and it hurts itself when it 'probes' (ܗܓܣ) and 'disputes' (ܕܪܫ) with the Medicine of Life. Ephrem uses different terms to describe the sickness of prying into the Divine Nature. The four words mentioned above appear both as nouns and verbs, and it is worth examining them at the outset.

The verb ܥܩܒ means 'to take by heel, follow closely', but in pa'el 'to trace, track, seek out, investigate'. In order to distinguish it from other related terms, ܥܩܒ will be mainly rendered by 'investigate', and ܥܘܩܒܐ by 'investigation'. Investigation can lead humans beyond the space of life, i.e. into death, but not into God. For Ephrem there is a 'chasm' (ܦܚܬܐ) between the Creator and Creation. While creation cannot cross this chasm, the Creator is able to cross it and enter into the life of humanity.[305] Spiritually, Scripture delineates the boundary of life.[306] Whoever investigates the Divine Power and thinks to cross the boundary will become spiritually disturbed and sick.[307]

The verb ܕܪܫ has the meaning of 'to find out, prepare [a path]; practice, train, instruct', and 'to dispute'. In the context of Ephrem's criticism of his opponents, ܕܪܫ means 'to dispute', corresponding in meaning to the nouns ܕܪܫܐ or ܕܘܪܫܐ 'disputation' and ܕܪܘܫܐ 'disputers'. Ephrem often links ܕܪܫ with ܕܠܚ, 'to disturb', and ܫܓܫ, 'to trouble'.[308] He uses the metaphor of a 'fountain' (ܡܒܘܥܐ) or 'spring' (ܡܥܝܢܐ) to explain the effect of disputation which disturbs the clear water.[309] Disputation may just refer to intellectual people, who are used to inquire instead

---

305 For ܦܚܬܐ see T. Koonammakkal, 'Ephrem's Imagery of Chasm', *VII Symposium Syriacum* (Orientalia Christiana Analecta 256, 1998), 175-183. In Nis 33.9, it is explicitly said that 'chasm' (ܦܚܬܐ) was caused by the Evil One: ܡܠܟܗ̇ ܒܦܘܚܬܗ ܠܦܚܬܐ ܕܥܒܕ ܒܝܫܐ ܦܣܩܐ ܦܣܩ ܪܒܐ ܕܢܦܣܘܩ ܗ̈ܘܘ ܠܚ̈ܝܐ ܒܦܘܚܬܗ ܫܪܝܘ ܘܥܒܕ ܐܘܪܚܐ ܠܟܠ ܡܢܗ.
The term ܦܚܬܐ is also used by Aphrahat (Aphr 20.9; 20.12) and in the Odes of Solomon 38.2.

306 Fid 46.1; 64.12.

307 Fid 65.12; 15.7. See further Fid 33.7; 47.11; 68.22; 72.12.

308 Fid 35.2; 35.8-9; 54.10; 59.11.

309 Fid 35.8-9; 59.11.

of believing, like certain 'teachers' (ܡܦܫܪ̈ܐ)[310] or some of Jesus' contemporaries.[311] Ephrem calls them ܣܟ̈ܠܐ, their wisdom is vanity.[312] Sometimes Ephrem uses 'investigation' (ܒܘܨܝܐ) and 'disputation' (ܕܪܫܐ) together, without any clear distinction.[313]

The verb ܒܨܐ is used often and means 'to pry into, inquire, investigate, examine'. The nouns ܒܨܝܐ and ܒܨܝܬܐ mean 'prying in, inquiry, search.' Ephrem speaks of 'defiled inquiry/prying into' (ܒܨܝܬܐ ܡܛܢܦܬܐ),[314] the 'boldness of those who pry into' (ܠܚܘܨܦܐ ܕܒܨܘ̈ܝܐ)[315] and the 'prying of the audacious' ( ܒܨܝܬܐ ܕܡܪ̈ܚܢܐ),[316] who try to pry into the 'Nature and Birth' of Jesus,[317] or into the 'Devouring Fire',[318] like a blind person prying into the light.[319]. Prying means dishonouring the Lord of All.[320]

The term ܗܓܣ can mean 'to meditate, muse upon, think upon', as well as, 'to seek, tempt, probe and attack'. Ephrem uses the noun ܗܓܣܐ, 'probing' or 'idea',[321] in a negative sense, and it is totally different from ܡܚܫܒܬܐ, 'process of thought', and ܪܥܝܢܐ, 'mind'. He says: 'an evil idea lies in the thought (ܡܚܫܒܬܐ); ... an [evil] idea (ܗܓܣܐ) disturbs everything at

---

[310] Fid 35.2; 35.8-9.

[311] Fid 54.10; 87.10.

[312] Fid 54.10: ܣܟ̈ܠܐ ܥܡܗܘ ܘܕܪ̈ܫܘ. See also Fid 28.11.

[313] Fid 68.22.

[314] Fid 28.16.

[315] Fid 28.9.

[316] Fid 28.11.

[317] Fid 5.19; cf. Fid 28.10.

[318] Fid 28.2: ܕܠܢܘܪܐ ܐܟܠܬܐ ܢܒܨܐ.

[319] Fid 65.10.

[320] Fid 28.13: ܡܢ ܢܒܨܐ ܢܒܨܪ ܠܡܪܐ ܟܠ.

[321] The translation of ܗܓܣܐ into English is very difficult, for there is no term in English that can be used constantly. In the context of the eye (ܥܝܢܐ), the term 'probing' is closer to ܗܓܣܐ; whereas in the context of the process of thought (ܡܚܫܒܬܐ, ܗܓܣܐ) has the meaning of an evil idea. Therefore, I prefer to use both terms, probing and [evil] idea.

any time'.[322] In a different sense, Ephrem uses ܗܡܣ in the context of the eye: 'it is not helpful for an eye if a finger probe it.'[323]

Let us look closer into Ephrem's theological understanding of prying into, investigating or meditating about God. It is clear that Ephrem does not mean that one should not seek and look for God, in terms of believing, praying and praising Him. Ephrem challenges and begs mankind to understand Scripture and Nature correctly, for these give evidence about God's existence and Majesty. But since Divinity and humanity differ in both name and nature, and a 'chasm' (ܦܚܬܐ) exists between them, human beings cannot go beyond creation and pry into and investigate the Only-Begotten-One, with the aim of defining and explaining Him, beyond what He has revealed to humanity by His grace. The boundary of humanity is defined as the boundary of a fish in water: just as the natural sphere of a fish is water, so Scripture provides an invisible boundary for humanity, particularly for the human intellect. Beyond the boundary, just as beyond the water, is death.[324] In Fid 64.12, Ephrem says:

ܡ̈ܝܐ ܒܪܐ ܘܝܗܒ ܠܢ̈ܘܢܐ ܠܬܘܬܪܢܐ
ܟܬܒ̈ܐ ܪܫܡ ܘܝܗܒ ܠܐܢܫܐ ܠܡܥܕܪܢܐ
ܘܦܣܩܗܝ ܚܕܐ ܠܚܕܐ ܐܝܟ ܠܚܢ ܒܚܪ[ܘ] ܢܘ̈ܢܐ
ܬܚܘܡܐ ܕܡܒܪܝܬܗܘܢ ܐܝܟ ܕܪܘܫܗܘܢ ܚܝܐ ܗܘ
ܘܐܦ ܒܚܪܘ ܒܢ̈ܝ ܐܢܫܐ ܬܚܘܡܐ ܕܟܬܒ̈ܐ
ܒܡܫܡܫܗܘܢ ܡܘܬܐ ܗܘ.

He created water and gave it to fish for [their] benefit.
He wrote the Scriptures and gave them to humans for
an assistance.

---

[322] Fid 45.2: ܗܡܣܢܐ ܗܘ ܕܝܢ ܒܥܝܢܐ ܕܪܡܐ ܒܗ̇ ܒܡܫܥܒܕܘܬܐ. ...ܗܡܣܢܐ ܡܫܟܚ ܟܠ ܒܟܠܥܕܢ.

[323] Fid 45.2: ܠܐ ܥܕܪܐ ܠܥܝܢܐ ܨܒܥܐ ܕܬܗܡܣܝܗ̇ ܒܗ̇. See further Fid 5.19; 46.1.

[324] Fid 46.1:
ܐܙܕܗܪܘ ܒܢ̈ܝܢܐ ܘܠܐ ܬܬܗܡܣܘܢ ܬܬܦܠܓܘܢ. ܢܘܢܐ ܬܚܘܡ ܢܗܪܐ ܥܒܪ ܘܠܐ ܚܒܪ. ܚܒܪܘܗܝ ܒܬܚܘܡܐ ܬܚܘܡܐ ܕܚܫܢ ܠܗ. ܗܘܝܐ ܗܘ ܕܗܡܣܬܐ ܠܡܢ ܠܗ. ܠܢܘܢܐ ܝܗܒ ܡ̈ܝܐ ܟܬܒ̈ܐ ܠܒܢܝ̈ܢܫܐ. ܠܟܘ ܡܢܗܘܢ ܚܝܐ ܠܒܪ ܡܢܗܘܢ ܡܘܬܐ.

They witness each one for [the truth of] the other. If
fish cross over
the boundary of their course, their leaping is a cause of
suffering,
and if human beings passed over the bounds of the
Scripture,
their investigation is a cause of death [for them].

*Fid 64.12*

The difference between divinity and humanity is real and always present. Divinity is hidden and invisible so that it cannot be investigated. If the Devil cannot be depicted with any pigments, how would it be possible for human beings to investigate the Divinity?[325] Ephrem prefers the simplicity of Faith instead of the profane wisdom that 'gains death'.[326] Faith brings humanity near to God, whereas prying into and inquiry cut humanity away from the Life-Giver.[327] Truth can also be learned through practising faith and it does not need 'investigation' (ܒܘܩܝܐ).[328] Prying into God is like a blind person prying into light.[329]

The consequence of investigation is immensely dangerous. Referring to the Old Testament, Ephrem demonstrates the incapability of human beings to investigate God. One of the examples he uses is the uplifted serpent of Moses' time (cf. Num

---

[325] Fid 33.7:
ܘܐܠܐ ܕܐܦ ܒܣܡ̈ܡܢܐ ܠܐ ܡܬܬܨܝܪ ܫܐܕܐ ܡܢܘ ܒܒܘܨܝܘܗܝ ܢܪܕܝܗ
ܠܐܠܗܐ ܡܘܕܝܐ. ܪܘܚܐ ܡܣܬܒܪܢܬܐ ܡܣܬܟܐ ܠܬܘܪ̈ܓܡܘܗܝ: Cf. Fid 50.7.
ܓܒܘ ܕܠܐ ܢܬܡܗ ܒܠܘܩܡ ܒܗܡܐ ܗܡܠܐ ܕܚܫܐ ܚܙܐ ܒܟܠܗ ܘܠܐ
ܡܪܟܢ ܒܠܘܩܡ.
ܠܐ ܡܬܚܙܝܐ ܠܚܝ̈ܘܗܝ ܘܠܐ ܡܬܟܢܫ ܠܐܝܕܗ̇. ܠܐ ܡܬܠܒܟ ܠܗ̇ ܒ
ܕܬܕܥ ܕܡܪ̈ܢܝܐ ܗܘ.
ܠܐ ܡܬܪܫܡ ܠܗ̇ ܒ ܕܬܘܟܢ ܕܐܝܟ ܕܦܪ̈ܐ ܗܘ ܕܟܠ ܟܠ ܕܡܢܐ ܓܡܝ
ܒܪܝܫ ܗܘ ܕܡܬܟܠܠ ܠܗ.

[326] Fid 67.14: ܦܫ ܗܘܐ ܬܘܒ ܕܦܫܩܬܐ ܢܦܠܐ ܫܢ̈ܝܐ ܘܠܐ ܒܣܡܡܬܐ ܡܘܬܐ ܠܡܩܢܐ.

[327] Fide 72.2: ܒܗܝܡܢܘܬܐ ܡܬܩܪܒ ܠܗ ܒܪܢܫܐ ܠܘܬ ܐܝܬ ܗܘ ܡܪܚܩ ܡܢ ܒܘܕܩܐ

[328] Fid 67.17: ܦܫ ܡܫܒܠ ܕܒܝܘܒܐ ܕܗܝܡܢܘܬܐ ܢܐܠܦ ܩܘܫܬܐ ܕܠܐ ܒܘܩܝܐ.

[329] Fid 65.10-13.

21:4-9). Investigation of the serpent did not heal the people, only the faithful gazing upon it as a type for Christ.[330] Such inquiry dishonours the Son of God, as did the stretching out of Uzzah's hands. Uzzah was cast down, because he did not obey the command of the Lord when his hands reached out and he held the Ark of the Lord (cf. 2 Sam 6:1-8).[331]

As a warning against prying into the divine Nature, Ephrem is fond of introducing Old Testament examples involving leprosy as a punishment for impiety. In Fid 28.9, Ephrem uses the illustration of the punishment of Miriam (Num 12:1-10) as an admonition to the Arians. Because Miriam criticised Moses for his Cushite wife and reproved him who was humble, her skin became diseased with leprosy: 'behold, leprosy, which reproved the talkers, reproves the impudence of inquirers; but Miriam, who spoke against the humble one, wove with her lips a robe of leprosy for herself'.[332]

Other examples used by Ephrem are Gehazi who lied to Elisha (2 Kgs 5:20-27)[333] and King Uzziah who entered the sanctuary in order to burn incense to the Lord as a priest. They were struck with leprosy for they scorned the Lord (2 Chr 26:16-

---

330 Fid 9.11: ܠܐ ܗܘܐ ܒܒܨܬܗ ܐܣܝܬ ܚܙܬܗ ܐܣܝܬ ܠܥܡܐ.

331 Fid 8.10-11. Instead of dishonour, we should show honour to the Ark. As the Ark was honoured (1 Sam 5:1-5), we should honour the Gospel which heals our wounds. Fid 8.12:
ܐܪܘܢܐ ܦܠܫ̈ܬܝܐ ܠܡܩܒܠܬܗ ܢܦܩܘܗ̇. ܟܕ ܢܩܫ ܣܠܩܗ̇ ܒܩܘܪܒܢܐ
ܣܓܕܘ ܠܗ̇. ܕܓܘܢ ܩܘܕܡܝܗ̇ ܐܫܬܛܚ. ܗܕܡ̈ܘܗܝ ܦܫܛܬ.
ܠܟܐ ܢܦܩ ܡܫܪܝܬܐ. ܕܢܚܙܐ ܩܘܕܡܝܗ̇ ܐܫܬܛܚ. ܗܐ ܡܫܐܠܬܗ
ܦܫܝܛܬܗ. ܒܩܘܪܒܢܐ ܠܐܘܢܓܠܝܘܢ ܕܒܡܣܡܢܘܗܝ ܐܣܝܬ.

332 Fid 28.9: ܗܐ ܓܪܒܐ ܕܐܟܣ ܠܡ̈ܠܠܐ ܡܟܣ ܠܗ ܠܚܨܝܦܘܬܐ
ܕܒܨܘ̈ܝܐ. ܕܐܦ ܡܪܝܡ ܕܡܠܠܬ ܒܡܟܝܟܐ ܟܘܬܝܢܬܗ̇ ܙܩܪ ܠܗ̇ ܣܦܘܬܐ
ܕܓܪܒܐ (Num 12:1-10). Since Miriam, as a prophetess, was afflicted with leprosy because of her words, Ephrem says: 'who will be blameless if he inquires into the Only-Begotten of Him Who exacts revenge from talkers?' (Fid 28.10: ܡܢ ܙܟܐ ܐܢ ܢܒܨܐ ܠܝܚܝܕܝܗ ܕܗܘ ܬܒܥ ܡ̈ܠܠܐ). In this context, Ephrem says: 'the inquiry of the insolent is like stubble before it [the fire], and disputation and strife are swallowed up [in it] like chaff and briars' (Fid 28.11: ܒܥܘܬܐ ܕܡܪ̈ܚܢܐ ܐܝܟ ܩܫܐ ܗܝ ܩܕܡܝܗ̇
ܘܕܪ̈ܫܐ ܘܚܪ̈ܝܢܐ ܐܝܟ ܥܘܪܐ ܘܐܝܟ ܟܘܒܐ ܡܬܒܠܥܝܢ).

333 Fid 28.12.

21).[334] Likewise, because of their boldness, the 200 sons of Aaron who dared to serve the Lord as priests did not become diseased with leprosy but were actually swallowed up by the earth (Num 16:1-35): 'the holy [fire] was jealous and the knowledge of the truth was zealous against the profane inquiry'.[335]

Scripture is clear to the clear-minded, but it is disturbed to the disturbed. Although the investigators reckon themselves wise, for Ephrem they are foolish and sick, and they are incapable of understanding the harmony of Nature and Scripture.[336] Ephrem delineates a picture of Nature and Scripture like clear waters which have been disturbed. Nature came into pain because of Adam's sin, as it is written in Genesis, and the Lord came to suffering, according to the Prologue of John. Both Moses and John rebuked the readers in order that they should not get sick when they hear this.[337] It is the sin of man which disturbs Nature, and disputation which upsets Scripture. This was prophesied by Ezekiel (Ez 34:19):

35.8

ܠܐ ܒܙܘ ܠܟܘܢ ܕܕܪ̈ܘܫܐ
ܕܠܡܒ̈ܘܥܐ ܫܦܝܐ ܕܠܚܬܘܢ
ܣܠܩܘܢ ܕܠܚܘܗ̇ ܠܟܝܢܐ
ܘܕܪ̈ܫܢ ܥܠܝܗ̇ ܠܟܬܒܐ
ܘܡܪ̈ܒܝܬܐ ܫܦܝܬܐ ܕܐܬܬ ܠܡܥܪܬܐ
ܐܬܕܠܚܬ ܕܐܫܬܝܗ̇ ܩ̈ܠܐ ܕܠܚ̈ܝܐ
ܐܬܬ ܠܟܝܢܐ ܘܣܟܠܘܗ̇ܝ
ܘܐܬܬ ܠܟܬܒܐ ܘܕܠܚܘܗ̇ܝ.
ܥܦܐ ܡܕܪ ܢ̈ܕܪܐ ܕܕܠܚܘ

[334] Fid 28.13: ܐܦ ܟܗܢܘܬܐ ܐܬܬܒܥܬ ܕܐܬܚܨܦܘ ܥܡ ܢܒܝܐ ܠܝܚܕ ܠܡܪܝܐ ܟܠ. ܠܐ ܬܦܪܘܥ ܠܓܪܡܗ ܕܠܐ ܬܐܟܠ: . On leprosy, see chapter IV, 1.2.

[335] Fid 28.16: ܘܛܢܬ ܩܕܝܫܬܐ ܘܝܕܥܬܐ ܕܫܪܪܐ ܛܢܬ ܒܗ̇ ܒܒܥܬܐ ܡܚܣܢܬܐ. While Ephrem speaks of 200 priests, Num 16:2 (and Num 16:17 and 16:35) has 250.

[336] Fid 35.10.

[337] Fid 35.2:

ܕܡܟܐ ܒܪܫܝܬ ܠܒܪܝܬ ܘܕܡܟܐ ܠܡܘܫܐ ܘܐܦ ܢܘܚܡ ܕܒܪܝܫ ܡܦܪ̈ܫܘܗܝ ܐܚܡܘ ܠܡܦ̈ܪܫܐ ܕܕܪܫܘ ܒܫܪܝܬܐ.
ܕܢܚ ܡܒܪ ܠܐܠܗܐ ܕܐܬܐ ܠܚܫܐ ܘܐܦ ܡܫܟܐ ܠܟܝܢܐ ܕܐܬܬܐ ܠܩܪ̈ܝܐ ܕܠܐ ܢܬܟܪܗܘܢ ܫܡ̈ܘܥܐ ܒܪܝܫ ܡܦܪ̈ܫܘܗܝ ܟܬܒܘ ܫܡ̈ܥܘܗܝ.

ܕܪ̈ܘܫܐ ܕܗܘܘ ܠܕܠܘ̈ܚܐ.

Disputers, is it not enough for you
that you have disturbed the clear springs?
Our sin has disturbed Nature
and our disputation has upset Scripture.
The innocent flock that came to drink has been disturbed
because we have watered it [with our] confused voices.
It came to Nature, but we have corrupted it;
it came to Scripture, but we have disturbed it.
My Lord, clear up the streams
which the disputers who are disturbers have disturbed.

35.9

ܠܗܢܐ ܕܪܫܐ ܥܟܪ ܟܠ
ܠܗܢܐ ܚܪܝܢܐ ܕܠܫ ܟܠ
ܚܙܩܝܐܝܠ ܩܕܡ ܨܪܗ̇
ܟܕ ܟܐܐ ܗܘܐ ܒܪ̈ܥܘܬܐ
ܕܥܢ̈ܝ ܠܟ ܪܥܘ ܪܥܝܐ ܕܕܫ ܒܪ̈ܓܠܝܟܘܢ
ܘܐܦ ܐܫܬܝܘ ܡ̈ܝܐ ܕܕܠܚ ܪ̈ܓܠܝܟܘܢ
ܗܐ ܩܠ̈ܐ ܘܗܐ ܣܘܥܪ̈ܢܐ
ܕܫܬܝ̈ܪܐ ܕܠܚܘܗ̇ ܠܒܪܝܬܐ.
ܢܘܕܐ ܕܥܕ ܩܕܡ ܕܪ̈ܘܫܐ
ܫܦܝܢ ܗܘܘ ܡܒܘ̈ܥܐ ܠܫܠܝ̈ܚܐ
ܫܦܐ ܡܪܝ ܫܦܝܐ ܕܕܠܚܘ
ܪ̈ܥܘܬܐ ܩܕܡ ܡܪ̈ܥܝܬܟ.

Ezekiel depicted beforehand
this disputation [which] troubles everyone,
this strife [which] disturbs everyone,
when he rebuked the shepherds:
»My sheep graze [on] pasture which your feet have trampled
and they also drink water your feet have disturbed« (Ez 34:19).
Behold, the voices, behold, the actions
with which the haughty have disturbed creation!
Let us give thanks that, before the disputers,
the fountains were clear for the Apostles!
My Lord, clear up the watercourse
which the shepherds have disturbed in the face of your flock.

*Fid 35.8-9*

All kinds of disputation disturb the never-disturbed clear Spring and the peaceful flock. In Fid 59.11, again Ephrem quotes Ezekiel as a witness who prophesied the harm and injury that would come to the weak and sick 'flock' (Ez 34:1-24).[338] Ephrem refers this to his time. All the contentious divisions, the various parties of the quarrel in the Church, are based on the misunderstanding of Scripture. False interpretation of it causes disturbance, like someone using medicine and drugs without knowing their effects.[339] As do the examples from the Old Testament, so also the oikonomia of Jesus gives witness to his Divinity and to his Father. Likewise, the Father bore witness to the Son in his baptism and revelation. The good deeds, like the healing of the man sick of the palsy and Peter's mother-in-law, are evidence for Jesus being the King's Son. Jesus as the Medicine of Life is present in his Church, but disputation can deprive people of this medicine and cause them to have doubt in His presence, as those who did not believe that He is 'able to give us his body' (Jn 6:52). Therefore, Ephrem says: 'their disputation deprives them of the Medicine of Life. Let not our disputation deprive us also because we do not trust'.[340]

In Fid 5.15-16, Ephrem says: if someone desires to investigate the fruit, inquiry will guide him to the root of the fruit. Jesus, the Son of God, descended from heaven as the fruit which can be

---

[338] Fid 59.11:
ܒܥܢܐ ܕܢܒܝܘܬܐ ܕܙܪܬ ܒܗ ܢܒܝܐ ܕܠܐ ܡܬܕܠܚܢ ܡܬܕܠܚܘܢ ܥܠܝܗ ܕܪ̈ܥܝܗܘܢ. ܘܒܗܢܐ ܡܫܬܥܝܢܬܐ ܐܬܬܥܝܬ ܕܠܫܘܥܝܬܐ ܘܐܬܕܠܚܬ ܐܦ ܗܝ ܕܠܐ ܬܬܕܠܚ ܬܪܥܝܬܐ. ܕܠܝܬܗ ܠܫܘܥܝܬܐ ܘܐܬܥܝܬ ܒܗ ܒܠܐ ܒܥܒܗܘܢ ܕܒܠ̈ܐ.

[339] Fide 53.6-7. As the weakness of man is feeble against natural things in their disorder, like thunder, earthquakes and storms, so too the power of drugs is harmful when it is not mixed: 'If weak things, without mixing, are hard, how hard will it be for a human to inquire into the devouring Fire, without order?' (Fid 28.2: ܘܐܢ ܕܝܢ ܡܚܝ̈ܠܬܐ ܥܫܝܢ ܕܠܐ ܡܘܙܓ ܟܡܐ ܥܫܝܢ ܕܠܐ ܛܘܟܣܐ ܕܠܢܘܪܐ ܐܟܠܬܐ ܢܒܥܐ ܐܢܫ).

[340] Fid 54.10:
ܝ̈ܢܒܐ ܥܒܟܘ ܘܕܪܫܘ ܕܐܝܟܢ ܡܨܐ ܗܢܐ ܦܓܪܗ ܕܢܬܠ ܠܢ ܕܪ̈ܫܗܘܢ ܟܠܐ ܐܢܘܢ. ܡܢܗ ܕܣܡ ܚ̈ܝܐ ܠܐ ܢܟܠܝܢ ܐܦ ܠܢ ܕܪܫܢ ܕܠܐ ܢܙܪ.

either the 'Medicine of Life' (ܣܡ ܚܝ̈ܐ) or the 'poison of death' (ܣܡ ܡܘܬܐ).[341] Because of investigation, Ephrem considers our broken state as very bitter (ܐܘ ܟܡܐ ܡܪܝܪ ܬܒܪܢ) and speaks of 'bruises on our bodies, scars on our souls, marks on our spirits'.[342] The injury of investigation is well illustrated using the metaphor of the eye, which serves a similar purpose to that of fish in the water, quoted above:

45.1

ܥܝܢܐ ܘܬܪܥܝܬܐ ܝܠܦܘ ܚܕܐ ܠܚܕܐ
ܕܡܕܡ ܙܥܘܪ ܐܢ ܗܘ ܕܢܦܠ ܒܓܘ ܥܝܢܟ
ܫܓܫ ܘܕܠܚ ܠܗ̇ ܘܗܟܢ ܠܬܪܥܝܬܟ
ܟܬܒܐ ܘܢܘܗܪܐ ܢܚܟܡܢܟ
ܢܘܗܪܐ ܦܐܐ ܠܥܝܢܐ ܘܫܪܪܐ ܠܬܪܥܝܬܐ
ܢܘܗܪܐ ܓܒܝ ܠܥܝܢܟ ܟܬܒ̈ܐ ܠܬܪܥܝܬܟ.

The eye and the mind teach one another
because [even] a little thing, if it falls into your eye,
upsets and disturbs it, and likewise your mind.
Let Scripture and light make you wise:
light is fitting for the eye and truth for the mind.
Choose light for your eye and the Scriptures for your
mind.

45.2

ܟܡܐ ܣܢܝܐ ܥܝܢܐ ܠܡܕܡ ܕܢܦܠ ܒܗ̇
ܡܚܫܒܬܐ ܗܘ ܕܝܢ ܒܝܫܬܐ ܐܝܬ ܒܗ̇ ܒܡܚܫܒܬܢ
ܢܬܪܐ ܡܥܐ ܠܥܝ̈ܢܐ ܟܡܐ ܕܝ ܡܥܐ ܠܢܦܫܐ
ܡܚܫܒܬܐ ܡܣܟܠ ܟܠ ܒܟܠܝܘܡ
ܠܐ ܒܙܪܐ ܠܥܝܢܐ ܨܒܝܢܐ ܕܬܗܡܘܣ ܒܗ̇
ܘܐܦ ܠܐ ܠܪܥܝܢܐ ܨܒܝܬܐ ܕܬܗܡܘܣܝܢ ܒܗ̇.

How the eye hates something that falls in it!
But an evil thought exists in our mind.

---

[341] Fid 5.16:
ܥܒ ܘܢܣܒܬ ܠܬܠܝܢ ܦܐܪܐ ܒܣܘܟܐ ܠܒܟܢܫܝܗ، ܫܠܝܘܬܗ ܬܫܪܝܢ. ܠܐ ܬܒܥܝܢ ܒܓܘܗ. ܣܡ ܚܝ̈ܐ ܗܘ ܕܡܬܒܥܐ ܐܦ ܣܡ ܡܘܬܐ ܠܡܣܘܒܐ.

[342] Fid 5.19:
ܬܡܗܐ ܘܬܗܪܐ ܒܕܪܢ ܕܣܢܝ̈ܩܬܐ ܒܥܘܩܒܝܢ ܥܘܩ̈ܒܬܐ ܒܠܦܬܢ ܒܘܬ̈ܬܐ ܒܢܘܣ. ܫܠܦ ܡܚܒܠ ܕܠܒܝܐ ܕܐܡܠܐ ܡܫܟܐ ܫܥܫ ܠܗ ܡܟܫܠܗ ܠܗ ܒܐܣܝܗ ܕܠܒܝܐ ܚܒܫܗ ܘܠܙܗ. ܐܘ ܟܡܐ ܡܪܝܪ ܬܒܪܢ ܕܐܣܝܐ ܕܪܕܦ ܠܐܒܢ ܫܠܚ ܒܗ ܡܚܫ ܡܠܘܟܢ.

> A hard crumb is in [our] eyes, but how much harder is
> it for the soul:
> an [evil] thought corrupts everything all the time!
> It is also no [help] for the eye [for] a finger to probe it,
> and it is no help for the mind for inquiry to attack it.
>
> *Fid 45.1-2*

Thus, the result of investigation can be death, or it may lead to being struck with sickness. Ephrem considers the Arians as wounded limbs in the body: as an injured limb, they need medicine from the 'Healer-of-all-pains'. But Ephrem indicates that even a good physician may give up on a bad case. That means that if the limb refuses to be healed, it should be amputated and thrown away, so that it will not harm the other limbs.[343] Referring to Ezekiel (Ez 34:1-24), because of their investigation the whole flock has been disturbed and wounded. Also the Greeks, at the time of Paul (Acts 17:16-34), were considered to be sick because they used to pry and investigate. Ephrem says that they 'rejected the Medicine of Life because they had been weakened for a long time by the disease of investigations'.[344] Instead of prying, mankind should seek the Lord's help,[345] for prying and investigation are sickness, and such

[343] Fid 15.17: ܐܝܟܐ ܕܡܟܡܟ ܗܕܡܐ ܗܘ ܕܐܬܡܚܝ. ܬܐܣܝܐ ܕܠܡܐ ܢܚܐ ܠܟܠܗ ܦܓܪܐ. ܘܡܛܠ ܕܟܠܒ ܢܟܘܪ ܢܫ̈ܘܗܝ ܡܢ ܡܪܚܒܬܐ ܡܐܣܐ ܥܠ ܟܐܒ̈ܝܢ. For a wound that is difficult to heal like a 'scar' (ܥܘܒܬܐ) or 'gangrene' (ܣܠܥܝܬܐ) see Aphr 7.5-6 and 7.17. A translation of Aphr 7.2-6 is provided in chapter II, 3.3.1.

[344] Fid 47.11: ܦܠܛܘܗܝ ܠܣܡ ܚܝܐ ܕܐܪܝܘܦܓܐ ܟܪܝܗܝܢ ܗܘܘ ܟܘܪܗܢܐ ܕܒܘ̈ܩܢܐ. Ephrem draws attention to the faith of the mysterious Dionysius 'the Areopagite' and a woman named Damaris who believed in God (Acts 17:16-34). Ephrem illustrates the significance of faith without investigation and inquiry. As types par excellence of the Old Testament, Ephrem emphasises Noah and Abraham. As apprentices trust their craftsmen, and sick people put faith in medicines and physicians, we should trust the Scriptures without investigation. Since the book of medicine has full authority for the physician, why not the holy Scripture for human beings? (Fid 56.11-12).

[345] Fid 72.12: ܠܗ ܦܬܚ ܗܘ ܡܘܬܒܗ ܠܟܢ ܗܘ ܫܠܝܛ ܗܘܬ. ܫܠܡ ܠܡܘܬܒܗ ܒܟܝ ܠܡܪܝܗ.

'sicknesses press hard' upon human beings.[346] Ephrem beseeches the Lord to heal 'our sickness' (ܟܘܪܗܢܢ) caused by investigation that has turned everything into bitterness: 'even honey is bitter to our sickness'.[347]

## 5.2 Healers and Healing Pre-Incarnation

### 5.2.1 Remedies from Paradise

As has been discussed in the exegetical chapter 'The Relationship of Paradise to the Earth', the world benefits from Paradise after the Fall. While earth was cursed resulting in pain and sickness, Paradise remained the garden of wellbeing from which, metaphorically speaking, a 'fragrance' (ܪܝܚܐ) and a 'perfume fountain' ( ܡܒܘܥܐ ܐܪܝܓܐ ܕܪ̈ܝܚܐ), as well as 'blossoms' (ܦܘܩܚܝ̈ܗ) and a 'river' (ܢܗܪܐ) issue forth into the world. Ephrem says explicitly that the fragrance of Paradise serves as a physician who is sent to give medicine to the sick state of the land that is under a curse.[348]

The breath of Paradise minimizes the sickness and pain of this world, by giving 'sweetness to the bitterness of this region' ( ܡܚܠܐ ܠܗ̇ ܠܡܪܝܪܘܬܗ ܕܗܢ ܐܬܪܐ). This healing, or restoration is not complete, but partial. The puff of air from Paradise does not heal humanity from its fallen state, but it 'gives medicine' (ܡܣܡܣܡ) and 'tempers the curse of this earth of ours' ( ܡܡܙܓܗ̇ ܠܗ̇ ܠܗ̇، ܠܘܛܬܐ ܕܐܪܥܢ).[349] The 'fragrance' (ܪܝܚܐ) or the light 'wind'

---

[346] Fid 68.22: ܬܒܥ ܟܘܪܗܢܐ ܒܟܠ ܡܠܟܘܬܗܘܢ ܘܒܝܢ ܡܢܝܐ ܟܘܒ̈ܝܗܘܢ ܘܕܪ̈ܫܗܘܢ.

[347] Fid 42.1: ܕܒܫܐ ܠܟܘܪܗܢܢ ܐܝܟ ܗܘ ܕܡܪܝܪܐ ܗܘ. In Fid 35.4, Ephrem says that sweetness becomes bitter to the sick ( ܐܝܟ ܚܠܝܘܬܐ ܕܐܦ ܠܟܪܝܗܐ ܡܪܝܪܐ ܗܝ).

[348] Parad 11.9:
ܡܢ ܒܘܣ̈ܡܝܗ̇ ܕܗܕܪܐ ܥܢܢܐ ܕܡܬܚܣܝܐ ܦܘܩܚܝ̈ܗ ܕܗ̇ܝ ܐܪܥܐ
ܡܣܬܡܟܝܢ ܘܠܝ̈ܬܝܢ ܘܡܚܠܡ ܕܗ̇ܘ ܪܝܚܐ ܕܦܐܫ ܒܠܒܘܬܐ
ܐܝܟ ܐܣܝܐ ܠܟܐܒܝ̈ܗ̇ ܡܫܬܠܚ ܕܐܪܥܐ ܕܠ̈ܘܛܬܐ ܒܪܝܫܐ
ܕܣܠܩܘܗܝ ܡܣܡܣܡ ܒܪܝܫܘܬܐ ܕܠܟܬ ܒܗ ܚܘܝܐ.

[349] Parad 11.10:

☞

(ܡܫܒܐ) of Paradise are understood as the 'life breath' (ܢܫܡܬܗ) of this world, so that man was not just kept alive in the hope of full recovery, but also the wind soothed his pains and kept him safe from the real curse and consequence of his prodigal action.

Based on Scripture (Gen 2:10), the metaphor of the river, which issues from Paradise and divides into the four rivers of the world, also explains the remedies of Paradise. The function of the river is to 'restore the fountains of it [the world] that have become polluted by curses' (ܬܫܠܡ ܠܡܒ̈ܘܥܘܗܝ ܡܪ̈ܥܝܢ ܒܠ̈ܘܛܬܐ). Ephrem compares this way of the restoration of the world's fountains to the sickly water that had been made wholesome by salt, mentioned in 2 Kgs 2:21.[350] Likewise, Ephrem compares the river of Paradise to the oil that is used in the sacraments of the church. While the function of Eden's river is the penetration of Paradise water into the sphere of earth, such as into the gardens and trees of the world, the oil illuminates the church and human bodies, by consecrating the churches and the altars, and anointing those baptised with oil.[351]

Finally, in Parad 11.12, the breath of Paradise mingled with 'our soul' (ܢܦܫܢ) so that 'our inhalation might be restored by this restored/sound breath from Paradise.'[352] Here the act of healing is

---

ܗܘܦܐ ܕܟܡ ܚܪ̈ܝܢܗ ܒܢܝܚܐ ܕܦܪܕܝܣܐ ܢܦܫ ܡܚܝܠܐ ܠܗ ܠܡܬܪܥܬܗ
ܕܗܘ̈ܢ ܐܬܪܐ ܗܘܐ ܡܟܟܟ ܠܗ ܠܗ̇، ܠܠܘܛܬܐ ܕܐܪܥܡ
ܗ̇ܝ ܚܝܘܬܐ ܐܝܬܝܗ̇ ܢܫܡܬܗ ܕܗܢܐ ܥܠܡܐ ܡܪ̈ܥܐ ܕܐܪܥܐ
ܒܟܘܪܗܢܐ ܐܐܪ ܕܗܘܐ ܚܢܐ ܐܫܬܠܝ ܠܡܚܘ̈ܬܗܘܢ.

[350] Parad 11.11:
ܡܠܚܐ ܚܘܠܡܐ ܗܘܬ ܐܪܒܥܐ ܕܟܡ ܬܘܠܡ ܢܙ̈ ܘܢܦܩܘ ܠܗ ܢܗܪܐ
ܕܡܬܦܠܓ ܐܠܐ ܕܡܬܚܠܛ ܒܡܪܚܬܐ ܒܝܫ̈ ܡܝ̈ܐ
ܘܬܦܩܘܕ ܠܥܡܘܬܗ ܕܚܠܦܐ ܘܬܫܠܡ ܠܡܒ̈ܘܥܘܗܝ ܡܪ̈ܥܝܢ ܒܠ̈ܘܛܬܐ
ܐܝܟ ܕܐܬܚܠܡܘ ܡܝ̈ܐ ܒܪ̈ܝܫܐ ܒܝܫ̈ ܡܠܚܐ.

[351] Virg 4.14:
ܢܗܪܐ ܕܒܗ ܡܬܦܠܓ ܒܐܪܥܐ ܠܐܝ̈ܠܢ ܦܐܪ̈ܬܐ
ܘܥܘܒܗ ܕܡܫܚܐ ܡܬܦܠܓ ܒܐܪܥܐ ܡܫܝܚܐ ܠܥܕ̈ܬܐ ܗ̇ܘ ܡܫܝܚܐ
ܚܠܬ ܒ̈ܬܝܐ ܗ̣ܘ ܡܢܗܪ ܒܕܬ ܩܘܕܫܐ
ܗ̇ܘ ܫܪܪ ܠܐܝܠܢܐ ܘܗܘܐ ܠܦܘܩܕܢܐ ܠܗܘ ܕܒܗ ܐܪܒܥܐ ܥܡ̈ܘܕܐ
ܒܪ̈ܘܐ ܕܢܗܝܪܘܬܐ ܘܠܡܫܝܚܐ ܥܡ̈ܘܕܐ ܬܠܬܐ ܫܦܘܪܐ ܕܡܥܡܘܕܝܬܐ.

[352] Parad 11.12:

☞

related to humanity, so that among all creation, human beings in particular might benefit from Paradise. All these metaphors, fragrance, breath, fountain and water, represent the remedies of the Medicine of Life, Who, as the Physician par excellence, is supposed to come and heal Adam's wound and the whole of creation.

### 5.2.2 The ܐܪܙܐ of the Medicine of Life and His Presence in the Old Covenant

Although the righteous of the Old Covenant did not see the Son of God personally, they did participate in Him through their hope and through the symbols for He was invisibly present in their days. In the exegetical chapter we saw that the Medicine of Life was hidden in the seed of the descendants of Abraham. Particularly, in the context of Thamar (Gen 38), it is said that she stole the Medicine of Life that was hidden in Judah.[353] Likewise, Ruth (Ruth 3) saw the hidden Medicine of Life in Boaz.[354] They risked their life, to benefit from the invisible Medicine of Life.

This hope of the messianic salvation is shared by some other Old Testament figures. Rahab (Jos 2; 6), for instance, risked her life too, to save her family in the hope of the final salvation through the Medicine of Life.[355] Sarah could see the birth of the Son of God in the birth of her own son, namely Isaak (Gen 22).[356] Furthermore, all the righteous people in the Old Testament perceived and desired to see the Medicine of Life and taste His sweetness.[357] The Lord was perceived by the prophets so that they could see His function as the Medicine of Life and Healer. Malachi

---

ܗܘܢ ܒܡܒܘܥܐ ܐܪܥܢܐ ܕܪ̈ܚܝܠܐ ܕܡܢ ܠܗ ܘܠܗ ܚܒ̣ܝ ܢܦܩ ܘܡܫܩܐ ܟܠܗ
ܐܐܪ ܗܘܦܐ ܕܦܪ̈ܕܝܣܐ ܘܒܗ ܠܒܗܐ ܢܦܫ

ܒܗ̣ ܡܬܚܠܛ ܗܘܘ ܒܡܥܒܕܗ ܫܠܝܚܐ ܕܦܪ̈ܕܝܣܐ ܘܡܬܒܪܟܝܢ ܢ̈ܦܫܬܐ
ܒܗ ܗ̇ܘ ܡܒܘܥܐ ܒܪܝܟܐ ܕܡܢ ܬܡܢ.

353 Eccl 11.10: ܘܓܢܒܬ ܡܢܗ ܣܡ ܚ̈ܝܐ ܕܟܣܐ ܗܘܐ ܒܗ.

354 Nat 1.13: ܪܥܘܬ ܚܙ̣ܬ ܒܗ ܢܦܠܬ ܗܘܬ ܕܣܡ ܚ̈ܝܐ ܚܙܬ ܕܟܣܐ ܒܗ.

355 Nat 1.33; 9.7; Virg 18.7; cf. Fid 87.3.

356 Nat 20.1-4; Eccl 11.3. In Eccl 51.5, Joseph is described as the symbol of the Son of God like Isaak.

357 Nat 1.52: ܢܦܫܐ ܕܐܒܪ̈ܐ ܪܓܝܓܬ ܒܗ ܒܒܪܐ ܕܐܬܝܗ̇، ܣܡ ܚ̈ܝܐ ܘܐܬܐܡܪܘ [ܘܐܬܐܡܪܬ] ܕܒܣܝ̈ܡܘܬܗ ܐܬܐ ܘܬܛܥܡ ܚܠܝܘܬܗ.

3:20 [4:2] illustrates Him as the sun that provides healing in its wings: 'He is the sun about which the prophets proclaimed: »Healing is in his wings« (Malachi 3:20 [4:2])'.[358]

The Son of Man served as the Medicine of Life in His ܐܪ̈ܙܐ, 'symbols'. As the Son of God saved humanity with His blood, so too, His symbols saved certain individuals as when 'His symbol saved the sons of Jacob'.[359] The unleavened bread, as a symbol for the Lord, served as the Medicine of Life for the People from Egypt until the Last Supper.[360] In the context of the paschal lamb, that also symbolizes the Lord, Ephrem explicitly speaks of the lamb which bound up the wounded; it is he [the lamb] who binds up the broken' (ܕܗܘܐ ܚܒܫ ܠܬܒܝܪ̈ܐ), and it is made to shine as the Medicine of Life' (ܕܗܘܐ ܘܗܘ ܐܝܟ ܣܡ ܚܝܐ).[361]

Hymn 12 On Faith is christological and includes many symbols and metaphors for the Son of God. One of them is the vine from Egypt (cf. Ps 80:8-13) that produces the cup of the Medicine of Life: 'You are a spring of the vine from Egypt which the wild boar of the wood ate (Ps 80:8-13) when it sprouted from the shoot that sent forth the blessed bunch [of grapes] and the cup of the medicine of life'.[362] This is compared to the bitter death of Jesus among His People from where He rose as a 'Sweet Fruit'

---

[358] Fide 4.4: ܗܘ ܢܗܘܪ ܒܥܠܕܐ ܕܐܠܝܨܘܗܝ ܕܢܫܠܡ ܠܥܡܗ ܒܥܠܡܗ ܡܫܬܡܫܝܢ ܫܡܫܐ ܗܘ ܕܐܟܪܙܘ ܢܒܝ̈ܐ ܐܣܝܘܬܐ ܒܟܢܦܘܗܝ ܘܫܒܚܐ ܒܟܠܗ ܒܟܢܦܗ . In Syriac ܟܢܦܐ could also means 'bosom'. The Peshitta has ܘܐܣܝܘܬܐ ܥܠ ܠܫܢܗ, whereas the Hebrew and Targum (ומרפא בכנפיה) and Septuagint (και ιασις εν τας πτερυζιν αυτου) correspond to ܐܣܝܘܬܐ ܒܟܢܦܘܗܝ. Ephrem might have taken it from a Syriac translation of a Greek writing which quoted the Septuagint.

[359] Azym 15: ܒܦܨܚܬܐ: ܥܘܒܝܐ ܠܗ ܠܒܪܐ ܕܒܘܟܪܗ ܦܪܩ ܐܝܟ ܕܦܪܩ ܐܪܙܗ ܠܒܢ̈ܝ ܝܥܩܘܒ.

[360] Azym 18.15: ܐܪܙܗ ܗܘ ܕܦܛܝܪܐ ܠܦܛܪ ܗܘܐ ܠܥܡܐ ܒܟܠܗ ܗܘ ܦܛܝܪܐ ܐܝܟ ܣܡ ܚܝܐ.

[361] Crucif 2.3-4.

[362] Fid 12.8:
ܥܒܘܒܐ ܐܢܬ ܕܓܦܬܐ ܗܝ ܕܡܢ ܡܨܪܝܢ. ܘܐܟܠܗ ܗܘܐ ܚܙܝܪܐ ܕܥܒܐ ܐܝܟ ܕܢܦܩ ܡܢ ܢܘܪܒܐ ܕܐܦܩ ܣܓܘܠܐ ܒܪܝܟܐ ܘܟܣܐ ܕܣܡ ܚܝܐ.

(ܦܐܪܐ ܚܠܝܐ) and as 'the Healer Who healed all' ( ܐܣܝܐ ܕܐܣܝ ܟܠ).[363]

In the context of healing the most developed symbol is the fixed serpent (Num 20:4-9). In contrast to the Serpent in Paradise that deceived Adam and Eve and symbolizes Evil, the fixed serpent symbolizes the Son of Man. Ephrem quotes from John's Gospel: 'Just as Moses lifted up the serpent in the desert, the Son of Man will be lifted up' (Jn 3:14). Both the Son of Man and the fixed serpent performed healing to those who believed: 'Just as those, who looked with bodily eyes at the sign which Moses fastened on the cross, lived bodily, so too, those who look with spiritual eyes at the body of the Messiah nailed and suspended on the cross, and believe in him, will live [spiritually]'.[364] As life granted by the fixed serpent was physical, so too, its healing was only physical. The healing was not as complete as that of Jesus: 'Moses saw the fixed serpent that healed the stings of basilisks, and he anticipated he would see the Healer of the first Serpent's wound'.[365] The fixed serpent is considered as the symbol of the First-Born ( ܐܪܙܗ ܕܒܘܟܪܐ) and it healed the wounds of those bitten by the other serpents.[366] The symbol of the Son of Man, namely the fixed serpent, could heal the present wounds of some individual people

363 Fid 12.9.

364 CDiat 16.15: ܐܝܟܢܐ ܚܘܝܐ ܠܐܕܡ ܒܦܪܕܝܣܐ ܘܩܛܠܗ. ܘܠܐܝܣܪܐܝܠ ܒܡܕܒܪܬܐ ܘܢܟܬ ܐܢܘܢ. ܘܐܝܟܢܐ ܠܗ ܕܐܪܝܡ ܡܘܫܐ ܚܘܝܐ ܒܡܕܒܪܐ. ܢܬܬܪܝܡ ܒܪܗ ܕܐܢܫܐ. ܐܝܟܢܐ ܓܝܪ ܕܚܙܘ ܢܟܝܬܐ ܕܡܚܒ ܡܘܫܐ ܒܥܝܢܐ ܗܘ ܦܓܪܢܝܬܐ ܗܢܘܢ ܕܦܓܪܢܝܬܐ ܚܝܘ ܗܘܘ ܒܗ. ܗܟܢܐ ܒܡܩܒܥܐ ܕܦܓܪܐ ܕܡܫܝܚܐ ܕܐܬܬܠܝ ܒܥܝܢܐ ܚܝܝܢ ܐܝܠܝܢ ܕܪܘܚܢܐܝܬ ܚܝܝܢ ܘܡܗܝܡܢܝܢ ܒܗ. ܐܬܚܙܝ ܒܗ ܕܝܢ ܒܠܚܘܕ ܗܘ ܕܠܐ ܚܙܐ ܒܥܝܢܗ. ܕܚܙܐ ܠܗ ܒܓܠܝܢܘܬܐ ܗܘ ܕܠܐ ܡܬܚܙܐ ܒܥܝܢܗ. Ephrem uses the term ܚܘܝܐ ܡܩܒܥܐ and is translated 'the fixed serpent', although the classic English term for this object is 'the brazen serpent'.

365 Nat 1.28: ܚܙܐ ܡܘܫܐ ܚܘܝܐ ܡܩܒܥܐ ܕܐܣܐ ܢܘܟܬܬܐ ܕܚܪܡܢܐ ܘܣܟܝ ܕܢܚܙܐ ܠܗܘ ܕܐܣܐ ܡܚܘܬܗ ܕܚܘܝܐ ܩܕܡܝܐ.

366 Fid 9.11: ܚܘܬܐ ܠܩܒܥܐ ܢܟܬܘ ܗܘܘ ܒܚܘܪܒܐ. ܩܒܥ ܚܘܝܐ ܐܣܝܢܐ ܕܢܘܟܬܐ ܒܗ ܘܚܝܘ. ܠܩܒܥܐ ܐܚܝܕܬ ܚܝܬܐ. ܗܝܡܢܘܬܐ ܠܩܒܥܐ. ܗܘ ܐܪܙܗ ܕܒܘܟܪܐ ܠܐ ܗܘܐ ܒܝܕ ܐܣܝܬ. ܚܝܬܗ ܒܠܒܗ ܐܣܝܬ. ܒܗܝܡܢܘܬܐ ܚܙܪ ܒܗ ܒܒܪܐ ܙܪܐ ܕܢܟܝܢ (ܕܢܫܝܢ)

who were wounded by the other serpents, but it could not heal the whole of humanity, i.e. the wound of Adam and man's fallen state. The latter could only be healed by the Son of God, the Medicine of Life, Whose coming the just were longing to see.

### 5.2.3 The Patriarchs and Prophets as Physicians of the World

God, by His mercy, used all sorts of ways and possibilities to heal man. Since the medicines provided through His prophets were not sufficient for the sickness of the world, God sent His Son as the Medicine of Life as the last opportunity to heal humanity.[367]

Referring to the time of Pre-Incarnation, though the just could not see the Son of Man being born as the Medicine of Life to grant healing to the whole fallen nature in their days, yet they were enabled by God to perform healing of individual sicknesses of their time. God sent them as physicians into the world to visit it, heal and restore it. But the healing that they performed was partial and limited, because the sickness of the world was grievous. Not one of them was able to heal the whole sick body of the world. Neither could they heal what was lacking in human nature.[368]

Nevertheless, the patriarchs and prophets were able to restore and heal partially, but what they restored was little compared to the healing ministry of Jesus, Who is the Physician par excellence. In Fid 36.1, it is said that the physicians before Jesus, namely the prophets and patriarchs, healed only a little, but left a lot without restoration and healing.[369] These physicians sent by God are called 'Hebrew physicians' (ܐܣܘ̈ܬܐ ܥܒܪ̈ܝܐ) whose medicines were

---

[367] Haer 33.

[368] Dom 12: ܢܒܝ̈ܐ ܕܝܢ ܟܠ ܐܬܘ̈ܢ ܒܥܕܢܗ ܗܘܘ. ܚܣܝܪܘܬܐ ܕܝܢ ܕܗܕܪ̈ܐ ܒܥܘܢ ܠܐ ܡܠܝܘ. ܐܬܡܠܝܬ ܕܝܢ ܚܣܝܪܘܬܐ ܕܦܓܪܐ ܕܥܒܕ: ܒܪܗ ܬܬܡܠܐ. In Dom 42, it is said that the prophets could not give life to sinners, by means of forgiving their sins, but the Lord of the prophets could forgive sins and heal.

[369] Fid 36.1:

ܒܪܐ ܢܚܬ ܗܘܐ ܕܢܣܒܘܪ ܒ̈ܢܝܐ ܕܢܚܘܪ ܘܐܣܝܘܪ ܒܪ̈ܘܚܗܘܢ
ܕܬܒܪܘ [ܕܬܒܒܘ] ܘܐܬܘ ܐܣܘ̈ܬܐ ܘܫܩܠܘ ܘܠܐܝܘ ܐܣܝܘ ܩܠܝܠ
ܘܫܒܩܘ ܣܓܝ.

the power of the miracles and visions God had revealed to them.[370] Ephrem also calls them the 'great physicians' ( ܕܐܣܘ̈ܬܐ ܪ̈ܘܪܒܐ)[371] of the world, that is described as a 'sick body'. The patriarchs and prophets are sent by God as the 'famous visitors, physicians, of it [nature]' (ܣܥܘ̈ܪܝܗ̇ ܡܫܒ̈ܚܐ ܐܣܘ̈ܬܐ).[372] They are the just (ܟܐ̈ܢܐ) whose medicine was divine and their ministry was spiritual.

Each of the prophets or patriarchs, was sent to a particular place to heal a particular part of the sick body of the world. In Nis 34, Ephrem draws a picture of the world in the form of a body; Babel as the head, Judaea as the middle part and Egypt forms the feet. For example, while the physician Joseph was sent to Egypt, Daniel was sent to Babel and other prophets visited Judaea to heal the body of the world. Nis 34 serves as a good illustration of the function of some of the patriarchs and prophets, and of their healing ministry:[373]

34.1

ܐܣܝܐ ܐܒܪܡ ܡܫܒܚܐ ܠܚܪܢ ܐܬܐ ܕܒܪܝܗܐ ܗܘܬ
ܒܨܗ̇ ܘܬܡܗ ܘܐܬܦܢܝ ܠܐܪܥܐ ܕܟܢܥܢ
ܡܛܐ ܠܡܨܪܝܢ ܠܟܠܗ ܦܓܪܐ ܣܥܪܗ ܘܢܚܬ
ܘܚܙܐ ܘܐܣܝ ܒܡܠܬܐ ܕܩܘܫܬܐ
ܕܐܒܪܡ ܠܐ ܣܦܩ ܠܟܝ ܟܠܗ ܕܣܦܩ ܠܟܝ
ܚܢ ܕܒܪܘܢܗ̇ ܒܨܡ ܠܗ̇܀

The glorious physician Abram came to Harran that was sick.
He explored it and was amazed, and turned to the land of Canaan.
He reached Egypt; he visited the whole body and went down,

---

[370] Haer 11.11:
ܘܟܕ ܚܙܘ ܟܐܢ̈ܘܗܝ ܠܬܘܪܬܗ ܦܘܐ ܠܟܠܐ ܠܐܣܘ̈ܬܐ ܒܪ̈ܝܬܐ
ܐܬܘ̈ܬܗܘܢ ܘܚܠܡ̈ܝܗܘܢ ܗܘܘ ܡܣܒܪܢܐ ܠܡܣܟܢ̈ܘܗܝ.

[371] Nis 34.6; cf Nis 34.7; 34.10.

[372] Nis 34.9; cf. Nis 34.1.

[373] Before dealing individually with those biblical figures who are explicity described as physicians, it must be said, that in Nis 34 Ephrem speaks not only about the time of the prophets, but also about early Christianity in the region of Harran, Babel, Egypt, etc.

he bound up and healed with the word of truth. Since
Abram was not sufficient for you, who will be
sufficient for you,
Harran, who enjoyed its sickness (Gen 11:31-13:18).
Refrain:

ܥܘܢܝܬܐ: ܒܪܝܟ ܗܘ ܕܠܐ ܡܢ ܫܒܩܗ ܥܒܘܕܗ
ܠܐܢܫܘܬܐ
ܕܐܣܓܝ ܒܟܠ ܕܪܝܢ ܡܣܥܘܪܢܘܗܝ܀

Blessed is He who never abandoned humanity
for He increased its visitors in all generations.

34.2

ܐܣܝܐ ܝܥܩܘܒ ܡܫܒܚܐ ܠܚܪܢ ܐܬܐ ܕܢܚܙܝܗ ܚܠܝܗ
ܒܨܗ ܘܒܣܝܗ ܘܐܪܦܝܗ ܕܠܐ ܢܒܛܠ ܒܗ
ܥܣܪܝܢ ܒܫܢܝܢ ܡܡܠܟ ܗܘܐ ܠܗ
ܘܕܚܙܐ ܕܫܢܝܬ ܐܦ ܡܚܫܒܬ ܒܗ
ܐܪܦܝܗ ܘܫܢܐ ܗܐ ܡܝܟܝ ܡܪܝܪܝܢ
ܘܦܣܝܩܝ ܒܢܝܟܝ ܚܪܢ ܐܬܒܣܡܝ ܒܨܠܝܒܐ܀

The famous physician Jacob came to Harran to gaze
upon it.
He explored, rejected and left it so that he might not
come
to nought in it. Twenty years (Gen 31:38) he was
moderating it;
and when he saw that it went on madly and thought
evil about him,
he left it and moved away. Behold, your waters are
bitter
and your children are cut off. Harran, become sweet by
the cross.

34.5

ܗܐ ܠܡܨܪܝܢ ܟܪܝܗܬܐ ܕܐܦ ܐܬܐܣܝܬ ܒܡܐܣܝܐ
ܟܠ
ܘܣܪܝܬܐ ܕܦܬܟܪܘܬܐ ܒܚܪܢ ܣܪܒܬ
ܘܡܟܐ ܕܐܬܐܣܝܬ ܠܝܬ ܬܘܟܠܢܐ ܒܗ ܒܐܣܝܘܬܗ
ܕܒܟܠ ܚܠܠܝ ܡܬܦܪܐ ܗܝ ܟܪܝܗܘܬܗ
ܒܟܠ ܘܐܦ ܚܢ ܘܡܨܪܝܢ ܬܠܬܝܗܝܢ
ܥܡܡܐ ܬܠܬܝܬܐ ܒܒܪ ܘܠܒܪ ܀

Behold, sick Egypt has been restored by the Healer-of-
All,
[but] the gangrene of idolatory crawled in Harran.
And even if it is restored, there is no reliance in its
restoration

for its wound breaks open from any cause.
O Babel, as well as, Harran and Egypt, all three,
be baptised and put on the Three Names!

34.6

ܡܐ ܕܕܡܐ ܕܝܢ ܥܠܡܐ ܠܨܠܡܐ ܪܒܐ ܕܚܙܐ ܛܘܪܢܐ
ܪܫܗ ܒܒܠ ܡܨܥܬܗ ܐܪܥܐ ܕܝܗܘܕ:
ܒܛܘܦܣܐ ܕܪ̈ܓܠܐ ܩܝܡܐ ܡܨܪܝܢ
ܓܘܫܡܐ ܗܘ ܪܒܐ ܕܐܣܘ̈ܬܐ ܪܘܪ̈ܒܐ ܥܡܠܘ ܒܗ
ܛܒܐ ܒܝܕ ܥܒ̈ܕܘܗܝ ܡܬܚܗ ܠܣܘܥܪܢܐ
ܐܝܟ ܐܣܝܐ ܪܒܐ ܠܟܠ ܦܢܝ̈ܢ ܀

How the world is similar to a great statue the tyrant
saw (Dan 2:31): Babel is its head, the land of Judaea its middle part,
Egypt is constituted in the type of the feet.
It is a great body on which great physicians laboured.
The Good One extended the visitation through His servants,
as a Great Physician, to all sides of the world.

34.7

ܘܐܝܟ ܐܒܪܗܡ ܐܣܝܐ ܡܢ ܪܝܫ ܪܫܐ ܐܣܝ ܘܢܚܬ
ܐܦ ܗ̇ܘ ܡܘܫܐ ܐܣܝܗ ܡܢ ܪܝܫ ܪ̈ܓܠܐ
ܐܘ ܠܟܪܝܗܐ ܕܐܣܘ̈ܬܗ ܡܢ ܟܠ ܓܒ̈ܘܗܝ
ܘܡܢ ܫܘܠܡܢܐ ܡܦܠܬܐ ܗܘ ܒܣܡ ܠܗ
ܒܪܝܟ ܗܘ ܕܠܐ ܡܢ ܡܬܘܡ ܫܒܩܗ̇ ܠܐܢܫܘܬܐ
ܕܐܣܓܝ ܒܟܠ ܕܪ̈ܝܢ ܒܥܘܕܪ̈ܢܗ̇ ܀

As the physician Abraham healed from the head and went
down, also Moses healed it from its feet. Behold,
the sick one whose physicians are surrounding him from all sides,
[but] instead of restoration, it enjoyed the fall.
Blessed is He Who never abandoned humanity
for He increased in all generations help for it.

34.8

ܘܐܝܟ ܕܠܒܣܡܐ ܒܪܝܬܐ ܐܣܝ ܘܣܦ ܠܐܪܥܐ
ܕܡܨܪܝܢ
ܢܒܝ̈ܐ ܠܝܗܘܕܝ̈ܐ ܐܣܝܘܗ̇ ܐܝܟ ܕܠܠܒܐ
ܐܦ ܕܢܣܐܠ ܠܟܠ ܒܢܝ ܐܝܟ ܕܠܥܪܐ
ܕܒܥܐ ܒܡܕܒܪܐ ܘܐܬܛܠܩ ܘܐܙܠ،
ܡܨܪܝܢ ܐܣܝܬܐ ܡܗܝܪܬܐ ܒܡܣܟ̈ܢܘܬܗ
ܒܐܪ̈ܥܬܗ ܡܪܚܝܢ ܐܬܦܢܝܘ ܀

And as a sick heel, Joseph healed the land of Egypt.
the prophets healed Zion as the heart,
Daniel, as well, moderated Babel as the head
which went mad in the desert and was restored and gave thanks.
The pains of the physician Egypt, famous in its medicines,
became grievous by its own free will.

34.9

ܟܪܝܐ ܟܠܗ ܐܬܪܗ ܒܕܡܘܬ ܠܓܘܫܡܐ ܒܟܘܪܗܢܗ̱
ܠܛܘܥܝܝ
ܬܒܥܘ ܗܘܘ ܡܣܥܪܢܘܗܝ܆ ܡܫܡܗܐ ܐܣܘܬܐ
ܕܬܬܐܣܐ ܗܘܐ ܡܢ ܒܘܪܗܢܐ ܟܣܝܐ ܕܢܦܫܐ
ܘܬܩܘܡ ܬܘܕܐ ܠܐܣܝܐ ܕܚܣܗ
ܫܘܒܚܐ ܠܗܘ ܕܐܕܒܪ ܠܟܐܢ̈ܐ ܒܟܠ ܦܢܝܢ
ܕܠܬܪܥܝܬܐ ܬܒܝܠ ܢܣܥܘܪ ܗܘܐ ܀

All nature became sick as a body with the sickness
of error. Its visitors, the famous physicians, pressed hard,
so that it might be healed from the invisible sickness of the soul,
and rise up to give thanks to the Physician Who had mercy on it.
Glory be to Him Who guided the just in all sites of the world,
so that He might visit the sick world.

34.10

ܠܐ ܣܦܩܘ ܠܗ ܕܝܢ ܠܥܠܡܐ ܐܣܘ̈ܬܐ
ܒܣܡ̈ܡܢܝܗܘܢ
ܚܙܗ̇ ܘܐܬܪܚܡ ܐܣܝܐ ܕܠܟܠ ܣܦܩ
ܠܒܪ ܡܢ ܦܓܪܗ ܗܘ ܟܠ ܟܐܒܗ
ܘܐܣܝ ܚܫ ܒܦܓܪܗ ܘܕܒܗ
ܐܫܠܡܗ̇ ܒܚܘܣܝܬ ܫܘܒܚܐ ܠܡܣܒ ܚ̈ܝܐ
ܕܗܘܘ ܣܦܩ ܘܐܣܝ ܒܐܒܐ ܕܢܦ̈ܫܬܐ ܒܝܘܠܦܢܗ܀

The physicians were not sufficient for the world
with their medicines.
The Physician Who is sufficient for everything saw it and had mercy.

> He cut off[374] from His body and put it on its [world's] pain.
> And He healed our suffering with His body and blood.
> He restored our wound. Glory be to the Medicine of Life
> for He was sufficient and healed the pain of souls.
> with His teaching.
>
> *Nis 34.1-10*

### *5.2.3.1 The Physician Abraham*

Only in Nis 34 does Ephrem speaks of Abram, or Abraham, as a physician, giving him this title, in stanzas, Nis 34.1 and 34.7. In the former, Ephrem describes Abraham as the 'glorious physician' (ܐܣܝܐ ܡܫܒܚܐ). In contrast to the other physicians, Abraham is considered to be a physician of the whole world for he lived in Harran, Judaea and Egypt. This is clearly said in both stanzas: while in Nis 34.1 attention is drawn to the regions where Abraham has been, resulting in visiting the whole body ( ܠܟܠܗ ܠܓܘܫܡܐ ܣܥܪܗ); in Nis 34.7 Ephrem says that Abraham 'healed from the head and went down' which implies Egypt (Gen 12:10) as the feet of the sick body. His healing activity is illustrated by three medical verbs: 'he visited' (ܣܥܪܗ), 'bound up' (ܚܒܫ) and 'healed' (ܐܣܝ). The verb ܓܫܗ, 'to touch, explore', might also be considered medical - it is also used in the context of Jacob.[375] Abraham performed his healing with the 'word of truth' ( ܡܠܬܐ ܕܩܘܫܬܐ) that indicates God's instruction. Without God's help, none of the prophets or patriarchs would have served as spiritual physicians for the soul. Being chosen by God, it is Abraham's duty to proclaim the truth in the world of error so that error might not grow stronger, so that those who have been led astray might believe and be restored.

---

[374] There is a contrast to what is said in Dom 11 where Ephrem says that the Lord did not need to cut off from His body to heal humanity.

[375] Nis 34.1; 34.7; cf. Nis 34.2.

### *5.2.3.2 The Physician Jacob*

The patriarch Jacob is described as the physician of Harran for he spent twenty years with Laban in Harran (cf. Gen 27:43-31:38). No medical terms are used to describe his healing activity, apart from the verbs ܒܨܗ̇, 'he explored it [Harran]', that is also used in the context of Abraham; and ܚܠܡ, 'to moderate', that is used in the context of Daniel.[376] Both Abraham and Jacob left Harran for they could not heal it, in contrast to Abraham, Jacob is only described as a physician of one region, namely Harran. While in the context of Abraham, Ephrem says that Harran enjoyed its sickness, in the context of Jacob, he says: Harran went mad. Thus, the 'famous physician Jacob' (ܐܣܝܐ ܝܥܩܘܒ ܡܫܡܗܐ) went to Harran to look after it and moderate it, but his labour was in vain.[377] He served as a physician of the Lord in his time, but what he restored was partial and only relevant to his time.

### *5.2.3.3 The Physician Joseph*

Joseph is the physician of Egypt which was famous for its medicines, but spiritually sick. Egypt is described as the 'sick heel' (ܥܩܒܐ ܟܪܝܗܬܐ) or 'feet' (ܪ̈ܓܠܐ) of the body. While at the beginning of Nis 34.8, Ephrem uses the verb ܐܣܝ, 'to heal', and explicitly says that Joseph healed Egypt, at the end of the same stanza he emphasises that Egypt's pains were increased by its free will which implies that Egypt was not healed at all. Ephrem does not contradict himself here: in the former he describes Joseph's activity and service, whereas in the latter, Ephrem refers to the reaction of Egypt. Egypt might have been healed for a while, but its restoration did not last for long. Furthermore, Ephrem draws a contrast: Egypt was famous for its medical skills, as it is called the 'physician Egypt famous for its medicines' ( ܡܨܪܝܢ ܐܣܝܬܐ ܡܫܡܗܬܐ ܒܣܡ̈ܢܝܗ̇), but it could not heal itself and it did not let itself be healed by others, for example by Joseph; in turn, it increased its pains as did Harran. Although Egypt was not healed,

---

376 Nis 34.8. Jacob is also mentioned in Virg 20.2 where Ephrem refers to the emigration of Jacob to Harran (cf. Gen 27:43).

377 Nis 34.2.

Joseph remains famous, particularly because of his victory over Potiphar's wife (Gen 39:1-20). The cry of Potiphar's wife is explicitly described as sin (cf. Gen 39.15), from which Joseph escaped.[378] Even after his death, Ephrem attributes victory to Joseph's bones which the Israelites had brought up from Egypt to Shechem (Jos 24:32).[379]

### *5.2.3.4 The Physician Moses*

Moses' name appears only once in Nis 34. He is described as the physician of the sick feet, namely Egypt, without any further references to him.[380] As has been said above, Egypt was not healed either by Joseph, or by Moses. However, on one occasion, Ephrem says that Egypt, in contrast to Judaea, went to Moses who healed its pains.[381]

With reference to Moses, in several passages he is mainly involved in the healing process of the Israelites, starting in Egypt and continuing through the Exodus, through the sea and desert. The title physician is only used one other time for Moses, where he is compared to Jonah, and the Israelites are contrasted with the Ninevites. Ephrem says: 'Moses taught, the People apostasized; the physician was irritated that his bandage/remedy did not avail.'[382] Ephrem often mentions Moses in the context of healing that was performed during his time. Like the Lord, Moses is described as a 'saviour' (ܦܪܘܩܐ) whom God chose and sent among the Israelites so that they might be healed. Through Moses, the Israelites 'were healed' (ܐܬܐܣܝܘ) at least for a while, when the 'evil spirit departed from them' (ܥܒܪܬ ܠܗ ܡܢܗܘܢ ܪܘܚܐ ܒܝܫܬܐ).[383] In the same context, Psalm 107:20 is cited: God 'sent His word and

---

378 Fid 14.7.

379 Virg 19:7; cf. Virg 21.11; 32.4; Nis 18.7; 21.3; Eccl 11.3; 27.4; 47.2; 51.1; 51.5.

380 Nis 34.7.

381 Haer 11.13: ܡܨܪܝܢ ... ܠܘܬ ܐܣܝܐ ܪܗܛܬ ܘܗܘܬ ܕܐܣܐ ܟܐܒܝܗ.

382 Virg 49.13: ܡܘܫܐ ܐܠܦ ܥܡܐ ܐܣܛܝ ܐܬܬܥܝܩ ܐܣܝܐ ܕܠܐ ܐܗܢܝ ܚܒܫܗ.

383 CDiat 11.7.

healed them, and rescued them from corruption'.[384] The term ܡܠܬܗ, 'His word', that is sent from God, is intriguing here. It seems Ephrem - probably based on Ps 107:20 - uses it for Moses, whereas in the New Testament, influenced by the prologue of John (Jn 1:1ff.), the term 'word' (ܡܠܬܐ) is a well-known title for the Son of God. Obviously, Moses has a high rank among the prophets. Therefore, Moses is a type of the Son of God par excellence. He was the man chosen by God to heal the Israelites. He was chosen and his eyes were illuminated supernaturally by the grace and power of the Lord that he saw on mount Sinai.[385] From there he took medicines for the invisible pain of the soul in the form of the Law written on the stones[386], as well as in that of fasting. Moses rejected the treasure of the Egyptians' medicine, and instead he used 'spiritual herbs' (ܥܣܒ̈ܐ ܪܘܚܢܝ̈ܐ) which he had received from God through his fasting on mount Sinai in order to heal the soul secretly.[387] In hymns 4 and 10 On Fasting, this medicine is described as 'fasting' (ܨܘܡܐ). Ephrem says:

ܗܘ ܨܘܡܐ ܡܐܣܝܢܐ ܢܪܚܡ ܒܣܡ̈ܡܢܘܗܝ ܘܢܣܒܐ
ܒܣܡ̈ܡܢܘܗܝ
ܨܘܡܐ ܗܘ ܓܝܪ ܢܚܬ ܗܘܐ ܡܢ ܛܘܪ ܣܝܢܝ
ܠܡܫܪܝܬܐ ܡܟܐܒܬܐ
ܘܐܣܝ ܟܐ̈ܒܐ ܒܢܦܫܐ ܕܟܣܝܐ
ܘܚܒܫܗ ܠܬܪܥܐ ܪܒܐ ܕܙܢܝܐ
ܨܘܡܐ ܡܫܡܫܗ ܠܡܫܠܡܘܬܗ ܕܗܘ ܚܟܡܐ ܒܒܪܐ
ܢܛܠ ܥܘܕܪܢܐ ܠܐܢܫܐ
ܕܨܘ̈ܡܐ ܛܒ̈ܐ ܗܘܘ ܠܗ ܐܝܟ ܡܫܡ̈ܫܢܐ.

This is the fasting that heals, let us love his remedies
and enjoy his medicines. It is the fasting
that came down from mount Sinai to the wounded
camp, and healed the invisible pains of the soul

---

[384] CDiat 11.7: ܫܕܪ ܠܗ ܡܠܬܗ ܘܐܣܝ ܐܢܘܢ ܘܦܨܝ ܐܢܘܢ ܡܢ ܚܒܠܐ.

[385] Dom 31: ܠܡܘܫܐ ܕܝܢ ܒܚܝ̈ܠܘܗܝ ܕܡܫܝܚܐ ܐܢܗܪܗܝ ܗܘ ܡܢ ܥܘܫܢܐ ܗܘ ܕܚܙܐ.

[386] For healing through the Law see the sub-section about 'Healing through the Law and the Commandments of God'.

[387] Iei 10.6.

and bound up the great wound of mind.
Fasting helped the fall of the People in the desert.
Let us give praise to the Grace,
for good fastings became like medicines for us.

*Iei 4.1*

Moses himself abstained and fasted while he was on mount Sinai. At the same time the Israelites were worshipping the golden calf.[388] Through his fasting, he learned the power of fasting so that, for example, he could divide the Red Sea and make a path through it.[389] Ephrem says: fasting acted as medicines for those who were led into error and were wounded by the calf.[390]

Furthermore, Moses did not only divide the Red Sea and offer fasting as medicines, but he also made sick/bitter water sweet through a piece of wood (Ex 15:25),[391] and his stick caused the rock to issue water for the People (Ex 17:6; Num 20:11).[392] Both of these aspects serve as a symbol for Jesus from whose side a fountain of the Medicine of Life issued for the pains of the

---

[388] Iei 10.4:
ܟܕ ܡܘܫܐ ܒܛܘܪܐ ܡܬܢܟܦ ܗܘܐ ܗܘ ܥܡܐ ܒܥܘܪܐ ܡܬܬܠܥܒ ܗܘܐ. ܠܡܘܫܐ ܕܝܢ ܨܘܡܐ ܕܚܣܝܐ ܘܠܥܡܐ ܒܣܘܥܪܐ ܕܦܬܘܪܬܐ. ܡܘܫܐ ܠܘܬ ܪܡܐ ܥܡܐ ܠܘܬ ܥܓܠܐ. ܪܘܚܐ ܒܟܠ ܡܘܫܐ ܘܠܟܠܗ ܒܟܠ ܥܡܐ. ܗܘܘ ܨܘ̈ܡܐ ܡܣܡ̈ܢܐ ܠܛܥ̈ܝܐ ܕܒܥܓܠܐ ܐܬܡܚܝܘ.

[389] Nat 14.19:
ܡܘܫܐ ܕܦܠܓ ܘܦܪܫ ܢܦܫܗ ܡܢ ܒܪܬ ܩܠܗ ܦܠܓܗ ܠܝܡܐ ܩܕܡ ܝܡܬܐ. ܦܘܪܫܐ ܢܛܪܬ ܩܕܝܫܘܬܐ ܟܕ ܒܪܬ ܒܡܕܒܪܐ ܗܝ ܒܟܠܠܐ ܠܒܪܬ ܒܪܬ ܐܒܪܗܡ.

[390] Iei 10.4.

[391] Virg 44.15: ܡܘܫܐ ܕܐܚܠܝ ܡܝ̈ܐ ܒܩܝܣܐ ܒܠܘܬܗ ܡܪܬ ܒܟܠܠܐ ܢܨܝܚܐ. In Epiph 8:22, the author refers to 2 Kgs 2:19-22 where Elisha caused the water to be healed through the salt: ܢܦܠܬ ܒܗܘܢ ܡܠܚܐ ܘܒܡܠܚܐ ܘܐܬܐܣܝܘ ܪ̇ܐܙܗ̇ ܕܗܝ ܡܠܚܐ ܣܠܝܬܐ ܕܗܢ ܡܪܝܡ ܕܒܢ̈ܝܐ ܐܬܡܫܠ ܘܣܝܬ ܒܗ̇ ܬܘܚܡܬܐ ܕܡܣܠܝܘܬܗ.

[392] Epiph 5.13: ܣܘܪܗ̇ ܕܡܘܫܐ ܬܪܥܗ ܗܘܐ ܠܐܦܐ ܘܐܪܕܝܬ ܡܒܘ̈ܥܐ ܘܐܬܦܪܥܒ [ܘܐܬܦܪܥܘܒ] ܗܘܘ ܡܢ ܥܡܘܕܗ ܕܡܢ ܓܗܝܐ ܐܬܦܪܛܘ ܗܘܘ. Cf. Nat 2.10.

gentiles.[393] The water from the rock refreshed the People for they were thirsty, whereas the Medicine of Life from Jesus' side was given to the pains of the gentiles.

The People repeatedly acted against Moses' healing activity. Ephrem strongly contrasts Moses' service with the actions, or better reactions, of the People. For example, while Moses sweetened the water, his People became bitter because of the fashioned calf (cf. Ex 32:4).[394] We find a similar contrast in the context of Jonah and Nineveh: Jonah is compared to Moses, and the People are contrasted with the Ninevites. The Ninevites believed Jonah, although he did not teach, but proclaimed the judgment of the Lord; whereas Moses taught and bound them, and he was willing to heal them as a physician, but they rejected his prophecy and sinned. Therefore, Ephrem says: 'the physician was irritated that his bandage did not avail'.[395]

Moses tried to heal the People through another three symbols of the Medicine of Life, namely through the 'unleavened bread' (ܦܛܝܪܐ), the 'lamb' (ܐܡܪܐ) and the 'fixed serpent' ( ܚܘܝܐ ܩܒܝܥܐ). In Azym 18.5, Ephrem says: 'Moses hid the symbol of the Son in the unleavened bread as the Medicine of Life.'[396] Eating the Medicine of Life contrasts with eating the forbidden fruit. While the result of the latter was the Fall including sickness and pain, the Medicine of Life has the function of restoration and healing. Likewise its symbol, the unleavened bread, served to provide medicine and healing for the People. However, the symbol of the unleavened bread was turned round. After the Last Supper, the eucharistic bread became the Medicine of Life, whereas the unleavened bread was turned into the poison of death.[397]

---

393 Epiph 5.14: ܗܐ ܡܢ ܣܛܪܗ ܕܡܫܝܚܐ ܪܕܐ ܡܒܘܥ ܕܣܡ ܚܝ̈ܐ ܘܐܬܝܗܒ ܠܥܡ̈ܡܐ ܕܐܬܛܪܦܘ ܘܦܠܛܘ ܒܗ ܐܦ ܠܟܐ̈ܒܝܗܘܢ.

394 Virg 44.15: ܡܘܫܐ ܐܚܠܝ ܡܝ̈ܐ ܒܩܝܣܐ ܘܐܘܡܬܗ ܡܪܬ ܒܥܓܠܐ ܢܣܝܟܐ.

395 Virg 49.13: ܡܘܫܐ ܐܠܦ ܒܥܡܐ ܐܘܣܦ ܐܬܬܚܝܡ ܐܣܝܐ ܕܠܐ ܐܗܢܝ ܚܒܫܗ.

396 Azym 18.15: ܪܙܗ ܗܘ ܕܒܪܐ ܛܡܪ ܗܘܐ ܡܘܫܐ ܒܓܘ ܗܘ ܦܛܝܪܐ ܐܝܟ ܣܡ ܚܝ̈ܐ.

397 Azym 18.16-17; 19.22-24.

Not only the Medicine of Life, but also its symbols have to be respected and honoured as long as they serve with the same intention as the Medicine of Life. Ephrem explicitly speaks of the lamb as a symbol of the Medicine of Life that bound up the wounded: 'the lamb warned its slaughterer so that no bone might be broken in it (Num 9:12; cf. Jn 19:36) for he is the one who binds up the wounded; thanks be to the Lord Who binds up all.'[398] Ephrem refers further to Ex 12:8-16 while he says: 'the lamb was teaching Moses not to be cooked in water ... but to be splendid as the Medicine of Life; blessed is the Lamb that made its symbol shine.'[399]

Finally, as has been discused above, healing actions are explicitly related to the fixed serpent.[400] Through the symbol of the Medicine of Life and Moses, the 'serpent healed the People and helped them'.[401] Moses saw how the fixed serpent healed some of those who were bitten by the other serpents, and he was longing to see the Medicine of Life heal the wound of the first serpent.[402]

Thus, Moses was a physician and healer for the People (and for Egypt). He also served as a mediator of healing through the miracles and symbols that revealed the coming Messiah. He offered the Law, fasting, water, the lamb and the unleavened bread to the Israelites as remedies and medicine for their sickness. Some of them were healed, - at least for a while.

### *5.2.3.5 The Physician Elisha*

The title physician is never used for the prophet Elisha, but he occurs as the subject of the verb 'to heal' (ܐܣܝ). Elisha is also

---

398 Crucif 2.3: ܙܗܪ ܐܡܪܐ ܠܢܟܘܣܗ ܕܠܐ ܓܪܡܐ ܢܬܒܪ ܒܗ ܕܗܘܝܘ ܚܒܫ ܠܬܒܝܪ̈ܐ ܬܘܕܝ ܠܡܪܐ ܚܒܫ ܟܠ.

399 Crucif 2.4: ܕܒܡ̈ܝܐ ܠܐ ܢܬܒܫܠ ... ܐܡܪܐ ܠܡܘܫܐ ܡܠܦ ܗܘܐ ܕܗܘܐ ܗܘܐ ܐܝܟ ܣܡ ܚ̈ܝܐ ܢܨܝܚ ܐܡܪܐ ܕܐܢܗܪ ܐܪܙܗ.

400 CDiat 16.15: ܘܐܣܝܡ ܠܗ ܕܐܪܝܡ ܡܘܫܐ ܚܘܝܐ ܒܡܕܒܪܐ. ܠܬܬܪܝܡ ܒܗܘ ܕܐܝܢܐ. ܐܝܟܢܐ ܚܪ ܕܒܗܘ ܚܝܐ ܕܡܚܒ ܡܘܫܐ ܚܝܠܢܝܐ ܗܘ ܦܓܥܬܐ .... See this chapter V, 2.2.

401 Haer 21.8: ܕܚ̈ܝܐ ܠܗܘ ܥܡܐ ܐܣܝ ܗܘܐ ܘܥܕܪܗ.

402 Nat 1.28: ܚܙܐ ܡܘܫܐ ܚܘܝܐ ܡܩܒܥܐ ܕܐܣܝ ܠܢܟ̈ܬܬܐ ܚ̈ܘܝܢܐ ܘܣܒܪ ܕܢܚܙܐ ܠܗܘ ܕܐܣܐ ܒܡܚܘܬܗ ܕܚܘܝܐ ܩܕܡܝܐ.

mentioned in the context of healing Naaman (2 Kgs 5:10) and the sick water in Jericho (2 Kgs 2:19-22) several times, but also in the reference to the revival of the son of the Shunamite woman (2 Kgs 4:34) and Elisha's sick hands that he puts on the hands of Jehoash King of Israel (2 Kgs 13:15-19).

Ephrem attributes the fact that Elisha asked Naaman to plunge himself seven times in the water (2 Kgs 5:10) to the seven spirits mentioned in the Gospel (Mt 12:45; Mk 16:9; Lk 8:2; 11:26).[403] The author of the hymns On Epiphany refers to the healing of Naaman by Elisha. He compares Elisha to Moses, and contrasts Naaman with the Israelites. While Elisha was able to cure Naaman of his leprosy, Moses could not cleanse the heart of the People. The purification of Naaman is performed through plunging Naaman into the water seven times,[404] so that he was 'consecrated' (ܩܕܫ) with the hidden Names. This way of healing is compared to the forgiveness of sin through the water of baptism upon which the names of the holy Trinity are invoked.[405] In CDiat 16.29, it is said that the healing, or purification, of Naaman was not just performed through the water of the river, but rather through the word of Elisha invoked upon the water.[406]

The author of the hymns On Epiphany also refers to 2 Kgs 2:19-22 and says: 'the prophet healed the sick water and restored the disease of the barren land ...'.[407] Based on the Bible, the healing was performed through the salt that the author of the hymns On Epiphany uses as a symbol for the Son of Mary.[408]

---

403 Nat 17.16-17:
ܒܠܘܫܐ ܬܘ ܢܒܝܐ ܘܐܠܐ ܒܡܠܐ ܫܒܥ ܕܘܟܝܐ ܠܐ ܒܢܝ ܫܒܥ ܐܝܟ ܐܠܝܫܥ
ܕܫܒܥ ܪܘܚܝܢ ܒܟܘܪܐ ܠܢܦܫܐ ܠܐ ܬܘܒ ܡܠܐܐ ܘܠܐܘ ܒܫܡܐ ܟܬܫܡܫܬܗܘܢ.
ܫܒܥ [ܕܐܠܝܫܥ] ܒܢܗܪܐ ܕܗܘ ܕܫܒܥ ܙܘܥܝܢ ܘܗܘܦܟܐ ܘܕܡܐ ܠܦܘܠܚܢܐ ܗܘ ܝܕܥ
ܠܐ ܐܝܬ ܐܚܪܬܐ ܠܡܪܕܘܬܐ ܠܐ ܡܬܒܥܝܐ ܒܪ ܡܢܐ ܟܠ ܡܢ ܡܢܐ ܟܠ.

404 Epiph 5.6-7.

405 Epiph 6.12; cf. Fid 28.12.

406 CDiat 16.29; cf. CDiat 16.13.

407 Epiph 11.7: ܡܝܐ ܒܪ̈ܝܗܐ ܐܣܝ ܢܒܝܐ ܘܐܫܠܡ ܗܘܐ ܡܪܥܝܬܗ ܕܐܪܥܐ ܡܚܝܠܬܐ ܕܟܠܠ ܡܟܘܬܗ ܘܪܡܙ ܐܬܪܗ....

408 Epiph 8:22: ܢܦܠܬ ܒܗܘܢ ܡܠܚܐ ܘܒܣܡܗ ܘܐܬܐܣܝܘ ܪܐܙܗ ܕܗܘ ܡܠܚܐ ܫܠܝܚܬܐ ܕܡܢ ܡܪܝܡ ܕܒܢ̈ܝܢܐ ܐܬܡܠܟ ܘܚܝܬ ܒܗ ܬܒܣܡܬܐ

☞

2 Kgs 4:34 is another biblical passage that includes a healing aspect. It says that Elisha stretched out his body upon the body of the son of the Shunamite woman and revived him. Ephrem compares the stretching out of the prophet's body to the shadow of Peter that healed people (Acts 5:14-16). Furthermore, it is compared to the oil that serves as a ܐܪܙܐ and 'shadow' (ܛܠܠܗ) for Jesus.[409] Also in Nis 42.6, Ephrem refers to the same biblical passage and speaks of the bones reviving the dead person.[410]

Finally, Nis 43.9-10 provides another aspect of healing in the context of Elisha putting his sick hands on the hands of King Jehoash who gained power. Ephrem is amazed that the hands of the prophet, even though they were sick and weak, became a 'fountain of restoration for the body of those who visited him'.[411] Ephrem goes further and says that the 'sickness [of the prophets] gave power to the kings'.[412]

### *5.2.3.6 The Physician David*

David is mentioned in only two passages in the context of healing. The most relevant passage is I Serm 7.109ff. - probably not genuine Ephrem - where David is presented as a physician. In this sermon about repentance, the author includes many healing aspects and refers to Jesus' healing ministry to indicate that through repentance humans can be healed.[413] The author also refers to some other biblical figures; Paul, Peter, Aaron and David. Among them, David is the only one who is described as a physician: he is a 'wise physician' (ܕܘܝܕ ܐܣܝܐ ܚܟܝܡܐ) who 'spoke, believed and

---

ܕܒܣܝܡܘܬܗܿ. Cf. Epiph 5:13 where Moses causes the water to become sweet by a piece of wood.

409 Virg 4.8: ܐܠܝܫܥ ܦܫܛ ܓܘܫܡܗ ܥܠ ܛܠܝܐ ܟܕ ܡܚܝܐ ܠܗ.

410 Nis 42.6; cf. Nis 43.12.

411 Nis 43.9: ܬܘܒ ܗܘܐ ܐܠܝܫܥ ܐܝܕܘ̈ܗܝ ܟܪ̈ܝܗܬܐ ܥܠ ܐܝ̈ܕܝܐ ܫܠܝ̈ܛܬܐ ܕܡܠܟܐ ܕܢܣܒ ܗܒܪܗ ܚܝܠܐ ܡܢ̈ ܘܗ̈ܒ، ܠܟܪܝܐ ܕܦܘܪܩܢܐ ܠܡܬܗܪ ܕܡܒܘܥܐ ܕܚܘܠܡܢܐ ܗܘ ܕܣܘܠܩܢܐ ܠܦܓܪܐ ܕܡܣܥܪ̈ܢܘܗܝ، ܠܡܣܬܥܪܢܘܗܝ ܐܫܬܚܠܦ ܗܦܟ ܠܡܣܥܪ̈ܢܘܗܝ.

412 Nis 43.10: ܟܪܝܗܘܬܗܘܢ ܗܘ ܡܚܝܠ ܠܡܠܟ̈ܐ ܝܗܒ ܚܝܠܐ.

413 I Serm 7.81-82: ܥܠ ܕܐܝܬ ܡܣܒܪܐ ܠܚܛܝ̈ܐ ܕܢܬܐܣܘܢ ܒܬܝܒܘܬܐ; cf. I Serm 7.136.

was healed' (ܡܚܠ ܘܗܘܢ ܘܐܬܐܣܝ).[414] Unlike the other prophets and patriarchs, the object of David's healing activity is himself. He sinned and healed himself through his repentance. Later his sin is described as sickness. Although he was victorious over the lion (1 Sam 17:34-36),[415] David was defeated by sin and was wounded on the roof when he saw Bathsheba the daughter of Eliam, the wife of Uriah (2 Sam 11:2-5).[416]

In Virg 30.2, David is mentioned in a totally different context. Hymn 30 On Virginity disproves Marcion's concept of an Alien coming into the world. Ephrem does this by referring to three harps, namely the Old and New Testament and Nature. Referring to the Old Testament, the harp of David played sound music which 'the sick ears of Saul' (ܐܕܢ̈ܝ ܫܐܘܠ ܕܟܪ̈ܝܗܢ ܗܘ̈ܝ) could not understand. Ephrem goes further saying that the harp of David illustrates the Son of David, whereas the sick spirit of Saul caused the ears of the 'tares' (ܕܙܝܙ̈ܢܐ) and 'scribes' (ܘܣܦܪ̈ܐ) to become sick.[417]

### 5.2.3.7 *The Physician Jonah (Jonah 1-4)*

Ephrem refers to Jonah and the city of Nineveh in several places, notably in the hymns On Nisibis, On Faith, On Paradise, Against Julian, I Sermo 8 and in the Commentary on the Diatessaron.[418] A developed discussion of the theme is to be found in the hymns On Virginity and in II Serm 1.[419] First, the latter will be discussed, then the former. In both, Ephrem speaks of the role of Jonah as physician sent to the sick town of Nineveh to heal the sickness and

---

414 I Serm 7.113-114: ܕܘܝܕ ܐܣܝܐ ܚܟܝܡܐ ܡܚܠ ܘܗܘܢ ܘܐܬܐܣܝ.

415 Cf. Haer 13.11; Nis 39.14.

416 I Serm 7.193-194: ܐܦ ܕܘܝܕ ܕܙܟܐ ܠܐܪܝܐ ܒܐܓܪܐ ܢܦܠܗܐ ܠܒܬܗ.

417 Virg 30.2: ܒܗܝ ܪܘܚܐ ܕܟܪܝܗܬ ܕܫܐܘܠ ܐܬܟܪܗ ܐܦ ܐܕܢ̈ܝܗܘܢ ܕܙܝܙ̈ܢܐ ܘܣܦܪ̈ܐ.

418 Nis 35.3; 43.22; 46.13; 55.3; Fid 20.9; 81.16; Epiph 3.19; 8.20; Parad 13.14; CJul 4.16-17; SFid 6.224; I Serm 8.135; 8.309-15; CDiat 11.1-4; 11.23-28.

419 Virg 42-50; II Serm 1.

iniquity of its people, the reaction of the inhabitants, and their penitence and healing.

The Peshitta narrative of Jonah does not include any terms concerning healing (Jonah 1-4). The author explicitly mentions the reason for sending Jonah to Nineveh (Jonah 1:1-2) as the 'wickedness' (ܒܝܫܘܬܗܘܢ) of the Ninevites which had risen up before the Lord.[420] Although the Ninevites' wickedness is the main reason for Jonah's commission (Jonah 3:8-10), the narrative does not provide any explanation of this wickedness, apart from what the last verse says (Jonah 4:11): 'and should not I have pity on Nineveh, that great city, wherein are more than twelve score thousand persons that cannot discern between their right hand and their left hand, ... ?'[421] This inability to discern the right from the left hand indicates the error and the sin of the Ninevites. The commission of Jonah is to preach the judgment of the Lord to them, so that everyone may turn away from his 'wickedness' (ܒܝܫܘܬܗ), his 'evil way' (ܐܘܪܚܗ ܒܝܫܬܐ) and from the 'violence that is in his hands' (ܚܛܘܦܝܐ ܕܐܝܬ ܒܐܝܕܘܗܝ).[422]

Ephrem, by contrast, often presents this wickedness as 'sickness' (ܟܘܪܗܢܐ) and 'pain' (ܟܐܒܐ). The source of sickness is the sin committed by free will.[423] Nineveh is a city 'full of debts' (ܕܡܠܝܐ ܚܘ̈ܒܐ) and "full of pains" (ܡܠܝܬ ܟܐ̈ܒܐ).[424] Its inhabitants suffer from the 'illness of desires' of various sorts.[425] Thus illness of desires refers to eating and drinking, as well as to wealth, acquisitiveness and sexuality. Therefore, there were among the Ninevites 'defiled' and 'lustful' people (ܛܡ̈ܐܬܐ, ܙܠܝ̈ܠܐ),

---

[420] Jonah 1:1-2: ܘܗܘܐ ܦܬܓܡܗ ܕܡܪܝܐ ܥܠ ܝܘܢܢ ܒܪ ܡܬܝ܆ ܠܡܐܡܪ. ܩܘܡ ܙܠ ܠܢܝܢܘܐ ܡܕܝܢܬܐ ܪܒܬܐ: ܘܐܟܪܘܙ ܥܠܝܗ: ܡܛܠ ܕܣܠܩܬ ܒܝܫܘܬܗܘܢ ܩܕܡܝ.

[421] Jonah 4:11: ܐܢܐ ܕܝܢ ܠܐ ܐܚܘܣ ܥܠ ܢܝܢܘܐ ܡܕܝܢܬܐ ܪܒܬܐ: ܕܐܝܬ ܒܗ ܣܓܝ ܡܢ ܬܪܬܥܣܪܐ ܪ̈ܒܘܢ ܒܢܝ̈ܢܫܐ: ܕܠܐ ܝܕܥܝܢ ܒܝܢ ܝܡܝܢܗܘܢ ܠܣܡܠܗܘܢ ....

[422] Jonah 1:2; 3:10; 3:8.

[423] Cf. II Serm 1.137-38.

[424] Cf. II Serm 1.112-118.

[425] Cf. II Serm 1.161-62: ܣܓܝ̈ܐܐ ܗܘܘ ܒܢ̈ܝ ܕܟܪ̈ܝܗܝܢ ܒܟܘܪܗܢܐ ܕܪ̈ܓܝܓܬܐ.

'thieves' (ܓܢ̈ܒܐ), the 'infatuated' (ܫܛܝ̈ܐ), 'sinners' (ܚܛܝ̈ܐ), the 'wicked' (ܒܝ̈ܫܐ), the 'lawless' (ܥܘ̈ܠܐ), etc.[426]

The commission and function of Jonah and his preaching to save the Ninevites from the 'punishment' (ܓܙܪ ܕܝܢܐ) of God allowed Ephrem to give him the title of 'physician' who was sent to Nineveh, 'the city full of pains/illnesses'.[427] Altogether in the long mimro 'On Nineveh and Jonah' the term 'physician' appears eight times,[428] where it refers not only to Jonah, but also to the king and to all the Ninevites. The health of Nineveh has been achieved through the efforts of these three different participants: the prophet of the Lord was sent as a surgeon to the disturbed city and he preached the judgment;[429] the king realised the truth of the physician and announced repentance as the medicine and the way of healing for all Ninevites;[430] finally, health is achieved when

---

426 Cf. II Serm 1.165-226. In the end of this mimro where the Ninevites praise the Lord, Ephrem contrasts their former status with that after their repentance. Before their repentance, there were among the inhabitants of Nineveh 'plunderers' (ܚܛܘ̈ܦܐ), the 'filthy' (ܛܢ̈ܦܐ), the 'grasping' (ܥܠܘ̈ܒܐ), 'drunkards' (ܪܘ̈ܝܐ), the 'insolent' (ܡܪ̈ܝܚܐ), the 'lustful' (ܙܠܝ̈ܠܐ), 'cursed people' (ܠܝ̈ܛܐ), and those who commit 'adultery' (ܓܝܪ̈ܐ), 'gluttons' (ܐܣܘ̈ܛܐ) and 'fornicators' (ܙܢ̈ܝܐ) (cf. II Serm 1.1973-2000). Later, when some of the Ninevites went with Jonah to his homeland, they saw many sinful deeds among the Israelites. In their astonishment they put the question: did the 'wickedness' (ܥܘܠܐ) of Nineveh flee and come to the promised land? (cf. II Serm 1.1735-1914). When the Ninevites find sinful deeds among the blessed people, they were reminded of the deeds that were practised in Nineveh before the Ninevites' repentance: 'idol-worship' (ܦܬܟܪ̈ܐ), 'oblations' (ܥܠܘ̈ܬܐ), 'Tammuz-worship' (ܬܡܘܙܐ), 'astrology' (ܟܘܟܒܘܬܐ), 'divination' (ܩܣܡܐ), 'paganism' (ܚܢܦܘܬܐ), 'star-worship/zodiacal signs' (ܡܠܘܫ̈ܐ), 'rebelliousness' (ܡܪܘܕܘܬܐ), 'lasciviousness' (ܦܚܙܘܬܐ), 'sun-worship' (ܫܡܫܐ), 'calf-worship' (ܥܓܠܐ), 'hateful things' (ܣܢ̈ܝܬܐ) and other forms of 'evil' (ܒܝ̈ܫܬܐ) and 'sins' (ܚܛܗ̈ܐ) (cf. II Serm 1.1819-42).

427 II Serm 1.117-120.

428 II Serm 1.117, 143, 151, 153, 164, 715, 737, 921. In II Serm 1.740 the plural form ܐܣܘ̈ܬܐ appears.

429 Cf. II Serm 1.117-20.

430 Cf. II Serm 1.918-24.

everyone becomes a physician to themselves and to each other.[431] They heal and were healed by each other.[432] Although the Ninevites had been healed through their own penitence, they accepted Jonah as their healer, who brought about the cure.[433]

While in II Serm 1.111-20, the title 'physician' describes the function and commission of Jonah,[434] later it is applied to everyone who heals himself.[435] There is an important process of development in the text. In the beginning, Jonah is the physician who heals through his words, whereas at the end, everyone who 'rebukes his own desires' will be his own physician. Jonah starts the healing process and points out the sickness through proclaiming the judgment of the Lord, but all those who had realised the truth in Jonah's words fulfilled the healing through their own deeds.[436]

While the healing method of an ordinary physician is soothing, Jonah uses the rigours of the sword and the 'rod of wrath' (ܫܒܛܐ ܕܪܘܓܙܐ).[437] He appears in Nineveh as a herald who 'disturbed' (ܕܠܚܗ) the city with his preaching and filled Nineveh with sadness and gloom.[438] Jonah is the 'fearful physician'

---

[431] Cf. II Serm 1.117-154; 1.163-64; 1.921-24.

[432] Cf. II Serm 1.147-8.

[433] Cf. II Serm 1.1357-58: ܗܡ ܒܪ̈ܝܐ ܠܗ ܕܐܣܝܘܬܐ ܕܒܥܝܢܐ ܟܠܗ ܐܘܕܝ ܠܗ; 1.1579-81: ܦܠܛ ܗܘܐ ܕܠܒܠܐ ܢܣܬܘܪ ܒܐܒܐ ܕܢܫܬܒܩ ܘܐܬܐܣܝ.

[434] II Serm 1.111-20: 'When Jonah was sent to that city full of debts, Justice armed him. She (justice) commissioned him with fearful words; she gave to him a stern decree for the pains with sharp medicines. The fearful physician was sent to the town full of pains. He opened and displayed to them his medicines, they were frightening and powerful.' ( ܝܘܢܢ ܟܕ ܒܗ ܐܫܬܕܪ ܠܗܝ ܩܪܝܐ ܕܡܠܝܐ ܚܘ̈ܒܐ. ܙܝܢܬܗ ܗܘܬ ܟܐܢܘܬܐ. ܒܡ̈ܠܐ ܕܚܝ̈ܠܐ ܥܙܝܙܬܗ. ܠܒܪܐ ܠܟܐ̈ܒܐ ܦܣܩܬ ܠܗ ܥܡ ܡܣܡ̈ܢܐ ܚܪ̈ܝܦܐ. ܐܣܝܐ ܕܚܝܠܐ ܐܫܬܕܪ ܠܡܕܝܢܬܐ ܕܡܠܝܐ ܟܐ̈ܒܐ. ܦܬܚ ܚܘܝ, ܗܘܐ ܣܡ̈ܡܢܘܗܝ, ܕܚܝܠܝܢ ܗܘܘ ܘܐܦ ܚܣܝܢܝܢ).

[435] II Serm 1.163-64: 'Every one rebuked his own desire and became a physician to himself' ( ܒܪܓܬܗ ܟܠ ܐܢܫ ܟܐܐ ܗܘܐ ܐܣܝܐ ܠܢܦܫܗ ܗܘ̇ܐ ܗܘܐ).

[436] II Serm 1.111-20; 1.153-64.

[437] Cf. II Serm 1.160.

[438] Cf. II Serm 1.11-14.

(ܐܣܝܐ ܕܚܝܠܐ) who received 'fearful words' (ܡ̈ܠܐ ܕܚܝ̈ܠܬܐ) and 'sharp medicine' (ܣܡ̈ܡܢܐ ܚܪ̈ܝܦܐ) from divine justice as a surgical instrument for pains ( ܣܡ̈ܡܢܘܗܝ، ܕܚܠܝܡ ܗܘܘ ܘܐܦ ܟܐܒܝܢ ).[439] Therefore, the justice of the Lord armed Jonah with severity and medicine for the 'pains' (ܟܐ̈ܒܐ) of Nineveh and sent him to the 'town full of pains'.[440] In contrast to an ordinary physician who 'soothes and heals' ( ܐܣܝܐ ܥܒܠ [ܡܥܒܠ] ܘܡܐܣܐ), Ephrem describes the voice of Jonah as a 'sword' (ܣܝܦܐ) and his visiting, as harsh preaching and rebuking.[441] Thus, Jonah cut away the 'pains of long-standing' and healed the 'sickness of the city'.[442] Ephrem used particular images of human diseases metaphorically in order to illustrate the healing of the sick Ninevites. Jonah shows a sword to the 'sick' (ܟܪܝܗܐ); 'the people lying sick' (ܟܪ̈ܝܗܐ ܕܪ̈ܡܝܐ) arose and hastened to repentance; 'the sick one left his bed' (ܢܦܩ ܗܘܐ ܟܪܝܗܐ ܒܥܪܣܗ).[443] Because the Ninevites were really sick, they were in need of a true physican.

After the king had examined Jonah, he draws attention to the consistency of the prophet's message. Fear, praise, wealth or force could not change Jonah's mind, for his preaching was not ordinary human skill.[444]

ܐܣܝܐ ܕܟܠܗ ܫܪܝܪܐ ܗܘ
ܫܪܪܐ ܗܘ ܐܡܪ ܠܟܪ̈ܝܗܐ
ܠܒܪܐ ܒܟܠ ܡܒܪ ܠܗ
ܒܟܠ ܒܝܬܗ ܠܐܢܫܐ ܕܟܪܝܗ
ܒܢ̈ܝܐ ܕܢܘܪܐ ܡܪ̈ܝܪܐ
ܒܟܠ ܡܝܬܘܬܗ ܡܟܐ ܠܗ
ܠܐ ܕܢܠ ܡܢ ܡܢ ܕܢܦܫܗ
ܕܟܡܐ ܟܪܝܐ ܢܟܪ ܠܗ

---

439 Cf. II Serm 1.113-120.

440 II Serm 1.113-18.

441 Cf. II Serm 1.149-156. Concerning rebuking, the same idea appears in Dom 16-17: Jesus heals Simon the Pharisee through 'rebuking' (ܒܘܐܪܐ); the Lord 'rebukes' (ܒܐܪ) Simon in order to help him.

442 II Serm 1.149-50; 1.924.

443 II Serm 1.144-162.

444 Cf. II Serm 1.657-704.

A physician, who is entirely truthful,
speaks the truth to the sick.
He proclaims a stern decree to the sick one
in his house, as he enters.
He prescribes in his room
bitter cauterization with fire.
He does not fear the one who is weak,
prescribing for him the extraction of a molar tooth.[445]

In this context, where the king of Nineveh gives evidence for the truth of Jonah's prophecy, he also compares Jonah's behaviour as a physician to that of other ordinary physicians and considers his rank higher than the other physicians.[446] It is interesting how Ephrem points out the fearlessness and truth of the good physician. The excellent physician always tells the 'truth' (ܫܪܪܐ) to the sick. Since he is a true and good physician, he does not fear proclaiming their present sicknesses, even if they are dangerous.[447] Jonah, described as 'this Hebrew', fulfils the conditions of being a good physician who risks his life for the truth. Jonah cannot be subdued with wages, wealth or any other profit. He acts because of God's judgment, the cause of which is the sin and iniquity of man.[448]

Sin caused the sickness of Nineveh, as sinful deeds cause punishment. The king of Nineveh realised this, and he became 'the physician who healed his city and knew the medicine that it needed'. He recognised that the punishment was proclaimed because of the 'folly' (ܣܟܠܘܬܐ) of man.[449] When he cut out the source of evil deeds, he also put an end to the punishment and to the sickness, healing it with a declaration of fasting: 'he is the

---

[445] II Serm 1.715-22. See further II Serm 1.723-735.

[446] II Serm 1.737-40: 'Although a physician is fearless, he is subordinate because of [his] wage. This Hebrew is more exalted than the rank of physicians' (ܟܕ ܛܒ ܐܣܝܐ ܠܐ ܕܚܠ ܡܛܠ ܐܓܪܐ ܡܫܬܥܒܕ.. ܗܢܐ ܥܒܪܝܐ ܪܒ ܗܘ ܡܢ ܕܪܓܐ ܕܐܣܝܘܬܐ).

[447] II Serm 1.715-18; 1.737-40.

[448] Cf. II Serm 1.715-48; 1.917-18.

[449] II Serm 1.841-60. See also II Serm 1.917-20: ܡܠܟܐ ܕܢܝܢܘܐ ܢܕܒ ܗܘܐ ܕܥܠܬ ܪܘܓܙܐ ܣܟܠܘܬܐ ܗܝ. ܦܣܩܗ̇ ܠܥܠܬ ܒܝܫ̈ܬܐ ܘܦܣܩܗ ܒܒܠ ܡܚܫ̈ܠܬܐ.

physician, who visited his town, and he knew the medicine which was proper for it; by fasting, the victorious medicine, he healed the sickness of the city'.[450] As the heralds proclaimed to the impure to put off their impurity, so the king walked in the city 'to cleanse their impurity'.[451] Thus, the affliction of Nineveh is the sickness of sin and evil deeds which the king healed by declaring fasting and penitence: 'and by the sackcloth and ashes he chased away the sin from the city.[452]

The case of Jonah and Nineveh indicates an excellent type of repentance for believers. When Jesus was asked for a sign, he referred to the sign of Jonah and Nineveh: 'the men of Nineveh shall stand up in judgment with this generation, and shall condemn it, for they repented at the preaching of Jonah.'[453] 'This generation' did not believe Jesus, whereas the Ninevites had faith in Jonah and, therefore, they repented. In the Commentary on the Diatessaron, where Ephrem comments on this passage (Mt 12:39-40; Lk 11:29), he compares the signs of Jesus among the Jews with Jonah's preaching in Nineveh. While Jesus 'healed their pains and revived

---

450 II Serm 1.921-24: ܐܣܝܐ ܗܘ ܕܩܪܒ ܠܡܕܝܢܬܗ ܘܝܕܥ ܣܡܐ ܕܝܐܠ ܠܗ. ܒܨܘܡܐ ܣܡܐ ܢܨܝܚܐ ܒܘܪܗܢܐ ܕܩܪܝܬܐ ܐܣܝ.

451 II Serm 1.841; 1.895-96: ܡܠܟܐ ܒܡܘܬܒܐ ܦܫܐ ܗܘܐ ܕܢܕܟܐ ܒܟܠܗܘܢ ܠܛܡܐܘܬܐ. The term 'impurity' (ܛܡܐܘܬܐ) is used in parallel to many others, such as 'greed/cupidity' (ܥܢܘܬܐ), 'fraudulence' (ܥܠܘܒܘܬܐ), 'gluttony/debauchery' (ܐܣܘܛܘܬܐ), 'drunkenness' (ܪܘܝܘܬܐ), 'adultery' (ܓܘܪܘܬܐ), 'harlotry/licentiousness/ immodesty' (ܙܢܝܘܬܐ), 'falsehood' (ܕܓܠܘܬܐ), 'theft' (ܓܢܒܘܬܐ), 'snake-charming' (ܐܫܘܦܘܬܐ), 'magic/witchcraft' (ܚܪܫܘܬܐ), 'astrology' (ܟܠܕܝܘܬܐ), 'divination' (ܩܘܣܡܘܬܐ), 'iniquity' (ܥܘܠܐ), 'impiety/wickedness' (ܪܘܫܥܐ) and 'deceit' (ܢܟܠܐ). All of these are described as the ܥܘܠܐ which exsisted in Nineveh before they repented (II Serm 1.1767-1810). Although Ephrem does not explicitly link each of these sinful deeds and thoughts with sickness, he relates them to the general sickness of sin which is the result of free will, and not of necessity (II Serm 1.137-38).

452 II Serm 1.923-26: ܘܒܣܩܐ ܘܒܩܛܡܐ ܛܪܕܗ ܠܚܛܝܬܐ ܡܢ ܟܠܗ ܟܪܟܐ.

453 Lk 11:32: ܓܒܪܐ ܢܝܢܘܝܐ ܢܩܘܡܘܢ ܒܕܝܢܐ ܥܡ ܫܪܒܬܐ ܗܕܐ ܘܢܚܝܒܘܢܗ܆ ܕܬܒܘ ܒܟܪܘܙܘܬܗ ܕܝܘܢܢ.

their dead' (ܒܟܠܠ ܕܐܝܟ ܒܐܒ̈ܝܗܘܢ ܘܐܝܟ ܒܡܝ̈ܬܝܗܘܢ), Jonah just proclaimed the overthrowing of the city, causing its inhabitants to fear. As a result, Ephrem emphasises that the pagan Ninevites repent, whereas the circumcised Hebrews, as blind people, did not believe in the Lord of the prophet.[454] But, according to Ephrem, both Jonah and the Ninevites fulfilled their repentance: the prophet in the whale at sea; and the Ninevites on the dry land, in the city of Nineveh. Both of them 'offered' (ܩܪܒܘ) 'repentance' (ܬܝܒܘܬܐ) to the Lord, and they were 'saved' (ܐܬܦܨܝܘ). Jonah's repentance was performed first and he was revived, he understood through the grace of the Lord that through repentance penitents would be 'revived' (ܕܢܚܘܢ). Thus, Jonah himself was an example for Nineveh.[455] The Ninevites found the 'key of repentance' through Jonah, so that they received good hope from the 'treasury of God'.[456] Their sustained repentance had an extraordinary power and brought about peace and reconciliation. The sea grew still because of prayer, so too did the dry land as a result of repentance.[457]

After Jonah had proclaimed the judgment of the Lord, the Ninevites 'strove' with the judgment of the Lord and 'dissolved it to show how much repentance is capable of reconciliation, and how much the penitent compels the bestowal of mercy through persistence'.[458] Through their repentance the Ninevites appeased the Lord so that he had mercy on them. Ephrem describes the repentance and supplication of the Ninevites as 'real', whereas the

---

454 Cf. CDiat 11.1.

455 II Serm 1.25-32: ܬܝܒܘܬܐ ܩܪܒܘ ܗܘܘ ܠܗ ܓܒ̈ܝܐ ܬܪ̈ܬܝܗܘܢ ܘܐܬܦܨܝܘ. ܒܝܡܐ ܠܢܘܢ ܢܦܩܬ ܗܘܬ ܘܠܢܝܢܘܝ̈ܐ ܒܝܒܫܐ. ܡܢܗ ܘܡܢܗ ܝܠܦ ܗܘܐ ܕܠܘܐ ܕܢܚܘܢ ܬܝ̈ܒܐ. ܕܒܥܘܬܐ ܒܦܩܕܗ ܢܦܩܬ ܠܗ ܠܬܝܒܘܬܐ ܚܠܦ ܢܝ̈ܢܘܐ.

456 II Serm 1.1345-48: ܐܕܪܟ ܗܘ ܒܪ ܐܫܟܚܘܗܝ, [ܐܫܟܚܘ] ܠܩܠܝܕܐ ܕܬܝܒܘܬܐ ܕܒܗ ܒܝܬ ܓܙܗ ܕܐܠܗܐ ܣܒܪܐ ܛܒܐ ܢܣܒܘܢ ܠ.

457 II Serm 1.15-16: ܫܠܐ ܗܘܐ ܝܡܐ ܒܨܠܘܬܐ ܐܦ ܝܒܫܐ ܒܬܝܒܘܬܐ.

458 II Serm 1.131-36: ܒܬܪ ܕܩܠܐ ܕܐܟܪܙ ܝܘܡ ܐܬܟܬܫܘ ܒܕܝܢܗ ܘܫܪܐܘܗܝ, ܕܢܚܘܐ ܕܟܡܐ ܡܨܝܐ ܬܝܒܘܬܐ ܠܬܪܥܘ ܘܕܟܡܐ ܚܐܦ ܬܝܒܐ ܕܒܚܘܨܦܐ ܪ̈ܚܡܐ ܢܣܒ.

repentance and supplication 'in our time' are just as a dream and shadow.[459] As soon as the Ninevites heard the true prophecy, they practised true penitence.[460] From 'lying sick' (ܟܪ̈ܝܗܐ ܕܪ̈ܡܝܐ) they arose and strove for repentance, for they trusted Jonah and feared the judgment of the Lord.[461] Thus, they were healed, and they healed each other through repentance:

ܝܕܥܢ ܗ̈ܘܝ ܕܚܠܦܝܗܝܢ
ܡܬܐܒܠܝܢ ܗܘܘ ܬ̈ܝܒܐ
ܐܦ ܐܣܝܘ ܐܦ ܐܬܐܣܝܘ
ܚܕ ܡܢ ܚܕ ܒܬܝܒܘܬܐ

195 They [fem.] knew that on their behalf
the repentant were mourning.
197 They were healed and they healed
each other through penitence.[462]

This is the only passage where Ephrem explicitly relates healing to repentance. Later on, the Ninevites said to Jonah that he had become victorious through their repentance. They asked him: 'Why are you sad, for you have healed us and the entire congregation is thanking you'.[463] The reputation of Jonah arose through the penitents (ܬ̈ܝܒܐ),[464] who understood repentance not just as a challenge to the judgment of the Lord, but also as a battle. The Ninevites, proud gentiles because of their power and victories, also wanted to win this war with different weapons: this war is not against the prophet and cannot be won with military weapons, but through repentance and fasting against one's 'own sins'.[465] The preachers, as well as the king, proclaimed and aroused everyone to

---

[459] II Serm 1.97-102: ܬܝܒܘܬܐ ܗܘܬ ܒܙܒܢܐ ܕܐܟ̈ܬܐ ܠܒܪ ܡܘܒܠܐ ܒܚܠܡܐ ܗ̄ܝ܆ ܬܝܒܘܬܐ ܗܕܐ ܕܠܝܬ ܐܝܟ ܚܠܡܐ ܗ̄ܝ. ܘܒܛܠܠܐ ܗ̄ܝ ܒܬܘܒܐ ܗܕܐ ܕܠܝܬ ܛܠܠܐ ܗ̄ܝ.

[460] Cf. II Serm 1.429-32: ܕܗܘܘ ܒܟܠ ܬ̈ܝܒܐ ܐܬܠܒܫܘ ܐܝܟ ܕܫܪ̈ܝܪܐ ܗܘܬ ܢܒܝܘܬܐ ܕܟܐܢܐ ܗܘܬ ܬܝܒܘܬܐ ܫܪ̈ܝܪܐ.

[461] Cf. II Serm 1.147-48.

[462] II Serm 1.195-98.

[463] II Serm 1.1355-58: ܡܢ ܕܝܢ ܬܬܥܝܩ ܗܫܐ ܕܒܬܝܒܘܬܢ ܐܬܚܝܠܬ. ܡܢ ܟܪܝܐ ܠܟ ܕܐܣܝܬܢ ܕܟܢܫܐ ܟܠܗ ܐܘܕܝ ܠܟ

[464] II Serm 1.1355-62.

[465] II Serm 1.763-68: ܠܘ ܕܝܢ ܒܚܪܒܐ ܕܢܒܝܐ ܢܬܟܬܫ ܒܬܝܒܘܬܐ ܠܐ. ܡܢ ܐܣܟܠܘ ܗܘ ܕܢܣܒܘܢ ܡܢ ܐܣܟܠ ܡܢܗ ܠܒܪ ܗܘܐ.

be repentant.[466] Repentance, which exists in the world for the sinner,[467] is depicted as a new weapon for the new war, and will not be turned back by divine justice and grace.[468] Instead, it will grant a victory (ܙܟܘܬܐ ܒܬܝܒܘܬܐ) to man and overcome Satan.[469] Because of repentance God has mercy on His people, so that He restores life to penitents.[470]

In the case of Nineveh, repentance is strictly linked with the wrath and punishment of the Lord. The seriousness of the punishment and the truth of the prophecy caused the Ninevites to repent and purify themselves.[471] In the beginning, the Ninevites fled from 'purity' (ܕܟܝܘܬܐ) as Jonah had fled from God.[472] But in the battle of repentance, it was necessary that the impure ones cast off their own impurity.[473] Also the king was eager to cleanse the impurity of his people.[474] While the Ninevites remained pure through fasting, the Israelites became defiled.[475] So the penitents and the penitent city replaced the symbolic character of the

---

466 Cf. II Serm 1.839-40; 893-94: ܠܚܛܝܐ ܟܠܗ ܦܬܚ ܗܘܐ ܕܬܪܥܘܗܝ ܠܬܝܒܘܬܐ.

467 II Serm 1.593-94: ܬܝܒܘܬܐ ܝܗܝܒܐ ܒܐܪܥܐ ܕܢܬܦܪܩܘܢ ܒܗ ܚܛܝܐ.

468 II Serm 1.569-74: ܚܝܠ ܟܐܢܘܬܐ ܠܛܝܒܘܬܐ ܬܝܒܘܬܐ ܠܐ ܡܬܟܠܝܐ. ܢܣܥܘܠ ܠܗ ܙܝܢܐ ܚܕܬܐ ܠܩܪܒܐ ܚܕܬܐ ܕܡܢ. ܘܐܪܗܛܐ ܗܘ ܚܣܡܐ ܣܢܐܝܬ ܐܝܬ ܚܣܡܐ ܗܘܐ ܢܣܒ ܠܗ.

469 II Serm 1.831-34: ܕܠܒܘܗܝ ܢܟܠܗ ܘܢܙܟܝܘܗܝ ܙܟܘܬܐ ܒܬܝܒܘܬܐ.

470 II Serm 1335-36: ܠܗܘ ܕܪܘܚܡܗ ܗܒ ܠܗܘܢ ܚܝܝܗܘܢ ܒܬܝܒܘܬܐ.

471 II Serm 1.357-60: ܟܕ ܠܘܣܛܐ ܕܐܟܪܙܐ ܦܬܚ ܠܗ ܠܬܝܒܘܬܐ ܘܟܕ ܪܘܓܙܐ ܚܙܘ ܡܟܐܒܐ ܠܗ ܥܕ ܕܟܝܘܬܐ.

472 II Serm 1.21-22: ܥܪܩ ܗܘܘ ܡܢ ܐܠܗܐ ܘܝܘܢܢ ܡܢ ܕܟܝܘܬܐ.

473 II Serm 1.841-42: ܠܛܡܐܐ ܢܥܠܘܢ ܠܛܡܐܘܬܗ ܕܠܛܡܐ ܬܕܟܝܘܗܝ ܒܩܪܒܐ.

474 Cf. II Serm, 1.895-96: ܡܠܟܐ ܒܥܘܩܐ ܦܫܐ ܗܘܐ ܕܢܥܒܪ ܒܥܡܗܘܢ ܛܡܐܘܬܐ.

475 Cf. II Serm 1.1017-18; 1.1105-06.

promised land, together with Zion and Jerusalem, where good deeds, such as justice and purity, were to be expected.[476]

The way of repentance was accompanied by weeping, sorrow, supplication, wearing of sackcloth, ashes, fasting and prayer.[477] Ephrem specifically links fasting and prayer with repentance, and he gives them occasionally a healing effect. Though he often draws attention to fasting,[478] there is only one sentence in the mimro in which Ephrem specifically attributes the healing of the town's sickness to fasting: 'by fasting, the victorious medicine, [the king] healed the sickness of the city.'[479] After the king saw the fasting of Jonah and he was reminded of the fasting of the prophets Moses and Elijah, he realised that fasting is the medicine for his city.[480] 'Victorious fasting' (ܨܘܡܐ ܢܨܝܚܐ) possesses the power of forgiveness[481] and is able to eliminate the invisible defilement of the city.[482] Fasting makes sweet the bitterness of the Serpent and of the mind,[483] and it also turns judgment away and the wrath of the Lord.[484] So fasting increased the Ninevites' hope for salvation.[485]

---

476 Cf. II Serm 1.1619-22; 1.1915-16; 1.1952; 1.1669-1702. After being saved by Jonah, some of the Ninevites wanted to accompany Jonah back to his homeland in order to be further perfected by the Hebrews. But after they were disappointed by the sinful deeds of the Hebrews, they said: 'the iniquity which the penitents had put off, the Hebrews have put it on' (II Serm 1.1923-24: ܥܘܠܐ ܕܫܠܚܘ ܬܝܒ̈ܐ ܠܥܒܪ̈ܝܐ ܗܘܘ ܠܗ ܠܒܘܫܐ).

477 Cf. II Serm 1.965-1022.

478 Cf. II Serm 1.106; 1.167; 1.437; 1.744; 1.751; 1.753f.; 1.810f.; 1.863; 1.890; 1.923; 1.931; 1.939; 1.958; 1.974; 1.982; 1.990; 1.1018; 1.1084; 1.1092; 1.1140; 1.1316; 1.1382; 1.1645; 1.1986; 1.2124.

479 II Serm 1.923-24: ܒܨܘܡܐ ܐܣܝܐ ܢܨܝܚܐ ܟܘܪܗܢܐ ܕܡܕܝܢܬܐ ܐܣܝ.

480 Cf. II Serm 1.743-64; 1.917-24.

481 II Serm 1.105-06: ܕܠܒܠܐ ܐܠܘ ܟܢ ܕܥܒܕܘ ܣܘܟ̈ܠܬܐ ܟܘܪܗܢܐ ܨܘܡܐ; 1.931-32: ܡܢܝܢ ܚܘ̈ܒܐ ܬܠܒ ܗܘܐ ܨܘܡܐ ܫܠܡܬܐ ܥܒܕ ܗܘܐ.

482 II Serm 1.809-12: ܐܬܠܐ ܣܘܦܐ ܚܠܝܐ ܘܟܒܫ ܨܘܡܐ ܢܨܝܚܐ ܕܢܣܪܘܦܗ ܕܨܘܡܐ ܦܣܩ ܠܗ ܠܬܘܠܐ ܟܡܝܢܐ ܕܒܚܪܝܢ.

483 II Serm 1.889-90: ܥܠܝܗ ܠܡܪܬ ܚܘܝܐ ܒܨܘܡܐ ܚܠܐ ܡܥܣܩܘܬܗ.

484 II Serm 1.939-42: ܕܒܨܘܡܐ ܨܘܡܐ ܥܢܐ ܠܗ ܠܚܘܪܢܗ ܕܐܠܗܐ ܗܪܐ ܢܝܢ ܠܐ ܒܥܐ ܕܢܦܠ ܗܘܐ ܡܢ ܥܘܕܡܐ.

When the 'bosom of Nineveh' was purified, fasting was victorious and became glorified in Nineveh.[486]

In the mimro, Ephrem often uses the term 'prayer' (ܨܠܘܬܐ)[487] in the context of repentance and fasting, but he never links it explicitly to healing. In the beginning of the sermo, Ephrem relates the salvation of Jonah to prayer, whereas he relates the salvation of the Ninevites to 'supplication' (ܒܥܘܬܐ).[488] Later, Ephrem personifies Nineveh as a penitent. The Ninevites were motivating each other to pray and to repent, for no one could be saved alone.[489] Like the limbs of a single body they prayed for each other.[490] The king also motivated the Ninevites to win the invisible war and to defeat Satan with prayers.[491] So prayer guided the Ninevites in the process of repentance. Even the infants were saved for they learned fasting and prayer in the bosom of their mothers.[492] Everyone cried out with prayers and took refuge in them.[493]

Also significant concerning healing is hymn 49 On Virginity. In this hymn, Ephrem contrasts the behaviour of Jonah with a

---

485 II Serm 1.957-58: ܒܪ̈ ܢܘܢ ܨܘܡ ܣܒܪܐ ܒܨܘܡܐ ܣܒܪܐ ܦܠܓܐ ܗܘܐ.

486 II Serm 1.1139-40: ܫܦܝܐ ܥܘܒܗ̇ ܐܬܕܟܝ ܨܘܡܐ ܒܟܠܗ̇ ܐܙܕܗܝ.

487 Cf. II Serm 1.15-20; 1.202; 1.209; 1.212; 1.226; 1.242; 1.483; 1.802; 1.808; 1.865; 1.960; 1.974; 1.1009; 1.1231, 1,1331.

488 II Serm 1.15-20: ܥܠ ܗܘܐ ܢܒܝܐ ܒܨܠܘܬܐ ܐܦ ܡܠܟܐ ܒܬܒܥܘܬܐ. ܗܘ ܥܠ ܟܪܣܐ ܪܒܐ ܘܢܝܢܘܐ ܒܪܒܐ ܪܒܐ. ܨܠܘܬܐ ܠܢܘܢ ܦܪܩܬ ܗܘܬ ܘܠܢܝܢܘܐ ܒܒܥܘܬܐ.

489 II Serm 1.201-04: ܟܠ ܐܢܫ ܚܒܪܗ ܢܟܙ ܗܘܐ ܠܨܠܘܬܐ ܘܠܬܒܥܘܬܐ. ܗܘܐ ܗܘܐ ܠܗ ܟܠܗ ܪܒܐ ܚܕ ܠܡܫܬܒܐ ܐܝܟ ܬܒܥܐ.

490 II Serm 1.209-12: ܠܐ ܐܢܫ ܥܠ ܗܘܐ ܬܒܥ ܕܠܢܦܫܗ ܚܝܐ ܒܠܚܘܕ. ܨܠܝܢ ܗܘܘ ܟܢ ܐܝܟ ܗܕܡܐ ܕܚܕ. ܟܠ ܚܕ ܥܠ ܟܠܢܫ.

491 II Serm 1.801-02: ܒܩܪܒܐ ܠܟܠܗܐ ܕܢܙܟܘܢ ܠܣܛܢܐ ܘܒܗ ܒܨܠܘܬܐ.

492 II Serm 1.973-74: ܥܘ̈ܠܐ ܒܥܘ̈ܒܐ ܐܬܝܠܦܘ ܕܠܦܘ ܨܘܡܐ ܘܨܠܘܬܐ.

493 II Serm 1.807-08: ܩܪܬ ܘܥܡܐ ܡܬܬܪܝܐ ܘܐܬܟܠܘ ܒܨܠܘܬܐ; 1.1231-32: ܟܠ ܐܢܫ ܠܒܪܐ ܒܨܠܘܬܐ ܦܘܡܗ ܡܦܩܐ ܩܠܐ ܗܘܐ.

series of images from the Old Testament. But Jonah, as a type of Christ par excellence, was more successful in his preaching than Joshua, Moses and Isaac. Jonah is considered as the 'circumcised healer' (ܐܣܝܐ ܓܙܝܪܐ), and his voice as the 'medicine of life' for repentance: 'the High One sent a circumcised healer to circumcise the heart of the uncircumcised people.[494] Jonah appears in Nineveh with terror (the same image as in II Serm 1) and caused the Ninevites to drink bitterness instead of sweetness.[495] As Isaac was lifted up to be sacrificed, so too Jonah 'lifted up' the city for forty days, in order to become 'empty'.

ܡܘܫܐ ܐܠܦ ܥܡܐ ܐܣܛܝ
ܐܬܬܥܝܩ ܐܣܝܐ ܕܠܐ ܐܗܢܝ ܥܩܪܗ
ܢܝܢܘܐ ܬܒܬ ܠܝܘܢܢ ܒܐܫܬ
ܐܬܬܥܝܩ ܐܣܝܐ ܕܙܟܝ ܣܡܡܗ ܀
ܣܡܐ ܕܐܝܢܐ ܡܢ ܐܣܘ̈ܢ
ܐܣܝ ܠܪܒܘ ܪ̈ܒܘܢ ܡܪ̈ܥܐ
ܣܡ ܬܝ̈ܒܐ ܢܚܬ ܡܢ ܪܘܡܐ
ܒܕܪ ܚܘܣܝܐ ܒܝܢܬ ܚܘ̈ܒܐ
ܟܕ ܡܬܬܥܝܩ ܐܢܬ ܝܘܢܢ ܚܕܝ
ܕܡܢ ܟܘܠ ܢܒ̈ܝܐ ܙܟܝܢ ܣܡ̈ܡܝܟ

[13] Moses taught; the people apostasised.
The healer was irritated that his remedy did not avail.
[14] Nineveh repented; it grieved Jonah.
The healer was irritated that his medicine triumphed.
[15] The medicine of which one of the healers
has healed ten myriads of the sick?
[16] The Medicine of penitents came down from the height.
He scattered pardon among the sins.
[17] While you are irritated, Jonah, rejoice
that of all the prophets your medicines are the most triumphant.[496]

---

494 Virg 49.1: ܐܣܝܐ ܓܙܝܪܐ ܫܕܪ ܪܡܐ ܕܢܓܙܘܪ ܠܒܗ ܕܥܡܐ ܥܘܪܠܐ.

495 Cf. Virg 49.10.

496 Virg 49.13-17.

One comes across different terms here: Jonah, as well as Moses, is described as a 'physician' (ܐܣܝܐ) whose 'medicine proved successful' (ܕܐܨܠܚ ܣܡ̇ܗ). The ensuing 'Medicine of Penitents' (ܣܡ ܬܝ̈ܒܐ) refers to Jesus rather than to Jonah. In Virg 42.5-6, where Ephrem discusses the entire narrative of Jonah, Ephrem speaks of the healing of Nineveh by the 'good one' (ܛܒܐ). Neither the subject of the second sentence, nor the meaning of ܚܕ ܛܒܐ is clear. The subject of this sentence can be both God and Jonah. The word ܛܒܐ can be read as ܛܒܐ (good), as well as ܛܶܒܐ (message, news) which would refer to the single sentence of Jonah's preaching in Nineveh (cf. Jonah 3:4).

ܒܢܝܢܘܐ ܕܐܣܝܗ̇ ܐܠܦ̈ܐ ܕܠܐ ܣܟ
ܙܪܘ ܗܘܘ ܥܠܘܗܝ ܟܠ ܩܘ̈ܠܣܝܢ
ܒܚܕ ܚܕ ܛܒܐ ܐܣܝ ܐܢܘܢ
ܘܪܣܡܬ ܫܘܒܚܗ ܥܢܢܐ ܕܦܘ̈ܡܐ

[5] In Nineveh that he healed, thousands without limit
poured upon him all kinds of praises.
[6] By means of one message he healed them,
and the cloud of mouths distilled his glory.[497]

However, in the first part of this passage it is very clear that Jonah is the healer of Nineveh: 'he healed it [Nineveh]' (ܐܣܝܗ̇). Since he had healed them, the Ninevites gave him praise and glory. It is very likely that the term ܛܒܐ also means 'news' or 'message' (ܛܶܒܐ) so that it would make sense that Jonah healed the Ninevites by his message.[498]

In contrast, in hymn 45 the idea of healing is introduced once. This time it is not Jonah who has healed the Ninevites, but rather the Ninevites who have cured Jonah: 'on the ship all the sailors

[497] Virg 42.5-6.

[498] Hymn 43 On Virginity compares Jonah with Peter. Both of them are described as 'fishermen' (ܨܝ̈ܕܐ), Peter willingly, Jonah against his will, who are to catch sinners for life. Ephrem does not use the word healing in this hymn; instead, he draws attention to 'life' (ܚܝ̈ܐ).

protected him; in Nineveh all the sinners cured him.[499] Here one should note that Ephrem uses the situation on the ship as a parallel: just as the sailors had 'protected' (ܣܬܪܘܗܝ) Jonah, Ephrem points out how the Ninevites, as sinners, also 'gave medicine' (ܣܡܣܡܘܗܝ) to Jonah. Jonah had expected the judgment of the Ninevites, rather than their healing and salvation. But his voice, as the medicine of life, caused, through sowing the threat of death, the flourishing of life.[500] Jonah himself was neither physically nor mentally ill, but his will contrasted with God's will. Against his free will, he was forced to travel to Nineveh. When he arrived there, he was concerned and in his anxiety he longed for death. For forty days he was watching the city, fearing that his preaching might be wrong.[501] But after the repentance and healing of the Ninevites, they praised him. Ephrem emphasises that his success and good reputation was through the Ninevites.[502] Thus, their repentance served as a witness to the truth of Jonah's preaching, so that he was cured from his worry and fear.

Finally, in hymn 17 On Virginity, where Ephrem gives a typological exegesis of the Scriptural passage on the city Shechem, he identifies the church with Shechem. Then, in stanza 9, he describes Jonah as the upright man who proclaimed his judgment in Nineveh and saved it. No healing imagery occurs here.[503]

### *5.2.3.8 The Physician Daniel*

The ministry of Daniel in Babel (Babylon), as well as of Moses in Egypt, is extensively described in Nis 30. His contest was against the Evil One, darkness, greed, error, oracle of the Chaldaean etc. However, Ephrem does not explicitly use any healing terminology in Nis 30. Likewise, in Iei 2.3, Ephrem refers to Daniel and illustrates the enormity of the bad effect of sin which 'tore in pieces

---

499 Virg 45.22: ܒܐܠܦܐ ܣܬܪܘܗܝ ܠܗ ܢܘ̈ܛܝܐ ܒܢܝܢܘܐ ܣܡܣܡܘܗܝ ܟܠ ܚ̈ܛܝܐ.

500 Virg 49.21: ܩܠܗ ܕܣܡ ܗܘܐ ܣܡ ܚܝܐ ܙܪܥ ܒܗ ܡܘܬܐ ܘܦܪܚܘ ܚ̈ܝܐ.

501 Cf. II Serm 1.1285-88.

502 Cf. II Serm 1.1349-72.

503 Cf. Virg 17.9.

the People' (ܒܣܒܣܬܗ ܠܥܡܐ) and its mouth is 'bitter and deadly' (ܡܪܝܪܐ ܘܩܛܘܠܐ) like that of wild animals. The wild animals that Daniel saw (Dan 7:3-7; 7:17-23) symbolise sin, and through them sin caused the great 'fracture of paganism' ( ܬܒܪܐ ܕܚܢܦܘܬܐ) in all the world.[504] Thus, Daniel's ministry was against sin that took place in Babel, and his conquest over sin made known through his fasting, described mainly in hymns 7 and 9 On Fasting. However, neither here is any healing terminology explicitly attributed to Daniel.[505]

Ephrem uses the name of the prophet Daniel only once in Nis 34. The title 'physician' is not attributed to him, neither does Daniel feature as the subject of any healing verbs, only of the verb 'to moderate' (ܡܟܝܢ). Babel is the region where the prophet Daniel was active and 'moderated'. Considering the context, Daniel's ministry was not different to the activity of the other prophets. His aim was to heal Babel that is described as the 'head' (ܪܫܐ) of the world. This head 'went mad in the desert' (ܕܫܢܐ ܒܡܕܒܪܐ). Contrasting Babel with Egypt, Egypt remained in its sickness, whereas Babel was 'restored and gave thanks' (ܘܐܬܚܠܡ ܘܐܘܕܝ). The verb 'to be restored' (ܐܬܚܠܡ) is passive, but since it refers to Babel as a head, and it occurs in the context of Daniel, he can be considered as the healer of Babel. This can only be the case if the restoration refers to Daniel's time. However, if Ephrem thinks of the restoration of Babel through conversion to Christianity, then the main Healer is the Lord. If the former is the case, through Daniel the restoration could not be complete, for all of the prophets and the patriarchs were not able to perform total healing. As Ephrem says: 'the physicians were not sufficient with their medicines for the world'.[506]

---

504 Iei 2.3.

505 Iei 7; 9.

506 Nis 34.10: ܠܐ ܣܦܩܘ ܠܗ ܕܝܢ ܠܥܠܡܐ ܐܣܘܬܐ ܒܣܡܡܝܗܘܢ.

### 5.2.4 Healing through the Law and the Commandments of God.

Instead of investigating the divine Essence, in SFid 3 Ephrem advises the Arians to study the 'commandments' (ܦܘܩܕ̈ܢܐ) and 'Law' (ܢܡܘܣܐ) of the Lord, and he also asks them to distinguish between the commandments. A commandment tells human beings 'what to do and what to leave'.[507] Ephrem considers the commandment of the Lord as 'sound/restorative' (ܚܠܝܡܐ) and 'true/sound/firm' (ܫܪܝܪܐ).[508] The Law, given by God, requires faith from human beings[509] in order to cure their pains.

The commandments were issued when they were required. Ephrem attributes the commandments not only to God, but also to the voices of the prophets which proclaimed medicine for the weakness, sickness and feebleness of their time.[510] All of the commandments did not exist at the beginning, and after their time some of them are not relevant either, for some of them were only temporary and just served for the pains of their times.[511] Some of the commandments by means of medicines are not relevant any more, for the relevant sickness has ceased and no longer exists.[512] Thus, some of the pains are universal, while others exist only in certain periods of time. Therefore, the commandments of the universal pains are always valued and are able to perform healing, whereas those of the past pains are irrelevant nowadays and, instead of healing, they can do much harm. Ephrem illustrates this by referring to the 'commandment of do-not-steal' ( ܦܘܩܕܢܐ ܕܠܐ ܬܓܢܘܒ) and the 'commandment of circumcision' ( ܦܘܩܕܢܐ ܕܓܙܘܪܬܐ):

---

[507] SFid 3.89-90: ܕܘܢ ܘܐܦ ܚܙܝ ܦܘܩܕܢܐ ܕܡܢ ܠܡܥܒܕ ܘܐܝܢܐ ܐܝܬ.

[508] Haer 32.2: ܫܠܡ ܒܪ ܦܘܩܕܢܐ ܚܠܝܡܐ ܘܫܪܝܪܐ.

[509] Fid 70.13: ܝܗܒ ܢܡܘܣܐ ܫܐܠ ܗܝܡܢܘܬܐ ܘܫܐܠ ܒܟܐܒܬܐ ܡܣܒܪܢܘܬܐ ܠܚܘܠܡܢܗܝܢ.

[510] SFid 3.145-148.

[511] SFid 3.91-120.

[512] SFid 3.149-152: ܐܝܬ ܡܢ ܦܘܩܕ̈ܢܐ ܕܒܛܠܘ ܕܠܡܘܬܗܘܢ ܒܟܐܒܐ ܘܕܡܝܐ ܐܝܬ ܕܐܢ ܡܚܘܢ ܕܡܣܝܡܝܢ ܡܛܠ ܟܐ̈ܒܐ ܕܡܢܝܚܝܢ.

There are pains of certain generations, and there are
pains of all generations.
They [the prophets and disciples] granted new
medicines to the new pains that they came across.
They granted permanent medicines to the permanent
pains that [exist] in all generations.
He [God] gave the commandment 'you should not
steal' (Ex 20:15); the pain is permanent and his
medicine is permanent.
He gave the commandment of circumcision, the pain
came to nought and so its medicine came to
nought.
He constructed instruments for the surgical operations
of the pains that were new.
[Concerning] the instruments, however, that were
constructed for the previous pains,
since the pain does not exist today, so too [its]
instrument becomes useless.
The fact that the harm has ceased, [its] instrument
became superfluous.
Today the commandments of Sabbath, circumcision
and purification have ceased.[513]

Obviously, the commandments served, and some of them still serve, as medicine for curing the pains of mankind. However, Ephrem draws attention to the right understanding and use of the medicine of the commandments. Once, all the commandments were used when they were required. Instead of healing, the use of the commandments at a time when they are not required will rather harm and injure. The commandments serve as medicine only for

---

[513] SFid 3.161-80:
ܐܝܬ ܟܐܒ̈ܐ ܕܕ̈ܪܝܢ ܐܝܬ ܟܐܒ̈ܐ ܕܟܠ ܕ̈ܪܝܢ ܠܟܐܒ̈ܐ ܚ̈ܕܬܐ
ܕܐܫܬܟܚܘ ܣܡ̈ܡܢܐ ܚ̈ܕܬܐ ܝܗܒܘ ܗܘܘ
ܠܟܐܒ̈ܐ ܐܡܝܢ̈ܐ ܕܟܠ ܕ̈ܪܝܢ ܣܡ̈ܡܢܐ ܐܡܝܢ̈ܐ ܝܗܒܘ ܗܘܘ ܝܗܒ
ܦܘܩܕܢܐ ܕܠܐ ܬܓܢܘܒ ܐܡܝܢ ܟܐܒܐ ܘܐܡܝܢ ܣܡܡܗ
ܝܗܒ ܦܘܩܕܢܐ ܕܓܙܘܪܬܐ ܐܒܕ ܟܐܒܐ ܘܐܒܕ ܣܡܡܗ ܡ̈ܐܢܐ ܬܩܢ
ܠܓܙܪ̈ܐ ܠܟܐܒ̈ܐ ܕܗܘܘ ܚܕ̈ܬܐܝܬ
ܡ̈ܐܢܐ ܕܝܢ ܕܐܬܬܩܢܘ ܗܘܘ ܡܛܠ ܟܐܒ̈ܐ ܕܩܕ̈ܡܝܐ ܕܠܝܬܘܗܝ ܗܘܘ
ܟܐܒܐ ܝܘܡܢ ܐܦ ܗܘ ܡܐܢܐ ܒܛܝܠܐ ܗܘ
ܕܒܛܠ ܠܗ ܓܝܪ ܢܟܝܢܐ ܗܘܐ ܠܗ ܡܐܢܐ ܝܬܝܪܐ ܒܛܠܘ ܝܘܡܢܐ
ܦܘܩܕ̈ܢܐ ܕܫܒܬܐ ܓܙܘܪܬܐ ܘܕܘܟܝܐ.

the 'wounded' (ܠܡ̈ܚܝܐ),[514] or for those 'wounded by paganism' (ܕܒܚܢܦܘܬܐ ܐܬܡܚܝܘ).[515] The remedies of the commandments are not only useless for the 'healthy in faith' ( ܕܚܠܝܡܝܢ ܒܗܝܡܢܘܬܐ), or for those who are 'healthy in knowledge' (ܕܚܠܝܡ̈ܐ ܗܘܘ ܒܝܕܥܬܐ),[516] but they will hurt, strike and wound the healthy. For this, both Nature and Scripture provide examples:

> Today, he who is using the commandments as instruments
> is the partner of that killer who cuts off the healthy limbs.
> Jeremiah might teach you this: 'the commandments are iron' (Jer 23:29),
> they were useful for the wounded; do not harm the sound person with them.
> They are formed because of the pains, do not strike the healthy with them;
> they are worse than visible surgical operations, for they harm the invisible soul.
> As they were helping the sick, so too, they harm the healthy.
> Do not torment the sound/firm body, just because there are medicines.
> Also at their times, the commandments ceased in certain places.[517]
> Where health existed, bandaging and medicine were deadly.
> Even nature's healing is useless among the healthy;
> if even during the time of pains medicine ceased in certain places,
> the fact that the People passed over along with their sicknesses, [so too] their medicines are useless.
> A pain ceases, [another] pains exists; a medicine ceased, [another] medicine exists.

---

[514] SFid 3.195; cf. Jer 23.29.

[515] SFid 3.188.

[516] SFid 3.184-86.

[517] Ephrem might have a particular biblical passage or historical event in his mind where, what ever the reason, some commandments were not considered as relevant.

Thus, the pains and medicines of offerings, Sabbath
and the tenth part ceased,
but the pains and medicines of 'you should not swear
(Ex 20:7), steal or commit adultery' (Ex 20:14-15)
exist.
Do not rush towards the commandment which ceased
and its pain has ceased.
Be aware about the commandment which is the
medicine of your wound.
Do not put on your bruises medicines which are
useless for you.
The pain upon pain will abound for you added iniquity
to hatred.
The Giver of Law will be angry, for He has loosed and
you bind up the [commandment].
You ignore the commandment which He gives, but
keep that which He loosed.[518]

---

[518] SFid 3.189-232:
ܐܝܟܢܐ ܕܡܬܚܣܢ ܢܘܟܡ ܒܦܘܩ̈ܕܢܐ ܐܦ ܒܟܐ̈ܒܐ ܒܪ ܙܘܓܗ ܗܘ
ܕܫܒܬܐ ܕܥܣܪ̈ܝܐ ܣܠܝ̈ܩܐ ܠܒܪ
ܦܬ̈ܓܡܐ ܐܢܘܢ ܦܘܩ̈ܕܢܐ ܢܠܦܝܢ ܗܕܐ ܐܪܡܝܐ ܠܡܣܡ̈ܢܐ ܡܣܝܢ ܗܘܘ
ܠܐ ܬܗܐ ܒܗܘܢ ܙܪܝܙܐ
ܡܛܠ ܕܐܝ̈ܢܐ ܐܬܬܦܠܘ ܠܐ ܬܗܦܟܐ ܒܗܘܢ ܠܣܠܝ̈ܩܐ ܡܢ ܠܒܪ̈ܐ
ܠܒܪ̈ܐ ܒܢܝ̈ܢ ܕܠܟܦܪܐ ܒܡܚܬܐ ܢܒܝܢ
ܒܟܐ ܕܒܕܘܪܐ ܗܘܘ ܠܒܪ̈ܝܬܐ ܡܢ ܢܒܝܢ ܠܣܠܝ̈ܩܐ ܠܗ ܡܛܠ ܕܐܝܬ
ܡܣܡ̈ܢܐ ܬܟܝܢ ܠܡܟܪܟܐ ܙܪܝܙܐ
ܐܦ ܒܪܒܢܝ̈ܗܘܢ ܦܘܩ̈ܕܢܐ ܒܒܘܣܐ ܕܒܘܣܐ ܥܠܝܡ ܗܘܘ ܐܝܟܐ ܕܐܝܬ
ܗܘܐ ܣܘܠܩܢܐ ܚܪܟܐ ܘܣܡܟܐ ܡܛܠ ܗܘܐ
ܐܦ ܐܣܘܬܐ ܕܒܝܫܐ ܒܢܬ ܣܠܝ̈ܩܐ ܒܛܠܟܐ ܗܝ ܐܢ ܗܡܝܠ ܒܢܝܢ
ܟܐܒܐ ܒܛܠ ܣܡܟܐ ܒܕܘܒܐ ܕܘܒܐ
ܕܒܢܝܢ ܒܢܒܐ ܘܒܘܪܗܢܗܝ ܠܐ ܣܥܝܢ ܡܣܡ̈ܢܝܗܘܢ ܒܛܠ ܟܐܒܐ
ܘܡܢܝ ܟܐܒܐ ܒܛܠ ܣܡܟܐ ܘܡܢܝ ܣܡܟܐ
ܒܛܠ ܠܗܢ ܟܐ̈ܒܐ ܘܣܡ̈ܡܢܐ ܕܕܒ̈ܚܐ ܫܒܬܐ ܘܡܥܣܪ̈ܐ ܐܝܬ ܕܝܢ
ܟܐ̈ܒܐ ܘܣܡ̈ܡܢܐ ܕܠܐ ܬܐܡܐ ܬܓܢܘܒ ܘܬܓܘܪ
ܠܐ ܬܪܗܛ ܠܘܬ ܦܘܩܕܢܐ ܕܒܛܠ ܗܘ ܘܒܛܠ ܟܐܒܗ ܗܘܬ ܙܗܝܪ
ܒܦܘܩܕܢܐ ܕܗܘܝܘ ܣܡܐ ܕܡܚܘܬܟ
ܠܐ ܬܣܝܡ ܠܡܚ̈ܘܬܟ ܣܡ̈ܡܢܐ ܕܠܐ ܡܥܕܪܝܢ ܠܟ ܟܐܒܐ ܥܠ
ܟܐܒܐ ܣܓܐ ܕܥܠ ܥܘܠܐ ܥܠܬܐ ܐܘܣܦܬ

☞

The commandments, as medicines, that are not relevant any more are basically those which only refer to the Old Covenant, and generally have been replaced by others of the New Covenant. For instance, Sunday took over the role of the Sabbath, and baptism the function of circumcision. In SFid 3.213-14, Ephrem speaks of the People, by means of the Hebrews, and their sickness that came to nought. Likewise, their medicine has ceased. In this passage, the examples given by Ephrem are limited: Sabbath, circumcision and the tithe.[519] However, some of the Old Covenant's commandments are still of value, for they are not limited to a particular time. Again, Ephrem only mentions three particular commandments based on Ex 20: do not swear, steal and commit adultery.

However, in the context of healing it is of interest to know that Ephrem attributes healing power to the heavenly commandments, and some of them are universal. They served, and some still serve, as medicine for the pains of humanity. Making a distinction between the commandments leads to the right use of their remedies and their curative power.[520] The commandments of God and His Law are written in the Bible. Ephrem is convinced that generally Scripture, and Nature as well, can heal if it is understood rightly.[521]

Particular examples for healing through the commandments do not occur explicitly in Ephrem, but indirectly some passages can be considered. In the Bible, the healing of Miriam, the Prophetess, is attributed to the commandment of the Lord to confine Miriam

---

ܪ̈ܓܫܝ ܗܘ ܦܣܩ ܠܡܣܟܢܘܬܐ ܕܗܘ ܙܒܢܐ ܘܐܬܬ ܐܣܪ ܐܬܐ ܦܘܩܕ̈ܢܐ
ܕܗܝܒ ܠܗ ܟܠܝܠ ܘܠܗܘ ܕܙܒܢܐ ܢܛܪ ܐܬܐ

[519] It is significant that Ephrem considers the commandment of the 'tithe' (ܡܥܣܪ̈ܐ) as past and as no longer relevant for Christians. I wonder, if this is based on the passage where a poor widow offered only two small copper coins (Lk 21:1-4), implying that everyone should donate as much as he can. However, the term ܒܡܥܣܪ̈ܐ only occurs several times in Hebr 7, while the verb ܥܣܪ is used in Mt 23:23; Lk 11:42; 18:12 and Hebr 7:9.

[520] This reflects the same idea as the use of medical herbs, and the right approach and interpretation of Scripture. Both of them can cure and harm. Therefore, Ephrem asks for the right balance and a discerning approach.

[521] Cf. Virg 1.3.

outside the camp for seven days (Num 12:14-15). Moses and Aaron followed the instruction of God, and so Miriam was healed. Ephrem, however, refers to the affliction of Miriam with leprosy in I Serm 2.1203-1342 and in Fid 28.10, but he mentions her healing only once, along with that of Naaman, in Haer 43.16. Here, the subject of healing is the Lord of the Law, namely God, and not just the Law.[522]

Finally, worth mentioning are the aspects of purification and cleansing through water/baptism and sprinkling of blood. Neither of them is directly linked with healing in the context of the Law, but since purification and cleansing are related to the forgiveness of sin, so they can be considered as spiritual healing from sin. As an example I just refer to Nat 17.16-17 and CDiat 16.13. In the former, based on the healing of Naaman who followed the commandment of the prophet Elisha to wash in the river (2 Kgs 5:1-17), Ephrem invites all lepers to be cleansed from their leprosy. Naaman serves as a type and example in that, when he was obedient to the word of the prophet and washed in the river, healing was achieved. Without any doubt, according to Ephrem, the power of healing is not in the substance of water, but in the name evoked upon them. However, through the water, or as Ephrem says, through the 'seven times' of his plunging in the water, the healing of Naaman was carried out.

Likewise, sprinkling with blood (Lev 14:1ff), not the element of blood itself, but the priestly ritual act performed in faith, had power to cleanse man from sin. Thus, in the Old Covenant, following the Law, burnt offerings and performing the sprinkling of blood, and washing in the water, had the power of cleansing and curing. For Ephrem all these served as symbols for Christ and they were replaced by Christian baptism.[523]

### 5.2.5 Healing through the Ark of God (1 Sam 6:1-12).

Only in Haer 51.4, does Ephrem use the Ark of the Covenant in the context of healing. The healing and medicine of the Ark are not attributed to the People, but rather to the Philistines. The historical background is depicted in 1 Sam 6:1-12, where the Philistines were

---

522 On Miriam, see further chapter IV, 1.2.1.

523 CDiat 16.13; Nat 17.16-17.

terrified of the Ark of the Lord, and they asked their priests and diviners what to do with the Ark of the God of Israel. Their advice is recorded in the Peshitta as follows (1 Sam 6:3): 'if you return the Ark of the Lord, the God of Israel, do not send it away empty, but in fact bring an offering to it; and then you will be healed and you will know why His hand has not been turned away from you.'[524] Ephrem is aware of this biblical passage and particularly of the verb 'to be healed' (ܬܬܐܣܘܢ) that is only once used in the entire context of the Ark. The healing of the Philistines was supposed to be from the wound that the Ark caused and the hand of the Lord that was heavy upon them (cf. 1 Sam 4-5).

Ephrem takes this narrative and uses it as an argument against the sickness of the People. In Haer 51.1, against the heresies of Marcion, Bardaisan and Mani, Ephrem rejects their doctrine and refers to the teaching of the prophets, particularly Isaiah, and the invisibility of the Lord in the Old Covenant. The prophets, like Isaiah, saw the sickness of the People, and provided medicine for it. Likewise, God provided medicines and he serves as the Physician for those who recognise Him. For Ephrem, based on 1 Sam 6, certainly the Philistines 'realised that medicines are necessary for their pains'.[525] Likewise, they realised that they could get medicine for their pains from the 'hidden Physician who dwelled in the Ark'.[526] The hidden Physician is certainly God the Father for 'the good Physician', namely Jesus, is called the 'Son of the hidden Physician'.[527] Thus, as the Philistines were wounded by the Ark of God, so too they were healed by it when they honoured it as they recognised the presence of the invisible Physician in it.

---

[524] 1 Sam 6:3: ܐܢ ܡܗܦܟܝܢܬܘܢ ܠܩܒܘܬܗ ܕܡܪܝܐ ܐܠܗܐ ܕܐܝܣܪܝܠ. ܠܐ ܬܫܕܪܘܢܝܗ̇ ܣܪܝܩܐܝܬ ܐܠܐ ܡܝܬܘ ܐܝܬܘ ܠܗ ܩܘܪܒܢܐ. ܘܗܝܕܝܢ ܬܬܐܣܘܢ ܘܬܬܝܕܥ ܠܟܘܢ ܕܠܡܢܐ ܠܐ ܬܗܦܘܟ ܐܝܕܗ ܕܡܪܝܐ ܡܢܟܘܢ. For the 'Ark', Ephrem uses the term ܐܪܘܢܐ, whereas 1 Sam 6 has both ܩܒܘܬܐ as well a ܐܪܘܢܐ.

[525] Haer 51.4: ܐܝܕܥܘ ܕܣܡ̈ܡܢܐ ܡܬܒܥܝܢ ܠܟܐܒ̈ܝܗܘܢ.

[526] Haer 51.4: ܐܣܝܐ ܟܣܝܐ ܕܫܪܐ ܒܐܪܘܢܐ.

[527] Haer 51.5: ܗܘ ܐܣܝܐ ܛܒܐ ܒܪܗ ܕܐܣܝܐ ܟܣܝܐ.

## 5.3 Jesus as the Medicine of Life: Healing in the Light of the Incarnation

While the healing achieved in the Old Covenant by the chosen people, or through the Law, Ark and the ܐܪ̈ܙܐ of the Medicine of Life, was partial and limited to individuals or to a particular time, Jesus performed complete healing for both individuals as well as for the whole of humanity and creation. With His healing ministry, Jesus made it clear that it is not just comparable to that of the prophets, but, as the 'Lord of the prophets' (ܡܪܗܘܢ ܕܢܒܝ̈ܐ),[528] He is the Healer of everything, as He came down from heaven as the Medicine of Life to heal humanity from its state of sickness which no one else was able to heal. Jesus, as the 'Medicine of Life' (ܣܡ ܚܝ̈ܐ)[529] and the 'Physician' (ܐܣܝܐ)[530] par excellence is the heavenly Medicine, the 'Word' (ܡܠܬܗ) and the 'Son of the Father' (ܒܪܗ ܕܐܒܐ),[531] Who is sent to fulfill what was deficient in human nature. With His 'good news' (ܣܒܪܬܗ), 'compassion' (ܡܪܚܡܢܘܬܐ)[532] and 'concern/caring' (ܒܛܝܠܘܬܗ),[533] Jesus performed healing, being 'our Lord' (ܡܪܢ),[534] 'Saviour' (ܦܪܘܩ)[535] and 'Creator' (ܟܒܘܠ).[536] He healed humanity from its 'state of sickness' (ܟܪܝܗܘܬܐ),[537] 'wound' (ܡܚܘܬܐ)[538] and 'sores' (ܫܒ̈ܪܬܐ)[539] that were effected by the enemy of humanity[540] and so

---

528 Dom 42.

529 CDiat 10.7; Dom 3; 15; 44; 42; 44; Nat 1.52; 3.19-20; 4.24; 6.8; 13.2; 24.27; Virg 49.16; Fid 36.1; Eccl 38 Ref.; 38.4; Nis 21.18; 34.10; 74.14; Haer 44.1ff.

530 CDiat 10.10; Dom 44; Nat 3.20; Nis 6.1; Eccl 12.9; 28.16.

531 CDiat 11.7; Eccl 38 Ref.; 38.4.

532 CDiat 13.1; Fid 8.12; Virg 26.6; 26.10; 31.13; Eccl 31.1; 38.4; Epiph 10.12.

533 CDiat 16.24; Nis 46.8; Haer 21.11; 33.3.

534 CDiat 16.10; Dom 21.

535 CDiat 16.32; Eccl 41.4.

536 CDiat 21.12.

537 Fid 79.7 (on ܟܪܝܗܘܬܐ, see further chapter III, 1.1).

538 Nis 19.11; 34.10; Nat 22.1-3; Fid 15.1; Epiph 10.12; 46.15.

539 Haer 33.1; 33.11.

through 'sin' (ܚܛܝܬܐ). Thus, as Jesus granted perfect 'healing' (ܐܣܝܘܬܐ)[541] and 'restoration' (ܚܠܝܡܘܬܐ)[542] to humanity, He also changed the 'bitterness' (ܡܪܝܪܘܬܐ) of the world into 'sweetness' (ܚܠܝܘܬܐ).[543]

The healing of individuals serves as evidence that Jesus is the Son of God Who came as the Medicine of Life to heal not only some individuals, but also the whole of humanity. It can be divided into those who were healed from physical sickness, those from demons and evil spirits, and those who were healed spiritually. All three sections are based on the Gospel. Here they are presented from a different aspect to those dealt with in the exegetical chapter. The aim here is to show the variety of Jesus' healing, as seen through Ephrem's eyes; they bear witness to His healing capability and to His divinity, He being One with the Father, the Creator of the World. Likewise, the healing of individuals shows the different sicknesses and man's need of the heavenly Medicine. Ephrem attributes healing not just to Jesus' word and hand, but also to His passion, cross, and even His garment.[544] Furthermore, Jesus' healing activity has not stopped with Him, but continues through His disciples, saints and martyrs, as well as being found in the sacraments of the Church through the priesthood and in acts of piety.

### 5.3.1 The Physical and Spiritual Healing of Individuals

In the context of salvation, this section includes most of the healing miracles that Jesus performed during His ministry (the miracles of giving sight to the blind and raising the dead have been left out). The exegetical chapter of this thesis covered three different aspects of Jesus' healing ministry. First, when Ephrem comments extensively on the woman with the haemorrhage, while he emphasises her physical healing, he goes beyond the biblical text

---

540 Nat 4.33; 13.2; 18.27; 26.9; Virg 37.8.

541 CDiat 12.24; 13.6; 16.31; Dom 13-14; Haer 38.13; 43.9; I Serm 6 App 3.13.

542 Virg 50.25.

543 Dom 4; 25; 44; Nat 1.52; Virg 31.13; Fid 5.16.

544 CDiat 4.13; 13.6; 13.24; Dom 49; Nat 19.15; 23.11-12; Fid 4.4; 10.6; 28.11; Nis 4.20; 27.3; Virg 34.3; Sog 1.22; Crucif 8.1.

and speaks of her spiritual healing. For Ephrem, perfect healing means being healed physically and spiritually. Secondly, in contrast to Simon the Pharisee, the comments on the sinful woman draw attention to spiritual healing from her previous sins. She was totally restored, for all her sins were forgiven. Thirdly, the section about blindness refers to the relationship of physical and spiritual healing and points to the healing of the whole of humanity. Jesus gave sight not only to the exterior eye, but also to the interior.[545] These three examples also illustrated the wide range of Ephrem's use of biblical references, and the way that Ephrem interprets and comments on Jesus' healing activity. In the present chapter, attention is drawn to the variety of sicknesses and the way that Jesus healed them according to Ephrem's view. It is interesting to look at the context in which Ephrem refers to Jesus' healing miracles and why he includes them in his work.

*5.3.1.1 Physical Healing*

Commenting on John's question as to whether Jesus is the One Who was to come, Ephrem refers to the answer given by Jesus and emphasises that John's aim was to manifest the faith of his disciples. They should not only hear from the others, but in particular see the miracles that Jesus performed, such as the blind receiving sight and the lame walking (Mt 11:4-5).[546] As an outstanding healing miracle, Ephrem considers the 'raising of the dead to be the first fruit of the goodness of the Only-Begotten-One, and the annuller and the destroyer of the wickedness which Adam caused to enter into the world.'[547]

---

[545] In order to avoid duplication, these three examples are not discussed again here.

[546] CDiat 9.2: ܗܟܢܐ ܐܦ ܒܗܕܐ ܨܒܐ. ܕܢܚܘܐ ܠܒܪܐ ܕܠܐ ܡܬܓܠܝܢ ܠܬܠܡܝܕܘܗܝ ܢܦܫܗ. ܟܕ ܡܒܪܪ ܠܗܘܢ ܒܗܢܐ ܐܣܟܡܐ. ܕܟܕ ܚܙܘ ܬܕܡܪܬܐ ܢܬܬܪܪܘܢ ܒܗܝܡܢܘܬܗ. ܘܐܡܪ ܠܗܘܢ ܠܡ ܢܗܘܐ. ܕܐܠܘ ܘܗܘܘ ܠܗܘܢ ܠܐ ܐܝܠܝܢ ܕܫܡܥܬܘܢ. ܐܠܐ ܐܝܠܝܢ ܕܚܙܝܬܘܢ. ܗܐ ܠܡ ܟܕ ܣܡܝܐ ܚܙܝܢ ܘܚܓܝܪܐ ܡܗܠܟܝܢ.

[547] CDiat 9.3: ܥܢܐ ܘܗܝܠ ܡܢ ܐܝܠܝܢ ܕܡܣܬܒܪܢ ܒܝܬܝܪܬܐ. ܟܕ ܬܕܡܪܬܐ ܪܒܬܐ ܘܪܫܝܬܐ ܚܕܐ ܥܒܘܬܐ ܡܢܗ. ܣܡܝܐ ܠܡ ܟܕ ܚܙܝܢ. ܘܚܓܝܪܐ ܕܡܗܠܟܝܢ. ܘܓܪܒܐ ܡܬܕܟܝܢ ܘܚܪܫܐ ܫܡܥܝܢ. ܘܠܡܝܬܐ ܐܝܟ ܕܠܣܘܬܪܐ ܕܟܠܗܘܢ. ܐܟܠ ܗܝ ܕܡܘܬܐ ܡܩܝܡ. ܕܐܝܬܝܗ̇ ܪܫܝܬܐ

☞

In Virg 19.2, Ephrem mentions the healing of the lame and deaf which happened in the city of Shechem. These miracles illustrated the good news indicating the joy and salvation which the Healer brought to the city: 'the lame who had been restored rejoiced and danced in you [Shechem]; the deaf shouted for joy; the mute sang praises.'[548]

The following section presents the healing of the paralytic (Mt 9:1-8; Mk 2:1-12; Lk 5:17-26; Jn 5:1-18), the Centurion's servant (Lk 7:1-10), Peter's mother-in-law (Mt 8:14-15; Mk 1:30; Lk 4:39), the leper (Mt 8) and the soldier's ear that was cut off by Simon when Jesus was arrested (Mt 26:51; Mk 14:47; Lk 22:51; Jn 18:10). Although they were healed and restored physically, spiritual healing was not totally excluded. Without the latter, the former cannot be perfect.

a) The Paralytic, ܡܫܪܝܐ (Mt 9:1-8; Mk 2:1-12: Lk 5:17-26; Jn 5:1-18)

Not only in the commentary on the woman with the haemorrhage, but also in some other healing miracles, Ephrem refers to both the visible and invisible healing through Jesus' divinity. Ephrem illustrates Jesus' healing miracles, such as the healing of the paralytic (Mt 9:1-8; Mk 2:1-12: Lk 5:17-26), as witnessing and manifesting Jesus' Sonship with His heavenly Father. In an anti-Marcionite polemic, Ephrem refers to the healing of the paralytic and says that Jesus' word healed first the paralytic spiritually, when He forgave his sins, and then He cured him

---

ܕܐܬܒܛܠܬܗ ܕܚܫܝܐ. ܘܥܘܪܬܐ ܘܡܫܬܠܛܢܘܬܐ ܕܡܝܬܘܬܐ ܕܐܟܠ ܐܕܡ ܠܟܠܗ ܥܠܡܐ.

[548] Virg 19.2 (cf. Mt 21:1-14; Jn 2:1-11):

ܛܘܒܝܟܝ ܟܠܬܐ ܘܡܫܠܠܬܐ ܕܟܠ ܠܟܝ ܣܘܬܪܐ ܕܫܪܬ ܝܫܘܥ
ܚܓܝܪܐ ܕܐܬܦܫܠܘ ܕܝܢ ܘܪܩܕܘ ܒܟܝ ܘܚܪ̈ܫܐ ܢܒܥܘ ܫܒ̈ܚܐ ܥܒܕܘ
ܒܫܠܘܬ ܡܢܗ ܗܘ̈ ܡܠܝܢ ܕܒܟܝ ܗ̈ܘܝ ܒܢ̈ܝܐ ܠܗ ܒܐܘ̈ܫܒܚܬܐ ܥܒܕܘܗܝ
ܕܝܫܘܥ ܐܬܒܪܘܗܝ ܐܕ̈ܢܝܗ ܒܡܘܟܟܝ ܕܡܠܟܝ ܡܠܟܐ ܝܐܝܕܗ.

In Crucif 2.4, Jesus is described as the 'Lord of binding up everything' for He 'bound up the wounded' (Crucif 2.4: ܕܗܘܐ ܚܒܫ ܠܬܒܝ̈ܪܐ ܬܘܒ ܠܡܪܗ ܚܒܫ ܟܠ).

physically.[549] The latter, the healing of the body, amazed the audience for it was a visible miracle, whereas the former was invisible and it could not be witnessed. Therefore, Ephrem says that the people would not believe that Jesus had forgiven the sins of the paralytic and had healed him spiritually, if He had not also healed him physically.[550]

Jesus must be the Son of God and have 'activity/power' (ܡܥܒܕܢܘܬܐ) according to His Nature, as well as according to the Law.[551] Obviously, perfect healing could not be achieved without spiritual healing, i.e forgiveness of sins. Furthermore, it seems Ephrem attributes the physical sickness to the fact that the paralytic sinned through 'his body' (ܒܦܓܪܗ). Based on the Gospel, Ephrem refers both the spiritual and physical sickness of the paralytic to his sin. Since the cause of both the spiritual and

---

[549] CDiat 5.19: ܘܣܥܪܬ ܘܐܣܝܬܗ. ܣܥܪܬ ܫܘܠܡܬܗ ܕܚܘܠܡܢܐ ܘܐܣܝܘܬ ܦܘܪܥܢܘܬܗ ܕܐܠܗܐ. ܘܐܬܗܝܡܢ ܒܗ̇ ܕܐܠܗܐ. ܐܦ ܥܠ ܕܚܘܠܡܢܐ. ܕܐܠܗܐ ܗ̇ܘ ܐܦ ܒܚܘܠܡܢܐ ܘܒܪܐܢܐ ܗܘ ܒܐܠܗܐ. ܕܡܛܠ ܐܢܫܘܬܗ ܕܠܒܪ ܐܬܝܗܒ ܕܒܪ ܐܢܫܐ ܗܘ. ܘܡܛܠ ܪܒܘܬܗ ܕܠܟܘ ܐܬܗܝܡܢ ܕܐܠܗܐ ܗܘ.

[550] CDiat 5.20a: ܫܒܝܩܝܢ ܠܟ ܚܛܗܝܟ. ܐܡܪܝܢ ܗܘܘ ܗܕܐ ܕܐܡܪ ܕܫܒܝܩܝܢ ܠܟ ܚܛܗܝܟ ܠܟܠ ܐܢܫ ܦܫܝܩ ܠܡܐܡܪ. ܐܠܐ ܕܐܡܪ ܕܩܘܡ ܫܩܘܠ ܥܪܣܟ ܬܡܝܗܐ (cf. Mt 9:5-6).

[551] This passage is very obscure, and it is difficult to understand. It seems some of the sentences are not completed, or are corrupted. Therefore, it is particularly difficult to analyse exactly what the teaching of the Marcionites was, or how they interpreted the healing of the paralytic. Ephrem uses the healing of the paralytic to illustrate the relationship of Jesus with the God of the Law, namely the God of the Old Testament. The Marcionites (see Chapter Four, 4.1.2.1; Chapter Five, 5.3.1.2a) separated strongly between the God of the Law and Jesus. According to the Marcionites, because of this fundamental difference, Jesus would not have been able to forgive sins committed against the God of the Law. Thus, Ephrem refutes this and must have held no differnce between 'the God revealed as Father by Jesus' (the one Marcion misrepresented as 'Stranger' or 'Alien', ܢܘܟܪܝܐ) and 'the God of the Law'. Jesus has healed the paralytic from his sins, although they were committed against the God of the Law, and not just against Jesus.

physical sickness was sin, sin needed to be forgiven in order to achieve perfect healing.[552]

In the next paragraph, based on the Gospel, Ephrem generalizes Jesus' function as the Physician Who came for the needy.[553] Thus, Ephrem confirms that there were spiritually sick people in the world and Jesus came to heal them. All healing miracles performed by Jesus give evidence about the sickness in the world on one hand, and Jesus being the Son of God Who came to heal, on the other.

In CDiat 13.1-7, Ephrem refers to the healing of the paralytic in Jn 5:1-18. While in the chapter about the leper Jesus Christ was asked about His will to heal the leper, in this chapter Jesus asks a paralytic if he wants to be healed. Ephrem underlines the importance of will. If the paralytic did not want to be healed the Lord would not heal him.[554] Since the Jews believe that the angel can heal illness through the water of Shiloah, how can they not believe that the Lord of the angels is able to purify the stain [of sin] through baptism? For Ephrem, baptism forgives sins, and so heals spiritually.

---

[552] CDiat 5.20b: ܡܟܐ ܒܪ ܡܬܒܥܝܢܐ ܗܘܬ ܗܝ ܕܫܒܝܩܝܢ ܠܟ ܚܛܗܝܟ. ܐܝܟܢܐ ܕܠܘ ܡܛܠ ܚܛܗܘܗܝ، ܡܟܪܗ ܗܘܐ ܡܟܪܝܐ. ܘܐܝܟ ܥܒܕ ܗܘܐ ܠܗܘܢ. ܐܠܐ ܠܗ. ܡܬܚܫܒ ܗܘܐ ܡܟܪܝܐ. ܐܘ ܡܟܐ ܬܟܪܘܗܝ ܗܘܬ. ܗܕܐ ܕܫܒܝܩܝܢ ܠܟ ܚܛܗܝܟ. ܕܗܐ ܐܦ ܠܐ ܢܬܒܥܘܢ ܠܗ. ܡܕܡ ܠܐ ܡܫܟܚܝܢ ܗܘܘ ܠܗ. ܕܐܟܢܝ ܠܗ ܚܙܐ ܕܝܢ ܡܢ ܬܒܥܬܐ ܠܘܬ ܚܝܠܐ.

[553] CDiat 5.21: ܕܠܐ ܣܢܝܩܝܢ ܚܠܝܡܐ ܥܠ ܐܣܝܐ. ܐܠܐ ܐܝܠܝܢ ܕܒܝܫ ܥܒܕܝܢ. ܘܠܐ ܐܬܝܬ ܕܐܩܪܐ ܠܙܕܝܩܐ ܘܗܕܐ ܕܠܐ ܫܘܐܠ ܬܬܗܘܢ. ܐܦ ܒܪ ܒܐܝܣܪܐܝܠ ܐܝܬ ܗܘܘ ܚܠܝܡܐ ܘܙܕܝܩܐ. ܗܐ ܠܐ ܢܘܟܪܝܐ ܠܐܬܘܬܗ ܕܝܫܘܥ ܠܙܕܝܩܘܬܐ. ܗܘ ܕܒܟܠ ܒܐܝܫ ܘܐܣܠܝܘܗ. ܘܒܝܕ ܙܕܝܩܐ ܘܐܦ ܕܝܢ ܒܢܒܝܐ. ܗܐ ܬܘܒ ܒܟܘܠ ܦܘܪܩܢ ܡܫܝܚ ܗܘܘ ܒܗ ܒܟܠܗܘܢ ܕܒܥܘܕܐ ܚܛܝܐ ܘܙܕܝܩܐ. ܘܟܠ ܗܠܝܢ ܕܗܫܐ ܐܬܐ ܠܐ ܣܢܝܩܝܢ. ܠܐ ܒܪ ܣܢܝܩܝܢ ܚܛܝܐ ܥܠ ܐܣܝܐ. ܘܐܦܠܐ ܙܕܝܩܐ ܥܠ ܬܝܒܘܬܐ.

[554] CDiat 13.1: ܐܝܬ ܗܘܐ ܠܗ ܬܡܢ ܓܒܪܐ ܕܬܠܬܝܢ ܘܬܡܢܐ ܫܢܝܢ ܟܪܝܗ ܗܘܐ. ܐܡܪ ܠܗ ܡܪܢ ܨܒܝܬ ܕܬܗܘܐ ܚܠܝܡ. ܘܐܠܐ ܠܐ ܨܒܐ...; cf. Jn 5:5-6.

Like the leper, the paralytic was healed through the compassion (ܐܣܝܬ ܡܪܚܡܢܘܬܐ ܠܘܬܗ) of the Lord.[555] The healing was not only corporal, but also spiritual; that means the Lord healed the paralytic totally, He granted him perfect healing (ܚܘܠܡܢܐ ܓܡܝܪܐ).[556] The spiritual restoration (ܚܘܠܡܢܐ) contrasts to sin: 'see you are restored, do not sin any more [again]' (ܗܐ ܚܠܝܡ ܐܢܬ. ܬܘܒ ܠܐ ܬܚܛܐ).[557] The healing is considered as a general good deed of the Father Who 'continues' His creation through His Son. Therefore, the Sabbath does not stop the process of healing, and likewise, it does not forbid people from breathing or bearing children.[558] Jesus showed through His healing that He is the Lord of the Law ( ܘܐܦ ܕܢܚܘܐ ܒܐܣܝܘܬܗ ܕܡܪܐ ܢܡܘܣܐ ܗܘ).[559] The paralytic trusted Jesus when He commanded him to take his bed and go. It was, likewise, with the blind man who was sent to go and wash himself in Siloam (Jn 9:7).[560]

---

[555] CDiat 13.1: ܐܣܝܬ ܡܪܚܡܢܘܬܐ ܠܘܬܗ. ܕܠܐ ܬܦܘܫ ܠܦܘܠܚܢܘܬܐ ܡܫܟܚܐܬ ܡܢ ܬܡܢ.

[556] CDiat 13.2: ܐܠܐ ܕܢܚܘܐ ܕܚܘܠܡܢܐ ܓܡܝܪܐ ܝܗܒ ܠܗ. ܕܐܦ ܦܓܪܗ ܐܚܠܡܗ. See further CDiat 13.3: ܘܕܢܒܘ ܕܢܦܫܗ ܠܬܕܟܪܬܐ ܕܐܘܣܦܬܗ. ܘܢܟܦܘܬܗ̇ ܕܐܠܝܡ ܒܢܝܗ̇. ܒܠܐܝܬܐ ܐܒܪܗ̇ ܠܗܘܢ ܠܐܘܣܦܬܗ. ܘܐܘܣܦ ܒܦܘܪܥܢܗܘܢ. ܐܡܪ ܠܗܘܢ ܒܢܝ. ܠܘ ܗܝ ܕܢܒܝܡ ܗܘܘ ܠܡܥܡܕ. ܐܠܐ ܗܝ ܕܡܫܬܠܡ ܗܘܘ ܠܡܫܡܫܢܘ. ܗܝ ܠܡ ܐܫܠܡܢ. ܗܘ ܐܡܪ ܠܗ ܕܢܥܘܠ ܒܪܘܚܗ.

[557] CDiat 13.3: ܘܟܠܗ ܚܘܝܗ ܘܐܡܪ ܠܗ. ܗܐ ܚܠܝܡ ܐܢܬ. ܬܘܒ ܒܬܪ ܠܐ ܬܚܛܐ. ܕܠܡܐ ܬܗܘܐ ܠܟ ܐܢܫ. ܠܡܡܚܠ ܗ̇ܝ ܕܠܝܬ ܠܗ̇ ܐܣܝܐ. ܐܝܟ ܕܝܢ ܗ̇ܘ ܠܓܒܪܐ ܘܐܡܪ ܠܡܘܪ̈ܕܢܐ. ܕܢܥܒܕ ܗܘ ܗ̇ܘ ܕܐܫܠܡܢ (Jn 5:14).

[558] CDiat 13.4.

[559] CDiat 13.6: ܘܐܦ ܕܢܚܘܐ ܒܐܣܘܬܗ ܕܡܪܐ ܢܡܘܣܐ ܗܘ. ܒܗ̇ ܕܡܫܬܒܚܝܢ ܗܘܘ ܠܗ ܒܫܒܬܐ. ܗܢܘ ܕܫܠܝܛ ܒܝ̈ܬܝܢ ܐܒܘܗܝ ܥܠ ܫܒܬܐ.

[560] CDiat 13.6: ܘܠܗܘ ܣܡܝܐ ܕܫܕܪܗ ܕܢܐܙܠ ܢܫܝܓ ܒܫܝܠܘܚܐ. ܕܢܚܘܐ ܕܠܐ ܦܠܝܓ ܗܘܐ ܥܠܘܗܝ ܕܡܐܡܪܗ ܠܗ. In Nis 39.9-10, Ephrem compares the deed of Joshua, the son of Nun, with the miracles of Jesus. While the former killed people (Jos 12:24) and filled Sheol with bodies, the latter emptied Sheol and filled up heaven with the raised bodies. In this context Ephrem mentions the healing of the paralytic and

☞

b) The Centurion's Servant (Mt 8:5-13; Lk 7:1-10)

Just before commenting on the healing of the centurion's servant (Mt 8:5-13; Lk 7:1-10), Ephrem contrasts Jesus' teaching with that of the teachers and Pharisees who based their authority on the Law. In comparison, while Moses' Law was shadow, Ephrem describes the 'teaching of Our Saviour' with the words of Malachi (Mal 3:20; 4:2) as the 'Sun of Justice' ( ܫܡܫܐ ܕܙܕܝܩܘܬܐ). For Ephrem, Jesus' healing ministry is evidence of His divinity. Before commenting on the healing of the centurion's servant and the raising of the widow's son (Lk 11-17), Ephrem summarized Jesus' healing activity with the words: 'He granted to the children of man restoration of the body and healing of the souls'.[561] Ephrem puts the healing of the centurion's servant in the context of the Sun of Justice Who is able to grant perfect healing to both bodies and souls. Although Jesus was not yet proclaimed to be the Son of God, Jesus' ministry illuminated the mind of the centurion so that he believed in Jesus being our Lord and God Who came to be among human beings. Not only the request to heal the servant, but even more so, the following conversation indicates the true faith of the centurion. The role of the centurion, in particular his faith, is significant, as Jesus comments: 'Amen, I tell you, never in a man of Israel have I found such faith as this'.[562] While at the beginning he asks for the reviving of his servant,[563] he

---

says: 'Jesus healed the one who was paralysed' (Nis 39.10: ܐܣܝ ܕܝܢ ܠܗܘ ܕܡܫܪܐ݂ ܐܝܟ ܗܘܐ).

[561] CDiat 6.21b: ܡܬܕܡܪܝܢ ܗܘܘ ܠܡ ܒܢܝܐ ܒܝܘܠܦܢܗ. ܕܐܝܟ ܣܦܪ̈ܝܗܘܢ ܘܐܝܟ ܦܪ̈ܝܫܐ. ܗܠܝܢ ܓܝܪ ܡܫܠܛܐ ܡܠܠ ܗܘܐ ܘܠܐ ܐܝܟ ܐܪ̈ܒܢܝܬܐ ܗܘ ܐܬܡܠܟ ܠܗܘܢ ܐܝܟ ܕܒܢܡܘܣܐ. ܡܢ̈ܝܢ ܕܝܢ ܡܠܦܢܘܬܐ ܕܫܡܫܐ ܐܫܬܘܕܝ ܠܬܠܡ̈ܝܕܘܗܝ. ܟܕ ܫܡܫܘ ܗܘܝܠ ܒܢ̈ܝܐ ܥܒܝܕܘܬܐ ܕܡܠܦܢܘܬܗ ܕܦܪܘܩܢ. ܢܗܘܐ ܕܗܠܝܢ ܕܫܡܫܐ ܠܟܠܗܝܢ ܐܣܝܘܬܐ ܐܝܟ. ܡܢ̈ܝܢ ܕܝܢ ܫܡܫܐ ܕܙܕܝܩܘܬܐ. ܢܗܒ ܓܝܪ ܠܒܢ̈ܝ ܐܢܫܐ ܚܘܠܡܢܐ ܕܦܓܪܐ. ܘܐܣܝܘܬܐ ܕܢܦ̈ܫܬܐ.

[562] CDiat 6.22.b: ܐܡܝܢ ܐܡܪ ܐܢܐ ܠܟܘܢ ܕܐܦܠܐ ܒܐܢܫ ܒܝܬ ܐܝܣܪܐܝܠ ܐܫܟܚܬ ܐܝܟ ܗܕܐ ܗܝܡܢܘܬܐ (Mt 8:10).

[563] CDiat 6.22a: ܐܬܐ ܠܡ ܠܘܬܗ ܟܕ ܡܬܚܢܢܐ ܘܒܥܐ ܗܘܐ ܡܢܗ ܕܢܚܐ ܠܗ ܠܛܠܝܗ. ܘܟܕ ܐܬܛܠܒܘܗܝ ܕܢܐܙܠ ܐܡܪ ܠܗ. ܡܪܝ ܠܐ ܬܬܥܡܠ (cf. Mt 8:5-7; Lk 7:3-6).

then defines his request and asks for only a small radiance from the Sun of Justice.[564] Based on the prophet Malachi,[565] if the Sun of Justice possesses the power of healing, so too its radiance. Ephrem develops the role of the centurion and considers his faith as the beginning of the faith of the gentiles.[566] Having emphasized the significance of the centurion's faith, Ephrem does not refer further to the fact that the servant was healed; instead he continues with his comment on the raising of the widow's son.[567]

c) Peter's Mother-in-law (Mt 8:14-15; Mk 1:30; Lk 4:39)

Ephrem refers to the healing of Peter's mother-in-law in several passages. In Virg 25.13-14, her fever is considered as 'hidden fire that cannot be seen' (ܢܘܪܐ ܟܣܝܬܐ ܕܠܐ ܡܬܚܙܝܐ), whereas the body of Jesus, her Physician, contains the 'fire of the height that only spiritual [beings] can see' (ܢܘܪܐ ܕܪܘܡܐ ܕܠܪܘܚܢܐ ܠܚܘܕ ܡܬܚܙܝܐ). Jesus is the 'Physician of the height' (ܐܣܝܐ ܕܪܘܡܐ) Who descended to visit her.[568] The

---

564 CDiat 6.22b:
ܘܗܕܐ ܗܝ ܬܕܡܘܪܬܐ ܕܐܦ ܩܕܡ ܫܠܝܚܘܗܝ ܕܛܠܝܐ ܛܪܝ̈ ܢܦܫܗ ܘܩܕܡܗ ܠܥܒܕܐ ܒܡܫܡܫܢܘܬܗ. ܠܐ ܠܡ ܫܘܐ ܕܬܥܘܠ ܬܚܝܬ ܡܛܠܠܝ. ܐܝܟ ܢܘܣܚ ܕܐܡܪ ܕܠܐ ܫܘܐ ܐܢܐ ܕܐܫܪܐ ܒܢܘ̈ܗܪܐ ܕܡܫܡܫܢܘ̈ܗܝ. ܐܠܐ ܢܘܣܚ ܢܒܥܐ [ܗ]ܘܐ. ܘܡܢ ܐܠܗܐ [ܐ]ܫܬܪܪ. ܗܢܐ ܕܡܢ [ܒ]ܪ ܐܢܫ ܠܐ ܐܡܪ [ܠ]ܗ. ܘܠܐ ܒܕܒܝܠ [ܐ]ܬܚܙܝ ܡܢܝ̱ ܕܐܠܗܐ [ܗ]ܘ. ܗܘܝܘ ܒܒܪܘ̈ܗܝ [ܕ]ܦܘܪܩܢ ܢܦܘܫܗܘܢ. [ܕ]ܐܠܗܐ ܐܬܐ ܠܒܝܬ [ܒ]ܪ̈ ܐܢܫܐ ܠܐ ܠܡ [ܫ]ܘܐ ܐܢܐ ܕܬܥܘܠ [ܠ]ܒܝܬܝ. ܠܐ ܠܡ [ܦ]ܩܘܕ ܐܢܐ ܕܐܥܘܠ [ܠ]ܒܝܬܗ ܥܒܕܐ ܕܕܚܝܠܘܬܐ. ܥܠ ܗܠܝܢ ܡ̈ܠܐ ܕܥܡܗ ܗܘܝ ܐܢܐ. ܕܐܚܝܕܘܗܝ ܠܣܘܪܚܢܐ ܐܝܟ ܕܠܚܣܝܐ.

565 Mal 4:2 (Pesh): ܘܬܕܢܚ ܠܟܘܢ ܠܕܚܠܝ ܫܡܝ ܫܡܫܐ ܕܙܕܝܩܘܬܐ ܘܐܣܝܘܬܐ ܒܟܢܦܝܗ̇.

566 CDiat 6.22b: ܘܕܝܢܐ ܕܡܫܡܫܢܘܬܗ ܕܩܛܪܘܢܐ ܪܫܝܬܐ ܗܝ ܕܗܝܡܢܘܬܐ ܕܥܡ̈ܡܐ.

567 Cf. CDiat 6.23; Lk 7:11-15.

568 Virg 25.13-14:
ܠܡ ܛܒܘ ܟܢܘܫܬܐ ܚܡܬܗ ܕܐܬܚܒܫܘ ܕܐܣܝܐ ܕܪܘܡܐ ܢܚܬ ܡܚܙܐ ܗܘܐ
ܠܐܝܕܝ ܒܗ ܦܓܪ ܠܐ ܗܘܐ ܕܢܓܘܫ ܕܗܘܘ ܕܬܫܒܘܚ ܠܗ ܥܠ ܙܕܝܩܐ

☞

phrases the 'fire of the height' and the 'Physician of the height' have almost the same connotation as the reference from Malachi 4:2, namely the 'Sun of Justice', that Ephrem uses in the context of the healing of the centurion's servant.[569]

The oikonomia of Jesus gives witness to His divinity and to His Father, as the Father bore witness to the Son in his baptism and revelation on the mountain. The healing of Peter's mother-in-law, along with that of the man sick with palsy (Mt 9:2-7), are evidence for Jesus being the King's Son.[570] The good news of Jesus and His good deeds brought joy to those who accepted and believed Him. His ministry healed and saved people from the hand of Satan and death. As with the raising of the dead, Sheol suffered, so too the healing of Peter's mother-in-law grieved Sheol.[571]

---

ܗܘ ܛܒܪܗ ܠܐܫܬܐ ܒܓܘܫܡܗܘܢ ܡܥܡܪ ܕܘܟܬܐ ܫܬܦܬ ܠܗ ܠܢܘܪܗܘܢ

ܒܡܪܐ ܕܡܪܘܗܘܢ ܐܦ ܪܚܡ ܘܡܪܕܚܡ ܬܪܥܗܘܢ ܒܚܝ ܠܒܥܬܐ.

ܒܦܓܪ ܟܪܝܗܬܐ ܫܪܬ ܐܫܬܐ ܢܘܪܐ ܟܣܝܬܐ ܕܠܐ ܡܬܚܙܝܐ

ܒܦܓܪܗ ܕܐܣܝܐ ܢܘܪܐ ܕܪܘܡܐ ܕܠܐ ܚܙܝܐ ܠܗܘܢ ܡܬܚܙܝܐ

ܬܗܪܐ ܗܘ ܗܢܐ ܘܡܢ ܢܦܩܘ ܠܡܐܡܪܗ ܕܪܬܝܚܐ ܕܐܫܡܥܐ ܥܠ ܦܘܪܪ ܘܐܣܝܢ

ܫܡܘܥܐ ܬܡܗܘ ܒܓܒܘܪܬܐ ܕܦܓܪܬ ܚܡܘܬܗ ܕܐܫܬܐ.

[569] CDiat 6.21-22. In Virg 25.13-14, Ephrem plays with the word 'fire' (ܢܘܪܐ). While in the body of the sick woman dwelt the fever, the hidden fire, in the body of the physician dwells the fire of the height (Ephrem also uses the term 'coal' as a title for Jesus; cf. Nat. 6.13; 9.15; 11.5; Fid 10.10).

[570] Fid 54.4:

ܡܢ ܗܘ ܥܒܕ ܛܒܘܬܗ ܡܬܕܪܝܢ ܕܒܪ ܡܠܟܐ ܗܘ ܕܐܝܟ ܢܬܪܐ ܛܒܐ ܚܝܦ ܕܒܝܬ ܐܒܘܗܝ

ܒܒܪܐ ܚܕܐ ܕܐܪܡܠܬܐ ܐܣܝܗ ܒܫܠܡܘܬܐ ܚܕܐ ܠܚܡܬܐ ܕܐܪܡܠܬܐ ܟܐܒܐ ܒܗ ܒܐܫܬܗ

ܠܚܡܬܐ ܚܕܐ ܕܢܦܠ ܘܫܡܫܬ ܒܢܬܗ ܘܐܘܕܝܘ ܠܥܠܘܝܐ.

[571] Nis 39.15: ܫܡܥܬܗ ܕܡܫܝܚܢ ܐܬܚܠܡܬ - ܠܫܝܘܠ ܕܝܢ ܐܟܪܝܗ ܠܟܐܒܐ ܕܚܘܠܡܢܗ. In Nis 40.2, Ephrem illustrates the contest of Satan with human beings and, particularly, with Jesus. Here he says: ܐܣܝܐ ܟܠ ܡܢ ܟܝܬ ܡܪܥܐ ܘܓܪܬ ܐܝܟ ܠܚܪܝܫܐ ܒܬܘܬܒܘܬܗ (Nis 40.2). In Parad 12.13, where Ephrem mentions some of Jesus' healing miracles, he

☞

d) The Leper (Mt 8)

Ephrem comments on the healing of the Leper in CDiat 12.21-24. All four paragraphs start with the biblical verse: 'if You are willing Lord, You can cleanse me'.[572] A part of this verse is also repeated in paragraph 22, and the whole verse is repeated three times in paragraph 23.

Ephrem explains the meaning of this verse according to the reasoning of the Leper and the Law. The Leper thought that either Jesus Christ observed the Law and would not approach (touch) him - like Elisha who had not gone forward to Naaman (2 Kgs 5:8-12) - or that He was a stranger to the Law. In other words, if Jesus Christ followed the Law He would not touch the Leper, and would be afraid of leprosy. On the other hand, if He approached the leper, He would not be observing the Law. However, Jesus Christ touched and healed the Leper secretly and openly - corporeally and spiritually, and the Leper's doubt was resolved. 'For [the Leper] was afraid to touch Him lest he defile Him. But [the Lord] touched him to show him that He would not be defiled, He, at whose rebuke the defilement fled from the defiled one.'[573]

As examples for this kind of healing, Ephrem mentions Moses who carried Joseph's bones (Gen 50:23-24; Ex 4:6), Samson who ate honey from the dead body of an impure animal (Judg 14:9) and drunk water from the jawbone of a dead ass (Judg 15:15-19). Ephrem confirms his argument with the words of St Paul: 'the Law

implies that all of them served as help/benefits for humanity: ܡܪ̈ܢ ܐܝܟܐ ܟܐܒܐ ܘܚܘܒ ܠܗ ܫܒܪ ܦܘܠܚܢܐ ܘܐܬܦܢܝ ܒܗܘ ܠܒܪܐ ܠܦܘܪܩܢܐ ܢܣܒ ܘܦܪܐ ܠܟܠܗܘܢ̈ ܕܟܠܬ̈ܪܬܐ ܚܝ̈ܘܬܐ ܒܪ̈ܐ ܒܢܝܢܐ ܘܠܬܠܬܐ ܒܢܝܢܫܐ ܐܘܬܒܘܗ̇ ܗܘܝ ܕܝܢ ܬܠܬܐ ܟܠܗܝܢ ܠܚܘܕܪ̈ܐ ܕܦܬܫ ܒܗܝܢ ܬܪ̈ܥܐ ܘܪ̈ܒܐ ܕܦܘܪܫܢܐ (Parad 12.13). It is important to point out that in Haer 18.3, Ephrem considers fever (ܐܫܬܐ) as something natural, such as darkness in the night, sleep, the venom of a serpent. Fever is not an act of free will, and it does not belong to the acts of will, such as sinful deeds.

[572] CDiat 12.21-24; Mt 8:2: ܐܢ ܨܒܐ ܐܢܬ ܡܪܝ ܡܫܟܚ ܐܢܬ ܠܡܕܟܝܘܬܢ.

[573] CDiat 12.21: ܕܚܠ ܓܝܪ ܗܘ ܠܡܩܪܒ ܠܗ ܕܠܐ ܢܛܡܐܝܘܗܝ. ܩܪܒ ܠܗ ܕܝܢ ܗܘ ܕܢܚܘܝܘܗܝ ܕܠܐ ܗܘ ܠܐ ܡܬܛܡܐ. ܕܐܦ ܡܢ ܛܡܐܐ ܥܪܩ ܡܢܗ ܛܡܐܘܬܗ ܒܟܐܬܗ.

was not laid down for the just'.[574] But still Jesus fulfilled the Law: 'therefore, by stretching out His hand, He showed His divinity and drove impurity away, and by the word of His mouth He showed His familiarity [with the Law] and put to flight the [possibility of] being a stranger [to it].'[575] Because he heard the dispute of the priests with Jesus, the leper thought Jesus might not be willing to heal the Jews. Paragraph 21 ends with this; but Jesus wanted to heal him. This healing was not natural, but it happened by the grace and mercy of God. It was not solely the healing of the body, but also of the soul and mind. Jesus cleansed the doubtful mind of the leper with the command 'go, show yourself to the priests, and make the offering as Moses prescribed'.[576] Moreover, Ephrem emphasises the keeping of the Law and of the commandments of Moses.

Paragraph 23 also deals with the doubtful attitude of the leper concerning the 'will' and 'ability' of Jesus. Here, Ephrem introduces two new points. Firstly, that the Lord was healing without discrimination of persons. Secondly, the leper was healed, because he believed that 'if You are willing, You can'.[577] Furthermore, paragraph 23 also deals with the commandments. According to the prescriptions, which were unable to procure any benefit, the one who approaches a leper becomes impure. Jesus stretched out His right hand that was full of healing, and He extended it to the leper. With His word Jesus bestowed healing and abolished these many precepts which the Law had reckoned should exist for leprosy. In the context of the healing of a paralytic Ephrem says:

Our Lord observed all the Law in its place, to show that it is to be observed, and to condemn, through His observance, those who destroy it. But He dispensed from certain [precepts] of it for

[574] 1 Tim 1:9: ܕܠܟܐܢܐ ܢܡܘܣܐ ܠܐ ܣܝܡ.

[575] CDiat 12.21: ܡܛܠ ܗܢܐ ܒܦܫܛ ܐܝܕܗ ܚܘܝ ܐܠܗܘܬܗ ܘܪܕܦܗ̇ ܠܛܡܐܘܬܐ ܘܒܡܠܬ ܦܘܡܗ ܚܘܝ ܒܝܬܝܘܬܗ ܘܪܕܦܗ̇ ܠܢܘܟܪܝܘܬܐ. In CDiat 12.24, Ephrem attributes the act of healing to Jesus' right hand that was full of healing (ܐܠܐ ܝܡܝܢܗ ܗܘ ܡܠܐ ܚܠܡܝܢܐ) and to the word by which He granted healing (ܘܡܠܬܐ ܝܗܒ ܐܣܝܘܬܐ). The healing of lepers is also mentioned in Hebd 5.242-43: ܘܠܓܪ̈ܒܐ ܕܕܟܝܬ ܬܪ̈ܝܨܬ.

[576] Mt 8:4: ܐܠܐ ܙܠ ܚܘܐ ܢܦܫܟ ܠܟܗ̈ܢܐ: ܘܩܪܒ ܩܘܪܒܢܐ ܐܝܟ ܕܦܩܕ ܡܘܫܐ.

[577] CDiat 12.23.

higher [motives], to show that higher [motives] prevail over everything, and also to show through His healing that He is the Lord of the Law.[578]

e) The Soldier's Ear (Mt 26:51; Mk 14:47; Lk 22:50-51; Jn 18:10, 26)

The importance of the healing of everyone and, particularly, of the whole body is illustrated in Nis 46, where Ephrem clarifies Jesus' attitude towards the human body, namely that Jesus cared about the body and provided remedies for it. Against the Marcionites, Ephrem refers to various passages of the Bible to emphasise that Jesus Himself became a man, taking a body from Mary. Jesus did not reject the body, instead He cleansed the human body and cured it, for the nature of the body is not impure. Therefore, salvation refers not only to the soul of man, but also to his body. In this context, Ephrem refers to the curing of a small limb of the body, the ear that was cut off by Simon when Jesus was arrested (Mt 26:51). In Nis 46.9, Ephrem says:

If the High One bent down and took the ear, which Simon cut off and threw away, and He fixed it lest it got lost, how much more He will search after all [the body] at the resurrection, so that nothing of its dust might stay away. Neither in the furnace did [the care of the Lord] forget a hair of the head (Dan 3.27), to indicate the care that He will show at the resurrection.[579]

According to Ephrem, the ear was cut off and fell on the ground. Jesus' bending down and picking up the ear shows His diligence and care about man's body. The healing of it is a result of His divine care. In the stanza before, Nis 46.8, Ephrem says that

---

578 CDiat 13.6: ܢܛܪܗ ܓܝܪ ܠܟܠܗ ܢܡܘܣܐ ܒܐܬܪܗ. ܕܢܚܘܐ ܕܡܬܛܪܢܐ ܗܘ. ܕܢܚܕ ܒܛܘܪܘܬܗ ܠܡܫܬܠܡܢܘܗܝ، ܘܫܪܐ ܒܗܘܢ ܡܕܡ ܡܕܡ ܒܥܒܝܕܬܐ. ܕܢܚܘܐ ܕܥܒܝܕܬܐ ܫܠܝܛܐ ܥܠ ܟܠ ܡܕܡ. ܘܐܦ ܕܢܚܘܐ ܒܐܣܝܘܬܗ ܕܡܪܐ ܢܡܘܣܐ ܗܘ.

579 Nis 46.9:
ܐܢ ܓܚܢ ܐܦ ܐܕܢܐ ܕܫܡܥܘܢ ܦܣܩܗ ܘܐܫܕܝܗ ܪܡܐ ܪܡ ܫܩܠܗ
ܘܩܒܥܗ ܕܠܐ ܬܐܒܕ
ܟܡܐ ܒܥܬ ܟܠ ܟܠܗ ܡܬܒܥ ܒܩܝܡܬܐ ܕܡܕܡ ܡܢ ܥܦܪܗ ܠܐ
ܢܦܘܫ
ܐܦ ܠܐ ܒܐܬܘܢܐ ܛܥܬ ܡܢܬܐ ܕܪܝܫܐ ܕܢܘܕܥ ܒܛܝܠܘܬܐ ܕܥܒܕ
ܒܩܝܡܬܐ.

the care of our Lord healed the whole man in every respect; His care baptized man with the Holy Spirit and nourished him with the Medicine of Life.[580] In Nat 18.27, Ephrem praises the restoration achieved through the Lord. The healing of the soldier's ear serves as an example that shows that the Lord defeated 'our enemy', whereas weapons and the sword never managed to kill the enemy.[581] Furthermore, the healing of the ear also serves as an example for the justice of the Law that has been removed and come to an end through the mercy of Jesus. According to the justice of the Law, the ear was justly cut off for it rejected the words of the Lord. As the ear was cut off by the sword that symbolizes justice, so too Jesus cut off justice tby the sword that cut off the ear of the soldier. Thus, through Jesus mercy took place instead of justice. Therefore, Ephrem says, the Merciful One (ܚܢܢܐ) came and healed the ear.[582]

### *5.3.1.2 The Healing from Demons and Evil Spirits*

This section contains the healing of the Gadarene demoniac (Mt 8:28-34), the daughter of the Canaanite woman (Mt 15:21-28) and the epileptic demoniac (Mt 17:14-21). Their healing from demons and evil spirits reflects the concern of the Lord to heal the People from the evil spirit that dwelt within them, as well as the healing of the gentiles. Beyond the Lord's care, faith plays an essential role.

---

[580] Nis 46.8: ܐܦ ܕܝܢ ܒܛܝܠܘܬܗ ܕܡܪܢ ܡܫܝܚܐ ܠܗ ܕܐܣܝܗ ܠܒܪܢܫܐ ܠܟܠܗ ܒܟܠ ܡܕܡ ܐܥܡܕܗ ܒܪܘܚ ܩܘܕܫܐ ܬܪܣܝܗ ܒܣܡ ܚܝܐ. For the caring of the Lord see further CDiat 16.24; Haer 21.11; 33.3.

[581] Nat 18.27:
ܒܥܠܬܐ ܕܚܣ̈ܡܝܢ ܘܬܪ̈ܬܝܢ ܢܕܪܐ ܙܝܢܐ ܘܣܝܦܐ ܠܐ ܫܦܩܘ ܩܛܠܘܗܝ ܠܒܥܠܕܪܢ
ܐܬܐ ܗܘ ܡܛܠܬܗ ܘܐܬܐ ܗܘ ܡܒܥܬܗ ܠܐܕܢܐ ܕܦܣܩܗ ܣܝܦܐ ܕܥܕܡܐ ܒܕܝܢ ܫܘܠܛܢܝ.

[582] Crucif 3.18:
ܠܘܩܒܠ ܕܘܟܬܐ ܕܟܝܦܐ ܐܬܬܪܝܡ ܥܡ ܒܐܢܘܬܐ ܒܥܒܕܐ ܕܫܡܥܐ
ܒܫܡܥܐ ܗܘ ܫܡܫܗ ܠܗܘ ܢܡܘܣܐ ܕܫܡܥܗ ܠܐܕܢܐ ܕܢܛܪܬ ܡ̈ܠܘܗܝ
ܐܬܐ ܕܝܢ ܚܢܢܐ ܘܐܣܝܗ̇ ܘܠܢܡܘܣܐ ܐܦܩ ܠܗ ܘܐܬܚܒܠ
ܐܢܐ ܢܡܘܣܐ ܗܘ ܗܘ ܚܙܝܐ ܕܐܬܒܛܠ ܒܕܝܢܗ ܕܡܫܝܚܐ.

a) The Gadarene Demoniac (Mt 8:28-34; Mk 5:1-20; Lk 8:26-39)

Ephrem refers to the narrative of the Gadarene demoniac in the context of arguing against Marcion's teaching. The Marcionites associated the God revealed as Father by Jesus with the Alien/Stranger god (ܢܘܟܪܝܐ). In order to disprove the Marcionite theory that the Creator is different from the Marcion's Alien, Ephrem uses the miracle of casting out the demons and causing them to enter into the swine which drowned in the sea.

According to Ephrem, if Jesus was not the Son of the Creator, He would not be able to cast out the demons which the Creator of the universe had created. The fact that Jesus cast the demons out and made them enter the swine, indicates that Jesus had power over them in the same way as He had the right to rebuke the wind and calm the sea (Lk 8:24),[583] or as He had the power to heal the paralytic (Mt 9:1-10).[584] Ephrem's logical argument is based on the supposition that no one can have authority over something that does not belong to him. Jesus drowned the swine of the Gadarenes to show His authority and force the Gadarenes against their will to come and see His miracles.[585] Since the legion had no choice about where to go, except with the permission of the Lord, and since the Lord commanded him to go into the swine instead of letting him dwell in human beings, Ephrem considers the Lord as the preserver and keeper of humanity: He saved the Gadarenes from the legion.[586] Jesus fights against the legion who symbolizes the

---

583 CDiat 6.25: ܗܘ̇ ܕܕܡܟ ܗܘ ܐܬܬܥܝܪ ܘܐܪܕܝܗ ܠܝܡܐ. ܕܡܪܘܬܗ ܕܝܡܐ ܕܕܡܟܬ. ܢܘܕܥ ܒܥܝܪܘܬܐ ܕܐܠܗܘܬܗ ܕܠܐ ܕܡܟܐ. ܒܥܐ ܠܗ ܒܘܝܢܐ ܘܫܠܝܬ. ܐܝܟ ܗܘܐ ܫܘܠܛܢܐ. ܐܘ ܐܝܟܐ ܗܝ ܗܕܐ ܠܒܥܠܘܬܗ ܕܝܡܐ. ܕܗܐ ܒܡܠܝܐ ܡܥܒܕ ܕܠܐ ܕܝܠܗ. ܒܘܝܢܐ ܗܒܠ ܕܝܡܐ. ܘܒܘܝܢܐ ܘܫܬܩܐ ܕܫܬܩ ܡܢ̈. ܗܘ ܕܒܪܗ ܗܘ ܕܒܪܘܝܐ.

584 CDiat 5.19-20 (see above, chapter V, 3.1.1.a).

585 CDiat 6.26:. ܓܕܪܝܐ ܬܗܘܡܐ ܗܘܘ ܠܗܘܢ ܕܠܐ ܢܦܩܘܢ ܘܠܐ ܢܚܙܘܢ ܐܬܘܬܗ ܕܡܪܢ ܒܠܓܝܘܢܐ ܒܚܢܩ ܚܙܝܪܝܗܘܢ ܕܢܦܩܘܢ ܟܕ ܠܐ ܨܒܝܢ

586 CDiat 6.26: ܘܠܓܕܝܐ ܕܐܬܟܠܝܘ ܐܪܘܚ ܗܘ ܕܠܓܝܘܢܐ. ܕܐܬܟܠܝܬ ܒܬܫܡܫܬܗ ܒܚܠܝܨܘ ܟܠ. ܐܢ ܒܚܙܝܪܐ ܒܥܝܐ ܕܢܥܠ ܒܡܢܫܐ ܠܐ ܟܠܗ. ܚܕ ܒܥܐ ܒܝܠܗ ܐܠܗܐ. ܘܕܒܥܝܐ ܗܠܝܢ ܒܡܘܪܐ. ܕܒܥܝܐ

☞

world and is the chief of Satan's force (Mk 5:13). Healing and saving the possessed man against the will of the legion indicates the care of the Lord towards man.[587]

Although Jesus saved the man and performed a healing miracle, the Gadarenes drove Jesus out of their region, as He drove out the demons. Ephrem plays with the terms 'to drive out' (ܪܕܦ) and 'to enter' (ܥܠ) and emphasises that the Gadarenes acted in exactly the opposite way to Jesus. Ephrem uses the term 'Physician' (ܐܣܝܐ) and 'their pain' (ܠܟܐܒܗܘܢ) to put the situation in the context of healing.[588] Although Jesus was their Physician and Healer, the Gadarenes rejected Him from their place. In Azym 15.23-24, Ephrem contrasts the fear of the devils, swine and legion with the impudence of Caiaphas and the servant who struck Jesus on His face. While the former feared Jesus, the latter treated Him badly without the deserved respect.[589] Ephrem considers all healing miracles of Jesus as helps and benefits for human beings.

---

ܡܦܩ ܡܢ ܚܕ ܘܡܥܠ ܒܐܚܪ̈ܢܐ ܘܢܦܫܗܘܢ. ܘܢܦܩܬܘܢ ܦܡ ܢܛܪ ܠܗܘܢ ܒܡܐܡܬ ܡܢ ܓ̈ܕܪܝܐ ܕܗܘ ܗܘ ܕܒܚ̈ܝܐ ܐܦܣ ܠܗܘܢ ܠܡܥܠ ܘܠܐ ܒܐܢܫܐ. ܗܘ ܕܐܡܪܘ ܥܠܘܗܝ ܕܒܒܥܠܕܒܒ ܡܦܩ.

587 CDiat 6.26: ܠܡܦܩ ܣܛܢܐ ܐܡܪ ܒܛܘܪܐ. ܘܠܡܦܩ ܠܓܝܘܢ ܪܒ ܚܝܠܗ. ܘܟܕ ܚܙܐ ܒܚ̈ܝܘܬܐ ܕܢܦܫܬܗ ܚܝܠ ܐܠܗܐ. ܕܢܦܩܢܝ ܡܛܪܐ ܡܪܫܥܢܐ. ܕܢܛܪ ܗܘܐ ܠܗ ܠܗܘ ܓܒܪܐ. ܘܟܕ ܗܘܘ ܠܟ ܡܢܗ ܕܠܐ ܢܦܩ ܐܢܘܢ ܡܢ ܐܬܪܐ. ܘܠܐ ܢܥܒܕ ܐܢܘܢ ܠܓܗܢܐ ܘܗܘ ܕܐܡܪ ܕܢܠܘ ܠܗܘܢ ܠܚܙܝܪ̈ܐ ܕܢܛܘܪܐ ܠܓܝܢܐ ܐܝܟ ܕܒܒܥܠܕܒܒ ܡܦܩ ܘܡܦܠܛ ܠܗ ܓܗܢܐ. ܘܦܣܩܐ ܗܘ ܕܠܐ ܠܟ ܢܥܒܕ ܐܢܘܢ ܠܓܗܢܐ.

588 CDiat 6.27: ܪ̈ܕܦܘ ܕܝܢ ܓܕ̈ܪܝܐ ܡܢ ܐܬܪܗܘܢ. ܠܗܘ ܕܡܣܝܐ ܗܘܐ ܪܕܦ ܓ̈ܕܪܝܐ ܡܢ ܐܬܪܗܘܢ. ܘܕܝܘܐ ܒܢ̈ܝ ܐܬܪܐ ܗܘ ܕܠܐ ܢܥܠ ܒܗܘܢ ܓ̈ܕܪܝܐ ܥܪܩܘܗ ܠܗܘ ܐܣܝܐ ܕܐܙܠ ܐܟܪܢ. ܕܗܘ ܠܗܘܢ ܕܡܫܟܐ. ܥܠܝܢ ܒܗܘܢ ܓ̈ܕܪܝܐ. ܕܡܬܪܕܦܝܢ ܡܢ ܟܠ ܕܘܟ. ܕܠܪܕܦ ܓ̈ܕܪܝܐ ܕܢܥܠ ܠܘܬܗܘܢ ܠܐ ܫܒܩܘ. ܢܛܪ ܒܪ ܫܠܝܡ ܒܟܐܒܝܗܘܢ ܕܗܢܘܢ ܕܠܐܣܝܐ ܕܢܥܠ ܠܘܬܗܘܢ ܠܐ ܫܒܩܘ. ܘܟܕ ܗܘܘ ܠܟ ܡܢܗ ܕܢܐܙܠ ܠܗ ܡܢ ܠܘܬܗܘܢ. ܘܐܦ ܛܒܐ ܒܪ ܢܘܟܪܝܐ ܗܘ. ܐܝܟܢܐ ܫܪ̈ܝܐ ܕܛܠܡܘܢ ܠܥܒܕܐ ܚܠܦ. ܘܟܕ ܟܝܢܐ ܐܦ ܠܓ̈ܕܪܝܐ. ܘܐܘܪܚ ܬܘܒܐ ܥܠ ܡܪܐ ܥܠܝܐ. ܘܓ̈ܕܪܝܐ ܒܥܘ ܠܡܫܢܝܘܬܗܘܢ.

589 Azym 15.23-24.

Nevertheless, some people often do not consider His healing miracles as such help.[590]

b) The Daughter of the Canaanite Woman (Mt 15:21-28; Mk 7:24-30)

The biblical narrative about the healing of the daughter of the Canaanite Woman occurs in Mt 15:21-28 and Mk 7:24-30. The former (Mt 15:21-28) describes the suffering of the Canaanite woman's daughter with the phrase 'she is terribly possessed by the Evil One' (ܒܝܫܐܝܬ ܡܬܕܒܪܐ ܡܢ ܫܐܕܐ) and explicitly speaks of her healing (ܘܐܬܐܣܝܬ ܒܪܬܗ), whereas Mark's narrative only uses the term 'impure spirit' (ܪܘܚܐ ܠܛܢܦܬܐ) that Jesus cast out.

Ephrem uses the terminology of Mk 7:24-30 in describing both the type of sickness and the healing.[591] He goes beyond the biblical text and draws a parallel between the impure spirit of the Canaanite woman and the impure spirit of the Canaanites at the time of Joshua, son of Nun (Num 13:32-14:38):

This name [Joshua] destroyed the giants before them, and this [impure] spirit went off to the Canaanites, who came then to do battle against Joshua, son of Nun. But when the true Jesus came, it was by means of the faith of the Canaanites that He drove out the spirit from the young girl, who was a symbol of the race of Canaan.[592]

Here Ephrem alludes to the faith of the Canaanite woman in contrast to the faith of the priests and the Pharisees. Her faith and

590 Parad 12.13; Virg 30.5; Hebd 1.125f.

591 CDiat 12.13-15.

592 CDiat 12.14: ܫܡܐ ܗܢܐ ܕܚܪܒ ܡܢ ܩܕܡܝܗܘܢ ܠܓܢܒܪܐ. ܘܐܙܠܬ ܠܗ̇ ܗܝ ܪܘܚܐ ܥܠ ܟܢܥܢܝ̈ܐ. ܘܐܬܘ ܠܗܘܢ ܕܢܩܪܒܘܢ ܥܡ ܝܫܘܥ ܒܪ ܢܘܢ. ܟܕ ܐܬܐ ܠܗ ܕܝܢ ܝܫܘܥ ܫܪܝܪܐ: ܒܝܕ ܗܝܡܢܘܬܗܘܢ ܕܟܢܥܢܝ̈ܐ ܐܪܕܦܗ̇ ܠܪܘܚܐ ܡܢ ܛܠܝܬܐ. ܕܐܝܬܝܗ̇ ܐܪܙ ܫܪܒܬܗ ܕܟܢܥܢ. In CDiat 12.15, Ephrem advises the reader/listener to accept fully the intention of this comparison and this parable, so that no one may be distracted with all parts of the comparison ( ܠܐ ܕܝܢ ܒܡܠܐܟܘܬ ܬܐܙܠ ܠܟ ܐܘ ܫܡܘܥܐ ܒܬܪ ܫܪܒܐ ܕܪܘܚܐ ܗܝ ܘܕܫܒܩ ܣܒܪܬܗ̇. ܐܠܐ ܣܘܟܠܗ̇ ܕܕܡܘܬܐ ܐܘ ܣܘܟܠܐ ܕܡܬܠܐ ܗܘܬ ܫܩܘܠ ܒܫܠܡܘܬܐ. ܘܠܐ ܗܘܬ ܦܗܐ ܒܟܠܗܘܢ ܠܡܢ̈ܘܗܝ ܕܕܡܘܬܐ. ܐܘ ܒܟܠܗܘܢ ܠܦܘܫܩܗ̇ ܕܡܬܠܐ).

humility is emphasised to illustrate her persistence through which she achieved the healing of her daughter. Jesus did not respond to her at first, instead, as Ephrem says, He spurns and despises her for honouring Israel and not the Canaanites (Mt 15:26-7). In contrast, she showed her insistent love to benefit from Jesus' word, and through her faith she honoured the Canaanites. The contrast is significant. In turn, Israel was not honoured for it spurned the Lord, and the woman was not ashamed for she showed her faith and her daughter was healed.[593]

c) The Epileptic Demoniac (Mt 17:14-21; Mk 9:14-29; Lk 9:37-43)

Those who rejected Jesus considered His healing ability to be a skill that could be learnt, and not as a divine power. The ability to heal was also given to the disciples. However, a man came to Jesus and told Him how His disciples were not able to heal his son (Mt 17:16). He thought the disciples had not learned perfectly the healing art of their Master at that time.[594]

After the disciples asked the Lord why they were unable to heal, the Lord says: 'because of your lack of faith' (Mt 17:20), or 'on account of the smallness of your faith' ( ܡܛܠ ܙܥܘܪܘܬ ܗܝܡܢܘܬܟܘܢ).[595] Thus, because of their faith, the disciples were not able to heal the epileptic demoniac, and not as the people thought, because they were not yet 'perfected in the [healing] art of their master' (ܕܠܐ ܥܕܟܝܠ ܐܬܓܡܪܘ ܒܐܘܡܢܘܬܗ ܕܪܒܗܘܢ), or 'they have not learned His art' (ܠܐ ܝܠܦܘܗ̇ ܠܐܘܡܢܘܬܗ).[596]

---

593 CDiat 12.13.

594 CDiat 14.14: ܒܗ̇ܝ ܕܝܢ ܕܐܦ ܫܪܒܬܐ ܡܚܝܠܬܐ. ܡܛܠ ܗ̇ܝ ܕܡܛܪ ܠܟ ܠܬܠܡܝܕܘܗܝ. ܕܠܐ ܠܡ ܐܫܟܚܘ ܠܡܐܣܝܘܬܗ. ܐܡܪ ܠܢ ܚܠܝܡܘܢ ܕܠܐ ܥܕܟܝܠ ܐܬܓܡܪܘ ܒܐܘܡܢܘܬܗ ܕܪܒܗܘܢ (Mt 17:16-17). The idea of considering Jesus' healing capability as a skill also appears in CDiat 16.31; Dom 36; 42.

595 CDiat 14.14.

596 CDiat 14.15: ܘܒܙܒܢܐ ܠܐܒܬܝ، ܐܘܗܐ ܠܬܘܒܢ. ܠܚܘܬ ܕܒܙܢܐ ܕܡܛܠܗܘܢ، ܫܡܥ ܠܗ ܠܥܡܗ ܒܕ ܚܕܐ ܫܢܝܐ ܘܬܡܗ̈ܬܐ. ܕܠܘ ܕܝܢ ܐܘܡܢܘܬܐ ܗܝ. ܐܡܪ ܠܗ ܠܗܘ ܕܠܟܝܢ ܕܡܗܝܡܢ ܟܠ ܡܕܡ ܡܫܟܚ ܠܗܘܡܐ ܠܗ. ܘܠܗܘܢ ܐܡܪ ܡܛܠ ܙܥܘܪܘܬ ܗܝܡܢܘܬܟܘܢ.

Jesus chose seventy-two and sent them to heal in order to refute the thought of the people.[597]

To heal people is not just a skill. Ephrem makes clear that Jesus performs His healing miracles not as a result of medical skill, but because He is the Son of the Creator, the heavenly Physician. Those who believe, like the twelve apostles and the seventy-two, are also able to heal in a miraculous way through the name of Jesus.[598] The healing of individuals continues. Healing is linked with salvation. As salvation has no end, so too healing did not come to an end with the death, resurrection and ascension of Christ to heaven.

### *5.3.1.3 Spiritual Healing*

Nicodemus' spiritual healing (Jn 3:1-21), Zebedee's sons (Mt 20:20-23; Mk 10:35-40), Saul (Acts 9:1-9) and the virgin Mary, the Mother of the Lord, illustrate healing from sin and error. In different ways, each of them were sick and in need of healing. Nicodemus was unable to understand the spiritual aspect of baptism for he was blind in his mind. Zebedee's sons were poisoned by the evil of greed. Likewise Saul (Paul) was 'sick' due to his pride and so blind, for he considered himself to be the persecutor of the Lord of heaven. The case of Mary is obscure for there is no clear evidence of her spiritual state before conceiving the Son of God.

a) Nicodemus (Jn 3:1-21)

For Ephrem faith is a source of all help, healing and understanding. Nicodemus considered Jesus Christ as a Rabbi, Master and good Teacher, but he is sick in his mind and unable to understand what Jesus says. Therefore, the Lord enlightens and heals him step by step. First of all, it is difficult to believe in heavenly things, if someone does not believe in earthly things. This is a general theory which Ephrem, referring to Jn 3:12-13, mentions at the beginning of this chapter.[599] Ephrem illustrates the inner

597 CDiat 14.14: ܘܡܛܠ ܗܢܐ ܓܒܐ ܫܒܥܝܢ ܘܬܪܝܢ ܡܢ ܥܠ. ܘܫܕܪ ܐܢܘܢ ܡܢ ܩܕܡܘܗܝ. ܘܐܣܝܘ ܬܡܝܗܐܝܬ. ܕܢܬܒܣܡܘܢ ܗܢܘܢ ܕܡܣܒܪܘ ܗܥܡܐ.

598 CDiat 14.15.

599 CDiat 16.11: ܘܗܝ ܕܠܐ ܐܢܫ ܣܠܩ ܠܫܡܝܐ ܐܠܐ ܕܢܚܬ ܡܢ ܫܡܝܐ ܒܪܗ ܕܐܢܫܐ. ܡܛܠ ܕܐܬܐ ܫܠܡ ܗܘܐ ܠܗ. ܐܡܪ ܠܗܘܢ. ܐܢ

☞

situation of Nicodemus and accuses him of not believing in Scripture. As a teacher of Israel, Nicodemus should actually have known the Scriptures - the Law and the prophets, and all matters concerning 'cleansing of hyssop, the waters of ceremonial sprinkling, and the baptism of purification'.[600]

Jesus treated Nicodemus justly, He reproached him, for the symbols of baptism were depicted in Scripture and he knew them.[601] Because Nicodemus did not think about these symbols, Ephrem considers him to be sick. Ephrem says that 'Our Lord shook him out of his sleep, and restored his sickness with His gentle voice, and reminded him of the baptism of expiation, which existed in Israel'.[602] The healing was caused through 'His humble word' (ܡܠܬܗ ܡܟܝܟܬܐ) after Jesus 'shook' (ܐܙܝܥ) Nicodemus from his sleep. In order to achieve perfect healing, Jesus 'reminded' (ܘܐܥܗܕܗ) Nicodemus of the symbols in Scripture, so that he might not fall back into his doubt and sickness. The act of reminding serves to explain and manifest the truths of baptism, and so the right understanding, i.e. the healing of Nicodemus.

However, before being restored totally, Nicodemus' sickness is compared to that of Zachariah when he doubted the word of the angel and his tongue was bound (Lk 1:20-22).[603] It is significant

---

ܥܠ ܐܝܠܝܢ ܕܒܐܪܥܐ ܐܢܫ ܐܡܪܬ ܠܟܘܢ ܘܠܐ ܐܗܝܡܢܬܘܢ. ܐܝܟܢ ܐܢ ܐܡܪ ܠܟܘܢ ܥܠ ܐܝܠܝܢ ܕܒܫܡܝܐ ܐܢܫ ܬܗܝܡܢܘܢ. ܘܠܐ ܐܝܟ ܗܠܝܢ ܠܥܡܐ ܕܒܝܬܐ ܘܢܡܘܣܐ ܠܗ ܓܐܪܒܝܟܘܢ ܣܗܕܐ.

[600] CDiat 16.12: ܬܘܒ ܢܐܡܪ. ܕܡܛܠ ܕܒܬܪ ܡܠܬܗ ܕܢܝܩܕܡܘܣ ܐܡܪ ܠܗ ܡܪܢ. ܕܐܢܬ ܗܘ ܡܠܦܢܗ ܕܐܝܣܪܝܠ. ܘܗܠܝܢ ܠܐ ܝܕܥ ܐܢܬ. ܐܝܠܝܢ ܕܝ ܦܠܐ ܗܘܐ ܠܗ ܠܡܕܥ. ܐܠܐ ܗܠܝܢ ܕܢܟܣܘܬܐ ܘܕܪܒܝܐ. ܫܘܠܠܐ ܕܙܘܦܐ ܘܡܝܐ ܕܪܣܣܐ. ܘܡܥܡܘܕܝܬܐ ܕܬܕܟܝܬܐ ܡܢ ܥܒܕܐ.

[601] CDiat 16.12: ܐܠܐ ܡܛܠ ܕܪܙܝܢ ܗܘܘ ܠܦܘܩܕܢܐ ܗܠܝܢ ܡܕܡ ܒܐܬܘܬܗ ܕܒܪܐ. ܡܛܠ ܓܠܝܗ ܡܪܢ ܠܢܝܩܕܡܘܣ.

[602] CDiat 16.12: ܐܢ ܕܝܢ ܠܡܫܬܝܢ ܗܘܘ ܠܗ ܒܟܬܒܘܗܝ، ܘܠܐ ܦܪܫ. ܥܝܪܗ ܡܢ ܫܢܬܗ. ܘܐܣܝܗ ܠܟܘܪܗܢܗ ܒܝܕ ܡܠܬܗ ܡܟܝܟܬܐ. ܘܐܥܗܕܗ ܡܥܡܘܕܝܬܐ ܕܚܘܣܝܐ. ܕܐܝܬ ܗܘܐ ܒܗ ܒܐܝܣܪܝܠ.

[603] CDiat 16.12: ܐܦ ܙܟܪܝܐ ܟܕ ܐܬܒܣܪ ܕܗܘܐ ܠܗ ܒܪܐ ܘܐܬܦܠܓ. ܐܬܐܣܪ ܠܫܢܗ ܗܘ ܕܒܗ ܦܠܓ ܗܘܐ ܠܐܫܬܢܝܐ. ܗܟܢܐ ܘܐܦ ܢܝܩܕܡܘܣ ܗܠܝܢ ܬܫܘܒܚܬܐ ܫܡܥ ܗܘܐ ܡܢܗܘܢ. ܘܠܐ ܗܝܡܢ. ܡܛܠ ܗܢܐ ܟܠܗ.

that the sickness of Nicodemus is not only his ignorance of the symbols and their meaning, but rather his doubt in not believing what they stand for. His sickness is his faith, or better, non-faith. Thus, Ephrem assumes that Nicodemus knew Scripture very well, but he did not believe, just as Zachariah did not believe what the angel revealed to him. Ephrem goes beyond this comparison and considers the dialogue between Jesus and Nicodemus as healing therapy. Ephrem is keen to draw attention to the fact that Jesus was concerned about the sick state of Nicodemus, and He wanted to heal him. Jesus knew that Nicodemus was close to being healed. Therefore, he reproved him for his lack of knowledge with gentleness. Because Nicodemus was ready to understand Jesus' words, He revealed the 'baptism of complete expiation for body and soul to him'.[604]

Furthermore, Ephrem refers to Scripture to illustrate how rebirth can take place. In CDiat 16.13, Ephrem demonstrates some examples from the Old Testament: Jacob acquired the right of the first-born (Gen 25:25) without entering his mother's womb a second time; Naaman was renewed and his flesh was cleansed through the word of Elisha (2 Kgs 5:14) without being born again; likewise Miriam was cleansed from her leprosy (Num 12:9-15) without receiving a new body. Ephrem considers Nicodemus' further questioning of Jesus as a sign of his sickness. In turn, Jesus' final answer and explanation indicates again the care of the Lord and His wish to heal Nicodemus. For Nicodemus was not completely healed at first, not understanding the revelation; Jesus, Ephrem says, 'did not abandon him in his weakness, but gave him a clear argument, »unless one is born of water and the spirit, he cannot enter the kingdom of God«' (Jn 3:5). Furthermore, 'that which is born of the flesh is flesh and that which [is born] of the spirit is spirit' (Jn 3:6).[605] According to Ephrem, Jesus was

---

[604] CDiat 16.12: ܗܘ ܕܝܢ ܡܟܝܟܘܬܐ. ܡܛܠ ܕܚܙܐ ܕܒܪܝܗܐ ܗܘܐ ܘܩܪܝܒ ܗܘܐ ܠܚܘܠܡܢܐ. ܘܕܠܐ ܐܬܟܡ ܒܡܕܡܝܢܘܬܐ ܕܒܠܡܘܣܐ ܕܬܝܡܢ ܗܘ̈ ܗܠܝܢ. ܚܘܝܗ ܡܢܗ ܡܥܡܘܕܝܬܐ ܕܚܘܣܝܐ ܡܫܠܡܢܐ ܕܦܓܪܐ ܘܕܢܦܫܐ.

[605] CDiat 16.14: ܡܢ ܕܝܢ ܠܐ ܐܪܦܝܗ ܒܟܘܪܗܢܗ ܐܠܐ ܝܗܒ ܠܗ ܦܬܓܡܐ ܢܗܝܪܐ ܕܐܠܐ ܐܢ ܡܬܝܠܕ ܡܢ ܡܝ̈ܐ ܘܡܢ ܪܘܚܐ. ܠܐ ܡܫܟܚ ܕܢܥܘܠ ܠܡܠܟܘܬܗ ܕܐܠܗܐ. ܗ̇ܝ ܕܐܠܘ ܓܒܪܐ ܡܫܬܟܚ ܗܘܐ ܡܢ ☞

instructing Nicodemus in the faith ( ܠܡܗܝܡܢܘܬܐ ܗܘ ܕܝܢ ܡܬܠܡܕ܆ ܗܘܐ ܠܗ), indicating that spiritual birth is invisible. Being restored means having the right faith and the right understanding. It was through Jesus' instruction, teaching and words that Nicodemus was healed.

b) Zebedee's Sons (Mt 20:20-23; Mk 10:35-40)

Just as withNicodemus' questions, so too the request of Zebedee's sons to be seated on each side of Jesus in His kingdom revealed their spiritual sickness. Ephrem considers evil pride as the cause of their question that entered their minds to poison not only both of Zebedee's sons, but also all of Jesus' disciples. In order to avoid this, healing was required. Ephrem highlights the aspect of healing and interprets Jesus' answer as medicine to heal the spiritual sickness of Zebedee's sons.

> When the wise Physician saw the venom of proudness
> that spread into the sons of Zebedee, He swiftly cut it
> off so that it might not also overspread
> into the body of His twelve who were threatened with
> all questions.
> The Physician cut off the cause of pain, and the
> fountain of harm dried up.[606]

Jesus is the wise Physician Who healed Zebedee's sons from their spiritual sickness. In the next stanza, Ephrem warns everyone to be aware about questioning and prying so that everyone should be aware of the reasons behind the asking of questions and prying. He advises everyone to consider that the 'Healer of the sons of Zebedee' (ܡܐܣܝܢܗܘܢ ܕܒܢ̈ܝ ܙܒܕܝ) is also capable of healing the fountain of all questions that cause harm.[607]

---

ܐܝܟ ܕܐܡܪܢܢ܆ ܘܗܟܢ ܬܫܥܝܬܐ. ܕܠܦܓܪܐ ܗܘ ܐܬܬܚܝܒܬ ܡܬܝܠܕܢܘܬܐ ܕܟܝܢܐ ܥܡ ܫܘܬܦܘܬܐ ܕܪܘܚܐ. ܡܛܠ ܕܐܝܟ ܗܝ ܕܒܪܐ ܒܣܬܪܐ ܗܘ. ܘܕܡܝܐ ܪܘܚܐ ܪܘܚܐ ܗܘ. ܠܡܗܝܡܢܘܬܐ ܗܘ ܕܝܢ ܡܬܠܡܕ܆ ܗܘܐ ܠܗ.

[606] Eccl 25.8:

ܗܘ ܕܝܢ ܐܣܝܐ ܚܟܝܡܐ ܕܚܙܐ ܠܟܐܪܬܗ ܕܫܘܒܗܪܐ ܕܦܫܬ ܠܗ̇
ܒܒܢ̈ܝ ܙܒܕܝ܆ ܪܗܛ ܦܣܩܗ̇ ܕܠܐ ܬܦܫܘܛ ܠܗ̇
ܘܐܦ ܒܦܓܪܐ ܕܬܪܥܣܪܬܗ ܕܒܨܝܢ ܗܘܘ ܠܗܘܢ ܒܟܠ ܫܐ̈ܠܢ
ܦܣܩ ܐܣܝܐ ܥܠܬ ܟܐܒܐ ܘܝܒܫܬ ܡܒܘܥܐ ܕܢܟܝ̈ܢܐ.

[607] Eccl 25.9:

☞

c) Saul (Acts 9:1-9)

The healing process of individuals has not come to an end with Jesus' death and resurrection. A good example of spiritual healing after the resurrection, is Saul's (Paul's) conversion (Act 9:1-9). Referring to Saul's vision on the way to Damascus, Ephrem emphasizes the significant role that Jesus' words play and the light of the vision. Ephrem explains the influence of Jesus' humble speech in Saul's conversion. He contrasts Saul's pride with the humility of our Lord. Ephrem also compares God's revelation to Moses with the revelation to Saul. The brilliant light was blinding Saul, because his inner eyes were blind; while the eyes of Moses radiated with the glory he saw. Another power lovingly reinforced the eyes of Moses beyond their natural power.[608] While the light struck Saul's weak eyes, injuring and blinding them, the voice passed through his ears and opened them, because through the speech our Lord was able to show that He was persecuted by Saul.[609] Ephrem does not speak of healing in this context, but he speaks of 'help' through humble speech:

---

ܐܦ ܐܢܬ ܗܟܝܠ ܫܐܘܠܐ ܡܪܢ ܕܐܬܚܙܝ ܠܟ ܒܝܕ ܢܘܗܪܐ ܚܘܪ ܒܗ
ܒܥܐܠܬܟ ܐܦ ܫܡܥܐ ܗܘ ܘܩܒܠ ܡܠܬܐ ܕܐܘܠܨܢܗ
ܐܦ ܚܢܢ ܠܗ ܬܐܠܬܟ ܡܠܬܐ ܗܝ ܡܥܕܪܢܘܬ ܡܘܟܟܐ
ܡܐܣܝܘܬܐ ܕܒܢ̈ܝ ܙܒܕܝ ܢܣܒ ܠܗ ܕܐܠܝܨ ܡܚܘ̈ܒܘܬܗ.

In some other passages, Ephrem refers to the request of Zebedee's sons positively. In Virg 15.7, Ephrem illustrates the twelve disciples as a body, of which Simon Peter is the head and the sons of Zebedee are the eyes (ܘܒܢ̈ܝ ܙܒܕܝ ܥܝ̈ܢܐ ܗܘܘ ܠܗ). Here Ephrem combines Mt 20:20-23 (Lk 10:35-40) with Mt 17:1-3 (Mk 9:2-4) saying, that they have asked for the thrones for they have seen the transfiguration of the Lord on the mountain (Mt 17:1-3; Mk 9:2-4). In Virg 34.8, Ephrem praises the place for which the sons of Zebedee asked the Lord. In the following stanzas, he explains the negative aspect of their request. The throne belongs only to the Lord and no one else; neither are the angels allowed to sit on the throne of the Lord. Here Ephrem does not consider the possibility of being seated on the other thrones, namely to the left and right side of the Lord. Generally, the divine grace and mercy have granted a high rank to man (cf. Virg 34.9-12).

608 Dom 31.

609 Dom 32. In Virg 30.2, Ephrem refers to David and Saul and emphasises that the playing of the harp made harmonious music pleasing ☞

Furthermore, this is why the humble voice accompanied the intense light, so that, from the combination of the humble and the sublime, our Lord might produce help for the persecutor, just as all His assistance is produced from a combination of the small and the great. For the humility of our Lord prevailed from the womb to the tomb. Observe how majesty accompanies and escorts His weakness, and the exaltation His humility.[610]

Ephrem understands Saul's conversion as a process of teaching. Generally, there are two ways of teaching, teaching by words or by deeds:

> Any master who intends to teach a person something teaches either by deeds or by words. If he does not teach by words or deeds, a person could not be instructed in his craft. And so, although it was with deeds that our Lord taught Paul humility, He taught him with words about that persecution of which He was unable to teach him with deeds. Before He was crucified, when He taught the persecution involved in humility, our Lord taught His disciples by deeds. After He completed His persecution on the cross, as He said, »every thing is fulfilled« (Jn 19:30), He could not go

---

to healthy ears, but unpleasant to the unhealthy: 'Already drawn on the harp of David was also the harp of the Son of David, for while he played and sang, Saul's melancholy ears could not endure [it] (1 Sam 19:9-10); by the spirit within him Saul was saddened. As Saul against David, therefore, the ears of tares and scribes stood on end against the Son of David'. (ܡܩܕܡ ܪܫܝܡ ܗܘܐ ܒܟܢܪܐ ܕܕܘܝܕ ܐܦ ܟܢܪܗ ܕܒܪ ܕܘܝܕ. ܟܕ ܓܝܪ ܢܩܫ ܘܙܡܪ ܠܐ ܣܝܒܪ ܗܘܝ، ܐܕܢ̈ܝ ܫܐܘܠ ܕܟܪ̈ܝܗܝ ܗܘܝ، ܒܗ̇، ܪܘܚܐ ܕܒܗܬ ܫܐܘܠ ܐܬܟܪܝܬ ܐܦ ܐܕܢ̈ܝܗܘܢ ܕܙ̈ܝܙܢܐ ܘܣܦܪ̈ܐ ܐܝܟ ܫܐܘܠ ܓܝܪ ܥܠ ܕܘܝܕ ܐܙܕܩܦܘ ܐܦ ܥܠܘܗܝ ܕܒܪ ܕܘܝܕ).

[610] Dom 34: ܬܘܒ ܕܝܢ ܐܦ ܡܛܠ ܗܕܐ ܠܘ̣ܐ ܗ̣ܘܐ ܠܗ ܠܢܘܗܪܐ ܚܣܝܢܐ ܩܠܐ ܡܟܝܟܐ. ܕܐܝܟ ܕܡܢ ܚܠܛ ܡܟܝܟܐ ܠܪܘܡܪܡܐ ܢܥܒܕ ܗܘܐ ܡܪܢ ܥܘܕܪܢܐ ܠܪܕܘܦܐ. ܐܝܟܢܐ ܕܐܦ ܟܠܗܘܢ ܥܘܕܪ̈ܢܘܗܝ ܡܢ ܒܝܬ ܙܥܘܪܘܬܐ ܠܪܒܘܬܐ ܡܬܥܒܕܝܢ ܗܘܘ. ܐܚܝܕܐ ܗ̇ܘܬ ܓܝܪ ܠܡܟܝܟܘܬܗ ܕܡܪܢ ܡܢ ܡܪܒܥܐ ܕܒܛܢܐ ܠܡܩܒܪܐ. ܚܙܝ ܕܠܘܝܐ ܗܝ ܠܗ ܘܐܙܠܐ ܪܒܘܬܐ ܠܟܪܝܗܘܬܗ ܘܪܘܡܪܡܐ ܠܡܟܝܟܘܬܗ.

> back again and foolishly begin something that once and for all had been finished wisely.[611]

d) Mary's Healing

The second hymn on the Nativity describes Jesus as the Inheritor of the tripartite leadership of the Old Testament: prophecy, priesthood and kingship. In Mary's exaltation in being His mother, she considers herself as a chosen one who rejoices more than all of those who have been healed:

> Most of all those healed, He causes me to rejoice, for I
> conceived Him;
> most of all those magnified by Him, He has magnified
> me, for I gave birth to Him.
> I am about to enter into His living paradise
> and in the place in which Eve succumbed, I shall
> glorify Him.[612]

It is difficult to know how to interpret the first sentence. Does Mary consider herself as healed, like all the others who were healed by Jesus? Or is she just comparing her joy to that of those who have been healed? In this context, the question of the immaculate conception is of significance. If she has been healed like the others, then she must have been spiritually sick before.

In Virg 25.8, Ephrem speaks of her 'sick womb' ( ܒܟܪܣܐ ܟܪܝܗܐ) in which the High One dwelt,[613] although it is compared

---

[611] Dom 36: ܚܕ ܡܢ ܬܪ̈ܬܐ ܕܝܢ ܕܢܣܒܐ ܕܢܠܦ ܡܕܡ ܠܐܢܫ. ܒܚܟ̈ܝܡܐ ܐܘ ܒܣܟ̈ܠܐ ܣܟܠܘ ܠܗ. ܐܢ ܕܝܢ ܠܐ ܒܣܟ̈ܠܐ ܘܠܐ ܒܚܟ̈ܝܡܐ ܚܟܡܘ ܠܗ. ܐܦ ܐܢܫ ܠܐܘܡܢܘܬܗ ܕܢܬܬܠܡܕ ܠܐ ܡܫܟܚ. ܐܝܟܢܐ ܕܐܦ ܡܢܘ ܐܦܢ ܠܐ ܗܘܐ ܒܚܟ̈ܝܡܐ ܐܠܦܗ ܡܗܝܡܢܘܬܐ ܠܫܠܝܚܘܗ. ܐܠܐ ܒܡܠܐ ܐܠܦܗ ܗ̇ܘܐ ܕܪܫܘܬܐ ܗ̇ܝ ܕܒܚܟ̈ܝܡܐ ܕܢܠܦܗ ܠܐ ܡܫܟܚ ܗܘܐ. ܡܕܡ ܠܒܪ ܕܢܕܘܦ ܗܘܐ ܡܢ ܕܪܫܘܬܐ ܕܡܗܝܡܢܘܬܐ ܗ̇ܝ ܕܐܠܦ ܗ̇ܘܐ ܠܬܠܡ̈ܝܕܘܗܝ ܒܚܟ̈ܝܡܐ ܠܗܘܢ ܐܠܦ ܗܘܐ. ܡܢ ܒܬܪ ܕܝܢ ܕܐܠܦܗ̇ ܠܪ̈ܫܘܬܐ ܒܡܫܘܬܐ. ܐܝܟܢܐ ܕܐܚܪܢ ܕܗܘܐ ܡܫܠܡ ܟܠ ܡܕܡ. ܠܐ ܬܘܒ ܡܚܡܣ ܗܘܐ ܕܢܗܦܘܟ ܢܫܪܐ ܣܟܠܐܝܬ ܡܕܡ ܕܚܕܐ ܙܒܢ ܐܫܬܠܡܬ ܚܟܝܡܐܝܬ.

[612] Nat 2.7:

ܡܢ ܟܘܠ ܕܐܬܐܣܝܘ ܚܕܝܐ ܕܐܢܐ ܒܛܢܬܗ ܡܢ ܟܠ ܕܪܒܘ ܒܗ
ܐܘܪܒܢܝ ܕܐܢܐ ܐܝܠܕܬܗ
ܠܦܪܕܝܣܗ ܚܝܐ ܕܐܥܘܠ ܥܬܝܕܐ ܐܢܐ ܘܒܐܬܪܗ ܕܢܦܠܬ ܒܗ ܚܘܐ
ܐܫܒܚܝܘܗܝ.

to the ark of the old covenant in which God was present for His People.[614] The sickness of the womb is not physical but spiritual. Compared to God's holy dwelling place in the highest heaven and Paradise, the womb of a human being can be only weak and sick. In particular this is the case, since humanity in general has fallen into the state of sickness. Humanity, and this includes the virgin Mary, has been healed by Jesus since His incarnation, but not before. Compared to other women, Mary's womb is considered 'pure' (ܕܟܝܐ). CDiat 7.15 contrasts Mary's 'pure womb' (ܡܪܒܥܐ ܕܟܝܐ) with the 'unclean womb' (ܡܪܒܥܐ ܠܛܡܐܐ) of the woman with a haemorrhage.[615] Taking Epiph 8.23-24 (although not genuine Ephrem) into consideration, the author has the same view as the later Syriac tradition. While he emphasises the necessity of baptism and holy ܩܘܪܒܢܐ for man's salvation, the author speaks of Mary's baptism[616] and her consuming of the Lord's consecrated body and blood. Although she gave birth to Jesus and He took body from her, in return, she put Him on spiritually at baptism and consumed Him in the eucharistic bread and wine as the Medicine of Life. In order to be saved, the virgin Mary must have been taking part in Jesus' salvation act, i.e, being spiritually re-born to a new life through baptism.[617] If she had to be baptised, then, even

---

613 Virg 25.8:
ܛܠܝܐ ܒܐܬܘܬܐ ܚܙܐ ܗܘܐ ܠܗ ܠܗܘ ܟܠܒܐ ܒܒܟܐ ܐܬܬܚܝܬ،
ܕܐܝܟ ܥܠ ܓܙܪܐ ܒܥܘܒܐ ܕܢܗܘܐ ܘܢܩܘܡ ܐܝܟ ܫܠܒܐ ܡܚܝܠܐ.

614 Virg 25.11: ܗܦܟ ܢܘܪܗ ܐܦ ܢܣܒ ܠܥܘܒܗ ܕܐܡܟܝܟ ܐܝܟ ܕܟܘܪܐ ܢܘܪܐ ܗܘ ܕܡܫܒܚܬܐ ܡܥܡܝܢ ܘܟܠܗ ܕܒܙܪܐ ܗܘܐ ܒܗ ܒܡܚܘܐܠ.

615 CDiat 7.15: ܡܛܠ ܗܢܐ ܥܙܪ ܚܠܡܗ ܠܡܪܒܥܐ ܠܛܡܐܐ. ܕܐܝܟ ܒܝܕ. ܠܛܡܐܐ ܢܣܒܘܢ ܒܡܗܡܢܘܬܗ ܕܠܗ ܕܗܝ ܡܪܒܥܐ ܕܟܝܐ. Here the author uses the term ܡܪܒܥܐ instead of ܥܘܒܐ.

616 Ephrem sees Christ's presence in Mary's womb as her baptism; see Nat 16:11.

617 Epiph 8.23-24:
ܘܐܦ ܐܡܗ ܒܥܡܕܗ ܩܒܠܬ ܒܪܬܗ ܘܡܢ ܡܪܗ ܠܒܫܬܗ ܠܒܘܫܬܗ
ܕܒܠܒܬܗ ܡܢ ܩܕܝܫ ܘܝܠܕܬܗ ܝܠܕܬܗ ܐܦ ܠܗ ܡܥܡܘܕܝܬܐ
ܝܠܕܬ ܘܐܬܝܠܕܬ ܕܦܓܪܐ ܕܢܦܫ ܡܢܗ ܗܦܟܬ ܢܦܫܬܗ ܗܝ ܒܠܫܡܐ
ܘܩܘܪܒܢܐ

☞

though she gave birth to the Son of God, she was in need of salvation. This goes against any idea of her immaculate conception. However, in order to define clearly Ephrem's view on this aspect, all his work needs to be examined.[618]

### 5.3.2 The Spiritual Healing of Human Nature and the Whole of Creation

God is the source of healing. He sent His Son into the world to heal humanity and fulfil what was lacking in nature. The fulfilling and healing of the world is considered to be a second creation (ܕܐܬܐ ܐܣܝܘܬܐ ܒܒܪܝܬܐ ܕܬܪܬܝܢ ܐܬܝܗܒܬ).[619] Healing is a divine act, so that Jesus' Healing shows that He is the Son of God,[620] Who has been sent as the 'Healer of all' (ܐܣܝܐ ܕܟܠ),[621] and as the 'Medicine of Life' (ܣܡ ܚܝܐ).[622] Jesus is the Physician Who heals everything by His 'medicine' (ܣܡܡܢܐ),[623] 'pity' (ܚܢܢܐ),[624] 'mercy' (ܪܚܡܐ) and 'compassion' (ܡܪܚܡܢܘܬܐ),[625]

---

ܒܗ ܦܓܪܗ ܗܝ ܕܠܒܫܬ ܣܡ ܚܝܐ ܕܒܠܥܕܘܗܝ ܡܚܝܐ ܠܗ̇. ܐܦ ܗܝ ܣܢܝܩܐ ܐܡܗ ܕܝܠܕܬܗ ܒܥܒܕܗ ܗܘܐ ܕܢܪܒܝܗ̇ ܒܗ ܒܢܝܐ
ܘܦܓܪܗ ܗܘ ܐܠܒܫܗ̇ ܒܗ ܠܫܒܐ ܘܚܟܡܗ ܗܘ ܐܪܘܒܗ̇ ܒܗ ܣܒܪܐ ܚܢܢ ܡܢܟ ܒܠܒܐ ܡܢܢܐ ܡܬܡܪܩܐ ܡܢܗ ܛܘܒ ܡܫܟܚܐ ܕܝܢ ܕܠܐ ܟܣܣ ܡܪܩܐ ܕܢܛܦܪܐ.

[618] The doctrine of the immaculate conception is based on a conception of what happened at the Fall which is considerably different from that of Ephrem and Syriac tradition - and indeed Eastern Christian tradition as a whole.

[619] Haer 43.9.

[620] CDiat 16.31: ܘܐܪܫܡ ܗܘܐ ܒܒܢܝ: ܐܣܝܘܬܗ ܐܪܙܐ ܕܒܪܗ ܗܘ ܕܒܪܘܝܐ.

[621] Eccl 28.16; 31.1; Fid 12.9; 15.7; Nis 4.16; 4.20; 34.5.

[622] For 'Medicine of Life' see chapter III, 2.2.3.

[623] Nis 4.16; 4.20.

[624] Eccl 31.1: ܡܐܣܝܐ ܕܟܠ ܒܚܢܢܐ ܘܠܐ ܒܐܓܪܐ ܣܠܩ ܦܓܥܐ ܒܥܘܪܐ ܘܚܓܝܪܐ ܕܡܟܐܒ ܐܝܬ ܠܗ ܚܢܢܐ ܪܚܡܐ.

[625] Virg 26.10; CDiat 13.1: ܐܣܝܬ ܡܪܚܡܢܘܬܐ ܠܗܘ. ܕܠܐ ܬܦܫܘܩ ܠܚܠܝܡܘܬܐ ܡܣܟܢܘܬ ܡܢ ܬܡܢ.

'goodness' (ܒܣܝܡܘܬܐ),[626] 'justice' (ܟܐܢܘܬܐ),[627] 'love' (ܚܘܒܐ),[628] and His 'providence/care' (ܒܛܝܠܘܬܐ).[629] Ephrem attributes the healing of man to the Lord's providence that 'healed the whole man in everything'.[630] Jesus healed humanity not only gratis,[631] but He also suffered for it, and His medicine is granted freely.[632]

In contrast to the prophets, only Jesus was capable of healing humanity from its fallen state. He was sufficient to heal 'our wound' (ܟܐܒܘܬܢ). The righteous of the Old Covenant desired to see Him come as the Medicine of Life.[633] He 'descended to heal those who engaged in all kinds of evil.'[634] Jesus is described as the 'Cluster of Mercy' (ܛܘܦܝܠܬܐ ܕܪ̈ܚܡܐ) that 'was trampled and gave the Medicine of Life to the people'.[635] As the Medicine of

---

626 Azym 1.3; 20.16-19; Nis 2.2; Haer 51.1 (cf. also Dom 1; CDiat 16.16; Haer 56.10).

627 Haer 51.1; Nis 11.3-4.

628 Haer 1.1; 1.8; 21.11; 39.6; I Ser 7.217-244.

629 Nis 46.8; CDiat 16.24 (cf. also Nachträge Auszug 2.184f.

630 Nis 46.8: ܐܦ ܕܝܢ ܒܛܝܠܘܬܗ ܕܡܪܢ ܡܦܝܣܐ ܠܝ ܕܐܣܝܗ ܠܒܪܢܫܐ ܠܟܠܗ ܒܟܠ ܡܕܡ.

631 Nis 2.2; 4.17.

632 Dom 14: ܡܫܝܚܐ ܗܘܬ ܠܗܘܢ ܚܢܢ ܠܬܚܠ ܐܣܝܗ ܒܡܓܢܐ ܕܡܓܢ. ܕܡܓܢ ܐܘܒܠ ܠܗ. ܡܫܚܬ ܣܘܠܦܢܐ ܠܡܐܣܝܘܗ̇.

633 Nat 1.52: ܢܦܫܐ ܕܟܐܢ̈ܐ ܪܓܬ ܒܗ ܒܒܪܐ ܕܐܬܝܬܗ، ܗܘ ܣܡ ܚܝ̈ܐ ܘܐܬܐܒܘ [ܘܐܬܐܒܬ] ܕܒܥ̈ܘܬܗ ܢܐܬܐ ܘܬܛܥܡ ܚܠܝܘܬܗ.

634 Dom 42: ܒܗ̇، ܒܪ ܕܠܐ ܦܣܩܘ ܢܒܝ̈ܐ ܠܡܚܣܘ ܠܚܫ̈ܝܐ. ܢܚܬ ܠܗ ܡܪ̈ܘܥܢ ܕܟ̈ܐܒܐ ܕܐܢܫܐ ܠܟܠܗܘܢ ܕܒܝܫ ܒܝܫ ܒܒܝ̈ܫܝܢ.

635 Virg 31.13:

ܛܘܦܝܠܬܐ ܕܪ̈ܚܡܐ ܕܐܬܕܝܫܬ ܒܡܥܨܪܐ ܕܦܘܠܚܢܐ ܛܠܡ ܗܘܐ
ܘܠܦܐܪ̈ܐ ܟܠܗ ܗܘܐ

ܠܕܗܒ ܠܗ̇ ܡܪܪܐ ܚܠܝܘܬܗ̇ ܦܠܓܬ ܐܬܓܪܬ ܘܚܡܒܬ ܣܡ ܚܝ̈ܐ
ܠܥܡܡ̈ܐ

ܠܦܘܡܗ، ܠܗܝ ܕܐܬܚܫܬ، ܡܢ ܚܙܘܪܗ̇ ܪ̈ܘܚܡܐ ܘܠܐ ܐܙܕܠܠ ܒܒܣܝܡܐ.

For Aphrahat's long allegory of the ܛܘܦܝܠܬܐ see R. Murray, *Symbols of Church and Kingdom*, 113-118; and Ephrem's other allusions see ibid., 118-120.

Life, He could heal the pains of the soul,[636] and the deadly wound.[637] He was sufficient for 'our pains' (ܟܐܒ̈ܝܢ),[638] and He 'chased away our pain'.[639] His medicine healed 'our sores' (ܫܘܚܢ̈ܬܢ),[640] while He approached 'our defilement' (ܬܘܡܣܬܢ).[641] Likewise, man's "mind" (ܬܪܥܝܬܐ)[642] and "free will" (ܚܐܪܘܬܐ)[643] were in need of healing, and Jesus provided medicine for the diseases caused by man's free will, such as 'paganism' (ܚܢܦܘܬܐ),[644] 'pride' (ܫܘܒܗܪܐ) and 'haughtiness' (ܪܡܘܬܐ).[645]

Jesus' incarnation and becoming a man like us plays an essential role in the healing of humanity. He lived among mankind in the manner of a human being to present Himself as Medicine of Life that they could understand Him. For example, His teaching

---

636 Nis 34.10; cf. Fid 15.1; Nat 22.1.

637 Nis 74.14: ܠܡܣܝ̈ܘܬܐ ܐܝܟ ܒܡܣܝ̈ܢܐ ܕܐܫܟܚ ܘܠܡܣܝܘܬܐ ܕܡܚܘܬܐ ܡܘܬܐ ܠܐ ܠܗ ܢܦܠ ܠܐܣܝܘܬܗ܆ ܗܘ ܚܢܢ.

638 Nat 22.1: ܕܢܕܒ ܐܢܕܪܐ ܡܣܝܘܬܐ ܐܝܟ ܠܕܪܐ ܕܐܫܬܠܚ ܟܐܒܝܢ ܗܘ ܕܣܦܩ ܠܟܐܒ̈ܝܢ.

639 Fid 5.19: ܐܘ ܡܢܐ ܡܢܘ ܛܪܕ ܟܐܒܢ ܕܐܣܝܐ ܕܪܕܦ ܠܟܐܒܢ ܚܝ ܒܗ ܡܚܝܢ ܘܠܘܡܢ.

640 Haer 33.1: ܒܪܢ ܡܢܢ ܕܐܣܐ ܫܘܚܢ̈ܬܢ.

641 Haer 33.11; I Ser 7.49.

642 Haer 11.2; cf. Fid 65.11-12; Parad 9.21.

643 Eccl 19.7; Haer 11.1; 28.5; 39.6; 51.2; Iei 6.6.

644 Nis 21.18:

ܟܠܟܐ ܟܠܗ ܐܝܟ ܠܡܫܟܐ ܒܡܘܪܒܐ ܪܟܐ ܢܦܠ ܗܘܐ
ܕܟܐܫܬܗ ܕܚܢܦܘܬܐ ܐܫܬܚܩ ܘܡܬܒܪ ܘܢܦܠ
ܡܣܝܢܐ ܕܐܝܩܪܐ ܠܫܬܗ ܘܡܫܦܬ ܢܦܫܗ ܒܣܢܝܐ ܦܫܦܫ ܒܟܠ
ܚܢܦܘܬܐ ܕܗܝ ܗܝ ܟܠܬ ܒܡܘܪܝܐ
ܘܐܬܠܦܝ ܘܐܒܬ ܘܦܣܩܐ ܫܘܒܚܐ ܠܐܒܪܐ ܕܡܫܒܚܬܗ.

645 Haer 51.2:

ܟܐܒܐ ܕܠܘܒܐ ܘܫܟܢܐ ܕܫܘܒܗܪܐ ܐܫܬܡܥ ܒܝܘܩܪܐ ܚܝܘܗܝ
ܐܣܝܐ ܠܣܟܢܐ ܕܟܐܒܐ ܗܘ ܕܗܘܪܪܐ ܘܡܘܟܟܐ ܕܫܘܒܗܪܐ
ܥܒܠ ܗܘ ܠܗ ܘܪܐ ܒܗܪܐ ܕܟܐܒܘܬܐ ܕܠܒܘܫ ܒܡܟܝܟܘܬܐ ܟܐܒܐ
ܕܪܡܘܬܐ ܕܟܝܢܐ ܒܚܐܪܘܬܐ.

served as Medicine of Life to them (ܘܠܟܠܗܘܢ ܐܝܟ ܣܡ ܚܝܐ).[646] As a human being, He talked and healed with His word (ܐܣܝܘܬܐ ܡܢ ܡ̈ܠܘܗܝ) which is more powerful than healing through His garments.[647] In CDiat 12.24, it is explicitly said that 'Jesus came [into the world] and granted healing by word'.[648] In particular His body, as a sign of His humanity, has a mediatory function. According to Dom 11, Jesus did not need 'to sever a part of His body to fill up the deficiency of other bodies', but still He separated from Himself what was needed, like the saliva for the pupils of the blind man.[649] In this context, Ephrem draws attention to Jesus' body that served as medicine for everyone. Since He became a man, people were encouraged to approach and touch His clothing (Lk 8:44) and His body (Lk 7:38) through which they were healed.[650]

---

[646] Dom 15: ܠܐ ܗܘܐ ܓܝܪ ܡܛܠ ܚܠܦ ܒܡܣܟܢܐ ܗܘܐ ܡܪܢ ܒܡ ܐܣܘ̈ܬܐ ܘܥܬܝ̈ܪܬܐ ܐܝܟ ܕܡܢ ܦܓܪܐ. ܐܠܐ ܕܒܡܐܣܝܘܬܗܘܢ ܕܟܠܗܘܢ ܕܡܣܝ̈ܢܘܬܐ: ܢܣܠܘܦ ܗܘܐ ܠܗܘܢ ܘܠܟܠܗܘܢ ܐܝܟ ܣܡ ܚܝܐ.

Nis 34.10: ܫܘܒܚܐ ܠܣܡ ܚܝܐ ܕܗܘܐ ܣܡܡ ܘܐܣܝ ܟܐܒܐ ܕܢܦ̈ܫܬܐ ܒܟܠܗܘܢ.

[647] Dom 14: ܐܦ ܓܝܪ ܡܢ ܒܠܒܘܫܗ ܐܣܝܘܬܐ ܕܐܝܟ ܗܕܐ ܒܠܒܘܫܐ ܐܬܝܗܒܬ. ܡܢ ܟܕ ܢܦܩܐ ܗܘܐ ܠܐܣܝܘܬܐ ܕܡܠܬܗ ܒܦܘܪܣܐ ܢܣܒܐ ܗܘܬ. ܘܐܦ ܒܠܘܚܡܬܐ ܕܡ̈ܠܘܗܝ ܡܫܘ̈ܚܬܐ ܠܡ̈ܐܟܬܐ ܐܬܚܙܝ ܗܘ̈ܝ. ܚܕ ܟܡܐ ܢܬܘܣܦ ܗܘ̈ܝ ܒܠܘܚܡܬ ܦܘܡܗ ܡܫܘ̈ܚܬܐ ܕܡ̈ܠܬܐ.

Virg 26.4: ܛܘܒ ܠܐܒܝ̈ܕܝܢ ܕܐܫܬܟܚܘ ܒܡܠܬܐ ܘܠܫܘ̈ܬܦܝܢ ܕܐܫܬܒܩܘ ܒܠܘܚܡܬܐ.

[648] CDiat 12.24: ܐܬܐ ܕܝܢ ܡܫܝܚܐ ܘܒܡܠܬܐ ܝܗܒ ܐܣܝܘܬܐ.

[649] Dom 11: ܠܐ ܓܝܪ ܣܢܝܩܐ ܗܘܬ ܕܢܦܣܘܩ ܡܢ ܦܓܪܗ ܢܡܠܐ ܗܘܐ ܡܢܗ ܘܢܡܠܐ ܚܣܝܪܘܬܐ ܕܦܓܪ̈ܐ ܐܚܪ̈ܢܐ. ܐܠܐ ܒܡܕܡ ܕܡܬܒܥܐ ܗܘܐ ܕܢܬܦܠ ܡܢܗ ܥܠ ܚܣܝܪܘܬܐ ܕܣܡ̈ܝܐ (Jn 9:6; Mk 7:33). Cf. Nis 34.10.

[650] Dom 13: ܠܐ ܗܘܐ ܓܝܪ ܦܓܪܐ ܒܠܚܘܕ ܠܒܪ ܡܢܗ. ܐܠܐ ܐܦ ܗܕ̈ܡܐ ܡܢ ܢܫܬܐ ܐܬܒܠܥ. ܕܟܕ ܗܕ̈ܡܘܗܝ، ܘܢܫܬܘܗܝ، ܢܬܠܒܒܘܢ ܡܬܚܝ̈ܢܐ ܠܡܩܪܒ ܠܘܬܗ ܕܐܣܝ̈ܘܬܐ. ܕܐܝܟܢ ܕܠܒܢ̈ܝܐ ܒܪ̈ܚܡܬܗ ܢܬܩܪܒܘܢ ܠܦܓܪܗ. ܘܐܝܟܢ ܕܗܕ̈ܡܝܢ ܒܫܠܝܗ ܢܬܩܪܒܘܢ ܠܠܒܘܫܗ. ܠܚܕܐ ܓܝܪ ܒܕܡܐ ܠܚܛܝܐ ܕܡܙܠܙܠܐ ܐܦܣܬ ܠܗ ܕܠܦܓܪܗ ܠܡܩܪܒ. ܠܐܚܪܬܐ ܕܝܢ ܒܕܡܐ ܠܚܫܗ ܐܪܗܛܬܗ ܕܬܬܩܪܒ ܠܠܒܘܫܗ. ܒܗ̇ ܕܝܢ ܕܡܠܟ ܐܣܝܘܬܐ ܡܢ ܢܫܬܘܗܝ، ܐܬܟܫܪܘ ܗ̇ܢܘܢ ܕܠܐ ܡܠܝܢ ܐܣܝܘܬܐ

☞

Furthermore, the Son of God dwelt in human nature to fulfil it and make it complete. The prophets did many miracles, but they were not able to fill up the deficiency as the Lord did. Neither were they able to heal the whole of humanity from its fallen state. Jesus is able to bring all creation to fulfilment, because He is the One Who holds the world and all creation in His hands:

The prophets worked all [sorts of] signs, but nowhere [is it recorded that] they filled up a deficiency in the parts of the body. Physical deficiency waited to be filled up by our Lord, so that souls would realise that every deficiency is filled up by Him.[651]

In Dom 11, Ephrem speaks of 'what was lacking in [human] nature' (ܚܣܝܪܘܬܗ ܕܟܝܢܐ). The man born blind was without eyes. The Lord created eyes for him and fulfilled what was lacking in his body. The deficiency of his body symbolises the deficiency of the whole of human nature and God's creation, that was caused by Adam's fall. Just as the Lord fulfilled what was lacking in the man born blind, He made known that He is the One Who fulfills the whole of nature.[652] Literally, the Lord's spittle (Jn 9:6; Mk 7:33), as

---

ܡܢ ܩ̈ܠܘܗܝ. ܘܒܗܝ، ܕܢܚܘܬ ܪ̈ܓܠܘܗܝ، ܐܬܚܫܒ ܗܘ ܕܠܐ ܥܝ̈ܢܐ ܗܘܐ ܕܢܫܠܡ ܡܫܡܠܝܘܬܗ.

[651] Dom 12: ܠܢܒܝ̈ܐ ܕܝܢ ܟܠ ܐܬܘ̈ܬܐ ܥܒܕ ܗܘܘ ܚܣܝܪܘܬܐ ܕܝܢ ܕܗܕ̈ܡܐ ܒܕܘܟ ܠܐ ܡܠܝܘ. ܐܬܟܠܝܬ ܕܝܢ ܚܣܝܪܘܬܐ ܕܦܓܪܐ ܕܒܝܕ ܡܪܢ ܬܬܡܠܐ. ܕܢܕܥܢ ܢܦ̈ܫܬܐ ܕܒܐܝܕܗ ܗܘ ܡܬܡܠܝܐ ܟܠ ܚܣܝܪܢ. Cf. Nis 34.10.

[652] Dom 11: ܘܐܦ ܗܪܟܐ ܟܝܢܐ ܚܣܝܪܐ ܐܬܡܠܝ ܡܢ ܡܪܢ. ܡܢ ܕܝܢ ܕܚܣܝܪܘܬܗ ܕܟܝܢܐ ܫܦܩ ܠܡܫܡܠܝܘ. ܐܚܝܕ ܕܒܐܝܕܗ ܗܘ ܦܐܡ ܡܘܠܝܗ ܕܟܝܢܐ. ܚܣܝܪܘܬܐ ܕܝܢ ܕܐܪܥܐ ܡܢ ܗܕܐ ܠܝܬ ܐܕܡܬܗ، ܕܐܝܟ ܕܠܐ ܡܠܬܐ ܢܬܠܕ. ܐܢ ܕܝܢ ܒܗ ܗܘ ܒܡܠܬܐ ܢܬܒܪܝ ܫܡ ܡܢ ܟܠ ܒܪ̈ܝܢ. ܕܒ ܗܘ ܫܘܦܪܗ ܡܢ ܒܥܠ ܫܘܦܪܝܗ. ܗܘ ܡܒܠ ܕܒܐܝܕܗ ܐܬܡܠܠܬ ܒܠܗ ܗܕܐ ܫܘܦܪܘܬܐ. ܐܚܝܕ ܕܒܐܝܕܗ ܗܘ ܡܒܥܐ ܒܠܗ ܡܠܠܘܬܐ. ܡܛܠ ܕܝܢ ܕܒܐܝܕܗ ܗܘ ܡܫܠܡ ܗܕ̈ܡܐ ܒܒܪ̈ܝܬܐ ܟܠ ܡܘܠ ܒܫܐܝܬ. ܐܬܡܠܝܬ ܒܐܝܕܗ ܚܣܝܪܘܬܗܘܢ ܠܟܠܝܬܐ. ܕܐܝܟ ܕܒܐܝܕܗ ܒܪܝܬ ܐܬܕܒܪ ܒܠܗ ܠܫܘܒܚܐ. Here, Ephrem sees language as an essential part of humanity. Language distinguishes human beings from the rest of God's creation. In the same way that God created Adam and bestowed on him language (i.e. He made him a rational human being), likewise Jesus gave the dumb the ability to speak and to glorify Him. This text touches on a major issue in Greek philosophy regarding man and animals, discussed at

☞

a material, shows that the fulfillment of what was lacking in human nature was achieved with what the Lord separated from Himself.[653] In Haer 20.4, it is said that Jesus healed the human body and restored it back to its original nature.[654]

In the Commentary on Diatessaron, where Ephrem deals with the man born blind, he uses the term 'fashioning' (ܓܒܝܠܬܐ) instead of 'nature' (ܟܝܢܐ) and says that the Lord 'brought to fullness what was lacking in the fashioning' ( ܘܡܠܝ ܚܣܝܪܘܬܗ ܕܓܒܝܠܬܐ). Here, however, even though the term ܓܒܝܠܬܐ might refer only to the man born blind as the 'fashioning' of a single person, it in fact refers to the whole of humanity, for the blind person symbolises the first Adam.[655] Nevertheless, Jesus' healing ability symbolises that He is the Son of the Creator, for

length by R. Sorabji, *Animal Minds and Human Morals: The Origins of the Western Debate* (London 1993).

653 Dom 11: ܪܩ ܠܗ ܒܝܬ ܨܒ̈ܥܬܗ ܘܣܡ ܒܐܕܢ̈ܘܗܝ ܕܚܪܫܐ ܗ̇ܘ. ܘܓܒܠ ܛܝܢܐ ܡܢ ܪܘܩܗ ܘܛܫ ܥܠ ܥܝ̈ܢܘܗܝ ܕܣܡܝܐ ܗ̇ܘ. ܕܢܐܠܦ ܕܐܝܟܢܐ ܕܚܣܝܪܘܬܐ ܐܝܬ ܗܘܐ ܒܒܒ̈ܬܗ ܕܣܡܝܐ ܗܘ ܕܡܢ ܟܪܣ ܐܡܗ. ܗܟܢܐ ܐܝܬ ܗܘܬ ܚܣܝܪܘܬܐ ܒܐܕܢ̈ܘܗܝ ܕܗܢܐ. ܒܚܣܝܪܐ ܗܟܝܠ ܕܡܢ ܦܓܪܗ ܕܡܫܡܠܝܢܐ. ܐܬܡܠܝܬ ܚܣܝܪܘܬܐ ܕܓܒܝܠܬܗ. ܠܐ ܓܝܪ ܙܕܩܐ ܗܘܬ ܕܢܣܒ ܡܢ ܦܓܪܗ ܠܫܘܡܠܝ ܗܘܐ ܡܢܗ ܘܡܟܠܐ ܚܣܝܪܘܬܐ ܕܦܓܪܐ ܚܝ̈ܐ. ܐܠܐ ܒܡܕܡ ܕܡܚܝܐ ܗܘܐ ܕܢܬܡܠܐ ܡܢܗ ܟܠ ܚܣܝܪܘܬܐ ܕܚܣܝܪܐ. Cf. Nis 34.10.

654 Haer 20.4:

ܘܐܝܟ ܕܐܣܝ ܦܓܪܐ ܘܠܟܝܢܗ ܦܢܝܗ ܥܘܦܪܐ ܡܕܡܟܐ ܬܟܝܢ ܩܕܡ
ܠܗ ܘܬܩܢܗ

ܘܐܦ ܠܗ̇ ܠܢܦܫܐ ܫܘܠܡܢܐ ܦܢܐ ܠܗ̇ ܕܐܘܒܕܬ ܗܘܐ ܗܕܡܝܢ ܦܓܪܐ
ܘܐܘ ܦܘܪܢܐ ܚܠܦ ܗܘܐ ܘܐܣܝܗ̇

ܐܝܟ ܐܣܝܐ ܕܚܠܦ ܡܟܬ̈ܫܢܐ ܠܐ ܕܝܢ ܠܡܟܬ̈ܫܝܢ ܡܟܬ̈ܫܢܘܗܝ
ܠܪܢܝܬܐ ܐܣܝܐ ܒܟܠ ܦܘܪ̈ܣܝܢ ܒܐܣܝܐ ܘܐܠܗܐ ܚܝܠܐ ܒܟܠ ܟܠܠ.

655 CDiat 16.28: ܗܟܢܐ ܘܐܦ ܗܪܟܐ ܓܒܠ ܛܝܢܐ ܡܢ ܪܘܩܗ. ܘܡܠܝ ܚܣܝܪܘܬܗ̇ ܕܓܒܝܠܬܐ. ܗ̇ܝ ܕܡܢ ܒܪܝܫܝܬ. ܕܢܘܕܥ ܕܗ̇ܘ ܕܒܐܝܕܗ ܐܬܡܠܝܬ ܚܣܝܪܘܬܗ ܕܟܝܢܐ. ܒܐܝܕܗ ܗܘ ܐܬܬܣܝܡܬ ܓܒܝܠܬܐ ܕܡܢ ܒܪܝܫܝܬ. ܘܕܠܐ ܢܒܗ ܕܢܬܗܡܟܘܢ ܕܩܕܡ ܐܒܪܗܡ ܐܝܬܘܗܝ، ܗܘܐ ܐܦܝܣ ܐܢܘܢ ܒܒܪܐ ܕܒܪܗ ܗܘ ܕܒܐܝܕܗ ܠܟܠܗ ܡܢ ܐܒܪܐ ܠܐܕܡ ܡܕܡܟܐ. ܕܗܢܐ ܚܣܝܪܘܬܗ ܟܕ ܦܓܪܐ ܟܠ ܗܘܐ

healing is something divine,[656] and it can be called a 'second creation'.[657] As God created the world, Jesus fulfilled it by His healing.

Thus, as when He gave sight to the man born blind, some of Jesus' healing miracles reflect the healing of the whole of humanity. Jesus' healing is considered to be a part of God's creation. Just as Jesus granted total and perfect healing to some specific individuals (ܚܘܠܡܢܐ ܓܡܝܪܐ),[658] so too He healed humanity from its fallen state.[659]

Nat 3 is a hymn of praise and thanksgiving for the incarnation. It glorifies the Newborn One Who fulfilled our need and tended to our sickness. Particularly, Nat 3.1 sees the healing of humanity in the light of the incarnation: 'His mercy inclined Him to visit our sickness', and 'He fulfilled our need'.[660] Man's sickness is the reason why the Lord descended and became a man. God's mercy (ܪ̈ܚܡܐ) caused Him to come and visit our sickness. According to the divine providence, God sent His Son into the

---

[656] CDiat 16.31: ܠܚܘܠܡܢ̈ܐ ܐܝܟ ܟܝ ܒܒܢ̈ܬ ܡܠܘܗܝ ܕܐܠܗܘܬܐ ܡܫܬ̈ܘܬܐ ܡܬܚ̈ܫܒܬܐ. ܘܐܪܝܟ ܗܘܐ ܒܒܪܐ ܐܣܝܘܬܗ ܐܘܪܐ ܕܒܪܗ ܗܘ ܕܒܒܪܐ. ܕܚܝ ܠܗ ܠܐ ܐܫܟܚ ܐܦ̈ܝܢ ܐܝܟ ܕܢܣܒܪ ܐܝܟ ܕܠܐܡܒܪܘܬܐ ܗܘ ܦܪܘܫܐ ܗܕܐ ܐܣܝܘܬܐ. ܬܒܥ ܡܢ ܕܠܫܠܡܐ ܚܕܪܗ ܟܝܢ ܕܐܢܫܐ.

[657] Haer 43.9: ܕܐܦ ܐܣܝܘܬܐ ܒܒܪܝܬܐ ܕܬܪܬܝܢ ܐܬܝܗ̇.

[658] For example see the healing of the paralytic in CDiat 13.2 (Jn 5:1-18).

[659] Healing is considered to be a general good deed of the Father who 'continues' His creation through His Son Jesus. Nothing could stop the process of healing, nor could the Sabbath forbid Jesus to heal, just as it does not forbid people from breathing or bearing children (CDiat 13.4). Jesus showed through His healing that He is the Lord of the Law (CDiat 13.6: ܘܐܦ ܕܢܝܚܐ ܒܐܣܝܘܬܗ ܕܡܪܐ ܢܡܘܣܐ ܗܘ). See also the Healing of the Man Born Blind, CDiat 16.28-32 (Jn 9:1-41); and cf. the Blind and Dumb Demoniac, CDiat 10.7.

[660] Nat 3.1: ܒܪܝܟ ܗܘ ܠܟܐ ܕܐܬܐ ܥܠ ܐܬܪܗ ܠܡܣܥܪܗ ܟܘܪܗܢܢ ܘܡܠܐ ܣܘܢܩܢܢ ܒܪܝܟ ܕܐܪܟܢܘܗܝ ܪ̈ܚܡܘܗܝ ܕܢܣܥܘܪ ܟܘܪܗܢܢ. It seems that the phrase 'He fulfilled our need' (ܡܠܐ ܣܘܢܩܢܢ) is related to the healing of the deficiencies of human nature (cf. Dom 11-12; CDiat 10.7; 16.28-32).

world to become the 'Fountain of Medicine of Life' ( ܡܒܘܥܐ ܕܣܡ ܚܝܐ).[661] Nat 3.18-19 gives some details of how the Medicine of Life affected mankind. The author refers to some essential aspects of Jesus' ministry and mentions the defeat of man's enemy:

Nat 3.18

ܢܘܕܐ ܠܗ̇ܘ ܕܡܚܐ ܘܐܚܝܢ ܒܡܚܘܬܗ
ܢܘܕܐ ܠܗ̇ܘ ܕܢܣܒ ܠܠܘܛܬܐ ܒܝܕ ܟܘ̈ܒܘܗܝ
ܢܘܕܐ ܠܗ̇ܘ ܕܐܡܝܬ ܠܡܘܬܐ ܒܡܡܝܬܘܬܗ
ܢܘܕܐ ܠܗ̇ܘ ܕܫܬܩ ܘܙܟܢ
ܢܘܕܐ ܠܗ̇ܘ ܕܩܥܐ ܒܡܘܬܐ ܕܒܠܥܢ ܗܘܐ
ܒܪܝܟ ܗ̇ܘ ܕܡܥܕܪ̈ܢܘܗܝ ܣܪܩܘܗ̇ ܠܣܡܠܐ.

Let us thank Him Who was beaten and Who saved us
by His wound.
Let us thank Him Who took away the curse by His
thorns.
Let us thank Him Who killed death by His dying.
Let us thank Him Who was silent and vindicated us
(Mt 27:14). Let us
thank Him Who cried out in death that had devoured
us (Mt 27:50).
Blessed is He Whose benefits have laid waste the left
[enemies of God].

3.19

ܢܫܒܚ ܠܗ̇ܘ ܕܫܗܪ ܘܕܡܟܗ ܠܫܒܝܢ
ܢܫܒܚ ܠܗ̇ܘ ܕܕܡܟ ܘܐܥܝܪܗ ܠܡܕܡܟܢ
ܫܘܒܚܐ ܠܐܠܗܐ ܐܣܝܗ̇ ܕܐܢܫܘܬܐ
ܫܘܒܚܐ ܠܗ̇ܘ ܕܥܡܕ ܘܛܒܥܗ
ܠܛܘܠ ܥܡܗ ܒܡܥܡܩܐ ܘܚܢܩܗ ܠܚܢܘܩܢ
ܢܫܒܚ ܟܠ ܦܘܡ̈ܝܢ ܠܡܪܐ ܕܟܠ ܦܘܪ̈ܩܢ.

Let us glorify Him Who watched and put to sleep our
captor.
Let us glorify the One Who went to sleep and awoke
our slumber.
Glory to God the Healer of humanity.
Glory to the One Who plunged/was baptised in and
sank

---

661 Nat 3.15: ܒܪܝܟ ܙܪܥܐ ܕܗܘܐ ܐܡܪܐ ܠܫܘܩܢ ܒܪܝܟ ܢܘܗܪܐ ܕܗܘܐ ܒܗܡܐ ܕܦܘܪܩܢ ܒܪܝܟ ܐܦ ܛܠܝܘܬܐ ܡܒܘܥܐ ܕܣܡ ܚܝܐ.

our evil into the depth and drowned our drowner. Let us
glorify with all our mouths the Lord of all means [of salvation].

3.20

ܒܪܝܟ ܐܣܝܐ ܕܢܚܬ ܘܓܙܪ ܕܠܐ ܚܫܐ
ܘܐܣܝ ܚܒܘܪܬܐ ܒܣܡܐ ܕܠܐ ܚܪܝܦ
ܝܠܕܗ ܗܘܐ ܣܡܐ ܕܚܐܣ ܠܚܛܝܐ
ܒܪܝܟ ܗܘ ܕܫܪܐ ܒܡܪܒܥܐ ܘܒܗ ܒܢܐ
ܗܝܟܠܐ ܕܢܥܡܪ ܒܗ ܢܘܣܐ ܕܢܗܘܐ ܒܗ
ܠܒܘܫܐ ܕܢܦܪܘܓ ܒܗ ܘܙܝܢܐ ܕܢܙܟܐ ܒܗ.

Blessed is the Physician Who descended and cut painlessly[662]
and healed the sores with a mild medicine.
His nativity was the medicine that takes pity on sinners.
Blessed is the One Who dwelt in the womb, and in it He built
a palace in which to live, a temple in which to be,
a garment in which to be radiant, and armour by which to conquer.

The first person plural includes everyone, all human beings. While stanza 19 glorifies God as the 'Healer of humanity' ( ܫܘܒܚܐ ܐܠܗܐ ܐܣܝܗ̇ ܕܐܢܫܘܬܐ), stanza 20 blessed Jesus as the Physician Who descended and healed our sores with His medicine, and He became Medicine for sinners. The 'curse' (ܠܘܛܬܐ) 'death' (ܡܘܬܐ), 'our captor' (ܫܒܝܢ), 'our slumber' (ܢܘܡܢ), 'our drowner' (ܛܒܘܥܢ) as well as 'our iniquity' (ܥܘܠܢ) have been taken away; all of these were a part of man's fallen state.

Hymn 19 On Faith deals with Jesus' incarnation. The divine nature is invisible and cannot be touched by human beings. However, the Hidden One revealed Himself in the clothing of human nature. He was revealed in robe and body, and is revealed in the Eucharistic bread. Ephrem describes the clothing of divinity in human nature (and in the Eucharistic bread) as the protection of mankind coming from the true strength of divinity, and so he emphasises the weakness of human nature, in which the Logos was

---

662 Cf. Nis 26.3-7; 27.1; 34; also see Murray, *Symbols of Church and Kingdom*, *Symbols*, 89-91; 199-204.

clothed. Although human nature is weak, the Son of God clothed Himself with it and suffered. With His suffering Jesus gave Himself as Medicine for human beings.[663] The Lord's medicines have a single power, but because of His love it has spread out into many for the sick and needy.[664]

Hymn 37 On Virginity describes Jesus as the Physician Who healed 'our sickness' (ܟܘܪܗܢ) with the medicines of wheat, olive and grapes:

ܚܛܬܐ ܘܙܝܬܐ ܘܥܢܒܐ ܕܐܬܒܪܝ ܠܚܘܫܚܢ
ܬܠܬܝܗܝܢ ܒܪܐܙܐ ܫܡܫܝܢ ܬܠܬܐܝܬ
ܒܣܡܡܢܐ ܬܠܬܐ ܚܠܡܬܝܗ̇ ܠܟܘܪܗܢ
ܡܚܠܬ ܚܫܬ ܗܘܬ ܐܢܫܘܬܐ ܘܐܫܦܬ
ܚܝܠܬܗ̇ ܒܠܚܡܟ ܡܒܪܟܐ
ܘܒܝܐܬܗ̇ ܒܚܡܪܟ ܡܢܟܦܐ
ܘܐܦܨܚܬܗ̇ ܒܡܫܚܟ ܡܩܕܫܐ.

Wheat, the olive and grapes, created for our use –
the three of them serve You symbolically in three ways.
With three medicines You healed our sickness.
Humankind had become weak and suffering and was
failing.
You strengthened it with Your blessed bread,
and You consoled it with Your sober wine,
and You made it joyful with Your sanctified oil.

*Virg 37.3*

Furthermore, Jesus healed humanity spiritually from its enemy, the Evil One, Death, Sin, etc. As Jesus defeated man's enemy, He also healed mankind from its wound. Since through

---

[663] Fid 19.10:
ܦܫܝܐ ܗܘ ܒܪ ܗܘܐ ܕܡܚܝܠܐ ܡܕܡ ܠܦܓܪܗ ܕܦܫܐ ܡܠܒܫ ܠܗ
ܐܠܐ ܚܫܐ
ܐܝܟ ܐܠܗܘܬܗ ܒܪ ܠܚܫܝܢ ܦܓܪܐ ܒܪܗܐ ܕܬܫܒܘܚ ܬܘܒ ܒܗ.

[664] Fid 19.11-12:
ܣܡܡܢܐ ܦܫܝܛܐ ܪܒܘ ܡܢܝܢ ܠܣܡܝܢܐ ܒܗ ܟܠܗܘܢ ܚܕ ܗܘ ܚܝܠܐ ܕܠܐ
ܡܬܦܠܓ
ܗܘ ܠܟܪܝܗܐ ܦܫܛ ܠܣܡܝܢܐ ܡܢ ܗܘܐ ܚܕ ܡܫܬܘܐ ܠܟܪܝܗܐ.
ܬܠܬܐ ܒܢܝ ܚܘܒܝ ܠܣܡܝܡܘܬܗ ܕܚܕ ܚܕ ܦܠܘܣܐ ܬܘܒ ܡܢ
ܡܬܗܘܝܢ
ܒܦܘܪܫܐ ܕܠܟܠ ܠܒܠܗ ܒܪ ܠܣܡܝܡܘܬܗ ܕܬܒܘܥ ܚܕ ܚܕ ܠܟܝ.

healing Sin was dead, so too Jesus' healing power killed 'our enemy' (ܠܒܥܠ ܕܒܒܢ).[665] By His fasting, Jesus defeated Satan and destroyed the 'gluttony' (ܐܣܘܛܘܬܐ)[666] and 'deceit' (ܙܐܦܐ)[667] that the Evil One put into human life.

Jesus' humanity was helpful for humans, but not for the Evil One. When the Evil One saw Jesus in a 'weak body' ( ܦܓܪܐ ܡܚܝܠܐ) and in 'sick nature' (ܟܝܢܐ ܟܪܝܗܐ), he erred, was disgraced and defeated for he treated Jesus just like the first Adam.[668]

The visible healing of sick bodies indicates Jesus' capability of healing spiritually and forgiving sins. Ephrem links the healing of the limbs with the forgiveness of sins in order to demonstrate the divinity of the Son.[669] As an example, Ephrem mentions the healing of the paralytic (Mt 9:1-8). Spiritual healing can only be

---

665 Nat 18.27:
ܒܥܢܬܐ ܕܒܣ̈ܡܝܢ ܘܬܐܪ̈ܝܢ ܢܘܕܐ ܙܠܝܐ ܘܣܘܣܝܐ [ܕ]ܠܐ ܣܓܝܘ ܩܛܠܘܗܝ ܠܒܥܠ ܕܒܒܢ
ܐܝܬ ܗ̣ܘ ܩܛܠܬܝܗ̇ ܘܐܝܬ ܗ̣ܘ ܡܚܝܬܗ ܠܐܕܢܐ ܕܒܣܡܗ̇ ܣܡܘܗ ܕܢܚܡܘܢ ܒܢܝ ܚܘܠܡܢܝ.

666 Virg 14.11:
ܒܐܪܐ ܕܒܢܝ ܓܕܐ ܠܣܡܐ ܗܘ ܕܓܒܠܐ ܙܐܪ ܒܚܢܘܬܐ ܕܠܘܬ ܐܕܡ
ܒܠܣܡܐ ܗܘ ܢܣܒܗ ܠܗ̇ܘ ܙܐܪ̈ܐ ܒܠ ܕܐܡܪ ܒܝܘܡܗ ܠܐܣܘܛܘܬܐ
----ܣܛܢܐ ---- ܬܠܡ̈ܝܕܘܗܝ ---- ܚܘܬܐ ܣܚܝܢܝ ܗܘܐ
ܬܢܢܐ ܒܣܛܢܐ ܚܝܠܗ ܗܘܐ ܕܠܐ ܢܓܒܐ ܕܢܥܬܝܚܘܢ ܒܐܦ̈ܐ.

667 Fid 38.7:
ܘܠܐ ܠܒܢܝ̈ܢܫܐ ܢܣܒܐ ܡܢܝ ܕܠܚܫ ܒܝܢܬܐ ܣܝܡܬ ܐܦ ܐܢܬ
ܙܐܦܐ ܕܐܝܬܘܗܝ ܒܐܒܐ ܒܝܫܐ ܒܚܠܬ ܘܡܢܬܐ ܒܙܪܬ ܢܥܝܬܘܗܝ
ܕܠܡܘܬ ܬܝܒܐ.

Cf. Fid 50.7; Haer 42.1.

668 Virg 14.13:
ܡܥܬܗ ܓܠܐ ܘܡܡܢ ܗ̇ܘ ܡܪܢܢܐ ܠܗܘܠ ܡܪܢ ܗ̇ܘ ܒܣܝܡܬܐ
ܛܒܐ ܒܗ ܘܐܬܓܠܝ ܕܚܝܘܗܝ ܕܠܒܫ ܦܓܪܐ ܡܚܝܠܐ ܟܝܢܐ ܟܪܝܗܐ
ܚܙܝܗܝ ܒܝܫܐ ܠܗ ܠܡܠܟܐ ܘܐܬܬܟܠ ܕܡܠܟܐ ܗܘܐ ܗ̇ܘ ܕܗ̇ܘ ܐܕܡ ܕܐܙܕܒܢ
ܙܟܐ ܗ̇ܝ ܒܗܬܬܗ ܕܒܝܫܐ ܕܒܗ ܙܟܐ ܚܒܠ ܚܬܝܬܗ.

669 Dom 21: ܡܢ ܕܝܢ ܐܝܬ ܗܘ ܕܝܢܐ ܕܚܛܗܝܢ. ܕܬܒܪ ܗ̇ܘ ܕܒܣܝܡ ܚܛ̈ܗܐ ܕܠܐ ܡܬܚܙܝܢ.

achieved when sin is forgiven. Therefore, with the spiritual healing 'deadly sin had been put to death'.[670]

The Lord, as the sun, dispelled the frost of hidden death from souls.[671] The dead son of the widow represents the dead world. By His mercy, the Lord healed the world as He healed the widow's son who was dead (Lk 7:11-17). His resurrection is reminiscent of the salvation of the creation:[672] Jesus came to die so that through His own death He would give life to Adam's children.[673] Jesus took

---

[670] Dom 21: ܕܢܘܕܥ ܐܢܘܢ ܗܟܝܠ ܡܪܢ ܕܫܒܩ ܚܛܗ̈ܐ ܗܘ. ܥܒܕ ܠܗ ܠܗܘ ܚܠܝܡܘܬܗ ܕܡܫܡܫܢܐ. ܘܐܚܠܡܗ ܒܪܘܚܗ ܒܚܠܝܡܐ ܕܒܪܢܫܐ ܠܚܘܠܡܢܐ ܕܐܬܚܠܡܬ. ܢܓܪܘܢ ܕܚܠܝܡܘܬܐ ܡܫܠܡܬܐ ܐܬܚܠܡܬ. Further, Ephrem says: 'Nor could it be proved that he had not forgiven sins, because he had (in fact) restored limbs. So our Lord linked hidden testimony to visible testimony, so that the infidels would choke on their own argument against them, because they did battle against the good one, who battled against their sickness with his cures'. Dom 21: ܠܐ ܕܝܢ ܡܬܕܟܝܐ ܗܘܬ ܕܠܐ ܫܒܩ ܚܛܗ̈ܐ. ܡܛܠ ܕܗܘܐ ܐܣܝ ܗܕ̈ܡܐ. ܐܘܦ ܚܒܪ ܡܪܢ ܠܣܗܕܘܬܗ ܟܣܝܬܐ ܒܓܠܝܬܐ. ܐܝܟ ܕܬܬܚܢܩܘܢ ܐܢܘܢ ܠܚܘܪܐ ܣܗܕܘܬܐ ܕܟܣܝܢ. ܠܚܘܫܒܢܝܗܘܢ ܗܟܝܠ ܚܒܪ ܡܪܢ ܕܢܦܪܥܘܢ ܠܡܚܠܗܘܢ. ܥܠ ܕܐܦܪܥܘ ܥܡ ܛܒܐ ܗܘ ܕܐܦܪܥ ܒܚܘܠܫܢܘܗܝ ܠܡܚܠ ܒܐܣܘ̈ܬܗ.

[671] Virg 26.6:

ܠܡܟܝܢ ܐܬܬܐ ܕܪܕܝܐ ܕܫܡܝܐ ܦܩܕ ܒܗ ܘܐܣܝ ܪ̈ܕܝܐ ܕܕܡܒܪ
ܥܡܝܩܐ ܗܘ ܕܡܐ ܥܒܪܐ ܡܪܝܘܬܗ ܕܡܠܟܘܬܐ ܒܫܡܝܐ ܡܢ ܢܦܩ̈ܬܐ
ܕܢܠܝܦܗ ܡܠܬܗ ܒܫܡܝܐ ܘܡܚܝܗ ܠܗܘ ܪܘܟܒܐ ܪܒܝܐ ܕܡܚܝܢܐ ܬܪܝܨܬܐ
ܒܪܗ ܝܚܝܕܝ ܠܡܚܝܘܗܝ ܫܘܠܛܢ ܡܟܝܟܘܬܗܝ ܕܡܚܝܐ ܕܟܘܪ̈ܗܐ.

[672] Virg 26.10:

ܠܡܟܝܢ ܐܦ ܠܟܝ ܐܘ ܐܪܡܠܬܐ ܕܓܠܝܬܐ ܡܝܬܬ ܘܟܪܝܬ ܡܝܬܬܐ
ܒܪܟܝ ܕܝܢ ܗܘܐ ܚܝܐ ܕܠܐ ܡܬܡܥܬܐ ܘܕܠܐ ܡܬܝܠܕܬ ܒܪܬܐ ܦܪܘܩܐ
ܠܐ ܒܡܘܬܟܝ ܡܪܬܗ ܗܘܬ ܠܐܘܠܨܢܐ ܘܐܦ ܠܐ ܝܠܕܬܟ ܐܪܒܥܬܗ ܠܦܪܩ
ܫܘܒܚܐ ܗܘ ܐܪܒܥܬܗܝ ܠܗܘ ܕܢܚܬ ܘܐܚܝܗ ܠܡܠܟܐ ܘܠܡܠܟܬܐ.

[673] Azym 14.1: ܫܘܒܚܐ ܠܡܫܝܚܐ ܕܐܬܐ ܠܡܘܬܐ ܕܒܡܘܬܗ ܢܚܐ ܠܒܢܘ̈ܗܝ ܕܐܕܡ.

body from the virgin Mary to be able to descend to Sheol.[674] He put on a body and was offered to both Adam and death: while Adam tasted Him and revived, 'the devourer ate Him and was destroyed'.[675] Through the human body Jesus fought against death; He was killed physically, but killed death in a supernatural way.[676]

The fixed serpent in the Israelite camp in the desert symbolises Jesus on the cross Who healed the wound of the first Serpent that wounded Adam. Jesus' suffering healed Adam's wound that was caused by the Serpent.[677] As the People who looked at the fixed serpent in the desert were healed, so too everyone who faithfully looks at Jesus on the cross can be healed.[678] Nat 1.28 is about the typology of the serpent at the time

---

[674] Dom 3: ܐܬܐ ܠܘܬ ܒܬܘܠܬܐ ܕܡܢ ܬܡܢ ܪܟܘܒܐ ܠܫܝܘܠ ܢܚܬ ܠܗ.

[675] Nat 26.9:
ܘܗܟܢܐ ܫܬܝܬܐ ܢܟܒܫ ܠܗܘ ܕܒܪܐ ܒܚܪܘܒܬܐ ܠܐܕܡ ܕܒܠܥܐ ܣܡܡ ܗܘܐ ܒܗ

ܐܝܟ ܪܚܡܐ ܢܛܠ ܐܦܝܣ ܘܐܘܫܛ ܠܗ ܣܡܐ ܒܡܐܟܘܠܬܐ
ܗܘ ܚܝܐ ܐܬܦܝܣ ܠܬܪܝܗܘܢ ܠܒܫ ܦܓܪܐ ܘܐܬܩܪܒ ܠܬܪܝܗܘܢ
ܡܝܬܘܬܐ ܛܥܡܗ ܘܚܝܐ ܒܗ ܟܠܒܐ ܕܐܟܠܗ ܐܬܚܒܠ.

[676] Dom 3: ܐܬܩܛܠܬ ܕܝܢ ܐܠܗܘܬܐ ܒܐܢܫܘܬܐ ܘܩܛܠܬ ܒܐܝܕܘܗܝ، ܩܛܠ ܘܐܬܩܛܠ ܩܛܠ ܡܘܬܐ ܚܝܘܬܐ ܕܟܝܢܐ. ܘܩܛܠܗ ܠܗ ܚܝܘܬܐ ܕܠܒܪ ܡܢ ܟܝܢܐ.

[677] CDiat 16.15: ܡܚܝܐ ܚܘܝܐ ܠܐܕܡ ܒܦܪܕܝܣܐ ܘܩܛܠܗ. ܘܠܐܝܣܪܐܝܠ ܒܡܕܒܪܐ ܘܚܪܒ ܐܢܘܢ. ܘܐܡܬܠܐ ܠܗ ܕܐܪܝܡ ܡܘܫܐ ܚܘܝܐ ܒܡܕܒܪܐ. ܢܬܬܐܣܘܢ ܒܗ ܕܐܝܠܢܐ. ܐܡܬܠܐ ܒܪ ܕܗܘܐ ܢܟܬܐ ܕܡܚܒ ܡܘܫܐ ܚܝܘܬܐ ܗܘ ܦܓܪܢܐܝܬ ܗܘ ܕܦܓܪܢܐܝܬ ܚܝܝܢ ܗܘܘ ܒܗ. ܗܟܢܐ ܒܡܚܙܝܐ ܕܦܓܪܐ ܕܡܫܝܚܐ ܕܐܬܬܠܝ ܒܙܩܝܦܐ ܚܝܝܢ ܐܢܫܐ ܕܪܘܚܢܐܝܬ ܚܝܝܢ ܘܡܬܚܠܡܝܢ ܒܗ. ܐܬܚܒܠ ܒܗ ܕܝܢ ܒܚܘܝܐ ܗܘ ܕܠܐ ܚܛܐ ܒܚܝܘܗܝ. ܕܢܚܐ ܠܗ ܒܡܠܝܘܬܐ ܗܘ ܕܠܐ ܡܐܬ ܒܚܝܘܗܝ.

[678] Fid 9.11:
ܚܘ̈ܬܐ ܠܥܡܐ ܢܟܬܘ ܗܘܘ ܒܚܘܪܒܐ ܡܚܕܐ ܚܘܝܐ ܐܣܝܐ ܕܚܘܪܘ ܒܗ ܘܚܝܘ

ܠܥܡܐ ܐܚܝܬ ܚܝܘܬܐ ܡܣܬܟܠܢܘܬܐ ܠܥܡ̈ܡܐ ܗܐ ܪܐܙܗ ܕܡܕܒܪܐ ܠܐ ܗܘܐ ܒܝܬܗ ܐܣܝܬ

ܚܬܗ ܒܠܒܗ ܐܣܝܬ ܒܡܣܬܟܠܢܘܬܐ ܚܘܪ ܒܗ ܒܡܕܒܪܐ ܪܙܐ ܕܚܝ̈ܝ (ܕܚܝܝ).

☞

of Moses, related to Paradise and Jesus as the Healer of the Serpent's wound: 'Moses saw the fixed serpent that healed the stings of basilisks, and he anticipated that he would see the Healer of the first Serpent's wound.'[679] This indicates the healing capability of the Son of God. He alone could heal humanity's wound that was caused by the Serpent. The Son of God suffered and took the pain of the world on Himself.[680]

The fig tree (ܬܬܐ) illustrates the healing of Adam and all mankind. Commenting extensively on the fig tree, Ephrem asks for the reason why our Lord caused the fig tree to dry out. Although it seems that the drying out of the fig tree contrasts with Jesus' good deeds and healing, Ephrem sees the healing of Adam and humanity in it. The fig tree was dried out 'because the time of His suffering was near'.[681] In Parad 12.13-14, Ephrem explicitly says that Jesus did everything, including the drying out of the fig tree, to help mankind.[682] Jesus suffered for Adam to restore and heal him. The fig tree symbolises Adam's nakedness and his need of the fig tree's leaves to cover his nakedness with them. Jesus dried it out to show

Cf. Haer 21.8-9; Jul Saba 20.18.

679 Nat 1.28: ܚܙܐ ܡܘܫܐ ܚܘܝܐ ܩܒܝܥܐ ܕܐܣܐ ܢܘܟ̈ܬܬ ܚܪ̈ܡܢܐ ܘܣܟܝ ܕܢܚܙܐ ܠܗܘ ܕܐܣܐ ܡܚܘܬܗ ܕܚܘܝܐ ܩܕܡܝܐ.

680 Sog 1.29:
ܛܠܝܗ̇ ܕܐܪܥܐ ܗܘܐ ܒܘܪܗܢܐ ܘܟܐܒ̈ܐ ܠܟܠܗܝܢ ܘܫܩܠܬ ܠܗ̇ ܟܐܒܐ ܠܡܘܬܐ ܘܟܠ ܕܢܫܗ̇
ܘܛܠܝܗ̇ ܕܡܪܝܡ ܒܡܘܟܟܗ ܦܓܥ ܒܐܒܝ̈ܢܗ̇ ܕܒܪܝܬܐ ܘܐܣܝܗ̇.

681 CDiat 16.8: ܣܢ̈ܐ ܟܢ ܕܟܠ ܐܝܟ ܐܡܪ ܗܘܐ. ܘܡܢ̈ܝܢܐ ܥܒܕܗ ܠܡܢܪܐ. ܘܡܢ ܠܡܬܐ ܠܒܘܪܐ ܟܕ ܡܥܝܢܐ. ܘܡܫ̈ܟܢܐ ܦܬܚ. ܘܠܐܪ̈ܙܐ ܕܟܪ. ܘܡܫ̈ܬܬܐ ܐܣܝ. ܘܟܠܝܢܕ ܬܬܐ ܗܘ ܐܬܒܝ ܕܐܘܒܫ. ܐܠܐ ܕܢܘܪ ܗܘܐ ܠܗ ܘܟܢܐ ܕܐܣܝܗ. See also Azym 15.22: ܬܬܐ ܕܐܣܬܗ ܡܥܫܬ ܟܡ ܥܠ. This interpretation of the figleaves is shared (surely independently) by St Cyril of Jerusalem. See, R. Murray, *Symbols of Church and Kingdom*, 256.

682 Parad 12.13:
ܘܠܬܬܐ ܟܢܥܐ ܐܘܒܫܗ̇ ܗܘܐ ܕܡ ܛܠ̈ܠܬܐ ܟܠܗܘܢ ܠܡܥܕܪܢܐ ܕܦܬܚ ܒܗܘܢ ܬܪ̈ܥܐ ܚܪ̈ܢܐ ܕܡܘܫܪܘܢܗ.
Parad 12.14: ܘܠܐ ܡܫܟܐܬܐ ܗܝ ܕܐܘܒܫ ܬܬܐ ܟܠܬܛܐ ܕܒܥܠܡܝܢ ܠܟܐ ܗܘ.

that He came to heal Adam, and so he does not need the fig tree's leaves anymore:

It was also said that, when Adam sinned and was deprived of that glory with which he was clothed, he hid his nakedness with the leaves of the fig tree (cf. Gen 3:7). Our Lord came and endured sufferings for him, to heal the wounds of Adam, and provide a garment of glory for his nakedness.[683]

Ephrem considers the loss of the paradise garment (glory) as a wound which Jesus Christ healed through his suffering. Through our Saviour, Adam was restored to his former glory, and his wound was healed. The leaves of the fig tree are no longer required for Adam is again clothed with the divine garment.

### 5.3.3 The Continuity of the Process of Healing in the Church

As Paul's case showed, the process of healing has not came to an end with Jesus' death, resurrection and ascension into heaven. In turn, it continues through the disciples and their successors to make it relevant for the faithful at any time. Everyone can take part in Jesus' healing process through the Church's sacraments, namely, by the water and oil of baptism and eucharistic bread and wine of the holy ܩܘܪܒܢܐ. Having accepted this, healing can be achieved through faith, as well as prayer, real repentance and fasting.

#### *5.3.3.1 Healing through the Disciples and their Successors*

In SFid 3.153-160, the title 'physicians' (ܐܣܘ̈ܬܐ) is used for the disciples, as it is used for the prophets. They are called 'the physicians of the souls' (ܐܣܘ̈ܬܐ ܕܢܦ̈ܫܬܐ) who provided remedies to heal the pains which they came across.[684] Based on the

683 CDiat 16.10: ܬܘܒ ܡܬܐܡܪܐ ܕܟܕ ܚܛܐ ܠܗ ܐܕܡ. ܘܐܫܬܠܚ ܡܢ ܬܫܒܘܚܬܐ ܗܿܝ ܕܠܒܝܫ ܗܘܐ. ܘܒܛܪ̈ܦܐ ܕܬܬܐ ܦܘܪܣܝܗ ܟܣܐ ܗܘܐ. ܐܬܐ ܡܪܢ ܘܣܝܒܪ ܚܫ̈ܐ ܚܠܦܘܗܝ. ܕܢܐܣܐ ܡܚ̈ܘܬܗ ܕܐܕܡ. ܘܬܬܒܫܬ ܫܘܒܚܐ ܠܦܘܪܣܝܗ ܢܬܠ.

684 S.Fid 3.153-160:

ܐܦ ܫܠܝܚܐ ܘܢܒܝ̈ܐ ܐܣܘ̈ܬܐ ܕܢܦ̈ܫܬܐ
ܐܝܟ ܚܫܐ ܗܘ ܕܐܢܫܘܬܐ ܗܟܢ ܡܙܓܘ ܒܣܕܪ̈ܢܐ
ܐܝܟ ܟܐ̈ܒܐ ܕܒܢܝ̈ܢܫܐ ܗܟܢ ܐܣܝܘ ܡܣܟ̈ܢܐ

☞

Gospel, in the context of the healing of the epileptic demoniac (Mt 17:14-21; Mk 9:14-28; Lk 9:37-43), the disciples have been criticised for not being able to heal a boy possessed by an evil spirit. Jesus, even during His ministry, sent His disciples (Mt 10:1; Mk 6:6-13; Lk 9:1-2) and the seventy-two (Lk 10:1-12) to heal. In CDiat 14.14, Ephrem considers the sending of the seventy-two as a reaction against the people's lack of faith and those who doubted the disciples' healing ability. Jesus sent them and 'they healed miraculously' (ܘܐܣܝܘ ܬܡܝܗܐܝܬ).[685]

In Virg 4.4, Ephrem refers to Mt 10:1 where the disciples are commissioned and authorised to drive out unclean spirits and to cure every kind of sickness and pain. Hymn 4 On Virginity is about oil, olives and the symbols of the Lord. Here Ephrem plays with the terms 'Christ, the Anointed One' (ܡܫܝܚܐ) and 'oil' (ܡܫܚܐ) which serves as a restorative substance. As oil symbolizes the Anointed One Who is the Medicine of Life, so too healing can be provided through oil that is considered as His 'shadow' (ܛܠܠܐ). This is illustrated by the image of a ship on the ocean, which symbolises oil. All the healing power is in the ship. The healing Spirit/wind draws the ship to the harbour of the sick in order to heal them.[686] The disciples are considered to be the 'merchants of all kinds of help' (ܬܓܪ̈ܐ ܕܟܠ ܥܘܕܪ̈ܢܝܢ) who sail on the sea with the 'healing Spirit/wind' (ܪܘܚܐ ܡܐܣܝܢܝܬܐ) to reach the harbour, i.e. the sick bodies to heal sick limbs. Their words, which

---

ܫܒܩܘ ܕܝܢ ܡܫܒܚܢܘܬܗܘܢ ܠܐܣܝܐ ܘܠܡܕܒܪܢܐ.

[685] CDiat 14.14:

ܘܡܛܠ ܗܢܐ ܠܒܢܐ ܫܒܥܝܢ ܘܬܪܝܢ ܡܢ ܥܠ.
ܘܫܕܪ ܐܢܘܢ ܡܢ ܩܕܡܘܗܝ. ܘܐܣܝܘ ܬܡܝܗܐܝܬ. ܕܢܬܒܣܡܘܢ
ܗܢܘܢ ܕܡܦܩܘ ܗܘܐ.(cf. Lk 10:1-12)

[686] Virg 4.4:

ܡܫܝܚܗ ܚܙܐ ܕܣܓܝܬ ܡܢܐ ܘܒܗ ܗܘ ܙܕܩ ܒܥܘܕܪ̈ܢܐ
ܠܡܪ̈ܥܐ ܐܝܟ ܠܠܡܐܢܐ ܠܡܬܠ ܬܓܪ ܚܘܠܡ̈ܢܐ
ܒܗܘܢ ܐܝܠܝܢ ܐܦ ܬܠܡ̈ܝܕܐ ܬܓܪ̈ܐ ܕܟܠ ܥܘܕܪ̈ܢܝܢ
ܕܪܘܚܐ ܡܐܣܝܢܝܬܐ ܦܪܫܘ ܝܡ ܡܪ̈ܥܐ
ܒܗ ܡܫܚܐ ܙܕܝ ܡܠܝܫܘܢ ܐܠܦܐ ܕܡܠܝܢ ܒܥܘܕܪ̈ܢܐ
ܘܟܠܗ ܦܓܡܗ ܚܘܠܡ̈ܢܝܗܘܢ ܒܗ ܦܓܪܐ ܠܟܐܒ ܟܐܒܐ.

are compared to the 'ships full of help' (ܐܠܦ̈ܐ ܕܡܠܝܢ ܥܘܕܪܢܐ), flowed within the oil, - the sea -, and entered the harbour of the sick bodies. The term 'their words' (ܒܡ̈ܠܝܗܘܢ) associates their healing with the preaching of the good news. Those who believed in what they preached were healed spiritually. Here oil symbolises the Anointed One, and it also refers to the anointing at baptism. In Virg 4.7, Ephrem explicitly speaks of oil as the substance for anointing through which the disciples healed: 'and when they [the disciples] anointed and healed by oil (cf. Lk 10:9; Jas 5:14), the Anointed One was portrayed in secret, and He chased away all harms.'[687]

Obviously, the Lord is the main Healer, and not the disciples. They perform healing through His Name, and the Name of the holy Trinity which accompanies the anointing at baptism.[688] Furthermore, the disciples did not only heal when they baptized and preached, but some people were also healed by just being physically close to the disciples. Ephrem demonstrates this on the basis of Acts 5:14-16 where the sick were carried out into the streets and laid there in order to be healed by Peter's shadow when he passed by: 'the shadow of Simon fell upon the sick, and they recovered'.[689] Thus, the disciples were able to heal in the Name of

[687] Virg 4.7:
ܥܡ ܡܫܝܚܐ ܠܒܪ ܐܝܟ ܪܐܘܪܐ ܗܘ ܘܟܕ ܗܘ ܢܦܩ ܫܡܫܐ ܡܫܝܚܐ
ܘܐܬܛܠܠ ܗܘ ܥܡ ܡܫܝܚܐ ܕܛܠܠܐ ܗܘ ܕܫܡܫܐ ܡܫܝܚܐ
ܕܐܦ ܪܘܫܡܗܘܢ ܗܘ ܕܬܠܡ̈ܝܕܐ ܠܘ ܗܘܐ ܠܗܘܢ ܒܪ ܐܫܬܪܪܘ
ܘܡܟܐ ܕܡ̈ܫܝܚܝܢ ܗܘܘ ܘܡܬܐܣܝܢ ܒܗ ܗܘ ܒܡܫܝܚܐ
ܡܬܛܝܪ ܗܘܐ ܡܫܝܚܐ ܒܡܫܚܐ ܘܪܕܦ ܗܘܐ ܟܠ ܢܟ̈ܝܢܝܢ
ܐܝܟ ܕܐܦ ܒܡܠܘܐ ܕܦܠܘܛܐ ܣܝܡܗ ܪܒܐ ܕܕܡܐ ܘܥܒܪ.

[688] Virg 4.14.

[689] Virg 4.8:
ܥܡ ܡܫܝܚܐ ܚܝܠܬ ܐܪܙܗ ܗܘ ܘܛܠܠܗ ܕܫܡܫܐ ܡܫܝܚܐ
ܛܠܠ ܫܡܥܘܢ ܚܝܠܬ ܢܦܠ ܗܘܐ ܥܠ ܕܟܪ̈ܝܗܝܢ ܘܡܬܚܠܡܝܢ ܗܘܘ
ܐܝܟ ܕܢܓܠܐ ܛܠܠܝܬܗ ܕܫܡܥܘܢ ܥܠ ܟܪ̈ܝܗܐ ܘܚܦܝܗ
ܛܠܠ ܫܡܥܘܢ ܐܝܟ ܪܫܘܡܗ ܡܫܒ ܠܥܠܝܫܘܗܝ
ܕܛܠܠܗܘܢ ܚܬܝܪ ܕܐܣܝܐ ܐܠܝܫܥ ܡܚܝܕ [ܗܘܐ] ܠܫܡܥܘܢ
ܥܠ ܛܠܠܐ ܒܪ ܚܝܐ ܠܗ ܫܡܥܘܢ ܕܝܢ ܛܠܠܝܬܗ.

the Lord when they preached the good news, called on the name of the Trinity, and when people believed through them.

Furthermore, this healing capability is not just limited to the disciples, the seventy-two and those who were contemporaries of Jesus, but it is also given to their successors and everyone who truly walks in the steps of Jesus. In Fid 2.15-16, Ephrem refers to those who gained the truth and justice of the Lord, so that they are able to sing songs that can heal the listeners. The words of the one who gained the truth becomes a lyre and sings songs that can heal the minds of weak people.[690]

With regard to individuals, Ephrem refers to the deeds of his bishops who served in Nisibis as spiritual healers. The truth and healing of bishop Abraham was guided by the words of Ez 34, to care and protect the healthy, to visit the sick and to bind up the wounded.[691] Therefore, Ephrem let Nisibis give praise to the Lord for the good deeds of its bishops Jacob, Babu, Vologeses and Abraham who served as medicine for the pains of the city.[692] Without their spiritual deeds, the faithful of Nisibis would suffer enormously under the circumstances of their time. It seems the bishops increased the people's faith, and provided spiritual remedies, restoring them spiritually.[693]

---

690 Fid 2.15-16:

ܛܘܒ ܠܐܢܫܐ ܕܗܘܐ ܠܟ ܡܪܝ، ܠܫܢܗ ܐܝܟ ܩܝܬܪܐ
ܘܙܡܪ ܒܗ ܩܠܐ ܕܟܐܢܘܬܟ ܕܢܐܣܘܢ ܫܡܘܥܘܗ̈ܝ.
ܛܘܒܘܗܝ ܠܐܢܫܐ ܕܩܢܐ ܡܪܝ، ܘܥܢܝܬܐ ܕܫܪܪܟ ܠܟܪ̈ܝܗܐ
ܘܗܘܐ ܫܪܪܗ ܐܝܟ ܩܝܬܪܐ ܠܐܢܫܐ ܕܪܥܝܢܗ ܪܟܝܟ.

Truth contrasts with error; knowing truth and living according to it, is like being spiritually saved and healed from the error that the Evil One caused to exist in the world. See Fid 2.16; Dom 15; Nis 34.10; I Serm 2.189.

691 Nis 19.4:

ܢܦܫܐ ܕܫܠܝܡ̈ܬܐ ܢܛܪ ܘܣܥܪ ܠܐܢܫܐ ܕܟܪܝܗܐ
ܘܚܒܫ ܠܐܢܫܐ ܕܬܒܝܪܐ ܘܦܩܕ ܠܐܢܫܐ ܕܐܟܝܢܐ.

692 Nis 16.21:

ܒܪܝܟ ܗܘ ܕܐܝܟ ܕܒܡܣܐܬܐ ܬܩܠ ܘܝܗܒ ܠܝ ܐܣܘܬܐ
ܕܠܘܩܒܠ ܪ̈ܒܘ ܟܘܪ̈ܗܢܝ ܘܠܘܩܒܠ ܟܐܒ̈ܝ ܣܡܡ̈ܢܝ.

693 In Nis 17.12, Ephrem uses the term ܣܡܡܢܐ in the context of referring to two of the bishops; but here ܣܡ̈ܡܢܐ has the meaning of ☞

In I Serm 6, healing is also attributed to the martyrs and their relics. The martyrs are described as 'physicians' (ܐܣܘ̈ܬܐ) who received healing freely from the Lord and are able to grant it freely to the sick at any time. This healing is spiritual ( ܐܣܝܘܬܐ ܪܘܚܢܝܬܐ), both of the body and soul ( ܐܣܝܘܬܐ ܕܢܦܫܐ ܘܦܓܪܐ).[694] They heal smoothly and do not hurt for their healing is different to that from the ordinary physicians.[695]

Finally, healing might also be attributed to the priesthood. Although it is not explicitly stated that the priests are physicians or healers, their function is compared, for example, to that of Moses who is called a physician. Their ministry can be described as a ministry of spiritual healing, for they provide the eucharistic bread as the Medicine of Life for the faithful, or they purify the soul from sins in baptism.[696] Through the priesthood the faithful can take part in Jesus' healing ministry so that they can be healed totally.

### *5.3.3.2 Healing through the Water and Oil of Baptism*

In several passages, certain aspects of baptism are mentioned in the context of healing. In Epiph 5.6 (Ephrem's authorship is doubtful), it says explicitly that the healing capability of baptism is always present so that the priests can grant it to the needy at any time.[697]

---

'pigments' instead of 'medicines': ܓܪܬ ܓܠܝܐ ܠܬܪܝܨܘܬܗܘܢ ܡܢ ܡܣܡ̈ܢܐ ܕܬܪܝܨܘܬܗܘܢ.

694 I Serm 6.447-52:

ܐܣܘ̈ܬܐ ܐܝܬܝܗܘܢ ܕܡܫܟܚܝܢ ܠܟܠ ܟܘܠܗܢܐ
ܕܒܡܪܐ ܕܫܢܝܐ ܠܚܠܝܡܝܢ ܐܣܝܘܬܐ ܕܢܦܫܐ ܘܦܓܪܐ
ܐܣܝܘܬܐ ܪܘܚܢܝܬܐ ܕܠܢܦܫܐ ܘܦܓܪܐ ܡܐܣܝܐ.

695 I Serm 6 App 5.1f:

ܕܠܐ ܟܐܒܐ ܘܕܠܐ ܠܒܪܐ ܡܐܣܝܢ ܟܐܒ̈ܐ ܘܡܟܐܒ̈ܢܐ
ܘܐܦ ܝܕܥܝܢ ܒܠܠܝܐ ܡܐܣܝܢ ܘܐܦ ܝܕܥܝܢ ܐܦ ܒܡܟܐܒܢܐ
.....ܫܘܠܚܢܐ ܗܟܝܢ ܡܟܝܠ ... ܕܠܗ ܐܝܬܘܗܝ ܐܣܝܘܬܐ ܕܡܢ
ܫܠܗ ܡܟܣܝܢ ܘܡܗܡܝܢ
.....ܪܢܝܢ ܠܐܣܝܘܬܐ ܕܢܦܫܐ ܕܠܗ ܗܘ ܪܫܡ ܐܠܗܐ.

696 Epiph 5.8; 11.6.

697 Epiph 11.6:

ܡܥܡܘܕܝܬܐ ܗܝ ܕܥܠܡܝܐ ܠܐ ܫܠܝܐ ܠܡܒܪܐ ܪܒܝܐ
ܕܬܠܬܝܢ ܘܬܫ̈ܥܝܢ ܥܬܝܕ ܗܘ ܕܢܣܒ ܒܐܦ̈ܐ ܗܘܐ ܕܠܘܬܐ

☞

Here, the author compares Christian baptism with the water of Shiloah. While the former can provide healing at any time, the latter was able to heal only once a year. The baptism of expiation, existing in Israel, was not complete (ܡܥܡܘܕܝܘܬܐ ܕܚܘܣܝܐ), whereas Christian baptism is a complete expiation for body and soul (ܡܥܡܘܕܝܘܬܐ ܕܚܘܣܝܐ ܡܫܡܠܝܐ ܕܦܓܪܐ ܘܕܢܦܫܐ),[698] as Jesus says: 'unless one is born of water and the spirit, he cannot enter the kingdom of God' (Jn 3:5).[699] The water of baptism is related to the water which came from Jesus' side on the cross (Jn 10:34) which is considered to be the fountain of the medicine of life.[700] Washing in the water of baptism is like being cleansed with the Holy Spirit.[701] Through the water, man's sins will be forgiven.[702]

The author of the hymns On Epiphany uses many references from the Old Testament as examples of types of Christian baptism. One of these is the event of the water of Jericho which was healed through mixing within it some salt (2 Kgs 2:20-22). The salt symbolises Jesus Who is called the 'sweet Salt from Mary' ( ܪܐܘܗ̇ ܕܗܘ ܡܠܚܐ ܚܠܝܬܐ ܕܡܢ ܡܪܝܡ). His baptism in the River Jordan, being comparable to the salt in the water, healed the 'pus of our wickness' (ܘܚܠܝܬ ܒܗ̇ ܬܡܘܣܬܐ ܕܡܚܠܘܬܢ).[703] Thus, Jesus cleansed the filth of our wound through His baptism, and fulfilled justice (Mt 3:15). The Lord's grace descended from heaven

---

ܠܡܒܥܝܘ ܕܐܣܝܘܬܗ ܒܟܠ ܗ̇ܝ ܒܠܚܘܕ ܘܡܫܝܚܐ ܢܦܩ ܘܡܬܝܕܥ
ܠܟܠ ܕܣܢܝܩ ܟܠ ܒܡܘܪܕܝܗ.

698 CDiat 16.12.

699 CDiat 16.14.

700 Epiph 5.14.

701 Hebd 3.157: ܡܢ ܕܣܚܐ ܒܡܥܡܘܕܝܘܬܐ ܘܡܩܒܠ ܗܘܐ ܒܪܘܚܐ ܕܩܘܕܫܐ ܠܐ ܣܚܐ ܠܗ ܕܢܣܚܐ ܟܠܗ ܐܠܐ ܕ̈ܟܠܗܝ ܟܠܗܘܢ.

702 Haer 2.3: ܢܣܒܘܢ ܒܗ ܡ̈ܪܝܐ ܫܘܠܗ̈ܐ ܕܚܘܣܝܬܐ.

703 Epiph 8.22:

ܥܡܕ ܕܝܢ ܒܢܗܪܐ ܠܐܢܫܘ ܠܟ ܥܘܪܝܗ ܘܐܣܝܗ ܠܡܚܘܬܗ
ܕܠܟ ܐܢܘܢ ܥܡܕ ܘܐܬܚܣܝܘ ܒܪܐܙܗ ܗܘ ܕܥܡܕ ܐܬܒܪܟܘ
ܢܚܬ ܒܗܘܢ ܡܠܚܐ ܘܒܣܡܗ ܘܐܬܦܫܘ ܪܐܘܗ̇ ܕܗܘ ܡܠܚܐ ܚܠܝܬܐ
ܕܡܢ ܡܪܝܡ
ܕܡ̈ܝܐ ܐܬܡܪܬ ܘܚܠܝܬ ܒܗ̇ ܬܡܘܣܬܐ ܕܡܚܠܘܬܢ.

For Christ as ܡܠܚܐ ܚܠܝܬܐ, see Nat 1.86.

and purifies the filth of Adam's wound.[704] When Jesus was baptised, rays flashed out from the water, so that everyone can be clothed with light.[705] Therefore, everyone is invited to be baptised and take part in this saving act of restoration.[706] Since Mary, the mother of the Lord, was baptised, no one can be sanctified without the spiritual rebirth at baptism.[707] As the blind man received sight from Shiloah, so too everyone baptised puts off darkness and puts on light.[708] Baptism cleanses man from sin as Elijah cured Naaman from leprosy (2 Kgs 5:10).[709]

In addition to water, oil is another important element for the sacramental process of baptism. The significant role of oil and its symbolic character is extensively illustrated in the hymns 4, 5 and 7 On Virginity. In particular, hymn 4 deals with both the natural restorative properties of oil and spiritual healing in the sacramental anointing at baptism. Playing with the terms ܡܫܚܐ (oil) and ܡܫܝܚܐ (the Anointed One, Christ), oil is considered to be the shadow of Christ. As Jesus Christ granted remedies and served as

---

[704] Epiph 10.12:
ܘܗܐ ܒܐܪܥܐ ܟܠܗ ܘܐܬܟܠܠ ܐܝܟ ܕܡ ܡܕܒܚܐ ܕܠ ܚܛܗ̈ ܗܘܐ
ܐܝܟ ܒܪܢܫܐ ܕܠܐ ܢܚܛܐ ܐܬܬ ܚܢܢ ܠܓܡܘܪܬܐ ܠܡܥܡܕܐ ܕܬܫܝܓ
ܘܐܟܘܬܗ̇ ܕܡܥܡܘܕܝܬܟ.

[705] Nat 23.12:
ܒܪܟ ܒܢܘ̈ܗܪܐ ܒܥܡܕܝܬܐ ܘܐܬܦܪܣܘ ܠܗ ܡܘ̈ܗܒܐ
ܠܟܠ ܢܫ̈ܬܐ ܒܟܠܝܠܘܬܐ ܘܠܒܫܘ ܡܠܘܗܝ ܒܥܕ̈ܢܐ
ܠܟܠ ܡܢ̈ܐ ܕܡܥܡܕܝܬܐ ܘܐܟܪܘܗ ܡܠܘܗܝ ܠܐܦ̈ܐ
ܠܟܠ ܒܬ̈ܐ ܒܡܫܝܚܘܬܐ ܘܐܬܚܘܝܘ ܒܗܘܢ ܠܢܘܚܐ
ܥܡ ܡܘܕ̈ܥܢܘܗܝ، ܘܡܕܪ̈ܫܘܗܝ، ܒܝܘܡ ܕܐܘܒܕ ܥܡܘܕܝܗ ܠܫܡܗ.

In Nat 19.15 the sweat of Jesus is considered as the water of baptism: ܘܐܦ ܗܘ ܕܘܒܬܟ ܠܐܝܠܢܐ ܕܫܘܐ ܡܥܡܘܕܝܬܐ ܗܘ.

[706] Epiph 8.23: ܐܬܥܡܕܘ ܐܚܝ̈ܢ ܒܦܘܪ̈ܩܢܐ ܐܘܪܚܬܐ ܥܡ ܦܘܪܩܢܐ.

[707] Epiph 8.23-24.

[708] Epiph 7.22:
ܒܡܥܡܘܕܝܬܐ ܕܫܠܝܚܐ ܐܝܟ ܗܕܝܐ ܕܐܬܦܬܚ
ܢܗܪ، ܒܟܠܗ ܡܢ ܡܢ̈ܐ ܫܠܚ ܚܫܘܟܐ ܕܚܠܝܡ
ܚܫܘܟܐ ܒܗܘܢ ܫܠܚܘ ܡܢ ܡܢ̈ܐ ܢܘܗܪܐ ܠܒܫܘ.

[709] Epiph 5.6-8; 8.23; Haer 2.3; Hebd 3.157; Nat 17.16f.

Medicine to heal the needy, so too oil heals those anointed with it. Oil is compared to an ocean on which all kinds of help and benefits, as in a ship, are driven to the harbour to grant healing. The disciples' words are fulfilled by actions and the use of oil.[710] Both oil and Christ sacrifice themselves, so that the sick may obtain help and healing.[711] Christ is a secret, hidden mystery, while His symbol, oil, is visible. Oil is a symbol and a shadow of the name of Christ and it portrays Him on those being anointed at baptism.[712] The shadow of the Name of Christ is able to heal, as the sick were restored by Peter's shadow (Acts 5:14-16),[713] for it is given by the Lord to His disciples as His pledge (ܛܠܠܐ ܫܡܗ ܐܝܟ ܪܗܒܘܢܗ). When people are anointed at baptism, 'sin is stolen from their bodies,[714] and sustains them in their youth like armour, in old age

---

710 Virg 4.4. It is already quoted, see above.

711 Virg 4.5:

ܝܗܒ ܢܦܫܗ ܡܫܚܐ ܠܡܪ̈ܥܐ ܕܢܥܕܪܘܢ ܒܗ ܟܠ ܒܥܘܕܪ̈ܢܝܢ
ܐܝܟ ܡܫܝܚܐ ܕܝܗܒ ܢܦܫܗ ܕܢܚܐ ܒܗ ܟܠ ܟܪ̈ܝܗܝܢ
ܡܫܝܚܐ ܚܕ ܗܘ ܘܦܘܢ̈ܝܘ ܘܫܡ̈ܗܐ ܠܗ ܣܓ̈ܝܐܐ
ܕܡܬܚܠܦܝܢ ܒܟܠ ܥܘܕܪ̈ܝܢ ܠܟܠ ܒܥܘܕܪ̈ܢܝܢ
ܐܦ ܡܫܚܐ ܟܕ ܗܘ ܚܕ ܗܘ ܫܡ̈ܗܐ ܡܫܡܠ ܣܓ̈ܝܐܐ
ܕܡܬܕܡܝܢ ܒܟܠ ܒܥܘ̈ܬܢ ܠܐܣܝܘܬܐ ܕܟܠ ܢܟ̈ܝܢ.

712 Virg 4.7:

ܫܡ ܡܫܝܚܐ ܟܣܐ ܐܝܟ ܪܐܙܐ ܗܘ ܘܟܣܐ ܗܘ ܢܗܝܪ ܫܡܐ ܡܫܝܚܐ
ܐܬܛܠܠ ܗܘ ܫܡ ܡܫܝܚܐ ܕܛܠܠܐ ܗܘ ܕܫܡܐ ܡܫܝܚܐ
ܕܐܦ ܪܫܡܘܗܝ ܗܘ ܕܬܠܡ̈ܝܕܐ ܠܦܐ ܗܘܐ ܠܗܘܢ ܟܕ ܐܫܬܪܪܘ
ܘܡܢ ܕܡ̈ܫܝܚܝܢ ܗܘܘ ܘܡܬܐܣܝܢ ܒܗ ܗܘ ܒܡܫܝܚܐ
ܡܬܬܝܪ ܗܘܐ ܡܫܝܚܐ ܒܡܫܚܐ ܘܪܕܦ ܗܘܐ ܟܠ ܢܟ̈ܝܢ
ܐܝܟ ܕܐܦ ܒܛܠܐ ܕܟܐܦܐ ܚܠܝܡܘ ܪ̈ܕܝܐ ܕܕܡܐ ܘܡܢܫ.

713 Virg 4.8:

ܫܡ ܡܫܝܚܐ ܚܝܠܬ ܪܐܙܗ ܗܘ ܘܛܠܠܗ ܕܫܡܐ ܡܫܝܚܐ
ܛܠܠ ܫܡܗ ܚܝܠܬ ܢܦܠ ܗܘܐ ܥܠ ܕܪ̈ܝܫܝܢ ܘܡܬܚܠܡܝܢ ܗܘܘ
ܐܝܟ ܕܢܦܠܬ ܛܠܠܬܗ ܕܫܡܥܘܢ ܥܠ ܡܪ̈ܥܐ ܘܩܡܘ
ܛܠܠ ܫܡܗ ܐܝܟ ܪܗܒܘܢܗ ܝܗܒ ܠܬܠܡܝ̈ܕܘܗܝ
ܕܛܠܠܗܘܢ ܚܠܦ ܕܐܠܗܐ ܐܠܝܨ ܡܚܝܒ [ܗܘܐ] ܠܫܡܗ
ܥܠ ܛܠܝܐ ܟܕ ܚܫܚ ܠܗ ܫܡܥܘܢ ܕܝܢ ܛܠܠܬܗ.

714 Virg 4.9:

☞

as a sceptre and 'it supports [against] sickness and is a bulwark of health'.[715]

Thus, oil serves to achieve perfect healing from all kinds of illnesses (ܠܐܣܝܘܬܐ ܕܟܠ ܟܘܪ̈ܗܢܝܢ), and it can be 'all with all' (ܘܡܫܚܐ ܕܥܡ ܟܠ ܟܘܠ ܢܗܘܐ).[716] Oil serves as visible pigments (ܣܡ̈ܡܢܐ) to portray the newly restored image, made available by Christ for the newly baptised, instead of the corrupt image of the old Adam. Virg 4.13 stresses the power of oil against diseases which are described as second demons. As the Lord chased away and punished the demon (Mk 5:1-20), so too, the power of oil acts against diseases,[717] and its natural substance helps the sick,[718] and oil blots out man's debts in baptism.[719]

---

ܡܫܚܐ ܫܒܠܐ ܕܦܘܬ ܦܘܠܚܢܐ ܠܐܣܩ̈ܝܢܐ ܕܠܐ ܗܘܐ ܠܗܘܢ
ܕܐܘܪܚܝܐ ܡܢܝܚ ܚܫ̈ܠܝܗܘܢ ܒܡܕܝܢܬܐ ܚܝܒ ܕ̈ܢܚܫܘܢ
ܐܝܟ ܕܐܠܝܫ ܡܪܗ ܒܟܠ ܕܘܟ ܠܡܦܪ̈ܩܐ ܕܠܘܩܡ ܗܘܘ ܠܗ
ܡܫܚܐ ܒܥܒܕܬܐ ܐܚܕ ܠܐܘܬܐ ܕܦܓܪܐ ܕܢ̈ܟܝܐ
ܘܗܘ ܒܪ ܗܘ ܡ̇ܫܝܚ ܐܚܕ ܠܫܠܝܛܘܬܐ ܒܡܕܒܪܢܘܬܐ
ܒܟܠ ܕܦܓܪ̈ܐ ܕܢ̈ܟܝܐ ܐܚܕ ܚܝ̈ܠܐ ܕܦܓܪ̈ܐ ܚܝ̈ܐ ܐܚܕ.

[715] Virg 4.10:

ܡܫܚܐ ܚܘܛܪܐ ܗܘ ܠܟܪܝܗܘܬܐ ܘܣܡܟܐ ܬܘܒ ܠܚܠܝܡܘܬܐ
ܗܘ ܡܦܫܩ ܠܟܪܝܗܘܬܐ ܘܗܘܐ ܥܘܕܪܗ ܕܚܠܝܡܘܬܐ
ܚܪ ܗܘ ܘܫܦܝܪ ܒܡܕܪ̈ܫܘܗܝ ܢܦܩ ܠܡܕܒ̈ܪܢܐ ܡܫܝܚܘܬܐ
ܘܠܒܫ ܡܘܪܫ ܬܪܥܘܬܐ ܘܡܢ ܢܣܒ ܠܗ
ܕܠܒܢ̈ܝܐ ܡܫܝܚ ܐܝܟ ܠܒܫܐ ܠܕܐܠܗܝܢ ܚ̇ܙܘܫ ܐܝܟ ܒܐܝܐ
ܕܐܝܟ ܡܪܗ ܦܬܚ ܒܝܬ ܩܡ ܠܡܠܟܐ ܡܫܝܚ ܟܠ ܒܙ̈ܢܝ.

[716] Virg 4.5-6. Furthermore, oil is used for the sacramental anointing of the sick, which is later called ܡܫܚܐ ܕܒܪ̈ܝܗܐ, or ܩܢܕܝܠܐ, and for the consecration of altars (see Virg 4.13-14; 5.11; 7.9).

[717] Virg 4.13:

ܡܠܦܪܗ ܕܡܫܚܐ ܐܝܟ ܕܡܫܝܚܐ ܕܪܦ ܡܘܪܥܐ ܕܒܟܘ ܦܓܪܐ
ܕܡܫܝܚܐ ܘܢܦܩ ܒܗܘܕܢܐ ܕܐܦ ܗܘ ܚܙܐ ܥܐܕܐ ܐܝܟܐ ܗܘ ܕܬܪܥ
ܘܡܫܝܚܐ ܕܡܫܝܚ ܡܫܪ̈ܐ ܩܒܐ ܗܘ ܚܝܠܗ ܠܡܩܒܠ ܟܐܒ̈ܐ
ܐܝܟ ܡܪܗ ܕܐܠܝܫ ܦܓܪܐ ܘܥܒܕ ܥ̈ܐܕܐ
ܚܝܠܗ ܠܦܓܪܐ ܐܠܝܡ ܠܠܥܝܘܢ ܕܪܦ ܥ̈ܐܕܐ ܒܦܓ̈ܪܐ
ܕܒܕܪܘܗܝ ܘܗܘ ܒܦܓܪܐ ܠܦܓܪܐ ܕܡܫܝܚܐ ܠܒܪܝܬܐ.

[718] Virg 5.11:

ܡܫܚܐ ܡܡܫܡܫ ܒܠܒܘ̈ܫܐ ܠܟܪ̈ܝܗܘܗܝ، ܒܡܫܡܫܬ ܡܪܗ

Although it is the water and oil that are the vehicles of baptism, the main agent is not the material element, but the 'invisible Name' (ܒܫܡܐ ܟܣܝܐ) evoked upon the water.[720] The significant role of the holy Names is found also in other texts. In CDiat 16.29, the author explicitly says that 'it is not the water of our atonement that cleanses us, but rather it is the Names pronounced over it which give us atonement.[721] The effect of the holy Names is compared to the creation of the world by the word of God. Creation sprang forth, light from darkness by the divine words (Gen 1:2-3),[722] in the same way the holy Names invisibly perform the spiritual act of baptism. The three Names are also mentioned in Virg 7.5 where Ephrem says that baptism portrays a new image and gives birth with the three names of the Father, Son and Holy Spirit,[723] in place of the corrupt image of the old Adam,

---

ܕܒܣܡ ܐܦ ܗܘ ܠܐܒܘܠܘܗܝ ܒܠܒܘܫܬܐ ܕܟܠ ܒܘܕܪ̈ܝܢ
ܡܫܝܚܐ ܓܝܪ ܠܓܪ̈ܒܐ ܦܘܫܐ ܕܡܢ ܒܝܬ ܡܥ̈ܠܬܐ
ܕܒܪܟܐ ܕܛܦܛܦ ܘܐܘܦ ܒܡܫܝܚܐ ܦܐܝ
ܘܠܡܦܩܕܐ ܕܐܠܝܫܥ ܗܘܘ ܒܡܫܝܚܐ ܦܝܗ ܡܢ ܡܘܬܐ
ܕܐܠܗܐ ܗܘܐ ܕܠܠܝܢ ܒܘܕܪ̈ܘܗܝ ܠܟ ܡܢ ܒܪ̈ܘܗܝ .

719 Virg 7.9.

720 Epiph 6.12:

ܡ̈ܝܐ ܚܣܝ̈ܢܐ ܩܕܫ ܗܘܐ ܐܠܝܫܥ ܒܫܡܐ ܟܣܝܐ
ܚܒܪ ܗܘܐ ܒܗܘܢ ܚܘܒܐ ܓܠܝܐ ܕܪܚܝܡܗ ܗܘܐ ܚܝܠܐ ܟܣܝܐ
ܐܬܓܠܝ ܚܘܒܐ ܒܡ̈ܝܐ ܐܝܟ ܚܘܠܐ ܒܡܥܡܘܕܝܬܐ.

721 CDiat 16.29: ܠܐ ܓܝܪ ܚܘܣܝܐ ܦܬܝܪ ܡܫܝܚܐ ܐܝܟ ܕܠܗ ܡ̈ܝܐ ܕܡܕܟܝܢ ܕܟܝܢ ܠܚܛܗܝܢ. ܐܠܐ ܦܘܪܩܢܐ ܗܘ ܗܢܐ. ܘܐܦ ܡ̈ܝܐ ܕܚܘܣܝܢ ܠܐ ܗܢܘܢ ܡܕܟܝܢ. ܐܠܐ ܫܡܗ̈ܐ ܕܥܠܝܗܘܢ ܡܬܩܪܝܢ. ܗܢܘܢ ܗܘܝܢ ܠܢ ܡܚܣܝܢܐ.

722 CDiat 16.28.

723 Virg 7.5:

ܒܡܫܝ̈ܚܢܐ ܡܬܚܕܫܢܐ ܡܬܨܝܪ ܨܠܡܐ ܕܡܠܟܘܬܐ
ܘܒܡܫܝܚܐ ܓܠܝܐ ܡܬܨܝܪ ܨܠܡܐ ܟܣܝܐ ܕܡܠܟܐ ܟܣܝܐ
ܒ̈ܢܝܫܡܐ ܕܡܥܡܘܕܝܬܐ ܕܡܫܚܠܦܐ ܠܗܘܢ ܒܗ ܒܗܘܒܗ
ܡܢ ܨܘܪܬܗ ܕܐܕܡ ܡܚܒܠܐ ܗܘ ܐܬܚܒܠ
ܝܠܕܐ ܒܗܘܢ ܨܠܡܐ ܚܕܬܐ ܘܝܠܕܐ ܠܗܘܢ ܒܫܡ̈ܗܐ ܬܠܬܐ
ܕܫܡ̈ܗܐ ܥܡܝܢܐ ܬܠܬܐ ܕܐܒܐ ܘܒܪܐ ܘܪܘܚ ܩܘܕܫܐ.

while sin has died in baptism.[724] Each of the three names of the Father, Son and Holy Spirit is active in baptism.[725] Finally, in Virg 4.14, the Names of the holy Trinity are compared to the metaphorical four rivers flowing out of Eden into the world (Gen 2:10-14). As the rivers serve as remedies for the world, so too the Names of the holy Trinity are called the 'trumpets of baptism' (ܫܝܦܘ̈ܪܐ ܕܡܥܡܘܕܝܬܐ).[726]

### 5.3.3.3 *The Eucharistic Bread and Wine as the Medicine of Life*

According to the biblical narrative of Genesis, at the beginning of human history, man was deceived and poisoned by the food offered by the Evil One. As a result, man fell into the state of sickness. Besides fruit, bread is a typical element of food. Through Jesus, the symbolic character of bread, representing the venom of the Evil One, particularly in the form of greed, has been reversed and changed.[727] At the Last Supper, Jesus offered Himself in the

---

[724] Virg 7.9:
ܡܫܝܚܐ [ܡܫܝܚܐ] ܡܚܘܒ ܚܘܕ̈ܝܐ ܠܘ ܐܠܐ ܠܡܦܪܥ ܡܚܘܒ ܚܘ̈ܒܐ
ܡܫܝܚܐ ܟܕ ܚܛܝܐ ܣܡ̈ܐ ܐܝܟ ܡܚܘܠܐ ܕܚܛܝܐ ܠܛܠܝ̈ܐ
ܛܘܦܢܐ ܟܕ ܐܝܟ ܒܐܢܐ ܒܐܢܬ ܚܛܝܐ ܠܒܢ̈ܝܢܐ
ܕܠܐ ܙܟܐ ܡܢܗܘܢ ܪ̈ܚܫܘܗܝ ܛܦܘ ܕܐܬܛܦܘ ܒܗ
ܡܫܝܚܐ ܕܝܢ ܒܡܘܬܗ ܛܒܥ ܚܛܝܐ ܣܡ̈ܐ ܒܡܥܡܘܕܝܬܐ
ܕܗܐ ܚܘܝܐ ܚܝܛܬܐ ܒܚܘ̈ܒܐ ܠܐ ܬܚܫ ܒܒ̈ܢܝܬܐ.

[725] Fid 67.10: ܗܢܘܢ ܫܡܗ̈ܐ ܕܬܠܝܬܝܘܬܗ ܚܕ ܒܬܪ ܚܕ ܒܡܚܣܢܘܬܐ ܠܡܥܡܘܕܝܬܐ.

[726] Virg 4.14:
ܢܗܪܐ ܕܒܗ݁ ܡܬܦܠܓ ܒܐܘܪܚܐ ܠܐܪ̈ܒܥ ܦܢܝ̈ܬܐ
ܘܫܡܗ ܕܡܫܝܚܐ ܡܬܦܠܓ ܒܐܘܪܚܐ ܥܡܝܩܐ ܠܬ̈ܠܬܐ
ܗ̇ܘ ܡܫܡܗܐ ܟܘܠܬ ܒܪ̈ܝܐ ܗ̇ܘ ܡܫܒܪ ܒܪܬ ܡܘܕܝܐ
ܗ̇ܘ ܡܪܘܐ ܠܐܝܠܢܐ ܘܗܘܝܐ ܠܡܦܐ̈ܪܐ
ܠܗ݁ܘ ܕܒܗ݁ ܐܪܒܥܐ ܫܡ̈ܗܐ ܒܪ̈ܘܐ ܕܢܗܝܪܘܬܐ
ܘܠܡܫܝܚܐ ܫܡ̈ܗܐ ܬܠܬܐ ܫܝܦܘ̈ܪܐ ܕܡܥܡܘܕܝܬܐ.

On remedies from Paradise, see chapter IV, 1.1.7.

[727] Virg 14.11; Dom 15: ܐܠܐ ܕܡܐܟܘܠܬܗܘܢ ܕܠܗܘܢ ܕܡܝ̈ܘܬܐ ܢܣܒ ܗܘܐ ܠܗܘܢ ܘܠܗܘܢ ܐܝܟ ܗܘ ܣܡܐ. ܐܡܚܠܐ ܟܕ ܕܒܠܬ ܡܐܟܘܠܬܐ ܗܘ ܢܗܒ ܗܘܐ ܒܝܫܐ ܡܠܗ ܡܒܪܐ ܠܒܝܬ ܐܕܡ.

☞

form of bread and wine to be consumed by His disciples. Thus, the bread and wine that He blessed became the medicine of life, just as He is the Medicine of Life. Likewise, the eucharistic bread and wine used today in the church are considered to be the medicine of life for the faithful, as Jesus became the Medicine of Life in the presence of His consumers (ܘܗܘܐ ܣܡ ܚܝܐ ܩܕܡ ܐܟܘ̈ܠܘܗܝ). For Judas Iscariot the blessed bread and wine became the poison of death, for the Medicine of Life was washed from it before he received it.[728] Through this spiritual bread (ܒܠܚܡܐ ܪܘܚܢܝܐ) everyone can enter into Paradise from which Adam was expelled. The 'Living Bread of the Son' (ܠܚܡܗ ܚܝܐ ܕܒܪܐ) grants spiritual wings to the faithful to fly and meet the Son of God in the clouds.[729] Unlike the unleavened bread of the old Pascha from which the Medicine of Life has been washed off and which has been changed into the poison of death, the new eucharistic bread serves as medicine of life in the new covenant and continues the healing providence of God to His people.[730] Therefore, Ephrem

---

ܗܢܝܐ ܒܥܠܬ ܡܐܡܘܢܘܬܐ ܢܣܒ ܗܘܐ ܠܓܒܐ ܡܠܚܡܗ ܚܝܐ ܠܒܢ̈ܝ ܐܕܡ.
On greed (ܥܠܘܒܘܬܐ), see chapter V, 1.4.2.

728 Azym 14.15-16:

ܝܗܒ ܢܣܒ ܠܗ ܠܚܡܐ ܠܓܢܒܬܐ ܒܟܣܝܐ
ܠܚܡܐ ܗܘܐ ܕܡܫܝܓ ܡܢ ܣܡ ܚܝܐ.
ܟܪܟ ܡܫܝܐ ܟܠ ܟܠ ܗ̇ܘ ܐܘܟܠܐ
ܘܗܘܐ ܣܡ ܚܝܐ ܩܕܡ ܐܟܘ̈ܠܘܗܝ.

729 Azym 17.12-13:

ܒܠܚܡܐ ܪܘܚܢܝܐ ܗܘܐ ܟܠ ܐܢܫ
ܢܥܪܐ ܕܡܟܠܠ ܓܢܬ ܦܪܕܝܣܐ.
ܡܢ ܕܐܟܠ ܠܚܡܗ ܚܝܐ ܕܒܪܐ
ܗܘ ܦܪܚ ܠܐܘܪܥܗ ܐܦ ܒܥܢ̈ܢܐ.

730 Azym 18.11:

ܗܐ ܠܒܪ ܢܣܒ ܠܗ ܡܢ ܦܛܝܪܗ
ܕܣܡܐ ܠܗ ܒܚܠܗ ܐܝܟ ܣܡ ܡܘܬܐ.

Azym 18.15-17:

ܙܪܗ ܗܘ ܕܒܪܐ ܠܦܛܝܪ ܗܘܐ ܡܘܫܐ
ܒܟܠܗ ܗ̇ܘ ܦܛܝܪܐ ܐܝܟ ܣܡ ܚܝܐ.
ܐܥܒܪܗ ܠܦܛܝܪܐ ܡܢ ܣܡ ܚܝܐ
ܢܣܒܗ ܠܝܗܘܕܐ ܐܝܟ ܣܡ ܡܘܬܐ.

☞

says that the holy blood of Jesus has been mixed with both unleavened and eucharistic bread: 'the one who has received It in the eucharist (ܩܘܪܒܢܐ) has received the medicine of life, the one who has received It with the People has received the poison of death.[731]

In the Church, the 'living body' (ܦܓܪܐ ܚܝܐ) is offered to be consumed by its children.[732] In Virg 37.3, Ephrem refers to the natural products of wheat, olives and grapes that are used in the ܐܕܪܐ of the Church. He says: 'With three medicines you bound up our sickness. Humankind had become weak and sorrowful and was failing. You strengthened her with your blessed bread, and you consoled her with your sober wine, and you made her joyful with your holy oil'.[733] Obviously, the wheat, olives and grapes imply their significant role and use in the Church. The medicine and healing that once Jesus provided continues to exist in the church through the use of these elements. As Jesus healed our pain through His body and blood when He was crucified,[734] so too His

---

ܣܡ ܡܘܬܗ ܡܚܠ ܕܐܘܟܪܝܣܛܝܐ

ܫܩܠ ܐܝܟ ܕܒܗ ܕܗܘ ܦܛܝܪܐ.

Azym 19.22:

ܠܐ ܢܐܟܘܠ ܐܢܫ ܥܡ ܣܡ ܚܝܐ

ܦܛܝܪܗ ܕܥܡܐ ܐܝܟ ܣܡ ܡܘܬܐ .

731 Azym 19.23-24:

ܕܥܡܗ ܠܒܪ ܕܡܥܡܕܢܐ ܡܥܒܪܝܢ ܘܥܪܐ

ܒܦܛܝܪܗ ܕܥܡܐ ܘܒܩܘܪܒܢܝܢ.

ܕܫܩܠܗ ܒܩܘܪܒܢܐ ܫܩܠ ܣܡ ܚܝܐ

ܕܐܟܠܗ ܥܡ ܥܡܐ ܫܩܠ ܣܡ ܡܘܬܐ.

732 Azym 21:25; Virg 16.5.

733 Virg 37.3:

ܬܠܬܐ ܐܣܘܬܐ ܘܚܠܫܐ ܕܐܬܒܪܝ، ܠܣܘܥܝܢ

ܬܬܚܝܠܝܢ ܒܪܐ ܫܒܝܚܢ ܬܬܠܬܐܝܬ

ܒܣܡܡܢܐ ܬܠܬܐ ܒܡܠܬܗ، ܠܒܘܪܗܢ

ܡܚܠܬ ܚܫܬ ܗܘܬ ܐܢܫܘܬܐ ܘܐܦܫܬ

ܚܝܠܬܗ ܒܠܚܡܟ ܡܒܪܟܐ

ܘܒܝܐܬܗ ܒܚܡܪܟ ܡܢܟܦܐ

ܘܐܦܨܚܬܗ ܒܡܫܚܟ ܡܩܕܫܐ.

734 Nis 43.10:

☞

holy body and blood in the form of the eucharistic bread and wine possess the power of spiritual healing.

In Virg 31.13, Jesus is considered to be the Cluster of mercy, full of sweetness, 'which was trampled and gave the medicine of life to the people'. Ephrem blesses him 'who has drunk from the sober grape and was not despised in secret'.[735] The Lord 'soothes its eaters with the tastes of all remedies'.[736] In Nat 3.15, Jesus is the Vine-shoot (ܢܘܪܒܐ) of the 'cup of our salvation' ( ܟܣܐ ܕܦܘܪܩܢ), the 'Cluster' (ܛܘܛܝܬܐ) of the 'source of the Medicine of Life' (ܡܒܘܥܐ ܕܐܣܝ ܚܝܐ), and the 'Ploughman' (ܐܟܪܐ) Who planted Himself as Wheat (ܚܛܬܐ) to become for us the Bread of Life.[737]

---

ܠܐ ܣܦܩܘ ܠܗ ܕܝܢ ܠܚܠܡܐ ܐܣܘܬܐ ܒܡܣܟ̈ܢܘܬܗܘܢ
ܚܝܘܗܝ ܘܐܬܪܘܡ ܐܣܝܐ ܕܠܟܠ ܦܩܕ
ܟܕ ܡܢ ܦܓܪܗ ܗܘ ܟܠ ܟܐܒܗ ܘܐܣܝ ܚܝܢ ܒܦܓܪܗ ܘܕܡܗ
ܐܫܠܡܗ ܡܚܝܘܬܗ ܥܘܒܕܐ ܠܣܡ ܚ̈ܝܐ
ܕܗܘܘ ܣܦܩ ܘܐܣܝ ܟܐܒܐ ܕܢܦ̈ܫܬܐ ܒܝܘܠܦܢܗ.

735 Virg 31.13:

ܛܘܛܝܬܐ ܕܪ̈ܚܡܐ ܕܐܬܥܨܪܬ ܒܒܪ̈ܝܬܐ
ܕܡܠܝܐ ܚܠܝܐ ܗܘܐ ܘܠܥܡܐ ܝܗܒ ܗܘܐ
ܠܕܝܫܗ̇ ܠܗ̇ ܡܪܝܪܐ ܚܠܝܘܬܗ̇ ܦܠܓܬ
ܐܬܒܪܟܬ ܘܫܒܚܬ ܣܡ ܚ̈ܝܐ ܠܥܡ̈ܡܐ
ܛܘܒܘܗܝ ܠܡܢ ܕܐܫܬܝ
ܡܢ ܣܓܘܠܗ ܢܟܝܦܐ
ܘܠܐ ܐܙܕܠܠ ܒܟܣܝܐ .

736 Virg 5.11:

ܡܒܣܐ ܡܒܣܡ ܒܛܥ̈ܡܐ ܠܐܟ̈ܘܠܘܗܝ ܒܕܡܘܬ ܡܪܗ
ܕܒܣܡ ܐܦ ܗܘ ܠܐܟ̈ܘܠܘܗܝ ܒܛܥ̈ܡܬܐ ܕܟܠ ܣܡ̈ܡܢ .

737 Nat 3.15:

ܒܪܝܟ ܙܪܥܐ ܕܗܘܐ ܐܡܪܐ ܠܚܘܣܝܢ
ܒܪܝܟ ܢܘܪܒܐ ܕܗܘܐ ܟܣܐ ܕܦܘܪܩܢ
ܒܪܝܟ ܐܦ ܛܘܛܝܬܐ ܡܒܘܥܐ ܕܐܣܝ ܚ̈ܝܐ
ܒܪܝܟ ܗܘ ܐܦ ܐܟܪܐ ܕܗ̣ܘ ܗܘܐ
ܚܛܬܐ ܕܐܙܕܪܥܬ ܘܚܨܕܐ ܕܐܬܚܨܕܬ
ܐܕܪܐ ܗܘ ܕܗܘܐ ܡܐܟܘܠܬܐ ܠܟܠܢ ܟܠܢ .

The human mind can consume the eucharistic bread, 'the bread of the Compassionate One' (ܠܚܡܐ ܗܘ ܕܚܢܢܐ), as the Medicine of Life.[738] Although it begins as ordinary bread, when it is 'broken' during the eucharist it becomes the medicine of life for the faithful, for when Jesus broke ordinary bread it became His body.[739]

In Fid 12.8-9, the cup of the Medicine of Life sprung from the vine of Egypt (Ps 80:8-13). Jesus is the 'Sprig' (ܥܒܘܒܐ) of the vine from which sprouted the 'Vineshoot' (ܢܘܪܒܐ) that brought the 'blessed Bunch [of grapes]' (ܣܓܘܠܐ ܒܪܝܟܐ).[740] The cup of the Medicine of Life refers to the eucharistic cup of the holy blood of our Lord. Likewise, Jesus is the 'Sheaf full of new Bread' ( ܟܦܐ ܕܡܠܝܐ ܠܚܡܐ ܚܕܬܐ), the 'sweet Fruit' (ܦܐܪܐ ܚܠܝܐ), and the 'Physician Who healed all' (ܐܣܝܐ ܕܐܣܝ ܟܠ).[741]

---

738 Nat 4.99: ܠܚܡܐ ܗܘ ܕܚܢܢܐ ܦܘܪܫܐܝܬ ܢܦܪܘܫ ܠܗ ܗܘܢܐ ܐܝܟ ܣܡ ܚ̈ܝܐ. The verb ܦܪܫ is used in 1 Cor 11:29 where Paul says: 'For anyone who eats and drinks of it [the body and blood of the Lord] without being worthy, he eats and drinks judgment on himself, for he did not discern the body of the Lord ( ܡܢ ܕܐܟܠ ܓܝܪ ܘܫܬܐ ܡܢܗ ܟܕ ܠܐ ܫܘܐ܆ ܚܘܒܐ ܗܘ ܠܢܦܫܗ ܐܟܠ ܘܫܬܐ܇ ܕܠܐ ܦܪܫ ܦܓܪܗ ܕܡܪܝܐ).

739 Nat 19.16: ܘܐܦ ܬܘܡܣܐ ܬܘܒ ܠܚܡܐ ܥܫܝܢܐ ܠܗ ܣܡ ܚ̈ܝܐ ܗܘ.

740 Fid 12.8:

ܥܒܘܒܐ ܐܢܬ ܕܡܢ ܗ̇ܝ ܓܦܬܐ ܕܡܢ ܡܨܪܝܢ
ܘܕܐܠܗ̇ ܗܘܐ ܫܘܪܝܐ ܕܟܒܐ
ܐܝܟ ܐܣܠܦ ܘܢܦܩ ܡܢܗ̇ ܢܘܪܒܐ ܕܐܝܬܝ
ܣܓܘܠܐ ܒܪܝܟܐ ܘܟܣܐ ܕܣܡ ܚ̈ܝܐ.

In Nat 16.7, Ephrem uses the term ܣܡ̈ܡܢܐ in the sense of 'pigments' in the context of bread and wine: ܗܐ ܦܪܫ ܦܠܚܝ ܒܕܡܐ ܕܚ̈ܒܐ ܠܟܠ ܡܢ ܠܚܡܐ ܘܦܪܫ ܟܠ ܠܒܐ ܦܝܦܝܐ ܕܣܘܟܐ ܡܢ ܣܡ̈ܡܢܐ ܕܗܝܡܢܘܬܐ ܒܪܝܟ ܗܘ ܕܐܒܕܪ ܦܠ̈ܚܐ ܠܟܦܢܐ ܒܦܠܓ ܘܫܬܗ.

741 Fid 12.9:

ܡܢ ܒܝܬ ܟܪ̈ܝܐ ܘܡܢ ܐܬܪܐ ܕܙܪ̈ܥܐ
ܢܦܩ ܠܟ ܟܦܐ ܕܡܠܝܐ ܠܚܡܐ ܚܕܬܐ
ܡܢ ܡܪ̈ܝܐ ܦܐܪܐ ܚܠܝܐ
ܘܡܢ ܡ̈ܠܬܐ ܐܣܝܐ ܕܐܣܝ ܟܠ.

Jesus gave Himself up to be consumed, so that His consumers might live through Him.[742] The consumers were not only the disciples who attended the Last Supper, but everyone can consume Him in the eucharistic bread and wine. Particularly, the author of Epiph 7 invites the faithful to consider themselves to be the 'consumers of the Medicine of Life Who gave life to all',[743] as he says: 'you shall consume the living Body, the Medicine of Life, which gives life to all'.[744] The author also refers to Mary; although she conceived Jesus and he took body from her, in return she received Him in the eucharistic bread and wine.[745]

### *5.3.3.4 Faith*

'Faith' (ܗܝܡܢܘܬܐ) plays a central role in religious life. It explains and defines the whole attitude of man towards his Creator. Faith can be the response to the divine call of the sovereign God; the total trust in His Majesty and the hope of God's merciful response to man's need. In the Gospel this word is used most obviously in relation to Jesus' healing miracles. Referring to these, Ephrem is not only aware about the aspect of faith, but he also draws attention to it, for faith is able to move mountains (Mt 21:21f.; Mk

---

742 Dom 50: ܐܫܠܡܗ ܠܒܪ ܕܢܗܘܐ ܦܓܪܗ ܕܢܬܐܟܠ ܕܒܗ ܡܬܐܟܠ ܢܚܐ ܠܐܟܠܘܗܝ.

743 Epiph 7.23:
ܐܝܕܘܗܝ ܐܫܝܛ ܦܠܛܘ ܕܠܐ ܢܗܘܐ ܡܢ ܡܬܓܠܐ
ܐܚܕܘܗ ܐܢܬܘܢ ܦܓܪܝܗܘܢ ܐܝܕܝܗܘܢ ܒܗ ܦܘܡܝܗܘܢ
ܒܗܘ ܗܘܘ ܡܢ ܐܟܘܠܘܗܝ ܕܗܘ ܗܘ ܣܡܐ ܕܐܚܝ ܟܠ.

744 Epiph 7.6:
ܒܪ ܚܕܐ ܒܡܢܐ ܘܒܗܕ ܩܠܝܠ ܚܕܐ ܠܚܡܐ ܘܐܚܝܕ
ܦܓܗ ܦܘܡܝܐ ܒܐܕܢܝܗܘܢ ܗܘ، ܡܠܟܐ ܒܟܠܗ ܡܐܢܝܗܘܢ
ܐܟܠܘ ܐܢܬܘܢ ܦܓܪܐ ܚܝܐ ܗܘ ܣܡܐ ܕܠܟܠ ܡܚܝܐ.

745 Epiph 8.23:
ܘܐܦ ܐܡܗ ܒܥܡܗ ܦܠܬ ܒܚܡܝܪܬ
ܘܡܢ ܡܢܐ ܠܒܥܬܗ ܠܒܣܝܡܘܬܗ
ܕܒܛܠܬܗ ܡܢ ܦܪܝܫ ܘܠܕܬܗ ܠܕܬܗ ܐܦ ܠܗ ܡܡܠܡܘܕܝܬܐ
ܠܕܬ ܘܐܬܬܠܕܬ ܕܦܓܪܐ ܕܢܣܒ ܡܢܗ
ܡܥܡܕܬ ܥܡܠܬܗ ܗܝ، ܠܕܬ ܗܘ ܣܡܐ ܕܠܚܝܡܗ ܡܚܝܐ ܠܗ.

11:22-24).[746] Thus having faith in the Physician of all can result in the restoration and healing of human beings from their spiritual sickness.

Faith is something divine and it is provided by the merciful God. Because of man's wickedness, God granted faith instead of questioning (ܒܥܬܐ), as He provided the Law instead of investigation (ܒܨܘܝܐ).[747] For Ephrem, faith is often contrasted with investigation and inquiry into the heavenly God, and doubt. Arguing against the inquiry of the Arians, Ephrem refers to the fixed serpent of Moses. As those who looked faithfully at the fixed serpent and lived (Num 21:4-9), likewise, faithfully looking on Jesus will give life and healing: 'Behold, the symbol of the First-Born! It was not inquiry into it that healed; it was the sight of it alone that healed. Look with faith on Him, the Lord of symbols, so that He can give you life'.[748]

Faith is considered to be the 'second soul' of man,[749] and it is a mediator between God and man. Ephrem makes a gradation in

---

[746] CDiat 16.5: ..... ܕܐܢ ܬܗܘܐ ܟܠܗܘܢ ܗܝܡܢܘܬܐ

[747] Fid 70.13: ܝܗܒ ܢܡܘܣܐ ܚܠܦ ܒܨܘܝܐ ܘܚܠܦ ܒܥܬܐ ܗܝܡܢܘܬܐ ܠܡܣܟܠܘܬܢ.

[748] Fid 9.11:

ܚܘ̈ܬܐ ܠܒܘܟܪܐ ܢܚܬܘ ܗܘܘ ܒܚܘܪܒܐ
ܡܟܝܠ ܚܘܝܐ ܐܣܝܢܐ ܕܚܘܪܘܢ ܒܗ ܘܚܝܘܢ
ܠܒܘܟܪܐ ܐܣܝܬ ܚܝܬܐ ܗܝܡܢܘܬܐ ܠܡܪ̈ܙܐ
ܗܐ ܪܐܙܗ ܕܒܘܟܪܐ ܠܐ ܗܘܐ ܒܨܬܗ ܐܣܝܬ
ܚܙܬܗ ܒܠܚܘܕ ܐܣܝܬ ܒܗܝܡܢܘܬܐ ܚܘܪ ܒܗ
ܠܡܪܐ ܐ̈ܪܙܐ ܕܢܚܝܟ (ܕܢܚܝܟ).

The same aspect also occurs in CDiat 16.15: 'Just as those who looked with bodily eyes at the sign which Moses fastened on the cross, lived bodily, so too those who look with spiritual eyes at the body of the Messiah nailed and suspended on the cross, and believe in him, will live [spiritually].' ( ܐܝܟܢܐ ܓܝܪ ܕܗܢܘܢ ܢܝܫܐ ܕܩܒܥ ܡܘܫܐ ܒܥܝܢ̈ܐ ܦܓܪܢܝ̈ܐ ܚܙܘ ܦܓܪܢܐܝܬ ܚܝܘ ܕܦܓܪܢܐܝܬ ܚܙܝܢ ܗܘܘ ܒܗ. ܗܟܢܐ ܒܥܝܢ̈ܐ ܕܦܓܪܐ ܕܡܫܝܚܐ ܕܐܬܬܠ ܒܥܝܢܐ ܚܝܝܢ ܐܝܠܝܢ ܕܪܘܚܢܐܝܬ ܚܝܝܢ ܘܡܗܝܡܢܝܢ ܒܗ).

[749] Fid 80.1: ܐܝܟ ܘܒܢܦܫܐ ܬܪܝܢܝܬܐ ܕܢܦܫܐ ܕܬܪ̈ܬܝܢ ܗܝܡܢܘܬܐ ܗܝ.

man: body, soul, faith, divinity, so that faith is the mediator between divinity and humanity.[750] Accordingly, Ephrem considers faith to be the eye which can see hidden things,[751] and serves as a 'balance' between the mind and thought.[752] Ephrem uses some examples from nature to explain the significant role of faith. Having faith and trust in an ordinary physician and the medicine book, is a natural example that Ephrem uses to illustrate the healing aspect of faith. Although an ordinary physician can cause pain, the sick person still believes and trusts the doctor and the medical book to restore him to health. Likewise a blind person believes the physician can heal his sickness with an instrument, as an apprentice trusts his craftsman.[753] A blind person cannot see light and the sun, but he has to take his fellows on trust when they talk about it.[754] Ephrem says: 'but if he were willing and believed,

[750] Fid 80.2:
ܦܓܪܐ ܗܘ ܡܚܝܠ ܗܘ ܒܗܝܡܢܘܬܐ ܬܠܐ ܒܢܦܫܐ ܘܢܦܫܐ ܬܠܝܐ
ܒܗܝܡܢܘܬܐ ܘܗܝܡܢܘܬܐ ܬܠܝܐ ܐܦ ܗܝ ܒܐܠܗܘܬܐ.

[751] Eccl 24.2: ܗܝܡܢܘܬܐ ܓܝܪ ܐܝܬܝܗ ܥܝܢܐ ܚܙܝܬ ܟܣܝܬܐ.

[752] Fid 5.20:
ܬܗܘܐ ܒܗ ܒܬܪܥܝܬܟ ܗܝܡܢܘܬܐ ܡܣܐܬܐ
ܬܫܩܘܠ ܪܥܝܢ ܐܡܝܢܐ ܥܡ ܡܘܠܟܐ ܘܦܘܫܐ.

[753] Fid 56.11-12:
ܟܠܗ ܟܡܐ ܕܐܝܟ ܠܐܣܝܘܗܝ ܕܕܐܝܟ ܒܗܠ
ܟܠܗ ܟܡܐ ܕܢܪܕܐ ܥܠܗ ܕܪܕܐ ܒܠ
ܗܐ ܠܐ ܒܟܐ ܣܡܝܐ ܡܣܬܡܟ ܠܐܘܡܢ̈ܐ
ܘܠܦܪ̈ܙܠܐ ܡܛܝܪ ܒܐܝܕܗ ܠܡܐܣܝܐ
ܗܐ ܛܠܒ ܡܟܣܟܣ ܠܗ ܡܛܝܪ ܐܦ ܠܟܘܐ ܗܐ ܛܠܒ ܡܒܝܠ ܠܗ .
ܟܠܗ ܕܠܐ ܢܬܟܣ ܕܟܠ ܐܝܟ ܡܣܡܝܡ ܠܗ
ܠܣܦܪܐ ܕܣܡܝܡ̈ܢܐ ܕܟܡܐ ܐܣܝܐ ܡܢܐ
ܘܬܠܐ ܘܡܠܦ ܠܗ ܕܢܛܪ ܠܦܬܓܡ̈ܘܗܝ
ܘܢܛܠܘ ܠܡܣܡܝ̈ܢܘܗܝ ܕܠܐ ܕܝܢ ܘܠܐ ܫܘܐܠ
ܘܡܦ̈ܩܘܕܘܗܝ ܕܐܠܗܐ ܠܐ ܗܘ ܫܦܝܘ ܘܐܣܝܘ [ܘܐܣܝܘܗ̈ܝ]
ܚܠ ܒܪܗ ܕܠܒܗ ܗܘ.

[754] Fid 65.10:
ܡܚܝܠ ܐܦ ܒܟܐ ܣܡܝܐ ܠܫܡܫܐ
ܗܐ ܠܐ ܚܙܐ ܕܢܘܗܪ ܥܡܝܩܐ ܘܠܝܬܗ
ܒܠܒܗ ܕܡܣܬܟܠ ܕܠܟܐ ܡܢܐ ܣܦܩ

☞

just persuasion would enlighten his faith.'[755] Ephrem advises everyone to have faith in God Who is capable of everything, and there is no reason to doubt. In this context the role of faith is not the healing of physical sickness, but rather protecting and healing man from the sickness of inquiry and investigation.

Like oil, faith is compared to a ship on which one can travel into Scripture and the right understanding of God, as a ship can travel on the ocean.[756] Faith is indeed better than a ship on the sea.[757] Faith enables man to approach Scripture and God in the right way.[758] Truth can be gained through experiment and faith.

---

ܕܢܣܝܘܗܝ ܠܠܝܫܗ ܘܠܒܪܗ ܕܗܘ ܥܒܕܐ
ܐܠܐ ܐܦ ܗܘ ܕܗܝܡܢ ܒܠܚܘܕ ܡܗܝܡܢܘ ܠܐܝܠܐ ܕܐܡܪ ܠܗ.
Fid 65.13:
ܡܢܘ ܕܠܐ ܢܕܥ ܕܐܦ ܡܬܪܥܐ ܡܗܝܡܢܐ
ܕܫܡܥ ܘܠܐ ܡܥܪ ܠܡܠܬܗ ܕܒܪܢܫܐ
ܕܟܝܢܐ ܕܢܐܡܪ ܠܗ ܢܗܘܪܐ ܕܐܡܝܢ ܗܘ
ܒܗܐ ܢܬܕܡ ܐܝܢܐ ܕܫܡܥ ܘܠܐ ܡܗܝܡܢ
ܠܡܠܬܗ ܕܐܠܗܐ ܕܡܠܐ ܕܝܠܕܗ ܐܚܪ ܕܗܘܐ ܒܪ.

755 Fid 65.11:
ܡܚܝܠ ܐܦ ܛܒܐ ܒܗܢܐ ܕܢܬܒܥܘܢ
ܕܫܡܥ ܘܠܐ ܡܗܝܡܢ ܒܪܗ ܢܦܠ ܒܢܝܢ
ܕܟܝܐ ܘܠܐ ܡܕܪܟ ܘܛܒܐ ܕܐܦ ܡܗܝܡܢܐ
ܢܬܒܥ ܒܬܪܬܝܗܝܢ ܒܟܝܢܐ ܘܬܪܥܝܬܐ
ܕܐܠܘ ܛܒܐ ܘܡܗܝܡܢ ܐܢܗܪܗ ܠܡܗܝܡܢܘܬܗ ܦܝܣܐ ܕܟܐܢܘܬܐ.

756 Fid 69.6: ܒܡܗܝܡܢܘܬܐ ܐܝܟ ܕܒܐܠܦܐ ܪܕܝ ܒܬܪܒܘܬܗ ܐܝܟ ܡܠܝܐ ܒܝܬ ܠܬܐܘܪܐ.

757 SFid 4.73:
ܛܒܐ ܠܝ ܡܗܝܡܢܘܬܐ ܡܢ ܐܠܦܐ ܕܥܠܗ ܝܡܐ
ܠܐܠܦܐ ܠܝܡܐ ܡܕܠܝܢ ܠܗ ܡܛܠܛܠܝܢ ܠܗ ܕܝܢ ܡܫܥܠܬܐ
ܠܐ ܛܒܐ ܡܗܝܡܢܘܬܝ ܐܦ ܛܒܥܝܢ ܠܐ ܝܡܐ
ܡܢ ܢܛܠ ܠܗ ܠܡܠܝܐ ܕܢܐܬܐ ܝܡܐ ܠܝܒܫܐ.

758 Fid 65.12:
ܡܢܐ ܥܣܩܝܢ ܐܢܫܝܢ ܐܦ ܐܢܫܝܢ ܒܫܐܠܬܐ
ܡܢܐ ܥܛܝܦܝܢ ܐܢܫܝܢ ܐܦ ܚܢܢ ܒܒܘܩܝܐ
ܡܗܝܡܢܐ ܗܝ ܬܪܝܨܘܬܐ ܕܬܚܝܬ ܒܗ̇ ܛܠܝܐ ܘܬܗܝܡܢܘܗܝ,
ܕܐܝܟ ܗܘ ܕܠܐ ܐܝܬ ܦܘܪܣܐ ܐܚܪܝܢ
ܐܠܐ ܕܐܢܫ ܒܠܚܘܕ ܢܗܝܡܢ ܡܗܝܡܢܘ ܠܡܠܬܗ ܕܫܪܪܐ.

However, man can gain divine truth, as much as God is willing to reveal, only through faith and its deeds,[759] whereas experiment cannot approach divinity.[760] In contrast to investigation, faith brings man nearer to God,[761] it links humanity with divinity.[762]

In order to benefit from divinity and its heavenly medicine it is necessary to have faith. Ephrem criticises the Pharisees and teachers who saw how Jesus healed sickness, but did not believe. In contrast, the crowds believed in Jesus. Commenting on the blind and dumb demoniac (Mt 12:22), Ephrem quotes Jesus where He said that the blind will see, and those who see will become blind (Jn 9:39),[763] and uses the healing of the blind and dumb demoniac as an example: '[the fact that] He healed him [the blind and dumb demoniac] and he could see and hear (Mt 12:22) is a symbol of those who have believed in Him.'[764] Seeing the healing miracles does not necessarily affect people, but having faith in Jesus can achieve both spiritual and physical healing.

The sinful woman (Lk 7:30f.) believed in Jesus as being 'Everything to everyone' (ܟܠ ܡܕܡ ܠܟܠ ܐܝܟ ܗܘܐ), and so her Healer: 'He became a physician to her who believed that He is the

---

[759] Fid 67.17: ܦܘܫ ܡܚܝܠ ܕܒܥܘܬܐ ܕܡܗܝܡܢܘܬܐ ܢܐܠܦ ܘܫܬܐ ܕܠܐ ܒܒܘܩܝܐ.

[760] Fid 36.17:

ܬܐܡ ܐܠܘ ܚܘܪܐ ܦܪ̈ܝܫܐ ܡܗܝܡܢܘܬܐ ܐܦ ܢܣܝܘܢܐ
ܐܘ ܠܘ̈ ܗܢܝܢ ܐܝܟ ܒܢܘܪܐ ܐܘ ܢܣܝܘܢܐ ܡܢܝܐ ܡܠܟ ܠܗ ܕܐܢܫ
ܐܝܬܘܗܝ.

[761] Fid 72.2: 'By faith he is brought near to you. For through inquiry you go far away from aid'. ( ܒܡܗܝܡܢܘܬܐ ܡܬܩܪܒ ܠܟ ܒܒܥܬܐ ܓܝܪ ܐܢܬ ܗܘ ܡܪܚܩ ܡܢ ܥܘܕܪܢܐ).

[762] S. Fid 2.485: ܚܝܬ ܐܠܗܘܬܐ ܠܐܢܫܘܬܐ ܡܗܝܡܢܘܬܐ ܡܚܒܟܬܐ.

[763] CDiat 10.8: ܗܝ ܗܝ ܕܣܡ̈ܝܐ ܢܚܙܘܢ. ܘܕܚܙܝܢ ܢܣܡܘܢ.

[764] ܘܐܣܝܗ ܘܚܙܐ ܘܫܡܥ: ܐܪܙ ܕܗܢܘܢ ܕܗܝܡܢܘ ܒܗ. The dumb, blind man who was possessed by a demon and brought to Jesus, was a symbol for the sickness of the People, as Isaiah 6:10: 'The heart of this people has become dull, and their ears heavy and they have covered their eyes, lest they see with their eyes and hear with their ears' (Isa 6:10; Mt 13:15; CDiat 10.7: ܐܝܟ ܕܐܡܪ ܐܫܥܝܐ ܕܐܬܥܒܝ ܠܗ ܠܒܗ ܕܥܡܐ ܗܢܐ. ܘܐܕܢܘ̈ܗܝ ܐܘܩܪ. ܘܥܝܢܘ̈ܗܝ ܥܡܨ. ܕܠܐ ܢܚܙܐ ܒܥܝܢܘ̈ܗܝ ܘܢܫܡܥ ܒܐܕܢܘ̈ܗܝ.

One Who heals everyone'.[765] Her faith contrasts with the faith of Simon the Pharisee. She shows her faith on entering Simon's house by pouring oil, drying and anointing Jesus' feet.[766]

Faith needs to be constant, otherwise future hope is lacking. Even though a man is healed for a while, later he can become sick and suffer. In the context of the unclean spirit (Mt 12:43-45), Ephrem says: 'Of what advantage is it to you if you are healed for a moment, but do not believe? For, if you are still in doubt after you are healed, something worse than the original pain may befall you'.[767]

Approaching Jesus with faith, man might be healed not only physically but also spiritually. Faith also achieves, along with the perfect healing of soul and body, perfect faith in order to sustain health. Thus, Jesus rewards perfect faith, as Ephrem says about the healing of the blind man at Bethsaida (Mk 8:25): 'when a little light had arisen in his eyes, a great light arose in his mind; his faith was made perfect within and his sight was crowned without'.[768] Along with sight, the blind man's faith was perfect and our Lord strengthened his weak faith (ܣܥܕܗ̇ ܡܪܢ ܠܗܝܡܢܘܬܐ ܡܚܝܠܬܐ).[769]

---

765 CDiat 10.10: ܘܗܘܐ ܐܣܝܐ ܠܗ̇ܝ ܕܗܝܡܢܘܬܗ̇ ܕܗܘܐ ܡܐܣܐ ܟܠ.

766 CDiat 10.8: ܗܝ ܕܒܕܡ̈ܥܝܗ̇ ܐܫܝܓܬ ܗܠܝܢ ܕܟܠ ܪ̈ܓܠܘܗܝ، ܘܗܘ ܒܪ̈ܓܠܘܗܝ، ܚܘܪ ܒܡܬܬ̈ܐ ܕܟܠ ܒܣܪܗ̇. ܐܣܝܬܗ ܗܝ، ܕܒܕܡ̈ܥܝܗ̇ ܠܚ̈ܛܗܬܐ. ܘܐܣܝܗ̇ ܗܘ ܒܪ̈ܓܠܘܗܝ، ܡܕܝ̈ܢܬܐ. ܚܣܐ ܗܘ ܗܘ ܡܢ ܚܠܐ. ܘܗܦܟ ܐܣܝܗ̇ ܠܗ̇ ܕܠܗ̇ ܡܢ ܚܘܠܐ. ܚܣܝ ܚܢܪ ܪ̈ܓܠܘܗܝ، ܒܕܡ̈ܥܐ. ܘܢܫܒ ܪ̈ܓܠܘܗܝ، ܒܥܘܦܡ ܚܠܗ̈ܡܐ. For more about the healing of the sinful woman see the exegetical section 2.1, New Testament. The parable of the two debtors, one of five hundred and the other of fifty, explains the relationship of Jesus to the sinful woman and Simon (Lk 7:41). Jesus forgave both, as a creditor annuls the debt of his debtors.

767 CDiat 11.5: ܕܡܢܐ ܬܬܐܪܘܢ ܐܢ ܬܬܐܣܘܢ ܕܫܥܬܐ. ܟܕ ܠܐ ܡܗܝܡܢܝܢ ܐܢܬܘܢ. ܒܬܪ ܟܢ ܕܬܬܐܣܘܢ ܐܢ ܬܬܦܠܓܘܢ، ܕܒܝܫ ܡܢ ܟܐܒܐ ܩܕܡܝܐ ܗܘܐ ܠܟܘܢ.

768 CDiat 13.13: ܟܕ ܕܢܚ ܠܗ ܢܘܗܪܐ ܙܥܘܪܐ ܒܥܝ̈ܢܘܗܝ، ܕܢܚ ܠܗ ܢܘܗܪܐ ܪܒܐ ܒܥܠ ܬܪܥܝܬܗ. ܐܬܓܡܪܬ ܗܝܡܢܘܬܗ ܡܢ ܠܓܘ. ܘܐܬܟܠܠܬ ܚܙܬܗ ܡܢ ܠܒܪ.

769 CDiat 13.13. In CDiat 14.14, Ephrem refers to Mt 14-20, when Jesus was asked about His disciples' inability to heal the possessed man ☞

In the context of the blind man of Jericho (Mk 10:47-52), Ephrem refers to Jesus' coming into the world to give sight and faith to the needy.[770] Ephrem draws parallels between sight (ܚܙܬܐ) and faith (ܗܝܡܢܘܬܐ). Sight should be understood more spiritually than physically. Therefore, Ephrem says: 'See, your faith has saved you (Lk 18:22). He did not say to him, it is your faith that has caused you to see'.[771] Faith gives life to people who trust Jesus. The priority is man's inner circumstance. If man is spiritually saved, then the physical healing will follow; likewise with the blind man of Jericho: '... that [faith] had first given him life, and then opening of his [physical] eyes' ( ... ܕܠܘܩܕܡ ܚܝ̈ܐ ܝܗܒܬ ܠܗ. ܘܒܬܪ ܦܬܚܘܬܗ ܥܝ̈ܢܐ).[772]

Nicodemus (Jn 3:1-21) was not physically blind, but Jesus enlightened his inner eyes and mind when He explained the meaning of spiritual baptism to him. Jesus introduced him into faith (ܠܗܝܡܢܘܬܐ ܗܘ ܕܝܢ ܡܥܠܬܢܝ: ܗܘܐ ܠܗ), for his faith was weak. Faith can become perfect through the Names of the

---

(Mt 17:14-18). The answer is that because of their lack of faith they were not able to heal (Mt 17:20): ܡܛܠ ܒܨܝܪܘܬ ܗܝܡܢܘܬܗܘܢ (CDiat 14.14).

[770] CDiat 15.22: 'The light came into the world to give sight to the blind and faith to those who lacked it' ( ܐܬܐ ܢܘܗܪܐ ܠܥܠܡܐ ܕܠܣܡ̈ܝܐ ܢܬܠ ܚܙܬܐ. ܘܠܚܣܝ̈ܪܐ ܗܝܡܢܘܬܐ).

[771] CDiat 15.22: ܚܝ̈ ܠܟ ܗܝܡܢܘܬܟ ܐܚܝܬܟ. ܘܠܐ ܐܡܪ ܠܗ ܕܗܝܡܢܘܬܟ ܐܚܙܝܬܟ.

[772] CDiat 15.22: ܗܕ: ܚܝܐ ܩܕܡ̣ ܕܚܝ̈ܐ ܕܠܟܘ ܗܟܢ ܠܥܝ̈ܢܐ. ܚܝ̈ܐ ܕܡ ܕܠܒܪ ܐܦ ܠܐ ܡܠܠ ܚܝܡ. ܐܡܗܪ ܚܝ̈ܐ ܕܠܒܪ ܐܝܟ ܚܝ̈ܐ ܕܠܟܘ. ܕܒܝܐ ܕܦܒܐ ܬܘܒ ܕܢܗܪܓ ܠܒܬܗ ܗܘܐ ܡܬܚܙܐ ܠܗ.

holy Trinity, which are fundamental at baptism.[773] Faith is also required for the holy eucharistic communion.[774]

Faith is not limited to God's chosen People any more, but is open to gentiles alike who might believe in God and achieve complete healing through their faith. The gentiles are represented by the Syro-Phoenician woman. Through her faith her daughter was healed: 'from afar your faith (Mt 15:28) healed your daughter in your house' (Mk 7:30).[775]

The woman with the haemorrhage (Mk 5:25-34) was afraid to approach Jesus, but she was encouraged to draw near to him because of her faith. The Lord recognized her will and faith and so went out to welcome her faith.[776]

---

[773] Fid 18.3:

ܘܐܦ ܗܝܡܢܘܬܐ ܐܬܬܠܝܬ ܐܬ ܠܒܪܬ
ܕܒܗ ܒܐܒܐ ܘܒܒܪܐ ܘܪܘܚܐ ܩܕܝܫܐ ܡܗܝܡܢܘ
ܡܢ ܗܘ ܦܪܫܬ ܒܪܘܪܘܬܐ ܠܐܪܒܥ ܦܢܝܢ
ܒܣܠܐ ܕܢܠܒܐ.

Fid 67.10: ܗܝܡܢ ܥܡܡܐ ܕܬܠܬܝܗܘܢ ܚܕ ܒܬܪ ܚܕ ܒܗܝܡܢܘܬܐ ܠܡܥܡܘܕܝܬܐ.

Also see Hebd 2.181: ܒܡܫܝܚܐ ܘܒܗܝܡܢܘܬܐ.

[774] Hebd 4.105:

ܕܢܗܘܐ ܚܝܐ ܠܢܦܫܬܗܘܢ، ܗܟܢ ܐܟܠܘ ܒܗܝܡܢܘܬܐ
ܘܠܐ ܬܬܦܠܓܘܢ ܕܗܢܐ ܦܓܪܝ،
ܘܕܐܟܠ ܠܗ ܒܗܝܡܢܘܬܐ
ܢܘܪܐ ܘܪܘܚܐ ܐܟܠ ܒܗ.

[775] Virg 26.9: ܗܝܡܢܘܬܟܝ ܡܢ ܪܘܚܩܐ ܗܘ ܐܣܝܬ ܠܒܪܬܟܝ ܒܒܝ ܬܟܝ.

[776] Virg 34.1:

ܕܕܡܗ̇ ܕܫܠܝܬ ܗܘܬ ܕܬܩܪܘܒ ܠܒܪܐ ܟܠ
ܐܬܠܒܒܬ ܡܢ ܗ̇ܘ ܡܠܒܒ ܠܚܠܫܐ
ܒܝܕܥܬܗ̇ ܐܪܓܫ ܕܢܓܥܐ ܗܝ، ܕܬܬܝܕܥܐ ܒܗ
ܠܗܝܡܢܘܬܗ̇ ܐܣܬܟܠ ܐܬܘܒܗ ܕܗ̇ܘ ܝܕܥ
ܕܡܗ̇ ܪܕܐ ܘܫܘܒܗ̇ ܬܚܝܬ ܗܘܐ
ܒܕܡܗ̇ ܚܙܬ ܗܘܬ ܕܐܬܒܣܡ
ܘܒܠܒܒܐ ܕܫܘܒܗ̇ ܕܐܪܕܝܗ.

Thus, to be healed, faith is required. The heavenly Medicine of Life and His spiritual physicians are waiting to see the faith of the spiritually sick people to heal their bodies and souls.[777] The sinners are encouraged to ask for healing faithfully through real repentance, prayer and fasting.[778]

### *5.3.3.5 Prayer*

Prayer (ܨܠܘܬܐ) is explicitly related to healing in only a few passages. The faithful can be healed through prayer not because it is a magical manipulation of the holy divinity, or asks for material possessions or reward; but because right prayer directs and corrects the whole of man's attitude towards his Creator, makes intercession and pleas spiritually for divine mercy, as well as gives thanks and praise for the splendour of the Lord's deeds and His majesty. The whole process of salvation and the healing of humanity did not start because of man's prayer, but because of God's compassion. In Virg 26.10, Ephrem refers to the resurrection of the widow's son in Nain (Lk 7:11-17). Ephrem compares the way Jesus reacted towards the widow's son to God's universal attitude towards humanity. As the boy was physically dead, so too, the whole world was spiritually dead. Jesus revived him 'without entreaty' ( ܕܠܐ ܒܥܘܬܐ), as He saved creation 'without prayer' ( ܘܕܠܐ ܨܠܘܬܐ):

ܠܒܪܟܝ ܐܦ ܠܟܝ ܐܘ ܐܪܡܠܬܐ
ܕܥܠܡܐ ܡܝܬܐ̇ ܘܒܪܟܝ ܡܝܬܐ
ܒܪܟܝ ܕܝܢ ܗܘ ܚܝܐ ܕܠܐ ܒܥܘܬܐ
ܘܕܠܐ ܨܠܘܬܐ̇ ܒܪܝܬܐ ܦܪܩܗ
ܠܐ ܒܥܘܬܟܝ ܪܬܚܗ ܗܘܬ ܠܐܣܝܐ
ܘܐܦ ܠܐ ܨܠܘܬܗ̇ ܐܪܡܠܬܗ ܠܦܪܩ

[777] I Serm 6.447:
ܐܣ̈ܘܬܐ ܐܝܬܝܗܘܢ ܕܣܦܩܝܢ ܠܟܠ ܟܘܪ̈ܗܢܐ
ܕܒܪܢܫܐ ܕܫܢܐ ܠܚܠܝܡܝܢ ܐܣܝܘܬܐ ܕܢܦܫܐ ܘܦܓܪܐ
ܐܣܝܘܬܐ ܪܘܚܢܝܬܐ ܕܠܢܦܫܐ ܘܦܓܪܐ ܡܐܣܝܐ
ܗܝܡܢܘܬܐ ܡܬܚܝܢ ܠܗ ܘܟܠܗܝܢ ܕܚܝܠܗ ܢܣܒܝܢ ܠܗ.

[778] I Serm 7.81: ܥܠ ܕܐܝܬ ܡܕܒܪܐ ܠܫܠܝܐ ܕܬܝܐܒܘܢ ܒܬܘܒܬܐ ܘܠܨܘܡܐ ܘܠܨܠܘܬܐ ܕܢܕܪܫܘܢ ܒܗܝܡܢܘܬܐ. See also S. Fid 2.489; IV Serm 1.479 and the next three sections.

ܪ̈ܚܡܐ ܗܘ ܐܪܟܢܘܗܝ، ܠܗܘ ܕܢܚܬ ܘܐܚܝܗ
ܠܥܠܡܐ ܘܠܥܠܝܡܐ.

Blessed are you, too, o widow,
for the world was dead, and your son was dead (Lk 7:11-17).
But your son revived without entreaty,
and without prayer creation was saved.
Your wailing did not summon the Physician,
nor did our prayer make our Saviour bend down.
Mercy made him condescend - the one who came down and gave life
to the world and to the youth.

*Virg 26.10*

Thus, Jesus' salvation and healing of humanity is not a reward or result of human prayer, but of His mercy, compassion and love towards us, as towards the dead boy whose mother did not pray for him. Even though it was not her prayer, or man's prayer that caused the Lord to act as the Physician, prayer still has a significant role in the religious context, and in the process of healing. Prayer has spiritual power. A good and right prayer can be the medicine of life, whereas wrong prayer is considered to be a fruit of sin.[779]

In Dom 41, Ephrem speaks about the power of humility (ܡܟܝܟܘܬܐ) that contrasts with pride: 'whenever pride caused divisions in the nation, humility through its prayer repaired their divisions'.[780] This refers to Moses' time when the People rebelled

---

[779] Iei 1.7:
ܢܗܘܘܢ ܠܟ ܕܝܢ ܒܥܘ̈ܬܐ ܒܕܡܘܬ ܡܚܣܝܢܘܬܐ ܘܚܣܝܐ ܒܗܘܢ ܨܘܡܢ
ܦܐܪܘ ܓܝܪ ܒܥܘ̈ܬܐ ܥܡ ܨܘܡܐ ܠܨܘܡܐ ܘܥܡ ܨܠܘܬܐ ܠܨܠܘܬܐ
ܒܥܘ ܓܝܪ ܠܨܘܡܐ ܘܐܫܠܡܘ ܠܨܘܡܐ
ܪܚܡܘ ܨܘ̈ܡܐ ܘܐܪܓܘ ܨܘ̈ܡܐ
ܐܝܬ ܨܠܘܬܐ ܕܚܛܝܬܐ ܗܝ، ܘܐܝܬ ܬܘܒ ܕܗܘܝ ܚ̈ܛܗܐ ܗܝ
ܡܢ ܠܚܕܐ ܒܨܘܡܢ ܐܝܟ ܡܢܐ ܕܒܙܝ، ܐܢܫ ܒܨܘܡܐ ܕܠܦܨܗ.

[780] Dom 41: ܐܡܬܝ، ܓܝܪ ܕܪܒܘܬܐ ܬܘܪ̈ܥܬܐ ܒܥܡܐ ܥܒܕܬ ܗܘܬ ܡܟܝܟܘܬܐ ܒܨܠܘܬܗ ܬܘܪ̈ܥܬܗܘܢ ܣܝܟܐ ܗܘܬ. After the long excursus about the conversion of Saul, Ephrem returns again to the pride of Simon the Pharisee: 'The one who used humble words with Paul, his persecutor, used the same humble words with the Pharisee. Humility is so powerful that even the all-conquering God did not conquer without it' ☞

against Moses and God. Ephrem emphasises that actually God does not need anything to save His people, but because of the 'stiff-necked nation' He 'found Himself in need of Moses' humility'. So Moses through his humility in prayer moved God to bind up the nation's wounds. Likewise, Jesus humiliated himself, fasted and prayed to cleanse the defilement of the first Serpent on the one hand, and to show that every human being needs to pray and fast.[781] As man's sin alienates human beings from God so that they become spiritually sick, so too man's prayer reconciles them with the Lord and restores them to health. Prayer has the power to bind and loose, as well as to destroy and save.[782] For example, concerning Nisibis, Ephrem says; 'your inhabitants' prayer was sufficient to save you; not because they were just, but because they were penitent.'[783] Prayer has the power to open and close heaven.[784] Therefore, right prayer can be a 'treasure of medicine' (ܨܠܘܬܟܝ ܣܝܡܬ ܣܡ̈ܡܢܐ). Prayer and fasting are two spiritual eyes that serve as baptism for the forgiveness of sin.[785]

---

(Dom 41: ܗ̇ܘ ܕܝܢ ܕܐܬܚܫܚ ܒܡ̈ܠܐ ܡܟܝ̈ܟܬܐ ܒܗ ܦܘܠܘܣ ܙܕܩܗ. ܗܘ ܐܬܚܫܚ ܒܗ ܦܘܪܫܐ ܒܒܥܘܬܗ ܩ̈ܠܐ ܡܟܝܟܘܬܐ. ܡܟܝܟܐ ܕܝܢ ܡܛܠ ܚܠܬܗ̇ ܕܡܟܝܟܘܬܐ. ܕܐܦ ܐܠܗܐ ܪܒܐ ܒܠ ܒܠܒܪܘܗ̇ ܠܐ ܐܪܓܐ).

[781] Eccl 13.21-25:

ܟܠ ܡܢ ܟܠܐ ܡܛܠ ܕܐܬܡܟܟܢ
ܣܥ̈ܝܡ ܗܘܐ ܒܒܪܘܗܝ ܒܚܕܐ ܐܦ ܒܚܕܐ.
ܦܫܛ ܗ̇ܘ ܥܒܕܢ ܡܛܠ ܦܐܪܗ ܚܝܐ ܕܐܒܐ
ܕܦܫܡ ܗܘܐ ܒܒܕܢ ܦܓ̣ܪܐ ܒܠ ܕܠܒܫܬܗ.
ܙܡ ܒܪ ܐܠܗܐ ܨܘܡܐ ܕܐܢܫܘܬܐ
ܨܠܘܬܐ ܕܒ̈ܢܝܐ ܢܓܠ ܥܡܒܕ ܨܠܘ̈ܬܐ.
ܨܘܡܢ ܬܪܥܡ ܠܟ ܨܠܘܬܢ ܕܡܟܝܐ ܗܝ
ܕܨܘܡܢ ܕܦܓܪܐ ܗܘܐ ܨܠܘܬܢ ܕܦܓܪܐ ܗܘܬ.
ܨܘܡܢ ܚܦܝ ܗܘܐ ܨܐܬܗ ܕܚܘܝܐ ܡܕܡܝܐ
ܨܠܘܬܢ ܗܘܬ ܒܘܪܐ ܕܢܦܫܬ ܥܘܡܝܬܐ ܕܠܒܡ.

[782] Haer 4.13: ܨܠܘܬܐ ܐܣܪܬ ܘܫܪܬ ܕܚܠܦܗ̇ ܚܝܪ ܘܐܚܝܢ.

[783] Nis 3.5:

ܨܠܘܬܐ ܕܒܡܘܬܒܝܟܝ ܣܦܩܬ ܠܦܘܪܩܢܟܝ
ܠܐ ܗܘܐ ܕܙܕܝܩܝܢ ܐܠܐ ܕܬܝܒܝܢ.

[784] Iei 9.13: ܕܒܨܠܘܬܐ ܠܫܡܝܐ ܐܚܕܘ ܘܦܬܚܘ.

[785] Abr Kid 4.1:

☞

### *5.3.3.6 Fasting*

Although fasting (ܨܘܡܐ) contrasts with eating and food, actually in their nature both of them are pure and fine. Eating and food are not defiled, if they are balanced.[786] While it is natural to eat, it is supernatural to fast, or as Ephrem says: 'it is according to nature to eat, [but] according to free will to fast'.[787] If eating and drinking are not balanced, they affect the body, as fire and flame affect wood;

---

ܠܡܟܝܢ ܗܟܢܐ ܕܐܬܚܠܫܬ
ܕܨܘܡܟܝ ܠܒܪܐ ܕܒܡܘܪ̈ܕܐ
ܨܠܘܬܟܝ ܗܫܟܚܬ ܗܡܟܝ̈ܢܐ ܬܪ̈ܬܝܢ ܒܬܢ̈ܝܢ ܗܘ̈ܝܢ ܠܟܝ ܡܒܡܕܪ̈ܝܬܐ ܕܢܚܫܐ.

See also Abr Kid 5.22:

ܗܒܒܗ ܐܝܟܝ ܚܙ ܠܝܫܢ̈ܝܟܝ ܫܦܝܪܐ ܠܨܘܡܐ ܡܨܝܒܬ ܗܘܐ
ܘܠܕܘܒܪ̈ܬܐ ܨܠܘܬܐ ܘܥܡ ܫܘܟܪ̈ܢܐ ܕܟܪ̈ܝܗܐ
ܪܘܫܡ ܬܘܠܡܕܐ ܕܫܠܝ̈ܚܐ.

See further Haer 11.14: ܘܗܘܢ̈ܝܐ ܕܒܨܠܘܬܗ ܕܐܗܒܐ ܢܦܠܘ ܗܘܘ.

SFid 2.489: ܗܝܡܢܘܬܐ ܗܝ ܘܨܠܘܬܐ ...

Haer 18.2:

ܕܡܠܐܟܘܬ ܕܝܢ ܢܬܒܥܘܢ
ܒܗܢܐ ܡܫܠ ܗܘ ܒܒܥܘܬܐ
ܕܟܪ̈ܝܗܐ ܗܐ ܢܦܫ ܒܗ ܘܒܕܘܪܗ
ܘܪ̈ܡܠܐ ܕܢܚܠܘ ܗܐ ܫܘܦܗܘܢ
ܒܠܘܗܝ ܗܐ ܪ̈ܡܠܐ ܐܪܡܠܘܬܗܘܢ
ܚܠ̈ܨܐ ܪܘܚܐ ܡܕܒܪܗܘܢ ܒܨܘܡܗܘܢ
ܗܡܝ̈ܢܐ ܘܪ̈ܐ ܗܠܠܗ ܘܒܡܫܡܗܘܢ
ܦܬܝ̈ܟܐ ܢܕܘ ܠܟܪ̈ܐ ܕܨܠܘܬܐ ܘܐܬܒܪܘ
ܟܪ̈ܝܗܐ ܗܘ ܕܝܗܒ ܠܗ ܚܠ̈ܨܐ ܡܠܐܟܐ ܠܗ ܪ̈ܡܠܐ ܘܪܚܡ ܠܗ.

II Serm 4.151:

ܘܟܠ ܗܝ ܐܝܟ ܗܘܐ ܡܢܗ̈ ܕܠܐ ܢܦܫ ܡܢ ܒܨܠܘܬܐ
ܕܠܐ ܢܥܒܕ ܡܕܡ ܡܟܠܠ ܘܢܦܪܘܩ ܢܗܘܐ ܫܘܟܠܠ.

IV Serm 1.479:

ܐܚܝܕ ܚܘܪܐ ܠܢܘܦܪܝܢ ܘܟܦܢܐ ܘܨܗܝܐ ܗܡܟܝ̈ܢܐ
ܘܗܝܡܢܘܬܐ ܬܘܟܠܢܐ ܕܗܒܐ ܚܝܠܐ ܒܨܠܘܬܐ.

786 Fide 79.7:

ܬܘܒ ܨܘܡ ܘܠܚܡ ܒܟܕܢܗ ܘܠܐ ܡܐܟܠ ܐܟܠ ܠܗ
ܨܘܡܐ ܒܐܟܘܠܐ ܠܡܐܟܠܐ ܘܨܘܡܐ ܒܪ ܬܪ̈ܝܢ ܕܝܢ ܘܦܐܝܢ.

787 Iei App 4.4: ܕܐܟܘܠ ܕܟܝܢܐ ܗܝ ܘܕܨܘܡ ܕܨܒܝܢܘܬܐ ܗܝ.

and so they disturb the mind and defile it.[788] Eating can be a sign of gluttony. Through eating man's fall was caused. Jesus healed the gluttony by His fasting (ܕܐܣܝ ܒܨܘܡܗ ܠܐܣܘܛܘܬܐ). When Jesus was fasting, Satan confronted and tempted Jesus with bread, the symbol of gluttony, as he tempted Eve with the fruit. In this context, Ephrem says:

ܓܐܪܐ ܕܫܕܐ ܒܟ ܠܚܡܐ ܗܘ ܕܒܥܐ
ܪܐܙܐ ܕܥܘܠܬܐ ܕܠܘܬ ܐܕܡ
ܒܠܚܡܐ ܗܘ ܢܣܝܗ ܠܗܘ ܙܐܢ ܟܠ
ܕܐܣܝ ܒܨܘܡܗ ܠܐܣܘܛܘܬܐ
----ܣܛܢܐ----
ܬܠܡܝ̈ܕܘܗܝ ---- ܚܬܢܐ ܣܡܝܟ ܗܘܐ
ܡ̈ܝܐ ܒܩܛܢܐ ܫܚܠܦ ܗܘܐ
ܕܠܐ ܨܒܐ ܕܢܫܚܠܦ ܟܐܦ̈ܐ.

The arrow he shot at you was the bread for which he asked,
symbol of the greed of Adam.
With bread he tempted the Sustainer of all,
Who by His fasting healed gluttony.
---- Satan ----
His disciples ---- the Bridegroom was reclining
He Who did not want to change stones
changed water at Cana (Jn 2:1-12).

*Virg 14.11*

Since the human body is weak and human nature sick, Satan saw Jesus as a man and tried to tempt Him; but Jesus defeated the Evil One by fasting.[789] Jesus fasted and prayed for He was born as

---

[788] Iei App 1.9:
ܒܕܡܘܬ ܡܫܚܐ ܕܡܫܟܚܝܢ ܠܢܘܪܐ ܫܠܡܘܬܐ ܗܟܢ ܠܦܓܪܐ
ܒܐܘܟܠܐ ܘܫܬܝܐ ܐܝܟ ܬܢܐ ܡܫܬܠܡܐ ܗܘ ܚܠܦܝܢ ܚܫܘ̈ܗܝ
ܘܕܠܚܝܢ ܠܗܘܢܐ ܒܝ ܫܘܪܬܐ.

[789] Virg 14.13:
ܡܫܬܗ ܟ̈ܠܐ ܘܚܙܐ ܗܘ ܒܪܢܫܐ
ܠܗܘܠ ܒܪܢ ܗܘ ܒܡܫܝܚܐ
ܛܒܐ ܒܗ ܘܐܬܓܒܪ ܕܢܣܝܘܗܝ ܕܠܒܝܫ
ܦܓܪܐ ܡܚܝܠܐ ܚܒܠܐ ܒܪܢܫܐ

☞

a man, and through His fasting He cleansed the defilement of the first Serpent.[790] Eating gives energy and power to the body, whereas fasting strengthens the spirit.[791] With His fasting, Jesus showed us the 'power hidden in fasting' (ܚܝܠܐ ܕܟܣܐ ܒܨܘܡܐ).[792] Fasting cleanses the soul and serves as wings with which the faithful can fly to meet God in heaven.[793]

Ephrem considers fasting to be a teacher (ܡܠܦܢܐ) that teaches one how to fight, just as Jesus' fasting shows us how to fast and defeat the Evil One. In the context of healing, Ephrem does not describe how and from what to fast, but he mentions eating

---

ܚܙܝܗܝ ܒܢܫܐ ܠܗ ܠܢܦܠܐ ܘܐܬܬܟܠ
ܕܢܦܠܐ ܗܘܐ ܕܗܘ ܐܕܡ ܕܐܙܕܟܝ
ܙܟܐ ܗܘ ܒܡܬܬܗ ܕܒܢܦܠܐ ܕܒܗ ܙܟܐ
ܣܚܦ ܚܛܝܬܗ.

790 Eccl 13.21-25:

ܟܠ ܡܢ ܟܠܐ ܡܛܠ ܕܐܬܡܚܝܢ
ܣܒܪܝܢ ܗܘܐ ܒܟܒܪܘܗܝ، ܒܟܒܪܐ ܐܦ ܒܟܒܪܐ.
ܦܓܪܐ ܗܘ ܥܒܕܢ ܣܦܩ
ܦܐܪܗ ܚܝܠܐ ܕܐܟܠܐ
ܕܦܓܡܝܢ ܗܘܐ ܒܟܒܪܝܢ
ܦܚܪܝ ܟܠ ܕܠܒܫܬܝܗ.
ܨܡ ܒܪ ܐܠܗܐ ܨܘܡܐ ܕܐܚܘܝܬܐ
ܨܠܘܬܐ ܕܟܒܪܐ ܢܨܠ ܥܒܕ ܨܠܘܬܐ.
ܨܘܡܟܝ ܬܪܬܝܢ ܠܝ ܨܠܘܬܟܝ ܕܡܟܠܐ ܗܝ
ܕܨܘܡܟܝ ܕܦܓܪܐ ܗܘܐ ܨܠܘܬܟܝ ܕܦܓܪܐ ܗܘܬ.
ܨܘܡܟܝ ܟܦܪ ܗܘܐ ܨܐܬܗ ܕܚܘܒܐ ܡܕܡܟܐ
ܨܠܘܬܟܝ ܗܘܬ ܒܘܪܐ ܕܨܦܪܬ ܚܘܫܒܬܐ ܕܢܦܫ.

791 Dom 15: ܨܘܡܐ ܡܚܝܠ ܢܦܫܐ ܡܐܟܠܐ ܡܫܡܢ ܦܓܪܐ.

792 Iei 1.1: ܠܗ ܗܘ ܚܘܝ، ܚܝܠܐ ܕܟܣܐ ܒܨܘܡܐ ܪܒܐ ܟܠ.

793 Iei 1.2:

ܨܘܡܐ ܒܟܣܝܐ ܦܪܚ ܠܫܡܝܐ ... ܒܢܝܗ ܗܘ ܕܝܗܒ ܠܗ ܨܘܡܐ ܠܓܦܐ
ܥܩܒܐ ܕܟܣܝܘܗܝ ܠܦܪܚ ܨܐܕܘܗܝ

In Abr Kid 4.1, fasting is described as the 'treasury of help':

ܠܟܢܝܢ ܣܝܡܐ ܕܐܬܟܢܫܬ ܕܨܘܡܟܝ ܓܙܐ ܕܡܥܕܪܢܐ
ܨܠܘܬܟܝ ܣܝܡܬ ܣܝܡܬܢܐ ܬܪܬܝܢ ܒܢܝܟܝ ܣܡܝ ܠܟܝ
ܡܟܢܘܫܬܐ ܕܚܘܣܝܐ.

(ܐܘܟܠܐ - ܡܐܟܠܐ - ܠܚܡܐ), drinking (ܫܬܝܐ)[794] and wine (ܚܡܪܐ).[795] However, Fasting is not just from food, but also from wrong thoughts; as well as our mouth, our heart needs to fast rightly.[796] As there is a difference between prayer and prayer, so too there is a difference between fasting and fasting.[797] The right fasting illuminates truth (ܩܘܫܬܐ) and rejects error that has grown strong in the fallen world,[798] and it strengthens man's weakness.[799] Fasting can serve as 'oars' (ܠܦ̈ܝܐ) to save and pull man from the destruction of this world, as the Ninevites performed pure fasting

---

794 Dom 15; Fid 79.7; Iei App 1.9.

795 Parad 7.18; cf. Haer 18.2:

ܕܡܠܐܟܘܬ ܕܝܢ ܠܬܚܘܡ ܒܕܟܐ ܡܣܝܠ ܥܠ ܒܬܘܠܘܬܐ ܕܒܢ̈ܝܗܐ
ܗܐ ܢܛܪ ܒܗ ܘܒܙܪܗ ܘܕ̈ܡܝܐ ܕܢܦܠܘ ܗܘܐ ܚܫܘܒܗ، ܒܠܗܘܢ
ܗܐ ܕ̈ܡܝܐ ܐܘܪܚܬܗ، ܣܓ̈ܝܐܐ ܢܘܩܦܘ ܡܕܒܪܗ، ܒܝܘܡܬܗܘܢ
ܗܡܝ̈ܢܐ ܘܚܢܝ ܗܠܠܘ ܘܒܡܗܘܢ، ܦܬܝ̈ܟܐ ܥܕܘ ܠܟܪ̈ܐ ܕܓܠܝܬܐ
ܘܐܬܒܣܪ

ܒܢ̈ܝܗܐ ܗܘ ܘܗܒ ܠܗ ܣܓ̈ܝܐܐ ܡܠܐܟܝܢ ܠܗ ܕ̈ܡܝܐ ܘܪܒܝܢ ܠܗ.

796 Iei 1.6:

ܗܠܝܢ ܝܘܡܐ ܡܠܦܢܐ ܡܠܦ ܠܐܬܠܝܛܐ ܥܢ̈ܕܗܘܢ، ܕܐܬܚܝܠܘܢ
ܐܬܦܪܣܘ ܠܗܬܠ ܘܡܠܦܠܘ ܘܐܬܠܒܫܘ ܬܠܡܝܕܘܬܐ ܕܦܘܪܫܢܐ
ܗܐ ܦܡܢ ܠܐ ܕܢܨܘܡ ܦܘܡܢ ܘܢܨܘܡ ܐܦ ܠܒܢ
ܠܐ ܢܨܘܡ ܠܫܡܝܐ ܘܢܪܢܐ ܒܡܪܢܝܬܐ ܕܒܣܝܐ ܒܗ ܗܘ ܡܘܬܐ
ܒܣܝܐ

ܢܗܪܐ ܒܨܘܡܐ ܠܒܡܪܢܐ ܕܢܣܒ ܠܢ ܡܐܡܪ ܚܘܐ ܕܢܬܗܦܟ ܒܗ.

797 Iei 1.7:

ܢܣܒܘܢ ܠܢ ܕܝܢ ܒܬܘ̈ܬܐ ܒܕܡܘܬ ܡܚܝܬܐ ܘܢܣܒܐ ܒܗܘܢ ܝܘܡܢ
ܦܪܫ ܒܝܢ ܬܘ̈ܒܬܐ ܒܝܬ ܨܘܡܐ ܠܨܘܡܐ ܘܒܝܬ ܨܠܘܬܐ ܠܨܠܘܬܐ
ܒܒܐ ܒܝܢ ܠܨܘܡܐ ܘܐܫܠܘ ܠܨܘܡܐ
ܕܒܢܐ ܨܘ̈ܡܐ ܘܐܪܒܥܘ ܨܘ̈ܡܐ ܐܝܬ ܨܠܘܬܐ ܕܡܫܬܠܝܐ ܗܝ، ܘܐܝܬ
ܬܘܒ ܕܣܡܟ ܫܢܐ ܗܝ،

ܡܢ ܠܣܕܐ ܒܝܘܡܢ ܐܝܟ ܡܐ ܕܝܕܝ، ܐܢܫ ܒܝܘܡܐ ܕܠܦܥܡܗ.

798 Iei 1.12: ܒܡܒܐ ܡܩܘܫܬܐ ܒܝܘܡܐ ܢܒܓܐ ܘܢܦܩܘܣ ܒܗ ܠܛܘܥܝܝܐ ܕܐܘܪ̈ܐ.

799 Iei 4.4: ܗܐ ܝܘܡܐ ܡܕܙܥܝܢܐ ܦܪܐ ܠܚܘܠܫܬܐ (ܡܚܝܠܘܬܐ)

and were saved.[800] Thus, man's fasting needs to be real and true in order to defeat error.[801]

Ephrem explicitly attributes healing terminology to fasting. He considers fasting to serve as a 'healer' (ܡܐܣܝܢܐ) that possesses a heavenly medicine (ܒܣܡܡ̈ܢܘܗܝ). Referring to Moses' time, fasting descended from mount Sinai to restore the wounded camp: 'it healed the hidden pains of the soul and bound up the great wound of the mind'. Fasting supported God's People when they fell in the desert. Ephrem describes 'good fastings' (ܨܘܡ̈ܐ ܛܒ̈ܐ) as 'medicines' (ܣܡܡ̈ܢܐ) that God provides for the faithful.[802] Moses rejected the Egyptian's ordinary medicine, for he had to deal with spiritual pain that needs a spiritual medicine, namely fasting. His own fasting on mount Sinai is illustrated as a 'fasting of atonement' (ܨܘܡܐ ܕܚܘܣܝܐ), and the 'fastings' (ܨܘܡ̈ܐ) of the People served as 'medicine' (ܣܡܡ̈ܢܐ) for those who were wounded by the golden calf.[803]

---

800 Virg 47.1: ܬܘܒ ܢܝܢܘܝ̈ܐ ܕܚܛܗܘ ܡܘܬܪܢܐ ܨܘܡܐ ܕܚܝܐ ܕܚܒ̈ܠܬܐ ܕܒܢ̈ܝܐ. Virg 47.19: ܗܘܘ ܗܘܘ ܨܘܡ̈ܐ ܠܢܦ̈ܫܐ ܘܐܣܝܘ.

801 Virg 40.8:

ܨܘܡܗ ܢܦܫܐ ܘܩܘܫܬܐ ܘܫܪܪܗ ܫܪܪܐ ܬܘܒ
ܕܨܘܡܐ ܐܦ ܫܪܪܐ ܕܠܒܝܫ ܡܗܝܡܢ ܗܘ ܕܐܝܬ ܗܘ ܢܨܚܬ
ܐܠܗܬ.

802 Iei 4.1:

ܗܘ ܨܘܡܐ ܡܐܣܝܢܐ ܢܚܬ ܒܡܪ̈ܘܡܘܗܝ܆ ܘܫܩܐ ܒܣܡܡ̈ܢܘܗܝ
ܨܘܡܐ ܗܘ ܟܕ ܢܚܬ ܗܘܐ ܡܢ ܛܘܪ ܣܝܢܝ ܠܡܫܪܝܬܐ ܡܡܚܝܫܬܐ
ܘܐܣܝ ܟܐܒ̈ܐ ܟܣ̈ܝܐ ܕܢܦܫܐ ܘܚܒܫ ܠܡܚܘܬܐ ܪܒܐ ܕܪܥܝܢܐ
ܨܘܡܐ ܣܡܟܗ̇ ܠܥܡܠܬܗ ܕܗ̇ܘ ܥܡܐ ܒܡܕܒܪܐ
ܢܬܠ ܫܘܒܚܐ ܠܐܣܝܐ ܕܨܘܡ̈ܐ ܛܒ̈ܐ ܗܘܘ ܠܢ ܐܝܟ ܣܡܡ̈ܢܐ.

803 Iei 10.4:

ܟܕ ܡܫܟܢܐ ܒܛܘܪܐ ܡܬܬܩܢ ܗܘܐ ܗ̇ܘ ܥܡܐ ܒܥܓܠܐ ܡܬܬܠܒܒ
ܗܘܐ
ܠܡܫܟܢܐ ܕܝܢ ܨܘܡܐ ܕܚܘܣܝܐ ܘܠܥܡܐ ܒܣܡܐ ܕܦܬܟܪܘܬܐ
ܡܫܟܢܐ ܠܗܬ ܪܡܐ ܥܡܐ ܠܗܬ ܥܓܠܐ
ܪܘܚܐ ܥܡܗ ܡܫܟܢܐ ܘܠܥܡܐ ܥܡܗ ܥܡܐ
ܗܘܘ ܨܘܡ̈ܐ ܣܡܡ̈ܢܐ ܠܡܚ̈ܝܐ ܕܒܥܓܠܐ ܐܬܡܚܝܘ.

☞

Beside Moses' fasting, Daniel's fasting is also significant. For as he fasted, he received divine help. The lions feared 'the fragrance of his fasting' (ܪܝܚܐ ܕܨܘܡܗ), and the angel caused the lions to fast.[804] Finally, in the context of Jonah, the Ninevites' fasting is described as the 'glorious medicine' (ܨܘܡܐ ܣܡܐ ܢܨܝܚܐ) through which Jonah 'healed the sickness of the town' ( ܟܘܪܗܢܐ ܕܡܕܝܢܬܐ ܐܣܝ).[805]

### 5.3.3.7 *Repentance*

The medicine of repentance is heavenly medicine that comes down from high to forgive sinners.[806] The heavenly medicine cannot be bought with any price, and no one is able to pay for it, but with repentance. According to Ephrem, repentance causes the Lord to be merciful. If someone repents, one drop of mercy annuls the book of his debts.[807] The divine mercy is medicine and it is free, so

---

See also Iei 10.6:

ܣܡ̈ܡܢܐ ܕܡܪ̈ܢܝܢ ܦܘܩܕܢ ܐܝܟ ܐܣܘ̈ܬܐ ܕܬܡܢ ܒܡܗܝܪܝܢ ܐܝܟ
ܥܠ ܡܘܥܐ ܡܣܬܟܠܬܐ ܕܣܡ̈ܡܢܐ ܕܠܐ ܒܟܐܒܐ ܗܘ ܕܦܓܪܐ ܐܠܐ ܕܢܦܫܐ

ܣܠܩ ܠܗ ܠܛܘܪ ܣܝܢܝ ܠܛܘܪܗ ܕܐܠܗܐ ܘܐܘܣܦ ܗܘܐ ܬܡܢ ܘܨܡ ܘܐܚܬ ܗܘܐ

ܒܣ̈ܡܐ ܪ̈ܘܚܢܐ ܕܠܢܦܫܐ ܡܐܣܝܢ ܗܘ ܒܡܫܟܢܬ.

804 Iei App 2.2: ܘܡܢ ܪܝܚܐ ܕܨܘܡܗ ܕܚܠܘ ܐܪ̈ܝܘܬܐ. See also Parad 6.20.

Iei App 2.9:

ܬܠܬܐ ܛܠܝ̈ܐ ܗܘܘ ܒܐܬܘܢܐ ܕܢܘܪܐ ܬܠܝܬܝܐ ܡܬܠܒܟܝܢ
ܗܐ ܪܘܚܐ ܘܨܒܥܐ ܦܓܪܐ ܬܠܝܬܝܐ
ܘܐܦ ܡܬܚܫܒ ܢܘܚܐ ܪܒܝܥܝܐ ܠܒܢܝܢܗ ܡܫܬܠܝܢ.

805 II Serm 1.921-24:

ܐܣܝܐ ܗܘ ܕܦܬܚ ܠܡܕܝܢܬܗ ܘܝܗܒ ܣܡܐ ܕܢܚܠܡ ܠܗ̇
ܨܘܡܐ ܣܡܐ ܢܨܝܚܐ ܟܘܪܗܢܐ ܕܡܕܝܢܬܐ ܐܣܝ.

806 Virg 49.16: ܣܡ ܬܡܢܐ ܢܚܬ ܡܢ ܪܘܡܐ ܒܪ ܚܘܣܝܐ ܒܝܢܬ ܚܛ̈ܝܐ

807 Eccl 5.16:

ܬܘ ܥܡܢ ܘܐܬܠܒܒܘ ܕܗܐ ܠܟ ܒܥܝܐ
ܬܟܬܒܬܗ ܕܚܘܒܬܐ ܐܢ ܗܘ ܕܐܢܫ ܬܐܒ
ܚܕܐ ܢܘܛܦܬܐ ܕܪ̈ܚܡܐ ܒܛܠܐ ܫܛܪ ܚܘ̈ܒܘܗܝ.

that everyone can take it freely through their tears.[808] In contrast to sin, repentance saves,[809] restores and heals.[810] Repentance is considered to be an ark of mercy[811] and the place for refugees, as it is called the 'town of refuge' ( ܬܝܒܘܬܐ ܩܘܪܝܬ ܒܝܬ ܓܘܣܐ).[812]

In Virg 7.1, repentance is compared to diligence (ܟܫܝܪܘܬܐ). As diligence is capable of doing business in the world to achieve wealth, so too repentance is required to achieve spiritual success to be victorious. In order to be successful in both worlds both diligence and repentance are needed.[813] Referring to other passages, diligence and repentance can be used only in this world, but they benefit both. In I Serm 5, the author personifies repentance:

ܟܕ ܕܝܢ ܗܕܐ ܚܛܝܐ ܬܝܒܘܬܐ ܠܐ ܐܡܪܬ ܗܘܬ
ܕܠܐ ܡܚܛܝܐ ܒܐܝܕܝ، ܐܘܬܪܬ ܠܚܛܝܐ ܡܚܕܐ ܬܡܢ

---

808 Nis 4.16-17:

ܐܝܬ ܗܘ ܡܐܣܝܐ ܒܠ ܡܫܪܬܠ ܒܡܘܪܗܢ
ܐܓܪܐ ܕܡܣܟܢܝܢ ܠܐ ܐܬܬܒܥܝܬ ܕܐܬܠ
ܕܕܡܥܝܢ ܠܝܬ ܠܗܘܢ.
ܘܥܡ ܠܡܣܟܢܝܢ ܕܥܝܢܝܢ ܚܠܝܪܐ
ܠܐ ܡܣܝܡ ܡܕܕܡܥܝܢ ܡܟܝܠ ܡܬܐܣܝܢ
ܒܕܡܥܐ ܗܘ ܡܬܠܚܡܝܢ.

809 CDiat 14.2: ܐܠܐ ܚܛܝܬܐ ܚܝܠܬ ܘܬܝܒܘܬܐ ܦܪܩܬ. ܗܘܐ ܕܝܢ ܕܕܘܟܝܬܐ ܫܘܪܒܬ.

810 Virg 3.10, I Serm 7.81; 7.249; 7.355; II Serm 1.197; cf. III Serm 4.599; IV Serm 3 (Epistola, p. 30).

811 Eccl 34.3: ܬܝܒܘܬܐ ܗܝ ܟܘܠܐ ܕܪܚܡܐ ܐܬܝܢ.

812 Eccl 34.1f. The whole hymn 34 is on repentance. For example Eccl 34.1:

ܩܪܝܬܐ ܩܘܪܝܬ ܒܝܬ ܓܘܣܐ ܐܬܝܗ. ܢܗܘܢ ܠܬܝܒܘܬܐ

or Eccl 34.2:

ܐܝܟ ܒܝܬ ܕܟܕ ܝܩܪܐ ܚܛܝܐ ܣܓܝܗ
ܘܐܦ ܕܚܛܐܒ ܒܟܠܬܐ ܕܒܢܝܐ ܡܢ ܒܐܦܐ
ܠܐܢܫܐ ܢܒܪܘܩ ܢܬܓܘܗ
ܐܠܐ ܒܒܠܥܗ ܕܬܝܒܘܬܐ.

813 Virg 7.1:

ܬܝܒܘܬܐ ܘܟܫܝܪܘܬܐ ܠܬܪܝܢ ܥܠܡܝܢ ܡܬܒܥܝܢ
ܠܥܘܠܡ ܐܪܒܐ ܒܫܝܢܐ ܠܥܘܠܡ ܕܪܘܚܐ ܬܗܢܐ.

> ܡܢ ܕܡܟܐ ܠܐ ܫܡܥ ܠܝ
> ܘܥܐܠ ܘܡܬܛܦܣ ܬܚܝܬ ܟܢܦ̈ܝ
> ܐܦܠܐ ܬܡܢ ܒܗܘ ܥܠܡܐ ܐܝܬ ܒܝ ܚܝܠܐ
> ܕܐܥܕܪܝܘܗܝ
> ܠܐ ܡܬܩܒܠܐ ܐܢܐ ܬܡܢ ܕܐܦܝܣ ܡܛܠ ܚܛܝ̈ܐ.
>
> You should know this, oh sinner, repentance has told me,
> it is not possible for me to be useful for sinners there.
> He who does not listen to me here,
> or enter and take supplication under my wings,
> in that world I have not power to help him.
> I am not accepted there to make supplication for sinners.[814]
>
> *I Serm 5.536*

It is in this world that sinners can hope to be healed through repentance.[815] Repentance can restore man from the pains of sin.[816] In I Serm 7, God invites everyone to heal himself through

---

[814] See III Serm 4.599:
ܘܩܕܡ ܕܢܐܬܐ ܗܘ ܝܘܡܐ ܐܬܟܫܦܘ ܒܬܝܒܘܬܐ
ܕܛܝܒܐ ܛܝܒܐ ܚܪ̈ܬܟܘܢ ܘܒܫܘܠܡܐ ܕܡܣܝܢܐ ܠܟܘܢ.

[815] I Serm 7.81:
ܟܠ ܕܐܝܬ ܡܣܒܪܐ ܠܚܛܝ̈ܐ ܕܢܬܐܣܘܢ ܒܬܝܒܘܬܐ
ܘܠܡܣܩ̈ܐ ܘܠܥܠܘ̈ܝܐ ܕܢܙܕܕܩܘܢ ܒܡܫܝܚܘܬܐ.

[816] I Serm 7.249:
ܠܐ ܢܙܘܥ ܒܝ ܦܘܪܫܢܐ ܡܟܐܒܘܬܐ ܘܡܘܬܒܐ
ܕܐܣܝܐ ܒܟܐܒ̈ܐ ܕܚܛܝܬܐ ܚܘܠܡܢܐ ܒܬܝܒܘܬܐ.

repentance.[817] Thus, through repentance everyone can be healed, and he can heal others.[818]

Sometimes Ephrem distinguishes between 'repentance' (ܬܝܒܘܬܐ) and momentary 'remorse' (ܬܘܬ ܢܦܫܐ) to emphasize the meaning of real repentance. While repentance (ܬܝܒܘܬܐ) heals for ever, remorse (ܬܘܬ ܢܦܫܐ) helps only momentarily:

Virg 3.10
ܩܢܝ ܬܝܒܘܬܐ ܕܡܬܡܪܐ ܘܠܐ ܬܘܬ ܢܦܫܐ ܗ̇ܝ
ܕܒܫܠܒ
ܬܝܒܘܬܐ ܓܝܪ ܡܐܣܝܐ ܒܡܩܝܡܘܬܗ̇ ܠܡܚ̈ܘܬܢ
ܬܘܬ ܢܦܫܐ ܕܝܢ ܗܕܐ ܗܘ̣ܝܐ
ܕܬܒܢܐ ܘܬܣܬܘܪ ܟܐ̈ܒܐ ܒܫܠܒ
ܦܓܪܐ ܐܢ ܬܡܪܬ ܕܬܬܘܒ ܘܬܚܘܒ ܬܚܒܠܐ
ܚܬܡܐ ܫܛܪܟ ܗܘ̣ ܬܘܬ ܢܦܫܐ.
Acquire repentance that persists and not momentary
remorse,
for repentance heals our bruises by its constancy,
but remorse has this [character]
that it builds up and tears down pains momentarily.
Body, if you are accustomed to repent and to sin again,
the seal of your letter of bondage is remorse.[819]

---

[817] I Serm 7.355:
ܘܪܒ ܠܚܛ̈ܝܐ ܕܐܬܚܫܚ ܒܬܪ ܕܐܬܗܦܟ ܡܢ̈ܝܢܘܬܗ̇
ܐܝܟܢܐ ܕܡܬܒܥܘܬ ܠܐ ܡܫܟܚ ܐܝܟܢܐ ܒܐܒ̈ܐ ܕܢܛܠܘܢ
ܗܟܢܐ ܕܘܪܒ ܚܛܝܬ ܒܡܫܟܢܐ ܚܘܒ ܒܬܝܒܘܬܐ ܕܢܥܒ̈ܕܬ
ܟܠܗ ܫܒܝܪ ܕܒܪܝܗܐ ܒܐܝܟܢܐ ܐܝܬܘܗܝ ܟܠܒ̈ܝ
ܐܦ ܗܘ ܡܠܬܗ ܕܚܘܒܐ ܠܡܒܥܐ ܠܐܣܝܐ ܕܒܪܝܗ
ܡܠܬܟ ܡܪܝ ܗ̇ܝ ܠܒܥܠܕܒܒ ܕܐܬܒܥܐ ܒܠ ܒܘܪܝܗܝܢ
ܬܘܒܘܢ ܒܢܝ̈ܐ ܬܝ̈ܒܐ ܘܬܝܒܘܬܟܘܢ ܡܐܣܝܐ ܐܝܢܐ
ܕܒܪܝܗܐ ܗܘ ܡܢܕܝܢ ܢܬܐ ܘܢܬܐܣܐ ܡܢ ܒܘܪܝܢܐ
ܘܕܬܒܥܐ ܗܘ ܠܣܘܐ ܒܐܝܟܢ ܢܫܒ ܫܒܝܐ ܠܚܘܒܗ.

[818] II Serm 1.197: ܐܦ ܐܣܝܘ ܐܦ ܐܬܐܣܝܘ ܚܕ ܡܢ ܚܕ ܒܬܝܒܘܬܐ.

[819] In III Serm 4.223, not by Ephrem, the author uses ܬܘܬܐ in the sense of ܬܝܒܘܬܐ: ܒܬܠܐ ܢܬܝܐ ܗ̇ܘ ܢܦܫܐ ܠܣܘܪ ܟܠܒܝ ܒܡܢܘܩܝܗ ܘܡܢ ܕܐܝܬ ܠܗ ܫܘܒܩܢܐ ܕܒܟܠܐ ܢܫܩܦ ܢܐܣܘܗܝ ܒܬܘܬܐ.

It is unlikely that momentary remorse will heal the wounds of sin, but lasting repentance can heal a person's bruises and sores.[820] In I Serm 1, the author explicitly says that repentance is required that lasts for months and years, not only for days.[821] Thus, real repentance implies that he who repents should not return again into his sin. Instead, he should constantly ask for the forgiveness of his debts and wickedness, so that he can be healed totally. In CDiat 11.5, although Ephrem does not use the term 'repentance' or 'remorse', he emphasises the necessity of constant repentance. Even after being healed, doubt can turn man back into spiritual sickness.[822] Ephrem also warns humankind not to misuse repentance with any wrong expectation. Because of the medicine of repentance, no one should increase his sin and wounds in the hope that God with His mercy will heal him.[823]

In Virg 47, Ephrem refers to the repentance of the Ninevites. Here Ephrem explains the effect of repentance metaphorically while he emphasises the importance of tears. The 'tears of repentance' (ܕܕܡ̈ܥܐ ܕܬܝܒܘܬܐ) are considered to be rain for the 'land of repentance' (ܐܪܥܗ̇ ܕܬܝܒܘܬܐ). Because of the tears, the land of repentance produces fruits that please the heavenly Father, so that He balances His mercy with the fruits. He takes fruits and grants mercy intead. Therefore, Ephrem says that the Lord is hungry for the 'tears of remorse' ( ܟܦܢ ܗܘ ܗܘܐ ܕܡܥܐ

[820] Virg 3.10: ܬܝܒܘܬܐ ܓܒܪ ܡܐܣܝܐ ܒܐܡܝܢܘܬܗ̇ ܠܫܘ̈ܚܢܬܗ.

[821] I Serm 1.150: ܕܬܝܒܘܬܐ ܡܬܒܥܝܐ ܠܐ ܬܝܒܘܬܐ ܕܝܘ̈ܡܬܐ ܐܠܐ ܕܝܪ̈ܚܐ ܘܕܫܢ̈ܝܐ.

[822] CDiat 11.5: ܕܡܢܐ ܬܐܬܪܘܢ ܐܢ ܡܬܐܣܝܬܘܢ ܕܫܠܡܬܐ. ܟܕ ܠܐ ܡܗܝܡܢܝܢ ܐܢܬܘܢ. ܒܬܪ ܓܝܪ ܕܡܬܐܣܝܬܘܢ ܐܢ ܬܬܦܠܓܘܢ ܕܒܝܫ ܗܘ ܟܐܒܐ ܘܡܪܥܐ ܗܘܐ ܠܟܘܢ.

[823] Eccl 5.6:

ܥܒܪܐ ܚܝܐ ܕܡܫܬܐ ܐܣܦܠ ܩܠܐ ܣܘ̈ܟܐ
ܕܚܙܐ ܕܐܝܬ ܡܫܬܐ ܕܡܠܝܢ ܡܐܣܝܐ ܠܗ
ܠܐ ܚܣ ܥܠ ܦܓܪܗ ܕܢܟܠܘܗܝ ܚܒܪ̈ܬܐ.

ܠܕܒܝ̈ܢܗ̇ ܕܬܘܬ ܢܦܩܐ ܠܒܪ ܗܘܐ ܒܡܐܪ̈ܘܗ̇).[824] The Ninevites repented and so they were healed.[825]

Beside the repentance of the Ninevites, the case of the sinful woman is the best example of healing through repentance. Ephrem considers the repentance of the sinful woman to be the reason for Jesus' invitation into Simon's house.[826] Jesus was not hungry for food, but for the tears of the sinful woman that indicated her repentance. Tears and oil, along with her action, showed her real repentance.[827] The oil she took with her when she went to Jesus became medicine for her. She offered oil gratis, and in return Jesus offered her the 'treasury of healing for her suffering' ( ܣܝܡܬ ܚܘܠܡܢ̈ܐ ܠܟܐ̈ܒܝܗ̇).[828] In Dom 44, Ephrem describes the oil of

---

824 Virg 47.1-11.

825 Virg 49.14: ܚܘܣܐ ܬܒܬ ܠܗܘܢ ܒܬܪ ܐܬܬܒܝܘ ܐܣܝܐ ܕܢܝܢܘܐ ܗܡܘܣ.

826 Dom 14: 'The one who fills the hungry was not invited on account of his stomach; the one who justifies sinners invited himself on account of the sinful woman's repentance' ( ܠܐ ܗܘܐ ܓܝܪ ܡܛܠ ܟܪܣܗ ܐܙܕܡܢ ܗܘܐ ܡܣܒܥ ܟܦܢ̈ܐ. ܐܠܐ ܡܛܠ ܬܝܒܘܬܗ̇ ܕܚܛܝܬܐ ܙܡܢ ܢܦܫܗ ܡܙܕܩ ܠܚܛܝ̈ܐ).

827 Dom 15: 'Our Lord was not hungry for the Pharisee's refreshments; he hungered for the tears of the sinful woman. Once he had been filled and refreshed by the tears he hungered for, he then chastised the one who had invited him for food that perishes, in order to show that he had been invited not to nourish the body but to assist the mind (soul). Nor was it as the Pharisee supposed, that our Lord mixed with eaters and drinkers for enjoyment, but rather to mix his teaching in the food of mortals as the medicine of life'. ( ܠܐ ܗܘܐ ܓܝܪ ܠܬܦܢܘܩܘܗܝ ܕܦܪܝܫܐ ܗܘ ܟܦܢ ܗܘܐ ܡܪܢ. ܐܠܐ ܠܕܡ̈ܥܝܗ̇ ܕܚܛܝܬܐ ܐܬܟܦܢ ܗܘܐ. ܟܕ ܣܒܥ ܓܝܪ ܘܐܬܬܢܝܚ ܡܢ ܕ̈ܡܥܐ ܕܠܗܝܢ ܟܦܢ ܗܘܐ. ܗܝܕܝܢ ܟܐܪܗ ܠܗܘ ܕܠܡܐܟܘܠܬܐ ܒܥܒܘܪܬܐ ܙܡܢܗ ܗܘܐ. ܕܢܚܘܐ ܕܠܐ ܗܘܐ ܡܛܠ ܡܣܝܒܪܬܐ ܕܦܓܪܐ ܐܙܕܡܢ. ܐܠܐ ܡܛܠ ܒܥܘܕܪܢܐ ܕܪ̈ܥܝܢܐ. ܠܐ ܗܘܐ ܓܝܪ ܡܛܠ ܒܘܣܡܐ ܚܠܛ ܗܘܐ ܡܪܢ ܥܡ ܐܟܘ̈ܠܐ ܘܫ̈ܬܝܐ ܐܝܟ ܕܣܒܪ ܦܪܝܫܐ. ܐܠܐ ܕܒܡܐܟܘܠܬܗܘܢ ܕܡ̈ܝܘܬܐ: ܢܚܠܛ ܗܘܐ ܠܗܘܢ ܡܘܠܦܢܗ ܐܝܟ ܣܡ ܚܝ̈ܐ).

828 Dom 14: 'She was graciously comforting the feet of her Physician with oil, who had graciously brought the treasury of healing for her suffering' ( ܡܢܝܚܐ ܗܘܬ ܠܗܝܢ ܓܝܪ ܠܪ̈ܓܠܐ ܐܣܝܗ̇ ܒܡܫܚܐ ܕܡܟܝܟ.

☞

the sinful woman as a 'bribe of repentance' ( ܫܘܚܕܐ ܗܘܐ ܕܬܝܒܘܬܐ) and as 'medicine' (ܣܡ̈ܡܢܐ) for her wounds.[829] The sinful woman became the scriptural example of repentance, and Ephrem advises every sinner to follow her. As the sinful woman was a cause of death (ܘܕܥܠܬ ܡܘܬܐ) for everyone through her sinful deeds, likewise through her repentance she has become a cause of repentance (ܥܠܬ ܬܝܒܘܬܐ) for sinners.[830]

---

ܕܒܟܝܟ ܐܘܒܠ ܠܗ̇ ܡܫܝܚܬ ܣܘܠ̈ܚܢܐ ܠܟܐܒܝܗ̇). Furthermore, the aspect of repentance is emphasised through her act. Dom 14: ܐܦ ܠܒܪ ܡܢ ܒܠܚܘܕ ܐܣܝܘܬܐ ܕܐܝܟ ܗܕܐ ܒܛܥܝܢܐ ܐܬܓܠܝܬ. ܡܢ ܕ ܢܫܩܬ ܗܘܐ ܠܐܣܝܘܬܐ ܕܠܬܗ ܒܦܘܪܣܢܐ ܢܣܒܐ ܗܘܬ. ܘܐܦ ܒܬܝܒܘܬܐ ܕܪ̈ܚܡܘܗܝ ܡܣܩ̈ܬܐ ܠܦܬܟܪ̈ܬܐ ܐܬܥܒܕ ܗܘ̈ܝ. ܚܙ ܒܝܕܐ ܢܬܩܪܒ ܗܘ̈ܝ ܒܡܠܘܬ ܦܘܡܗ ܡܣܩ̈ܬܐ ܕܫܢ̈ܝܬܐ.

[829] Dom 44: 'The precious oil of the sinful woman proclaimed that it was a "bribe" for her repentance. These were the medications the sinful woman offered her physician, so that he could whiten the stains of her sin with tears, and heal her wounds with her kisses, and make her bad name as sweet as the fragrance of her oil. This is the physician who heals a person with the medicine that that person brings to him!' ( ܡܫܝܚܗ̇ ܛܒܐ ܕܚܛܝܬܐ ܡܟܪܙ ܗ̤ܘܐ ܕܫܘܚܕܐ ܗܘܐ ܕܬܝܒܘܬܐ. ܗܠܝܢ ܣܡ̈ܡܢܐ ܩܪܒܬ ܚܛܝܬܐ ܠܐܣܝܗ̇. ܕܒܕ̈ܡܥܝܗ̇ ܢܚܘܪ ܟܘܬ̈ܡܬܗ̇ ܘܒܢܘܫ̈ܩܬܗ̇ ܢܐܣܐ ܚܒ̈ܘܪܝܗ̇. ܘܒܡܫܝܚܗ̇ ܒܣܝܡܐ ܢܒܣܡ ܫܡܗ̇ ܒܝܫܐ ܐܝܟ ܪܝܚ ܡܫܝܚܗ̇. ܗܢܐ ܗܘ ܐܣܝܐ ܕܒܣܡ̈ܡܢܐ ܕܡܝܬܐ ܠܗ ܐܢܫ. ܒܗܘܢ ܗ̣ܘ ܡܐܣܐ ܠܗ). For the importance of tears for real repentance see further Dom 44: ܠܐ ܕܝܢ ܡܫܝܚܐ ܗܘܬ ܫܦܝܪܬܐ ܕܡܦܣܬܗ̇ ܬܥܠܝܗܘܝ ܗܘܬ ܠܡܪܢ. ܡܛܠ ܕܗܝܡܢܘܬ ܕܝܕܥ ܗܘܐ ܐܝܟ ܐܠܗܐ ܥ̈ܠܬܐ ܕܒܠܒܗ̇ ܒܕ̈ܡܥܝܗ̇. ܐܦܠܐ ܡܢ ܥܐܠܬܗ̇ ܕܒܟܝܐ ܒܒܟ̈ܬܗ̇. ܡܛܠ ܕܝܕܥ ܗܘܐ ܕܒܬܝܒܘܬܗ̇ ܕܚܛܝܬܐ ܣܘܟ̈ܠܗ̇ ܠܬܐܪܬܐ ܦܪܥܐ ܗܘܬ. ܗܝ ܗܘ ܡܛܠ ܕܗܝܡܢܘܬ ܕܝܕܥ ܒܬܝܒܘܬܐ ܗܘ. ܓܠ̈ܝܬܗ̇ ܒܠܒܗ̇ ܗܘ ܡܬܪܥܐ ܗܘܬ ܠܗ. ܝܕܥ ܒܬܝܒܘܬܐ ܒܪ ܟܠ ܡܦܩܬܐ ܒܪ̈ܬܐ ܠܐ ܡܫܝܡ. Dom 49: ܫܦܝܬܐ ܡܛܠ ܒܡܠܐܐ ܕܕ̈ܡܥܐ ܥܘܒܝܢ ܣܘܓܐܐ ܡܢ ܠܘܬ ܪ̈ܓܠܘܗܝ ܒܦܪܘܣܝܐ ܐܬܬܟܪܬ. ܘܗ̇ܝ ܕܬܪܒܝ ܗܘܐ ܕܡܫܝܚ ܣܘܠܚܢܐ ܡܢ ܦܘܪܢܐ ܕܡܪܓܠܘܗ̇ ܟܢܫܬ.

[830] Virg 35.6:

ܒܡܪܢ ܥܒܠܬ ܗܘܬ ܡܢ ܕܒܥܠܬܗ ܒܦܪܥܬܐ
ܥܬܐ ܕܡܢ ܦܓܪܟ ܡܢܘܬܗ ܠܬܪܝܥܘܬܗ̇
ܘܕܥܠܬ ܡܘܬܐ ܠܟܠܢ ܚܒܝܒܐ ܗܘܬ

☞

---

ܚܠܦ ܬܘܒܬܐ ܠܢ̈ܦܫܐ ܗܘܬ ܗܘܬ
ܠܟܐ̈ܒܐ ܕܚܐܘܗ̇ ܒܚܘܒܗܘܢ
ܘܢ̈ܫܐ ܚܐܘܗ̇ ܘܫܠܡܘܢ
ܘܡܪ̈ܥܐ ܬܪܣܘ ܒܗ ܘܚܠܠܘܢ.

# 6 CONCLUSION

Summarizing, one can say that Ephrem's works portray a comprehensive theology of healing, where God is the ultimate Healer Who cares about humanity in general, and about the individual in particular. God is the only One Who is capable of healing mankind totally, spiritually, physically and mentally; and He does it as He cares and provides medicine for man. Since the creation of the world God provides the Medicine of Life, first hidden in the paradisiacal Tree of Life that was placed in the centre of Paradise. The eating of the Tree of Knowledge opened man's eyes to see the loss of his healthy state (i. e. Paradise) and almost total separation from the Medicine of Life. In order to keep man alive, in the hope of being healed and restored to good health, God acts in His mercy and invents physical death to limit man's suffering and pains in his Fallen state, the state of sickness. He also sends the fragrance of Paradise into earth's air to act as a physician on behalf of the true Medicine of Life for man's life on earth. The fragrance from the Garden of Eden minimizes pains and suffering, but it does not heal and restore, for it was not the Medicine of Life Himself. Furthermore, God sends His mediators, the patriarchs and prophets, to act as physicians, to visit and heal the sicknesses of their time with His medicine, but their healing was temporary and limited. God's commandments that particularly took shape in Moses' Law have a medical function. Likewise, God's creation, visible to man, proclaims the right way in which to benefit from divine medicine.

Since all of these metaphors and ܐܪ̈ܙܐ of the real Medicine of Life were not sufficient for humanity, God sends the Medicine of Life in person, His beloved Son, into the world, so that mankind may eat from this Tree of Life and be healed and totally restored. This Medicine of Life is Jesus Christ Himself. Through His birth, baptism, crucifixion and resurrection, He has healed humanity as such, and in His ministry He granted perfect healing to particular individuals, to those who approached Him with faith and truth. Jesus has not limited His medicine to those in His time, to those who could see Him clothed in a human body, but He granted healing power to His disciples and their successors to heal in the Name of the Trinity. In addition, He makes Himself, as the Medicine of Life, present in particular in the Church's sacraments. For example, consuming Him in Holy Communion means, for the faithful, consuming the Medicine of Life.

This healing is basically spiritual, it is the restoration of man into his primordial state before the Fall; and beyond this, it is a restoration to good health that man will be aware of (unlike Adam and Eve, who were in good health, but did not know it until it was too late, having been expelled from the Garden of well-being). In other words, this is the ideal eschatological restoration into a perfect state of good health. Humanity as such is restored, because the process, as the process of salvation, has started and the way is open, and Medicine is provided. The Medicine of Life has acted against man's enemy and defeated the source of man's sickness, i.e. sin. With His Bread of Life, He has neutralized the poison and venom of the Evil One, and has defeated Satan who poisoned humanity with his deceitful advice. The Medicine of Life has healed the first wound that affected everyone. Mankind does not live anymore under the curse that was the consequence of the disobedience of the divine commandment, but everyone can live in participation of the eschatological restoration, that is the destiny of humanity.

Even though humanity is still in its fallen state, the condition of life has fundamentally changed. As mankind was condemned to death after the Fall, but did not die totally, so too God has restored humanity, but this restoration will be realized totally in the eschaton, in the second coming of Christ, and not in this world. This spiritual healing will be complete, including mental, psychological and physical healing - all visible and unvisible. Restoration of man means total restoration and taking him into a state of good health. This process starts with the Medicine of Life that is provided for believers. Everyone can take part in Him, consume Him in faith and be spiritually healed. Jesus Christ healed individuals from various sicknesses, evil spirits, visible and invisible sicknesses. In most of these cases, although Jesus healed physical sicknesses, He indicates the healing of the mind and soul as well. Thus, total spiritual healing cannot be separated from physical healing. Equally, total physical healing cannot be achieved without spiritual healing.

Jesus Christ's healing action and His healing miracles were the result of His will to heal man and the faith of those who believed in Him. The healing actions were carried out in response to the faith of individuals as they believed that He was capable of healing. Ephrem makes this relevant to his time, and implies its relevance to all times. Divine healing power was given to the Apostles and they healed. Likewise, their successors are able to heal, such as the bishops of Nisibis who provided spiritual medicine for the spiritual wound of their times. Ephrem goes further and challenges all shepherds to look after and visit the sick sheep, as he challenges the sick to have faith in God and in the Medicine of Life that is present in the Church, that can be taken by faith, accompanied by repentance, fasting and praying. In both baptism and the Eucharist, the Medicine of Life is present at any time for anyone.

Even though the Lord's medicine is free and accessible to everyone, healing can only be achieved if man approaches Him in the right way: this is faith, with repentance, fasting and prayer, including charitable work. Pious acts can serve as medicine that man is able to bring with him in order to be healed; such as in the case of the sinful woman: her oil, tears and real repentance served for her as medicine that she took with her to visit the heavenly Physician; and He healed her through the medicine that she brought with her. Although perhaps shocking for us, Ephrem makes it clear that the wrong approach to the Medicine of Life may result in the poison of death, such as was the case with Judas Iscariot; or relating to Ephrem's contemporaries, the Marcionites and Arians who are described as a sick limb in the body, because they misunderstand Scripture and the essence of the Incarnated Logos.

So far, it is clear that spiritual sickness is caused by sin that is the result of the Evil One and man's free will, and God's intention is to heal man from this sickness. Where would Ephrem place physical sickness and disease? Are the physical afflictions also caused by sin? The answer is yes and no. In Ephrem's theology, physical sickness can be an expression of spiritual sickness. If the soul is sick, the body cannot remain healthy, for they are related to each other. As an example we need just to refer to the leprosy of King Uzziah, the prophetess Miriam and Gehazi. All three were afflicted with leprosy because their mind and soul were sick. Thus physical sickness can be the consequence of spiritual sickness. However, Ephrem also accepts the fact of pure natural sicknesses, such as the fever of Peter's mother in law which was natural. The fact that man can become physically sick is attributed to the general condition of humanity after the Fall. Humanity's fallen state is a state of sickness where individual sicknesses, pains and suffering can be experienced by individuals. Had the Fall not taken place, pain and suffering would not be a part of human life. Since the Fall is real, all kinds of sicknesses, pains and suffering, along with natural death, indicate the imperfect situation of humanity and the need for salvation (i.e. healing and restoration).

Presenting Ephrem's theology of healing like this, one might leave a wrong impression, namely, that his concept of sickness and healing is purely abstract and irrelevant for practical life. Probably if we look at the contexts where Ephrem makes use of his healing terminology, this might give us a different view. Thus, often aspects of healing theology occur in the form of prayers and giving praise to God. Likewise they appear when he comments on and explains certain biblical passages. Again, he uses healing imagery to argue against heresies and to illustrate the correct understanding of Scripture and the Divinity. In other words, he is concerned about right faith in God, how to believe and how to worship the Creator of humanity Whose healing activity is considered to be a second creation. In Christianity there has always been a tension between 'orthodoxy' and 'orthopraxy' (the two cannot be separated). Ephrem's concept of sickness and healing served as an answer to this problem in his time, and it can equally be considered as an answer to some of our questions today, such as how does God allow so much pain for mankind.

The description above of Ephrem's theology of healing has been pieced together from all his writings. There is no single work that just presents the concept of sickness and healing in its totality. Elements are to be found in all his works, commentaries, madroshe and mimre. It is a significant theme, but not the only one through which he speaks about the inter-relationship between divinity and humanity, and explains their different natures. Other themes may characterise Ephrem's theology of salvation too. When Ephrem makes use of the imagery of sickness and healing, he rarely means it to be taken literally. For him, this image, like many others, is an approach to explain the incomprehensibility of the supreme God, His supernatural existence and His merciful acts, as He reveals Himself to man in their ways, i.e. allowing Himself to be spoken of in their language insofar as they can comprehend. All images and metaphors, as used by Ephrem, aim to delineate a way to explain the salvation of man that is initiated by the grace of the heavenly God. For example, the key term 'chasm' serves to distinguish between the state of humanity and divinity, and implies that only divinity could cross over to humanity and bring mankind salvation in the sense that man may be enabled to cross over to divinity. Or the imagery of the garment of light - put off during the Fall and put on in baptism through Christ, and to be realized at the second coming of Christ - encompasses the whole process of salvation too. And many other examples can be found. However, the healing imagery is readily accessible to readers and easy to follow, for almost everyone experiences pain and suffering in this life and values health. It is a natural metaphor taken from everyday life, understandable, and it has its place in the life of every individual.

Saying this, it is easy to assume that Ephrem's healing imagery is based on Nature.[1] On the one hand this is true, but at the same time Ephrem also uses Scripture, and so it is equally a biblical theology, incorporating all the divine revelations. Throughout his work, we see that Ephrem refers frequently to both Scripture and Nature, and he brings examples from both to illuminate his arguments. This can be found not only in the concept of sickness and healing, but also in the other metaphors and theological aspects.

Ephrem's healing terminology is biblical, based on both the Old and New Testaments. From the instances that have been

---

[1] Ephrem's 'book of Nature' is something quite different from 'natural theology' that is the philosophical investigation of how far the human mind can argue to the existence of God and other transcendental truths without appeal to divine revelation or grace. Ephrem does use arguments of this kind in his prose controversial works, but obviously he preferred to contemplate the 'two books' of Nature and Scripture as full of ܐܪ̈ܙܐ.

discussed in the thesis, it is clear that Ephrem is well aware of the various biblical healing passages, and he refers to them at different lengths. He does not just cite them, but goes further and develops them in the context of his argument. For example, the term ܟܘܪܗܢܐ does not only refer to the spiritual and physical sickness of man, but also to the sickness of the universe, the whole of human nature and the entire world; likewise he attributes the term ܟܐܒܐ not only to body and soul, but also to Sheol, man's free will, and to the whole of creation. It is not only these terms and their derivatives, but also others, such as ܟܪܝܗܐ, ܚܠܡ, ܬܒܪ and their derivatives that become key terms in the context of Ephrem's healing imagery. Less biblically based are the following terms: ܚܒܪ̈ܬܐ, ܬܒܣܘܬܐ, ܫܘܚܢܐ, ܫܘܡ̈ܬܐ and ܣܠܝ̈ܬܐ, the last two terms (ܫܘܡ̈ܬܐ and ܣܠܝ̈ܬܐ) characterizing Aphrahat's healing theology.

The verb ܐܣܐ, apears almost in all its forms in the Bible, and Ephrem uses it to describe God's action as the ultimate Healer, and the healing ministry of His mediators. While the terms ܣܡܐ and ܣܡ̈ܡܢܐ are very rarely used in Scripture, Ephrem uses them with a specific meaning. The singular ܣܡܐ has the meaning of medicine; and so Jesus Christ is the 'Medicine of Life', His nativity is considered to be 'medicine' and divine Justice acts as a 'sharp medicine'. It also has the sense of poison, particularly when it is used with 'death', ܣܡ ܡܘܬܐ, and then it characterizes the evil venom that has poisoned humanity. The plural ܣܡ̈ܡܢܐ is used in the sense of pigments, portraying a new spiritual image for Adam, or for everyone at the baptismal font; and it is used in the sense of medicines that can be attributed to an ordinary physician, as well as to God, to those authorized by Him and individuals. Also the verbs ܐܚܠܡ, ܚܒܫ and ܣܒܪ are biblical, but Ephrem incorporates them totally into his healing vocabulary and uses them in a much stronger healing sense.

It is very difficult to say for certain whether Ephrem has used any other sources, such as those studied in the second chapter. On the theological level, there are some similarities between Ephrem and the Acts of Thomas, as well as Aphrahat's Demonstrations. The Acts of Thomas clearly distinguish between the role of the Apostle as a physician and Jesus Christ as the Physician par excellence. As Jesus was sent into the world to heal mankind, so too the Acts of Thomas presents the mission of the Apostle, as being sent to India to heal the people there. And indeed he heals them in the Name of the Lord. This is comparable with Ephrem, as he considers all of God's mediators, both the patriarchs and prophets, and the Apostles and their successors as physicians. In the Acts of Thomas, the title Medicine of Life occurs once, but is not given the same attention as in Ephrem. As in Ephrem, the author of the Acts of Thomas highlights the aspect of spiritual healing and restoration from spiritual sickness. In common also is the teaching that spiritual medicine is free, without payment. However, the main concern of the Acts of Thomas is the mission of the Apostle, and his healing miracles, like those of Jesus, are part of his ministry. Thus, it can be said that the Acts of Thomas is biblical, but its healing theology is not as developed as that of Ephrem.

Aphrahat's Demonstrations display Aphrahat's healing theology in the context of repentance and the metaphor of 'battle' that is used to explain the seriousness of penitence and its effect. The idea of the healing power of repentance can also be found in Ephrem, but it is not at all a central point of his healing theology, or healing terminology. The metaphor of war and battle for describing the life of Christians also introduces a distinctive terminology, and one that cannot be found nearly so dominantly present in Ephrem. This is characterized by the terms gangrene, scars, wound, and repentance as medicine. The spiritual medicine is also free here, and those with authority are provided with heavenly medicine and are enabled to act as physicians. Aphrahat's Demonstrations are referring to his contemporary Christians, probably in particular to the ܒܢ̈ܝ ܩܝܡܐ ܘܒܢ̈ܬ ܩܝܡܐ, and he encourages them to be strong in their spiritual life. Aphrahat makes them aware that their enemy is invisible, it is the Evil One, and if they are not awake to fight against Satan, he will harm and hurt them greatly.

Theologically, Ephrem would agree with both the Acts of Thomas and Aphrahat's Demonstrations, as well as with the Odes of Solomon. However each of these is different. While their healing theology is limited in its range (probably it could be described as one-sided), Ephrem has a much wider spectrum of the concept of healing which is developed so that the whole history of salvation can be covered by it.

Ephrem's texts, both the authentic and non-authentic, reveal different aspects of healing theology. It is very difficult to discern any development of the healing terminology or the healing imagery in Ephrem's writing. His various works seem to complement each other, and those which are not authentic often display similar healing imagery. It is not the main concern of this dissertation to answer questions about the authenticity of Ephrem's works, in particular, of the Commentary on the Diatessaron, but as far as the aspect of healing is concerned, there is nothing that can be said definitely not to be Ephrem's, and there is nothing obvious that would disagree with the genuine Ephrem. Although the Commentary on the Diatessaron sometimes approaches some biblical narratives in a different way and draws attention to other issues than those which occur in Ephrem's certainly genuine texts (such as the healing miracle of the sinful woman), it does not mean that it is definitely not written by Ephrem. The biblical narratives are used differently in different contexts and different genres, and the author highlights different aspects of the same narrative. Likewise concerning the other texts which are questionably genuine Ephrem, on the basis of their healing theology, it cannot be said that they differ markedly from those which are genuine Ephrem. Thus, it appears that judgments on questions of authenticity need to be based on criteria other than those of healing terminology and theology.

Does Ephrem reveal anything about the role of an ordinary physician in Syrian Christian society? Can we find any hellenistic influence in his theology, such as the incorporation of Graeco-Roman scientific medicine into his theological thought, or does he reject ordinary medicine, as Tatian, Arnobius and Marcion do? Certainly it can be said that ordinary medicine is not a part of Ephrem's concern, and he does not comment on it as such. However occasionally he mentions it, in two ways: either by comparing or contrasting spiritual medicine and the heavenly Physician with the role and function of an ordinary physician and herbal medicine. Once he also speaks about the book of medicine in which people put their trust and believe totally in what it says. The use of herbal medicine and its power is used as a metaphor to describe the importance and effect of a right understanding of

Scripture. This might possibly indicate one of Galen's medical books and how he illustrates the power of herbs and plants, and emphasises the importance of correct usage. Almost certainly Ephrem did not read Greek, and it is unlikely that hellenistic medical works were translated into Syriac by Ephrem's time, but nevertheless Ephrem was living under the rule of a western power that went back there over half a millennium before him, and the famous Galen lived two centuries before him. Even though he has not read Hippocratic medicine, surely he might have heard of it.[2] The question of how much hellenistic medicine was practised in Syrian Christian communities remains unsolved. However, in general, it can be said that this is not relevant for Ephrem, for he is concerned about spiritual sickness and its medicine. When Ephrem speaks about the fame of Egyptian medicine, he says that Moses rejected it and went to Sinai, for the People were afflicted with a spiritual sickness, not a physical one. So here, when Ephrem contrasts the effect of spiritual medicine with that of ordinary physicians, he limits their function and and considers their medicine as useless. Likewise, in such comparisons he shows a negative attitude towards ordinary physicians, for they are unable to heal certain sicknesses, even though they are physical sicknesses, such as the haemorrhaging woman. Finally, it can be said that all in all Ephrem distinguishes radically between the role of the heavenly Physician Who is able to heal everything, both spiritual and physical, and the function of the ordinary physician who can only treat a certain number of physical diseases. Certainly an ordinary physician does not have a mediatory function in Ephrem's healing imagery, such as some scholars attribute to Ben Sira. In his theology, Ephrem is certainly concerned about both the body and soul. Ephrem defines Peter's mother-in-law's fever as a natural sickness, and the healing of the ear that was cut off was physical. Jesus healed both of these for He is the Healer of all mankind, and the destiny of man is the perfect restoration of both body and soul.

---

2 U. Possekel's recent study *Evidence of Greek Philosophical Concepts in the Writings of Ephrem the Syrian* (CSCO 580; Subsidia 102; Louvain 1999) has shown that Ephrem must have had a more extensive knowledge of Greek philosophy than was previously thought.

The usage of oil in the context of healing can be found in the Bible. Oil is also used in the Church's sacraments. For Ephrem, 'oil' (ܡܫܚܐ) represents 'Christ' (ܡܫܝܚܐ), because it has many functions and different powers, as Christ does. Beside the sacramental use of oil and its symbolic spiritual power, Ephrem also speaks of the natural power of oil. This indicates that oil was used to treat sick people. L. Wells says: 'Anointing with (olive) oil (Mk 6:12-13) was a common therapeutic practice in the ancient world. It had several functions. If the skin was broken it served as an antiseptic by providing an effective barrier against harmful bacteria, and as an emollient, preventing bandages sticking to the wound. Also it was used extensively to treat skin disorders, and as the emollient agent for massage, particularly in the treatment of muscular complaints and bruising'.[3] Beside playing with the terms ܡܫܚܐ and ܡܫܝܚܐ Ephrem uses oil in both senses: sacramental and natural. The natural aspect is a sign of his natural theology, that Nature in general, just as Scripture, gives evidence about Divine existence.

A further minor aspect might be worth mentioning. Ephrem uses the serpent as a symbol for the Evil One, not because it is evil in its nature, but because it was misused by the Evil One to deceive humanity. In turn, in a number of cult legends the serpent is associated with healing. In particular, Asclepius, who is described as the pagan 'Saviour and Healer', appeared in the shape of a serpent and possessed extraordinary healing power. In the second and third century, Arnobius scorns and reviles Asclepius who, while he was supposed to be a god and the giver of health, 'is enclosed in the shape and compass of a serpent, crawling along the ground after the fashion of worms which spring from mud'.[4] It is conceivable that Ephrem's development of the theme of the bronze serpent was aimed at countering the attractions of the

---

[3] Wells, 128. See the bibliography given there.

[4] Arnobius of Sicca, *Arnobii Adversus Nationes*, libri VII, 44f.; R. Arbesmann, 'The Concept of »Christus Medicus« in St. Augustine', *Traditio* 10 (1954), 1-28. For Asclepius and his representation in the form of a serpent, see E. Küster, 'Die Schlange in der griechischen Kunst und Religion', *Religionsgeschichtliche Versuche und Vorarbeiten* 13.2 (Giessen 1913), 133-37.

pagan cult of Asclepius, but this must remain very hypothetical since there does not seem to be much evidence for this cult in Syria.

Finally to conclude, Ephrem's healing imagery and the healing terminology in the Odes of Solomon, Acts of Thomas and Aphrahat's Demonstrations give clear evidence about the popularity of the theology of healing in early Syrian Christendom. The fact that each of them - and very likely independently - expresses his healing imagery in a different way, shows how much this theme was widespread among Syrian Christians. Although we do not know when and where the Odes of Solomon and the Acts of Thomas were written, we know that Aphrahat wrote his Demonstrations in the first half of the fourth century in the Persian Empire, and Ephrem wrote in Nisibis and then in Edessa, during the last ten years before his death in 373 A. D. Thus, Aphrahat represents healing imagery that was probably familiar to the Syrian Christian under the Persian Empire, and Ephrem shows a concept of healing that, at least partly, might have been well known to the Syrian Christians under the Western rulers. It is particularly interesting that Ephrem should have paid so much attention to precisely the same three Gospel healing narratives that feature so commonly on fourth-century sarcophagi:[5] though there is obviously no direct influence either way, their common interest in these episodes indicate that a concern with the Gospel's healing miracles was very much 'in the air' in Ephrem's time.

Ephrem's much more developed theology of healing has had great influence on the Syriac writers after him. In particular, Jacob of Serugh must have studied Ephrem's texts very well, as he often reflects Ephrem's phraseology, including features of his healing imagery. Healing terminology, not very different from that of Ephrem, can also be found in the prayer books of the West Syrian Church, such as in the weekly prayer book, or breviary (ܫܚܝܡܐ).

[5] P. D. E. Knipp, *'Christus medicus' in der frühchristlichen Sarkophagskulptur: ikonographische Studien der Sepulkralkunst des späten vierten Jahrhunderts* (Leiden 1998). Knipp studied these three biblical miracles: giving sight to the man born blind (Jn 9), healing the haemorrhaging woman (Lk 8:43-48), and healing the man sick for 38 years in Bethesda (Jn 5:1-9).

It needs further research and careful study in order to define the extent of Ephrem's true impact and great influence on the Syriac liturgy and on Syriac writers in general. Such a study would reveal how Ephrem's healing imagery has been understood and how it has been developed in later Syriac tradition. It would also indicate the value given to the healing imagery among Syriac writers and in Syriac theology in general.

Further work should also be carried out to compare Ephrem's concept of healing with that of other early Christians writers, above all Greek and Latin, but also Coptic and Armenian as well, to see how their healing imagery compares with or is different from that of Ephrem. One could mention in particular here the Cappadocian Fathers, John Chrysostom, Ambrose of Milan, Jerome and Augustine, all from the fourth and beginning of the fifth century. It is to be hoped that this work opens up a way to such studies by presenting the significance of Ephrem's healing imagery and how it is characteristic of the early Syriac theology of healing in general.

# BIBLIOGRAPHY

## Primary Sources


E. Beck, *Des Heiligen Ephraem des Syrers Hymnen contra Haereses* (CSCO 169/170; SS 76/77; Louvain 1957).

E. Beck, *Des Heiligen Ephraem des Syrers Hymnen de Paradiso und contra Julianum* (CSCO 174/175; SS 78/79; Louvain 1957).

E. Beck, *Des Heiligen Ephraem des Syrers Hymnen de Nativitate (Epiphania)* (CSCO 186/187; SS 82/83; Louvain 1959).

E. Beck, *Des Heiligen Ephraem des Syrers Hymnen de Ecclesia* (CSCO 198/199; SS 84/85; Louvain 1960).

E. Beck, *Des Heiligen Ephraem des Syrers Sermones de Fide* (CSCO 212/213; SS 88/89; Louvain 1961).

E. Beck, *Des Heiligen Ephraem des Syrers Carmina Nisibena I* (CSCO 218/219; SS 92/93; Louvain 1961).

E. Beck, *Des Heiligen Ephraem des Syrers Hymnen de Virginitate* (CSCO 223/224; SS 94/95; Louvain 1962).

E. Beck, *Des Heiligen Ephraem des Syrers Carmina Nisibena II* (CSCO 240/241; SS 102/103; Louvain 1963).

E. Beck, *Des Heiligen Ephraem des Syrers Hymnen de Ieiunio* (CSCO 246/247; SS 106/107; Louvain 1964).

E. Beck, *Des Heiligen Ephraem des Syrers Paschahymnen (de azymnis, de crucifixione, de resurrectione)* (CSCO 248/249; SS 108/109; Louvain 1964).

E. Beck, *Des Heiligen Ephraem des Syrers Hymnen de Fide* (CSCO 154/155; SS 73/74; Louvain 1955/1967).

E. Beck, *Des Heiligen Ephraem des Syrers Sermo de Domino Nostro* (CSCO 270/271; SS 116/117; Louvain 1966).

E. Beck, *Des Heiligen Ephraem des Syrers Sermones I* (CSCO 305/306; SS 130/131; Louvain 1970).

E. Beck, *Des Heiligen Ephraem des Syrers Sermones II* (CSCO 311/312; SS 134/135; Louvain 1970).

E. Beck, *Des Heiligen Ephraem des Syrers Sermones III* (CSCO 320/321; SS 138/139; Louvain 1972).

E. Beck, *Des Heiligen Ephraem des Syrers Hymnen auf Abraham Kidunaya und Julianos Saba* (CSCO 322/323; SS 140/141; Louvain 1972).

E. Beck, *Des Heiligen Ephraem des Syrers Sermones IV* (CSCO 334/335; SS 148/149; Louvain 1973).

E. Beck, *Nachträge zu Ephraem Syrus* (CSCO 363/364; SS 159/160; Louvain 1975).

E. Beck, *Ephraem Syrus, sermones in hebdomadam sanctam* CSCO 412/413; SS 181/182; Louvain 1979).

R. Beshara, *Mary Ship of Treasures* (Brooklyn NY 1988).

S. P. Brock, *The Harp of the Spirit: 18 Poems of St Ephrem* (Studies supplementary to Sobornost; 2nd ed., London 1983).

S. P. Brock, *Sogiatha. Syriac Dialogue Hymns* (The Syrian Churches Series; Kottayam 1987).

S. P. Brock, *A Garland of Hymns from the Early Church* (St Athanasius' Coptic Publishing Center; Mclean Virginia 1989).

S. P. Brock, *St. Ephrem the Syrian, Hymns On Paradise* (New York 1990).

S. P. Brock, *Bright of Light. Hymns on Mary from the Syriac Churches*, Moran 'Ethō 6 (Kottayam 1994).

H. Burgess, *Select Metrical Hymns and Homilies of Ephrem Syrus* (London 1853).

H. Burgess, *The Repentance of Nineveh: a Metrical Homily on the Mission of Jonah by Ephrem Syrus* (London 1853).

J. H. Charlesworth, *The Odes of Solomon* (Montana 1977).

H. Grimme, *Die Oden Solomos* (Heidelberg 1911).

J. Gwynn, *Selections translated into English from the Hymns and Homilies of Ephraim the Syrian* ..., in A Select Library of Nicene and post-Nicene Fathers, Second series, 13 (Oxford/New York 1898).

J. R. Harris, *The Odes and Psalms of Solomon* (Cambridge 1911).

J. R. Harris and A. Mingana, *The Odes and Psalms of Solomon II* (London 1920).

A. F. J. Klijn, *The Acts of Thomas* (Leiden 1962).

T. J. Lamy, *Sancti Ephraem Syri Hymni et Sermones I-IV* (Malines 1882-1902).

M. Lattke, *Die Oden Solomos in ihrer Bedeutung für Neues Testament und Gnosis* (OBO 25/1; Göttingen 1979).

L. Leloir, *Commentaire de L'evangile Concordant I-II* (Louvain 1963; 1990).

S. C. Malan, *Meditations for every Wednesday and Friday in Lent on a Prayer of St Ephrem…* (London 1859).

C. McCarthy, *Saint Ephrem's Commentary on Tatian's Diatessaron* (Oxford 1993).

K. E. McVey, *Ephrem the Syrian Hymns* (Classics of Western Spirituality; New York 1989); contents: hymns On the Nativity, Against Julian, On Virginity, On the Symbols of the Lord.

K. E. McVey (ed.), *Selected Prose Works, St. Ephrem the Syrian*; translated by E. G. Mathews, Jr. and J. P. Amar (Washington 1994); contents: Commentary on Genesis, Commentary on Exodus, Homily on Our Lord, Letter to Publius.

P. Mobarak and S. E. Assemani, *Sancti Patris Nostri Ephraem Syri Opera Omnia quae exstant Graece, Syriace, Latine* I-VI (Rome 1732-46).

J. B. Morris, *Select Works of St Ephrem the Syrian* (Oxford 1847).

J. Overbeck, *St. Ephraemi Syri Rabulae Episcopi Edesseni Balaei Aliorumque Opera Selecta* (Oxford 1865).

J. Parisot, *Aphraatis Sapientis Persae, Demonstrationes, PS I* (Paris 1894); PS II (Paris 1907), 1-489.

P. S. Russell, *Ephrem the Syrian, Eighty Hymns On Faith* [unpublished typescript] (1995).

R. M. Tonneau, *Sancti Ephraem Syri in Genesim et in Exodum Commentarii* (CSCO 152/153; SS 71/72; Louvain 1955).

W. Wright, *The Homilies of Aphraates, the Persian Sage I* (London 1869).

W. Wright, *Apocryphal Acts of the Apostles I and II* (London 1871).

## Secondary Sources

S. AbouZayd, *Ihidayutha. A Study of the Life of Singleness in the Syrian Orient. From Ignatius of Antioch to Chalcedon 451 A.D.* (Oxford 1993).

A. Adam, 'Grundbegriffe des Mönchtums in Sprachlicher Sicht', *ZKG* 65 (1953-54), 209-39.

D. W. Amundsen, *Medicine, Society, and Faith in the Ancient and Medieval Worlds* (Baltimore 1996).

R. Arbesmann, 'The concept of 'Christus medicus' in St Augustine', *Traditio* 10 (1954), 1-28.

P. Bachmann, 'Galens Abhandlung darüber, daß der vorzügliche Arzt Philosoph sein muß', in *Nachrichten der Akademie der Wissenschaften in Göttingen* (Göttingen 1965), 1-67.

E. Beck, 'Ein Beitrag zur Terminologie des ältesten syrischen Mönchtums', in *Antonius Magnus Eremita* (St. Ans. 38, Rome 1956), 254-67;

E. Beck, 'Asketentum und Mönchtum bei Ephräm', *OCA* 153 (1958), 341-62.

P. Bedjan, *Acta Martyrum et Sanctorum III* (Parisiis 1892), 1-175. [Acts of Thomas].

C. Booth, 'History of science in medicine', in G. Teeling-Smith (ed.), *Science in medicine: how far has it advanced?* (London 1993), 11-22.

S. P. Brock, 'Early Syrian Asceticism', *Numen* 20 (1973), 1-19.

S. P. Brock, Spirituality in the Syriac Tradition, *Moran 'Etho* 2 (Kottayam 1989).

S. P. Brock, 'A brief guide to the main editions and translations of the works of St Ephrem', *The Harp* 3 (Kottayam 1990), 7-29.

S. P. Brock, *The Luminous Eye. The Spiritual World Vision of St Ephrem* (Rome 1985, Kalamazoo 1992).

C. Brockelmann, *Lexicon Syriacum* (2nd ed., Halle 1928).

E. A. W. Budge, *Syrian Anatomy, Pathology and Therapeutics or "The Book of Medicines"* I and II (London 1913).

J. H. Charlesworth, *The Odes of Solomon* (Montana 1977).

J. H. Charlesworth, *Critical Reflections on the Odes of Solomon* (JSPS 22; Sheffield 1998).

L. Cohn-Haft, *The Public Physician of Ancient Greece* (Northampton 1956).

R. Degen, 'Ein Corpus Medicorum Syriacorum', *Medizin historisches Journal* (Hildesheim) 7 (1972), 114-22.

R. Degen, 'Galen im Syrischen: eine Übersicht über die syrische Überlieferung der Werke Galens', in V. Nutton (ed.), *Galen: Problems and Prospects* (London 1981), 131-166.

R. Degen, 'Das Verzeichnis der Schriften des Hippokrates in der Überlieferung des Barhebraeus. Ein kritischer Bericht', in R. Schulz and M. Görg (eds.), *Lingua Restituta Orientalis. Festgabe J. Assfalg* (Ägypten und Altes Testament 20; Wiesbaden 1990), 79-88.

K. Deichgräber, *Medicus gratiosus* (Wiesbaden 1970).

M. Dols, 'The origins of the Islamic hospital: myth and reality', *Bull Hist Med* 61 (1987), 367-90.

M. Dols, 'Syriac into Arabic: the transmission of Greek medicine', *Aram* 1:1 (1989), 45-52.

L. Edelstein, *The Hippocratic Oath* (Baltimore 1943).

L. Edelstein, *Asclepius: A Collection and Interpretation of the Testimonies* II (Baltimore 1945).

L. Edelstein, 'The professional ethics of the Greek physician', in *Bull Hist Med* 30 (1956), 391-419.

L. Edelstein, 'Greek Medicine in its Relation to Religion and Magic', in *Ancient Medicine* (Baltimore 1967), 217-46.

N. El-Khoury, *Die Interpretation der Welt bei Ephrem dem Syrer* (Mainz 1976).

G. Fichtner, 'Christus als Arzt: Ursprünge und Wirkungen eines Motivs', *FMS* 16 (Berlin 1982), 1-18.

H. J. Frings, *Medizin und Arzt bei den griechischen Kirchenvätern bis Chrysostomos* (Bonn 1959).

H. Grimme, *Die Oden Solomos* (Heidelberg 1911).

L. Haefeli, *Stilmittel bei Aphrahat dem Persischen Weisen* (Leipzig 1932).

G. Harig and J. Kollesch, 'Der Hippokratische Eid', in *Philologus* 122 (1978), 157-76.

J. R. Harris, *The Odes and Psalms of Solomon* (Cambridge 1911).

J. R. Harris and A. Mingana, *The Odes and Psalms of Solomon* II (London 1920).

R. F. Hau, 'Gondeschapur - eine Medizinschule aus dem 6. Jahrh. nach Chr.', *Gesnerus* 36 (1979), 98-115.

J. Hempel, 'Ich bin der Herr, dein Arzt', in *ThLZ* 82 (1957), 809-826.

J. Hempel, 'Heilung als Symbol und Wirklichkeit im biblischen Schrifttum', *Nachrichten der Akademie der Wissenschaften in Göttingen* (Göttingen 1958), 237-314.

L. P. Hogan, *Healing in the Second Temple Period* (Freiburg 1992).

K. Hoheiel, H. J. Klimkeit, *Heil und Heilung in den Religionen* (Wiesbaden 1995).

M. Honecker, 'Christus medicus', in P. Wunderli (ed.), *Der kranke Mensch in Mittelalter und Renaissance* (Düsseldorf 1986), 27-43.

I. Illich, *Limits to Medicine. Medical Nemesis: the Expropriation of Health* (Middlesex 1977).

T. Jansma, 'Aphraates' Demonstration VII. 18 and 20. Some observations on the discourse of penance', *PdO* 5 (1974), 21-48.

W. A. Jayne, *The Healing Gods of Ancient Civilization* (New Haven 1925).

W. H. S. Jones, *The Doctor's Oath* (Cambridge 1924).

H. C. Kee, *Miracle in the Early Christian World* (New Haven 1983).

H. C. Kee, *Medicine, Miracle and Magic in New Testament Times* (Cambridge 1986).

C. Kerenyi, *Asklepios: Archetypal Image of the Physician's Existence* (New York 1959).

Helen King, *Greek and Roman Medicine* (1999).

P. D. E. Knipp, *'Christus medicus' in der frühchristlichen Sarkophagskulptur: ikonographische Studien der Sepulkralkunst des späten vierten Jahrhunderts* (Leiden 1998).

T. Koonammakkal, 'Ephrem's Imagery of Chasm', *VII Symposium Syriacum* (OCA 256, 1998), 175-183.

T. Kronholm, *Motifs from Genesis 1-11 in the Genuine Hymns of Ephrem the Syrian with particular Reference to the Influence of Jewish Exegetical Tradition* (Lund 1978).

T. Kronholm, 'Holy Adultery. The Interpretation of the Story of Judah and Tamar (Gen 38) in the Genuine Hymns of Ephraem Syrus (ca. 306-373)', *Orientalia Suecana* 40 (1991), 149-63.

E. Küster, 'Die Schlange in der griechischen Kunst und Religion', *Religionsgeschichtliche Versuche und Vorarbeiten* 13.2 (Giessen 1913), 133-37.

P. Lain' Entralgo, *The Therapy of the Word in Classical Antiquity* (New Haven 1970).

M. Lattke, *Die Oden Solomos in ihrer Bedeutung für Neues Testament und Gnosis* (OBO 25/1 - 25/4; Göttingen 1979-98).

M. Maroth, 'Ein Fragment eines syrischen pharmazeutischen Rezeptbuches aus Turfan', *Altorientalische Forschungen* 11 (1984), 115-25.

T. McKeown, *The origins of human disease* (Oxford 1988).

J. Melki,'Ephrem le Syrien: bilan de l'édition critique', *PdO* 11 (1983), 3-11.

B. M. Metzger, *The Early Versions of the New Testament* (Oxford 1977).

R. Murray, 'The exhortation to candidates for ascetical vows at baptism in the ancient Syriac Church', *New Testament Studies* 21 (1974), 59-80.

R. Murray, *Symbols of Church and Kingdom* ( ܪ̈ܙܐ ܕܥܕܬܐ ܘܕܡܠܟܘܬܐ) (Cambridge 1975).

R. Murray 'Some rhetorical patterns in early Syriac Literature', in R. H. Fischer (ed.), *A Tribute to Arthur Vööbus: studies in early Christian Literature and its environment, primarily in the Syrian East* (Chicago 1977), 109-31.

J. Nasrallah, 'Médecins melchites de l'époque ayyubide', *PdO* 5 (1974), 189-200.

S. Noorda, 'Illness and sin, forgiving and healing: the connection of medical treatment and religious beliefs in Ben Sira 38:1-15', in M. J. Vermaseren (ed.), *Studies in Hellenistic Religions* (Leiden 1979), 215-24.

R. J. Owens, *The Genesis and Exodus Citations of Aphrahat the Persian Sage* (Leiden 1983).

M. F. G. Parmentier, 'Non-medical ways of healing in Eastern Christendom', in *Fructus Centesimus: Mélanges offerts à G. J. M. Bartelink* (ed. A. A. R. Bastiaensen et. al; Dordrecht, 1989), 279-95.

U. Possekel, *Evidence of Greek philosophical Concepts in the Writings of Ephrem the Syrian* (CSCO 580; Subsidia 102; Louvain 1999).

J. Preuss, *Biblische - Talmudische Medizin* (Berlin 1911).

W. H. R. Rivers, *Medicine, Magic and Religion* (London 1924).

H. Schipperges, 'Zur Tradition des "Christus Medicus" im frühen Christentum und in der älteren Heilkund', in *Arzt und Christ* (Salzburg 1965), 12-20.

N. Séd, 'Les Hymnes sur le paradis de Saint Éphrem et les tradtions juives', *Le Muséon* 81 (1968), 455-501.

J. P. Smith, *A Compendious Syriac Dictionary* (Oxford 1903).

R. P. Smith, *Thesaurus Syriacus* I (Oxonii 1879), II (Oxonii 1901).

R. Sorobji, *Animal Minds and Human Morals: The Origins of the Western Debate* (London 1993).

H. L. Strack & P. Billerbeck, *Kommentar zum Neuen Testament aus Talmud und Midrash* I (München 1922).

O. Temkin, *Galenism: Rise and Decline of a Medical Philosophy* (Ithaca, New York 1973).

O. Temkin, *Hippocrates in a World of Pagans and Christians* (Baltimore 1991).

M. Ullmann, 'Yuhanna ibn Sarabiyun. Untersuchungen zur Überlieferung seiner Werke', *Medizin-historisches Jahrbuch* 6 (1971), 278-96.

H. Urs von Balthasar, 'Casta Meretix' in his collection *Sponsa Verbi* (Einsiedeln 1961), 205-305.

S. A. Vardanyan, 'Ancient Armenian traslations of the works of Syrian Physicians, *REA* 16 (1982), 213-19.

G. Vermes, *Jesus the Jew* (New York 1973).

A. Vööbus, *History of Asceticism in the Syrian Orient* I-III (CSCO 184, 197, 500; Louvain 1958, 1960, 1988).

D. J. Weatheral, *Science and the Quiet Art. The Role of Research Medicine* (New York 1995).

M. Weizman, *The Syriac Version of the Old Testament* (Cambridge 1999).

L. Wells, *The Greek Language of Healing from Homer to New Testament times* (Berlin 1998).

A. O. Whipple, *The Role of the Nestorians and Muslims in the History of Medicine* (Princeton 1967).

G. Widengren, *Mesopotamian Elements in Manichaeism* (Uppsala/Leipzig 1946).

P. Yousif, *L'Eucharistie chez Saint Ephrem de Nisibe* (OCA 224; Rome 1984).

## Printer's Note

The Syriac text is set in 'Estrangelo Talada' (version 1.20, 2001), an OpenType digital font designed by George A. Kiraz. The font derives from types based on drawings by William Morley, and cut for the London typefounders William Watts & Co. ca. 1851. Morley's drawings follow the script of a seventh-century manuscript (British Library Add. 14640). 'Estrangelo Talada' is named after the Syrian Orthodox monastery at Talʿada, Syria. It is part of the *Meltho Fonts* family [see www.bethmardutho.org].

The English text is set in Monotype Garamond (version 2.30, 1998), a TrueType digital font based on roman types cut by Jean Jannon in 1615. Jannon followed the designs of Claude Garamond in the previous century.